Beyond the Yellow Badge

Brill's Series in Jewish Studies

VOLUME 37

Beyond the Yellow Badge

Anti-Judaism and Antisemitism in Medieval and Early Modern Visual Culture

Edited by

Mitchell B. Merback

TUTA SUB AEGIDE PALLAS · 1683 ·

BRILL

LEIDEN • BOSTON
2008

Cover Image: Württembergische Landesbibliothek, Stuttgart, Cod. brev. 125, 91v.
Image Editing: Bruce Corbett

This book is printed on acid-free paper.

Library of Congress Cataloging-in-Publication Data is available on http://catalog.loc.gov.

ISSN 0926-2261
ISBN 978 90 04 15165 9

PRINTED IN THE NETHERLANDS

CONTENTS

CONTRIBUTORS
(in alphabetical order)

Eva Frojmovic is a lecturer in the School of Fine Art, History of Art and Cultural Studies at the University of Leeds, and is Director of its Centre for Jewish Studies. She is the editor of *Imagining the Self, Imagining the Other: Visual Representation and Jewish-Christian Dynamics in the Middle Ages and Early Modern Period* (Leiden, 2002), and is currently writing a book on the earliest illustrated Hebrew manuscripts in thirteenth-century Germany.

Anne F. Harris teaches at DePauw University in Indiana, and has published on the interactions of stained glass and popular culture at Canterbury Cathedral, as well as Chartres. Her current research on the intersection between stained glass and liturgical drama encompasses other sites within the medieval archbishopric of Sens, including Auxerre and Saint-Julien-du-Sault. Issues of identity, devotion, and popular manipulations of visual culture inform her work.

Jacqueline Jung, a specialist in the sculpture and architecture of later medieval Germany, teaches in the department of History of Art at Yale University. Her first art historical article, on the unifying role of Gothic choir screens (*Art Bulletin*, 2000), received the Arthur Kingsley Porter Prize from the College Art Association; she is now completing a book on the Naumburg west choir screen, from which the present essay is drawn. Her new project, pursued while a Fellow at the American Academy in Berlin in spring 2006, focuses on the expressive uses of the body in German Gothic figural arts.

Paul Kaplan is Professor of Art History in the School of Humanities at Purchase College, State University of New York. He is the author of *The Rise of the Black Magus in Western Art* (Ann Arbor, 1985) and many essays on the political context and content of Italian, and especially Venetian, Renaissance art. He is currently working on a study of images of black Africans in Italian art between 1500 and 1700, and will be a Fellow at the W.E.B. DuBois Center for African and African-American Research at Harvard University in 2008.

Vivian B. Mann is the Feld Chair in Judaica at New York's Jewish Museum, and Advisor to the Masters Program in Jewish Art at the Graduate School of the Jewish Theological Seminary. Her latest book is *Art and Ceremony in Jewish Life: Essays in Jewish Art History* (London, 2005). She has been the recipient of numerous fellowships and was a Fellow at The Institute for Advanced Studies, The Hebrew University. In 1999 she received the Achievement Award in Jewish Thought from the National Foundation for Jewish Culture.

Mitchell Merback teaches Art History at DePauw University, and is a Fellow at the Radcliffe Institute for Advanced Studies at Harvard University (2007–08). He is the author of *The Thief, the Cross and the Wheel: Pain and the Spectacle of Punishment in Medieval and Renaissance Europe* (Chicago, 1999), with a second book, *Pilgrimage and Pogrom: Anti-Jewish Myth, Memory and Visual Culture in Germany and Austria, 1300–1520*, soon to appear. His current research examines the responses of German and Swiss Renaissance artists to the radical sectarianism of the early Reformation era.

Elizabeth Monroe is Assistant Professor of Art History at Stern College for Women in New York City. A former editor at George Braziller publishers, she has received fellowships from the Kress Foundation, the Getty Research Institute, and Fordham University's Center for Medieval Studies. Her current work investigates medieval reading habits combined with a broader reconsideration of the relationship between devotional imagery and spectatorship.

Kara Morrow is Assistant Professor of Art History at Albion College in Michigan. She recently completed her dissertation at Florida State University on the visual narratives of Saint Stephen in medieval architectural sculpture. She is currently working on the hagiographical imagery of Saints Ursin and Stephen in the programs of Bourges Cathedral.

Pamela A. Patton is Associate Professor of Art History at Southern Methodist University in Dallas, and is a specialist in the art of medieval Iberia. Her first book, *Pictorial Narrative and the Romanesque Cloister: Cloister Imagery and Religious Life in Medieval Spain*, appeared in 2004; her current book project explores representations of Jews and Judaism in the visual culture of Spain's Christian kingdoms during the High Middle Ages.

Nina Rowe is Assistant Professor of Art History at Fordham University in New York City. She is co-author of *Manuscript Illumination in the Modern Age: Recovery and Reconstruction* (2001) and co-editor of *Excavating the Medieval Image: Manuscripts, Artists, Audiences* (Ashgate, 2004). Her forthcoming monograph examines sculptural representations of Synagoga and Ecclesia in the High Middle Ages, and she has recently published on this subject in the journal *Gesta*.

Shalom Sabar is Professor of Jewish Art and Folklore and Chair of the Department of Jewish and Comparative Folklore at The Hebrew University of Jerusalem. His fields of teaching and research encompass the art, material culture, daily life and rituals of Jewish communities in Christian Europe and in the Islamic East. Among other works, he is the author of *Ketubbah: The Art of the Jewish Marriage Contract* (Rizzoli, 2001); his most recent book (in Hebrew) deals with the life cycles of Jewish communities in the lands of Islam.

Debra Higgs Strickland is Deputy Director of the Glasgow Centre for Medieval and Renaissance Studies at the University of Glasgow and an Honorary Fellow in History of Art at the University of Edinburgh. She is the author of *Medieval Bestiaries: Text, Image, Ideology* (Cambridge, 1995; published under the name Debra Hassig), and *Saracens, Demons, and Jews: Making Monsters in Medieval Art* (Princeton, 2003). Her current research focuses on images of non-Christians in the paintings of Hieronymus Bosch and their multiple meanings in the early modern period.

Annette Weber received her Ph.D. in Art History from the University of Freiburg im Breisgau, and is Chair for Jewish Art at the Hochschule für Jüdische Studien Heidelberg. Her research interests, covered by numerous publications, include the image of Jews and Judaism in medieval and early modern Christian art; Jewish culture in Germany; and the impact of Jewish collecting in nineteenth- and twentieth-century Europe. Between 1986 and 2004 she served as curator for Jewish Art at the Jüdisches Museum in Frankfurt am Main.

LIST OF FIGURES

Chapter One

Chapter Two

Chapter Three

Chapter Four

Chapter Five

Chapter Six

Chapter Seven

Chapter Eight

Chapter Nine

Chapter Ten

Chapter Eleven

Chapter Twelve

Chapter Thirteen

ACKNOWLEDGEMENTS

Scholars who give their work over to anthologies, though they may never meet one another, form a virtual community, and often find themselves sharing more than they bargained for. In the case of the present group of contributors one of these things was the challenge of dealing with a zealous first-time editor given to lengthy emails and, at times, imperious directives. For rising to this challenge, for displaying saintly patience through the long editorial process, but moreso for bringing to the project the best of their learning and experience, each of these authors has my deepest gratitude. Another thing the group shares are the many debts accumulated by each of them individually. To take in the full panorama of persons and institutions who have helped make this volume possible, dedicated readers are asked to peruse the footnotes of the essays that follow, for it is there the particulars of each author's debts are acknowledged, and their feelings of gratitude expressed in their own words. As one among the contributors I have done likewise—while as editor I enjoy the special privilege of thanking those who graciously gave their time, effort, expertise, and counsel to the project as a whole. Julian Deahl of Brill Publishers offered inspiring encouragement from the start, and along with Marcella Mulder shepherded the project through its nascent stage. My editorial assistant, Amira Korkor, brought diligence, high aptitude and an enviable calm to the job when mountains of work threatened to engulf us. Jacqueline Jung kindly offered hours of assistance in the preparation of the bibliography and sage advice throughout. Brooke Cox and Jessica Bozeman of the Visual Resources Center at DePauw University assisted in preparing many of the digital image files. Mike Mozina and his production staff at Brill performed miracles in giving crisp final form to a motley collection of texts and images; and Michiel Swormink, our series editor, captained the heavily laden ship safely into harbor. It has been a pleasure working with everyone connected with this volume. I hope that all of them, along with our future readers, will find the completed whole worthy of their efforts.

—M. B. M.

INTRODUCTION

Mitchell B. Merback

I

This collection of essays takes its title from the yellow Star of David that Jews in Germany and in German-dominated territories were forced to wear during the Nazi era as a badge of infamy—a visual sign that worked as a quarantine for Jews and an ominous warning to non-Jews as well.[1] In making the yellow badge compulsory the Nazis were reviving one of the notorious regulations of medieval Jewry law, first decreed on November 11, 1215 by an illustrious assembly of 412 bishops, 800 abbotts and priors, numerous and sundry prelates and representatives of cathedral chapters, as well as deputies of virtually every prince in Christendom, convened inside the Church of San Giovanni Laterano in Rome. Canon 68 of this assembly, the Fourth Lateran Council, famously ordained that, "Jews and Saracens of both sexes in every Christian province and at all times shall be marked off in the eyes of the public from other peoples through the character of their dress."[2] Ostensibly

---

[1] Citations for this essay are limited to what is necessary for documenting my own discussion and supplementing the sources provided by the contributors where I thought this necessary. Aside from those cited below, works that I found helpful in preparing this overview include: Amos Funkenstein, "Basic Types of Christian Anti-Jewish Polemics in the Later Middle Ages," *Viator* 2 (1971): 373–82; Jeremy Cohen, "Scholarship and Intolerance in the Academy: The Study and Evaluation of Judaism in European Christendom," and the comment by Gavin Langmuir, both in *American Historical Review* 91, no. 3 (1986): 592–613 and 614–24 respectively; David Berger, "From Crusades to Blood Libels to Expulsions: Some New Approaches to Medieval Antisemitism," Second Annual Lecture of the Victor J. Selmanowitz Chair of Jewish History (New York: Touro College, Graduate School of Jewish Studies, 1997), 1–29; Johannes Heil, "'Antijudaismus' und 'Antisemitismus': Begriffe als Bedeutungsträger," *Jahrbuch für Antisemitismusforschung* 6 (1997): 92–114; Zygmunt Baumann, "Allosemitism: Premodern, Modern, Postmodern," in *Modernity, Culture and 'the Jew'*, ed. Bryan Cheyette and Laura Marius (Stanford: University Press, 1998), 143–56; and Ivan G. Marcus, "Medieval Jewish Studies: Toward an Anthropological History of the Jews," in *The State of Jewish Studies*, ed. Shaye J. D. Cohen and Edward L. Greenstein (Detroit: Wayne State University Press, 1990), 113–27.

[2] Guido Kisch, "The Yellow Badge in History," *Historia Judaica* 19, no. 2 (October 1957): 89–146, at 102; and Shlomo Simonsohn, *The Apostolic See and the Jews: History*

adopted to prevent sexual promiscuity across religious boundaries, the measure went much further, as popes long after Innocent III's reign continued to request its enforcement by Christian rulers. Its effects are captured in the phrase *in the eyes of the public*, which made clear the badge's double function in medieval society. For Jews it meant restriction and repression, a visual token of their reprobate status within the Christian world order, a humiliation writ large across the body of every living member of the community. For Christians, especially those who might waver in their faith, potentially "backsliding" toward Judaism, or consort too brazenly with their Jewish neighbors, the badge was a warning and a reproach, a glimpse of their own potential misfortune outside the saving benefactions of the Roman Church.

One may also take this phrase, *in the eyes of the public*, as a modern academic allegory. It evokes a peculiar disciplinary stance on the question of how the visual arts registered anti-Jewish perceptions, attitudes, ideas and doctrines during the long era stretching from the Middle Ages to the Emancipation of European Jewry (the period covered by the present volume). For just as the implementation of the badge after Fourth Lateran allowed for a more precise social labelling and tracking of Jews within a society already organized hierarchically, the special recognition given by art historians to those forms of *pictorial* labelling that first emerged in the High Middle Ages—not only the circular badge but the conical hat, the hooked nose and bulbous eyes, pseudo-Hebrew letters, Mosaic Tablets, and so on—offered an earlier generation of scholars the promise of being able to track Jews, Judaism, and the image of "the Jew" through every relevant pathway of Christian art. In both instances, medieval and modern, "the Jew" becomes a special object of the gaze, the negative centerpiece of an entire regime of representation, the very image of alterity, or "Otherness."

There is no need to wonder at the initial timing of the scholarly discovery of Christian art's stereotyped image of "the Jew" and Judaism. In 1942 Joseph Reider completed a short pioneering study of Jews in medieval art. With sharp rhetoric and a sense of moral indignation that seems restrained given the historical emergency swirling around, Reider opened his short survey with these words:

(Toronto: Pontifical Institute of Medieval Studies, 1991), 135–37. Still useful is Joseph Jacobs, "Badge," in *The Jewish Encyclopedia*, vol. 2 (New York: Funk and Wagnalls, 1902), 425–27.

> It is well known that art in the Middle Ages, like so many other disciplines, was chiefly religious, ancillary and subservient to the all-powerful *ecclesia*, and consequently it reflected the ideas and ideals of the regnant Catholic Church. Now since this Church is known to have been antagonistic and hostile to the Jews, it is not at all surprising that art, its protégé, should have proved anything but sympathetic to them. And indeed we find art playing a very important role in disseminating distorted conceptions and false notions of the Jews, often depicting them in unnatural colors and derogatory poses, sometimes even as frightful monsters without any redeeming virtues. The artists thus helped to fan the bias and hatred of the populace, who knew them for the most part from these misrepresentations and caricatures and not from close personal contact. In an age of rampant ecclesiastical and furious sacerdotalism, when reason was garrotted and superstition held full sway, it was not unnatural that art should contribute its share in formulating and promulgating the well-known myth of His Satanic Majesty, the medieval Jew.[3]

Today it is possible to read Reider's opening statement, point by point, as an unintended prolegomenon to an entire trajectory of research. Each of the themes he sounds—medieval art's subservience to religion, the Church's hostile stance toward the Jews, the defamatory and dehumanizing effect of images, popular culture's captivity to superstition, distortions and lies, the artist as paid accomplice—reverberate throughout much of the post-war discourse.

What we should also bear in mind, however, as we cast a glance back on this tradition of liberal scholarship, is that, for Anglo-American art history, the years encompassing the systematic destruction of European Jewry were not only a time of deep disillusionment over Europe's descent into barbarism; they were also boom years for the discipline. Following the lead of Jewish-German emigré scholars whose posts were terminated by the Nazis—most prominent among them Erwin Panofsky, who had settled in Princeton by 1934—American art historians in the postwar period invested heavily in the new "method" of iconography, which promised a privileged access to symbolic meanings through a transposition of literary and visual artefacts. In line with this new amalgamation of German *Kunstgeschichte* and American empiricism, scholars

---

[3] Joseph Reider, "Jews in Medieval Art," in *Essays on Anti-Semitism*, ed. Koppel S. Pinson (New York, 1942), 45–56, at 45. Seven years before this, two antisemitic German scholars drew upon the corpus of medieval Christian anti-Judaic iconography to illustrate in positive terms the longevity of antagonism toward Jews and Judaism; see Robert Körber and Theodor Pugel, eds. *Antisemitismus der Welt in Wort und Bild* (Dresden, 1935).

widened the scope of their inquiry into the particulars of medieval and Renaissance works—this in order to account for images and motifs whose explanation lay beyond the reach of canonical sources. Such efforts relied upon, and in turn reinforced, a distinctly modern notion of subject matter,[4] and it was not long before "Jews and Judaism" had come into its own as a distinct area of iconographic inquiry.

This paved the way for a fertile reception of the efforts already being undertaken in Europe, in particular by Jewish historians working in the spirit of the *Wissenschafts des Judentum*, the scientific study of Judaism and Jewish history, of which the history of antisemitism was an important part. In 1963 the Austrian historian Bernhard Blumenkranz gave a series of lectures at the University of Münster on the representation of Jews and Judaism in medieval art, concentrating almost entirely on religious imagery and almost exclusively on manuscript evidence. Already established as the author of the seminal study of Augustine's *Tractatus adversus Iudaeos*, as well as a pioneering assessment of Jewish-Christian relations in the early Middle Ages, Blumenkranz organized his survey to cover Old and New Testament themes, the allegories of Church and Synagogue, and the pictorial treatment of anti-Jewish legends. The rise of hostile antisemitic imagery he traced to the religious enthusiasms and violences occasioned by the Crusades; the decline of hateful stereotypes, by contrast, he attributed to the power of Renaissance realism, which broke the spell of irrational perceptions under which medieval Christendom's "picture-Gospel of hate" had flourished.[5] Between Blumenkranz's Münster lectures and their publication in German two years later, Wolfgang Seiferth published his foundational study of the Church-Synagogue antithesis, revealing both the pernicious and

---

[4] A point usefully made by Alfred Acres, "Porous Subject Matter and Christ's Haunted Infancy," in *The Mind's Eye: Art and Theological Argument in the Middle Ages*, ed. Jeffrey F. Hamburger and Anne-Marie Bouché (Princeton: Department of Art and Archaeology, Princeton University, and Princeton University Press, 2006), 241–62, though the author's central argument must be approached with some reservation.

[5] Bernhard Blumenkranz, *Juden und Judentum in der mittelalterlichen Kunst* (Stuttgart: Kohlhammer, 1965); translated one year later as *Le juif médiéval au miroir de l'art chrétien* (Paris: Études augustiniennes, 1966). Blumenkranz published a preliminary report on anti-Jewish imagery, "Das Bilderevangelium des Hasses," in the important collection, *Judenhass—Schuld der Christen?* ed. W[illehad]. P[aul]. Eckert and E. L. Ehrlich (Essen: Hans Driewer, 1964), 249–56. His crucial early works are *Die Judenpredigt Augustins. Ein Beitrag zur Geschichte der jüdisch-christlichen Beziehungen in den ersten Jahrhunderten* (Basel: Helbing & Lichtenhahn, 1946) and *Juifs et chrétiens dans le monde occidental, 430–1096* (Paris: Mouton, 1960).

conciliatory dimensions of this long-running allegorical-polemical theme in art and literature.[6]

A few exemplary studies may be cited to show the trajectory of this research after Blumenkranz and Seiferth. Owing much to, but also departing from, these earlier efforts, the medievalist Henry Kraus devoted an illuminating chapter to the subject in his *Living Theatre of Medieval Art* (1967), a study widely admired for its pioneering fusion of art and social history. In the same year the *Art Bulletin* published Marilyn Lavin's brilliant analysis of the host-desecration legend scenes in Paolo Uccello's predella panels for the Corpus Christi Altar in Urbino. The 1970s saw the appearance of an exhaustive and scrupulously researched American dissertation by Eric Zafran (1973), Isaiah Schachar's impassioned exploration of the "Jewish sow" (*Judensau*) motif (1974); and the beginning of spate of studies by independent art historian Ruth Mellinkoff, whose work has in many ways dominated the field since then (1970; 1981; 1993).[7] Especially influential toward the end of this period was James Marrow's elaboration of traditional iconographical method to penetrate the density of negative signifiers in late medieval Passion imagery. Marrow's application of a philological approach—pioneered by F. P. Pickering—explained the bestial attributes of Christ's Jewish tormentors, for example, in terms of a transformation of metaphorical Old Testament imagery into narrative details, an exegetical method employed by the authors of late medieval Passion tracts (and one that mirrored the spinning of prophecy into history in the composition of the Gospels themselves).[8]

---

[6] Wolfgang S. Seiferth, *Synagoge und Kirche im Mittelalter* (Munich: Kösel, 1964); translated as *Synagogue and Church in the Middle Ages: Two Symbols in Art and Literature*, trans. Lee Chadeayne and Paul Gottwald (New York: Frederick Ungar, 1970).

[7] Henry Kraus, *The Living Theatre of Medieval Art* (Philadelphia, 1967), esp. ch. 7, "Anti-semitism in Medieval Art," 139–62; Marilyn Aronberg Lavin, "The Altar of Corpus Domini in Urbino: Paolo Uccello, Joos van Ghent, Piera della Francesca," *Art Bulletin* 49, no. 1 (March 1967): 1–24; Eric M. Zafran, "The Iconography of Anti-semitism: A Study of the Representation of the Jews in the Visual Arts of Europe 1400–1600" (Ph.D. dissertation, New York University; repr. Ann Arbor, 1973); and Isaiah Schachar, *The Judensau: A Medieval Anti-Jewish Motif and its History* (London, 1974). The significant studies by Ruth Mellinkoff are *The Horned Moses in Medieval Art and Thought* (Berkeley: University of California Press, 1970); idem, *The Mark of Cain* (Berkeley: University of California Press, 1981); and her magnum opus, *Outcasts: Signs of Otherness in Northern European Art of the Late Middle Ages*, 2 vols. (Berkeley: University of California Press, 1993).

[8] James H. Marrow, "*Circumdederunt me canes multi*: Christ's Tormentors in Northern European Art of the Late Middle Ages and Early Renaissance," *Art Bulletin* 59 (June 1977): 167–181; and then in expanded form in his monumental *Passion Iconography in*

Since the mid-1980s the discourse of anti-Jewish iconography has burgeoned into a fully fledged corpus of articles, dissertations, monographs, anthologies, reference works, exhibition catalogues and conference sesssions, a discourse with its own authoritative voices and youthful interventionists, peopled by Jewish and Christian authors alike, and dominated by American, British, German and Israeli scholars. In sum, we have a well-seeded field of inquiry and a rich harvest of research and synthesis. Art historians have catalogued every type of defamatory caricature and stereotyped "sign of otherness," every pictorial projection of monstrosity and diablery in which Europe's construction of "the Jew" as Other has rooted itself. The relevant literature—theological, polemical, legendary and folkloric—has been sifted for sources, analogies and parallel conceptions. With the taxonomy all but complete, we are confronted with a veritable "iconography of antisemitism" within European art, horrible yet fascinating, ordered and bound between glossy covers, and available on library shelves and coffee tables throughout the civilized world. Standing before such an achievement, it seems fair to ask whether we have yet arrived at an accurate, realistic and honest picture of art's place in the history of anti-Judaism and antisemitism, or whether that picture remains obscure in some fundamental ways.

II

Medieval art has perenially served enlightened minds as the poster-child for premodern unreason, religious tyranny and repressive exclusionism, as Joseph Reider's statement of 1942 showed so clearly. So it has also played perfectly into the hands of those who would also look for the "roots" of modern antisemitism, the origins of Auschwitz as it were, in the anti-Judaic policies, polemics, myths and perceptions of the Middle Ages. Expressing a commonly held view about the tilt toward exclusionary categories, one expert explains, "Medieval drama and art are didactically, rather than esthetically, oriented and structured, and the dualistic typological system determines their thematic choices

Northern European Art of the Late Middle Ages and Early Renaissance (Kortrijk, Belgium: Van Ghemmert, 1979). For an introduction to this exegetical technique in the writing of the Gospels, see John Dominic Crossan, *Who Killed Jesus? Exposing the Roots of Anti-Semitism in the Gospel Story of the Death of Jesus* (HarperCollins, 1995).

as well as their formal solutions."[9] What such statements show is that, in their commitment to aligning the traditions of polemical texts and polemical images, art historians have installed inside the iconographic enterprise that defines this field a model for explanation and interpretation. Though its contours are rarely made explicit, this model treats all stereotyped images as repositories of negative attitudes, symbolic vehicles that reflect either the theological interpretation of Judaism stretching back to the Gospels and patristic thought, or one of the many popular tropes surrounding the "demonic Jew" (described so compellingly in Joshua Trachtenberg's famous 1943 study, *The Devil and the Jews*).[10] Because it accepts the premise that Christian art and culture knew a Jew when it saw one (or when it depicted one), I propose to call this, borrowing the concise German term, the *Judenbild* model. Under its auspices, visual images are reduced either to propaganda or the pictorial equivalent of what anthopologist Alan Dundes, writing about ritual murder, calls "evil folklore."[11] Interpretation operates under a limiting set of assumptions, mainly psychological, about the mechanisms that allowed images of Jews, regardless of their context, to function as symbolic vehicles of hatred, reflections of intolerance, or even catalysts of repression and persecution. These assumptions cluster around terms like *defaming, marginalizing, scapegoating, demonizing, dehumanizing, stigmatizing, victimizing*—each with its own shades of belief about social psychology, judgments about the pathology of inter-religious conflict and the inability of medieval people to disentangle image from reality. Exemplary are the conflations made in the following passage by Moshe Lazar:

> Marked with the sign of Cain or the seal of Antichrist on his forehead—later to be made visible and explicit through the yellow badge of

[9] Moshe Lazar, "The Lamb and the Scapegoat: The Dehumanization of the Jews in Medieval Propaganda Imagery," in *Antisemitism in Times of Crisis*, ed. Sander L. Gilman and Steven T. Katz (New York: New York University Press, 1991), 38–80, at 51, an assertion for which the author cites his own previous studies.

[10] Trachtenberg sifted through a stunning range of historical sources to confront a specifically demonological conception of the Jew, rooted in medieval Christian culture and patterns of thought; see Joshua Trachtenberg, *The Devil and the Jews: The Medieval Conception of the Jew and its Relation to Modern Antisemitism* (Philadelphia, 1983). This work was preceded by the author's foundational study of *Jewish Magic and Superstition: A Study in Folk Religion* (1939; repr. New York, 1982).

[11] Alan Dundes, "The Ritual Murder or Blood Libel Legend: A Study of Anti-Semitic Victimization through Projective Inversion," in *The Blood Libel Legend: A Casebook in Anti-Semitic Folklore*, ed. Alan Dundes (Madison, 1991), 336–60.

> infamy on his garment—branded as Christ killer and possessed by the devil, hated by God and his preachers, the mythical Jew of Christian theology became superimposed on the real Jew living in the shadow of the church. The lines of demarcation between reality and myth concerning the Jews and the synagogue were further blurred by translating the metaphors of hatred and contempt, elaborated in patristic literature, into codified systems of social vilification and juridical ghettoization of people who had been stripped of their human features.[12]

Foundational for all these diverse notions about the negative power of images is an overly rigid concept of the *stereotype* and its function. Without being aware, scholars of an older generation reproduced in their writing about anti-Jewish stereotypes something of the original technical meaning of the term—invented in the late eighteenth century, it denoted a relief plate cast from printer's type, capable of producing multiples of the same image (the French *cliché* once denoted the same thing).[13] Absorbed into common usage, the term came to denote any kind of fixed collective idea, belief or perception. Incessant social reproduction and redistribution lend the stereotype is power to compel thought and behavior, and eventually its contours become indistinguishable from common sense. As integral mental representations of the world, stereotyped anti-Jewish images certainly index collective perceptions. But does our acknowledgement of this baseline fact force us to view these stereotypes as immutable fixtures of thought, beliefs that are culturally unshakeable?

With the rise of academic interest in cultural encounters, cultural difference, and cultural identity in the last two decades of the twentieth century, the nature of the stereotype, as a representation *sui generis*, at last began to receive the theoretical attention it deserved.[14] Part of this reconsideration was an understanding of the shifting, contingent and unstable character of all images of "the Other." As Sander Gilman explains, stereotypes

---

[12] Lazar, "The Lamb and the Scapegoat," 49.

[13] In some sources the word refers to a papier-maché cast for copying printing type.

[14] Among many statements of the problem, see esp. Sander Gilman, *Difference and Pathology: Stereotypes of Sexuality, Race and Madness* (Ithaca: Cornell University Press, 1985); and more recently, Peter Burke, *Eyewitnessing: The Uses of Images as Historical Evidence* (Ithaca: Cornell University Press, 2001), 123–39. I thank Guy Tal for his insights and many helpful suggestions on this topic.

> perpetuate a needed sense of difference between the "self" and the "object," which becomes the "Other." Because there is no real line between the self and the Other, an imaginary line must be drawn; and so that the illusion of an absolute difference between self and Other is never troubled, this line is as dynamic in its ability to alter itself as is the self…paradigm shifts in our mental representations of the world can and do occur. We can move from fearing to glorfying the Other. We can move from loving to hating. The most negative stereotype always has an overtly positive counterweight. As any image is shifted, all stereotypes shift. Thus stereotypes are inherently protean rather than rigid.[15]

What factors, then, determine the meaning of a stereotyped *pictorial* image for individuals and social groups at a given time and place? Cultural encounters set the stage for a wide range of possible reactions, but tend to polarize, according to Peter Burke, into those that either collapse cultural differences, assimilating the other to the self, or those that magnify them, turning the other into an "Other," a threatening opposite, a reified inversion of the self.[16] Here another pivotal concept comes into play, that of the *scapegoat* mechanism. In discussions of premodern Jewish-Christian relations it is frequently this concept that is given interpretive pride of place; though here again researchers are too often content to allow catchwords to perform the labor of analysis for them, rather than unravel what anthropologists have long recognized as a complex and shifting set of cultural mechanisms for maintaining the cohesion of ingroups at the expense of outgroups.[17] Art historians have not considered until recently how one might locate stereotyped representations, or the scapegoating mechanism itself, along a continuum of representations and behaviors between the positive and negative poles of cultural encounter. Should we expect all of the stereotyped figures and motifs of "the Jew" to tend toward the pole of magnified threat, where they endanger the fragility of the projected-inverted self, thus engendering fear and hatred? Or are some of these familiar *Judenbilder*

---

15 Gilman, *Difference and Pathology*, 18.

16 Burke, *Eyewitnessing*, 122–24.

17 Central to the topic after the pioneering work of Sir James Frazer (in *The Golden Bough*) has been René Girard, *The Scapegoat.* trans. Yvonne Freccero (Baltimore: Johns Hopkins University Press, 1986); see the valuable reflections on Girard's theory by Masao Yamaguchi, "Towards a Poetics of the Scapegoat," in *Violence and Truth: On the Work of René Girard*, ed. Paul Dumouchel (Stanford: University Press, 1988), 179–91. For a useful, if somewhat tendentious, application of the scapegoat thesis to the history of antisemitism, see Hyam Maccoby, *A Pariah People: The Anthropology of Antisemitism* (London: Constable, 1996).

more or less benign, threatening nothing of great importance, engendering something more akin to mockery, bemused contempt, or simple condescension? Such alternatives rarely receive the close consideration they deserve. They trouble the aura of moral seriousness under which discussions of cultural encounter in its darker aspects—colonialism, xenophobia, racism, antisemitism—are carried on.

Built into the the *Judenbild* paradigm, then, is precisely that tendency to read every stereotyped representation rigidly and through a glass darkly. This turns out to be liberal art history's version of another cliché: the tendency to subsume the varied streams of Jewish-Christian conflict into an engulfing torrent of constant persecution, fed at its historic source by Christianity's doctrine of supersession, and driven inexorably downstream by powerful undercurrents of irrationality, fear, enmity, and the will to dominate. Arranging the real diversity of representational strategies and contexts into an unbroken geneaology of racist images, the *Judenbild* paradigm constructs its own continuum along similar lines: stereotyped images and motifs become reflections of an undying (Christian) enmity toward Jews. In the eyes of antisemites, of course, this genealogy, this "iconography of antisemitism," would look like a visual archive of Judaism's undying enmity toward God and man, fleshed out in lurid shapes and colors.[18]

However it is understood, the result is the art-historical equivalent of what Hannah Arendt critically labelled "eternal antisemitism."[19] Adapting her definition, we might characterize the orthodoxy this way: stereotyped depictions of Jews "need no special explanation because they are natural consequences of an eternal problem."[20] Concomitantly, it happens that when all negative images of Jews find berth in the "persecuting discourses" of theology or folklore, scholars are often looking

[18] Michael Camille spelled out the danger inherent in art history's lavish display of racist caricature in a most memorable book review of Ruth Mellinkoff's two-volume survey, *Outcasts* (*Art Bulletin* 77, no. 1 [March 1995]), cited above, which he called an "expansive encyclopedia of infamy"; in his view, the book not only reproduces and analyzes, but enacts an "aestheticization of hate."

[19] Hannah Arendt, *Antisemitism*, part one of *The Origins of Totalitarianism* (San Diego, 1979), 7.

[20] See, for an example of the continuity thesis, Lazar, "The Lamb and the Scapegoat," 49, esp. his apologia in note 46: "In spite of the differences between the traditional articulations of antisemitic propaganda and modern ones which include racial overtones, the commonality of ideas and imagery as well as their dehumanizing purpose and effect are a clear testimony of continuity rather than rupture."

for origins and endpoints, that is, a kind of teleological development.[21] Despite its good intentions, liberal scholarship winds up containing premodern Jewish social realities inside the very prison of "Otherness" built and furnished with the propaganda imagery it sets out to study. Within the polemical spaces of Christian art, art history has discovered its own "lachrymose conception" of Jewish history (as the great Jewish historian Salo W. Baron famously characterized it) and its own sense of purpose in upholding the varieties of Holocaust piety that inform so much contemporary culture.

Over the past two decades this rigid conception has slowly eroded, replaced by understanding of cultural encounter, difference, interaction and exchange that is more flexible, more nuanced, and yet still sensitive to the terrors of history. This reorientation has been undertaken by a diversity of critical voices, both within and without Jewish studies—by historians, cultural theorists, and art historians as well. And it has been accompanied by a frank awareness that Jews were not the only group whose *difference* became an obsession for Christian image-makers. Highly influential in this respect, and widely admired beyond its own discipline, has been Michael Camille's brilliant study of the idolatry trope in medieval Christian visual culture, *The Gothic Idol: Ideology and Image-Making in Medieval Art* (1989).[22] Although Camille did not go so far as to explicitly challenge the idea of an "iconography of antisemitism," his work represents the earliest and boldest effort to resituate anti-Jewish (and anti-Muslim) imagery within an expanded semiotic field of visual signs and image-making practices, and within the broader ideological field of hegemony and social controls. Visual allegories and tropes of Jewish "idolatry," paradoxically imbricated within tales of Jewish iconoclasm, were at the very heart of an emergent Gothic visual regime in the thirteenth century, argued Camille, a culture which both thrived on, and fretted over, its new commitments in a rapidly expanding economy of the visible. Riffing on Lester K. Little's theory about the medieval Christian inability to adapt to a rapidly changing money economy, and its consequences for Jews, Camille conjectured that Jews likewise

[21] Compare the introductory remarks in David Nirenberg, *Communities of Violence: Persecution of Minorities in the Middle Ages* (Princeton, 1996).

[22] Michael Camille, *The Gothic Idol: Ideology and Image-Making in Medieval Art* (Cambridge: University Press, 1989). Ironically, his iconoclastic chapter on "Idols of the Jews" (pp. 165–94) has made him, I believe, one the most widely quoted Anglophone authorities on Jews in medieval art.

"functioned as a scapegoat for Christian concern about adapting to an expanding economy of images, which allowed greater access by more segments of the Christian community to a whole gamut of representations, private, public, and cult."[23] An expanded facility with images also meant a more thoroughgoing domination of this aniconic minority, this "nation without art" within Christian society. In an increasingly visual world, Camille realized, Christendom's containment of the troubling ambivalence Jews represented could only be achieved by extending its hegemony across the whole domain of the visual:

> The stigma the Jews had to bear in thirteenth-century Christian societies was often a visual sign and can be seen as part of the new emphasis on visual organization and order of society. The most extreme form that visual control of the Other took in this period was making the Jews themselves into images, into spectacles of alterity.[24]

Within this new Gothic visual economy, living bodies as well as mute stone and painted images bore the burdens of signification. As "spectacles of alterity," medieval Jews were themselves the screens for a shifting spectrum of projections and displacements, fears and fascinations, both judeophobic and—if we recall the nature of stereotypes—judeophilic as well.

How might such insights help us grapple with the real diversity of images and experiences connected with medieval and early modern Jewish-Christian relations, and do so in a way that spares the premodern period the double-burden of guilt for its own persecutions and those of our own era? Hoping to see this and other questions addressed in ways that were no longer beholden to outmoded models and conceptions, I organized a conference session—bearing the title of this anthology—at the 2003 meeting of the College Art Association. Those papers formed a starter crop for the present volume, and subsequently a number of others were commissioned to round out the selection. At the time I was convinced of the topicality of any endeavor focusing on anti-Judaism and antisemitism in history, despite my skepticism about the post-9/11 rumblings regarding a "new antisemitism" (a canard aimed

[23] Camille, *The Gothic Idol*, 185; cf. Lester K. Little, *Religious Poverty and the Profit Economy in Medieval Europe* (Ithaca: Cornell University Press, 1978), esp. 42–57, where the author advances the theory that anti-Jewish hatred and persecution were based on "projection"—ie. that Christians resented Jews for doing what they themselves were doing and feeling guilty about, calculating for profit.

[24] Camille, *The Gothic Idol*, 180.

at leftist critics of Zionism and a blanket thrown over the multifarious expressions of anti-Israel animus in the Arab world). Today I remain convinced of its topicality. Whatever the continuities or discontinuities we may discover in its long history, antisemitism remains, as Max Horkheimer and Theodor Adorno described it in 1944, "a deeply imprinted schema, a ritual of civilization."[25] Yet topicality alone does not amount to a rationale for focusing historical work. Scholars must always be on their guard against inadvertantly replicating the very "historical structures of marginalization and exclusion" they study, as so often happens when the victimization of a single group becomes the sustained (or sole) focus of investigation. In the academy one finds today a growing insistence that the harrowing histories of anti-Jewish polemic, antisemitic stereotyping, and interreligious conflict should not be regarded as phenomena unto themselves, let alone foundation stones for a monolithic "history of hate." Rather, a new consensus is taking shape within and beyond Jewish Studies, one which sees anti-Judaism and antisemitism as integral parts of a broader field of Jewish-Christian relations. Antagonistic representations *of* Jews by non-Jews, the new paradigm suggests, are always interconnected with Jewish self-representations, an insight which compels art history to look for new ways to bring together the study of Christian arts and Jewish arts strictly speaking. The recent vigor of this enterprise recommends it as a compelling future direction for research.[26]

The aims of the present volume are perhaps more modest, but of course no less important. Undoubtedly the moral urgency that animated earlier scholarship on the legacy of Christian anti-Judaism, mythmaking and persecution, the spirit of outrage that produced epochal works of reproach and correction like Trachtenberg's *The Devil and the Jews* (1943) and Jules Isaac's *Jésus et Israël* (1948), has faded, despite the persistence of certain forms of antisemitism.[27] The historical and cultural circumstances under which scholars in the western democracies now

[25] Max Horkheimer and Theodor Adorno, *Dialectic of Englightenment*, trans. John Cumming (New York: Continuum, 1987), 171.

[26] Eva Frojmovic, ed., *Imagining the Self, Imagining the Other: Visual Representation and Jewish Christian Dynamics in the Middle Ages and Early Modern Period* (Leiden: Brill, 2002); the reference above to "historical structures of marginalization..." comes from the editor's thoughtful forward, at xvii.

[27] Jules Isaac, *Jésus et Israël*, 2nd edn. (Paris: Fasquelle Éditeurs, 1959); translated as *Jesus and Israel*, ed. Claire Huchet Bishop, trans. Sally Gran (New York: Holt, Rinehart & Winston, 1971). Trachtenberg as cited above.

approach the history of Jewish-Christian conflict encourage a dispassionate attitude similar to the one attending the critical study of religion, or the history of culture, in general. Among a younger generation of academics, direct or personal experiences with antisemitism are less likely to serve as touchstones for research or cornerstones of identity. Yet the conviction remains that the long and bitter "sibling rivalry" between Judaism and Christianity is a special case in the history of religion, no less an unresolved problem of modernity, thus demanding special attention from the historian. As a working premise, this conviction will continue to generate new insights and useful work, despite its potential for abuse. The present volume, it is hoped, will demonstrate the ongoing need to scrutinize the changing dynamics and consequences of a historic rivalry that has seen intolerance and misunderstanding turn virulent, and to do so in a way that encourages neither exaggerations of its dimensions, nor illusions about its passing.

III

Assembled under the rubric "Stages of Conversion," the first suite of essays explores several important cultural and artistic vectors emerging from Christendom's long-standing preoccupation with the overcoming of Jewish disbelief. Ever since the earliest rabbinical rejections of the "good news" about Jesus, Christian efforts to extend universal mission to the Jews were marked by tensions, ambivalences about its meaning and purpose, and open skepticism about its probability. It may be that the hope of leading Jews to baptism, individually and collectively, has long amounted to little more than that, a pious and sometimes impatient hope, programmed into the head of every devout Christian regardless of real prospects—but no less a powerful hope for all that. Only recently have researchers begun to realize that active missionary effort was not the routine concomitant of such a hope. Nor was it the necessary counterpart to anti-Jewish polemic, which was, before the thirteenth century, written for the purpose of refuting "Jewish error" among real Jews in only the rarest cases. We know that Jews in the Middle Ages remained extremely vigilant in the face of proselytizing where and when it did occur, and struggled creatively to reverse the losses—material, human, symbolic—that followed from the violence of forced conversion campaigns, such as that accompanying the onset of the First Crusade in 1096. Meanwhile, protectionist Church policies, grounded in the Augustinian rationale for tolerating Jewish survival in Christian society, enshrined a contradiction, according to David Berger, "between the theoretical goals of a universal Christian mission and an argument for toleration that came close to discouraging Jewish conversion."[28]

Recognizing these contradictions, the contributors here also reveal the ways "conversion" became a defining trope in Christian *representations* of their relationships with Jews. In Chapter One, "'Fair and Friendly, Sweet and Beautiful': Hopes for Jewish Conversion in Synagoga's Song of Songs Imagery," Elizabeth Monroe exposes a vein of tension and ambivalence around hopes for conversion in several early medieval manuscripts depicting the allegorical figures of Ecclesia and Synagoga. Earlier scholars such as Blumenkranz and Seiferth already saw in the pair a reflection of the symbolic harmony, or *concordia*, of Old and New Testaments; but they also recognized its polemical and denunciatory aspects. While acknowledging how her manuscript evidence fits into the *contra Judaeos* tradition, Monroe taps farther than any previous researcher into a key exegetical tradition that profoundly influenced the figurative arts in this and other iconographic domains: the bridal mysticism arising from learned commentary on the Song of Songs. In this tradition Synagoga is promised the bridgegroom's love if she abandons disbelief and, like the Sulamite woman of verse 6:13, heeds the call to "return, return... that we may behold you." A surprising number of illuminators were responsive to this typological conflation, and Monroe's close reading of the images reveals places where illuminators deviated from the anti-Jewish elements found in the commentary. Her emphasis on the contextual determinations of imagery, the divergent of attitudes toward Synagoga imagery among different audiences, lay and monastic, pointedly reminds us of what is lost when the iconographer's "method" for interpretation demands that themes and motifs be isolated from their matrix, their lineages traced from one example to another, regardless of context.

Likewise responsive to the need for deeper contextual analysis, Kara Ann Morrow offers a rich reading of a pivotally important sculpture ensemble in her essay, "Disputation in Stone: Jews Imagined on the

[28] David Berger, "Mission to the Jews and Jewish-Christian Contacts in the Polemical Literature of the High Middle Ages," *American Historical Review* 91, no. 3 (June 1986): 576–91, at 576.

St. Stephen Portal of Paris Cathedral." Two events take center stage in her account: first, the famous "trial" of the Talmud staged by King Louis IX and Blanche of Castile, an event that pitted Rabbi Yehiel ben Joseph of Paris against the Dominican Nicholas Donin, a convert from Judaism credited with instigating the affair. The second event is Louis's acquisition of the large carved Roman gem known as the Grand Camée de France. Morrow's analysis makes the tympanum a charged site where the embedded meanings of hagiographical narrative are activated and directed toward a kind of theatricalization of Jewish-Christian conflict. In the reception of the image ecclesiastical authority, royal Jewry policy, and popular resentments mingled and merged.

When Stephen rails against the rabbis for remaining "uncircumcised in heart and ears" (Acts 7:51), we are hearing a common late antique trope and a defining issue of *Adversus Judaeos* polemic: Jews erred in interpreting Scripture "carnally" rather than "spiritually." With the Paris Disputation and those staged through a collusion of secular authorities and mendicant preachers elsewhere in Europe (Barcelona in 1263, Tortosa in 1415), Christian polemic was being sharply refocused on the rabbinical exegesis of the bible and, concomitantly, on the beliefs and practices of *post-biblical* Jews. In a profound sense an older Christian stereotype of the Jews as a people in whose culture time stood still was being overthrown, preparing the way for new mental representations and a new "cultural encounter." Questions about the Talmud, seen as a deep well of distortion into which the post-biblical Jews had fallen, would henceforth hold center stage in the confrontation between Synagogue and Church. As Jeremy Cohen has persuasively argued, the mendicant orders, charged with combating heresy, fatefully abandoned the Augustinian rationale for preserving the Jews—a people "stationary in useless antiquity"—as witnesses to the Christian truth embedded in Hebrew Scripture, in large part because they no longer accepted the identity of biblical and contemporary Jews. In other words, once the Talmud began to be regarded as the preeminent text of a thriving, post-biblical religion, Judaism could no longer be seen as an lifeless relic; rather, it had become a subversive force, a menace akin to heresy, forfeiting its place in the Christian world order, and requiring proactive response by Christian authorities.[29]

---

[29] Jeremy Cohen, "Introduction," in *Essential Papers on Judaism and Christianity in Conflict: From Late Antiquity to the Reformation*, ed. J. Cohen (New York: University Press, 1991), 1–36, at 20–21.

For historians a thorny problem remains in assessing the degree to which the growing familiarity with Hebrew sources, which formed the scholarly basis for the increasingly aggressive critique of contemporary Judaism, giving birth to the Jewish-Christian *disputatio*, affected the tenuous balance between the theory and practice of the Church's mission to convert the Jews. What is clear is that Christian knowledge of Hebrew was not sufficiently widespread or advanced in these transitional centuries to dispense with the idealization of the "knowing Jew" as a facilitator of Christian pursuits of the "Hebrew Truth" (*Hebraica veritas*). This is why Jewish apostates like Donin, who brought their own knowledge of Talmud into the arena of confrontation, however tendentiously, could exert the influence they did.

As Eva Frojmovic's contribution makes clear, these developments must be set against the backdrop of medieval systems of learning, in particular, the growing prominence of urban schools and universities, high medieval institutions that were rapidly eclipsing the monastery as the primary site of learning and intellectual creativity. In "Taking Little Jesus to School in Two Thirteenth-Century Latin Psalters from South Germany," Frojmovic presents a nuanced reading of the anti-Jewish undercurrents in two south German prayerbooks, where the apocryphal story of young Jesus's first day in school prefaces the Psalter proper. In the Waldkirche Psalter, one of her key examples, the illuminator's young Jesus knowingly struggles to flee from a classroom depicted with the trappings of a scholastic institution, though its faculty are shown wearing pointed Jewish hats (*Judenhut*) and working with scrolls instead of codices. As negative tropes for "worldly learning," such characterizations went beyond suspicions of a Jewish blindness that leads to error (or a paradoxical failure of Jews to "understand" their own language). Once again we are in the presence of a fear that Judaism is far from being the dead-letter of the official, Augustinian conception, but a cancer-like peril that will spread through Christian society if left unchecked. Frojmovic nevertheless resists the temptation to equate what she reads as "judaizing" signs, and all that they *may* connote, with active antagonism toward Jews; rather, she wants us to see the iconography of the Jew and Judaism "as a trope that helped Christians think through anxieties arising out of historical change."

A similar assumption threads through Anne Harris's chapter, "The Performative Terms of Jewish Iconoclasm and Conversion in Two Saint Nicholas Windows at Chartres Cathedral," which turns our attention to the visual language of stained glass. Focusing on a climactic scene from the *vita* of Nicholas, in which the saint's statue bears the violent brunt of Jewish resentment after the moneylender's ill-gotten gains are stolen, Harris finds the story depicted in two different locations at Chartres, and argues for their interaction with liturgical performances. Despite the specific inflections of each mode of representation, pictorial and performative, Harris stresses an underlying unity, a "dynamic of violence" that plays out in the conversion of the Jew, a spiritually edifying outcome to a narrative that addresses not Jewish problems but Christian ones, in particular those arising from the money economy. Cast in the light of the priest's performative conversion of bread into body, the pictorial and para-liturgical evocations of the baptizing saint's conversion of Jew into Christian become, in Harris's analysis, a "sign of reconciliation" broadcast to the community of the faithful. Whether this helped resolve clerical—or communal—misgivings about how Christians might handle money's labile forms in the emerging mercantile economy may have to remain an unanswered question, but Harris's essay opens the door to further productive thinking.

IV

A set of troubling contradictions accompanied the thirteenth century's project of turning the existing tradition of anti-Jewish polemic into concerted missionary action, led by the Church's new preaching orders. Long at issue for churchmen was the nature and scope of the so-called *culpa Iudaeorum* the collective guilt of the Jews for killing Christ; a guilt sealed in blood for generations by the famous lines spoken by the Jewish crowd in Matthew 27:25 ("His blood be upon us and our children"); a guilt manifested, according to countless Christian polemicists, in the unending Jewish rejection of Jesus as the messiah. During the twelfth century's great reawakening of intellectual creativity, which brought with it a deeper conviction that matters of faith could be proven empirically and through rational argument, medieval schoolmen transformed the basis for evaluating Jewish guilt. In a world perfectly bounded and determined by God's will, the ultimate cause of all things, what room, they asked, was there for human agency, good and evil intentions? What were the moral principles underlying free will? To the point: Did God will the Jews to kill Christ? If so, how could they be blamed, let alone condemned and punished by God himself? Peter Lombard, in his authoritative theological textbook, the *Sentences*, articulated the problem with the scholastic academician's finest tool, the distinction:

> We say that it should be conceded that God wanted Christ to suffer and die, since his suffering was good and was the cause of our salvation. But when we say, 'He wished him to suffer and die at the hands of the Jews,' we must make a distinction. If this statement is taken to mean that God wanted him to undergo suffering and death, which was brought about by the Jews, then this is true. If however the statement is taken to mean that God wanted the Jews to kill him, this is false. For God did not will the action of the Jews, which was evil. Rather, he desired the good of Christ's suffering, and this wish was fulfilled through the evil desires of the Jews.[30]

Along with the Christian discovery of the Talmud, and the realization that contemporary Judaism was not the timeless embodiment of biblical Israel, the turn toward an ethical conception of human action undertaken by Peter Lombard (and before him, Peter Abelard)[31] meant that it could no longer be argued that an involuntary "blindness" kept Jews from the truth; rejection of God in the here and now must be born instead of an inherent wickedness. From this realization a new perception of the medieval Jew was fatefully born, one posessing the features of a two-headed monster. One head was possessed of reason, capable of sharp cunning, and knowledgeable of the truth but rejecting it out of malice; the other was bestial, incapable of reason, a monstrous deformity of God's image in man, now turned sinister and deadly.

Among the leading religious personalities in an era marked as much by irrational xenophobia as rational inquiry, Peter the Venerable, the influential abbot of Cluny, ranks as the earliest and most vitriolic exponent of this perception. Despairing over the failure of empirical proofs and argument to dislodge the Jews' disbelief, Peter concluded in his treatise, *Against the Inveterate Stubbornness of the Jews* (written between 1144 and 1147), that there could only be one explanation:

> It seems to me, Jew, that I... judge in these matters... as do all men. And if all men, then you also—if, nevertheless, you are human. For I dare not declare you are human lest perchance I lie, because I recognize that reason, that which distinguishes humans from... beasts, is extinct in you or in any case buried.... Truly, why are you not called brute animals?

[30] Peter Lombard, *Sententiae in IV Libris Distinctae* (Rome, 1971), Liber I, Dist. XLVIII, Cap. 2; quoted in translation and discussed in John Y. B. Hood, *Aquinas and the Jews* (Philadelphia: University of Pennsylvania Press, 1995), 69–70.

[31] Most importantly, Abelard's work of c. 1140, the *Ethics*, ed. and trans. D. E. Luscombe (Oxford: Clarendon, 1971), esp. 53–71.

> Why not beasts? Why not beasts of burden?... The ass hears but does not understand; the Jew hears but does not understand.[32]

In the face of overwhelming evidence from their own prophecies, Jewish refusal to embrace the true meaning of Scripture was more than involuntary blindness, more than sinful stubbornness, more than an immoral exercise of free will: it was an inexplicable abomination, worthy of the fiercest condemnation by those who loved God. It was a sign that the Jews were not quite human. A Pandora's box had been opened, releasing new stereotypes to infest the European-Christian imagination. In their collective guilt brought on by their role in the Passion of Christ, the Jews were cursed by God and disfigured in the eyes of men. In matters of anti-Jewish mythmaking all roads lead back to the deicide charge and the *culpa Iudaeorum*. So it is not surprising that the critical mass of Christian art's dehumanizing portrayals of "the Jew"—the bestial, the grotesque, the demonic, the polluted and the polluting—find berth in visual (and theatrical) representations of the Passion. Yet the development was anything but linear, and stereotypes of the "demonic Jew" shifted along with the changing terrain of Christian self-understanding, as the essays in this volume's second section, "The Image of the Jew and its Public," show.

In her contribution to the volume, "The Passion, the Jews, and the Crisis of the Individual on the Naumburg West Choir Screen," Jacqueline E. Jung challenges the routine assumption that, when telling the story of Judas's betrayal at the Last Supper, or his selling out of Jesus to Caiaphas, medieval artists felt compelled to invest their Jewish characters, specifically their Jewish men, with physiognomic "signs of otherness" and thereby participate in an "iconography of rejection."[33] Appealing to the aristocratic laymen who formed one principal audience for the reliefs, the Naumburg sculptors refocused the familiar story through a reflexive lens of ethical choice and action, leaving aside the

---

[32] Peter the Venerable, *Adversus Judaeorum inveteratum duritiem*, ed. Yvonne Friedman, Corpus Christianorum, Continuatio Mediaevalis, vol. 58 (Turnhout, 1985), 125; quoted in translation in Gavin I. Langmuir, "Peter the Venerable: Defense Against Doubt," in *Toward a Definition of Antisemitism* (Berkeley: University of California Press, 1990), 197–208, at 207.

[33] The two phrases belong, respectively, to the discussions of anti-Jewish imagery in Mellinkoff, *Outcasts*, and Debra Hassig, "The Iconography of Rejection: Jews and Other Monstrous Races," in *Image and Belief: Studies in Celebration of the Eighteenth Anniversary of the Index of Christian Art*, ed. Colum Hourihane (Princeton: University Press, 1999), 25–37.

commonly employed forms of visual differentiation—the grotesque, hooked-nose countenances and wild, bestial gesticulations found in other contemporary programs. In doing so they set themselves an extraordinary challenge, and Jung's sensitive reading reveals multiple moments of artistic self-awareness as they navigated around the existing visual language of anti-Jewish invective. Reflecting this strategy in the art historian's here and now, her essay also puts forth an implicit methodological challenge: to read medieval anti-Jewish imagery beyond the "immutable" stereotype, and reconstruct meanings around the embodied experiences of actual viewers in their own social reality, where the lines between self and other are constantly shifting. Only a nuanced visual analysis, as Jung's essay demonstrates, can accomplish this.

Medievalists today are more aware than ever that, as the *sine qua non* of public art, architectural sculpture demands an understanding of both its political context and the ritual uses that actualized power and authority. Aligned in this respect with Jung's analysis of the Naumburg Passion, Nina Rowe's essay in Chapter Six, "Idealization and Subjection at the South Façade of Strasbourg Cathedral," gives us a powerful reinterpretation of a canonical monument that has been misunderstood for what it reveals about the nexus between anti-Jewish imagery and the social reality in which it was viewed. Rowe asks us to marvel at the aesthetic grandeur and courtly elegance the Strasbourg sculptors imparted to the allegorical figures of Christ's beloved and scorned brides—proud Ecclesia and dejected Synagoga—but not as an edifying sight in itself. Rather, for Rowe, the striking versimilitude of the sculptures contributed to a performance of ecclesiastical power. Drawing on Louis Althusser's theory of ideology as a mechanics of power that produces the individual's self-recognition as a subject, Rowe highlights the contradiction between Synagoga's idealized beauty and Jewish subjection within the Christian world order, a contradiction actualized as Ecclesia confronts her counterpart across the open space of the porch. With this emphasis Rowe ably raises the question of the continuities between symbolic representations of Jews and Judaism and the actual conditions of Jewish communities; between theological constructions of the Jewish-Christian relationship and the comprehension of that relationship by the various classes within a Christian majority who, like the Jewish minority, had little choice but to accede to their place in the structures of power. The hardening terms of Christian hegemony in the turbulent German empire extended not only to the Jews.

Debra Higgs Strickland, in "The Jews, Leviticus, and the Unclean in Medieval English Bestiaries," discovers the operative power of anti-Jewish ideology in an unlikely genre: the allegorical animal tales of the English bestiaries, which became an independent genre in the twelfth century. Recognizing the manifold ways these moralizing texts filtered contemporary social and theological concerns; and noting the wide array of "judaizing" traits grafted onto animals like the owl and the hyena, Strickland sees the bestiaries as an unacknowledged channel for transmitting some of the major themes of *Adversus Judaeos* theology, in particular, Jewish blindness, idolatry and perversity, and the supersession of the Old Law by the New. A peculiar strategy of Christian polemic, a value-inversion played out in text and image, is revealed when Strickland takes this analysis a step further. According to the bestiarists, the prohibitions of Leviticus 11 bore witness to the Jew's inborn desire to violate (or failure to follow) their own laws, relying instead on the "blasphemous" Talmud. Strickland's revisionist impulse is striking: from being an overlooked source for anti-Jewish sentiments, she wants to rank the bestiaries "among the most popular and widely-disseminated of Christian polemical texts directed against Jews." This occurs, she points out, during a time of escalating tensions between Christians and Jews in England, tensions unresolved until the expulsion from England in 1290.

Can artists and artisans be counted as especially sensitive barometers of anti-Jewish trends in Christian society overall; do they reproduce the point of view of their socio-economic class; or do they faithfully transmit the biases of their patrons? Several essays in this volume can be read as posing careful solutions to this question. Pamela Patton's study of the scholar-king Alfonso X of Castile's (1252–84) famous collection of over 400 Marian miracle legends, the *Cantigas de Santa María*, is especially keen on what the discrepancies between text and image in illuminated manuscripts can tell us about diverging attitudes toward Jews among elites and other social classes. In her essay "Constructing the Criminal Jew in the *Cantigas de Santa María*: Theophilus's Magician in Text and Image," Patton shifts the framework of explanation from Alfonso's Jewry policy to the "ideological points of intersection between the king's presumed tolerance toward Jews and the increasingly hostile outlook of the society that surrounded him." Although conditions in Alfonso's Castile were favorable to Jewish economic and intellectual enterprise, the surviving Cantigas maunscripts are rife with anti-Jewish legends and demonizing portrayals. To explain this Patton takes up the legend of the vicar Theophilus, whom the Virgin's intervention rescues from an ill-advised pact with the Devil. Whereas the Cantigas poet gives Theophilus's advisor, a Jewish magician, little play in the text, the illustrators, as her analysis reveals, give the figure real narrative prominence. This visual rescripting of the part suggests that Alfonso's court artists were, in their own way, an avant-garde of anti-Jewish resentment (eventually Castillian Jewry would witness a sharp decline, and even Alfonso's own toleration policies would be rolled back). But they are also, Patton reminds us, representatives of their class. Her analysis rightly urges us to remain attentive to the flow of multiple streams of anti-Judaism in a single society at any given time.

Similar issues animate Vivian Mann's case study of a latter-day "Jewish magician" and the defamatory images made to commemorate his deeds and celebrate his death. "Images of 'Jud Süss' Oppenheimer, an Early Modern Jew" brings us into the eighteenth century and examines the role of printed broadsheets in constituting a Christian public for verbal-visual storytelling, an early form of tabloid journalism shot through with antisemitic tropes. Mann surveys a corpus of astonishing variety: printed images devoted to the life and times of Joseph Oppenheimer (1698/9–1738), known as "Jud Süss," who rose to exceptional prominence in the service of the Duke of Württemberg, Carl Alexander (r. 1733–37), only to be arrested immediately upon his patron's death, charged and hung from the gallows in Stuttgart on 4 February 1738. In addition to broadsheets commemorating the hanging, publicists fed the public appetite by issuing several kinds of defamatory portraits of Jud Süss, for example, allegorical images depicting Oppenheimer on the Wheel of Fortune. Unlike the broadsheets that introduced a wider public to the perversities and diabolical crimes of Jews during the first two centuries of printing,[34] however, several of the broadsheets studied by Mann offer relatively neutral portraits of the condemned man, even while the accompanying texts cast Oppenheimer as an enemy of the state and a menace to Christian morality. As other essays in this volume also reveal, *foregoing* antisemitic visual stereotypes could amount to a conscious choice by

[34] For recent developments in this important field, see Christine Mittlmeier, *Publizistik im Dienste antijüdischer Polemik: Spätmittelalterliche und frühneuzeitliche Flugschriften und Flugblätter zu Hostienschändungen* (Frankfurt am Main: Peter Lang, 2000); and Petra Schöner, *Judenbilder im deutschen Einblattdruck der Renaissance: Ein Beitrag zur Imagologie* (Baden-Baden: Valentin Koerner, 2002).

artists and publicists, a choice motivated, it would appear, by a close gauging of audience interests and a careful calibration of the rhetoric of the image.

As is well known, the phenomenon of the Court Jew was closely tied to the rise of the absolutist state, elevating a small number of prominent Jews far above the socio-economic status of their co-religionists. Oppenheimer's demise shows how, in the political atmosphere of the eighteenth-century state no less than in the Middle Ages, antisemitic canards could become channels for resentments of other kinds (Oppenheimer aroused popular hatred not only because of his wealthy lifestyle and penchant for Christian mistresses, but because he was a Jew serving a Catholic ruler of a largely Protestant duchy). Mann's essay is particularly valuable, therefore, in documenting how prints and print culture disseminated antisemitic tropes which were largely secular in nature. Animated by the discourse of *conspiracy* (a defining theme of both medieval and modern antisemitisms, one that has only recently begun to receive the attention it deserves),[35] these tropes ultimately triumphed over the outmoded "religious" accusations leveled against Jews—a sign, some would say, of the advent of a very different species of Jew-hatred, one peculiar to the modern world.

V

It is fascinating to note that, in the entire corpus of images devoted to Oppenheimer and his fate, only one presents him in a monstrous guise, bearing the stereotyped attributes of the Other. Rather than the hooked nose, bulging eyes or horns of traditional anti-Jewish caricature, however, the broadsheet's creator gives us a Jud Süss of ruddy complexion, short, curly hair, and shows him wearing conch shells—all in the manner of a Native American Indian. This appeared at a time when the "discovered" inhabitants of the New World were still widely regarded as one of the Ten Lost Tribes of Israel (a belief so entrenched by the late fifteenth century it prompted Columbus, anticipating a cultural encounter of historic significance, to bring along the converted Jew

[35] As in the important recent study by Johannes Heil, *Gottesfeinde—Menschenfeinde. Die Vorstellung von jüdischer Weltverschwörung (13.–16. Jh.)*, Antisemitismus: Geschichte und Strukturen, Bd. 3 (Essen, 2006). An English translation is in preparation.

Luis de Torres as an interpretor).[36] Juxtapose this line of representation with another broadsheet in the Jud Süss corpus, this one depicting Oppenheimer as the scheming Persian vizier Haman from the Book of Esther—thereby casting the Protestant population of Württemberg as the oppressed Children of Israel!—and we are breathing the atmosphere of a distinctively early modern ambivalence about the "Hebrew Truth" (*Hebraica veritas*) as a mediating force in both Christian self-understanding and in the precarious balance between tolerance, persecution and mission. This ambivalence is the common thread in the selections for our volume's third section.

Paul Kaplan's essay "Old Testament Heroes in Venetian High Renaissance Art" examines the various ways Old Testament personages—Moses, David, Solomon, Judith—were enlisted by the leaders, artists and propagandists of the Italian city-states as points of emulation and identification. With only a few notable exceptions, Old Testament subjects were relatively scarce in Venetian Quattrocento art (in contrast, Florentine and Mantuan artists produced a wide variety of images depicting biblical heroes and heroines). Kaplan shows how this situation changed with the onset of the Italian wars in 1494. In paintings from this era the Israelites wear "ancient" robes—mixtures of Venetian and Levantine (Ottoman and Greek) fashions, some of which may have suggested to viewers a connection with contemporary Jews. Among the artists venturing into this iconography, Giorgione emerges in Kaplan's account as one of the most innovative, though the author dismisses speculation that a Jewish or crypto-Jewish identity lead the artist to this fund of subjects. Giorgione's self-portrait as David posed with the monstrous enemy's severed head, a work known only through a fragment in Braunschweig, stands not only as one of the first independent self-portraits made by an Italian artist (c. 1508–10), but as arresting evidence for the penchant among patricians during wartime to identify with Old Testament heroes.

Should it surprise us that all of this transpired at a time of worsening conditions for the Jews of Venice, a community barred from living in the city since 1397 and readmitted only as refugees in the first decade of the sixteenth century, their existence hemmed in by mendicant preaching,

[36] See the fascinating discussion in David Katz, "The Phenomenon of Philo-Semitism," in *Christianity and Judaism: Papers Read at the 1991 Summer Meeting and the 1992 Winter Meeting of the Ecclesiastical History Society*, ed. Diane Wood (Oxford: Blackwell, 1992), 327–61, at 338.

attempts at ghettoization, and general ill-will? Ideological heirs to the ancient claim that God's covenant with his chosen people had passed to the Christian Church, the *verus Israel*, leaving the Synagogue reprobate and cursed, Venetians clung to the appropriated mantle of the "chosen people" while real Jews in their midst endured a benighted existence. And yet this is not a story of triumphalism pure and simple, for as Kaplan's essay shows, despite the one-sided political relationship in the city at the time, the Christian appropriation of Old Testament models in Venice did not go uncontested. As paradigms of virtue the same biblical figures resonated loudly in Venetian *Jewish* art as well as its hegemonic counterpart. Future researchers will want to examine the extent to which competing interpretations of such paradigms are better understood as components of a Jewish-Christian *dialogue*, and as a shared set of symbols, rather than fixtures in a common strategy of mutual negation.

My own contribution to the volume, "Cleansing the Temple: The Munich Gruftkirche as a Converted Synagogue," represents a case study in another kind of Jewish-Christian encounter, one in which the "Hebrew Truth" assumes a less familiar form: the adaptive reuse of synagogues (and the sites of destroyed synagogues) for Christian chapels and churches, in particular those dedicated to the Virgin Mary. As in the famous pilgrimage to the *Schöne Maria* of Regensburg (1519), it was a territorial expulsion (this one in 1442) that set the stage for the creation of the Munich "Gruftkapelle" from that city's only recorded medieval synagogue. I argue that each historical moment in the church's 350-year career, from its initial conversion and establishment as a public pilgrimage shrine, through its Counter-Reformation renewal, finally to its historicization in the mid-eighteenth century, when a kind of cult archaeology allowed for the re-identification of the site as a former place of Jewish sacrileges—each of these moments was marked not only by changes to the physical fabric of the building, but by a shifting constellation of cult imagery and devotionalia, legend motifs and propagandistic claims. The picture that emerges of clerical and popular attitudes toward the Jewish "prehistory" of the building is anything but homogenous or exclusively negative. Viewing the legends that accrued around the shrine critically, as ciphers of a kind of Christian exegesis of the site itself, reveals a range of cultic and ethnographic preoccupations with Jewish presence, Jewish rites, and Jewish "sacred space"—Christian fictions into which cult planners could ask pilgrims to enter imaginatively.

Annette Weber's essay, "New Attitudes towards Jews in the Era of Reformation and Counter-Reformation: The Patronage of Bishop Julius Echter von Mespelbrunn," likewise considers the projection of anti-Judaism into the interlocking spheres of Christian devotionalism, pilgrimage, and the shaping of a sanctified landscape. Focused on the period preceding the Thirty Years War, Weber considers the policies of the powerful prince-bishop of Würzburg, Julius Echter von Mespelbrunn (1573–1617), who made the retrofitting of medieval pilgrimage shrines the linchpin of an aggressive policy of Catholic renewal in his episcopal territory (*Hochstift*). Prominent among these shrines were places associated with fabulous Jewish sacrileges against the sacramental body of Christ—so-called "host-desecration churches" (*Hostienfrevelkirchen*)—some traceable back to the fourteenth and fifteenth centuries. Revitalization efforts aimed at pilgrimages such as Röttingen on the Tauber (embarkation point for the horrific "Rintfleisch" pogroms that swept Franconia in 1298), or Marian shrines such Maria Buchen (where the devout worshipped a wonder-working image of the Pietà allegedly stabbed by a Jew), became a cornerstone of pastoral renewal under Echter, for they drew all classes within Christian society into a closely administered annual calendar of local processions.

Weber's study helps us see the continuities, but moreso the discontinuities, in the maintenance of communal memory in places where episodes of Christian violence were turned on their heads and refashioned as memories of Jewish sacrileges. Where the propagandistic requirements of cult are at issue, the recrudescence of memory goes hand in the hand with the appropriation of sacred space, as if filling a void created by an enforced Jewish absence. To put it another way: just as, in the Augustinian version of *Adversus Judaeos* theology, the world-order of Christendom required, as a testament to its truth, a Jewish presence, but only so long as the living forms it took were nothing but frozen anachronisms—so too did a type of Christian conception of sacred space receive its validation from a dead presence that was nothing more, but also nothing less, than a reification of Jewish absence. Once holy places as well as holy texts were safely delivered into Christian hands; once a scholarship pursuant of a "Hebrew Truth" freed itself from dependence on actual Jewish interlocutors; once these reifications took hold, an anti-Judaism rooted in the soil no longer needed real Jews as living witnesses, not even as actual victims.[37]

Elsewhere in early seventeenth-century Europe, Christian Hebraism pursued its ambivalent embrace of whatever thriving, post-biblical Jewish culture it could find. Shalom Sabar's essay, "Between Calvinists and Jews: Hebrew Script in Rembrandt's Art," examines the evolution of Rembrandt van Rijn's (1606–1669) incorporation of Hebrew words and passages into this paintings, and reveals a new stage in the Christian artist's point of view vis-à-vis biblical history, Judaism, and contemporary Jewish culture. Unlike most of his late medieval—and many of his Renaissance—predecessors, who inserted Hebrew or pseudo-Hebrew scripts into their pictures as decorative elements to conjure up the exotic world of the ancient Levant, or to evoke the "secret language of the Jews," Rembrandt's use of Hebrew inscriptions was genuinely informed by the humanist rediscovery and reevaluation of Hebrew, and designed to imbue his works with a measure of "historical authenticity." Early in his career the great Dutch artist's effort to incorporate his own observations of Jewish life tended to be superficial, but after he moved to Amsterdam in 1632 this superficiality vanished; the artist's life and activities were, in fact, centered upon the "Breestrat" (the Jews' street) in close proximity to the Sephardic community's leading families and intellectuals. This development culiminates in Rembrandt's most sophisticated use of Hebrew in *Moses Holding the Tablets of the Law* (1659). Here the peculiar ordering of the Decalogue is unlike the ones favored solely by Jews or solely by Protestants (Lutherans or Calvinists) in Rembrandt's time. Rather, as Sabar deduces, the peculiar order expresses Rembrandt's own fusion of Calvinist and Jewish sources, imbued with a personal feeling for the tragic aspect of the theme.

Shalom Sabar's essay is a fitting capstone to this collection, I believe, for his conclusions open onto a crucial set of questions: to what degree had the Hebraism of Rembrandt's time—equal parts biblical scholarship, ethnographic curiosity and popular eschatology—transcended the medieval paradigm that saw Judaism as a religion intrinsically hostile

---

[37] The question of how anti-Judaism and antisemitism continue to operate under social conditions in which Jews are marginally invisible has been more germane to debates about the trope of "the Jew" in contemporary German art, literature and thought; on this issue, see Sander L. Gilman and Steven T. Katz, "Introduction," in Gilman and Katz, eds., *Antisemitism in Times of Crisis* (as cited above), 1–19, at 4. One hopes that historians of pre-modern culture will contribute more to exploring this question of an "antisemitism without Jews."

to Christianity? Was Rembrandt's art progressive in this regard? Can it be called *philosemitic*? Was it aimed, ultimately, at the dispensationalist dream of a final ingathering of the Ten Lost Tribes and the conversion of the Jews at the Second Coming? Or can we glimpse in it the murmurings of an enlightened culture of toleration and ecumenicism? The editor and contributors of this entire volume sincerely look forward to answers posed, and new questions asked, by future researchers and commentators.

PART I

STAGES OF CONVERSION

CHAPTER ONE

'FAIR AND FRIENDLY, SWEET AND BEAUTIFUL': HOPES FOR JEWISH CONVERSION IN SYNAGOGA'S SONG OF SONGS IMAGERY[1]

Elizabeth Monroe

The iconography of Ecclesia and Synagoga is perhaps best known through Crucifixion scenes that allude to the Christian Church's birth on earth and Judaism's demise. Medieval artists in the Latin West frequently juxtaposed the two personifications at the base of the cross according to the concept, famously articulated by Augustine, that the New Law reveals and perfects what the Old Law conceals: "For what does the term Old Covenant imply but the concealing of the New? And what does the term New Covenant imply but the revealing of the Old?"[2] Christ's sacrificial death inaugurates a New Law, often symbolized by Ecclesia's collecting of Christ's blood in her chalice in an enactment of the Eucharist. At this same moment Synagoga, the embodiment of God's Old Covenant with the Jews, is rendered obsolete. The Crucifixion miniature from a luxurious gospel book commissioned by duke Henry the Lion of Saxony (d. 1195) and his wife Matilda (d. 1189), for example, typifies this antithetical relationship.[3] Underneath the Flagellation, which occupies the folio's upper zone, Ecclesia, in a sumptuous

---

[1] This paper has profited from the suggestions of Christopher Heuer, Carolyn Malone and Diane Reilly, who critiqued earlier drafts. I dedicate this essay to Helen, *dilecta mea*, in honor of her third birthday.

[2] "Quid est enim quod dicitur testamentum vetus nisi novi occultatio? Et quid est aliud quod dicitur novum nisi veteris revelatio?" *De civitate Dei. Libri XI–XXII* (Corpus Christianorum Series Latina 48), ed. B. Dombart and A. Kalb (Turnhout, 1955), 16.26, 531.

[3] This folio is one of eight, full-page miniatures that accompany the text of John's Gospel, the last book in the manuscript, and lead up to the Easter celebration. For a facsimile edition, see *Evangeliarium Heinrici Leonis: autorisiertes vollständiges Faksimile des Codex Guelf. 105 Noviss. 2° der Herzog August Bibliothek, Wolfenbüttel, und zugleich CLM 30055 der Bayerischen Staatsbibliothek, München* (Frankfurt, 1988). Also see Sotheby Parke and Bernet & Co., *The Gospels of Henry the Lion.* Sales cat. London, December 6, 1983 (with an analysis by Christopher de Hamel); and Elisabeth Klemm, *Das Evangeliar Heinrichs des Löwen* (Frankfurt am Main, 1988).

gown, is crowned as a queen and stands at the foot of the cross (fig. 1). With her outstretched hands reverently covered, she lifts a chalice to catch the blood pouring from Christ's wound. Synagoga, however, on Christ's left, remains obdurate, refusing to acknowledge him as Savior and turning away from the cross. The crown that tumbles from her head and her upside-down banner testify to her status as Ecclesia's forerunner and to her repudiation under the New Law. In addition, Synagoga appears to curse Christ; inscribed on the banderole that she unfurls in her left hand is the malediction, "Cursed is everyone that hangeth on a tree" (Gal. 3:13).[4] In his Letter to the Galatians, Paul argues that Christ, by allowing himself to die in a cursed manner (Deut. 21:22–23), redeems the faithful from that same curse. Read strictly at face value, however, the Galatians inscription would probably be seen as an offensive, anti-Christian imprecation and a potent sign of Synagoga's intransigence to the Christian message. This verse seems to situate her squarely within the *contra Judaeos* literary tradition, as though she has been given the text to mark her as both an embodiment of and a mouthpiece for Jewish disbelief and blasphemy.[5] That Synagoga is the only figure in the miniature's central zone who carries a text scroll makes her execration all the more arresting. Indeed, one viewer of this page was so incensed by her image that he scratched away at her mouth, as though to deny her a voice in this disputation and perhaps to silence her for eternity.

On the facing page, however, Synagoga appears a second time in a surprisingly different manner (fig. 2). Here she and Ecclesia express their mutual love for Christ. From corner medallions at the bottom of the folio, the two women converse with one another across the miniature, raising their left hands and holding scrolls clearly inscribed with verses from the Old Testament nuptial poem, the Song of Songs. Ecclesia laments to Synagoga: "On my bed through the nights I sought him

---

[4] *Maledictus omnis qui pendet in ligno.*

[5] Deut. 21:22–23 was crucial polemical evidence for both Christian and Jewish disputants; the former used the verse to assert the "curse" ancient Jews put on Jesus at the Crucifixion, and the latter to deny Christ as Messiah. I am grateful to Mitchell Merback for this observation. For an overview of Christian polemical literature, see Bernhard Blumenkranz, *Les auteurs chrétiens-latins du moyen âge sur les juifs et le judaïsme* (Paris, 1963); and Heinz Schreckenberg, *Der christlichen Adversus-Judaeos-Texte (11.–13. Jh.) mit einer Ikonographie des Judenthemas* (Frankfurt am Main, 1991). For Jewish anti-Christian polemics, see Robert Chazan, *Fashioning Jewish Identity in Medieval Western Christendom* (New York, 2004).

whom my soul loves" (3:1).[6] In reply, Synagoga not only praises Ecclesia's beauty but also clearly expresses her willingness to join the Bridegroom, Christ: "Where is your beloved gone, O fairest of women?...and we will seek him with you" (5:17).[7] Because she yearns for Christ in this illumination, Synagoga merits a crown, wears similarly rich garments as Ecclesia and lacks any of the degrading attributes so common in Crucifixion imagery, such as an upside down banner, fallen crown or broken tablets of the Law. Significantly, then, Synagoga appears on this page not so much as Ecclesia's foil (as she is on the facing page at the Crucifixion) as her honored predecessor and mirror image. In fact, were it not for their identifying inscriptions (*Ecclesia Sponsa* and *Synagoga*), one would have difficulty distinguishing between the two personifications.

For those familiar with Ecclesia and Synagoga's iconography, few elements of Synagoga's depiction in the Crucifixion illumination described above will seem extraordinary. Postwar scholars of Synagoga's imagery have tended to focus on Crucifixion iconography in order to demonstrate the ways ecclesiastical officials positioned the Jews as a humiliated out-group, often interpreting such depictions against the backdrop of medieval Jewish history. Within one year of each other, for example, Wolfgang Seiferth and Bernhard Blumenkranz pointed to the Crusades (particularly the First Crusade of 1096) as both initiating and providing an outlet for widespread anti-Jewish enmity.[8] In an overview of Ecclesia and Synagoga's iconography, Seiferth analyzed several examples in which the two women symbolized the harmony between the Old and New Testaments (*Concordia Veteris et Novi Testamenti*), but largely ignored Song of Songs contexts.[9] Blumenkranz, meanwhile, investigated depictions of Jews to demonstrate the pervasiveness of their denigration in Christian art. Though he briefly touched upon settings other than the Crucifixion, Blumenkranz focused upon Synagoga as Ecclesia's foil, obsolete and spiritually bankrupt. This line of inquiry has proven

[6] *In lectulo meo per noctem quesivi quem diligit anima mea.*

[7] *Quo abiit dilectus tuus o pulcherrima mulier et queremus eum tecum.*

[8] Wolfgang Seiferth, *Synagoge und Kirche im Mittelalter* (Munich, 1964), esp. chap. 7; and Bernhard Blumenkranz, *Juden und Judentum in der mittelalterlichen Kunst* (Stuttgart, 1965), 57, as well as "Géographie historique d'un thème de l'iconographie religieuse: les representations de *Synagoga* en France," in *Mélanges offerts à René Crozet l'occasion de son soixante-dixième anniversaire*, ed. Pierre Gallais and Yves-Jean Riou, vol. 2 (Poitiers, 1966), 1143. For a re-evaluation of the impact of the 1096 pogroms on Ashkenazic Jews, see: Robert Chazan, *European Jewry and the First Crusade* (Los Angeles, 1987).

[9] Seiferth, *Synagoge und Kirche*, esp. chap. 2.

especially enduring in the past decades, as evinced by a multitude of studies that focus mainly upon Synagoga's rejection.[10] Interestingly, some of these have interpreted what might now be called "standard" motifs signifying Synagoga's denigration (blindfolded and turning away from Christ while holding a broken banner and upside down tablets of the Law) within an eschatological framework of redemption. In discussions of Strasbourg cathedral's south portal, for instance, Adolf Weis and Otto von Simson situate Synagoga as Christ's first Bride, on the verge of reuniting with him as Bridegroom, despite the fact that she retains attributes of blindness, error and defeat.[11] More recently, Sara Lipton has recognized the possibility of Synagoga's reconciliation with the Christian faith as portrayed in a wide variety of narrative contexts in the thirteenth-century *Bible moralisée*.[12]

Still, there have been no significant challenges to the traditional assumptions that Ecclesia and Synagoga are antithetical figures. One result is that Synagoga's image today is more often than not seen as emblematic of defamed medieval Jewry. Many scholars, ignoring the multiple roles Synagoga plays within salvation history, assume that her image necessarily signaled degradation to medieval viewers. Certainly, at the Crucifixion she embodies the Jews as a people, who refuse to accept Christ as Messiah; in some particularly harsh depictions she also bears the guilt of those who provoked his death. Although medieval

[10] For instance, Marie-Louise Thérel, "L'Origine du thème de la 'Synagogue répudiée,'" *Scriptorium* 25 (1971): 285–89; Herbert Jochum, *Ecclesia und Synagoga: Das Judentum in der christlichen Kunst. Ausstellungs Katalog, Alte Synagoge Essen, Regionalgeschichtliches Museum Saärbrucken* (Essen, 1993); Heinz Schreckenberg, *The Jews in Christian Art: An Illustrated History*, trans. John Bowden (New York, 1996); Ruth Mellinkoff, *Outcasts: Signs of Otherness in Northern European Art of the Late Middle Ages*. 2 vols. (Los Angeles, 1999); and Achim Timmerman, "The Avenging Crucifix: Some Observations on the Iconography of the Living Cross," *Gesta* 40 (2001): 141–60.

[11] Adolf Weis, "Die 'Synagoge' am Münster zu Strassburg," *Das Münster: Zeitschrift für christliche Kunst und Kunstwissenschaft* 1 (1947): 65–80; and Otto von Simson, "Le programme sculptural du transept méridional," *Von der Macht des Bildes in Mittelalter: Gesammelte Aufsätze zur Kunst des Mittelalters*, ed. Reiner Haussherr (Berlin, 1993), 77–99. Both essays have added considerably to our understanding of Synagoga within Song of Songs exegesis, although I find Weis's interpretation more compelling. Also see Bernd Nicolai, "Orders in Stone: Social Reality and Artistic Approach. The Case of Strasbourg South Portal," *Gesta* 41 (2002): 111–128.

[12] "The Temple is My Body: Gender, Carnality, and Synagoga in the *Bible Moralisée*," in *Imagining the Self, Imagining the Other: Visual Representation and Jewish-Christian Dynamics in the Middle Ages and Early Modern Period*, ed. Eva Frojmovic (Boston, 2002), 129–63. Notably, Lipton's study is one of the first to consider gendered motifs in Synagoga's depictions with any depth, although more work in this area is surely needed.

artists frequently denigrated her in this context in precisely this way, Christians were also capable of conceiving other, equally important roles for Synagoga. One of these was to signal the Jews' conversion and union with the Church at the End of time. In this essay, I explore this other role and posit an alternative reading to the more common understanding of Synagoga as belittled at the Crucifixion. In certain contexts, such as the Old Testament nuptial poem, the Song of Songs, Synagoga carries "positive" connotations, albeit from a Christian point of view. During the twelfth century, at the same time that Christian anti-Jewish polemical literature proliferated and manifested increasing viciousness, artists, commentators and dramatists seem to have been particularly responsive to the idea of Jewish conversion and reconciliation with the Christian majority. This essay will mine both visual and textual evidence (including commentaries, drama and sermons) for high medieval conceptions of Synagoga as Christ's Bride in order to highlight a new emphasis on the Jews' conversion in Christian art.

Synagoga in the Song of Songs: Exegetical and Pictorial Traditions

Pauline thought, fundamental to all subsequent Christian thinking on Judaism's place within the world, accorded the Jews an integral function within God's divine plan. The Apostle's notably ambivalent position recognized the Jews' status as original custodians of sacred Scripture, even though their adherence to the letter and not the spirit of the Law led them to error and rejection of Christ as Savior, as well as their supercession by Christians as God's new elect.[13] Concomitant with this purpose as holders of the first Covenant was the expectation that the Jews would ultimately regain God's favor; at the end of time, a remnant will convert and "all Israel should be saved" (Rom. 11:26).[14] Patristic authors employed imagery from the Old Testament

---

[13] See the general discussions of Paul's thinking on the Jews in Miriam Taylor, *Anti-Judaism and Early Christian Identity: A Critique of the Scholarly Consensus* (New York, 1995); and A. Andrew Das, *Paul and the Jews* (Peabody, Mass., 2003).

[14] Paul implies that part of God's plan is for the Israelites to become "enemies" of the Christian faith so that they can aid the conversion of the Gentiles (Rom. 11:11–12); Heikki Räisänen, "Paul, God, and Israel: Romans 9–11 in Recent Research," in *The Social World of Formative Christianity and Judaism: Essays in Tribute to Howard Clark Kee*, ed. Jacob Neusner, Ernest Frerichs, Peder Borgen and Richard Horsley (Philadelphia, 1988), 178–206. Put another way, the enormity of their error increases the enormity

nuptial poem, the Song of Songs, to elaborate on these ideas of Jewish conversion. Usually grouped in the Bible with the Wisdom books and also known as the Song of Solomon, since the king was its presumed author, the Song of Songs reads as a dialogue between at least two lovers, the Bride (*Sponsa*) and the Bridegroom (*Sponsus*). Capitalizing on the Song's dramatic appeal, patristic commentators copied its text with rubrics that defined the different voices as *dramatis personae*, and many commentaries read as a passionate dialogue. The first verse, "Let him kiss me with the kisses of his mouth" (Osculetur me osculo oris sui), typifies the sensuousness of the Song's lyrics, and yet biblical commentators long considered the poem to glorify divine, not earthly, love. Rabbinical scholars, for instance, interpreted the Bride as Israel and the Bridegroom as Yahweh and understood the poem as expressing God's love for Israel.[15] Medieval Christians, however, following the tradition established by Origen (d. c. 254), commonly reinterpreted the Song of Songs as an allegory of the mystical marriage between Christ and the Christian soul, or the Church, Ecclesia.[16] Hence it is not surprising that Christ and Ecclesia often figure as the *Sponsus* and *Sponsa* in eleventh- and twelfth-century Song of Songs illuminations (fig. 3).

Many theologians also associated Synagoga with particular passages of the Song, usually in the context of emphasizing a familial relationship between Ecclesia and Synagoga as Christ's Brides. Origen, in his *Homilies* on the Song, for instance, conceives of Ecclesia and Synagoga as sisters and Christ as the son of Synagoga.[17] In the late fourth to early fifth century Ambrose, one of the earliest commentators to expand Synagoga's role in the drama, gives her a voice as interlocutor. Thus, Synagoga speaks verses 1:4–5 of the Song: "I am black but beauti-

---

of the importance of their salvation; see Jeremy Cohen, *Living Letters of the Law: Ideas of the Jew in Medieval Christianity* (Los Angeles, 1999), 8.

[15] For an introduction to the Song of Songs in the Hebraic tradition, see Gerson D. Cohen, "The Song of Songs and the Jewish Religious Mentality," in *Studies in the Variety of Rabbinic Cultures*, ed. Gerson D. Cohen (New York, 1991), 3–17; and Elliot R. Wolfson, "Asceticism and Eroticism in Medieval Jewish Exegesis," in *With Reverence for the Word: Medieval Scriptural Exegesis in Judaism, Christianity and Islam*, ed. J. D. McAuliffe et al. (Oxford, 2003), 92–118.

[16] Two essential starting points for any study of the Song of Songs in the Middle Ages are Friedrich Ohly, *Hohelied-Studien: Grundzüge einer Geschichte der Hoheliedauslegung des Abendlandes, bis um 1200* (Wiesbaden, 1958); and Helmut Riedlinger, *Die Markellosigkeit der Kirche in den Lateinischen Hoheliedkommentaren des Mittelalters* (Münster, 1958).

[17] *The Song of Songs: Commentary and Homilies* (Ancient Christian Writers Series 26), trans. R. P. Lawson (New York, 1957), 287.

ful daughters of Jerusalem"; meaning that she is "darkened" by her disbelief and error, yet beautiful through the law and because she will eventually rejoin the faith.[18] Indeed, many theologians explicitly predict Synagoga's conversion and assimilation into the Christian faith when discussing her in Song of Songs contexts. The Carolingian exegete Haimo of Auxerre (d. 875), whose *Commentarium in Cantica Canticorum* remained one of the most popular commentaries in the medieval period, expands upon the motifs of harmony and love and meditates upon the reconciliation between Synagoga and Christ/Ecclesia as allegorically predictive of Judaism's assimilation into Christianity. In regards to verse 3:4 ("I held him nor will I let go, until I lead him into the house of my mother"), Haimo conceives of Synagoga as Ecclesia's "spiritual mother," who will be led into the Christian fold at the end of time:

> That is, until I proclaim him above Synagoga, who is my mother spiritually, and lead her also into the faith. This will happen on the day of judgment, when (as the Apostle says) "the fullness of the people will have entered, and then all of Israel will be saved." Therefore the Church promises itself so much concerning the love of its bridegroom that it even believes that it is able to convert Synagoga.[19]

Moreover, Haimo associates Synagoga with the last verses of Songs 6: "return return, Sulamite... that we may behold you," and indeed it became common to interpret the Sulamite (alternatively, Sunamite) woman with the Synagogue, Bride of the Old Alliance. Haimo, for instance, glosses verse 6:12 so that it is clearly Ecclesia who speaks to Synagoga, exhorting her to leave hatred for love, to abandon disbelief and to return to God's grace.[20]

Although many patristic theologians envisioned Synagoga's eventual conversion and assimilation with Christ and the Church in their Song of Songs commentaries, the earliest artists to include Synagoga in their illustrations of the poem reproduce the defamatory imagery commonly found in Crucifixion scenes. In late-eleventh and early twelfth-century

---

[18] "Fusca per incredulitatem, decora per legem: fusca per lapsum, decora quia dilexit me sol, et prior facta sum congregatio Dei." *Commentarius in Canticum Canticorum*, PL 15, col. 1956.

[19] "Hoc est, donec illum Synagogae, quae est mater mea spiritualiter, praedicem, et eam quoque ad ejus fidem perducem. Hoc fiet in die judicii, quando (ut ait Apostolos) 'plentitudo gentium introierit, tunc omnis Israel salvus fiet.' Tantum ergo sibi de charitate sponsi sui Ecclesia promittit, ut etiam se credat Synagogam posse convertere." PL 117, col. 310.

[20] PL 117, col. 341.

manuscripts, for example, Synagoga walks away from Christ and Ecclesia—recalling the design of Carolingian ivories in which she at once refuses to participate in the historic moment of Christ's death on the cross yet turns her head to witness it—or even removes her own crown to signal her defeat by Ecclesia.[21] The artist of the *Bible of Stephen Harding* (c. 1109) also conceived of Ecclesia and Synagoga as adversarial brides, although in the initial it is Christ himself who rejects Synagoga (fig. 4).[22] Enthroned in the center of the *O* of the Songs' first line, Christ crowns Ecclesia while shoving away Synagoga, who is hunched over as though collapsing. This miniature represents the earliest surviving example in the West in which violence is enacted against Synagoga, an important watershed that I have explored more fully elsewhere.[23] It must be emphasized here, however, that this conception of Ecclesia and Synagoga as rival brides is not found in the literal, biblical text of the Songs. The nuptial poem neither explicitly refers to bridal discord nor mentions Synagoga at all. Early Christian commentators were the first to include her within their allegorical interpretations of the Song, while later exegetes gave her a more distinct voice by including her in rubrics identifying the speakers.

Despite the design of these two early initials, it is relatively uncommon to see Synagoga defeated or rejected in Song of Songs contexts. During the twelfth century, when Song of Songs imagery became increasingly popular in a variety of media (illustrated Bibles, commentaries, public sculpture) artists more frequently emphasize Synagoga's conversion and acceptance by Christ, as in Henry the Lion and Matilda's *Gospels*. Given that the royal couple probably commissioned their manuscript soon after their marriage in 1168, it is not surprising that images referencing the

---

[21] *Bible of Saint Bénigne* (Dijon, Bibliothèque Municipale, 2, fol. 301r), repr. in Marie-Louise Thérel, *Le triomphe de la Vierge-Église: à l'origine du décor du portail occidental de Notre-Dame de Senlis: sources historiques, littéraires et iconographiques* (Paris, 1984), 191; and Cambridge, Trinity College, MS. B. 1. 16, fol. 173r, repr. in Michael Gullick, "Manuscrits et copistes Normands en Angleterre (XIe–XIIe siècles)," in *Manuscrits et enluminures dans le monde normand (X^{e}–XVe siècles). Colloque de Cerisy-la-Salle, Octobre 1995*, ed. Pierre Bouet and Monique Dosdat (Caen, 1999), 90.

[22] Significantly, the manuscript's scribe changed the text's rubrics, so that Synagoga is the speaker of verse 1:5 ("My mother's sons fought against me"), rather than Ecclesia, as is standard in this particular variant. Hence, as Diane J. Reilly notes, both the illuminator and the scribe underscore Synagoga's anguish. "Picturing the Monastic Drama: Romanesque Bible Illustrations of the Song of Songs," *Word and Image* 17 (2001): 6–7.

[23] Elizabeth Monroe, "Images of Synagoga as Christian Discourse (1000–1215)," Ph.D. diss. (University of Southern California, 2003), esp. chap. 3.

Song of Songs, a passionate nuptial poem, feature prominently in its pages. The *Sponsus* and *Sponsa* address each other in many of its miniatures, but fol. 171r (fig. 2) is the only one to include two Brides (rather than the Bride and Bridegroom) and to label them *Ecclesia Sponsa* and *Synagoga*. Notably, in all other instances the more generic designations *Sponsa* and *Sponsus* appear in their frames.[24] The manuscript's designer, therefore, consciously honed the Brides' identities for this particular illumination, which focuses on events in the life of Mary Magdalene, the former sinner who became one of Christ's most devoted followers.[25] The page's central narrative commences in the lower right, where Mary, crying because she cannot find Christ, implores two angels seated on the empty tomb to divulge to her where his body has been taken (John 20:15 and 20:13). Next, Christ himself appears to the kneeling Magdalene and instructs her to announce to the Apostles that he has risen and will ascend to his Father (John 20:17). This Mary does in the illumination's upper register, underneath the kings David and Solomon, who address each other with scrolls that both amplify the joyousness of the Resurrection and advocate steadfast devotion to Christ.[26] Because this entire folio commemorates his Resurrection, it would be appropriate for the Easter season when his rebirth through death, and hence mankind's salvation, is celebrated. Therefore, by positioning Ecclesia and Synagoga as Brides from the Song of Songs in the corner medallions, the designer of this folio reinforced Mary Magdalene's fervent pursuit of Christ, a context quite different from the Crucifixion.

The association of Mary Magdalene with the Church, Ecclesia, as well as the Bride from the Song of Songs was not unusual in Christian exegesis. Gregory the Great (d. 604) initiated a tendency to interpret the *Sponsa* as a prefiguration of the Magdalene, specifically in reference to verse 3:1, the same verse that was inscribed on Ecclesia's scroll

[24] The verses in which the Bride and Bridegroom "speak" to each other throughout the manuscript seem neither to have been arranged in any order, nor reflect the tenor of a single commentary. Instead, they frequently highlight the illumination's central narrative(s).

[25] Two solid introductions to the Magdalene's identity and significance within the Christian West are Ingrid Maisch, *Between Contempt and Veneration. Mary Magdalene: The Image of a Woman Through the Centuries*, trans. Linda Maloney (Collegeville, Minn., 1998), 30–42; and Katherine Jansen, *The Making of the Magdalen: Preaching and Popular Devotion in the Later Middle Ages* (Princeton, 2000).

[26] David holds a verse from Psalm 44:2 (*Eructavit cor meum verbum bonum*) that plays off of Mary Magdalene's good news to report to the disciples, while Solomon admonishes: *Invenientur ab his qui non temptant eum* (Wisd. of Sol. 1:2).

in Henry's *Gospels*.[27] Just as the *Sponsa* seeks the one whom her soul loves, Mary Magdalene, an embodiment of the Church, searched for Christ at his empty tomb. Moreover, the ancient ecclesiological tradition associated Mary, sister of Lazarus, with the Church and Martha with the Synagogue. In a Song of Songs commentary predating that of Origen, Hippolytus (d. c. 235) considered the Bride who seeks her beloved in verse 3:1 as a prefiguration of both Mary and Martha; for him these two women represent the Synagogue, Bride of the Old Testament, who announces to the Apostles the news of Christ's Resurrection.[28] The themes of penitence and conversion, as well as the repetition of female imagery in Henry and Matilda's manuscript, are certainly exciting avenues for further research. Important to emphasize in this discussion, however, is that Synagoga longs for Christ after his Resurrection. This expectation that the Jews would convert toward the end of days remained prevalent in twelfth-century theology. The Benedictine scholar Honorius Augustodunensis, for instance, predicted that Synagoga would eventually receive Christian salvation. Specifically in reference to Song of Songs 5:17 (the same verse Synagoga speaks in Henry's *Gospels*), Honorius asserts that when Christ departs from his bodily incarnation and ascends in his spiritual form, "Synagoga will come to Ecclesia through grace."[29] The designer of Henry and Matilda's manuscript, therefore, represents Synagoga differently on facing folios because in each image her theological context is different. At the Crucifixion, the birth of the Church on earth, Ecclesia supersedes Synagoga, who rejects Christ. At the Resurrection, however, when Christ defeats death, Synagoga abandons disbelief and joins Ecclesia.

[27] Gregory the Great, *XL Homilarum in Evangelia libri duo, Homilia XXV*, PL 76, cols. 1189–90.

[28] *Traités d'Hippolyte sur David et Goliath, sur le Cantique des cantiques et sur l'Antichrist* (Corpus Scriptorum Christianorum Orientalium, Scriptores Iberici 264), trans. Gérard Garitte (Leuven, 1965), 43–44. Also see Giles Constable, "The Interpretation of Mary and Martha," *Three Studies in Medieval Religious and Social Thought* (Cambridge, 1995), 15–16, 45.

[29] "Christus corporaliter abiit, cum videntibus discipulis coelos ascendit...cum de Synagoga in Ecclesiam per gratiam venit." *Expositio in Cantica Canticorum*. PL 172, col. 445. For general discussions of Honorius's work on the Song, see Ohly, *Hohelied-Studien*, 251–62; Valerie I. J. Flint, "The Commentaries of Honorius Augustodunensis on the Song of Songs," in *Ideas in the Medieval West: Texts and Their Contexts* (London, 1988), 196–211; and by the same author (briefly), in *Honorius Augustodunensis of Regensburg*. Authors of the Middle Ages 6 (London, 1995), 40–42 and 52–53.

When interpreting Synagoga's imagery, it is therefore crucial that modern viewers remain as sensitive to context as were medieval artists.

Synagoga as Sulamite, Bride of the Old Alliance

Another figure to embody Christian hopes for Jewish conversion was that of the Sulamite woman addressed in the Song of Songs (6:12). As noted above, many commentators from Bede onward considered the Sulamite as representative of the primitive Church and hence associated her with Synagoga. Although she was once mired in error for rejecting Christ, the Sulamite, Bride of the Old Alliance, would eventually acknowledge him as Savior and join the community of the faithful.[30] Here again, the ideas of Honorius Augustodunensis are particularly relevant since he conflates the Sulamite with the Synagogue in both of his widely copied Song of Songs commentaries, the *Sigillum beatae Mariae* of c. 1100 and the *Expositio in Cantica canticorum* of c. 1135. In the *Sigillum* Honorius interprets the Song as relating primarily to the Virgin Mary and explicates the lessons for the Feast of her Assumption for a clerical audience.[31] Here the Sulamite is representative of the penitent Church, that which is to be converted from the Jews (poenitentis Ecclesiae, quandoque de Judaeis convertende). Toward the *Sigillum*'s conclusion, the Sulamite laments to the Virgin that her "zeal for the law" has caused her to stray from the true faith, and in response the Virgin urges her to return from captivity through hope and faith in Christ.[32] When he later returned to the Song of Songs, Honorius this time expounded upon the theme of Christ's marriage to his Church and hardly mentions the Virgin. Instead, the *Expositio* describes four ages through which Christ and his Church must pass: *ante legem* (before the Law is given to Moses), *sub lege* (under the Law), *sub gratia* (under Christian grace), and *sub antichristo* (under Antichrist prior to the final

---

[30] For instance, Bede, *In Cantica Canticorum libri VI*. CCSL 119B, ed. D. Hurst (Turnhout, 1983), 314–315; and Robert of Tombelaine (d. c. 1090), *Commentariorum in Cantica Canticorum*. PL 79 (as Gregory the Great), col. 533.

[31] PL 172, cols. 495–518, translated by Amelia Carr as *The Seal of Blessed Mary*, Peregrina Translation Series 18 (Toronto, 1991).

[32] PL 172, col. 512, as cited by Rachel Fulton, *From Judgment to Passion: Devotion to Christ and the Virgin Mary, 800–1200* (New York, 2002), 279.

redemption).[33] Similarly, Christ's Bride appears in four manifestations, each illustrative of the different phases of salvation history; from the four corners of the earth they travel to greet Christ the Bridegroom in Jerusalem. The Sunamite, representative of the age under grace (*sub gratia*), arrives from the west in the Quadriga of Aminidab, the cart used to transport the Ark of the Covenant. Like Synagoga, she was once captive of the devil and despised but will eventually convert at the end of days (*in fine mundi*).[34] Hence the Sunamite is an exultant figure in illuminations of the *Expositio* who carries Ecclesia's victory banner in the company of the four Evangelists (fig. 5).[35] The Jews following her, marked with pointed hats and labeled *Iudei*, are those among her people who have already suffered martyrdom for their new-found belief during Antichrist's reign and hence accentuate the Sunamite's eventual conversion.[36]

The illuminator of one copy of Honorius's *Expositio* and *Sigillum* (Munich, Bayerische Staatsbibliothek, Clm. 4550) seems to have been particularly sensitive to the exegete's conflation of the Sunamite with Synagoga. In his frontispiece, the *Sponsa* and *Sponsus* (labeled above their heads) share a throne within the high walls of a towered city (fig. 6). Pressing a book inscribed with the Song's first verse to her chest, the Bride gazes into the eyes of her Bridegroom and inclines her head toward him. She is haloed as well as crowned and holds a scepter in her left hand. The *Sponsus* (also haloed and crowned) looks heavenward and embraces the *Sponsa* with his right hand while caressing the cheek of a

[33] PL 172, cols. 347–496. For an overview of Honorius's intricate exegetical strategy, see E. Ann Matter, *The Voice of My Beloved: The Song of Songs in Western Medieval Christianity* (Philadelphia, 1990), 58–85.

[34] PL 172, col. 353. This point was also made by Jeremy Cohen, "*Synagoga conversa*: Honorius Augustodunensis, the Song of Songs, and Christianity's 'Eschatological Jew,'" *Speculum* 79 (2004), 309–340, who highlights the novelty of Honorius's commentary, which envisions Synagoga's conversion before that of the Gentiles and hence breaks with traditional eschatological roles assigned to the Jews. Cohen's characteristically rich and thorough treatment of this material came to my attention, unfortunately, while I was preparing the final version of this essay and hence too late to be given full consideration.

[35] Eight extant copies of Honorius's *Expositio* incorporate drawing cycles of Christ's Brides en route to Jerusalem, and a general treatment of their pictorial programs can be found in Gertrud Schiller, *Ikonographie der christlichen Kunst*. 7 vols. (Gütersloh, 1966–91) vol. 4.1, 102–4.

[36] Michael Curschmann, "Imagined Exegesis: Text and Picture in the Exegetical Works of Rupert of Deutz, Honorius Augustodunensis, and Gerhoch of Reichersberg," *Traditio* 44 (1988), 156. This perceptive essay scrutinizes what has traditionally been assumed as a close text/image relationship in depictions of the Sunamite.

second woman who genuflects before the bridal pair outside of their architectural enclosure. An inscription along the edge of the window through which the *Sponsus* extends his left arm is the initial section of verses 2:6 and 8:3 ("His left arm under my head"), which continues over the shoulder of the *Sponsa* ("his right arm will embrace me"). Blood pouring from a wound in the *Sponsus*'s hand flows in rivulets down the front of the kneeling woman's dress. She wears a veil that covers her hair and raises a scroll that describes her reaction to the Bridegroom's gesture: "my beloved put forth his hand through the hole and my belly trembled at his touch" (5:4). Behind her, a verdant tree grows almost as tall as the highest city walls surrounding the embracing couple, and a final verse winds up its trunk: "under the apple tree I aroused you" (8:5).

Given established Song of Songs discourse, we can be confident in interpreting the *Sponsus* as Christ, crowned, haloed and enthroned in Heaven with his Bride, who might represent the Church, Ecclesia. Few, however, have speculated on the kneeling woman's identity. Josef Endres understands the theme of the entire illumination as Christ reviving humanity from its sinfulness, and several subsequent scholars concur that the woman under the apple tree is representative of redeemed humanity, the Church born from the Crucifixion.[37] Humankind's redemption through Christ's death on the cross is indeed a natural and legitimate general framework in which to interpret the illumination as a whole, but we can get at something even more specific, I believe, through further analysis of Honorius's Song of Songs commentaries. For instance, he associates Christ's left hand with the Old Law and the right with the Gospel, perhaps influenced by Robert of Tombelaine (d. c. 1090), whose commentary on the Songs was attributed to Gregory the Great in the Middle Ages.[38] Robert distinguishes between

---

[37] Josef Endres, *Das St. Jakobsportal in Regensburg und Honorius von Augustodunensis: Beitrag zur Ikonographie und Literaturgeschichte des 12. Jahrhunderts* (Kempten, 1903), 34. This image has also been identified as a precursor to the apse mosaic at Santa Maria Trastevere in Rome; see G. Wellen, "Sponsa Christi: Het Absis mosaïek van de Santa Maria in Trastevere te Rome en het Hooglied," in *Feestbundel F. van der Meer: Opstellen aangeboden aan Prof. Dr. F. G. L. van der Meer ter gelegenheid van zijn zestigste verjaardag op 16 november 1964* (Amsterdam, 1966), 148–59.

[38] PL 172, cols. 386–87. Robert's commentary appears in the PL in two partial versions: one in Robert's name (PL 150, cols. 1361–70 for the text only to Song of Songs 1:11) and the other attributed to Gregory the Great (PL 79, cols. 493–548 for 1:12 to the end of the text). Also see Dom Paul Quivy and Dom Joseph Thiron, "Robert de Tombelaine et son commentaire sur le *Cantique des Cantiques*," *Millénaire*

Christ's right and left hands specifically in reference to Ecclesia and Synagoga; regarding Song of Songs verse 8:3, he asserts that Christ's left hand holds present life, and his right hand holds saintly life: "It is said, therefore, that Synagoga by the preaching of Ecclesia converts in the future."[39] I would thus like to suggest that the kneeling woman represents Synagoga as the Sunamite.

Additional passages from Honorius's commentaries explicating verse 8:5 (a portion of which is inscribed on the tree growing behind the kneeling woman) are of particular import for an identification of the kneeling woman in Clm. 4550's frontispiece. The biblical passage reads:

> Who is this who comes up from the desert,
> flowing with delights and leaning on her beloved?
> Under the apple tree I aroused you,
> there your mother was corrupted,
> there she who bore you was violated.

Earlier theologians interpreted the first half of this verse as praise for Ecclesia, often conceiving of Synagoga as its speaker and therefore as admiring the Church.[40] Significantly, Honorius deviates from this tradition and reverses it somewhat; in his *Expositio* the members of the Church marvel, "Who is this?" in admiration of Synagoga after her conversion.[41] Moreover, in regards to the second line of verse 8:5, Honorius explains:

> The apple tree is the cross of Christ...The Sunamite slept beneath the tree, when Synagoga lay down dead from guilty collusion under the tree...Under the apple tree I revived you, just as if he said to the converted Synagogue: Deservedly I am to be loved by you, because I loved you before, and I redeemed you by my death by the cross. Then your mother was corrupted, certainly Synagoga up to the time of the cross was damned in hell and shouted out the words: "His blood be on us and upon our sons" [Matt. 27:25].[42]

---

monastique de Mont-Saint-Michel: vie Montoise et rayonnement intellectuel du Mont Saint-Michel 2 (1967): 347–56.

[39] "Laeva Christi vita praesens, dextera vero vita beata habetur. Caput autem nostrum spiritualiter mens esse perhibetur. Dicit ergo Synagoga praedicationibus Ecclesiae jam conversa." PL 79, col. 539.

[40] For instance, Haimo of Auxerre, PL 117, col. 352.

[41] PL 172, col. 480.

[42] "Arbor mali, est crux Christi...Sunamitis sub abore dormivit, quando Synagoga de arbore praevaricationis mortua jacuit...Sub abore malo suscitavi te, quasi conversae Synagogae dicat: Merito diligendus sum a te, quia prior dilexi te, et morte mea

Honorius therefore forges an explicit connection between Synagoga and the Sunamite who sleeps under the apple tree, under the cross. In her former incarnation, prior to redemption through Christ, she is corrupted and condemned as an embodiment of the Jews who called for Christ's execution, an association also made in the *Sigillum*.[43] Hence the invocation of Matthew 27:25, a passage that Christian theologians traditionally associated with the Jews' recognition of their own accursedness for killing the Messiah.[44] Christ, however, defeats death through his sacrifice on the cross, revives Synagoga and saves her from damnation. Meanwhile, on the frontispiece of Clm. 4550, Synagoga as the Sunamite is situated on Christ's left (as is common in her depictions), kneeling in deference to him under the apple tree/cross and covered in his blood. Moreover, she is plainly dressed and wears a modest head covering rather than revealing her hair, just as in the Resurrection page in Henry the Lion's Gospel book. Prominently displaying a scroll that proclaims her excitement at his arrival, Synagoga longs to join Christ and his Bride the Church, and it seems that Christ welcomes her into his realm. He reaches out to her, caressing her cheek and inviting her to join him and Ecclesia.

Today, a level of ambiguity is inherent within this drawing; the fascinating play on themes of interiority and exteriority, inclusion and exclusion render it impossible for a modern viewer to determine precisely the meaning behind Christ's gesture and the kneeling woman's identity. Clearly, however, she must be connected with Synagoga as the Sunamite, awakened under the apple tree and redeemed by Christ, admiring him and his Bride Ecclesia, who is seated with her beloved. As Honorius himself declares, both the primitive Church (that which existed during the time of the prophets, before Christ's advent) and the present Church are united through Christ into a single faith.[45] An instructive contrast can be made between this miniature and the Crucifixion illumination from Herrad of Hohenbourg's celebrated

redemi te in cruce. Ibi corrupta est mater tua, scilicet sub cruce Synagoga in inferno damnata, quae clamavit dicens: Sanguis ejus super nos, et super filios nostros (Matt. 27:25)." PL 172, col. 481.

[43] PL 172, col. 515.

[44] Matt. 27:25 was used within the context of the Jews' eventual conversion as early as the late fourth or early fifth century; see Rainer Kampling, *Das Blut Christi und die Juden: Mt 27,25 bei dem lateinischsprachigen christlichen Autoren bis zu Leo dem Grossen*. Neutestamentliche Abhandlungen 16 (Münster, 1984), 104–109.

[45] PL 172, col. 379.

Hortus deliciarum (c. 1175–1190),[46] in which similar inscriptions, including Songs 8:5 and Matt. 27:25, clearly label Ecclesia as Christ's Bride and Synagoga as the Sulamite and suggest her future union with the Church. Despite Ecclesia and/or Christ's call for her to rejoin the faith (revertere Sunamitis), however, Synagoga ignominiously flees the cross with multiple signs of Jewish blindness, stupidity and obstinacy. Herrad cites Honorius extensively in her encyclopedic work and, as I demonstrate elsewhere, was certainly influenced by him in this particular illumination.[47] Nonetheless, within the context of the Crucifixion, she positions Synagoga as defeated and rejected, the antithesis of her role in many Song of Songs illuminations.

Synagoga's Conversion in Troyes, Bibliothèque Municipale, MS. lat. 1869

Miniatures such as the Clm. 4550 frontispiece suggest an association between the redeemed Sulamite of the Song of Songs and the converted Synagoga, but later illuminations portray the latter's acceptance by Christ in an even more blatant fashion. For example, a composite manuscript produced most likely in the Cistercian monastery of Clairvaux in the late twelfth or early thirteenth century includes sections from both Gregory the Great's sixth-century commentary on the Song and Robert of Tombelaine's eleventh-century commentary that was attributed to Gregory in the medieval period.[48] On fol. 173r, Ecclesia and Synagoga sit next to each other within the *Q* for verse 5:17, the same verse that Synagoga speaks to Ecclesia in the *Gospels of Henry the Lion*: "Where is your beloved gone, O fairest of women?... We will seek him with you" (fig. 7). Wearing a crown that resembles a helmet, Ecclesia holds both a chalice and a book. To her left, Synagoga, wearing a blue headdress

---

[46] *Herrad of Hohenbourg. Hortus deliciarum*, ed. Rosalie Green et al., 2 vols. Studies of the Warburg Institute 36 (London, 1979). Also see two studies by Fiona Griffiths, "Nuns' Memories or Missing History in Alsace (c. 1200): Herrad of Hohenbourg's *Garden of Delights*," in *Medieval Memories: Men, Women and the Past, 700–1300*, ed. E. van Houts (New York, 2001), 132–149, and "Herrad of Hohenbourg and the Poetry of the *Hortus deliciarum: Cantat tibi cantica*," in *Women Writing Latin From Roman Antiquity to Early Modern Europe*, Medieval Women Writing Latin 2 (New York, 2002), 231–263.

[47] An essay on this topic, currently in preparation, presents an extensive analysis of this miniature and the complexity with which Herrad interwove Song of Songs verses to define *both* Ecclesia and Synagoga as Christ's Brides, which is, to my knowledge, unparalleled in twelfth-century art.

[48] Troyes, Bibliothèque Municipale, MS. lat. 1869 (hereafter lat. 1869).

that partially obscures her eyes, unfurls an uninscribed scroll and holds the tablets of the Law. In an extraordinary gesture, she places her right hand on Ecclesia's shoulder in what could be a poignant overture towards reconciliation, or at least a direct attempt to communicate with Ecclesia. As discussed above, verse 5:17 is traditionally rubricated so that Synagoga asks Ecclesia, "Where has your beloved gone?" and Robert's *Commentary* is also based on this designation. Importantly, he contextualizes their dialogue in terms of Synagoga's conversion: "This can be understood about Synagoga, so that when she is at last converted she may ask the Church, ['Where has your beloved gone?'] and the Church will reply at once."[49] Yet the artist of the corresponding miniature depicts Synagoga as though unconverted, seemingly endowed with attributes of incredulity, and hence contrary to the spirit of the commentary. It appears, for example, that Synagoga inserts her left hand into a vessel fashioned out of the same gold leaf as Ecclesia's book. A precise assessment is difficult to make, though the object is evocative of the bucket of vinegar offered to Christ during the Crucifixion. The sponge-bearer's vinegar bucket, referred to by some medieval exegetes as "the container for the accumulated iniquity of the world,"[50] does in fact become Synagoga's attribute in twelfth-century Mosan enamels.[51] On the other hand, the vessel might allude to a situla or an ointment jar and hence be suggestive of a penitential attitude, in keeping not only with associations between Synagoga and Mary Magdalene seen earlier in the *Gospels of Henry the Lion*, but also with Synagoga's partial embrace of Ecclesia. Given the precious material chosen to depict the object, however, it seems to denote earthly wealth and hence carry primarily negative associations. Since early medieval theologians repeatedly linked Jews with monetary excess, avarice and worldly riches, Synagoga could perhaps be seen as wearing a golden moneybag.[52]

---

[49] "Quamvis hoc de Synagoga intelligi valeat, ut aliquando conversa Ecclesiam interroget, cui protinus Ecclesia respondet." PL 79, col. 525.

[50] See William Jordan, "The Last Tormentor of Christ: An Image of the Jews in Ancient and Medieval Exegesis, Art, and Drama," *Jewish Quarterly Review* 78 (1987): 31, who is here paraphrasing Augustine (PL 186, col. 582).

[51] For example, the c. 1170–80 Scheldewindeke processional cross; see *La Salle aux Trésors: Chefs d'oeuvres de l'art Roman et Mosan* (Turnhout, 1999), 28–29.

[52] And yet, no earlier, extant image depicts her with this sign of greed. Blumenkranz conjectures that the moneybag as Synagoga's attribute was an invention of the thirteenth-century *Bibles moralisées*; "La représentation de *Synagoga*," 81. See, for instance, Vienna, Österreichische Nationalbibliothek, Cod. 1179, fol. 74r; repr. in Sara Lipton, *Images of Intolerance: The Representation of Jews and Judaism in the Bible moralisée* (Los

Her pink costume conveys further derogatory overtones. Although its right sleeve fits tightly (along the arm with which she reaches out toward Ecclesia), the sleeve of her left arm (in which she cradles the tablets of the Law) extends to the ground and is conspicuously knotted in the middle, a feature of twelfth-century luxury dress.[53] That Synagoga's sleeve is knotted while Ecclesia's is more modestly arranged may be a signal of Synagoga's profligacy.[54] Synagoga in the Troyes initial could therefore be interpreted as if mired in error: stubbornly clinging to the Old Testament Law that leads her and the Jews to reject Christ and to offer him vinegar from a golden bucket during his execution, Synagoga flaunts her vain attachment to luxurious dress and monetary excess through her knotted sleeve (and, possibly, a moneybag). The illuminator thus creates a distinction between Synagoga's left arm, which might represent the materialism of the Jews, and the right, which could signal her desire to join the Christian community. But because she has not yet abandoned the Old Law, she cannot join the Christian faith and hence remains blinded by her mantle. The Cistercian artist, in other words, deviates from the commentary text on this page that clearly interprets verse 5:17 as Synagoga "at last converted" and offers the viewer a more ambivalent assumption regarding her relationship to the Church at the end of days.

In the manuscript's next miniature (on fol. 176v), Christ and Ecclesia, who is crowned and holds a model of a church, embrace and share a passionate kiss (see fig. 3). This illumination accompanies verse 6:2 ("I am my beloved's and my beloved is mine"), and, notably, omits Synagoga, despite the fact that Robert's commentary explicitly mentions her and again asserts her conversion:

Angeles, 1999), 40. For broader discussions of the Christian identification of the Jews with money and moneylending, see Lester K. Little, *Religious Poverty and Profit Economy in Medieval Europe* (Ithaca, 1978), esp. chap. 3.

[53] Two useful sources for medieval costume are Françoise Piponnier and Perrine Mane, *Dress in the Middle Ages*, trans. Caroline Beamish (New Haven, 1997); and Jennifer Harris, "'Estroit vestu et mensu cosu': Evidence for the Construction of Twelfth-Century Dress," in *Medieval Art: Recent Perspectives. A Memorial Tribute to C. R. Dodwell*, ed. Gale Owen-Crocker and Timothy Graham (New York, 1998), 89–103.

[54] The Devil dressed in women's clothing in the c. 1150 *Winchester Psalter* provides an instructive comparison. While his right sleeve hangs loosely as though improperly sewn, his left sleeve is conspicuously knotted. Eunice Goddard suggests that this difference between the Devil's sleeves probably denoted slovenliness and extravagance respectively; *Women's Costume in French Texts of the Eleventh and Twelfth Centuries* (Baltimore, 1927), 159–60.

> It must of course be noted that Synagoga will at some time be converted to the faith by the preaching of Ecclesia, in such a way that... she will follow Christ and love him with the same desire that Ecclesia loves him... The bridegroom speaks to her now that she has become his friend and bride who is united with him, congratulating her and saying, "You are fair my friend, sweet and beautiful as Jerusalem."[55]

The Latin text is ambiguous as to which Bride Christ is speaking and congratulating; the object of *alloquitur* (speaks to) is the feminine *eam*, which could refer either to Synagoga or Ecclesia. Therefore, it is possible that Robert envisioned Christ speaking to Synagoga "now that she has become his friend and bride." Although the commentary text beside the miniature celebrates the moment when Synagoga follows and loves Christ "with the same desire that Ecclesia loves him," the artist chose to depict only Christ and Ecclesia passionately holding each other.

Nonetheless, the very next initial, that which accompanies verse 6:3 ("You are fair my friend, sweet and beautiful as Jerusalem") does indeed show Christ embracing Synagoga (fig. 8). Here, Synagoga is modestly dressed; her blue mantle is similar to the one she wears on fol. 173r, and her red cloak is without knotted sleeves. In a motion expressive of submission and intimacy, she bows her head and rests against Christ. Most remarkably, Synagoga is also haloed, a signal that Christ has accepted her into the Christian community, and that she has received divine grace.[56] Unlike her previous depiction in this manuscript, in which she holds the tablets of the Law and a golden bucket/moneybag, Synagoga in this miniature is without denigrating attributes. Now her only attribute is a halo, signaling that she has abandoned Judaism and assimilated with Christ. The accompanying commentary compares Synagoga to Ecclesia and joyously proclaims her ultimate conversion:

> Fair and friendly, sweet and beautiful, Synagoga will be said to be; because when at last converted she will follow the four holy Gospels just as Ecclesia... Holy Ecclesia is well prefigured by Synagoga, because while

[55] "Notandum quippe, quod Synagoga per praedicationem Ecclesiae ad fidem quandoque convertetur, ita ut se abnegans, Christum solum sequatur, et eodem desiderio diligat Christum, quo eum Ecclesia diligit, quem caeteris postpositis solum amat. Quam jam amicam factam, jam sponsam sibi conjunctam Sponsus alloquitur, congratulans et dicens: Pulchra es, amica mea, suavis et decora sicut Jerusalem." PL 79, col. 526.

[56] Although the Song of Songs is the only context in which I have seen Synagoga endowed with a halo, this example is not unique. See fol. 75 of a late-twelfth century, French copy of Origen's *Commentary* on the Song (Paris, BN, MS. lat. 1636); repr. in Blumenkranz, "Géographie historique," 1150 and 1156.

> she is in the world she always suffers oppression...and contemplates the peace of her heavenly home which is her goal...Yet Synagoga will be converted worthily, just as Jerusalem is called fair and friendly and sweet and beautiful; because she imitates holy Ecclesia.[57]

Significantly, this is Synagoga's last depiction in the manuscript. The monastic reader would therefore be left with a striking image of Christ lovingly embracing the Jewish church, just as he embraces his Bride Ecclesia in earlier initials, including fol. 176v. Moreover, the accompanying text clearly establishes Synagoga as an image of the Church (*Ecclesiam imitator*). Robert of Tombelaine interprets the Song of Songs explicitly in terms of Synagoga's conversion and repeatedly stresses that, although at one time captive and despised for her rejection of the Savior, she will convert at the end of time, called to the faith by Ecclesia, from whom she will receive her earlier dignity.[58] Whereas in the *Q* initial she longs for reconciliation with Ecclesia, it is not until she abandons her adherence to Mosaic Law that she joins the Christian community. Importantly, therefore, some Christian viewers might have seen a sort of progression in the manuscript's depictions of Synagoga, her transformation from Other to welcomed member of the Church.

Because lat. 1869 was created within a Cistercian milieu and was most likely read primarily by monks of that order, mention must be made of Bernard of Clairvaux, the dynamic founding abbot of Clairvaux and one of the Song of Songs' most powerful medieval commentators. Bernard wrote over eighty sermons on the Song that celebrate the love between God and the individual, human soul and are frequently referred to as "spiritual" more than allegorical.[59] Throughout his sermons, one

---

[57] "Pulchra et amica, suavis et decora sicut Jerusalem, Synagoga esse perhibetur; quia sancta quatuor Evangelia, aliquando conversa sicut Ecclesia sectabitur...Per quam bene sancta Ecclesia figuratur; quia dum in mundo semper pressuram patitur...quae sit pax patriae coelestis currendo contemplatur...Digne autem Synagoga conversa, sicut Jerusalem pulchra et amica et suavis et decora dicitur; quia dum sanctam Ecclesiam imitator." PL 79, col. 526.

[58] For example, PL 79, col. 533. Also see cols. 539–40, in which Robert predicts Synagoga's conversion after the trials of Antichrist.

[59] Jean Leclercq, *Recueil d'études sur Saint Bernard et ses écrits*, 4 vols. (Rome, 1962–87). For the Latin texts of his sermons, *Sancti Bernardi opera*, ed. J. Leclercq, C. Talbot, and H. Rochais, vols. 1–2 (Rome, 1957–1958). English translations can be found in *On the Song of Songs*, trans. Kilian Walsh, vols. 2–3 (Spencer, Mass., 1971); and *On the Song of Songs IV*, trans. Irene Edmonds, vols. 3–4 (Kalamazoo, 1979–1980). Two more recent studies that focus on his Song of Songs sermons and include earlier bibliography are: Kilian McDonnell, "Spirit and Experience in Bernard of Clairvaux," *Theological Studies*

finds an emphasis on the soul's quest for union with God, what has been called "a high point of mystical contemplation particularly adapted to the cloister."[60] They had a direct and almost immediate impact on the Cistercian community, inspiring at least six other "mystical" commentaries during the twelfth century alone. Given Bernard's stature and erudition, it is probable that any Cistercian cleric at Clairvaux (where lat. 1869 seems to have been produced) who commissioned a Song of Songs commentary in the late twelfth or early thirteenth century would have been aware of the revered abbot's thought on this subject. Although it is fairly certain that his *Sermons*, as they survive today, were intended as literary works, Bernard doubtless also preached their content to the Clairvaux community. Hence monks of all positions in the monastery could have been familiar with Bernard's essential ideas regarding this text. Perhaps his emphasis on the human soul searching and longing for union with God sparked an association with Synagoga, Christ's first Bride, within the Cistercian mind. As Church authorities such as Gregory the Great taught, Synagoga was thought to be initially mired in worldliness and sin but would renounce her past error to join Christ. Meanwhile, Cistercian commentaries distinctly meditate on the human soul's unworthiness and imperfections, which necessitate spiritual ascent. One can therefore speculate whether the monks of Clairvaux might have been particularly sensitive to those conceptions of Synagoga in which she rejects her past error and ultimately achieves spiritual union with Christ.

At the same time, several of Bernard's sermons on the Song of Songs employ distinctly anti-Jewish tropes. For example, in sermon 14, "Concerning the Church of the Faithful Christians and the Synagogue of the Perfidious Jews," he argues that although the Gentiles desired Christian enlightenment, it was the prideful, envious Synagogue that stood in their way.[61] The abbot's ambivalent position towards the Jews manifested itself in other contexts, such as his counter-preaching during the Second Crusade, for which he is often credited with mitigating violence against Jews. Despite his vigorous prohibitions against anti-Jewish violence, however, Bernard was just as emphatic about the Jews' subservience, which he considered a just reward for their crime

58 (1997): 3–19; and Jacques Blanpain, *S'ouvrir au désir: En lisant le Cantique des Cantiques avec Bernard de Clairvaux*, Cahiers Scourmontois 4 (Begrolles-en-Mauge, 2004).

[60] Matter, *The Voice of My Beloved*, 14.

[61] *Sermones super Cantica canticorum*, 14:1.2 in *Sancti Bernardi opera*, vol. 1, 76.

of deicide.[62] This ambivalence might explain, to a degree, why the illuminator of lat. 1869 shows Synagoga both blind and haloed. At the very least, text and image in this captivating manuscript reveal an emphatic yet ambivalent discourse on the Jews and Judaism; the illuminated initials respond directly to, yet in some aspects chafe against, the accompanying commentary, therefore suggesting a tension between authoritative, patristic tradition and popular sentiment.

Synagoga's Conversion: Public Statements

Thus far, my attention has been focused on Synagoga's imagery within manuscripts, objects that communicated to a relatively circumscribed readership. Importantly, however, Christian writers and artists also drew upon Synagoga's personification to emphasize the Jews' eventual conversion in considerably more public forums such as monastic drama, stained glass and stone sculpture. The anonymous Bavarian monk who composed the *Ludus Antichristo* (*Play of Antichrist*), for instance, also envisioned Synagoga's conversion within an eschatological context.[63] Writing in c. 1160 (only about ten years before Henry commissioned his *Gospels*) for a learned, clerical audience, the dramatist predicts the unification of the Christian world under the Last Emperor, his abdication, and Antichrist's rise and fall as a precursor to Christ's Second Coming. During the second half of the *Ludus*, Antichrist deceives secular world rulers and representatives of the leading faiths, including Ecclesia and Synagoga, into worshipping him as their savior. Immediately after the prophets Enoch and Elijah expose him as a false messiah, Synagoga renounces Antichrist (this happens, notably, even before Ecclesia renounces him) and converts to Christianity, enraging Antichrist, who sentences her to death. The *Ludus* dramatist was certainly indebted to

---

[62] David Berger, "The Attitude of St. Bernard of Clairvaux Toward the Jews," *American Academy for Jewish Research* 40 (1972): 89–107.

[63] Munich, Bayerische Staatsbibliothek Cod. lat. 19411, which has been studied most thoroughly by Helmut Plechl, "Die Tegernseer Handschrift Clm. 19411, Beschreibung und Inhalt," *Deutsches Archiv für Erforschung des Mittelalters* 18 (1962): 418–501. Karl Young, *The Drama of the Medieval Church*, vol. 2 (Oxford, 1933), 371–87, includes the Latin text of the play; for an English translation, see *The Play of Antichrist*, trans. John Wright (Toronto, 1967). Regarding its historical background and staging, see Markus Litz, *Theatrum sacrum und symbolische Weltsicht: Der staufische ludus de antichristo* (New York, 1990).

Adso of Moutier-en-Der's tenth-century *Libellus de Antichristo*, but he deviates noticeably from Adso in the solemnity and respect with which he treats Synagoga and the Jews.[64] Although the playwright's relative tolerance towards the Jews is striking, it is not as rare or as unusual as previous authors have assumed, given the widespread Christian expectation of their conversion at the end of time.

This more benign attitude, moreover, is manifested in part through a Song of Songs lyric delivered at a climactic moment of the drama. While Antichrist's servants execute Synagoga for her new acceptance of Christianity, Ecclesia sings, "A little bundle of myrrh is my beloved to me" (1:12). The inclusion of this verse (the only Song of Songs excerpt in the *Ludus*) at such a critical juncture signals its importance and provides a crucial link between Jewish conversion, Synagoga's martyrdom and Christ's eschatological union with his Brides. Commentators such as Origen, Apponius and Bede interpreted the Song's many references to myrrh in terms of Christ's suffering during his Passion as well as to the sweetness of his Resurrection, to the hardship that the Church endures on earth, as well as to the joyousness of its redemption.[65] The "little bundle of myrrh" of which Ecclesia sings might therefore have sparked an association both with Christ's death and his Resurrection, as well as his union with the *Sponsa* in Paradise. This lyric is thus a fitting reminder that both Ecclesia and Synagoga are Christ's Brides, and, importantly, that "at the moment of her death, following her conversion, Synagoga, so to speak, *becomes* Ecclesia."[66] The drama indicates the pervasiveness of the belief that Synagoga, and hence the Jews, would join the Christian majority at the end of time. In the *Play of Antichrist* she dies as a martyr for the Christian faith, just as in Honorius's *Expositio* the converted Sunamite leads a procession of martyred Jews to meet Christ in Jerusalem.

[64] Wright, *The Play of Antichrist*, 60–61. For surveys of the Antichrist legend, see *The Apocalypse in the Middle Ages*, ed. Richard Kenneth Emmerson and Bernard McGinn (Ithaca, 1992); and Kevin L. Hughes, *Constructing Antichrist: Paul, Biblical Commentary, and the Development of Doctrine in the Early Middle Ages* (Washington, D.C., 2005).

[65] Virginie Minet-Mahy, "Étude des métaphores végétales dans trois commentaires sur le Cantique des cantiques (Origène, Apponius, Bernard de Clairvaux)," *Cahiers de civilisation médiévale* 46 (2003): esp. 174–176.

[66] Richard Axton, Review of *The Play of Antichrist*, trans. John Wright (as cited above), *Medium aevum* 38 (1969): 187, as cited by Amelia Jane Carr, "Visual and Symbolic Imagery in the Twelfth-Century Tegernsee *Ludus de Antichristo*," Ph.D. diss. (Northwestern University, 1984), 216.

The *Ludus Antichristo* also demonstrates that medieval conceptions of Synagoga's conversion were not exclusive to Song of Songs illustrations. Nor, in fact, were they regionally confined to the German empire; in mid-twelfth-century France, for example, Abbot Suger publicly stressed Synagoga's assimilation in his famous ambulatory windows at Saint-Denis. At the apex of a series of panels based upon the Pauline exegesis of the harmony between Old and New Testaments, Christ radiates the seven gifts of the Holy Spirit and crowns Ecclesia at the same time he removes Synagoga's blindfold so she may bear witness to Christ and receive his grace (fig. 9).[67] Clearly resonant with 2 Corinthians 3:14–16, this stained glass medallion shows Ecclesia and Synagoga as Brides of the Song of Songs united by Christ as the Apocalyptic Lamb.[68] While Suger was certainly not the first to express a hopeful final outcome for Synagoga, he makes an original visual statement by portraying the Christian Church as a presence, however mysterious and hidden, within the Old Law.[69] By unveiling Synagoga, Christ exposes this hidden aspect of the Old Covenant, thereby uniting the Old and the New in a manifestation of the mystery of the Alliance.

Significantly, Suger's artistic declaration concerning the revelation and assimilation of the Synagogue is a public one, visible to anyone visiting the church at Saint-Denis and therefore accessible to a larger cross-section of medieval viewers than were manuscript illuminations. Admittedly, the entire window's program would have eluded uneducated viewers, just as modern scholars today still debate its nuances. But Suger's conception of Synagoga unveiled as a visual metaphor for her conversion did inspire artists in northern France who repeated this motif in other mid-twelfth-century, public works. On either side of a stone baptismal font from the Premonstratensian abbey Sainte-Larme de Sélincourt, for instance, angels descend from heaven with crowns, offering eternal rewards for those who join the Church.[70] Christ appears

[67] By far the most comprehensive iconographic treatment of Suger's windows must be credited to Louis Grodecki, and I have relied heavily on his essay "Les vitraux allégoriques de Saint-Denis," in *Études sur les vitraux de Suger à Saint-Denis (XIIe siècle)*, ed. Catherine Grodecki, Chantal Bouchon and Yolanta Załuska (Paris, 1995), 51–83.

[68] Grodecki was the first to advance an Apocalyptic connection in this panel, positing that Suger drew inspiration from the theme of the *Sponsus* glorifying the *Sponsa* in the presence of the Old Testament Bride at the end of time; "Les vitraux allégoriques," 74.

[69] Thérel, *Le triomphe de la Vierge-Église*, 219.

[70] The font appears to be the only surviving work from this monastery; see Grodecki, "Les vitraux allégoriques," 73.

twice on the third side, first baptized by John and then crowning his Bride the Church (who shares his throne), while pulling off Synagoga's veil (fig. 10). Holding a scroll and perhaps, originally, a scepter, Synagoga walks toward Christ and Ecclesia as though she were about to take her place beside them. Like Suger's medallion, this image publicly emphasizes the revelation of the New Law within the Old.[71] Its placement on a baptismal font, a site where one's sinful past is erased, is unusual, and this fascinating iconographic juxtaposition seems closely related to the font's liturgical function. Just as a new convert to the Church would renounce Original Sin before his baptism, Synagoga comes to Christ to be unveiled and received within the Church. It is interesting to speculate what sorts of meanings these panels would have stimulated in a medieval Christian viewer. Seeing Synagoga's unveiling and assimilation with the Christian Church might have suggested to potential converts the universality of Christian salvation, perhaps reminding the members of the monastery that the whole world is united in Christ.

Conclusion

With this essay, I have tried to expand an awareness of Synagoga's meaning beyond the degradation common in Crucifixion imagery. Of course, depictions of Synagoga converted to Christianity, however "positive" from a Christian, missionizing perspective, would have been distasteful to a Jewish viewer. Yet, the Christian audience for these illuminations, windows and carvings, on seeing Synagoga joined with the Church, would have reacted to her image differently than to those in which she is shown as hostile to Christ. Because Synagoga is the only one who "speaks" in the Crucifixion miniature from the *Gospels of Henry the Lion*, her curse against Christ is highlighted all the more and hence probably stimulated anger toward the Jews. As already mentioned, Synagoga's presence on this folio was so vexing to one unknown reader that he defaced her visage, an almost unimaginably audacious act given the illumination's costliness. However, this same reader refrained from mutilating her image on the facing page, which shows Synagoga

[71] For another public example of Christ crowing Ecclesia while removing Synagoga's veil, see the façade of Berteaucourt-les-Dames; reproduced in André Lapeyre, *Des façades occidentales de Saint-Denis et de Chartres aux portails de Laon: Études sur la sculpture monumentale dans l'Ile-de-France et les régions voisines au XIIe siècle* (Paris, 1960), 33–40.

bridging the Old Law and the New. Unmistakably associated with the Old Testament kings David and Solomon, Synagoga at the same time is allied with Christianity's New Covenant in that she speaks to Ecclesia about their mutual love for Christ, and therefore merits a crown. Together, these two folios from Henry's manuscript are clear evidence that Synagoga had at least two simultaneous functions, both of which were consistent with ideals of the medieval Church.

In contrast to Synagoga's Crucifixion imagery, which remained relatively static during the twelfth century, portrayals of her conversion and assimilation in Song of Songs contexts vary markedly from one another.[72] In attempting to identify their exegetical roots, I have linked such depictions with Honorius Augustodunensis's conceptions of Jewish conversion as embodied by the Sulamite. Significantly, Synagoga's laudatory visual iconography of assimilation also coincides with broader trends concerning the role of the Jews in late-medieval millennialism, particularly within the realm of Franciscan apocalypticism. Recent work on the Franciscan abbot, Joachim of Fiore (d. 1202), for example, draws attention to the privileged position he afforded the Jews in his eschatology, and, importantly, that this attitude was upheld by his followers.[73] According to Joachim, the Jews' conversion would usher in a new "status," equal to humanity's greatest fulfillment, and he believed that some converted Jews would even "provide a refuge for just Christians during Antichrist's tyranny."[74] Almost contemporaneous depictions of Synagoga as honored Bride of the Old Covenant, haloed, crowned and expressing her desire to join Christ, might have served as

[72] By the mid-thirteenth century, Synagoga only rarely appears in Song of Songs initials. Parallel with the rise of Marian devotion, it became more common for illuminators to focus on the Virgin and Christ child in this context. For instance, Orléans, Bibliothèque Municipale, MS. 13, p. 95, reproduced in Isabelle Malaise, "L'Iconographie Biblique du *Cantique des cantiques* au XIIe siècle," *Scriptorium* 46 (1992), pl. 8b. For further discussions, see Philippe Verdier, *Le couronnement de la Vierge: Les origines et les premiers développements d'un thème iconographique* (Paris, 1980), 81–112; Ann W. Astell, *The Song of Songs in the Middle Ages* (Ithaca, 1990), esp. chap. 2; and Ruth Bartal, "Le Cantique des Cantiques: Texte et images," *Les Cahiers de Saint-Michel de Cuxa* 25 (1994): 121–8.

[73] Robert E. Lerner, *The Feast of Saint Abraham: Medieval Millenarians and the Jews* (Philadelphia, 2001). Also see Cohen, "*Synagoga conversa*." For further discussions of Franciscan apocalypticism, see E. Randolph Daniel, "Abbot Joachim of Fiore and the Conversion of the Jews," in *Friars and Jews in the Middle Ages and Renaissance*, ed. Steven J. McMichael and Susan E. Meyers (Boston, 2004), 1–21; and within the same volume, David Burr, "The Antichrist and the Jews in Four Thirteenth-Century Apocalypse Commentaries," 23–38.

[74] Lerner, *The Feast of Saint Abraham*, 31–32.

visual reminders of the Jews' important function at the end of time, and certainly anticipated the moment when Paul's prophecy would be fulfilled and Israel "saved."

The provocative question of how the Song of Songs resonated within the different monastic orders deserves further consideration and exceeds the scope of this essay. It is apparent, however, that the majority of Synagoga's Song of Songs imagery was produced by and for monastic viewers from a variety of orders (Benedictine, Cistercian, Premonstratensian). Jean Leclercq attributes the Song's popularity among monks in part to its personal, compelling expression of their desire for union with God in the form of alternating intimacy and separation. Indeed, he says, the Song of Songs "is the poem of the pursuit which is the basis for the whole program of monastic life: *quaerere Deum*."[75] As an embodiment of the Old Testament, Synagoga is therefore an indispensible and honored actor within the drama of salvation. The fact that she is often shown accepted by Christ in Song of Songs illuminations implies a degree of universality to the anticipation of Jewish conversion, but it is difficult to distinguish general pictorial trends within these examples. For instance, even though one of Synagoga's earliest surviving Song of Songs appearances is in the context of defeat (Christ shoving her away) and was produced for the Cistercian abbot Stephen Harding, later extant Cistercian works such as the Troyes manuscript show her conversion and assimilation. In Honorius's frontispiece, Synagoga as the Sunamite remains in a subordinate position, kneeling outside the walls of the Heavenly Jerusalem as Christ the *Sponsus* reaches out to caress her cheek. If one senses ambivalence on the part of the illuminators and designers, perhaps it is because the conciliatory emphasis put upon the Jews' eschatological function was innovative in the twelfth century, and hence its iconography was likewise novel.

It may be more profitable to speculate about the reception of Synagoga's conversion imagery on the level of the individual viewer. Monks reading commentaries on the Song or hearing them read aloud could have identified themselves with the *Sponsa*, Christ's Bride. Not only does the structure of the Song of Songs as a rubricated dialogue lend itself to an identification with the speakers; the *Sponsa* is a model of devotion to Christ. Origen's conception of the Song as celebrating God's love

[75] Jean Leclercq, *The Love of Learning and the Desire for God: A Study of Monastic Culture*, trans. Catharine Mishrahi (New York, 1982), 85.

for the human soul also personalizes the biblical poem, allowing the reader to associate the *Sponsa* with his own, individual soul on its spiritual journey toward union with God. Moreover, as Caroline Walker Bynum has so perceptively articulated, the use of feminine, maternal imagery to describe both God and Christ became extremely popular during the twelfth century, particularly within Cistercian communities.[76] Bernard of Clairvaux, she notes, far exceeds his contemporaries in assigning maternal characteristics (nurturing, suckling) to male figures, including himself, and it is not surprising that this language is most prevalent and complex in his sermons on the Song of Songs.[77] Cistercian monks could have therefore performed a kind of reverse identification when listening to or reading the abbot's sermons, imagining themselves as the Bride, nurtured by the maternal Bridegroom. On a more fundamental level, those meditating upon these passionate dialogues (textual or visual) between the *Sponsus* and his Brides would have perceived a harmony between the speakers.

This underscoring of the harmony between Ecclesia and Synagoga as Christ's Brides can also be related to larger socio-religious developments. Since the eleventh-century Reform movement, the western Church had been striving for unity within Latin Europe. André Vauchez has suggested that this preoccupation with unity intensified during the late-twelfth century to the point of obsession; he characterizes the end of the twelfth and beginning of the thirteenth centuries as encompassing a hardening (*durcissement*) of the Church's attitude against Jews and all other deviants from the Christian message.[78] The principal goal of clerics, he argues, was the pursuit of a perfect, unified Christian society lead by a single authority, the pope. Within this ideological framework, diversity or deviance from this goal was linked to evil.[79] Perhaps it is no coincidence that church art used Synagoga's assimilation imagery to stress Christian unity at this same moment. In fact, when we review some of the visual and exegetical tropes discussed in this essay, we are reminded of how often during the second half of the twelfth century Synagoga is lovingly embraced by Christ (Clm. 4550 and lat. 1869)

---

[76] See her classic study: Caroline Walker Bynum, *Jesus as Mother: Studies in the Spirituality of the High Middle Ages* (Los Angeles, 1982), esp. chap. 4.

[77] Bynum, *Jesus as Mother*, 115–20.

[78] André Vauchez, "L'Historiographie des hérésies médiévales," in *L'ogre historien: Autour de Jacques Le Goff*, ed. Jacques Revel and Jean-Claude Schmitt (Paris, 1998), 243–58.

[79] Vauchez, "L'Historiographie des hérésies médiévales," 258.

or unveiled by him and hence entering the community of the faithful (Suger's window and the Sélincourt font). In *Henry the Lion's Gospels* she is even shown as Ecclesia's mirror image, and one can imagine the Christian audience for this manuscript contemplating Synagoga's status as Bride of the Old Covenant with hopeful expectation, perhaps anticipating the time when, in the words of Robert of Tombelaine, Synagoga will be "fair and friendly, sweet and beautiful... because when at last converted she will follow the four holy Gospels just as Ecclesia."[80]

[80] PL 79, col. 526.

CHAPTER TWO

DISPUTATION IN STONE: JEWS IMAGINED ON THE ST. STEPHEN PORTAL OF PARIS CATHEDRAL

Kara Ann Morrow

Medieval visual narratives of Saint Stephen, the Christian protomartyr, have been addressed by scholars whose primary interest is the elucidation of hagiographical imagery derogatory toward a cultural or religious Other. However, the prevalence of iconographic and text-driven interpretations has hampered our understanding of the role of anti-Judaism in the formation of hagiographic imagery.[1] This approach has relegated iconographic anomaly to the realm of coincidence, and figurative eccentricity is often dismissed as charming anecdote. Meanwhile, anti-Jewish visual imagery has often been judged according to a litany of readily identifiable attributes: differentiating headgear, grotesque physiognomy, and classifying badges on clothing. While important for cultural or religious designation, the text-driven iconographic approach to the visual codes of anti-Judaism can distract us from the compositional elements and relationships that are more artistically and historically relevant.[2] References to the "readability" of

[1] My choice of the term anti-Judaism is informed by the work of scholars such as Salo Baron, David Berger, and Gavin Langmuir. Like Sander Gilman and Steven Katz, I see the shifts in attitudes that informed the treatment of European Jews in the Middle Ages as "shifts in the articulation of perception, not in the basic perception itself." See Sander L. Gilman and Steven T. Katz, "Introduction," in *Anti-Semitism in Times of Crisis* (New York, 1991), esp. 5; Gavin I. Langmuir, *Toward a Definition of Antisemitism* (Berkeley, 1990), esp. 311–340; Salo Baron, *A Social and Religious History of the Jews*, 2nd edn., vol. 11 (New York, 1967), 191–201; and David Berger, "From Crusades to Blood Libels to Expulsions: Some New Approaches to Medieval Antisemitism," *Second Annual Lecture of the Victor J. Selmanowitz Chair of Jewish History* (New York, 1997), 1–29. For a review of the historiography, Johannes Heil, "'Antijudaismus' und 'Antisemitismus': Begriffe als Bedeutungsträger," *Jahrbuch für Antisemitismusforschung* 6 (1997): 92–114.

[2] That the iconographic model falls short in considering the compositional nuances informed by oral and performative medieval practices has been recognized by, among others, Michael Camille, "Mouths and Meanings: Towards an Anti-Iconography of Medieval Art," in *Iconography at the Crossroads*, ed. Brendan Cassidy (Princeton, 1993), esp. 43–45.

visual narrative permeate our vocabulary and approaches to art history even though scholars who have examined the interaction of word and image in medieval art have convincingly argued that it is not solely texts that give narratives meaning.[3] Rather, meaning is constructed. The patron's agenda often subjugates the artist's expression and strives to manipulate viewer reception. Each time a story is retold, meaning is reinvented. Even well-known hagiographic narratives are constantly renewed. Similarly, anti-Jewish expression is particularized within varied narrative and artistic contexts. Medieval visual narratives of Stephen, which accompanied the cult of the first martyr across France and form the foundation of my study, are not static, uniform compositions, slaves to texts or iconographic types.

When considered alongside images of Saint Stephen from the tympana of other French ecclesiastical buildings, the composition made for the south transept at Notre-Dame, Paris (c. 1258), the subject of my investigation, offers a unique opportunity to study the constructed nature of visual hagiography in high medieval art (fig. 1). The goal of this paper is to situate the intricately sculpted Stephen tympanum on Notre-Dame within the historic circumstances and interests of Christian hegemony that informed its conception and reception in thirteenth-century Paris.[4] Outside the bishop's private entrance to his cathedral, artistic production and viewer reception were highly influenced by the self-interests of this powerful patron. Specifically, I propose that the imagery on the Paris tympanum is the corollary—perhaps also the result—of a new and specific form of anti-Judaic practice, the so-called "trial" of the Talmud, and is directly informed by the combats staged

[3] For the importance of differentiating between literary and oral communities, see Peter J. Rabinowitz, *Before Reading: Narrative Conventions and the Politics of Interpretation* (Ithaca, 1987), esp. 58–64 and 185–191; Walter J. Ong, *Orality and Literacy: The Technologizing of the Word* (London, 1982); and Michael Camille, "Seeing and Reading: Some Visual Implications of Medieval Literacy and Illiteracy," *Art History* 8, no. 1 (1985): 26–49. However, St. Gregory's designation of visual images in liturgical contexts as "books of the illiterate" still dominates the historiography of medieval art even though the formulation has been effectively challenged; see Lawrence G. Duggan, "Was Art Really the Book of the Illiterate?" *Word & Image* 5, no. 3 (1989): 227–251. Camille, "Mouths and Meanings"; Richard Brilliant, *Visual Narratives: Storytelling in Etruscan and Roman Art* (Ithaca, 1984); Evelyn Vitz, *Medieval Narrative and Modern Narratology: Subjects and Objects of Desire* (New York, 1989); Cynthia Hahn, *Portrayed on the Heart: Narrative Effect in Pictorial Lives of Saints from the Tenth through the Thirteenth Century* (Berkeley, 2001).

[4] For another sculptural program considered in conjunction with medieval anti-Judaism, see Laurence Brugger, *La façade de Saint-Étienne de Bourges: le Midrash comme fondement du message chrétien*, Civilisation médiévale 9 (Poitiers, 2000).

between Jewish scholars and their Christian counterparts in Paris in 1240. Alongside this context, I will discuss the acquisition by the organizer of the disputation, King Louis IX of France (St. Louis), of the large carved Roman gemstone known as the *Gemma Tiberiana*, or the Grande Camée de France, an ancient object that provided a formative model for the retelling of Stephen's martyrdom and for updating it in relation to events in the capital. By considering the variations in the contemporary visual narratives of Stephen and reviewing the anti-Judaism inherent in the primary texts; by exploring the history of the Stephen cult in Paris; by analyzing the disputation of 1240; and, finally, by considering the tympanum as a "disputation in stone," this paper offers an alternative construction of anti-Jewish meanings in the Saint Stephen narrative of Paris Cathedral.

Variations in the Narratives of Saint Stephen

Saint Stephen, differentiated from his numerous saintly namesakes by the designation proto-martyr, was the first Christian witness to follow the example of Christ by enduring torture and death at the hands of unbelievers. The hagiographical construction of his martyrdom at the hands of the Jews in particular provided a unique opportunity for medieval Christians to focus their own contemporary anti-Judaic preoccupations. Stephen's secondary title was proto-deacon, or the first deacon. According to Acts, when the needs of the Greek congregation became too great for the twelve Apostles, they searched among the disciples for seven men who could be appointed to minister to the widows of the followers. The first among these men was Stephen, "full of faith, and the Holy Ghost." Peter and the Apostles laid hands upon him while praying (Acts 7:1–6).[5] Thus, the ecclesiastical hierarchy was established and the office of the deacon would be forever linked to the power and privilege of the bishop. While the deaconate and its relationship to ecclesiastical prerogative would be refined throughout the Middle Ages, Stephen's cult enjoyed a special status because he was the only saint whose *vita* could be established as hagiographic dogma; his was the only saintly martyrdom included in Scripture. No less an authority

[5] All biblical texts in English come from the Douay-Rheims translation of the Vulgate; online source at http://www.drbo.org.

than Augustine, Bishop of Hippo, attested to the veracity and efficacy of his relics, miraculously discovered in 417 and widely disseminated.[6] According to Acts, Stephen performed great works but found his calling as a preacher to the Jews. The saint's vitriolic speech so enraged them that they took him from the city of Jerusalem and stoned him in the presence of Saul, the unconverted Paul. Stephen's last words were prayers for his persecutors. On the topic of his burial the Vulgate only reveals that "devout men took order for Stephen's funeral" (Acts 8:2).

Where the Vulgate ends, the thirteenth-century compilation of saints' lives, the *Golden Legend* by Jacobus de Voragine, picks up the narrative thread. It also provides an explanation for the dissemination of the martyr's relics: Stephen was buried by Gamaliel and Nicodemus in Gamaliel's tomb.[7] The invention of the saint's body is said not to have occurred until 417, when Gamaliel appeared in a dream to a priest named Lucien in the territory of Jerusalem. He told the priest to "open our tombs with the greatest care, for it is not seemly that we should lie in a lowly place! Go therefore to John the bishop of Jerusalem, and tell him to transport us to an honourable resting-place..."[8] Jacobus goes on to explain that after the Jews stoned Stephen, Gamaliel and his nephew, Nicodemus, gathered the remains, even though they had been "thrown outside the city to be devoured by beasts and birds of prey," and buried them in his new tomb.[9] In time, Gamaliel, Nicodemus and Gamaliel's son Abibas joined Stephen in the tomb. Lucian, after receiving the vision three times, rushed to Jerusalem and, with the assistance of John and other bishops, recovered the relics of the saint. Eventually they would be translated all over Christendom. Within the environs of northern France, ecclesiastical powerhouses such as the cathedrals at Paris, Sens, Bourges, Caen, Orléans, Meaux, Nevers and Auxerre identified Stephen as their patron saint in the Middle Ages. The cathedrals at Châlons-sur-Marne, Rouen, Reims, Soissons, Chartres, and Bayeux were also major cult centers for the martyr, and

---

[6] Augustine of Hippo, *City of God Against the Pagans*, ed. and trans. R. W. Dyson (Cambridge, 1998), 1120–1134.

[7] Jacobus de Voragine, *The Golden Legend*, trans. Granger Ryan and Helmut Ripperger (London, 1941), 56.

[8] *The Golden Legend*, 408. The author refers here to John II, Bishop of Jerusalem (386–417).

[9] *The Golden Legend*, 408.

most of them promoted this association in visual narratives of the saint's story.[10]

The Stephen tympanum on the south transept of Paris Cathedral (c. 1258) is one of the most detailed visual narratives still extant on a French cathedral (fig. 1). The cycle begins on the lower left, where the saint is shown disputing with the rabbis. His sermon extends across most of the lowest register of the tympanum, which terminates on the right in the arrest of Stephen at the hands of a Roman soldier with African features. A nursing woman is found in the center of the register. Moving up the composition to the middle register, we see Saul sitting on the garments of the executioners who stone Stephen on the left side. The narrative terminates in the right half of this register, in the entombment of the saint. At the apex of the tympanum, in a small upper register, Stephen's vision is depicted.

Other examples contrast sharply with this disposition. The mid-thirteenth-century Stephen tympanum carved above the south portal of the west façade of Bourges Cathedral (fig. 2), for example, provides a revealing foil for the Paris tympanum. The first scene on the bottom left is devoted to the ordination of Stephen and the first seven deacons at the hands of the Apostles. On the right half of the register, Stephen is led from the city in two scenes. Above, Saul, in a similar compositional position as at Notre-Dame, reaches for a witness's cloak and gestures toward the martyrdom. Stephen kneels, isolated in the center of the composition, and an angel descends with the crown of martyrdom. The executioners extend across the tympanum beneath the saint's vision. A second example is found on the west portal of the south transept façade at Chartres Cathedral (c. 1215), where Stephen's vision dominates the composition spatially (fig. 3). Only a small ribbon of space below the celestial revelation is devoted to the narrative in which Stephen is led from the city gates and stoned. Saul and the executioners are relegated to the first level of archivolts to the right. In the imagery on the south portal of the west façade of Rouen Cathedral (c. 1240), my third comparison, the stoning dominates the composition (fig. 4). Saul,

---

[10] Romuald Bauerreiss, *Stefanskult und frühe Bischofsstadt* (München, 1963), esp. 30–40. For explanations of comparable subject matter in eastern France and Germany see Robert Will, "L'ancien portail roman de l'église Saint-Étienne de Strasbourg," *Cahiers alsaciens d'archâeologie, d'art et d'histoire* 24 (1981): 59–70; Annette Weber, "Die Entwicklung des Judenbildes im 13. Jahrhundert und sein Platz in der Lettner- und Tympanonskulpture: Fragen zum Verhältnis von Ikonographie und Stil," *Städel-Jahrbuch* 14 (1993): 35–54.

sitting high upon the garments, witnesses from the left and is balanced by an open door on the opposite side of the register. The executioners loom over Stephen, bracketing him in the center of the tympanum, gazing at his vision above.

In each of these compositions Stephen's disputation and preaching are omitted in order to emphasize the martyrdom and the vision of the saint. While images depicting Stephen with the rabbis are not unheard of, they are far less common than those showing his martyrdom. Louis Réau identifies only two images of Stephen's discussion with the rabbis in the thirteenth century: a window at Chartres and the Paris tympanum.[11] The scenes unique to Paris south—the preaching sequence, the nursing mother, the African soldier, and the saint's entombment[12]—suggest that the patron's motivations were not governed solely by artistic convention or fidelity to a text.

In the Middle Ages a number of ecclesiastical buildings, including the bishop's palace, surrounded the south transept portal and created a rather private informal court for the bishop, his entourage, his clerics and his guests. The Stephen portal (fig. 5), the only entrance on the south transept, therefore was (and still is) the bishop's entrance. Access to this and the north side of the cathedral was otherwise restricted in the thirteenth century. The gated "court of the Archbishop" can be seen in a eighteenth-century drawing by Abbé Delagrive that identifies the "cour de l'Archêveché" surrounding the Stephen portal (fig. 6).[13] Thus the intended audience of the tympanum was the bishop and his politically and theologically savvy associates. The north side of the cathedral was similarly configured for the canons of Notre-Dame, a scheme that suggests the apportioning of the ecclesiastical powers in the city.[14] Indeed, for centuries the transept portals had been the symbolic battlegrounds for the canons and the bishops. Each group asserted its claims to authority through art at their exclusive entrances to the church.

---

[11] Louis Réau, *Iconographie de l'art chrétien*, tome 3 (Paris, 1959), 451.

[12] Réau, *Iconographie de l'art chrétien*, 444–456; Engelbert Kirchbaum, *Lexikon der christlichen ikonographie*, 8 vols. (Freiburg im Breisgau, 1976), 395–404; for a review of the traditional iconography of Stephen, Michel Pastoureau, "De l'hagiographie à l'iconographie," in *La légende de saint Étienne* (Avignon, 1997), esp. 1–76.

[13] The diocese of Paris did not become the seat of the archbishop until 1622.

[14] Thierry Crépin-Leblond, *Paris: La cathédrale Notre-Dame* (Paris, 2000), esp. 19, 24, 47–49; Françoise Bercé et al., "Dossier: Notre-Dame de Paris," ed. Françoise Bercé and Claude Eveno, in *Monumental Annuel 2000* (Paris, 2000), esp. 8–87. For an early, but important, historiographic review, Francis Salet, "Notre-Dame de Paris: état présent de la recherche," *La sauvegarde de l'art Français* 2 (1982): 89–113.

The resulting sculptural programs conform to the agendas of their patrons. The canons' portal, facing the canons' close on the northern transept, is associated with the Virgin. The bishop's entrance, emerging from the southern transept and facing the episcopal palace, is devoted to Stephen. The reinvention of the Stephen narrative gave ecclesiastical authorities the opportunity to assert their specific religious and political ideologies in a highly visible, permanent, public form.[15]

The Cult, the Bishop, and the Jews

It is important to note that a great deal of Stephen's attraction for Early Christian and medieval churches must have been the pedigree of his *vita*, bolstered by its foundations in the Bible. Similarly advantageous was the provenance of his relics, advocated in a Church Father's writings, and distributed at a time when relics were needed to consecrate churches for the growing religion.[16] The *Golden Legend* explains that initially Stephen's remains were deposited in the church of Sion in Jerusalem.[17] However, they were destined to travel far and often. The early management of Stephen's relics seems to have been dominated by women and imperial officials in Constantinople.[18] A new church devoted to Stephen was

[15] The renovation of the transepts was expensive and daring, lengthening each transept by one rib. The plan, begun by Jean de Chelles, required a massive and intricate stained glass rose window on each transept and, of course, an intricately carved portal. Upon Jean de Chelles's death, the bishop's new entrance on the southern transept was still only in the design stages. The plan would again be reconsidered and finally completed around 1258 by the master mason Pierre de Montreuil. See Alain Erlande-Brandenburg, *Notre-Dame de Paris*, trans. John Goodman (New York, 1997), 158; and Allan Temko, *Notre Dame of Paris* (New York, 1952), 255.

[16] On the establishment of Stephen's cult, Micheline Durand, "'Le tré glorieux Etienne': la naissance du culte," in *Histoire de Saint Etienne: la tenture de choeur de la cathédrale d'Auxerre* (Auxerre, 2000), esp. 13–16.

[17] The *Golden Legend* (410) also acknowledges the Venerable Bede's account of the invention and translation in his *Chronicle*. For variations on the story and influence of Anastasius see Laura Weigert, *Weaving Sacred Stories: French Choir Tapestries and the Performance of Clerical Identity* (Ithaca, 2004), 91, n. 18.

[18] On the first association, Maribel Dietz, "Women as Patrons and Promoters for the Cult of St. Stephen the Protomartyr," paper delivered at the International Medieval Studies Congress, Kalamazoo, MI, May 7, 2005; on the latter, Ioli Kalavrezou, "Helping Hands for the Empire: Imperial Ceremonies and the Cult of Relics at the Byzantine Court," in *Byzantine Court Culture from 829 to 1204*, ed. Henry Maguire (Cambridge, 1996), 53–79; and Kenneth G. Holum and Gary Vikan, "The Trier Ivory, Adventus Ceremonial and the Relics of St. Stephan," *Dumbarton Oaks Papers* 31 (1979): 115–33.

built in Jerusalem by a Constantinopolitan Senator, Alexander. Upon his death, he wished to be interred near the saint, whose relics were translated to the new church. Seven years after his death, his widow, wishing to return to her home, sought the permission of the bishop to remove her husband's coffin for the voyage to Constantinople. The bishop gave her permission but could not testify which silver coffin contained her husband. She assured him that she knew, and unknowingly returned to Constantinople with the relics of Stephen. This was surely not a mere mistake; in the view of the storyteller, Stephen's will was at work in choosing his earthly dwelling.[19] Speaking through Eudoxia, the possessed daughter of Emperor Theodosius, Stephen demanded to be delivered to Rome and placed next to Saint Lawrence;[20] this was done by the authority of Pope Pelagius around 425.[21] The *Golden Legend* also acknowledges the translation of the relics into the control of western ecclesiastical officials. The relics of Stephen were delivered to St. Augustine by Orosius, who had received them from St. Jerome.[22]

But it was Augustine, Bishop of Hippo, who was most instrumental in the proliferation of the cult of Stephen in the west. In the *City of God* he noted the movement of relics across northern Africa, always under the direction of bishops. The bishop Praejectus brought the relics of Stephen to "the waters of the Tibilis." A blind woman was healed after she "begged that she might be led up to the bishop who was carrying" them. Stephen's remains were placed in the castle of Sinity by the bishop Lucullus, who was miraculously healed in the process.[23] Augustine exclaimed, "What am I to do? I am so much driven by the need to fulfill my promise of completing this work that I cannot record all the miracles [performed by the relics of St. Stephen] of which I have knowledge."[24] While his enumeration of miracles served to advocate the veneration of relics whose authenticity and efficacy was vouchsafed by orthodox bishops, his chronicle also associated the relics of Stephen

---

[19] Patrick Geary explains that saints were believed to take an active role in movement of their relics; *Furta Sacra: Thefts of Relics in the Central Middle Ages*, rev. edn. (Princeton, 1990).

[20] For a critical analysis see Renate L. Colella, "Hagiographie und Kirchenpolitik: Stephanus und Laurentius in Rom," *Pratum Romanum: Richard Krautheimer zum 100. Geburtstag*, ed. R.L. Colella (Wiesbaden, 1997), 75–96.

[21] While sparing an arm, which was left in Capua; see Jacobus de Voragine, *The Golden Legend*, 409–412.

[22] *The Golden Legend*, 57.

[23] Augustine, *City of God Against the Pagans*, 1128–1129.

[24] Augustine, *City of God Against the Pagans*, 1130.

with the ecclesiastical sees. This connection has not gone unnoticed by scholars.[25] The dissemination of Stephen's cult—and by extension his relics—through Europe and France is difficult to date with specificity, except for the occasional mention in other hagiographic texts, treasury records, and of course through the inferences of visual culture.[26] For example, St. Ursin, the first bishop of Bourges, deposited a reliquary containing Stephen's relics into a model of the church on the façade of Bourges Cathedral (fig. 7).[27]

The fourth-century basilica that was the first Cathedral of Paris had been dedicated to Saint Stephen as early as the seventh century, and his relics were probably introduced to the church not long after their discovery.[28] The antique church housed Stephen's relics and functioned as a focal point for his cult; as such, both were closely associated with the bishop.[29] In the mid-eighth century, significant political and organizational changes were underway, resulting in the formation of a chapter of canons linked to the cathedral.[30] The canons' influence was spatially manifested in the northern section of the cathedral and associated artistically with the Virgin. Her name was often found alongside

---

[25] Bauerreiss, *Stefanskult und frühe Bischofsstadt*, 35–36 for Paris.

[26] For the relics, Renate Kroos, "Vom Umgang mit Reliquien," in *Ornamenta Ecclesiae: Kunst und Künstler der Romanik*, ed. Anton Legner, 3 vols. (Köln, 1985), 3:25–49, esp. 29, 30, and 35 for mentions of Stephen's dalmatic, relics built into architecture, and stones, respectively; Claire Wheeler Solt, "Romanesque French Reliquaries," *Studies in Medieval and Renaissance History* 9 (1987): 165–236, at 186 and 193 for a tomb and a vial of blood; and idem., "Byzantine and Gothic Reliquaries," *Byzantinoslavica* 45 (1984): 212–216. For maps of Stephen cult sites with generalized dates indicated, Matthias Zender, *Räume und Schichten mittelalterlicher Heiligenverehrung in ihrer Bedeutung für die Volkskunde* (Köln, 1973).

[27] For the St. Ursin portal tympanum on the west façade of Bourges, see Laurence Brugger and Yves Christe, *Bourges: La cathédrale* (Saint-Léger-Vauban, 2000), esp. 272–278; for other examples see Hans Belting, "Appendix C: Western Art after 1204: The Importation of Relics and Icons," in *The Image and its Public in the Middle Ages* (New Rochelle, 1990), 203–222, esp. 204–205 and 212; and Willibald Sauerländer, "Reliquien, Altäre und Portale," *Römisches Jahrbuch der Bibliotheca Hertziana* 33, supplement (1999–2000): 121–134.

[28] For the architectural relationship between the church of Notre-Dame and the old Cathedral of St. Stephen, M. Marcel Aubert, "Les anciennes église épiscopales de Paris, Saint-Etienne et Notre-Dame, au XI siecle et au début du XII," *Comptes rendus des séances de l'Académie des inscriptions et Belles-Lettres* (1939): 319–327. For the cults of the city, Dom Jacques Dubois, "L'organisation primitive de l'Église de Paris du III au V siècle," *Cahiers de la Rotonde* 1 (1988): 5–18, esp. 5–7.

[29] Pierre Batiffol, "L'église Cathédrale de Paris au VI siècle," *Journal of Theological Studies* (1916): 354–370; Victor Mortet, *Étude historique et archéologique sur la cathédrale et le palais épiscopal de Paris du VI au XII siècle* (Paris, 1888).

[30] *Cartulaire général de Paris*, ed. Robert de Lasteyrie (Paris, 1887), 49–50.

that of Stephen as co-patron of the diocese.[31] In the course of the late tenth century, as the privilege and influence of the chapter soared, the Virgin became designated as the sole patron of the cathedral, but Stephen remained closely associated with the place and privilege of the bishop. Finally, in 1196, the altar of the Gothic edifice, begun by Maurice de Sully in the twelfth century, was dedicated to the favored patroness of the canons. The change in dedication reflected not only the movement in popular devotion toward the cult of the Virgin but also the shifting politics of Paris, where the influence of the canons often outstripped that of the bishop.[32] However, the bishop did not shy from using Stephen's prestige to bolster his power.

Anti-Judaism in the Martyrdom of St. Stephen

Conflict between Christian and Jewish groups is at the center of the scriptural account of Stephen's martyrdom. As already noted, it was the Jews of Jerusalem to whom Stephen made his impassioned and vitriolic speech, calling them "stiffnecked and uncircumcised in heart and ears." To introduce Stephen's sermon, the author of Acts draws upon a term used by God himself to chastise the Israelites for their abrogation of the covenant, a choice that would come to exemplify the Christian view of Judaism through the Middle Ages. As Stephen concludes his sermon, he is rewarded with a private revelation of God and the Son of Man. He is then seized by his Jewish auditors, led from the city and stoned to death in the presence of Saul.

> You stiffnecked and uncircumcised in heart and ears, you always resist the Holy Ghost: as your fathers did, so do you also. Which of the prophets have not your fathers persecuted? And they have slain them who foretold of the coming of the Just One; of whom you have been now the betrayers and murderers: Who have received the law by the disposition of angels, and have not kept it. Now hearing these things, they were cut to the heart, and they gnashed their teeth at him. But he, being full of the Holy Ghost, looking up steadfastly to heaven, saw the glory of God, and Jesus standing on the right hand of God. And he said: Behold, I see

[31] *Cartulaire général de Paris*, 2, 17, 21, 35, 36, 38, 49 and passim. Stephen's name and designation as the proto-martyr were consistently acknowledged when officials addressed the cathedral in Paris or a bishop in particular.

[32] Erlande-Brandenburg, *Notre-Dame of Paris*, esp. 18–20.

> the heavens opened, and the Son of man standing on the right hand of God. And they crying out with a loud voice, stopped their ears, and with one accord ran violently upon him. And casting him forth without the city, they stoned him; and the witnesses laid down their garments at the feet of a young man, whose name was Saul. And they stoned Stephen, [as he was] invoking, and saying: Lord Jesus, receive my spirit. And falling on his knees, he cried with a loud voice, saying: Lord, lay not this sin to their charge (Acts 7:51–60).

At the heart of Stephen's sermon is the Christian belief that Jews no longer interpreted scripture correctly.[33] Rather, Jews read the text too literally, or too "carnally."[34] By clinging obstinately to the letter of the law, they are unable to understand that the true mark of God's chosen was not a physical mark upon the body but a spiritual mark, or "circumcision," upon the heart. In the Augustinian tradition Jews remained among Christians as witnesses of the Old Law, to be converted at the end of days.[35] Physical circumcision became a sign not of piety but of blindness. The call to Christians for a new circumcision was used by Justin Martyr in his *Dialogue with Trypho*,[36] and the metaphor is reiterated by St. Augustine, who references the sermon of Stephen when he describes the Jews as "the people from whom the kingdom would be taken away when Christ Jesus our Lord should come to reign not carnally, but spiritually, through the new covenant."[37] Justin Martyr's disputation ends with the conversion of the targeted disputant; Stephen's conflict ends with his martyrdom.[38]

---

[33] On St. Stephen, his speech and the Christian shift away from Jewish communication and tradition, see Gilman and Katz, "Introduction," 16–17.

[34] Anna Sapir Abulafia suggests that the contrasting characterizations are too restricting for both sides. Jewish scholars only refused metaphorical interpretations that required a christological interpretation, and Christians were certainly capable of reading a text literally if it supported their beliefs; see her "Jewish Carnality in Twelfth-Century Renaissance Thought," in *Christianity and Judaism: Papers Read at the 1991 Summer Meeting and the 1992 Winter Meeting of the Ecclesiastical History Society*, ed. Diane Wood (Oxford, 1992), 59–75.

[35] David Berger, "Mission to the Jews and Jewish-Christian Contacts in the Polemical Literature of the High Middle Ages," *American Historical Review* 91, no. 3 (1986): 576–91.

[36] Justin Martyr, "Dialogue with Trypho," *The Writings of Saint Justin Martyr*, ed. Thomas B. Falls (New York, 1948), 165–166; Amos Funkenstein, "Basic Types of Christian Anti-Jewish Polemics in the Later Middle Ages," *Viator 2* (1971): 373–82, esp. 374–377.

[37] Augustine of Hippo, *City of God Against the Pagans*, 788.

[38] On general interpretations of Stephen's story see, most recently, Alan Watson, *The Trial of Stephen: The First Christian Martyr* (Athens, GA, 1996); L. W. Barnard, "Saint

Augustine's interest in Stephen's association with Jewish "blindness" is not limited to the spiritual/carnal disputation. He relays the story of a great lady named Petronia, whose name is a play on the Latin word for rock, *petra*, the instrument of Stephen's martyrdom. Seeking a cure for an illness, Petronia was instructed by a Jew to set a little stone into a ring, and wear it against her skin tied in a hair circlet. After preparing the little rock she headed for Stephen's shrine nearby, but the stone fell from her body. When she looked to find the break in the ring or circlet, however, she found them both intact.[39] While the generalized metaphor of sightedness versus blindness, spirituality versus carnality, and even conversion versus obstinacy remained in force as elements of anti-Judaic attitudes in the Middle Ages, a more specialized set of concepts informed the trial of the Talmud in thirteenth-century Paris.

The Talmud on Trial

Beginning in Paris in 1240, the forced public debates over the Jewish texts collectively known as the Talmud announced a new era in anti-Jewish action and ideology among medieval Christians.[40] Like much Christian knowledge of Judaism, the medieval understanding of what the Talmud encompassed was skewed. Instead of a veritable library of books chronicling hundreds of years of Jewish experience—from legal, ethical and medical commentaries, to historic, folkloric, and comedic notations—Christians believed the Talmud was "a text" that had come to rival the place of the Old Testament in Jewish philosophy.[41] In the words of Pope Gregory IX in a letter to French ecclesiastical officials, "For they, so we have heard, are not content with the Old Law which God gave to Moses in writing: they even ignore it completely, and affirm

Stephen and Early Alexandrian Christianity," *New Testament Studies* 7 (1960): 31–45; Marcel Simon, *St. Stephen and the Hellenists in the Primitive Church* (London, 1956).

[39] Augustine of Hippo, *City of God Against the Pagans*, 1130–31. The miracle is also retold in the *Golden Legend*.

[40] Samuel Krauss, *The Jewish-Christian Controversy from the Earliest Times to 1789* (Tübingen, 1996), 150.

[41] Hyam Maccoby, *Judaism on Trial: Jewish-Christian Disputations in the Middle Ages* (Rutherford, NJ, 1982), 19–20 and 31; Alexander Patschovsky, "Der 'Talmudjude': Vom mittelalterlichen Ursprung eines neuzeitlichen Themas," in *Juden in der christlichen Umwelt während des späten Mittelalters*, ed. Alfred Haverkamp and Franz-Josef Ziwes (Berlin, 1992), 13–27.

that God gave another law which is called 'Talmud'..."[42] Thus if the Talmud was accepted as the preeminent text of Judaism by Jews, their role as witnesses to the authenticity of the Old Law would be nullified. In the Christian understanding of Jewish identity, it would follow that Jews had no place in the medieval world.

The terms "trial" and "disputation" are problematic as descriptions of the 1240 conflict over the Talmud from any perspective other than that of the medieval Christian majority. The rabbis, representatives of a precariously situated minority, could hardly have been expected to mount an aggressive, effective defense of the text against the charges of blasphemy. The readily apparent concern of the rabbis for their safety surely would have prevented such an effort. The rabbis actually requested assurance from Blanche of Castile that Christian forces would be kept in check.[43] Moreover, the verdict of the "trial" was a forgone conclusion; the winner of the disputation was established before the leaders were summoned. The confrontation was staged for the sake of reinforcing Christian hegemony and, at least ideologically, encouraging Jewish conversion.

Given the staged nature of the conflict, it is surprising that the king did not order the Talmud texts seized and burned until a full year after the disputation. The burning did not actually take place until 1242. Some scholars suggest that Blanche of Castile was a tempering force, having been raised in a more tolerant region of Christendom. Others suggest that time was needed to search for copies, scrutinize the texts, and consult with papal authorities. Possibly, further testimony concerning the alleged blasphemies was collected over the next year and thus finally tipped the scales against the Talmud in royal policy.[44]

The disputation was contrived when Pope Gregory IX sent letters to royal and ecclesiastical officials across Europe, after being informed of the alleged blasphemous content and the erroneous place the Talmud

[42] Solomon Grayzel, *The Church and the Jews in the Thirteenth Century*, rev. edn. vol. 1 (New York, 1966), 241.

[43] William Chester Jordan, "Marian Devotion and the Talmud Trial of 1240," in *Religionsgespräche im Mittelalter*, ed. Bernard Lewis and Friedrich Niewöhner (Wiesbaden, 1992), 68–69; Jeremy Cohen, "Towards a Functional Classification of Jewish Anti-Christian Polemic in the High Middle Ages," in *Religionsgespräche im Mittelalter*, 107.

[44] Jordan, "Marian Devotion," 69.

had achieved in the lives of European Jews.[45] The allegations by a Jewish convert to Christianity, the mendicant friar Nicholas Donin, ranged from the substitution of the Talmud for the Old Testament to blasphemies against Christ, irreverence toward God, and slurs about the Virgin.[46] This final category took the form of allegations that Mary was not in fact a virgin, and that her conception of Christ was not miraculous, but adulterous. Mary was even associated with a thinly veiled reference to a woman named Miriam who took a lover in the Talmud text.[47] William Chester Jordan points out that both the Latin and Hebrew transcripts indicate that the only display of Christian indignation arose in light of the presumed attacks against Mary.[48] The belief that the Talmud contained such blasphemies was of primary concern to the organizers of the Paris disputation.[49] While Mary's virginity was a subject of some ridicule in a variety of Jewish texts, it was her association with the Talmud in particular that encouraged the burning of those texts in 1242.[50] It should be recalled that the Virgin was the primary patroness of Paris Cathedral in the thirteenth century. A visual focus for her cult, the portal of the north transept, balancing the Stephen narrative on the south, was devoted to her role as the Mother of Christ and intercessor for the repentant faithful.

Renowned for his devotion to the Virgin and notorious for his anti-Jewish ideology and rhetoric,[51] Louis IX was moved to action in conjunction with ecclesiastical officials from the royal demesne. Donin, an apostate and mendicant friar,[52] would be the primary witness and disputant for the Christian position. The Queen Mother Blanche of

[45] Isidore Loeb, "La controverse de 1240 sur le Talmud," *Revue des études juives* 1 (1880), 246–62; 2 (1881), 248–70; 3 (1881), 39–57.

[46] Funkenstein, "Basic Types of Christian Anti-Jewish Polemics," esp. 379–381; Berger, "From Crusades to Blood Libels to Expulsions," 8–12.

[47] William Chester Jordan, *The French Monarchy and the Jews: From Philip Augustus to the Last Capetians* (Philadelphia, 1989), 137–41; Maccoby, *Judaism on Trial*, 156–65, who believes thirteenth-century Jews actually did conflate Miriam of the Talmud with the Christians' Virgin Mary.

[48] Jordan, "Marian Devotion," 66–67.

[49] "Talmud, Burning of," *Encyclopedia Judaica* 15, 16 vols (Jerusalem, 1972), 768–71; Maccoby, *Judaism on Trial*, 216, n. 4.

[50] Jordan, "Marian Devotion."

[51] William Chester Jordan, *Louis IX and the Challenge of the Crusade: A Study in Rulership* (Princeton, 1979), 56.

[52] For the involvement of the mendicant orders in the harassment and conversion efforts of thirteenth-century Jews, Jeremy Cohen, *The Friars and the Jews: The Evolution of Medieval Anti-Judaism* (Ithaca, 1982). There is presently no consensus on whether Donin belonged to the Franciscan or Dominican order.

Castile would preside and the event would be held at the royal palace, with various Christian clerics, including William of Auvergne, the Bishop of Paris, serving as judges.[53] Highly respected rabbis from the region were brought to Paris where they were forced to answer to the charges presented. While the formal organization of the encounter is still uncertain,[54] there is no doubt that this was staged as an adversarial confrontation in which Donin faced off with his opponent, Rabbi Yehiel ben Joseph. The Christians assumed the offensive, while the rabbis were placed in a defensive position.

Latin and Hebrew accounts survive, though both are as much propaganda—full of epithets, stock exaltations, and religious topoi—as they are historic records of an actual event.[55] Nevertheless, they are valuable descriptions of how each side interpreted and regarded the conflict. According to the Hebrew account, Rabbi Yehiel "faced his antagonist" and "answered him directly."[56] The disputation was confined to the translation and veracity of the allegedly anti-Christian sections of the Talmud. Donin sat before Rabbi Yehiel and read passages from the Talmud, demanding his acknowledgment of the correctness of the translation and his explanation for its content. According to the Latin account, the rabbi sat in silent consternation, or simply lied.

[53] The number of bishops and royal clerics present is noteworthy: Geoffrey of Belleville, the chaplain to the Louis IX; Walter, the Archbishop of Sens; Adam de Chambly, the Bishop of Senlis; and the Chancellor of the University of Paris. Interestingly, Bishop William of Auvergne drew heavily on the work of Ibn Gabriol and Maimonides for his own theological work and is noted as strongly anti-Jewish by modern scholars. Maccoby, *Judaism on Trial*, 22.

[54] Jordan, *Marian Devotion*, 65–66; Robert Chazan, "The Condemnation of the Talmud Reconsidered," *Proceedings of the American Academy for Jewish Research* 55 (1998): 19; and Maccoby, *Judaism on Trial*, 20–23. Judah Rosenthal, "The Talmud on Trial," *Jewish Quarterly Review* 47, (1956–57), 145–69, argues for a historical face-to-face confrontation as communicated in the Hebrew account. Maccoby notes that Yitzhak Baer suggests an inquisitorial format, Yitzhak Baer, "On the Disputations of R. Yehiel of Paris and R. Moses ben Nahman," [in Hebrew], *Tarbiz* 2 (1930–31): 172–87.

[55] For mutual polemical attitudes around the time of the disputation, Cohen, "Towards a Functional Classification," esp. 104–109.

[56] Rosenthal, "The Talmud on Trial," 145–69; Maccoby, *Judaism on Trial*, 23. The Hebrew account was documented 20 years after the debate took place by Rabbi Joseph ben Nathan Official. For mutual conceptions of the other, Ivan G. Marcus, "Jews and Christians Imagining the Other in Medieval Europe," *Prooftexts* 15, no. 3 (1995): 209–226; Grayzel, *The Church and the Jews*, Appendix A "Nicholas Donin," 339–340.

Disputation in Stone

The trial of the Talmud informed the patronage and reception of the Stephen tympanum at Paris Cathedral in several ways. The involvement of the patron in the disputation, the unique choice of and emphasis on Stephen's role as preacher and disputant, and the structural relationships in the tympanum itself all made Stephen's efforts to convert the Jews a type for the 1240 Parisian trial. In the first scene on the tympanum (fig. 8), Stephen sits opposite the older Jew, who, like Rabbi Yehiel, "faces his antagonist" (the friar Donin), and "answers him directly." The seated figure of the saint references passages from a book and encourages a response from the Jew before him. Stephen, with his tonsure and dalmatic, anchors the composition, and is framed by the presence of another cleric. He gestures with his right hand to the figure seated opposite him, a bearded Jew identified by his Phrygian cap. The older Jew rebuts the saint's demonstration with his gestures.

By the thirteenth century Stephen was consistently depicted with the tonsure; as an anachronistic detail,[57] it is presented here as a visual foil to the Phrygian cap on the head of his Jewish opponent, and deserves our closer attention. In the Middle Ages the monastic tonsure, as James Marrow explains, was symbolically associated with the torments endured by Christ. The agonies related in the Gospels were only a part of the abuse that medieval Christians understood Christ to have endured. Added to the traditional list that included the mocking, flagellation, and bearing of the cross were the plucking and pulling of Christ's hair.[58] The meaning of this indignity, especially as it applies to the fate of a martyr, can be gleaned from biblical text, "He shall be led as a sheep to the slaughter, and shall be dumb as a lamb before his shearer (Isaiah 53:7)." However, it is to the medieval understanding of the plucked head that one must turn for a deeper understanding of the Stephen tympanum at Paris. Around 1130 Rupert of Deutz composed an explanatory text "On the Shaving of Heads" in his *De divinis officiis* (Book 12):

> Notwithstanding our being so adorned, we prefer the head untouched, and the tonsure that we call the crown, we cover with no ornament. For

[57] Louis Trichet, *La tonsure, vie et mort d'une pratique ecclésiastique* (Paris, 1990).

[58] James H. Marrow, *Passion Iconography in Northern European Art of the late Middle Ages and Early Renaissance* (Kortrijk, Belgium, 1979), 68.

> our joy is not full since we rejoice not in this of the present, but in the hope of the future. Therefore, however, we are shaved, because...of our Lord Jesus Christ who was crucified in the place of Calvary... [We] have decided against hair, because the Lord Christ, leader of the Nazarenes, was shorn; that is, crucified in the place of Calvary where the heads of the condemned are cut off. Dalila, that is the poor and stupid synagogue, shaved the head of the most brave Samson...Although we may rejoice at His victory in the above-mentioned ornamentation, we still mourn His shearing out of compassion in the shaving of our heads. However we call this sign of humility a crown, that is a victory, because that faithful shearing of our Lord, of which this shaving is a sign, is a victory beyond doubt; it is a triumph, it is our honor and glory![59]

The tonsure, or as Rupert calls it, *the crown*, worn by late medieval clerics is therefore maintained in order to mimic and rejoice in Christ's victory through martyrdom. As the first of all the martyrs to follow Christ, Stephen's name, explains Jacobus de Voragine in the *Golden Legend*, is Greek for *crown*. "He was the crown of the martyrs, for he was their forerunner under the New Covenant."[60] Upon his martyrdom, he was crowned by angels, as is literally communicated on the tympanum at Bourges (fig. 9). In the Paris narrative his tonsure is contrasted with the Phrygian cap on the head of the Jew opposite. This latter head-covering does not necessarily communicate anti-Jewish ideals, but designates a religious ideology that, in this context, contrasts with Stephen's sign of blessedness.

In his lap the saint holds a book (fig. 8). The artist has placed it on a dramatically tilted plane to make it more readily visible to the Jew in front of Stephen as well as the viewer in front of the portal. Stephen points to the text demonstratively. His hands create a physical link between the text and the Jewish man's hands that work to refute the words. Only Stephen has physical contact with the codex. While Stephen is framed by another standing cleric, the Jew, or rabbi, before him is accompanied by a standing figure who scratches his head and pulls his beard in consternation. The fact that Stephen and the deacons are all rendered with youthful, clean-shaven faces, in contrast to the images of the mature, bearded Jews, is significant. The Christian response to the Jew's perceived preference for the Talmud is here being explained

[59] Rupert of Deutz, *De divinis officiis libri* (12.2.25), in J.-P. Migne, ed., *Patrologiae cursus completus, Series Latina*, 221 vols. (Paris, 1844–55), 170: 54–56 [hereafter cited as PL]; trans. from Marrow, *Passion Iconography*, 69–71, 277 and n. 275.

[60] Jacobus de Voragine, *The Golden Legend*, 54, 57.

in "familial" terms. While the Jews were seen as the "parents" of the Christian tradition, still to be convinced of Christianity's validity, they were also, in their perceived preference for the Talmud, seen as denying the truth of their own legacy, the Old Testament. As such, relations between Christians and Jews were wrought with "Oedipal anxiety."[61] The *Golden Legend* contributes to our understanding of this by relating Stephen's name to his association with his mature auditors. In reviewing origins for his name, Jacobus explains that "Stephen comes from *strenue fans anus*, he who speaks with zeal to the aged."[62] The conflict between the clerics and the rabbis on the Paris tympanum is communicated in terms of age. As the Jew pulls his beard, his mouth gaping indecorously, he looks out from the portal at the spectator; the viewer witnesses the debate between a young, angelic,[63] tonsured cleric in a medieval vestment with an old, capped, bearded Jew. Behind them other bearded, Jewish men congregate in various states of attention, hearing Stephen's argument, discussing among themselves and, importantly, consulting their own text. Their text, however, is not a codex like Stephen's book. Rather it is depicted in the ancient format of a scroll. The scroll, traditionally the attribute of Old Testament prophets who foretold the coming of Christ,[64] carries an altogether different meaning on the Stephen tympanum at Paris, where Jewish writings had recently become the focus of debate and destruction. Presented as a textual Other, the Jew cannot find the answer in his scroll to satisfy Stephen's logic, rooted in his codex. Rabbi Yehiel could not by definition defend the Talmud from Donin's attack. Just as the Old Testament had been superseded by the New, the Talmud would now be confiscated and destroyed.

Ancient Iconography and Subjugated Peoples

In the next scene (fig. 8), Stephen stands to address his auditors in a more active and formal manner. His congregation is expanded and

---

[61] Hyam Maccoby, "Did Antisemitism Begin in the Middle Ages?" in *A Pariah People* (London, 1996), 169–172.

[62] Jacobus de Voragine, *The Golden Legend*, 54.

[63] Stephen's face is often referred to as angelic. "[They] saw his face as if it had been the face of an angel (Acts 6:15)."

[64] James Hall, *Dictionary of Subjects & Symbols in Art* (New York, 1974), 275–76.

diverse; the reactions of the Jewish audience members are different from the disputants' responses in the first scene; rapt attention is no longer predominant. They listen now with apprehension. They begin to turn away. Along the bottom, an older man in left profile sits dejectedly with his head in his right hand, a gesture of melancholy. Another man, his hand on his chin, stares blankly. A woman looks on as she nurses a child on the left side of her body. Certainly no nursing mothers were present at the disputation. However, neither these figures nor the Roman officer arresting Stephen (discussed below) are merely quaint details or charming anecdotes, injected into the scene in order to make it more accessible, as some scholars have suggested.[65] The inclusion of a familial group in the center of the lintel not only suggests Stephen's ministration to the widows but also visually associates all medieval Jews with the conquered and the vanquished, the tragically excluded exiles seated at the feet of their conqueror. The figural type is, I argue, derived directly from antique Roman sources of captured barbarians to which the thirteenth-century French authorities who organized and supervised the Paris disputation, the very same officials who commissioned the tympanum, would have had direct access.

A 1279 inventory of the treasury of the Sainte Chapelle, Louis IX's royal chapel, verifies the presence of just such an antique source. The *Gemma Tiberiana*, known as the Grand Camée de France, was acquired by Louis IX from Constantinople around 1247 (fig. 10).[66] The acquisition of such an important and visually remarkable relic—it is truly grand at 31 × 26 cm.—could easily have influenced the bishop's portal at Notre-Dame. Conspicuously visible in the center of the bottom register, a woman sits holding her child to the left of her body. To the right a bearded man sits with his right hand pensively to his cheek. Above the two, a bearded figure sits dejectedly in a melancholic pose and wears a Phrygian cap. The gem's conquered Gauls sit dysphoric on the ground line of the lowest register, corresponding to the tympanum's lowest compositional space. The mother and child, seated in the center, are emphasized within the composition, just as the mother and child at Stephen's feet are punctuated by the portal's trumeau (figs. 1 and 5). In the center of the gem the victory of the conquerors is celebrated for

[65] Erlande-Brandenburg, *Notre-Dame of Paris*, 184.

[66] Mathilde Avisseau-Broustet, "Le Grand Camée de la Sainte-Chapelle," in *Le Trésor de la Sainte-Chapelle*, ed. Jannic Durand and Marie-Pierre Laffitte (Paris, 2001), 90–95.

posterity as a worldly testament in historic, terrestrial time and space, just as Stephen preaches the word of God and triumphs as the first martyr. The Romans sit triumphantly beneath a celestial vision; they gaze up at the Apotheosis of Augustus but the conquered barbarians all stare unseeing at the ground. Stephen experiences his own divine vision, a private revelation denied to his Jewish persecutors who are metaphorically blind.

According to Nicolas-Claude Fabri de Peiresc, the seventeenth-century discoverer of the antique *Gemma Tiberiana*, medieval viewers understood the gem's imagery not as the Apotheosis of Augustus but as the triumph of Joseph at the court of Pharaoh in Egypt. Even without this *interpretatio christiana*, however, the clerical iconographers would not have hesitated to borrow motifs from the Grand Camée de France, which was housed in the Sainte Chapelle on the Île de la Cité, where the bishop's preoccupations interacted with the king's interests. The proximity of the bishop's portal to the king's treasury as Delagrive's plan illustrates (fig. 6), is compelling. Moreover, Pierre de Montreuil, the architect and master mason of Notre-Dame's south transept, was rumored to have built the Sainte Chapelle.[67] When one considers the charged imperial imagery and extraordinary appearance of the Grande Camée, there is no wonder that Louis IX arranged for its acquisition from Constantinople. Its connections to the Roman imperial past and its figural representation of the Phrygian-capped Gauls would have appealed to his Capetian sense of might.

As the story on the tympanum continues, one man, his back turned to Stephen, notes the offences uttered against the Jews by the Christian preacher. He provides a visual and narrative link to the next scene in which Stephen is arrested. A Roman guard with stereotypically African facial features, dressed in a beautiful field uniform, holds the saint by a fistful of hair and presents him for judgment to the Sanhedrin and two Jewish witnesses (fig. 11). Stephen's hands are symbolically crossed before him, referencing the Crucifixion, the sacrifice Stephen's arrest and martyrdom mirror. There is no reference in the textual sources to the presence of a Roman soldier with African features at the arrest of Stephen.[68] The Roman presence should be seen as a reference to

[67] Erlande-Brandenburg, *Notre-Dame of Paris*, 163.

[68] Again, see Réau, *Iconographie de l'art chrétien*, 444–56; Kirchbaum, *Lexikon der christlichen Ikonographie*, 395–404; Pastoureau, "De l'hagiographie à l'iconographie"; and Hall, *Dictionary of Subjects & Symbols in Art*, 290–91.

Christ's Passion, where Roman guards and officials accomplished the Arrest and Crucifixion at the behest of the Jews.

Thirteenth-century Christian ideology concerning "blackness" was greatly influenced by the writings of the third-century Alexandrian, Origen. As Jean Devisse explains in his monumental work, *The Image of the Black in Western Art*, Origen proposed that, upon the Second Coming, the damned cast into darkness would be clad in bodies that would echo their spiritual state and outcast condition. That is to say, they would be wrapped in a skin of darkness.[69] Following Origen's analogy, medieval artists depicted spiritually dark beings, demons and devils, with blackened skin and hair.[70] Neither the antique sources nor Origen related the allegorical equation of evil and darkness to African people or the stereotypically "negroid" facial features often seen in later medieval art and even the modern era: heavily ridged brows, round cheeks, short flat nose, and full prominent mouth.[71] However, the author had indicated the presence of an African—specifically, Egyptian—executioner in the *Passion of Perpetua* in the second century.[72] Gregory the Great, in his *Moralia on Job*, commented that Ethiopia represents the blackness that is a sign of evil among the sinful of the world. He also told of an abbot who saw that "a little Negro was tugging at the cloak of the monk who could not stay at prayer." The monk was struck with rods so that "the ancient Enemy, as if he himself had been whipped, no longer dared to disturb thoughts."[73] Thus, not only was evil associated with blackness, it could also be associated with sub-Saharan African people in literary texts. Nonetheless, the association of spiritual darkness with dark complexions and African features would not become fixed in the iconography of medieval art until the twelfth century. One must consider the face-to-face encounters experienced by medieval Christians

---

[69] Jean Devisse, *The Image of the Black in Western Art, vol. 2: From the Early Christian Era to the "Age of Discovery,"* Pt. 1: *From the Demonic Threat to the Incarnation of Sainthood*, trans. William Granger Ryan (New York, 1979), 11–12, citing and translating Origen, *Peri Archon* 2.10.8, in J.-P. Migne, ed., *Patrologiae Cursus Completus, Series Graeca*, 161 vols. in 166 parts (Paris, 1857–66), 2:240.

[70] Jan Nederveen Pieterse, *White on Black: Images of Africa and Blacks in Western Popular Culture* (New Haven, 1992), esp. 24.

[71] David Brion Davis, *Slavery and Human Progress* (New York, 1984), 36–38.

[72] Devisse, *The Image of the Black in Western Art*, 72–78, citing and translating chapter three of *Passio sanctarum marytrum Perpetuae et Felicitatis*, associated with Tertullian (PL 3:40–41).

[73] Devisse, *The Image of the Black in Western Art*, 69, citing and translating Gregory the Great, *Dialogi* 2.4, 87–88.

in order to understand the exact context in which the African soldier was sculpted.

The most significant encounter western Europeans had with Africans in the Middle Ages was through the conflicts between Christians and Muslims in the struggle over the Iberian Peninsula. Soldiers within the Moorish ranks were often of sub-Saharan origin, having not only dark complexions but also stereotypically "African" features.[74] The black personification of evil was assigned to the Muslim,[75] especially the Muslim soldier or executioner. Black Africans became associated with the tormenters of Christ, as per the executioner of Perpetua in the early hagiography. Sculpted images of the African executioner can be seen on the Cathedrals at Chartres, Rouen, Auxerre, Reims and in the form of the arresting soldier in Paris (fig. 11). At Chartres an African male stands ready in a long tunic in the Judgment of Solomon on the north transept. At Rouen an African in a belted knee-length garment holds John the Baptist by the hair, poised with his sword for the fatal blow. At Auxerre an African soldier in a highly detailed Roman cuirass, similar to the one depicted on the Stephen tympanum in Paris, holds the infant before the judging Solomon.[76]

The fact that African physiognomy is exploited on the same portal where undercurrents of Christian xenophobia toward Jews informs the meaning of a narrative should not be surprising. The combination of stereotyped "Jewish" and "African" physiognomies appeared in roughly contemporary Parisian manuscripts,[77] and the first of the executioners to stone Stephen in the middle register of the Paris tympanum seems to bear just such a conflated facial type. Biblical exegesis supported the

---

[74] Peter Mark, *Africans in European Eyes: The Portrayal of Black Africans in Fourteenth and Fifteenth Century Europe* (Syracuse, 1974), esp. 5–10.

[75] Positive images of black Africans certainly existed in the Middle Ages. An African Christian officer in the Roman Theban Legion, St. Maurice, the patron saint of the crusade against the Slavs, was conceived as a black African in the dress of western crusaders. At Chartres Cathedral, an African servant or supplicant accompanies the Queen of Sheba, depicted in this instance as a white woman. On the Klosterneuburg Altarpiece she has a distinctly dark complexion. In the later Middle Ages the conception of the black African Magus who paid homage to the Christ Child at Epiphany also inspired cults that honored the Royal saint.

[76] Devisse, *The Image of the Black in Western Art*, 73–75.

[77] In the 1280–1290 manuscript *Images de la vie du Christ et des saints*, the "Stoning of Stephen" and the "Carrying of the Cross" include tormenters that conflate Jewish and African physiognomy and dress; Devisse (76–77) sees the imagery as particularly African. Paris, Bibliothèque nationale de France, MS. fr. 16251, fols. 76r and 37v.

comparison of obstinate Jews with the sinful Ethiopians. According to the medieval Christian interpretation of Psalms 67:32, even the sinful Ethiopians will convert before the Jews.[78]

The Jews on the Paris tympanum avoid conversion. On the left side of the second register Stephen is stoned by the Jews as Saul witnesses from the far left and points to the execution (fig. 1). His position on the tympanum echoes Stephen's just below him, and their gestures, each pointing with his right hand, reflect one another. Stephen, stretched across the scene, looks up into the faces of his persecutors, who grin with malice. At the peak of the tympanum Stephen's private divine vision is depicted for all viewers. As the gaze of the viewer is lifted, the mind and spirit are edified in anagogical fashion. Here Christ's appearance between two angels breaks with the literal translation of the story.[79] Stephen cries out, "Behold, I see the heavens opened, and the Son of Man standing on the right hand of God (Acts 7:55)." This vision breaks the boundaries of time and space; it is at once Stephen's vision according to the text and the vision of the living observer. In the final scene the proto-martyr's body is lowered into the casket from which relics will be exhumed in 417 for dissemination, making their way eventually to Paris Cathedral. Gamaliel and Nicodemus appear as witnesses. Above the saint's body, the righteous Christian codex again appears.

Conclusion

While religious conflict is at the heart of the story of Stephen's martyrdom in Acts, it is not only the scriptural source that informs the meaning of anti-Jewish ideology in the tympanum devoted to the saint. The inclusion of Stephen's disputation, the incorporation of stereotyped physiognomies, and the juxtaposition of Jewish and Christian elements encourage a metaphorical equation of Stephen with the Christian antagonists in the Paris Talmud trial of 1240, of the Jewish

---

[78] Pieterse, *White on Black*, 18–19, 24; Davis, *Slavery and Human Progress*, 36; Ephraim Isaac, "Genesis, Judaism and the 'Sons of Ham'," *Slavery and Abolition* 1 (1980): 3–17; and Winthrop D. Jordan, *White over Black: American Attitudes Toward the Negro, 1550–1812*, (New York, 1968), 18 and 36.

[79] For variations of Stephen's vision in medieval art see François Boespflung, "'Voici que je contemple ses cieux overts...' Sur la lapidation d'Etienne et sa vision dans l'art médiéval," *Revue des sciences religieuses* 66, nos. 3–4 (1992), 263–295.

disputants with the Parisian rabbis, and of the dejected auditors with real thirteenth-century Jews. Both the staged trial of the Talmud and the acquisition of the visually powerful Grand Camée de France interpose a lens through which the designers of the tympanum interpreted the original hagiography. The royal and ecclesiastical involvement with the disputation indicates that it was the intention of the tympanum's patron that Stephen's narrative be conflated with contemporary events, and suggests the intersection of royal authority with an ecclesiastical agenda, creating an iconographically rich and politically meaningful interpretation of the *vita* of Saint Stephen at Paris Cathedral.

Ultimately the *vita* of any martyr is about the relevance of the Passion and the miracle of the Resurrection that the saint's sacrifice mirrors, but by highlighting the "uncircumcised hearts" of the persecutors, the truth of the martyr's sacrifice and the sacrifice of Christ becomes heightened. In such a conception, the Jew has again turned his back on the divine word, this time by defending the Talmud. As the anti-Jewish tide rose in medieval France, the traditional Jewish role as witness to the veracity of the Old Testament was being denied on the bishop's portal. Blind to the celestial vision, Jews cannot witness. On the tympanum, as the Jews of the scene become more overtly vilified and blind, Stephen's piety and vision is heightened. Stephen's peaceful faith is contrasted with the obstinate, murderous disbelief of the Jews. While medieval Jews—persecuted through constraints on dress, vocation, speech, and now literature—were threatened with exile, abduction, torture and death, hagiographic images of Saint Stephen reversed the actuality of events so that the persecutor became the persecuted.

CHAPTER THREE

TAKING LITTLE JESUS TO SCHOOL IN TWO THIRTEENTH-CENTURY LATIN PSALTERS FROM SOUTH GERMANY[1]

Eva Frojmovic

From early Christian times, the gap in the Gospel narrative between Jesus' infancy and his appearance during a disputation in the Temple at the age of twelve called for the writing of apocryphal narratives about Jesus' childhood. These apocryphal childhood gospels invented an uncanny child hero who threatened and subdued those who slighted him, manifesting his divine nature in miracles that set him apart from his playmates. Such a story is the one that recounts how Joseph tried to subject his little boy to primary schooling. The early apocryphal gospels tell how an aggressive Jesus duels with his increasingly exasperated teachers, who finally expel him as unteachable, but not before the boy has put them in their place as the guardians of an Old Law he has overcome. Apocryphal gospel stories such as this one were revived and retold in Latin versions and vernacular translations from the twelfth century on. The versions that will occupy us here rewrite the plot in transferring the responsibility of parenthood from Joseph to Mary, and toning down the violence of Jesus' behavior. Nevertheless, they retain the basic plot of the unchildlike altercation between Jesus and his would-be teachers that results in Jesus' expulsion. This altercation, hinging on the opposition between the Old Law and the New Law, and the supersession of the former by the latter, harbored the potential for anti-Jewish invective.

[1] This research has been supported by a Research Fellowship from the Leverhulme Trust and by the School of Fine Art, History of Art and Cultural Studies at the University of Leeds. I owe debts of gratitude to Philip Alexander, George Brooke, Richard F. M. Byrn, Michael Clanchy, William Flynn and Mitchell Merback, as well as the librarians and curators at the National Museums of Merseyside Liverpool, Stiftsbibliothek Klosterneuburg and Württembergische Staatsbibliothek Stuttgart.

The apocryphal first schoolday of Jesus was rarely represented in the visual arts. It appears for the first time in two South German Psalters of the early thirteenth century that are the subject of the present chapter.[2] My interest in this iconography was aroused by the Waldkirch Psalter's characterization of the schoolteachers as "Jewish" by means of "Jews' hats." I wondered whether this "Jewish" school may have originated in Christian observations of real Jewish schools, the Yeshivot or Talmudic academies that flourished in France and south Germany at the time. Studying this extraordinary manuscript further, my attention was arrested by another "judaized" scene, the trial of Pilate, which I shall explore in more detail later (cf. fig. 6); in this image, Pilate is assisted by men in "Jews' hats" who confront Jesus with an aggressive display of written documents. So in two scenes Jesus is opposed to hostile textualities that are marked as "Jewish." Although the contrast between the Old Law and the New Grace is as old as Paul's letters, the specific visual articulation in the Waldkirch Psalter poses an inevitable question: what is the significance of the "Jewish" school and the "Jewish" courtroom, and are these images clear statements of anti-Jewish sentiment? This question becomes even more pressing if one considers that the Liverpool Psalter, which is the only other object from this period that includes the scene of Jesus' first schoolday, and which was produced in the same general area perhaps only a decade or so later, is entirely devoid of these anti-Jewish accents.

Hope that the details of as well as the differences between the two Psalter images might be satisfactorily explained by specific textual sources is quickly disappointed. The differences between the images and the known texts are at least as significant as the differences between the two images. These divergences from the texts concern the role of the parental protagonist and the choice of the narrative moment to be illustrated. A study of these divergences will reveal the creativity and multi-layeredness of the images.

[2] The isolated close-up group of Mary leading a more or less unwilling Jesus along the way appears also separately from the school context. A fresco in the choir of the Marienkirche, Gelnhausen (ca. 1235) appears to be among the earliest instances of this iconography, which becomes more common from the late thirteenth century onwards. Mary pulls a resistant Jesus, who carries a writing tablet, along towards the right. The adjacent arcade features the twelve-year-old in the Temple; see Hans Wentzel, "Maria mit dem Jesusknaben an der Hand. Ein seltenes deutsches Bildmotiv," *Zeitschrift des Deutschen Vereins für Kunstwissenschaft* 9 (1942), 203–50.

My contention is that the opposition of the Old Law and the New Grace is deployed in the Waldkirch Psalter in order to articulate tensions within Christian society between an essentially monastic ideal of learning and those new forms of learning informed by scholasticism. The Waldkirch Psalter, I propose, includes a polemic against the new schooling, which draws on Psalm commentaries, and pushes this polemic by visually "judaizing" the environment where this new learning takes place. The "Jewish school" then becomes a trope for worldly learning.

Taking Little Jesus to School in the Waldkirch and Liverpool Psalters

The two manuscripts discussed here are typical luxury psalters made for aristocratic lay use, produced in south German lands in the years 1220–40.[3] Both preface the Psalter proper with a picture quire containing a sequence from the life of Jesus, and that is where the scenes of Jesus being taken to school find their place. I shall begin with a discussion of the Waldkirch Psalter, because it is the older of the two manuscripts and because it is here we find the denigration of certain forms of learning and textuality represented as "judaized".

The position of the Schooling scene at the end of the prefatory picture cycle of the Waldkirch Psalter draws attention to the strategic importance of the image (fig. 1). In terms of Jesus' biography, the Schooling scene should be placed between the Flight into Egypt and the Baptism. Instead, it interrupts the flow of this chronological sequence. The Schooling scene comes after the Presentation in the Temple (fol.

[3] The dating and exact origin of both manuscripts, especially the Waldkirch Psalter, are contested. The Waldkirch Psalter has in fact been variously ascribed to the Upper Rhine, Switzerland, Bavaria (Regensburg), and Central Franconia; see Hanns Swarzenski, *Die lateinischen illuminierten Handschriften des XIII. Jahrhunderts in den Ländern an Rhein, Main und Donau* (Berlin, 1936), cat. no. 51, 45; Ellen J. Beer, "Der Rheinauer Psalter. Ein Werk des Zackenstils in Bayern vor der Mitte des 13. Jahrhunderts," in *Studien zur Buchmalerei und Goldschmiedekunst des Mittelalters. Festschrift für Karl Hermann Usener zum 60. Geburtstag am 19. August 1965*, ed. Frieda Dettweiler, Herbert Köllner and Peter Anselm Riedl (Marburg an der Lahn, 1967), 265, n. 39; *Codices breviarii (Cod. brev. 1–167)* [*Die Handschriften der Württembergischen Landesbibliothek, Stuttgart*], ed. Virgil Ernst Fiala and Wolfgang Irtenkauf (Wiesbaden, 1977), ser. I, 3:16. The problems of localizing thirteenth-century German psalters are summarized in Christine Sauer and Ulrich Kuder, *Die gotischen Handschriften der Württembergischen Landesbibliothek Stuttgart* (Stuttgart, 1996–), vol. 1: *Vom späten 12. bis zum frühen 14. Jahrhundert* (1996), 21–5; the Waldkirch Psalter is cat. 16, (77–80), pl. I and II, (247–8), and figs. 47–62, (272–87).

10 verso), and opposite this, on folio II recto, the Psalter opens with an elaborate Beatus initial that fills most of the page. Additional full-page Christological miniatures articulate the tenfold division of the Psalter, and these (surprisingly) return us to the moments before Jesus was taken to school: the Massacre of the Innocents prefaces Psalm 38, and the Flight into Egypt Psalm 51; only then, the Baptism (placed opposite Psalm 52) forms the transition to the Passion. The theological significance of this position of the Schooling scene, which makes it into a programmatic frontispiece to the Psalter, will be further explored below.

A curious anticipatory moment is chosen for the representation of Jesus' first day of school in the Waldkirch Psalter: the resistance of the divine pupil to his schooling. While Mary enters the school gate and points to the busy classroom on the right, little Jesus pulls her away to the left. Mary does not hold his hand but grabs his wrist—a gesture that clearly indicates disagreement or even the use of force. Jesus, meanwhile, while still holding an object that looks like his lunch basket, has reached, even breached, the frame. The monogram "IHC," which makes reference to the boy's messianic status, is inscribed on the dark framing border above his halo, which protrudes outside the painted frame of the miniature. The entire weight of his little body leans left; in an energetic movement he has bent his right leg and planted his left one; he looks back at his mother and strains to pull her back, or break free. Mary, in a symmetrical turn of her body and head, comes to confront not Jesus but the viewer.

The interior of the school is laid out in two superimposed registers—the teachers at the top, the pupils at the bottom. Perhaps as a consequence of this layout, teachers and pupils do not interact but work separately. Inside the school we see two teachers, contrasted by age and the writings they hold, engaged in a disputation, presumably about the text held by the younger teacher at the right. Both teachers wear white "Jews' hats," the one on the right being tied under the chin with a black string. Their disputation is carried out in vivid gestures, and the younger scholar, with his hand pointing to heaven, appears to be winning the argument. The older teacher on the left, a white-haired and bearded old man, argues with both hands in the rhetorical gesture of an advocate, as if to reason with a superior adversary. A hinged writing tablet in the form of a rectangular diptych, colored a dull gray brown, lies in front of him on the desk. It is inscribed on two transverse lines with a nonsensical sequence of golden letters.[4] The writing tablet identifies the older man as the teacher of grammar. The younger, brown-haired and short-bearded teacher holds a scroll whose shape approaches that of a tablet, inscribed in golden letters on a parchment ground (left bare): "Diligis dominum tuum et viv[as]." The source of this text is most likely Deuteronomy 30:15–16:

> See, I have set before thee this day life and good, and death and evil, in that I command thee this day to love HaShem thy G-d, to walk in His ways, and to keep His commandments and His statutes and His ordinances; then thou shalt live and multiply, and HaShem thy G-d shall bless thee in the land whither thou goest in to possess it.[5]

The subject of the disputation therefore identifies the teachers as engaged in an exposition of theology.

Meanwhile, the two pairs of bareheaded boy pupils, seated on the floor and separated from their elders by a large desk, are engrossed in their own textual study.[6] The texts studied by the pupils form two parts of a syllogism. The left pair of students jointly hold a scroll that reads *Nullum malum bonum est* ("No evil thing is good"), while the right pair hold *Nullum bonum malum. bonum est*—presumably an erroneous transcription of *Nullum bonum malum est* ("No good thing is bad"). Clearly, the two pairs and their respective texts relate to each other in a paired group study that serves as training for the mastery of the disputation technique. The source can almost certainly be identified as Boethius' *De Syllogismo Categorico*, an authoritative explication of

---

[4] "P h k" and "cf.fcy" or "cf.fiy". The penultimate letter may be a "c" or an "i", since the dot is ambiguously positioned between the penultimate and last letter, which is also surmounted by an abbreviation mark.

[5] Translation from the Jewish Publication Society Bible of 1917, online resource [http://www.mechon-mamre.org/e/et/et0530.htm]. The painted scroll does not correspond exactly to any of the invocations of the love of God in Deuteronomy. Jerome's version of Deuteronomy 30:15–16 reads: "Considera quod hodie proposuerim in conspectu tuo vitam et bonum, et e contrario mortem et malum, ut *diligas Dominum Deum tuum*, et ambules in viis ejus, et custodias mandata illius et caeremonias atque judicia, *et vivas*, ac multiplicet te, benedicatque tibi in terra, ad quam ingrederis possidendam." *Patrologia latina database* [electronic resource], ed. J. P. Migne (Cambridge, 1993), 28: col. 454C. I have italicized the segments quoted in the Waldkirch Psalter. The Psalter's scribe has changed "diligas" to "diligis."

[6] The head of the fourth pupil is damaged, but can be seen at the extreme right.

Aristotle's *Categories*.[7] This text therefore places the scene firmly in the context of the discipline of Dialectic (Logic).[8] Given its preoccupation with good and evil, its inclusion in the Psalter makes sense.

The school in the Waldkirch Psalter is marked as a particular type of school. Both by its study techniques—study in pairs, disputation of the masters—and by its curriculum—training in Dialectic in the service of theology—it is characterized as a scholastic institution of learning. For the thirteenth century, this type of school was exemplified by the French cathedral school and above all by the pinnacle of scholastic learning, the university. These were very different types of schools from the older monastic or cathedral grammar schools that were traditional in the Holy Roman Empire.

But this modern school is clearly depicted in a negative light. If Jesus resists it, it must *a priori* be evil. To drive the value judgement home, the teachers are dressed in "Jews' hats." The scholastic seat of learning is characterized as a "Jewish" school. So when the reader opening the Psalter reaches the verse "[Blessed is the man...] who does not sit in the chair of pestilence," the association between the chair of teaching and the chair of pestilence is easily made. After considering the corresponding scene in the Liverpool Psalter, I will offer some suggestions as to why the scholastic school in the Waldkirch Psalter should be so represented.

The scene of Jesus' first school day in the Liverpool Psalter (Liverpool, National Museums of Merseyside, Ms Mayer 12004, on deposit at the Walker Art Gallery) appears at first sight to follow a very similar iconography (fig. 2). Mary pulls a resistant Jesus along by the wrist towards a school on the right. The interior of the classroom is visible

---

[7] A. M. Boethius, *De Syllogismo Categorico*, book 2, in *Patrologia latina* database, vol. 64, col. 816B ff. See also M. Bernhard, "Boethius im mittelalterlichen Schulunterricht," *Schule und Schüler im Mittelalter. Beiträge zur europäischen Bildungsgeschichte des 9. bis 15. Jahrhunderts*, ed. M. Kintzinger, S. Lorenz and M. Walter (Cologne, 1996), 11–27; A. J. Minnis, ed., *Chaucer's "Boece" and the Medieval Tradition of Boethius* (Cambridge, 1993).

[8] *De Syllogismo Categorico* was introduced into the medieval logic curriculum in the late eleventh and twelfth centuries. It was part of the core curriculum of Dialectic, together with Aristotle's *Categories* and *Peri hermeneias* (*De Interpretatione*), and Porphyry's *Isagoge*. When the remaining Aristotelian texts on logic were discovered around 1150, Boethius's *De Syllogismo Categorico* remained part of the the *Ars Vetus* or *Logica Vetus*; see S. Ebbesen, "Medieval Latin Glosses and Commentaries on Aristotelian Logical Texts of the Twelfth and Thirteenth Centuries," in *Glosses and Commentaries on Aristotelian Logical Texts*, ed. Charles Burnett, Warburg Institute Surveys and Texts 23 (London, 1993), 129 ff.

there, with a teacher instructing a group of four pupils. Even the tower above the gateway and the double arch of the school room correspond to the architecture in the Waldkirch Psalter. But the differences are just as significant as the similarities.

The Liverpool Psalter was most likely written and illuminated for a lay owner in the diocese of Constance before the middle of the thirteenth century.[9] Of the original prefatory picture quire (which apparently once contained four bifolia), the first three folia are lost, leaving five painted folia in place (i.e. twenty out of the original thirty-two half-page images). As it stands now, the Schooling scene comes at the beginning of the surviving picture quire, in the upper register of folio 7 recto; it is combined with the Baptism in the lower half of the page. The remaining painted folios cover the Passion, and the cycle ends with the Last Judgment on folio 11 verso, followed by the large Beatus initial opening the Psalter on folio 12 recto.[10] So in this manuscript, the Schooling scene evidently took its natural biographical place at the transition from the infancy cycle to the Passion.

The Liverpool image of Jesus' schooling is composed of two units: at the extreme left, Jesus, holding a rectangular green object (a writing tablet?) is pulling away, while Mary pulls him forward and raises a birch rod, a threatening gesture at odds with the comparatively timid resistance of Jesus. On her right, a school building encloses four pupils facing their teacher, who grabs the nearest pupil by the hair and raises

---

[9] My thanks to Dr. Xanthe Brooke of the Walker Art Gallery, Liverpool, for enabling me to study the original manuscript. In addition to Margaret Gibson and Martin Kauffman, eds., *Medieval Manuscripts on Merseyside* (Liverpool, 1993), cat. no. 3, 3–4, see also N. R. Ker, *Medieval Manuscripts in British Libraries* (Oxford, 1969–2002), vol. 3, 216–8; Nigel F. Palmer, "*Parzival* Fragments from the Binding of a Latin Psalter in Liverpool," in *Joseph Mayer of Liverpool, 1803–1886*, ed. Margaret Gibson and Susan M. Wright (London, 1988), 145–51; idem, "Zum Liverpooler Fragment von Wolframs *Parzival*", in *Studien zu Wolfram von Eschenbach*, ed. Kurt Gärtner and Joachim Heinzle (Tübingen, 1989), 151–81; idem and K. Speckenbach, *Träume und Kräuter. Studien zur Petroneller "Circa instans"-Handschrift und zu den deutschen Traumbüchern des Mittelalters* (Cologne, 1990), 129–31.

[10] There is clear evidence of a division of labor, with different specialists working simultaneously on different parts: the artist(s) of the prefatory picture quire worked in a classicizing style indebted to the Ingeborg Psalter; painted somewhat hastily in pale pastel colors with copious white highlights against a matt gold ground. By contrast, the historiated initials of the Psalter and the Calendar were executed with great precision by an artist trained on the Saxonian early *Zackenstil*. This artist(s) used a brilliant primary palette, in which strong reds and blues predominate, framed by burnished gold. A number of strange iconographical choices, together with gross negligence in the text (fol. 100!), indicates a lay workshop.

his own birch rod. Mary reflects the punitive gesture of the teacher, while Jesus' resistance contrasts with the submissiveness of the four pupils. As Jesus looks up at Mary while pulling her back, she turns around to him and, at that moment, establishes eye contact with the book's beholder. This configuration of opposing impulses is indeed very reminiscent of the Waldkirch Psalter. But in terms of methods of instruction and curriculum, this is a very different institution from the school represented in the Waldkirch Psalter: it is, rather, a secular grammar school. Mary's gesture echoes and amplifies the punitive pedagogy familiar from the iconography of Grammatica, who is routinely shown wielding the birch rod.[11] While the rest of the picture cycle abounds in men wearing pointed hats, this schoolmaster is bareheaded. This school is not depicted as a "Jewish" school.

By now it is clear that there are significant differences between the two early thirteenth-century versions of the Schooling scene in the Waldkirch and Liverpool Psalters. The main difference concerns the characterisation of the school, a scholastic institution teaching Logic and theology in the Waldkirch Psalters, a secular grammar school in the Liverpool Psalter. If we may consider the Liverpool Psalter as a control sample, we can see all the more clearly that the artist of the Waldkirch Psalter (or his model or advisor) made a deliberate choice in the specific visual definition of the school as "Jewish." Another difference lies in the level of Jesus' resistance: whereas in the Waldkirch Psalter, his whole body speaks of his vehement rejection of the school, in the Liverpool Psalter his body language reads more like mere childlike shyness. Finally, whereas Mary appears to counter Jesus' recalcitrance in the Waldkirch Psalter with verbal arguments only, in the Liverpool Psalter she threatens him with a birch rod that would offer a bitter foretaste of the schooling he was destined never to undergo.

Before we turn to the textual sources, it is also worth dwelling on what the two versions of the Schooling scene have in common. In narrative terms, the images allude to but do not tell the story of a confrontation. No real action is depicted in these images. Everything is suspended in anticipation, in a delicate balance that invites the viewer's participation and prompts and relies on his extrapictorial knowledge. It is all

---

[11] See Michael Camille, "Illuminating Thought: The Trivial Arts in British Library, Burney Ms. 275," in *New Offerings, Ancient Treasures: Studies in Medieval Art for George Henderson*, ed. Paul Binski and William Noel (Stroud, 2001), 347.

too easy to take the mother-and-child group for granted, steeped as we are in the maternal stereotypes of the nineteenth century: who else if not the mother should take the small child to school? But a survey of the textual sources will disrupt this expectation.

Images and Texts

There can be little doubt that medieval images of Jesus' first school day are broadly based on the accounts in the early apocryphal Infancy gospels of Pseudo-Thomas and Pseudo-Matthew as well as their medieval elaborations, as previous scholarship has shown.[12] Yet any expectation of finding in texts an exhaustive explanation for the iconographic particularities of the images is disappointed by careful comparison. For example, the role of Mary in the two Psalter images is contrary to the older textual sources, which had put Joseph firmly in charge of Jesus' education. In the various versions of the Infancy Gospel of Pseudo-Thomas, the responsibility for Jesus' education rests clearly with Joseph, who dominates as a father figure. Mary is virtually invisible.[13] The Psalter miniatures constitute a mariological reformulation that is in line with the high medieval privileging of Mary.

In the texts, the schooling episode focuses on the extraordinary debates between Jesus and successive teachers, a series of exchanges that invariably end with the humiliation of the latter. The account of this event insists on the contrast between the miraculous nature of little Jesus' wisdom and the ordinary knowledge of the schoolmasters.

---

[12] Ewald Vetter, "Maria mit dem Kind an der Hand," *Wiener Jahrbuch für Kunstgeschichte* 56–7 (1993): 775–96, 899–902, sp. 784, tries to match the elements in the Waldkirch Psalter miniature with the apocryphal source(s). Wentzel, "Maria mit dem Jesusknaben an der Hand," 227, was more cautious and drew attention to the innovation of Mary's role. Clanchy, "Icon of Literacy," discusses the Tuse fresco of Jesus going to school as a visualization of Luke 2:40 and the Pauline Epistle to the Galatians 3:24–6, and only secondarily as an illustration of the apocryphal infancy gospels.

[13] Achim Masser, *Bibel, Apokryphen and Legenden: Geburt und Kindheit Jesu in der religiösen Epik des deutschen Mittelalters* (Berlin, 1969), 290–291, 296–300. According to O. Cullmann ("Infancy Gospels," in *New Testament Apocrypha*, 2 vols., ed. Wilhelm Schneemelcher, trans. Robert McLachlan Wilson [Cambridge, 1991–92], 414–69, esp. 439–41 and 441–53), the textual tradition of the Greek Pseudo-Thomas is so complicated as to preclude a reconstruction of an ancient prototype. The original may have been known in the late second century. The late (post-Carolingian) version of the Latin Pseudo-Matthew in *Los Evangelios apocrifos*, ed. A. de Santos Otero (Madrid, 1963), mentions "Joseph and Mary."

In the Pseudo-Thomas, the miracles wrought by Jesus in order to confound the schoolmasters are described with a violence that is at odds with his divine wisdom. The Gospel of Pseudo-Thomas features two, in some versions three, teachers. First, Zachyas approaches Joseph to entrust Jesus to him—there is no mention of a school, only of a (private) tutor. When Zachyas tries to teach Jesus the alphabet, the latter challenges him with a trinitarian interpretation of the first letter.[14] At that, Zachyas is overawed and begs Joseph to take Jesus away. After some time, Joseph seeks the services of another teacher, who again attempts to teach Jesus the alphabet. Again, Jesus challenges his teacher by demanding an allegorical interpretation of the alphabet. In exasperation, this teacher actually hits him, so Jesus in turn "hurt and cursed him, and he immediately fainted and fell to the ground on his face."[15] Finally, Joseph makes a last attempt with a friend, who offers to teach and promises to be patient. After warning him of the child's supernatural powers, Joseph "took him with fear and anxiety, but the child went gladly."[16] This time, Jesus enters a recognizable school setting, and, taking up the book placed on the lectern, proceeds to teach a rapidly assembling crowd. The teacher submits to Jesus' authority, and Jesus is reconciled with the teachers and departs.

In the Latin Gospel of Pseudo-Matthew, Jesus rejects Zachyas' authority to teach by asserting that:

> The precepts of the law which you have just spoken of, and all the things that you have named, must be kept by those who are instructed in human learning; but I am a stranger to your law-courts, because I have no father after the flesh. You who read the law, and are learned in it, abide in the law; but I was before the law.[17]

[14] "How do you, who do not know the Alpha according to its nature, teach others the Beta? Hypocryte, first if you know it, teach the Alpha, and then we shall believe you concerning the Beta. [...] Hear, teacher, the arrangement of the first letter, and pay heed to this, how it has lines and a middle mark which goes through the pair of lines which you see, (how these lines) converge, rise, turn in the dance, three signs of the same kind, subject to and supporting one another, of equal proportions." *New Testament Apocrypha*, 445.

[15] Ibid. 447.

[16] Ibid. 447–8.

[17] "Praeceptor legis: quae paulo ante dixisti et omnia quae nominasti oportet servari ab his qui hominum docentur institutis; sed extraneus sum a foris vestris, quia parentem carnalem non habeo. Tu qui legem legis et instructus es, in lege permanes; ego autem ante legem eram." *Los Evangelios apocrifos*, ed. de Santos Otero, 222.

Zachyas then hands Jesus over to the aged alphabet teacher Levi. Provoked by Jesus' refusal to repeat the alphabet, Levi hits him in exasperation. Jesus then proceeds to teach the teacher his own alphabet, and the teachers submit to Jesus' uncanny wisdom. None of this agonistic narrative is pictured in our two Psalter miniatures!

The early Christian apocrypha described a world very different from—and unacceptable to—the high medieval one. Mary is barely mentioned in this episode; instead Joseph appears as Jesus' father, and Jesus acts with a violence suited to an antique demi-god, not the mild mannered *Jesuskind* of high medieval devotion. So when these ancient apocrypha became the basis of literary elaboration in Latin and the vernaculars, the plots and characters had to be modified in order to create an affectively satisfying narrative of Jesus' childhood, a childhood that could appropriately address a new public.[18] Thus arose epics devoted to the life of Mary and the infancy of Jesus, some of which appeared in the vernacular during the twelfth and thirteenth centuries: Frau Ava's (d. 1127?) *Leben Jesu*,[19] the Old French *Évangile de l'enfance*,[20] Ælred of Rievaulx's (1109–66) *De Jesu puero duodenno*,[21] Wernher the Priest's *Driu liet von der maget* (Three songs about the Virgin) of 1172, Konrad von Fussesbrunnen's vernacular *Kindheit Jesu*, dated ca. 1190–1200,[22]

[18] Maureen Barry McCann Boulton, ed., *The Old French Évangile de l'enfance* (Toronto, 1984), who is content with a dating to the thirteenth century (already proposed by Paul Meyer in the late nineteenth century) and offers no suggestions about either authorship or readership, nor any suggestion of why this vernacular literature arises in the twelfth century.

[19] *Die Dichtungen der Frau Ava*, ed. Friedrich Maurer (Tübingen, 1966); *Ava's New Testament Narratives: When the Old Law Passed Away*, ed. and trans. James A. Rushing, Jr. (Kalamazoo, 2003).

[20] *The Old French Évangile de l'enfance*, ed. Boulton, 46–51, verses 769–910. As a counterpoint, the author sought to integrate moments of affective intimacy between Mary and Jesus. These are clearly inserts which are there to balance Joseph's unfashionable predominance and give some space to the cult of Mary, who was virtually absent from the apocryphal gospel narratives; see E. B. Vitz, "The Apocryphal and the Biblical, the Oral and the Written, in Medieval Legends of Christ's Childhood: The Old French *Évangile de l'enfance*," in *Satura: Studies in Medieval Literature in Honour of Robert R. Raymo*, ed. Nancy M. Reale and Ruth E. Sternglantz (Donington, 2001), 124–149. Vitz reads the *Evangile de l'enfance* as very close to the ancient prototypes in its non-conformity to normative theology.

[21] I am grateful to Mitchell Merback for bringing this text to my attention.

[22] Konrad von Fussesbrunnen, *Die Kindheit Jesu*, eds. H. Fromm and K. Grubmüller (Berlin and New York, 1973), verses 2945–3008. In Konrad's work, the school visit stands at the end of the entire narrative. This position is significant, since it corresponds to the placing of the same story at the end of the infancy cycle in the Waldkirch Psalter. But there the similarities end.

and finally the Latin *Vita beate virginis Marie et Salvatoris rhythmica*, dated towards 1230.[23] Surprisingly, most of these high medieval versions retain Joseph's paternal role. The schoolmasters negotiate only with him; and only he takes Jesus to school. Only the latest of these works, the Latin *Vita beate virginis Marie et Salvatoris rhythmica*, finally transfers this parental obligation to Mary. She, not Joseph, is described there as taking Jesus to school. But this action occupies the space of only one line.[24] So while the *Vita* registers the elevation of Mary to Jesus' sole guardian, it too cannot be seen as a determining source for Mary's expanded role and monumentalized figure in the Psalter images.

These high medieval versions rework their sources by downplaying the violent behavior of Jesus and instead highlight affective and even sentimental motifs. They substantially abbreviate the exchanges between Jesus and his teachers. Yet even in Konrad of Fussesbrunnen's *Kindheit Jesu*, Jesus still impresses us as a—by human standards—very naughty child indeed, a bit of a bully in fact. Only in the *Vita beate virginis Marie et Salvatoris rhythmica* is his appearance in school so brief that such a negative impression does not take root. The bulk of this stanza is made up of Jesus' exchange with the one teacher present about the hidden meaning of the letter J, and the teacher's expulsion of his pupil. None of the surviving versions of the Schooling episode, whether ancient or medieval, mention Jesus' resistance to being taken to school in the first place. None of the texts mention any other pupils; none define the school as either a grammar school or a scholastic school, nor cite the passages inscribed in the Waldkirch Psalter's schooling scene; none of the texts prefigure the effective avoidance of the pupil-teacher confrontation, or the interaction between Mary and Jesus that is so striking in the two Psalters' images.

In sum, while the Psalter images of Jesus' abortive school visit are informed by the apocryphal tradition in a general way, they refashion it. This visual rewriting takes the form of the elevation of Mary to protagonist, and a narrative focus on an early and seemingly peripheral

---

[23] *Vita beate virginis Marie et Salvatoris rhythmica*, ed. A. Voegtlein (Tübingen, 1888).

[24] "Maria Ducens filium ad scolas commendavit / Magistro, quod litteras docent hunc rogavit." *Vita beate virginis Marie et Salvatoris rhythmica*, verses 2784–5. The debate about the alphabet follows, and the 18-line episode ends at v. 2801 with Jesus' expulsion by the unnamed "magister/doctor." As Masser, *Bibel, Apokryphen and Legenden*, 81, and Vetter, "Maria mit dem Kind an der Hand," 776, point out, this work was read aloud during meals in Kloster Tegernsee, thus indicating its intended monastic audience.

moment in the plot. The confrontation between the precocious Jesus and the Pharisaic teachers is not actually staged in either the Waldkirch or the Liverpool Psalter. Instead, both images home in on a naturalistic depiction of Jesus' childlike behaviour, that of the shy, unwilling schoolboy. The two images are to some degree parallel developments to the progressive textual rewriting of the apocryphal Schooling scene, though the main narrative moment of Jesus' resistance—which they stage in a most original fashion—is not paralleled in any of the texts. Both images, while based on a narrative tradition, are independent interpretations of textual sources. My contention is that their interpretative force derives from their multilayered character. Next to the apocryphal story, they visualize elements of Psalm exegesis, and they register anxieties about the changing nature of education under the sign of scholasticism.

The Chair of Pestilence

Having broached the iconographic confrontation between images and possible source texts, we need to set up a different text-image confrontation, that between the images and their own (con)text—the Psalter—and its medieval exegesis. Having considered the inscriptions from Deuteronomy and Boethius in the Waldkirch Psalter, we now turn to the beginning of Psalm 1, which comes into view opposite the picture:

> *Beatus vir qui non abiit in consilio impiorum et in via peccatorum non stetit et in cathedra pestilentiae non sedit, sed in lege Domini voluntas eius; et in lege eius meditabitur die ac nocte* (Blessed is the man who hath not walked in the counsel of the ungodly, nor stood in the way of sinners, nor sat in the chair of pestilence; But in God's law is his will; and he will meditate on His law day and night).

The associative links between the beginning of the Psalm and the painted texts in the Schooling scene opposite are the Deuteronomic exhortation to love God and the syllogism on good and evil. Together, they pose the choice between good and evil, and associate divine law with goodness. But to say this is to only skim the surface of this intertextuality, for the Psalter as a medieval devotional book with its Old Testament text juxtaposed with its New Testament images is always already a typological construction. And this is certainly true, as our further investigation will show, of such a contested concept as divine law.

The Deuteronomic exhortation that links the love of God with the observance of his laws and the practice of rituals was a fundamental and controversial text from the very foundation of Christian theology, which claimed superiority over Judaism in its spiritual (rather than literal) understanding of those very "commandments and ceremonies and judgments." Therein lay, in fact, one of the fundamental hermeneutical differences between Judaism and Christianity. The page layout and image-text juxtaposition in the Waldkirch Psalter creates an exegetical framework in which the scene of Jesus' first day at school constitutes a visual gloss on Psalm 1. The reader is practically invited to meditate on image and text as a unit: is this "Jewish" school a "council of the ungodly," and the chair of the teachers a "chair of pestilence"? The use of the term *cathedra*, with its obvious overtones of clerical and didactic institutional authority, only draws attention again to the seated teachers behind the large table as the intended target of the psalmist's critique. Within this framework, the deuteronomic exhortation held by one of the teachers in the Waldkirch Psalter miniature forms a textual gloss to the second verse of the Psalm, "But in God's law is his will."

Commentaries on the first two verses of Psalm 1 explicated the meaning of the phrases "counsel of the ungodly" and "chair of pestilence" and glossed the reference to God's law. That the *cathedra pestilentiae* of Psalm 1 was commonly understood as a reference to "bad" schooling and teaching, shading into the heretical, and that the concept of God's Law was interpreted figuratively, can be evidenced from Psalm commentaries of the twelfth and thirteenth centuries. Three authoritative examples may suffice. Peter Lombard, Magister Sententiarum and Bishop of Paris, compiled before 1160 the Psalms commentary he had come to use in his cathedral school. He glosses Psalm 1:1 by first comparing the "ungodly" to "Adam, who consented to his wife who was deceived by the devil." Peter then proceeds to equate the "ungodly" with the Scribes and Pharisees, a common circumlocution for Judaism. Finally, he comments on the *cathedra pestilentiae*:

> "The seat of pestilence" is understood as evil and dangerous teaching that spreads like a cancer. And "does not sit in the seat of pestilence," that is: does not teach dangerous but wholesome teaching.[25]

[25] "'*Et in cathedra pestilentiae non sedit*':... accommodatius accipitur prava, et perniciosa doctrina, quae ut cancer serpit. 'Et in cathedra pestilentiae non sedit,' id est non perniciosam doctrinam docuit, sed salubrem." Peter Lombard, *In Totum Psalterium Commentarii*, in *Patrologia Latina* database, vol. 191 col. 61B. Translation mine.

Hugh of St. Cher (1200–1263), in his *Postille super totum Psalterium*, similarly attacks non-orthodox teaching, though the overall thrust of the postilla to Psalm 1 appears to be an exhortation to penitence. Following Peter Lombard, Hugh also associates the *cathedra pestilentiae* with the teaching of Scribes and Pharisees. He then offers three examples: "Error in teaching, like heretics. Incitement to evil, like false Christians. Offering a bad example, like bad prelates."[26] Hugh's argument starts out where Peter's reasoning had arrived. He first reiterates the latter's understanding of the *cathedra pestilentiae* as heretical teaching, but finally brings the argument back home by inveighing against "bad prelates." In the final analysis, "bad prelates" are tarred with the twin brushes of heresy and "Judaism." This association of "false Christians" and "bad prelates" with heretics, and all three with "Judaic" scribes and Pharisees, was a strong concern of the Paris university theologians of the first third of the thirteenth century.[27] It gives us a glimpse into the logic by which the schoolteachers in the Waldkirch Psalter could have been visually "judaized." Authority in teaching was a very hot issue in the anti-heresy wars.[28] In this perspective, the judaized *cathedra pestilentiae* points us to the pervasive joint classification of Jews and heretics during the period of these campaigns.[29]

Thomas Aquinas's commentary on the Psalms postdates the period of the Liverpool and Waldkirch Psalters, but it is nevertheless useful to see how self-evidently Thomas assumes the equation of *cathedra* and school:

---

[26] "De tertio [Et in cathedra pest] vel derisorum alia littera [non sedit] Mar. 1. Erat docens in ptate [pietate] hns [hominis]: non sicut scribe et pharisei... et ph[ar]i[sei]. Jere. 2. Dabo vobis pastores iuxta cor meum; et pascent vos scientia et doctrina. Et dicitur cathedra pestilentie tribus modis: Errorem docendo ut heretici. Ad malum incitando ut falsi christiani. Malum exemplum prebendo ut mali prelate." Hugh of St. Cher, *Postille super totum psalterium* (Venice: per Iohannnem et Gregorium de Gregoriis fratres impensis Stefani et Bernardini de Nallis, 1496), 1 ad Ps 1:1.

[27] As Sara Lipton has documented in her *Images of Intolerance: The Representation of Jews and Judaism in the Bible moralisée* (Berkeley, 1999), 83–111.

[28] Germany, too, had its own anti-heresy crusade in 1233. In this context, heretics were believed to transmit their erroneous teachings in schools. Gregory IX's Bull of 1233, addressed to the Archbishop of Mainz and the inquisitor Conrad of Marburg, specifically describes the heretics' *school*; see Joshua Trachtenberg, *The Devil and the Jews: The Medieval Conception of the Jew and its Relation to Modern Antisemitism* (Philadelphia, 1983), 205–6; Lipton, *Images of Intolerance*, 45; Richard Kieckhefer, *The Repression of Heresy in Medieval Germany* (Liverpool, 1979).

[29] See Cohen, *Living Letters*, 147–312 and 317–63, for a detailed discussion of Judaism qua heresy. Cohen dates the equation of Talmud with heresy from the late 1230s.

> "in the chair [of pestilence]": this is the third element, that is, to induce others to sin. Therefore it says "in the chair" like a teacher who teaches others to sin; and therefore [the Psalmist] says "pestilence," because pestilence is an infectious illness.[30]

Perhaps this is the point to return to the deuteronomic text held by the younger schoolteacher in the Waldkirch Psalter, and see it in relation to commentaries on Psalm 1:2. The Deuteronomic exhortation to love God and the divine law was indeed cited in Psalm commentaries since the Church fathers, but was progressively allegorized. Peter Lombard, in juxtaposing with the evils of verse 1 the willingness of the good person to place his will "in the law of the Lord" and to meditate on the Lord's law by day and night, is quick to impose a christological interpretation:

> "But in the Lord's law"—this points to Christ full of all good in himself... It is one thing to say "in the law," another thing to say "under the law." Whoever is in the law acts according to the law, obeying the law voluntarily. But whoever is under the law acts according to the law, forced by fear of necessity. The former is free, the latter a slave. Furthermore: the law of the letter, written for the slave, is one thing, the law of sanctity, which is perceived in the mind by the son and which does not need the letter, is something else.[31]

So Peter distinguishes between the law of the letter for the unfree slave (that is, the Old Testament for the servile Jews) and the law of sanctity for the free son (that is, God's new chosen people, Christians). The effect of the gloss is to abolish the letter of the law in favor of a spiritual understanding.

It is worth contrasting the Christian exegesis of the Psalms with that of the Jewish scholar Rashi (d. 1104), the founder of the Jewish

---

[30] "*et in cathedra*": ecce tertium, id est inducere alios ad peccandum. In cathedra ergo quasi magister, et alios docens peccare; et ideo dicit, *pestilentiae*, quia pestilentia est morbus infectivus." St. Thomas Aquinas, *Opera omnia*, 25 vols (New York, 1948–1951), 14:150.

[31] "Aliud est esse in lege, aliud sub lege. Qui est in lege, secundum legem agit, voluntarie legi obediens. Qui autem sub lege est, secundum legem agit, necessitatis timore coactus. Ille liber, iste vero servus. Iterum: Aliud est lex litterae, quae scribitur servo; aliud lex sanctitatis, quae mente conspicitur a filio, qui non indiget litteris." Petrus Lombardus, *Commentarius in Psalmos*, in *Patrologia Latina* vol. 191 col. 62. Thomas Aquinas' gloss, *Opera Omnia*, vol. 14, 151, points in the same direction: "*Sed in lege Domini*; et hoc spetialiter pertinet ad Christum... Et dicit *in lege*, per dilectionem, non sub lege per timorem."

counterpart to the scholastic movement. In his commentary on Psalm 1, Rashi takes a moralistic direction: he chastises the conduct of people who "walk in the counsel of the wicked" and warns that to "sit in the seat of scorners" leads to the "neglect of Torah" (which includes the study of Talmudic law).

> For as a result of the fact that "he did not walk [in the counsel of the wicked]," "he did not stand [in the path of habitual sinners]," and as a result of the fact that "he did not stand [in the path of habitual sinners]," "he did not sit [in the seat of scorners]." ... Note [that on the basis of the antithetic parallelism of verses 1 and 2] you learn that the "seat of scorners" leads to neglect of Torah.[32]

The emphasis is on a person's moral conduct as conducive (or not) to the study and cultivation of Torah, whose study is seen as the supreme good. In fact, verse 2 of Psalm 1 is interpreted with a view to the pedagogical development of the Torah student:

> "And he thinks about his Torah." One who is beginning [the study of Torah], it is called "the Lord's Torah" but a person who has exerted himself over it, it is called his [the student's own] Torah.[33]

A few of the manuscripts conveying Rashi's commentary also include anti-Gentile polemic:

> Some say that it ["the laudations of the man"][34] refers to Abraham, "who did not walk in the counsel of the wicked." The latter are the generation of the division [of humankind into different nations and languages; i.e. the people who conspired to build the tower of Babel: Nimrod and his associates]. "And he did not stand in the path of habitual sinners." The latter are Abimelech's people..., for they are suspected of adultery... "And he did not sit in the seat of scorners." The latter are the people of Sodom... they were scoffers... for they were making fun of him.[35]

The equation of the "wicked," "habitual sinners" and "scorners" with various Gentile peoples—the builders of Babel, Abimelech's people, and Sodom—would surely have been understood as negative allusions

---

[32] Rashi, *Commentary on Psalms*, trans. and ed. Mayer I. Gruber, (Leiden, 2004), 173. The last square bracket is an explanatory gloss supplied by the editor; the other square brackets supply the quoted Psalm texts.

[33] Rashi, *Commentary on Psalms*. The explication hinges on the ambiguous pronoun "his Torah."

[34] This is Rashi's alternative formulation, which interprets the first words of the Psalm not as "Happy is the man" but as "These are the commendations of the man who does not walk..."

[35] Rashi, *Commentary on Psalms*, 174–77.

to contemporary Gentiles. But nowhere in Rashi's Psalm commentary is schooling itself connoted negatively.

To sum up: Psalm commentaries worked to allegorize the Psalmist's dialectic between the evils of the counsel of the ungodly and the chair of pestilence on the one hand, and the good of God's law on the other. High medieval commentators equated the "chair of pestilence" with error of teaching, and interpreted divine law spiritually. The Schooling scene in the Waldkirch Psalter articulates some of the concerns of these Psalm commentaries. The "Jewish hats" of the teachers identify their chairs as the *cathedra pestilentiae*, and place the deuteronomic verse they debate into a new, figurative light. The judaization of scholastic learning is complemented by a judaization of judicial textuality in the full-page miniature of Jesus before Pilate. Pilate is assisted by a number of men in "Jews' hats." The table between Jesus and his adversaries is littered with aggressively writhing scrolls covered with texts. Threatening textuality overwhelms the bodily rhetoric (and implied orality) of the courtroom, and once more Jesus' hidden divinity is opposed to the tangible physicality of text.

Scholastic Anxieties

> Blessed is not the man who heard Master Anselm, nor he who has pursued knowledge in Laon or Paris, but "Blessed," it is written, "is the man whom you instruct, Lord, and whom you teach your law" (Ps. 93.12).[36]

Thus wrote the twelfth-century Premonstratensian abbot Philip of Harvengt to a canon regular who boasted of having studied with the great theology teacher Anselm of Laon. In a clever allusion to the Psalter, Philip puts the eminent scholars of his time in their place. Although Philip draws on Psalm 93, the resonance of its "Beatus homo" with the "Beatus vir" of Psalm 1 is strong. High medieval exegetes of the Psalms attacked schools as places of erroneous teaching and immoral conduct. Among their targets were not just heretical movements; during the twelfth century even eminent theologians came under heavy fire. In this section, I want to argue that the schooling scenes in our two psalters, and the Psalm commentaries we have discussed, allude

[36] Philip of Harvengt, *Epistola* 7, *Patrologia Latina* 203, col. 59A (between 1157 and 1182). The translation is that of Stephen C. Ferruolo, *Origins of the University: The Schools of Paris and their Critics, 1100–1215* (Stanford, 1985), 89.

to common anxieties about the changing nature of schools, and about scholasticism specifically as a new approach to learning.

As demonstrated above, the two images of Jesus being taken to school show us the interior of two quite different schools. In the Liverpool Psalter, we observe a classical grammar school, that is, an elementary school where children learned reading and writing in Latin. A lay teacher staffs the school; his instruction methods encompass the book and the rod. The rod was recognised as having mnemonic functions since pain was believed to aid memory.[37] In many medieval paintings and sculptures, the personification of Grammatica was equipped in just the same way. The raised rod in Mary's hand serves a naturalistic function—Mary seems to be threatening her recalcitrant child—but it also amplifies the theme of Grammatica. Similar school scenes can be found in textbooks of the time. As an example, we may take the frontispiece of a grammar treatise of ca. 1210–1220, in which the seated Magister threatens to discipline a pupil with the rod (fig. 3).[38] The kneeling pupil, who has stripped to his underwear, is clasping his hands imploringly or in submission. In a lower register, five more pupils witness the scene of discipline. The representation of spoken text forms an important part of the image. While the five squatting students study a book, the teacher forces the sixth student (note that the class would consist of three pairs) to repeat after him the promise *Volo studere pie magister* ("I will study, O venerable master"), inscribed twice—in the teacher's voice and in the pupil's voice—in the picture. In this grammar school picture, the teacher performs the role of Grammatica.

This authoritarian approach to learning serves as a useful foil to the Waldkirch Psalter's image of scholastic *disputatio*, which introduces us to a scholastic school. We have noted that both the method of study and disputation in pairs, and the curriculum leading from Dialectic to Theology, are typical of the new scholastic learning of the twelfth and thirteenth centuries. There can be little doubt that *disputatio*, with the

---

[37] My thanks to Mitchell Merback for reminding me of the pain-memory nexus, elaborated in his "Torture and Teaching. The Reception of Lucas Cranach the Elder's *Martyrdom of the Twelve Apostles* in the Protestant Era," *Art Journal* 57, no. 1 (Spring 1998), 14–23.

[38] For catalogue information, see M. Pippal, *Illuminierte Handschriften aus Österreich*, Vienna [http://homepage.univie.ac.at/Martina.Pippal/Wien.htm], and basic information in my list of figures. Because the kneeling student has stripped to the waist, I believe the rod is being wielded for a lashing, not just to impress. The miniature is also reproduced in Vetter, "Maria mit dem Kind an der Hand," 899, fig. 2. I have not been able to identify the text inscribed in the book.

aim of public *praedicatio*, the core activities of scholastic secular clerics, is exactly what is going on in the Waldkirch Psalter's image of a "Jewish" school. The simultaneous presence of two teachers who are engaged in a theological disputation, while students train in Dialectic, far exceeds the requirements of fidelity to a text. For while most of the apocryphal texts speak of two teachers, sometimes three, in the texts these teachers take turns at trying to teach Jesus; they do not dispute with each other, as they do in the Waldkirch Psalter's image. This *disputatio* is connoted negatively, not least by means of the judaization of the teachers with their pointed hats.

That the artist of the Waldkirch Psalter saw fit to judaize and thereby denigrate a scholastic school draws attention to the controversies surrounding the new cathedral and high schools of the twelfth and thirteenth centuries. Since late antiquity, schools had been run by monasteries. This institutional framework, already challenged in theory during the Carolingian reform, changed dramatically during the twelfth century under the pressure of two independent developments: monastic reform and the rise of scholasticism.[39] Among the monastic reform orders it was especially the Cistercians who advocated that schools be removed from monastic premises, so as to remove the monasteries from the world. Monastic reforms also meant that child oblation (that is, the placement of minors in monasteries by their parents) was effectively abolished by the twelfth century, so that monastic schools in any case would not have taken in *nutriti* (small children). Now, monasteries admitted adults who were expected to have already graduated from elementary grammar schools (though in practice, many illiterate adults entered the monasteries and required elementary teaching). It is in the spirit of monastic reform that formerly renowned monastic primary or grammar schools were taken out of convents and were handed over to the administration of secular clerics.

Despite pressure to renounce the teaching of the laity altogether, many monasteries were not going to renege on their obligation to educate the children of laymen who were associated with them, because this primary education was also a religious one. Despite the apostolic

---

[39] For the following I am indebted to P. Johanek, "Klosterstudien im 12. Jahrhundert," in *Schulen und Studium im sozialen Wandel des hohen und späten Mittelalters*, ed. J. Fried (Sigmaringen, 1986), 35–68.

ideal, monasteries and canonical foundations had become an integral part of the social fabric of medieval Europe, and unbreakable ties bound them to lay society. Monasteries accepted the children of benefactors and employees as *nutriti*, even when there was no intention for these children to "leave the world" and take vows. And these children, including girls, required schooling, so that, as a donation document of 1228 stipulated, "she would be able to read the Psalter."[40] This persistence was bound to generate ideological tension.

The twelfth century saw the rise of new schools and high schools for the so-called secular clerics, mainly in the urban precints of the cathedrals. This is where the new scholastic learning was cultivated, and France was its center. The new learning encompassed a curriculum based on the rediscovery of Aristotle and his Arabic and Jewish commentators and translators, and on a new method of study and teaching, *disputatio*, that is, the systematic exposition and resolution of contrary arguments around a *quaestio disputata*. The theoretical framework of the *disputatio* was Logic (also called Dialectic), which scholastic teachers elevated to a master discipline that threatened to topple the status of Theology.

Sustained resistance to the proliferation, aims, methods and morals of the schools arose above all from the Cistercians, beginning with Bernard of Clairvaux's conflict with Peter Abelard around 1140. From that time on, the battle lines between the monastic and the scholastic worlds of learning were clearly drawn.[41] Twelfth-century monastic theologians were quick to paint contrasting pictures of scholastic and monastic modes of knowledge. On the monastic side, *lectio* (study of the sacred scriptures) was intended to lead to *meditatio* (meditation) and thence to *oratio* (prayer). This was the monk's curriculum that would enable him to leave the world behind. By contrast, in scholastic studies *lectio* leads to *disputatio* (disputation) and thence to *praedicatio* (preaching), that is, public instruction. Reformist clerics such as Bernard of Clairvaux and Gerhoch of Reichersberg (an Augustinian canon) were quick to point out the sinful roots of *disputatio* in the evil curiosity that had brought Adam and Eve to perdition.

---

[40] Ibid. 65. Ulrich of Dagsberg's daughter's education in a canonical foundation was paid for by a donation of lands to the monastery.

[41] See above all Ferruolo, *Origins of the University*, especially chapter 3.

In the Holy Roman Empire cathedral schools had been well established since the late eleventh and early twelfth centuries.[42] By the late twelfth century, the old-style cathedral schools had become centers of administrative training. Their remit was essentially that of training the clergy in the service of the empire. Traditionally strong in grammar and rhetoric, these characteristically German schools went into stasis and crisis around 1200 because they failed to adopt the new scholastic emphasis on Logic and Theology (the two disciplines pictured being taught in the "Jewish" school in the Waldkirch Psalter).[43] There were exceptions: Prevostin of Cremona (ca. 1150–1210), an eminent scholastic teacher in Paris, was *scholasticus* at the cathedral school of Mainz during the 1190s, before becoming chancellor of Paris university. His conflicts with the cathedral chapter were indicative of the resistance of the old cathedral schools against the new schools.[44] For the most part, scholasticism struggled to become established in the Holy Roman Empire, and whoever desired to stay abreast of international scholarship and reap its intellectual and temporal rewards had to go to France. This new academic demand to study abroad conflicted with the monastic *stabilitas loci*, the requirement to stay in one place. On a more popular level, this conflict and the monastic opposition to the new schools register in Caesarius of Heisterbach's *Dialogus Miraculorum*, in which the prize of success at the schools is bought at the price of the scholar's soul, which can only be redeemed at the twelfth hour by entry into the Cistercian order.[45]

But despite the vehement polemics issued by authors of the monastic reform against the worldliness of schools, schooling and teaching, in Germany and Austria a total separation between the urban schools

---

[42] In south Germany, the most eminent cathedral school was Bamberg, elevated to a bishopric by Henry II in 1002. For its traditionalism and slow reception of scholasticism, see Johannes Fried, "Die Bamberger Domschule und die Rezeption von Frühscholastik und Rechtswissenschaft in ihrem Umkreis bis zum Ende der Stauferzeit," in *Schulen und Studium*, ed. J. Fried, 163–201.

[43] Fried, "Die Bamberger Domschule," 171, who writes, "Das Fehlen der Dialektik als hochentwickelte Spezialdisziplin ist ein Wesenszug der deutschen Domschulen."

[44] Paul Pixton, "The Misfiring of German Cultural Leadership in the Twelfth Century: The Evidence from the Cathedral Schools," *Paedagogica historica* 34, no. 2 (1998), 347–63.

[45] Caesarius of Heisterbach, "Of the conversion of the abbot of Morimond, who died and returned to life," in *Dialogus Miraculorum*, ed. J. Strange, 2 vols. (Cologne 1851), 1:36–9 (Bk. 1, ch. 32); for English translation of same, *The Dialogue on Miracles*, trans. H. von E. Scott and C. C. Swinton Bland, 2 vols. (London, 1929), 1:39–42; see also Ferruolo, *Origins of the University*, 67.

and the reformed monastic ideal of total withdrawal from the world was never totally enacted.

The widespread ambivalence toward scholasticism as a curriculum, a method and a lifestyle also manifested itself in the visual arts of the twelfth and early thirteenth centuries, the formative period of scholasticism. A range of articulations is traceable, from a harmonizing attitude to outright hostility. It is worth comparing the school image in the Waldkirch Psalter, which I consider hostile, with the self-representation of the quintessential scholastic institution of the time, the University of Paris, in its thirteenth-century Great Seal (fig. 4).[46] At the bottom, six students, dressed in hooded robes, dispute in pairs. Above them, two Masters dispute "in cathedra." In the heavenly realm above, dialectic is sublated, as Saints Nicholas and Denis flank a centrally enthroned Virgin and Child, who is pictured as the final authority of scholastic disputation. Her baldachin, decorated with the apocalyptic sun and moon, unifies the school's "dialectical" architecture of superimposed double arches. The Great Seal seeks to reconcile the dialectical principle of scholastic teaching with an authoritarian worldview; it does that by placing the institution of scholastic learning under the patronage of the heavenly court, and by imaginatively subordinating Dialectic (the schools) to Theology (Virgin, Saints).

This hierarchical relationship between Dialectic, taught in the Arts Faculty, and the Faculty of Theology is evocative of the similar hierarchy in the Waldkirch Psalter school. So is the consistency with which both the school and the university carry out their work by means of the scholastic technique of *disputatio*. Needless to say, the Great Seal of the University of Paris, the *universitas magistrorum et scolarium parisius*, was bound to be a harmonizing and celebratory representation, yet not entirely devoid of tension.

A more ambivalent visualization of disputation as indissolubly linked with Dialectic is suggested by Michael Camille's analysis of a tympanum relief from Reims, datable ca. 1160 and probably originally located

[46] Paris, Archives Nationales, D 8015, inscribed "s[igillum] universitatis magistror[um] et scolariu[m] parisius". The *universitas* had used an unauthorized seal at least since 1215; see H. Boockman, "Ikonographie der Universitäten. Bemerkungen über bildliche und gegenständliche Zeugnisse der spätmittelalterlichen Universitätsgeschichte," in *Schulen und Studium*, ed. J. Fried, 569 and fig. 8; and Pierre-Marie Auzas and André Tuilier, eds., *La vie universitaire parisienne au XIIIe siècle* (Paris, 1974), 41 cat. No. 49.

above the bifora window of a house owned by the cathedral chapter.[47] The figures in this sculptural representation of disputation perform Dialectic by means of a triple pairing: a dragonfight and an embracing couple in the two small semicircles at the bottom of the tympanum perform negative and positive exchanges. Their correspondence is emphasized by the repetition of oral contact: while the young man and woman kiss, the dragon lashes out its tongue towards the closed mouth of its human opponent. These opposing affects are kept in an unstable balance by the two disputing masters in the larger semicircle above. It is possible to see the dragonfight and embrace as illustrating the opposing statements presumably made by the disputants above. If there is a center to this composition, it is, as Camille pointed out, the gutter of the open book—a profoundly unhierarchical, dialectical middle. To look at this relief together with the later Waldkirch Psalter is instructive, because the latter image of the "Jewish" school also lacks a center. In parallel fashion, its pairing of masters and students performs the deferral of authority that was the hallmark of scholastic disputation. The ease with which both the dragonfight and the kiss invite negative moralization is indicative of the ambivalence, even unease, with which it is possible to invest this image of scholastic disputation.

Another image that negatively connotes disputation can be found in an extraordinary double-page, two-tone drawing in a twelfth-century manuscript of Hugo of St. Victor's *De Sacramentis* made at the Klosterneuburg monastery, an important foundation of Augustinian canons near Vienna.[48] On the final double page of the manuscript a

---

[47] Michael Camille, "'Seeing and Lecturing': Disputation in a Twelfth-Century Tympanum from Reims," in *Reading Medieval Images: The Art Historian and the Object*, ed. Elisabeth Sears and Thelma K. Thomas (Ann Arbor, 2002), 75–87 and fig. 6.1 on 76.

[48] Stiftsbibliothek Klosterneuburg, manuscript CCl 311, ca. 1150–75, fols 82v–83r; for catalogue information, see M. Pippal, *Illuminierte Handschriften aus Österreich (ca. 780–ca. 1250), Klosterneuburg Stiftsbibliothek*, [http://homepage.univie.ac.at/Martina.Pippal/Klosterneuburg.htm]; cf. E. Winkler, *Die Buchmalerei in Niederösterreich von 1150–1250* (Vienna, 1923), 11–13; and Anton Legner ed., *Ornamenta Ecclesiae: Kunst and Künstler der Romanik*, exhib. cat., 3 vols. (Cologne, 1985), 1:79–80, cat. no. A 24. Winkler was puzzled by the apparent disjuncture between the textual content of the manuscript and the drawing, which he suggested was added ca. 1200. Pippal equally sees a disjuncture between text and drawing, without offering a separate date for the latter. The authors of *Ornamenta Ecclesiae* agree that the drawing is not an illustration of the text, but believe it to be coeval; the catalogue description explains the image in terms of scholastic *disputatio*, but makes no reference to the gendering of the disputants. See Johanek, 52, on this scene as one of *disputatio*; Johanek's description diverges sharply from Winkler's and Pippal's in that he reads the double-page drawing as an all-male (!) school scene and

disputation is in progress, this time across genders: on the left page, a man in secular dress is seated crosslegged on a *faldistorium* and argues with a laywoman seated on a backless stone throne (a *cathedra*?) on the opposite page (fig. 5). She alone holds a book, drawn with its cover and jewelled spine visible. Each disputant is accompanied by a youth of the same sex; these are labelled *fautores* (supporters, fans). The disputation is performed through the gestures of argument and by means of the inscribed speech: the man's "est / est," to which the woman opposes "non est / non est."[49] The *fautores*, too, participate with their gesturing hands in the disputation; the young man is labelled as *male dicit*, the young woman *bene dicit*. Thus a chiastic relationship links the seated woman with the young man on the opposite page, and the mature man with the young woman.

In this monastic manuscript, the vanity of the new schools is condemned by staging the disputation as a wholly secular activity of questionable morality, one that is opposed to the strict gender separation practiced in schools and monasteries. The lady and the young girl bring the world into the school. They are marked by their lack of restraint, which flouts norms of feminine behavior: the seated woman's long hair flows down her shoulders in an unruly manner, while her emphatic profile position makes her demonstrative gesture, and above all her open "loudly" speaking mouth, stand out. All of these physical markers defy the norms of courtly *maze*, or restraint, prescribed to women at the time. The young girl's teaching gesture (index and middle finger of her right hand tapping against the palm of her left hand) would have been considered inappropriate, and to drive the negative point home, it contrasts with the way her tunic has parted to reveal both her thighs. Despite the powerful visual presence of these women, whose equal status as disputants may be unprecedented, the moralizing misogynistic innuendo is quite clear. The feminization of the disputation in the Klosterneuburg manuscript, and by extension the scholastic learning espoused by the Victorines, served a polemical purpose comparable to the judaization of the school in the Waldkirch Psalter, where the

---

interprets the man on the *faldistorium* as the Magister, insisting that this is a hierarchically structured conventional school. My thanks to Dr. Heinz Ristory, Stiftsbibliothek Klosterneuburg, for his generous assistance.

[49] Each utterance is written once in red ink and once in sepia ink; even the script differs slightly. I have not yet been able to unravel the relationship between the red and sepia ink in this two-tone drawing.

scholastic *disputatio* is imaginatively judaized precisely in order to be denigrated. Although by other means, the Klosterneuburg manuscript and the Reims tympanum—as much as the Waldkirch Psalter—cast the seated disputants negatively, or at least ambivalently, referencing the dispersal of divinely sanctioned authority that was attributed to scholasticism by its opponents.

Jewish Images of Schooling

It is important to include brief discussions of both Jewish Psalm exegesis and images of schools because they show the extent as well as the limits of the cultural affinities that bound together Jews and Christians. The cities of France, south Germany and Austria boasted eminent Jewish schools and scholars at that time. Among the Jewish minority the literacy rate was high; books and schooling were highly prized.[50] Jewish primary schooling was apparently less institutionalized than higher schooling. Communities did not organize primary schools; rather, private elementary teachers were hired by fathers, thus introducing social inequities. On the status of the primary teachers, medieval Ashkenazic sources conflict. While the practice was often lowly and poorly paid, some sources insisted that the primary teacher's work was the "work of heaven" (*melekhet shamayim*).[51] Despite the apparent absence of public primary schools, the Jewish child's first day of schooling was symbolically invested and marked by a special ritual that coincided with the Festival of Shavuot, on which the Revelation of the Torah at Sinai is commemorated. Beyond primary schooling, the Yeshivot of France, south Germany and Austria formed the backbone of the Jewish equivalent of scholasticism, which consisted of Talmudic scholarship, especially the study of Halakhah (Jewish law). The commitment to Talmudic scholarship formed the normative core of rabbinic culture in high medieval Europe, but this norm was not uncontested. Mystical

[50] Christoph Cluse, "Jewish Elementary Education in Medieval Ashkenaz," in *Seriis Intendere: A Collection of Essays Celebrating the Twenty-Fifth Anniversary of the Centre for Medieval Studies*, ed. Sharon Abra Hanen (Leeds, 1994), 7–14; and Ephraim Kanarfogel, *Jewish Education and Society in the High Middle Ages* (Detroit, 1992).

[51] Kanarfogel, *Jewish Education*, 29, citing a Tosafist Talmud commentary of the twelfth century. The existence of communal primary schools had been assumed in the older literature.

movements, such as the south German Hasidei Ashkenaz, opposed the exclusive focus on legal studies.[52]

In a rare image of the schooling ritual, found in a late thirteenth-century manuscript called the Leipzig Mahzor (High Holiday Prayer-book), both ritual and symbolism are visualized in marginal illustrations to the Shavuot liturgy.[53] On folio 130 verso, Moses hands down from the mountaintop a pair of gilded tablets in the form of hinged writing tablets to four Israelites below (fig. 7). On the opposite page, folio 131 recto, three children are received by their new teacher with symbolic foods (cakes and eggs) and a gilded writing tablet that mirrors the tablets in Moses' hands (fig. 8). Then two of the children are taken to a river whose water symbolizes Torah and protects against forgetting. The school initiation ceremony is mirrored in the giving of the Torah at Sinai in such a way that the contemporary schoolteacher is a "new Moses," and Moses becomes the teachers' teacher; the parallelism is reinforced in that the moment chosen for illustration is not Moses' *receiving* the Torah from Heaven, but his *transmission* of the Torah to the Israelites. The initiation into schooling renews the revelation at Sinai; the sweet food offered by the teacher to the children glosses Torah as being food for the mind.

A second illumination that thematizes schooling (fol. 52r) is part of an Esther sequence illustrating the festival of Purim (fig. 9). In the Midrash Rabbah on the book of Esther, Mordechai flees from Haman's wrath to the house of study. Not knowing that Haman has been forced by the king to lead him around town in a royal procession, Mordechai first tries to save his students by sending them away, and when they refuse to abandon him they pray together "so that we may die praying." Having finished their prayers, they settle down to study and are interrupted by Haman coming in with the royal steed and accouterments.[54] Mordechai is pictured as a teacher examining three students in a formal setting. All hold open books. Given that the Leipzig Mahzor was

---

[52] I thank Philip Alexander for sharing this insight with me.

[53] Descriptions of the ritual speak of a child being brought to the teacher or rabbi on its first day of school, and of the ritual foods that the teacher fed the child in an enactment of transferred parentage; see Ivan G. Marcus, *Rituals of Childhood: Jewish Acculturation in Medieval Europe* (New Haven and London, 1996). The school initiation scene in the Leipzig Mahzor, discussed by Marcus on 81–2, accompanies "Adon Imnani," literally translatable as "The Lord has been my nurse," a hymn extolling the antiquity of the Torah, sung on the first day of Shavuot.

[54] *Midrash Rabbah*, ed. I. Epstein (London, 1983), vol. 9, 116–117.

a book used by adults, not children, it is significant that the schooling scenes are considered so important. In these miniatures, we find little of the ambivalence towards schooling that we encountered in the south German Latin Psalters.

Beyond the modest realities of the "kiddies' teacher," a more lofty, symbolic truth about primary teaching comes into view here, one that enabled the Ashkenazic community to construct an image of itself as guardians of scriptural learning—a self-image not so far removed from Christian notions of Jews as *bibliothecarii* (librarians). The image of the "Jewish" school in the Waldkirch Psalter, too, references the trope of the Jews as biblical *capsarii* (bookbearers) or *librarii* (librarians).[55] If so, the Waldkirch Psalter introduces a negative distancing where the Leipzig Mahzor insists on a positive identification.

Conclusion

Both the Waldkirch and Liverpool Psalters picture the same apocryphal episode from Jesus' childhood, in which his parents attempt to have him schooled; yet these two images arrive at quite independent figurations that gloss the apocryphal texts and translate them into their own world of the early thirteenth century. Through its image of a "Jewish" school, the Waldkirch Psalter uniquely articulates the monastic opposition to scholastic learning. The visual argument of that miniature equates the Old Law with the New Learning of the urban schools and universities. The Liverpool Psalter makes this polemical point less clearly, in that it seems to visualize opposition to secular schooling through the image of a generic grammar school.

The scene of taking Jesus to school is not the only place in the Psalter where textuality is imaginatively judaized. A similar concentration of painted writing occurs in the trial scene of Jesus before Pilate on folio 91 verso of the Waldkirch Psalter (fig. 6). Here Jesus confronts a massive assault of written documents held mostly by men in "Jews' hats." Pilate wears a fancy hat that, although not a "Jews' hat," associates him broadly with the Jews "on his side." The trial before Pilate especially associates

[55] On these Augustinian tropes, see Cohen, *Living Letters of the Law*, 36; and on their legacy, Y. Friedman, "Anti-Talmudic Invective from Peter the Venerable to Nicholas Donin (1144–1244)," in *Le brûlement du Talmud à Paris 1242–1244*, ed. Gilbert Dahan (Paris 1999), 171–89.

textuality with bureaucracy and secular learning. It is easy to see here too a monastic condemnation of secular clerics and their conduct in wordly affairs. "Jewish" literacy and clerical literacy are perceived in this image as equally negative, even threatening. It remains a paradox that such monastic preoccupations and anti-scholastic prejudices were woven into a Psalter for lay use—the book that more than any others stands for lay as well as clerical education during this period. But perhaps this ideological tension between the iconography of the book and its presumed audience tells us something about the openness of viewing and reading with which illuminated Psalters were received.

The opposition to the "Jewish" school must not be confused with an antagonism to Jews—although there is clearly an anti-Judaic undercurrent in the Waldkirch Psalter that negatively tropes certain forms of literacy as Judaic. When I set out to research the "Jewish" school in the Waldkirch Psalter, I thought I could discern in it a malevolent observation of the realities of Jewish schooling in high medieval Ashkenaz. I hypothesized that the artist had depicted the real Jewish school, the *Yeshiva*, with its method of learning in pairs and rabbinic disputation (the latter an ancient Jewish tradition). I believed that the Waldkirch Psalter visualized an early attack against Talmudic "hairsplitting" even before the concerted anti-Talmud campaign of the late 1230s. I intended to link the association of the new scholastic learning with Judaism and the discovery of the Talmud as *nova lex*. Having arrived at the end of my winding path of investigation, I am no longer convinced of this possibility.

I now see "The Jew" as a trope that helped Christians think through anxieties arising out of historical change. "The Jew" was also a figure of foreclosure for all that was uncanny and threatening in Christian society. As Sara Lipton has argued,

> Once again, the site of danger is not where Judaism is most specifically Jewish but where it intersects with and spills over into Christianity. Jewish literalistic interpretation and Maimonidean rationalist explication threaten... not because they constitute deviations from age-old or internal Jewish traditions... but because they parallel and on occasion overlap with current Christian preoccupations and controversial developments.[56]

[56] Lipton, *Images of Intolerance*, 75. I am indebted to this line of thought, in which the author shows how the new learning of secular schools and university faculties could be denigrated through the association of Philosophers and Jews, secular and rabbinic learning.

While the representation of the Jewish school discussed in this chapter deploys the verisimilitude characteristic of some thirteenth-century art, the Jewish figures remain tropes; Jewish schools were not necessarily perceived as a serious threat to Christendom, but the rise of scholastic learning elicited resistance, and this resistance could imagine the scholastic learning of secular clerics as figuratively "Jewish."

If we consider the imaginative judaization of the scholastic masters in the Waldkirch Psalter within the context of modern theories of medieval anti-Judaism, we encounter a paradox. It has been especially R. I. Moore's argument that the developed high medieval anti-Judaism was part of a range of exclusionary discourses practiced by the urban secular clerics as they rose into the royal bureaucracy.[57] They refigured the margins of society and thereby produced new margins. The same scholar has elsewhere argued that the ecclesiastical reform movements of the late eleventh and twelfth centuries entailed a return to patristic theologies and policies towards the Jews, including the harsh legislation of the Theodosian *Codex Juris Civilis*.[58] Clearly, in the Waldkirch Psalter the scholastic language of exclusion has been turned against the school itself, in the name of a new wave of monastic reforms. The reform orders of the twelfth century have traditionally not been implicated as spreaders of anti-Judaism. Bernard of Clairvaux is remembered for his determined opposition to the work Radulph's anti-Jewish rants. The Victorines are studied for their embrace of the *Hebraica veritas* and their scholarly return to the Hebrew scriptures. And yet, as I have argued here, the image of the "Jewish" school emerges from a monastic reform sensibility.

That references to Jewish schooling could be deployed polemically, but in the opposite direction from that encountered in the Waldkirch Psalter image, is indicated by a well-known passage from the Abelardian or Cambridge Commentary to Paul's Letter to the Ephesians:

> The Jews, out of zeal for God and love of the law, put as many sons as they have to letters, that each may understand God's law.... A Jew, however poor, even if he had ten sons would put them all to letters, not

[57] R. I. Moore, *The Formation of a Persecuting Society: Power and Deviance in Western Europe, 950–1250* (Oxford, 1987), 27–45 and passim.

[58] R. I. Moore, "Anti-Semitism and the Birth of Europe," in *Christianity and Judaism: Papers Read at the 1991 Summer Meeting and the 1992 Winter Meeting of the Ecclesiastical History Society*, ed. Diane Wood, Studies in Church History 29 (Oxford, 1992), 33–57.

> for gain as Christians do, but for the understanding of God's law, and not only his sons but his daughters.[59]

Here, Jews are upheld as putting Christians to shame. Whether or not it can be cited as evidence of Jewish educational practices, this passage is extraordinary for the stress it places on the love and understanding of God's law as the goal of Jewish primary education. In our survey of Psalm commentaries above, we have seen the theological and polemical potentials of invoking God's law. Here Jewish schooling becomes instead a stick with which to castigate the perceived weaknesses of Christian schooling. Once again, rather than a realistic depiction, the Christian image of the Jewish school serves as a trope, a metaphor that enables the exploration of a problem in Christian education.

---

[59] *Commentarius Cantabrigiensis in Epistolas Pauli e Schola Petri Abelardi*, ed. Artur Landgraf, 4 vols (Notre Dame, 1937) vol. 2, 434. See Beryl Smalley, *The Study of the Bible in the Middle Ages*, 2nd edn. (Oxford, 1952), 78; Kanarfogel, *Jewish Education and Society*, 16.

CHAPTER FOUR

THE PERFORMATIVE TERMS OF JEWISH ICONOCLASM AND CONVERSION IN TWO SAINT NICHOLAS WINDOWS AT CHARTRES CATHEDRAL*

Anne F. Harris

Jewish iconoclasm took center stage in thirteenth-century Chartres by means of a representation in stained glass, depicting the whipping of a statue of Saint Nicholas by a Jew, an image that makes visible the climactic scene of a liturgical play known as the *Iconia* (fig. 1). In the same window, assimilated visually within the same quatrefoil pattern, is another depiction of the abuse of an image, this one by a Christian who falsely swears the repayment of a loan to a Jewish moneylender before a statue of Saint Nicholas (fig. 2). What is rendered visible in this latter representation is a popular *exemplum* from a contemporary sermon. The contrast between the two images is striking: the complex liturgical play of the *Iconia* is reduced to one, stark image, while the sermon, simpler in narrative terms, is given three panels; the violence of the *Iconia* miracle is exacted upon the statue of Saint Nicholas, while the violence of the sermon is meted out upon the body of the False Borrower, the character after whom the tale is known. The purpose of this essay is to understand these two scenarios of insult paid to images through their representation in both stained glass and images and in performative texts, and to place these representations within the context of the anxiety provoked by money and moneylending for the cathedral chapter at Chartres. The volatility and danger of money was a concern to the cathedral chapter in the absence of any firm means of control over both monetary value and exchange; and both the *Iconia*

* I would like to thank Linda Seidel for years of encouragement and inspiration—the ideas and explorations presented here would never have flourished without her; Mitch Merback for his wise and patient editing, and very generous mentoring; and Donna Sadler and Michael Mackenzie for making sense of it all. A grant from the National Endowment for the Humanities in Summer 2000 provided much welcome support for archival and on-site research. I dedicate this work to my daughter, Iris Evelyn Mackenzie, and to the memory of Michael Camille.

Jew and the Jew in the tale of the False Borrower (henceforth referred to as the Borrower's Tale) convert to Christianity after money crises. Both narratives were therefore instrumental in articulating the personage of the "converting Jew," whose reconciliation to Christianity put not only religious matters but money in its place, i.e., in subservience to the Church.

Using the preacher's tale of the False Borrower as both a visual and ideological contrast to the *Iconia* image, I will show in what follows how the interaction of characters, images, and settings of the *Iconia* at Chartres established what I will call a dynamic of desecration and consecration, and further, how this dynamic functioned as a set of performative terms for the provocative Christian fantasy of Jewish iconoclasm. The performance of the *Iconia*, culminating in the solemn conversion of the Jew to Christianity, projected a vivid drama of conversion into church space, one ultimately concerned with the reassertion of a homogeneous Christian community. Violence and iconoclasm were reconfigured as humility and sanctification through a violent but ultimately reconciliatory performance. Was this reconciliation meant to mend actual tears in the social fabric caused by money and its conflicts, or was it a more allegorical projection of sin and redemption? Another purpose of this essay will be to discern the tensions between the social reality of a Jewish presence in Chartres and its allegorical representation and manipulation in the cathedral's stained glass program.

The early appearance of the *Iconia* image (between 1210 and 1235)[1] in the glass program at Chartres, an image that involves a Jewish figure in a violent iconoclastic act, and the rare presence of a saintly figure other than Mary or Christ bearing the brunt of iconoclastic violence,[2] merit our attention. That a liturgical drama and a sermon became iconographic sources for stained glass windows is also cause for con-

[1] Colette Manhes-Deremble, *Les vitraux narratifs de la Cathédrale de Chartres*, Corpus Vitrearum Medii Aevi Étude Iconographique 2 (Paris, 1993), 9–17, discusses the controversies and evidences for dating the windows between 1210 and 1235. See also "Chartres" in *Les vitraux du Centre et des Pays de la Loire*. Corpus Vitrearum Medii Aevi—Recensement II (Paris: Editions du Centre National de la Recherche Scientifique, 1981), 25–26; Brigitte Kurmann-Schwarz, "Récits, programmes, commanditaires, concepteurs, donateurs: Publications récentes sur l'iconographie des vitraux de la Cathédrale de Chartres," *Bulletin Monumental* 154 (1996): 55–71; and Claudine Lautier, "Les vitraux de la Cathédrale de Chartres: Reliques et images," *Bulletin Monumental* 161 (2003): 3–96. All translations, unless otherwise noted, are my own.

[2] Bernhard Blumenkranz. *Juden und Judentum in der mittelalterlichen Kunst* (Stuttgart: Kohlhammer, 1965).

sideration, not so much for its rarity,[3] as for what it indicates about the relationship between stained glass programs and the *spoken* word of performative text. Far from simply illustrating biblical passages for the illiterate, and far from being a kind of "Bible for the Poor,"[4] these windows were a projection of contemporary concerns as expressed in contemporary performative texts. As such they intersected with the performance of these texts both literally, in that the location of the windows positioned viewers and participants of the liturgical drama during its performance in church space, and structurally, in the reliance of both the narrative and the image on the performance of the text for the realization of its full meaning.

The *Iconia* miracle is deployed across *two* stained glass windows at Chartres, both strategically placed to intersect with the performance of the liturgical play. The one with which we begin our investigation resides at the very top of a window in the nave, establishing (but not completing) the action of the story within a uniquely condensed single panel.[5] The other, located in the ambulatory, concludes the narrative with similar visual economy (fig. 3). Such intense narrative concentration in the single *Iconia* panel and this kind of narrative suspension—in which the story is begun in one window in the nave but only completed in another in the ambulatory—operating across church space are quite unusual in medieval stained glass cycles; most windows of the *Iconia* miracle present developed and self-contained narratives, such as those we see in the windows of Auxerre[6] (displayed across nine panels) and

[3] There are other instances of stained glass windows inspired by and intersecting with liturgical drama; indeed, the entire Nicholas window depicts various tales found first, and sometimes only, in liturgical drama (the *Tres Filiae*, the *Tres Clerici*, the Borrower's Tale and the *Iconia* miracle). There is the possibility, still not investigated, that the Joseph window at Chartres may be related to the *Joseph* play.

[4] See the critique of this notion by Madeline Caviness in "Biblical Stories in Windows: Were They Bibles for the Poor?" in *The Bible in the Middle Ages: Its Influence on Literature and Art*, ed. Bernard S. Levy (Binghamton, NY, 1992), 103–48.

[5] By the late fourteenth century, the reduction of an entire miracle play into one image would be commonplace, but the phenomenon is unique to Chartres in the thirteenth century. John Wesley Harris, *Medieval Theatre in Context* (London, 1992). "[T]he plays present the viewers with extremely strong visual images that they can remember...if the cycle-plays indeed sprang from the pictures and tableaux carried in the Corpus Christi procession, this was a continuous tradition" (106).

[6] See Virginia Chieffo Raguin, *Stained Glass in Thirteenth-Century Burgundy* (Princeton, 1982), 71, for a diagram and discussion of the Saint Nicholas and Saint Eloi window. For further basic iconographic information about the stained glass windows of the cathedral, G. Bonneau, "Description des verrières de la Cathédrale d'Auxerre," *Bulletin de la Société des Sciences Historiques et Naturelles de l'Yonne* 39 (1885): 296–348.

Saint-Julien-du-Sault (six panels).[7] The images narrating the Borrower's Tale also follow this pattern of narrative displacement from nave to ambulatory, emphasizing its role as visual foil to the *Iconia* image. In the nave, as mentioned above, the Borrower's Tale takes up three of the four panels it shares in a quatrefoil with the *Iconia* miracle. In the ambulatory (fig. 4), the tale is deployed in three of four small quatrefoils grouped around a central diamond depicting the baptism of the Jew. Thus, with an elegant and seamless visual structure, the stained glass panels inextricably bind the two tales of the *Iconia* and the False Borrower in their inevitable endings: the conversion of the Jew. The power of this assimilation will be discussed later in this essay; for now, it is crucial to enter the fray of our narratives.

Narrative, Image, Text

For the sake of argumentation and analysis, I would like first to isolate narrative from image and text, before engaging those narratives in the intersection of stained glass and performance. Here I present the story of the *Iconia* miracle, told without the elaborations or specificities of different versions of the play (which are addressed below). A foreigner is the owner of a treasure and has brought a statue of Saint Nicholas into his home as booty. Convinced of the apotropaic power of the statue, he entrusts his treasure to it, but is robbed by thieves in his absence. He whips the statue of Saint Nicholas for its inefficacy and laxity in this crucial matter of pledges and promises, and threatens to burn it. Saint Nicholas then appears to the thieves "in the flesh," cut and bruised, and threatens to turn them in to the authorities. The thieves return the treasure, and the owner of the treasure is astounded at the power

Raguin utilizes Bonneau's numbering system within her diagram. Window 67 in the eastern ambulatory depicts the miracle of the Boiling Baby as well as Nicholas's episcopal ascent. Nicholas shares window 67 with Saint Germain (pp. 336 and 339); *Corpus Vitrearum, Recensement III: Les vitraux de Bourgogne Franche-Comté et Rhône-Alpes* (Paris, 1986), 113–8.

[7] The image is reproduced in Raguin, *Stained Glass in Thirteenth-Century Burgundy*, 92. For further discussion of the windows of Saint-Julien-du-Sault see Gabrielle Rheims, "L'eglise de Saint-Julien-du-Sault et ses verrières," *Gazette des Beaux-Arts* 13–14 (1926): 138–162 (the Saint Nicholas window is discussed on 156–157), and Jean Lafond, "Les Vitraux de Saint-Julien-du-Sault," *Congrès Archéologiques de France* (1958): 37–54.

of the saint, converts to Christianity, and is baptized.[8] There are two important elements to note in the structure of the narrative because of their manipulation in different versions of the tale: the openness of the identity of the foreign treasure owner, and the dynamic of violence and redemption.

In the Borrower's Tale a dishonest Christian swears before a statue of Saint Nicholas to return the full amount he has borrowed from his Jewish moneylender. Called before a court after he fails to repay his growing debt, the borrower asks the moneylender—there in the courtroom—to hold a stick into which he has already secreted the money. When asked to swear before a statue of Saint Nicholas that he has returned the money owed to the moneylender, the borrower, at that very moment when the moneylender holds the stick with the secreted money, swears (honestly) that he has. The borrower is soon punished for his lies by being run over by a chariot, but Saint Nicholas appears and resurrects the false borrower in the presence of the Jewish lender, who instantly converts to Christianity. The tale ends with the saint baptizing the Jewish lender.[9] The dynamic of violence and redemption is at work again, this time upon the body of the Christian—but the narrative structure is clear: it is the Jew's moneylending that is the cause of the crisis and the motivation of the Christian's lies. In contrast to the *Iconia* tale, the Borrower's Tale is much more fixed in its character identities: the borrower is Christian and the moneylender is Jewish. This contrast stems, I believe, from the tale's intended use as an *exemplum* within a sermon,[10] a more prescriptive oral text, whereas the *Iconia* tale is by nature the kind of text that is revised and reinvented with each dramatic rendition (and arguably with each performance).

In contrast to the text of the play, the *Iconia* panels at Chartres fix the identity of the foreign treasure owner, perhaps reflecting the version of the play known to the stained glass programmers: characterized by

[8] The foreign identity of the borrower (and perhaps his treasure) ranges from Barbarian (in the earliest versions of the tale, before it became a play), to Jew (in the Fleury Playbook and Hilarius version) to Muslim (in the 1200 version by Jean Arras). For more on the pre-dramatic history of the *Iconia* miracle, see Charles W. Jones, *Saint Nicholas of Myra, Bari, and Manhattan: Biography of a Legend* (Chicago, 1978), 45–49, and 79–82 (translation of the earliest version of the *Iconia* miracle).

[9] As retold in Jones, *Saint Nicholas of Myra*, 307.

[10] For an analysis of the inclusion of *exempla* in sermons as "attention grabbing" elements of oral discourse, Jean-Claude Schmitt, "Receuils franciscains d'*exempla* et perfectionnement des techniques," *Bibliothèque de l'École des Chartres* 135 (1977): 5–21.

his *Judenhut*[11] and beard, he is identified as Jewish. Amazingly, when we consider the complex narrative of the *Iconia* miracle described above, the iconoclastic panel in the nave (fig. 1) presents no narrative establishment or dénouement, only the aggressive, violent imagery of the humiliation of a saint. In the nave, the viewer enters the story at its highest pitch, just as the Jew steadies the icon of saint Nicholas in preparation for another beating. A continuity of the violence is signaled in the stop-action pose of the Jew. The straps of the whip he holds undulate with the force of his blows; his bright red cloak swings with his body's movement against the statue, his right leg extends beyond the representational space, signaling the powerful lunge of the figure as he throws himself upon the icon, while his eyes seem to seek out those of the statue, willing it to speak in its defense. Prescribed structures of demarcation, such as the pillars that frame the statue of the saint and the bright red doorway that would otherwise separate him from the Jew, are violated with every repetition of the violent attack. The scourging and desecration of the statue is relentless. Its violence steps out of narrative time: it offers neither explanation nor resolution, neither motive nor ending. It is pure dramatic action.[12] The ambulatory window (fig. 3) repeats this visual structure "verbatim": the Jew steadies the statue, which is again presented in iconic form; his robes billow about him with the exertions of the blow, and his right leg once again crosses the boundary of the floor.[13]

[11] Distinctive clothing and marking for Jews had been decreed in 1215 at the Fourth Lateran Council; see Bernhard Blumenkranz, "Louis IX ou Saint Louis et les juifs," *Archives Juives* 10:2 (1973–74), who specifies that neither Philip Augustus nor Louis VIII went to any great pains to see the Council's decree enforced: "Il restera à Louis IX d'imposer aux Juifs de France cette marque d'infamie" (19). See also Gérard Christmann, "L'image du juif dans la société chrétienne de la fin du moyen âge," *Saisons d'Alsace* 20 (1975): 55–56.

[12] Jody Enders, *The Medieval Theater of Cruelty: Rhetoric, Memory, Violence* (Ithaca, 1999). This isolation of violence invites associations with other "pure" moments of action, other instances of violence: "[M]oments of extreme violence are always 'decontextualized.' It is not the literary critic who selects them out but rather the scourging scenes that select themselves out. To a medieval audience as to a modern one, a beating was never associated exclusively with the theater. Instead, it recalled other spectacles of punishment (legal or illegal) in which bodies in pain were displayed" (6). For a treatment of pictoral images with this spectacular power, see Mitchell B. Merback, *The Thief, the Cross, and the Wheel: Pain and the Spectacle of Punishment in Medieval and Renaissance Europe* (Chicago, 1999).

[13] One intriguing addition, that of a door to the left of the Jew (and to the right of the baptism of the Jew) indicates a sense of movement and passage, one I will eventually

The Borrower's Tale follows the same dynamic of violence (in the nave) and redemption (in the ambulatory) established by the *Iconia* images. The three panels of the nave quatrefoil (fig. 3) read counter-clockwise, starting in the right middle panel. There we see a Jewish moneylender, closely resembling the protagonist of the *Iconia* miracle panel above, and a Christian borrower sealing a loan before the icon of Saint Nicholas. The Jew sits in a position of authority while the borrower, in a short tunic, stands and gestures in deference to him. The backdrop to the scene is marked as urban, with architectural elements of a roof and doorway visible at the left of the panel. This urban element indicates that the space of the image is controlled by the presence and practices of the Jew. The story continues in the bottom panel, where the borrower and the moneylender both have their hands on the stick containing the money (a fact only known to the Christian debtor—and the viewer/auditor, of course). The Christian deceiver is thus able to swear before the icon that in this precise moment he has indeed returned the money owed. The borrower's stance is complicitous as his body twists and turns to negotiate the space between the Jew and the icon. The posture of the Jew is no longer confident and commanding: he leans forward awkwardly and points questioningly to the stick while staring at the icon. The final panel of the Borrower's Tale leaves the story at its most disastrous moment. In the left panel, the Christian is run over by a cart, which crushes him to death but also reveals the money stashed in the stick. The clear visibility of money, aligned in a well-ordered row below the wheels of the cart, is unique among images depicting this legend.[14] The body of the Christian in

connect with the movement from the nave to the ambulatory during the performance of the liturgical play.

[14] The only known earlier example of the Borrower's Tale in stained glass is found in 1170–80 at York Minster, where the demise of the borrower is the focus and the money is nowhere to be seen. This window is discussed in Richard Marks, *Stained Glass in England during the Middle Ages* (Toronto, 1993), plate 5. Through stylistic similarities and the claims of other scholars, Marks argues that the York Minster glass may have been executed by workshops shared with sites in France, specifically at St-Denis and St-Rémi at Reims. This French connection would seem to underscore the popularity of the legend in the regions surrounding Chartres. Only images of the scene which were made after Chartres's, such as those of Auxerre Cathedral from 1235–40 (see *Recensement III*, fig. 101; p. 118) visually emphasize the coins by arranging them in a clearly defined row; see Meredith Parsons Lillich, *Rainbow Like an Emerald: Stained Glass in Lorraine in the Thirteenth and Early Fourteenth Centuries* (University Park, 1991), who cites a series of renditions of this scene of the Borrower's Tale: they are found in York Minster, the nave and ambulatory windows of Chartres Cathedral, Beverley Minster

the bottom panel at Chartres is broken in three places, his legs flung out at awkward angles. In a similarly exacting manner, the ambulatory window panels depicting the Borrower's Tale (fig. 4) follow the same narrative order (three panels depicting the moments of loan, lie, and punishment) as those of the nave window. The counterclockwise narrative disposition of the panels in the ambulatory, however, is grouped around the central culminating image of the Jew's baptism, visually eliding with the ending of the *Iconia* tale.

Finally we must examine the performative texts (plays and sermon) with which the *Iconia* miracle and the Borrower's Tale co-existed. The *Iconia* miracle first[15] appears in the form of a play in France in the twelfth-century Fleury Playbook.[16] It is this telling of the *Iconia* Tale that

---

and Auxerre Cathedral; sculptural examples exist in a cloister capital of Tarragona Cathedral and a relief on the façade of San Nicola church in Bari; and a fresco example remains on the wall of Hunawir church in Haut-Rhin. Lillich also mentions, but does not reproduce, a panel from Dreux, a town near Chartres, that includes a representation of the Borrower's Tale.

[15] Though it is elaborated and expanded upon only in the thirteenth century, the *Iconia* miracle is as old in the West as the first Latin life of Saint Nicholas. It was appended to the biography written by John, Deacon of Naples, around 880; see Jones, *Saint Nicholas of Myra*, 45–49. John based his addition upon a Greek miracle story from around 900, now known as *Thauma de imagine*, which characterized the treasure owner as a vandal. Jones provides a translation of this earliest text (79–82) and dates the earliest Greek version to around 900, citing the Muslim invasion of Calabria (871–923) as a historical (and inspirational?) backdrop. We know that John of Naples's work was present in the library of Chartres (Yves Delaporte, *Les vitraux de la Cathédrale de Chartres* [Chartres, 1926], 262) but it obviously was not the primary text used in conjunction with the image, since the owner of the treasure in the Chartres window is depicted as a Jew and not a Vandal.

[16] Other renditions of other Saint Nicholas miracle stories had been written in the meantime; see Grace Frank, *The Medieval French Drama* (Oxford, 1954). The German nun, Hrotvitha, wrote a version of the *Tres Filiae* miracle story in the Benedictine community of Gandersheim in the tenth century within what she called a "dramatica series." Both inspired by and writing in resistence to Terence, Hrothvita was interested in those plays that would reveal the "heroic adherence of saintly women to their vows of chastity" (10). The Anglo-Norman poet Wace wrote a first French version in the twelfth century, but it is in the form a *vita*; see Wace, *La vie de Saint Nicolas*. ed. E. Ronsjö (Lund, 1942). This version could assuredly be considered a transitional piece to the Fleury Playbook, especially in questions of character development, but it is still an oral text perfomed by one voice. For an interesting discussion of the various incarnations of the story leading up to the play, see Lynette R. Muir, "The Saint Play in Medieval France," in *The Saint Play in Medieval Europe*, ed. Clifford Davidson, Early Drama, Art, and Music Monograph Series 8 (Kalamazoo, MI, 1986), 123–180. Otto E. Albrecht, *Four Latin Plays of St. Nicholas from the 12th Century Fleur Playbook* (Philadelphia, 1935), makes the distinction between the Fleury Playbook's theatricality and that of past versions of the miracle stories: "It is in our MS that we have the first mention of the miracle-play as a dramatic form" (107). What is especially convincing about Fleury's

changed the identity of the treasure owner to a Jew, whereas he had been a pagan, or simply "Barbarus" in all earlier versions. It is remarkable that the cathedral chapter of Chartres, and every French cathedral stained glass cycle thereafter, adopted this change. Throughout this dramatic telling of the *Iconia* tale,[17] the Fleury Playbook fleshes out the characters: the thieves speak one by one of their desires for the wealth made available to them through the Jew's absence; the Jew's devastation over his lost loot is characterized as comic when he is shown literally "hopping mad" at his fate; the Jew's iconoclasm enacted upon the statue is also expanded when the Jew tells it exactly what it "deserves" for its shortcomings: "You deserve to fall under my whip" (*Tu meritris subdare probris tondere flagellis*) (verse 64) and threatens to throw the statue into a fire. After being chastised by the saint, the thieves decide "that we should go back and give it back" (*Redeamus et reddamus*) and thus restore the treasure to its proper place in the Jew's home. The final four stanzas of the play project the Jew's rejoicing, punctuated by cries of "Let us rejoice!" (*Gaudeamus!*) which flow excitedly into the *Statuit ei dominus*, the introit of the Mass of Saint Nicholas, which would have been celebrated immediately after the play's performance.[18]

By the thirteenth century, the *Iconia* miracle existed in at least two additional well-known dramatic versions: as a play by the twelfth-century wandering scholar Hilarius,[19] and as the much-heralded *Jeu de saint*

dramatic intention is the presence of an explanatory text summarizing the action to follow, to be read before the play begins. This text begins, "Aliud miraculum de sancto Nicholao et de quodam iudeo" ([Here follows] another miracle of Saint Nicholas and a certain Jew) and seems to invite the audience to gather round.

[17] The most helpful editions of this play can be found in Karl Young, *The Drama of the Medieval Church*, 2 vols. (Oxford, 1932), 2:344–348; and Albrecht, *Four Latin Plays*, 129–134. Albrecht provides more stage directions and codicological information. The lay-out of his text also makes the internal rhymes of certain speeches more legible. For a general introduction to the codicological problems of the Fleury Playbook manuscript, Solange Corbin, "Le manuscrit 201 d'Orléans; drames liturgiques dits de Fleury," *Romania* 74 (1953): 1–43. For its relationship to and place within the history of drama, Clifford C. Flanigan, "The Fleury *Playbook*," in *The Traditions of Medieval Latin Drama and Modern Scholarship*, ed. Thomas P. Campbell and Clifford Davidson, Early Drama, Art and Music Monograph Series 7 (Kalamazoo, MI, 1985), 1–25.

[18] The Jew's conversion is not made readily apparent through baptism, but he does joyfully renounce the error of his ways for believing in false gods in his final lines: "Ut, error sublato mencium,/ Nicholai mereamur consorcium./ Gaudeamus!" (Thus, I lived in error, Nicholas is whose company's I should keep).

[19] The most comprehensive edition is found in J. B. Fuller, *Hilarii versus et ludi, edited from the Paris Mss.* (New York, 1929). The full text of the *Ludus super Iconia* is also found in Young, *Drama of the Medieval Church*, 2:337–340. The earliest edition was by

Nicholas by Jean Bodel, composed around 1200.[20] It is not the purpose of this paper to establish exactly which specific version of the play was the inspiration for the iconography of the window. The windows, I argue, are not based on one textual source, but rather take varying elements from multiple sources. Dramas were, we cannot forget, oral and visual performances not just texts. As such, they were more volatile than written texts, more susceptible to their performers' interpretations and circumstances.

The oldest extant version of the Borrower's Tale is found in the so-called Battle Abbey Life, a manuscript which dates to the late eleventh century. The manuscript presents five miracles in rhyming Latin verse, ostensibly meant to be read aloud.[21] In this early version of the tale, no mention is made of the icon of Saint Nicholas, just of his altar.[22] The only other manuscript of equally early date containing the tale was once preserved in the city library of Chartres. Lost in the 1944 bombing, the manuscript apparently displayed a prose Latin version.[23]

Champollion-Figeac, *Hilarii versus et ludi* (Paris, 1838). The manuscript from which all these editions are culled is Paris, Bibl. Nat. MS lat. 11331.

[20] The play exists in multiple editions. The most complete in French was edited by A. Henry, *Le jeu de Saint Nicolas de Jehan Bodel*. 3rd edn. (Bruxelles, 1980). An English translation, with a very general introduction to a series of plays, is *Medieval French Plays*, trans. Richard Axton and John Stevens (Oxford, 1971), 71–130. An excellent analysis of the play's sources in older legends and themes can be found in Patrick R. Vincent, *The* Jeu de Saint Nicolas *of Jean Bodel of Arras: A Literary Analysis* (Baltimore, 1954). See also, for the historical context of the Crusades, Charles Foulon, "La représentation et les sources du 'Jeu de Saint-Nicolas'," in *Mélanges d'histoire du théâtre du Moyen Age et de la Renaissance offerts à Gustave Cohen* (Paris, 1950), 55–66.

[21] Jones, *Saint Nicholas of Myra*, 307. This illuminated manuscript is in the British Museum, Cotton Tiberius B V. The Borrower's Tale is found on folios 55r–56r, 73r–v, and 77r; also Walter de Gray Birch, "The Legendary Life of St. Nicholas," *Archaeological Journal of the British Archaeological Association* 44 (1888): 222–234. Birch was the first to edit the saint Nicholas miracles found in this manuscripts.

[22] Birch, "The Legendary Life of St. Nicholas," 223, lines 11–12. The miracle's action is established very quickly: within the first ten lines, the Jewish moneylender and the impoverished Christian have struck up their bargain. The moneylender imposes one condition, that a pledge be made. The Christian responds: "Nothing is nearby that I can make a pledge to, says the Christian, but the altar of the archbishop. I give my pledge in this place."

[23] Jones, *Saint Nicholas of Myra*, reports on the manuscript's destruction in a footnote: "According to Meisen, a prose version existed in a Chartres MS almost contemporary with the Battle Abbey Life; but we cannot examine it, for all Chartres MSS were destroyed in a night bombing in 1944." Meisen, writing in 1931, may well be referring to the manuscript Delaporte (in *Les vitraux de la Cathédrale de Chartres*) identifies as "manuscrit 27," a lectionary from Saint-Père. Delaporte reports that the eleventh-century manuscript contains all the canonical miracles of the saint. He adds, "There follows an epilogue, written in a hand of the twelfth century, the beginning of the

In the 1140s, Honorius of Autun presented the miracle in a sermon.[24] At this point, the Borrower's Tale and the *Iconia* miracle were being juxtaposed to form a grouping we now know as the "Icon of Saint Nicholas" stories, even though Honorius makes no mention of the image of Saint Nicholas in the Borrower's Tale.[25] In the later twelfth century, we once again find the tale within a sermon, this time in a manuscript from Namur, in modern Belgium.[26] In the twelfth century, the Borrower's Tale had become a staple of vernacular lives of the saint.[27] By the late thirteenth century, the tale was also a fixture of Jacobus de Voragine's *Golden Legend*, where it immediately preceded the *Iconia* miracle, a coupling that endured for the rest of its medieval tradition.[28]

The Performance and Reality of Jewish Identity in Thirteenth-Century Chartres

Now that we have laid out all of the representational forms of our miracle stories (narratives, imagery, and text), we can intersect these with the experience of the medieval viewer before our stained glass windows. The archival process of recovering texts and visual artifacts, for our modern audience, differs radically from the seamless assimilation of narrative and image, propelled by physical movement and liturgical acts, characteristic of medieval viewing practices. Narrative, image and

---

miracle of the borrower" (262). The discrepancy between Delaporte's identification of the Borrower's Tale as twelfth-century writing and Meisen's as eleventh century is one of many reasons to mourn the loss of this manuscript. For our purposes, it serves to know that an early version of the Borrower's Tale was present at Chartres.

[24] *Patrologiae cursus completus, Series Latina*, ed. J.-P. Migne, 221 vols. (Paris, 1844–55), 172:1035–1036 [herafter cited as PL].

[25] Honorius of Autun, *De sancto Nicolao*. "Then coming before the altar he [the borrower] swore that in placing his pledge he would return the gold to him [the moneylender] from whom he had accepted the loan." (Quo perveniens super altare jurat quod in vadimonium posuerat se aurum reddidissse quod mutuo acceperat) in PL, 172:1036. The other interesting difference in Honorius's account is that the owner of the treasure is a pagan.

[26] Jones, *Saint Nicholas of Myra*, 228. The full version of the text can be found in *Analecta Bollandiana* 2 (1883): 153–156. The sermon again posits the altar as the site of the pledge. The Jewish moneylender addresses the saint directly (as opposed to through his image) for the duration of the story. The innovation of this sermon seems to be that saint Nicholas works to avenge the wronged moneylender, as much as he strives to restore justice.

[27] Jones, *Saint Nicholas of Myra*, 228.

[28] Jacques de Voragine, *La Légende Dorée*, trans. J.-B. M. Roze (Paris, 1967), 51–52.

performance operated together to gather viewers before provocative images of the Jewish antagonist's iconoclasm and the culminating images of his baptism. Understanding how this worked is our first task. Our second is to discern the disparity between the performances played out in window and spoken word, both sanctified within the church space, and the social reality of a Jewish presence in the city of Chartres. I will be arguing that the windows are not mirrors of social reality, but rather projections of a clerical anxiety about money and a consequent desire to convert both money and those dealing with money into the life of the Church. Rather than seeking for continuities between performance, image, and lived experience, we will need to investigate the discontinuities.

Both Karl Young and Otto E. Albrecht agree that the performance of material from the Fleury Playbook plays would have taken place in the church space itself.[29] The liturgical introits with which the miracle plays end indicate their integration into the longer feast day celebrations for the saint on December 6.[30] All the festivities surrounding Saint Nicholas's day, such as the election of the Boy Bishop and the coming of Christmas, resulted in large audiences for these plays and services, as marked in space and guided in ritual by our stained glass windows (fig. 5). Albrecht and Young both suggest that the plays *initiated* the mass. Young goes on to argue for two *sedes* in the staging of the play: one standing for the house of the Jew, where the statue of Saint Nicholas

[29] I must acknowledge the critique of dramatic performance by Thomas P. Campbell in "Liturgical Drama and Community Discourse," in *The Liturgy of the Medieval Church*, ed. Thomas J. Heffernan and E. Ann Matter (Kalamazoo, MI, 2001). "The Nicholas plays may have been monastic in origin, if the attribution of the Playbook to the abbey at St. Benoît sur Loire is accurate, but they were most certainly scholarly productions, intended for the refectory, not the church... There is no guarantee, after all, that a drama must be performed; and in a work as self-consciously literary as the Fleury Playbook, it may be possible to argue that we have a set of signals which are to be interpreted by either an audience or a reader" (643). But Campbell fails to take into account the many visual depictions of the miracle tale in stained glass, a medium profoundly implicated in the experiences of the popular viewer within the church. There are many more "signals" (such as money, thievery, and financial redemption) within the Fleury play that would have appealed to a lay, urban audience in a cathedral than to a monastic audience in a refectory.

[30] Young, *The Drama of the Medieval Church*, writes, "The closing rubric [of the *Iconia* play] directs the choir to sing the introit of the Mass of St. Nicholas, *Statuit ei Dominus*" (2:351). Corbin, "Le Manuscrit 201 d'Orléans," explains, "We have the liturgical program of a full day, complete with the solemn celebration of the hours. The other dramas, with the exception of the Pilgrims, finish with the 'Te Deum' which calls for the end of Matins" (27).

would appear where the beating occurs, and one for the house of the thieves, where the "actual" Saint Nicholas would make his appearance.[31] On the basis of the narrative deployment of the *Iconia* tale in the nave window, that is, the fact that the story is left incomplete at its most violent moment, I would locate the first *sedes* in the space near the northern nave window of Saint Nicholas. Similarly, because the narrative concludes in the window in the ambulatory, and because the saint appears "in person" for the baptism of the Jew, I argue that the second *sedes* would have been placed in the ambulatory before the Saint Nicholas window in the Chapel of the Confessors. These stations establish one of the key elements of the *Iconia* play: movement within and across the church space. The central window of the Chapel of the Confessors, where I believe the play culminated, was that of Saint Nicholas, directly above the altar.

Admittedly, nowhere in the city's archives, much of which were destroyed during the Second World War, has the tell-tale text confirming the performance of the *Iconia* play within the cathedral space been found. But the windows themselves and their placement provide the best evidence that the figures within the windows were meant to intersect with a performance in the church space. Chartres's *Ordinal* also gives indications about performances of the play by outlining the processions and performances of the liturgical celebrations in the cathedral.[32] The writing of the *Ordinal* is more notational than descriptive; but embedded within the abbreviations and rubrics for hymns is a strong clue about the movement of the Saint Nicholas liturgy, suggestive of a trajectory of reconciliation from the space of the nave (symbolizing chaotic urban and monetary scenarios) to the space of the ambulatory (where the religious community is reaffirmed through the Jew's baptism).[33]

The introit which ends the *Iconia* play initiates a series of hymns. When the hymns cease, it is time for readings about Saint Nicholas to be performed, described as "reading nine of his life and appropriate tales" (Lect. ix. de vita eius et hystoria propria sicut est.) Identifying

[31] Young, *The Drama of the Medieval Church*, 2:351.

[32] Delaporte, *L'Ordinaire Chartrain du XIIIe siècle*, "The clergy of the period sought in its ordinal information about the liturgy of a practical order" (23). The *Ordinal* is thus a type of liturgical "prompter" book.

[33] The celebration of Saint Nicholas was a "festum duplex," signaling his importance within the hierarchy of saints. The celebration would have begun the night before and lasted throughout the next day, continuously punctuated by hymns and prayers. The full text of the liturgy can be found in Delaporte's edition of the *Ordinal*.

these "appropriate tales" as our miracle plays is certainly an inviting notion. This is a moment when Chartres's stained glass windows would have come into play for the mass. The Nicholas windows were located in two crucial places along the processional path of the celebrants from the nave to the ambulatory, initiating an almost seamless movement from the performance of the play to that of the mass.[34]

The reading of the "appropriate tales" is preceded by the notation "by coming forward" (de adventu) signaling an approach, a movement within the church. At this point, the procession culminated in the choir and, we are told, "At the beginning of the *Te Deum*, uncovered the cloth" (Dum incipitur *Te Deum* discooperiatur capsa), in other words at the singing of the *Te Deum*, the Holy Mantle, Chartres's most precious relic housed in the choir, was uncovered. The transformations and translations which the windows had projected and promised are now fulfilled in this final, resplendent image revealing the relic of the Virgin, site and sight of divine presence at Chartres. It is at this point that the *Ordinal* calls for the celebration of Mass, the ultimate transformative miracle of the liturgy, and the most resplendent image of Christian cult. At this culmination, performed on the saint's feast day, the viewer experienced a powerful association of vibrant images: the Nicholas windows, the Eucharist,[35] and the relic of the Virgin. All three of these images were calls to unity, homogeneity, and continuity in that all three asserted the ideal of a unified Church sanctified by ritual: the windows through the image of the Jew's baptism and his ritualized integration into a Christian community; the Eucharist through its celebration of Christ's universal body; and the relic of the Virgin through its miraculous power within the local community. By following the trajectory of the Nicholas windows and the liturgical play from nave to ambulatory, partaking in the Eucharist, and venerating the relic of the Virgin, the medieval viewer

---

[34] R. N. Swanson, "Medieval Liturgy as Theater: the Props," in *The Church and the Arts*, ed. Diana Wood (London, 1992). "[Visual] decoration placed many vestments in the category of 'books for the unlearned,' their depictions of saints and significant events in the lives of Christ and his mother matching similar portrayals in stone, glass and wood" (248). With many such examples of liturgical furniture, Swanson demonstrates the fluidity of imagery from depictions in church space to those used in liturgy.

[35] Davidson, "Space and Time in Medieval Drama," 64. "The liturgical play, as closely related to ritual form, is itself an invocation of divine power... the dramatic spectacle is designed to bring the audience within a circle of action that transcends aesthetics in its function. By bringing spectators into the scene, the vernacular play is ultimately part of the redemptive pattern which is characteristic of the cult." This redemptive pattern is instigated by the positioning of the Nicholas windows in the nave and ambulatory, and by the liturgical movement towards the east of the cathedral.

became a participant in a multivalent incorporation ritual, designed to reaffirm a Christian spiritual and social body.

The Jew's baptism in the ambulatory window (fig. 6) becomes the focal point within the stained glass panels of this complex alignment of incorporation images. The window's imagery, placement, and liturgical connection culminate where the Jew's body emerges from the baptismal font, a vulnerable presence compared to his authoritative stance in the surrounding scenes. He is naked now, stripped of his identifying garb, his head tilted to one side, his left hand drawn in to his body. The resonance of baptism here includes the Eucharist, since the window is stationed directly above an altar: as a result, the sacrifice of the Jew's identity is absorbed into the sacrifice that is perceived to be the Eucharist. The Jew's naked body thus begins a complex play of *incorporations* ending in the loss of Jewish identity and an assertion of Christian homogeneity. The emphasis on the transformed body, both in the theology of baptism and that of the Eucharist, creates a powerful connection between the two rituals. The medieval viewer saw the image of the Jew's baptism at the end of the liturgical play and just before the performance of the Eucharist. Understood within this para-liturgical and liturgical context, the image of the Jew's baptism therefore takes on greater significance: it becomes a sign of reconciliation, not just for the Jew, but for the whole Christian community, including the viewer before the window. The viewer's body had experienced the movement of the play, symbolic of a transformation; the body of Nicholas had been transformed from statue to saint; the body of the Jew had become that of a Christian; and the bread of the Eucharist had become the body of Christ. All of these incorporations, these miraculous transformations, reasserted the powerful community of the Christian Church.

But were actual Jews perceived as such a threat to the social body of Chartres? A common interpretation of images depicting identifiable groups such as Jews is to think of them in terms of a cause and effect relationship between social reality and representation.[36] I would argue,

[36] Manhes-Deremble, *Vitraux narratifs*, "On a social level, we find ourselves, during the reign of Philippe Auguste, in an era of confrontation against Judaism" (127). In her discussion of the Borrower's Tale, Manhes-Deremble argues for a connection to a general anxiety about usury, and presents a short series of antisemitic texts as evidence. She cites a passage from the *Philippide* praising Philippe Auguste's persecution of pagans and Jews alike, as well as the Third Lateran Council's 1179 invective against Jewish communities, the sermons of Foulques de Neuilly and Pierre de Roissy, and the writings of John of Salisbury. The stained glass windows of Chartres then become, too simplistically I think, reflections and illustrations of these texts.

however, that these images of Jews and the whipping of images are not a mirror image of a social reality. There are no specific texts in the annales of Chartres which would indicate an anxiety about Jews in the city, and thereby "explain" the special violence of these images. In fact, Chartres was a town remarkably *un*populated by Jews.[37] The small Jewish community recorded in the lands of Chartres and Blois at the end of the twelfth century was continuously hounded by local lords. In 1172, count Thibaud V of Chartres burned the houses of the Jews of Blois following an accusation of ritual murder.[38] The noted nineteenth-century historian of Chartres, J.-B. Souchet, relates with disturbing glee a series of acts committed against the Jews of Chartres ordered by Philippe Auguste in 1179, which resulted in their expulsion from the city. The synagogue was converted into a hospital under the protection of St. Hilaire and the goods and properties were given over to the then fledgling order of the Fransiscans (*Cordeliers*) for the foundation of their priory.[39]

Presumably, then, the thirteenth-century chapter of Chartres was not dealing with local or contemporary personages in their representations of Jewish protagonists in the Nicholas tales. Why then, use this new imagery of the wronged and converting Jew for the money miracles? I argue that the antisemitism of Chartres's imagery begins with its use of the Jew as a "vehicle" for monetary anxieties. Stephen Spector has indicated the symbolic potential of absent persons for the purging of present social problems.[40] The anxieties that money presented to the cathedral chapter at Chartres are projected elsewhere within the windows,[41] and were principally concerned with the issue of "just price"[42]

[37] Chédeville, *Chartres et ses campagnes (XIe–XIIIe s)* (Paris, 1973). "In the majority of medieval cities, Jews were often the first to handle money. In the city of Chartres, there is nothing to indicate that they ever formed an active community" (474).

[38] Chédeville, *Chartres*, 475.

[39] J.-B. Souchet, *Histoire du diocèse et de la ville de Chartres* (Chartres, 1868), 508.

[40] Stephen Spector, "Time, Space and Identity in the *Play of the Sacrament*," in *The Stage as Mirror: Civic Theatre in Late Medieval Europe*, ed. Alan E. Knight (London, 1997). "[T]he Jews, even—or especially—in their absence... could be symbolic vehicles for qualities or beliefs that needed to be localized and rejected" (198).

[41] Specifically in the so-called windows of the trade. See my doctoral dissertation, "Giving Gifts and Taking Chances: a Reconsideration of the Trade Windows," in "The Spectacle of Stained Glass in Modern France and Medieval Chartres" (University of Chicago, 1999), esp. 115–161.

[42] The "Just Price Doctrine" called for a fair assessment of the value of a product when making a sale. A kind of formula was worked out in which the price of a good was calculated according to the price of the materials necessary for its production in

and the Church's ability to incorporate the secular power of money into its spiritual realm.[43] As we have already seen, the Borrower's Tale had, since its twelfth-century invention, featured a Jewish moneylender, but the owner of the treasure in the *Iconia* miracle had been alternately Jewish, Saracen, and pagan. Why would the chapter make this careful choice of using a Jew and repeat it for both of the money miracles? I suggest that the chapter's anxiety about its ability to adapt to the repercussions of money and its practices to the devotions of the Church[44] is what motivated them to use the ambivalent figure of the converting Jew. As Lester K. Little has succinctly stated, "The Jews functioned as a scapegoat for Christian failure to adapt successfully to the profit economy."[45] As this foreign figure is ultimately reconciled to the Christian fold, so too must money practices must be integrated into Church practices. The dynamic of chaos and re-established order is once again both narrative and visual. Instead of blunt and brutal violence against the Jews in body, the images of Chartres show Jews *causing* violence in scenarios involving money (the Christian borrower is killed and the statue of Nicholas is beaten). The libelous quality of these images is less blatant and more insidious than most other forms of medieval anti-Semitism: the Jew is wronged and humiliated, and his

addition to the cost of the human labor for its manufacture or transport. It was the act of fixing a price on human labor (an aspect of the human experience which had, since Adam's fall, been under God's purview) which proved so problematic for the Church. For a full exploration, see John W. Baldwin, "The Medieval Theories of Just Price: Romanists, Canonists, and Theologians in the Twelfth and Thirteenth Centuries," *Transactions of the American Philosophical Association* 49, no. 4 (1959): 1–92.

[43] We can witness this anxiety in the many innovative ways in which the Church changed its donation practices. Before money was appropriated by the merchant class emerging in the thirteenth century, we see donation of land and serf's labor in both images and texts of the Church; after money became an instrument of the merchant class, cash donations appear much more frequently. We see this contrast at Chartres in the older, aristocratic donations of Thibault de Champagne in the Zodiac window (which feature him before his serfs), and in the newer, merchant-class donations of the tradesmen, such as the shoemakers, butchers, bakers, etc.

[44] Jean Ibanès, *La Doctrine de l'église et les réalités économiques au XIII*[e] *siecle: l'intérêt, les prix et la monnaie* (Paris, 1967). "Truth be told, canonists and theologians sought less, in principle, to harmonize their theses with economic realities, than to influence these by guiding the behavior of economic agents" (33). Ibanès indicates an even more forceful stance by canonists and theologians who wished to influence monetary practices not just reconcile them. At Chartres, we are confronted with the pragmatic decisions of a chapter rather than the ideological position of the Church.

[45] Lester K. Little, *Religious Poverty and the Profit Economy in Medieval Europe* (Ithaca, 1978), 55. For Little's discussion of the invention and configuration of Jews as moneylenders see esp. 42–58.

suffering is at the center of violence provoked by mishandled money. But his humiliation and suffering is necessary to the narrative in that it prompts the much sought-after reconciliation with Christianity that his baptism and conversion afford.

These visual and performative images thus work to *construct* a social and theological truth. And they are enlisted by the Church, I have suggested, in order to create a coherent stance on the still incoherent, *undefined*, and volatile issue of money.[46] The hovering anxiety still surrounding the worship of images becomes a conduit to the emerging anxiety of possessing money—both anxieties involve the relationship between subjectivity (human identity) and objectivity (a thing in the world), and both anxieties, often characterized as sins by Christian theology, are embodied to the fullest degree by the Jewish character. The violent imagery of the stained glass windows and the iconoclastic performances of the play can therefore be understood as initiatives taken by the Church to give ideological and moral coherence to a still theologically and socially murky set of practices involving money.

If we may see visual form and performance as *productive* of meaning instead of reflective of social reality, we can work towards the associations, and the multiplicity of meanings, that the intersection of iconoclasm and the anxiety over money produced. The desecration of the statue by the Jew allegorically functions as an assault on the Church by a figure who had already become associated with money. The conversion of the Jew into a humble servant of Saint Nicholas then functions as an allegory of the conversion of money into pious gifts to the Church (a practice actively encouraged at Chartres and exemplified by the trade images in the bottom panels of stained glass windows). The conversion of the Jew through baptism signals the reconciliatory power of liturgical ritual for any member of the Christian community.

[46] Jean-Pierre Torrell, "Les Juifs dans l'oeuvre de Pierre le Vénérable," *Cahiers de civilisation médiévale* 30 (1987): 331–346. Earlier attempts had been made by Church writers such as Peter the Venerable to codify the relationship of Jews to money, and Christians to Jews through the problem of money. In three texts, the *Vita* of Matthew of Albanos, the *Adversus Judaeos*, and in a letter to Louis VIII, Peter outlines a program of separation meant to bar all relations betwen Christians and Jews, especially commercial ones, which have a profound theological dimension for Peter. Contemporary with his pronouncements are decrees by Philippe Auguste prohibiting clerics from standing in the way of commerce between Jews and Christians; see Blumenkranz, "Louis IX ou Saint Louis et les Juifs," 20.

The Performative Terms of Jewish Iconoclasm and the Body of the Jew

Despite the lack of historical evidence about a Jewish community in Chartres, the cathedral chapter had ample occasion—and, arguably in the thirteenth century, urgency—to reflect on the social *and* symbolic reality of Jews, through debates which intersected money, usury and Jewish socio-political identity within both the discourse of canon law[47] and the rhetoric of secular decrees. The few Jews of Chartres and its surrounding regions lived under the protection of its bishop,[48] which was a rather unusual situation in France, as most Jewish communities "belonged" to secular, feudal lords.[49] The social and legal status of "protector" of the Jews may have been more important to the bishop and chapter than the actuality of "protecting" them. The Jews, in their physical reality, were much less interesting to the cathedral chapter

---

[47] The classic analysis of Church policy toward Jews (with translations of original sources) is Solomon Grayzel, *The Church and the Jews in the Thirteenth Century* (New York, 1996), esp. 41–75. Another helpful comparative discussion is Kenneth R. Stow, "Papal and Royal Attitudes toward Jewish Lending in the Thirteenth Century," *Association for Jewish Studies* 6 (1981): 161–184. For treatment of secular decrees throughout Europe, James Parkes, *The Jew in the Medieval Community* (New York, 1976) esp. 101–154, and 273–383. For analysis specific to France, William Chester Jordan, *The French Monarchy and the Jews: From Philip Augustus to the Last Capetians* (Philadelphia, 1989). For further analyses of the issue of Jewish legal status, Gavin I. Langmuir, "*Tanquam Servi*: The Change in Jewish Status in French law about 1200," in *Les Juifs dans l'histoire de France*, ed. Myriam Yarden (Leiden, 1980), 24–54; and Aryeh Grabois "Les Juifs et les seigneurs dans la France septentrionale aux XIe et XIIe siècles," in *Les Juifs dans l'histoire de France*, 11–23.

[48] Chédeville, *Chartres et ses campagnes*, 475. Citing letter no. 33 from an abbot Geoffroy (also cited in Lucien Merlet "Lettres d'Ives de Chartres," *Bibliothèque de l'Ecole des Chartes* 1885, 443–471), Chédeville writes, "In addressing the monks of Notre-Dame about this matter, bishop Geoffroy uses the formula *our Jews*, which allows us to suppose, at this time, that the Jewish community was under the chapter's protection" (476). Later, in 1265, and in Bonneval (not Chartres), a charter of the monks of Saint Florentin gave the local count rights over Jews to "exploit them, treat them according to his will, and expel them if he thinks it best" ("les exploiter, les traiter à sa volonté, et de les expulser s'il le juge bon") (quoted in ibid.).

[49] Langmuir, "*Tanquam Servi*," traces the struggles to identify both the identity and obligations of Jews to their feudal lords by the French nobility and aristocracy. Secular lords had a much greater interest in the financial gain of "their" Jews than the Church was allowed to have, and were consequently in fierce competition with each other over the possession of Jews. "In France, because of the weakness of the Capetian monarchy and the extreme fragmentation of secular authority before 1200, full jurisdiction over Jews pertained to any lord with high justice who permitted them to reside under his jurisdiction" (44). Royal and aristocratic lords even made special pacts: "Philip Augustus and Thibaut III of Champagne mutually agreed not to retain each other's Jews" (45). The competition between secular lords and the Church for Jews could become quite fierce.

than the Jews in their symbolic possibility. The symbolic body of the Jew, subjected to image, performance and ritual, as we have seen, was the ideal vehicle through which the Church could enact its projects of reconciliation, and solidify the definition of a Christian community. The bishop and chapter exercised their ownership of Jews by manipulating the image, performance and rituals enacted upon the body of Jew. In conceiving these stained glass images[50] and in anticipating their effect, the chapter was confronting a broad and consequential issue: the challenge which the town's emerging urban and monetary economy presented to the chapter's way of life and its understanding of the world order.

The brilliance of the stained glass programmers lay in their ability to parallel the bodily experience of the Jew with the bodily witness of the audience: as the Jew beat the image of Saint Nicholas in an area of the nave marked by the stained glass window depicting the same scene, the spectator became both viewer (of the window) and participant (in the play) in the act. Viewer-participant subjectivity is evoked again as the Jew is baptized at the very end of the play in a space in the ambulatory marked by the window. Because the spectator is now before an altar in a chapel, the participatory element is much more profound and ritually implicated. By "simply" following the story (i.e. participating in the images and movements of the stained glass windows and the liturgical play), the spectator engages with Christian corporate identity at its most fundamental level, that of Eucharistic ritual.[51] That engagement, of course, is predicated upon the rejection of money and its conflicts, and the denial of Jewish identity.

A performative dynamic also exists between the body of the Jew and the dual bodies of Saint Nicholas (icon and the saint himself): while at the climax of the play—here projected at the apex of the window in the nave—it is the body of the saint that is desecrated, at the end of the play—here shining forth in the ambulatory—it is the body of the Jew that kneels, stripped and naked. The Jew is humiliated after his act of

[50] There is long-lasting debate about the programmers of the stained glass cycles of Chartres cathedral; see my "Giving Gifts and Taking Chances" esp. 115–8.

[51] It is important to point out that this dynamic of viewer-to-participant can operate even without the presence of liturgical drama. Those visitors to the cathedral who traced the Borrower's Tale from its violence in the nave to its reconciliation in the ambulatory did so with the same liturgical ending: the trajectory delineated by the narrative suspension of the stained glass windows "inevitably" ends before an altar and its associations with, if not performance of, the Eucharist.

humiliation and iconoclasm upon the statue of the saint. The Jew's humiliation of the saint is thus reformulated as his *humility*, and his consecration in baptism, his conversion, occasions the reconciliation of a Christian community. What is a restorative ending for the Christian community is, however, a loss of self and identity for the Jewish character.[52]

These symbolic exchanges of the body of the Jew were increasingly exercised not just in the religious realm, but in the socio-economic realm as well. Jews and their financial transactions were a significant source of wealth to the secular and clerical lords who "owned" them.[53] As such, Jews were often given as gifts, loaned, exchanged, or even redeemed at a later time.[54] The chapter's awareness of these types of scenarios need not have been specific to the region or any social reality experienced by the canons: the symbolic logic of the body of the Jew as an object of exchange was enough to have facilitated their exploitation of the image and performance of the Jew's body. Ensnared as it was in issues of money in both the *Iconia* miracle and the Borrower's Tale, the Jew's body was itself an object of economic exchange, reconciled and redeemed in the act of baptism.

The conversion of money to a more spiritual benefit is the precondition of the conversion of the Jew to Christianity. The powerful metaphor and act of conversion is the final performative term enacted upon the Jew's body in our investigation of these windows. The principal protagonists of the *Iconia* play at Chartres are the character of the wronged, awed, and eventually converted Jew, and that of the desecrated, righteous, and ultimately conciliatory Saint Nicholas. Miri Rubin has discussed the usefulness and volatility of the character of the converting Jew, a figure whose motives and movements were being

[52] Parkes, *The Jew in the Medieval Community*, 143, who notes, "But the greatest weapon against conversion was the fact that a Jew on baptism forfeited all his property." Once a Jew became a Christian subject, his feudal lord took possession of all of his belongings (whereas before he had laid claim to all, or almost all, of "his" Jew's profit).

[53] Grayzel, *The Church and the Jews*, 54, n. 66.

[54] Parkes, *The Jew in the Medieval Community*, 113, who describes several of these scenarios, including one involving Emperor Henry VII who "stated in some of his grants of Jews the price at which he might redeem them." The symbolic logic of the wordplay around "redeeming" and "redemption" in these texts might be well-worth pursuing as we inquire about the symbolic treatment of Jews in the emerging discourse of medieval economics.

defined with increasing precision at the turn of the thirteenth century.[55] The *Iconia* play, as we have seen, was instrumental in articulating this personage of the converting Jew, so useful for the coalescing of an urban Christian community. There is further evidence that the dynamic of desecration and reconciliation around conversion transcended the cathedral walls and engaged the social mission of the pope and the archbishop of Sens. In an extraordinary letter of 1213 from Innocent III to Pierre Corbeil,[56] the pope praises the latter for the diffusion of a miracle in his archdiocese in which a Jew, having deviously arranged for a consecrated host to be stolen from a church, secrets the precious token away in his coffer, which otherwise contained "seven Parisian pounds." The Jew soon thereafter discovers that every coin in his coffer has been miraculously transformed into a host: "they were no longer coins, but hosts" (eam non utique denariis, sed hostiis). Once he abandons hope that the hosts would revert (reconvert) to money, he and his family convert to Christianity in awe of the power of the Eucharist, and are baptized. The intention to desecrate is here thwarted by the movement to consecrate. The pope goes on to entreat the archbishop to look out for the needs of this converted Jew and his family, in order to insure their proper integration into the Christian community.[57]

Through the liturgical conclusions visualized at the stories' end in the ambulatory, the Nicholas windows at Chartres were positioned to reconcile social bodies. The "narrative suspension" of the stained glass windows whose violence and iconoclasm are displayed in the nave, and whose conversion and reconciliation are projected in the ambulatory, along with the drama of iconoclasm and conversion within those same cathedral spaces, provided an immediacy and level of participation for viewers rarely witnessed in thirteenth-century religious experience.

---

[55] Miri Rubin, *Gentile Tales: The Narrative Assault on Late Medieval Jews* (New Haven, 1999), 6–39, which traces the early, "happy ending" tales of Jewish conversion to Christianity, and 84–88, which specifies the volatility of loyalties converts from the Jewish faith to Christianity embodied. "Converts appear in the host desecration narrative as morally ambiguous figures…converts were the carriers of knowledge of the secret actions of Jews" (84–85). The much-desired reconciliation of the Jew to Christian society was also a dangerous one, revealing the fragility of the "reconciled" community.

[56] PL, 217:885–886.

[57] See my article, "St. Nicholas in Context: Stained Glass and Liturgical Drama in the Archbishopric of Sens," in *Proceedings from the 2004 Corpus Vitrearum Medii Aevi Colloquium in Nürnberg* (Freiburg im Breisgau, 2006), 89–99, in which I address the *Iconia* miracle windows of both Chartres and Auxerre within the larger context of the archbishopric of Sens.

Rather than serving to confirm a social reality, the windows and their performance through liturgical drama authenticated the *symbolic* reality of Jews in a Christian world and social order increasingly threatened by money. The Jew's violence in image and performance was emblematic of that threat. The Jew's conversion, by contrast, stood for the redemption of that social order. This seductive dynamic of violence and conversion was to have a long-lasting, and increasingly literal, interpretation throughout the later Middle Ages.[58]

[58] For example, in the 1290 accusation of host desecration which was used to persecute Paris Jews; cf. Rubin, *Gentile Tales*, 84–88.

PART II

THE IMAGE OF THE JEW AND ITS PUBLIC

CHAPTER FIVE

THE PASSION, THE JEWS, AND THE CRISIS OF THE INDIVIDUAL ON THE NAUMBURG WEST CHOIR SCREEN*

Jacqueline E. Jung

Marking the boundary of nave and choir, respective domains of laity and clergy in medieval churches, the Gothic choir screen at once reinforced social distinctions and provided a stable, unifying focus during liturgical rituals.[1] Yet to cast these structures in strictly binary terms, as has often been the case in earlier scholarship, is to risk oversimplifying a situation that was far more complex. First, the binary approach concentrates solely on the solid frame of the screen while ignoring its points of permeability; the Gothic screen was, after all, as important for its capacity for (controlled) passage as it was for its exclusions. Second, this approach implicitly assigns a static, inflexible character to liturgical spaces that is belied by documentary and pictorial evidence

* This essay is a substantially revised version of chapter seven of my dissertation, "The West Choir Screen of Naumburg Cathedral and the Formation of Social and Sacred Space" (Columbia University, 2002). For their thoughtful comments on that redaction, I thank Caroline Bynum, Jeffrey Hamburger, David Freedberg, Keith Moxey, and Stephen Murray. A version of this paper was presented during my fellowship period at the American Academy in Berlin in March 2006, where it was graciously introduced by Dr. Gerhard Lutz, and again, in German, at the Naumburg-Haus in Naumburg in May 2006. The latter engagement took place at the joint initiative of Dr. Henry Sapparth and Dr. Susanne Kröner of the Naumburg Stadtarchiv, who on several earlier occasions facilitated my research on local history with unstinting graciousness and generosity. I owe them both, and all the respondents at these venues, my sincere thanks. My deepest gratitude goes to Mitchell Merback for his lively company during research trips through Germany in spring 2006, for the probing questions and illuminating insights he offered on my paper in its later stages, and for his patience throughout the long revision process.

[1] See Jacqueline E. Jung, "Beyond the Barrier: The Unifying Role of the Choir Screen in Gothic Churches," *Art Bulletin* 82, no. 4 (Dec. 2000): 622–57; and idem, "Seeing through Screens: The Gothic Choir Enclosure as Frame," in *Thresholds of the Sacred: Architectural, Art Historical, Liturgical and Theological Perspectives on Religious Screens, East and West*, ed. Sharon Gerstel (Washington, D.C., 2006), 188–213. For German screens through to the end of the Middle Ages, see Monika Schmelzer, *Der mittelalterliche Lettner im deutschsprachigen Raum: Typologie und Funktion* (Petersberg, 2004).

alike; just as members of the clergy performed many services outside the choir—at altars distributed throughout the nave, in side chapels, or in elevated galleries—so were at least some laypeople allowed to venture into the clerical sanctuary.[2] The possibility of selective access points to the third inadequacy of the binary approach: that is, its effacement of the internal diversity of the social groups in question. For all the insistence in contemporary writings on the sharp divide between clergy and layfolk, members of both groups were well aware that the subtler distinctions within their own cohort—in social status, institutional affiliation, education, gender, and so forth—were no less visible, consequential, and crucial to maintain.[3]

These more specific social identities not only determined people's physical access to the spaces demarcated by a choir screen, but also must have inflected understandings of the pictorial programs displayed thereon. In sartorial details, gestural conventions, material accessories, and even stylistic modes, the narrative sculptures embellishing the great stone screens of the thirteenth century—whether scenes from sacred history (as at Amiens, Chartres, Bourges, Modena, and Naumburg), depictions of virtuous behavior in the present (as at Strasbourg), or renderings of persons' fates in the future (as at Mainz and Gelnhausen)—are packed with social commentary that would have been immediately recognized, if variously understood, by contempo-rary beholders of diverse social origins.[4] One group particularly well-represented in the imagery of Gothic choir screens was, paradoxically, a group without access to the screens at all—Jews.

This paper concentrates on the portrayal of Jewish men in the Passion narrative on the finest thirteenth-century choir screen to have survived *in situ*: the *Westlettner* of Naumburg Cathedral (fig. 1), fashioned around 1250 by a group of sculptors previously responsible for the (now

---

[2] On the complex nature of Gothic choirs, see the essays in *Kunst und Liturgie: Choranlagen des Spätmittelalters—ihre Architektur, Ausstattung und Nutzung*, ed. Anna Moraht-Fromm (Ostfildern, 2003); and my review in *KUNSTFORM* 5 (2004), Nr. 7/8 [15.07.2004], www.kunstform.historicum.net/2004/07/5073.html.

[3] Especially useful on the question of social definition and distinction in the High Middle Ages are Giles Constable, "The Orders of Society," in *Three Studies in Medieval Religious and Social Thought* (Cambridge, 1995), 249–360; and Caroline Walker Bynum, "Did the Twelfth Century Discover the Individual?" in *Jesus as Mother: Studies in the Spirituality of the High Middle Ages* (Berkeley, 1982), 82–109.

[4] See Jung, "Beyond the Barrier," for discussion of these monuments and further bibliography.

destroyed) choir screen at the metropolitan cathedral of Mainz.[5] The stone reliefs at Naumburg, carved with exceptional verve and composed with unusual dramatic force, have long been extolled as embodiments of the "new individualism" characteristic of high medieval intellectual culture.[6] Not bound to an exclusively didactic function, each figure in the program seems conceived as a character, his (or, in one case, her) gestures, physiognomy, and facial expression conveying something of a personality that gave new inflections to the well-known stories.[7] For all their seeming spontaneity and naturalism, however, the figures' social identities are consistently fixed—and thus their degree of individualism checked—through costume elements, bodily comportment, and other material details.[8] In some cases these elements of local meaning have led to modern misunderstandings of the scenes' social content; for example, despite many commentators' conviction that the Apostles appear here as rustic folk—especially in the first relief, which shows Christ's companions eating with their fingers at the Last Supper (fig. 2)—their luxurious clothing, modish hairstyles, and stylized gestures

[5] On the Naumburg choir screen progam, Ingrid Schulze, *Der Westlettner des Naumburger Doms: Das Portal als Gleichnis* (Frankfurt, 1995); Antje-Fee Köllermann, "Die Darstellung der Passion Christi am Naumburger Westlettner," and Anja Rasche, "Die Passionsreliefs am Naumburger Westlettner: Beobachtungen zur Erzählstruktur und Einbeziehung des Betrachters," both in *Meisterwerke mittelalterlicher Skulptur*, ed. Hartmut Krohm (Berlin, 1996), 349–64 and 365–76 respectively; Jung, "West Choir Screen"; and Michael Viktor Schwarz, "Retelling the Passion at Naumburg: The West-Screen and Its Audience," *Artibus et historiae* 51 (2005), 59–72. For its architecture, see Schmelzer, *Der mittelalterliche Lettner*, 124–28. On the Mainz screen, completed in the 1230s, Kathryn Brush, "The West Choir Screen at Mainz Cathedral: Studies in Program, Patronage, and Meaning" (Ph.D. diss., Brown University, 1987); and Christine Kitzlinger and Stefan Gabelt, "Die ehemalige Westlettneranlage im Dom zu Mainz," in Krohm, ed., *Meisterwerke*, 205–44.

[6] For the current state of the question of individualism in this period, see esp. Susan R. Kramer and Caroline W. Bynum, "Revisiting the Twelfth-Century Individual: The Inner Self and the Christian Community," in *Das Eigene und das Ganze: Zum Individuellen im mittelalterlichen Religiosentum*, ed. Gert Melville and Markus Schürer (Münster, 2002), 57–85; and the essays collected in *Individuum und Individualität im Mittelalter*, ed. Jan A. Aertsen and Andreas Speer (Berlin, 1996).

[7] See, for example, Peter Kidson, "A Note on Naumburg," in *Romanesque and Gothic: Essays for George Zarnecki* (Woodbridge, Suffolk, 1987), 143–46. On individuality in the Naumburg donor figures, Ernst Schubert, "Individualität und Individualisierung in der Mitte des 13. Jahrhunderts: Die Naumburger Stifterstandbilder," Dritte Sigurd Greven-Vorlesung gehalten am 4. Mai 1999 im Schnütgen-Museum Köln (Cologne, 1999).

[8] The tension between "bildnishafter, individualisierender Charakterisierung... und idealisierender Typisierung" is also noted by Rasche, "Passionsreliefs," 367.

would have instead defined them as noble in the eyes of contemporary viewers, as I have shown elsewhere.[9]

Such misattribution is impossible with regard to the Jewish characters. Of the thirty-one figures populating the screen's six original reliefs, thirteen wear the funnel-shaped hats that had come to signify Jewishness in medieval iconography well before the thirteenth century. These figures play leading roles in three of the reliefs: the second in the sequence, showing Judas' receipt of the thirty silver pieces from the High Priest Caiaphas (see fig. 8); the third, Christ's Betrayal and Arrest in Gethsemane (see fig. 10); and the fifth, Christ's Trial before Pilate (see fig. 15).[10] Two additional Jewish men, each brandishing a pole, occupy the otherwise empty ground to the right of the portal's central gable, compositionally balancing the image of Peter's Denial on the left-hand side and forming a transition to the Trial scene on the right. The last two reliefs in the sequence, showing the Flagellation and the Carrying of the Cross, are roughly carved wooden replacements of originals badly damaged in a fire in 1532; although many of the attendant figures in these scenes were given updated costumes by their eighteenth-century designer, the appearance of pointed hats on several suggests that the original models also featured Jewish men.[11]

As we shall see, for all its quantitative emphasis on Jewish involvement in Christ's Passion, the Naumburg program is unusual, if not unique, among contemporaneous monumental depictions of the subject in its refusal to cast the Jews consistently and unambiguously as malevolent "others." Not only do most of the Jewish characters appear physically interchangeable with the Apostles or the Romans, but also, far from heaping crass and violent abuses on Christ, they conduct themselves according to the legal conventions and behavioral codes of thirteenth-century Saxon laypeople. Through this pictorial strategy, I argue, the critique of the Jewish establishment in the Passion narrative, while

[9] Jacqueline E. Jung, "Peasant Meal or Lord's Feast? The Social Iconography of the Naumburg Last Supper," *Gesta* 42 (2003): 39–61. For closer views of these figures, see the photographs by Janos Stekovics in Ernst Schubert, *Der Naumburger Dom* (Halle an der Saale, 1997), 137–41.

[10] For detailed images, see Schubert and Stekovics, *Naumburger Dom*, 143–63.

[11] Ibid., 162–63. The wooden reliefs were fashioned over the course of three weeks (!) in 1747 by a local turner named Johann Jacob Lütticke as replacements for the damaged originals. The contract (quoted at 160), specifies only that Lütticke adhere to certain drawn designs (*Risse*). For further discussion of these reliefs and their iconography, Jung, "West Choir Screen," 295–96.

certainly acknowledged, is also dispersed onto the Christian lay elite who comprised a primary audience for the reliefs. Thus, rather than acting as demonizing devices aimed at chanelling fear and hostility onto a collective religious "other," the depictions of Jews at Naumburg were designed so as to compel beholders to turn scrutiny back upon the self.

In light of then-current representational practices for rendering Christ's Jewish antagonists during the Passion, this choice is surprising; its very singularity, I suggest, reveals something about the local political conditions of this provincial bishopric and about the engagement of the cathedral clergy with the ethical concerns that characterized much social thought in the twelfth and thirteenth centuries.[12] On the one hand, as we shall see, the patron of the Naumburg west choir, Bishop Dietrich II von Wettin (act. 1242–72), had practical reasons for downplaying the role of the Jews as unambiguous enemies; anti-Jewish activity was flaring elsewhere in the Empire, and Dietrich depended on the financial resources of local Jews for the construction of his church and the defense of his territory against the heavy-handed incursions of his half-brother, Margrave Henry the Illustrious of Meissen (1218–88).[13] On the other, the removal of primary responsibility for Christ's death from the collective shoulders of the Jews throws the actions of the individuals into higher relief, calling attention to the sometimes devastating consequences of personally motivated actions within rigorously structured social codes. As we shall see, beneath what scholars have long celebrated as the newly personalized conception of the Passion narrative at Naumburg there lies a darker subtext, a critique of the "new individual" who breaks established conventions governing public behavior. Whereas the concern with the motivations and intentions of individual agents characteristic of mid-thirteenth-century ethics is

[12] The new ethics, articulated earliest and most explicitly in Peter Abelard's *Scito te ipsum* ("Know Yourself") and evident in various cultural domains, from confessional practices to devotional exercises and legal processes, placed emphasis on the personal internal intentions behind outer deeds; see Peter Abelard, *Ethical Writings: His Ethics or "Know Yourself" and his Dialogue between a Philosopher, a Jew and a Christian*, trans. by Paul Vincent Space (Indianapolis, 1995). The literature on the larger phenomenon is too expansive to cite comprehensively here, but a useful overview of the issues is Colin Morris, *The Discovery of the Individual, 1050–1200* (1972; repr. Toronto, 1987), esp. 64–75. For more specialized studies on individuality and intention in the philosophy and ethics of the late Middle Ages, see Aertsen and Speer, ed., *Individuum* (as n. 6).

[13] On Dietrich's troubled tenure, Heinz Wiessner, *Das Bistum Naumburg I: Die Diözese*, Germania Sacra, N.F. 35 (Berlin, 1998), 2: 801–10; and Jung, "West Choir Screen," 9–30.

present here, it is, paradoxically, instrumentalized to reinforce group solidarity and existing social mores for a target audience of high-status Christians.

Beyond the Pointed Hat: Anti-Jewish Polemic in Monumental Narrative Sculpture

For modern-day viewers, all-too aware of the tragic consequences of government-imposed clothing restrictions, it is easy to regard the funnel-caps balanced on the heads of the Naumburg figures as an essentially derogatory sign forced on Jews by a hostile Christian establishment[14]—an assumption that seems confirmed by Canon 68 of the Fourth Lateran Council (1215), which stipulated that Jews and Muslims "of either sex, in all Christian lands and at all times... easily be distinguished from the rest of the population by the quality of their clothes."[15] The main purpose of this canon was to prevent sexual intermingling between persons of various religious groups; in certain lands, the clerical drafters complained, "there has arisen such confusion that no differences are noticeable."[16]

It was not only Christian authorities who worried over the lack of visual differentiation among members of diverse religious communities; the danger of blurred boundaries was also sensed by Jewish men and women, who, despite close interactions with their Christian neighbors, were equally averse to being mistaken for them.[17] Just as living together

---

[14] See, for example, Ruth Mellinkoff, *Outcasts: Signs of Otherness in Northern European Art of the Late Middle Ages*, 2 vols. (Berkeley, 1993), 1: 65–73, 91–94. A more nuanced approach is taken by Sara Lipton, *Images of Intolerance: The Representation of Jews and Judiasm in the* Bible moralisée, (Princeton, 1999), 15–19.

[15] Original Latin and translated text in Solomon Grayzel, *The Church and the Jews in the XIIIth Century: A Study of Their Relations During the Years 1198–1254, Based on the Papal Letters and the Conciliar Decrees of the Period*, rev. ed. (New York, 1966), 308–309; for further analysis, see Allan Cutler, "Innocent III and the Distinctive Clothing of Jews and Muslims," *Studies in Medieval Culture* 3 (1970): 92–116.

[16] Grayzel, *Church and the Jews*, 309.

[17] For an excellent account of the social life of Jewish communities in Christian towns in the High Middle Ages, see John Y. B. Hood, *Aquinas and the Jews* (Philadelphia, 1995), 19–37; for the later period, Dean Phillip Bell, *Sacred Communities: Jewish and Christian Identities in Fifteenth-Century Germany* (Boston: Brill, 2001). For further remarks on religious definition in Germany, Ivan G. Marcus, "Hierarchies, Religious Boundaries, and Jewish Spirituality in Medieval Germany," *Jewish History* 1, no. 2 (1986): 7–26; and Yacov Guggenheim, "Meeting on the Road: Encounters between German Jews and Christians on the Margins of Society," in *In and Out of the Ghetto: Jewish-Gentile*

in specially designated streets was sometimes understood by medieval Jews less as a form of "ghettoization" than as a means of protection and community,[18] so could the wearing of distinctive tokens, paradoxically, serve to forge and reinforce group solidarity. Numerous Hebrew manuscripts, as well as the coats of arms and seals of some prominent Jewish families, included emblematic images of pointed hats.[19] While, in social practice, some medieval Jewish communities seem to have adopted the conical hat "of their own will as a national custom," others mandated that their members "not cut [their] hair or shave [their] beard[s] after the manner of the gentiles."[20] Such stipulations indicate both that visual distinctions were important to some Jews, and that a slippage, "a tendency...for the younger and more prosperous Jews to catch up with the prevalent [Christian] styles," was desirable to others.[21]

Nonetheless, the evidence that medieval Jews wore distinctive caps after Lateran IV, or that the Christian establishment took pains to impose them, is slim. The pointed cap had signified Jewishness in the pictorial arts long before 1215—indeed, during that very time prior to the Council when Jewish and Christian communities were supposedly threatened by their lack of discernable difference. The drafters of Canon 68 were surely familiar with such sartorial coding from pictures of Old Testament Jews in manuscripts, on liturgical paraphernalia, and in monumental public sculpture programs,[22] and it is possible that their idea of imposing distinct iconographic markers on real bodies was inspired by the clarity such images provided. On the other hand, it is important to keep in mind that the canon leaves unspecified the precise nature of the clothing to be regulated. Those prelates who did obey it often chose other markers such as badges, earrings, or colored cloaks;[23]

Relations in Late Medieval and Early Modern Germany, ed. R. Po-Chia Hsia and Hartmut Lehmann (Cambridge, 1995), 125–36.

[18] For the (often slippery) distinctions between "voluntary" and "compulsory" forms of Jewish settlement, see Alfred Haverkamp, "The Jewish Quarters in German Towns during the Late Middle Ages," in Hsia and Lehmann, eds., *In and Out of the Ghetto*, 13–28, esp. 13–16.

[19] Lipton, *Images of Intolerance*, 18.

[20] On hats, see Grayzel, *Church and the Jews*, 67, n. 114; on beards, 66, n. 112. This was a precept from a rabbinical synod held by Rhineland Jews in 1220.

[21] Grayzel, *Church and the Jews*, 66, n. 112.

[22] See Lipton, *Images of Intolerance*, 18. For hats on positive figures, see Bernard Blumenkranz, *Le juif médiéval au miroir de l'art chrétien* (Paris, 1966), 117–34.

[23] Grayzel, *Church and the Jews*, 67. For one alternative, see Ariel Toaff, "The Jewish Badge in Italy during the Fifteenth Century," in *Die Juden in ihrer mittelalterlichen Umwelt*, ed. Alfred Ebenbauer and Klaus Zatloukal (Vienna, 1991), 275–80.

but enough churchmen disregarded the precepts altogether that Gregory IX lamented in 1233 that "a disgraceful situation still obtains in some parts of Germany, namely that no difference [between Christians and Jews] is discernible."[24] We do not read of the Jews of Naumburg wearing special hats until 1454, when anti-Jewish sentiments, motivated by political as well as religious factors, flared in the region.[25]

Whereas the pointed hat was not, in itself, an unambiguous mark of denigration, it became one when conjoined with the patently negative motifs that played a growing part in imagery of the twelfth and thirteenth centuries and reached a particularly ugly nadir in the Late Gothic screen at Havelberg Cathedral (to be discussed below). Not content with using neutral accessories to identify the Jews of the Gospels, Christian artists in these contexts imbued their characters with bodily signs—wild gesticulations, contorted facial expressions, and a stereotyped physiognomy—to brand them as "other" in a clearly negative sense.[26] The combined modernization and demonization of biblical Jews in medieval art represented, as Joshua Trachtenberg put it, a "conscious effort" on the part of churchmen to present them "not as... historical figure[s] but as the contemporary Jew[s] with whom the audience was more or less familiar. The sins of Jesus' contemporaries were deliberately piled upon the collective head of medieval Jewry."[27] Medieval liturgical dramas, sermon exempla, and a wide variety of images—from abstruse visual commentary in moralized Bibles to monumental public narratives on portals and choir screens—are filled with anonymous figures who serve no narrative purpose beyond displaying signs of Jewish perfidy, blindness, and guilt.[28]

---

[24] Grayzel, *Church and the Jews*, 198–99.

[25] Discussed further below.

[26] A survey of negative attributes is in Mellinkoff, *Outcasts*, 1: 111–227. For anti-Jewish signs and their relation to strategies for demonizing other groups, see Debra Higgs Strickland, *Saracens, Demons, and Jews: Making Monsters in Medieval Art* (Princeton, 2003), esp. 105–55.

[27] Joshua Trachtenberg, *The Devil and the Jews: The Medieval Conception of the Jew and its Relation to Modern Anti-Semitism* (1943; repr. Philadelphia, 1983), 13.

[28] See Henry Kraus, *The Living Theatre of Medieval Art* (Philadelphia, 1967), 139–62. On the modernization of biblical Jews in liturgical plays, Heinz Pflaum, "Les scènes de juifs dans la littérature dramatique," *Revue des Études Juives* 89 (1930): 111–34; and Winfried Frey, "Zur Rolle der Juden in mittelalterlichen deutschen Texten des Weihnachtsstoffkreises," in *Spannungen und Konflikte menschlichen Zusammenlebens in der deutschen Literatur des Mittelalters*, Bristoler Colloquium 1993, ed. Kurt Gärtner, Ingrid Kasten, and Frank Shaw (Tübingen, 1996), 125–41. For exempla, Joan Young Gregg, *Devils, Women, and Jews: Reflections of the Other in Medieval Sermon Stories* (Albany, NY, 1997),

A veritable encyclopedia of anti-Jewish caricature appears in the twelfth-century sculpture program on the west façade of the abbey church of St-Gilles-du-Gard, a cycle possibly known to the designers of the Naumburg choir screen.[29] In the relief showing the Payment of Judas, two bearded figures press close together in a corner, apparently commenting on the transaction unfolding beside them (fig. 3). The distance of this pair from the main action gives their conversation an air of secrecy; the gesture of the figure on the right, busily counting his fingers, suggests that it concerns money. Like the two attendants who shove an apparently reluctant Judas toward the High Priest's throne, these men wear the knee-length tunics of medieval servants, though their fashionably gathered sleeves and short capes suggest employment in a home of high rank.[30] And although the faces, like many in the series, are badly eroded, it would take a good deal more rain to wear away the counting figure's huge hooked nose, angular cheekbones, and jutting jaw.

In the adjacent relief, showing the Betrayal and Arrest of Christ, Jesus is confronted by a motley procession of characters whose faces—marked by furrowed brows, hooked or porcine noses, leering mouths and double chins—brand them as aberrant by nature and not only for what they do (fig. 4).[31] In contrast to the tall, elegantly attired Christ and Judas, these men wear the knee-length sheaths and saggy boots of the servile. Whereas this band of rogues also includes Roman soldiers, the peaked hats of the two bearded, hook-nosed henchmen who flank Christ and Judas mark them as specifically Jewish.[32]

169–235; and Ivan G. Marcus, "Images of the Jews in the *Exempla* of Caesarius of Heisterbach," in *From Witness to Witchcraft: Jews and Judaism in Medieval Christian Thought*, ed. Jeremy Cohen (Wiesbaden, 1996), 247–56.

[29] The connection between Naumburg and St-Gilles was first drawn by Richard Hamann, *Die Abteikirche von St. Gilles und ihre künstlerische Nachfolge*, 3 vols. (Berlin, 1955), 1: 416–23; for the Judas scenes, see 1:84–86; and for photographic details, 2: plates 54–55. For close stylistic analyses of these scenes, Whitney S. Stoddard, *The Façade of Saint-Gilles-du-Gard: Its Influence on French Sculpture* (Middletown, Conn., 1973), 95–96. The central tympanum of this program also included an early depiction of Ecclesia and Synagoga flanking the crucifix; see Henry Kraus, *Living Theatre*, 150, 152.

[30] Uncharacteristically, the High Priest appears in the guise of a generic kingly figure, positioned frontally with splayed limbs and long garment. Evidently it was his haughtiness rather than his social identity that was the artist's main concern; bodily signs of Jewishness were reserved for servile figures.

[31] Hamann, *Abteikirche*, 1: 84–86 and 3: plates 73–75; Stoddard, *Façade*, 95.

[32] For further examples of stereotyped Jews in Payment, Arrest, and Trial scenes, Gertrud Schiller, *Ikonographie der christlichen Kunst*, 4 vols. (Gütersloh, 1968), 2: 62–69, 71–76.

Such derogatory motifs were hardly alien to artists active in later medieval Saxony. The sculptors who, between 1395 and 1411, fashioned the reliefs for the H-shaped screen ensemble in Havelberg Cathedral exploited and expanded the established range of physiognomic and expressive devices for degrading Jews in order to visualize more clearly that paradoxical combination of ignorance and malevolence attributed to Christ's persecutors.[33] Throughout the program's twenty Passion reliefs, Jesus is confronted by male figures whose aggressive gestures and grotesque features strike a contrast with the mild manners and noble faces of himself and his apostolic cohort. Such visual denigration, at times, even rubs against the grain of the biblical text and longstanding iconographic traditions; in the Entry into Jerusalem, for example, Christ's donkey pulls back on stiffened forelegs as a spindly man in a funnel-cap crawls toward him on all fours, more like a nasty dog than a person paying homage, while a tall, nattily dressed man brandishes a cloak in front of Christ's path as if to impede, rather than encourage, his progress.[34]

The anti-Jewish message in this relief is subtle, however, compared to that apparent in scenes of overt violence. Christ's Flagellation and

[33] This unusually large ensemble consists of a lateral screen with a central pulpit flanked by two small doors, attached to two longitudinal walls that separate the choir and crossing from the side aisles; for this and other so-called *Kanzellettner*, Schmelzer, *Der mittelalterlicher Lettner*, 41–64; and Jung, "Seeing through Screens," 205–7. The outer surfaces of the north and south enclosing walls also contain narrative scenes, but the Passion reliefs I discuss here are located on the walls facing the Cross Altar and thus would have been visible during lay services. For a concise overview of the screen and its imagery, Harald Wildhagen and Torsten Buchholz, *Der Lettner im Dom zu Havelberg* (Halle an der Saale, 1995). For a stylistic analysis of the reliefs, Ingrid Schulze, "Böhmischer Einfluß in der Plastik des fortgeschrittenen 14. und 15. Jahrhunderts in Barby und Havelberg," in *Skulptur des Mittelalters: Funktion und Gestalt*, ed. Friedrich Möbius and Ernst Schubert (Weimar, 1987), 255–79, esp. 266–79; and idem, "Die Havelberger Lettner- und Chorschrankenreliefs: Inhaltliche Problematik und stilistische Kriterien," in *Die mittelalterliche Plastik in der Mark Brandenburg*, ed. Lothar Lambacher and Frank Matthias Kammel (Berlin, 1990), 93–99. On the use of the screen in liturgical dramas, Claudia Lichte, "Der Havelberger Lettner als Bühne: Zum Verhältnis von Bildprogramm und Liturgie," in *Mittelalterliche Plastik*, 101–7. The only monographic study of the screen and its context is idem, *Die Inszenierung einer Wallfahrt: Der Lettner im Havelberger Dom und das Wilsnacker Wunderblut* (Worms, 1990). The studies by both Schulze and Lichte sidestep the question of anti-Judaism in the reliefs, placing emphasis rather on formal and stylistic qualities of the representations. Lichte insists that the contemporary garb of the monstrous Jewish characters served primarily to make them more effective vehicles of identification for Christian pilgrims (!), who would have been warned away from similarly bad behavior (*Inszenierung*, 119).

[34] See Lichte, *Inszenierung*, 51, fig. 31.

Crowning with Thorns are accomplished by exclusively Jewish men, most wearing foppish contemporary clothing that reveals large expanses of their legs and buttocks.[35] Although the Jewish antagonists are unified by their oversized peaked caps crowned by a ball, distinctions of status are drawn through the figures' clothing and gestures. Whereas the Crown of Thorns is affixed to Christ's head by a pair of dwarfish ruffians who must be physically supported in order to accomplish their goal, this action is framed by two stately Elders or Pharisees in long formal robes, who, resting their hands on the backs of their servants, tacitly give their approval (and assistance) to the proceedings.

In this image it is the figures' gestures and placement, more than their facial features, that lend the scene its polemical edge; in others, Christ is attacked by persons barely recognizable as human at all. Placing one hand on the shoulder of a dapper henchman, Caiaphas—his huge beaked nose overhanging a mustachioed upper lip—watches approvingly as another pair of Jewish brigands manhandle their meek captive (fig. 5).[36] One, in the long robe of an Elder, crawls on the floor, jerking his head back to reveal his tongue and teeth as he swings his club against Christ's thigh. As if the stereotyped physiognomy left any doubt as to this character's affiliation, the sculptor has drawn further attention to his hat by including an additional henchman who fondles its crowning knob from behind. Meanwhile, Christ's right arm and shoulder are grasped by an armed figure with scraggly hair and bulldog-like features; cocking his lantern-jaw and stretching his thick lower lip toward his nose, the figure gazes into distant space from eyes pressed deep within skull-like sockets. His strictly tactile engagement with Christ, the strange positioning of his head, and his deeply sunken eyes suggest that this man is blind, making his juxtaposition with the literally blindfolded Jesus all the more poignant.[37] Indeed, the chain of touch that links all the Jewish figures in this scene—a chain whose center is occupied by Christ, although, his hands being tied, he is not an active participant—reinforces the impression that the figures' knowledge is gained

[35] See Lichte, *Inszenierung*, 55, fig. 39 (Flagellation), 56, fig. 40 (Crowning with Thorns).

[36] Lichte, *Inszenierung*, 54, 67–68 identifies this relief as Christ before Herod. The fact that the main figure's clothing and physiognomy are identical to those of Caiaphas in the preceding relief, which depicts the High Priest rending his garments while accusing Jesus of blasphemy, suggests that the two images are meant to form a continuous scene.

[37] On blindness motifs in the Middle Ages, see Moshe Barasch, *Blindness: The History of a Mental Image in Western Thought* (New York, 2001), 67–114.

by blind groping rather than insight, and that their communication occurs through carnal contact rather than through intelligible speech.

The suggestion in the Havelberg relief that Christ's Jewish persecutors were at once blind, dumb, and malicious is accentuated by its contrast with the adjacent image of Christ before Pilate. Here, communication does take place through speech—exceptionally loud speech, to judge from the gaping mouth of Christ's accuser, who tilts his oversized head back to shout his complaints from grotesquely distended lips (fig. 6). Although the angle of Pilate's head, the shape of his long beard, and the sharp lines of his cheekbones make him resemble Christ, his prominently hooked nose aligns him with the stereotyped Jews shown elsewhere. Indeed, the fact that he wears both a hat and a long, buttoned robe almost identical to those worn by Caiaphas shows him to be cut, as it were, from the same cloth. In this case, stereotypical anti-Jewish attributes are translated onto the Roman character so as to highlight his guilt—this despite the fact that long-entrenched interpretations of the Passion (visual and textual alike) tended to mitigate Pilate's agency so as to amplify Jewish calls for blood.

Recent scholarship on the Naumburg west choir screen gives the impression that attitudes toward Jews were no less hostile there than in the St-Gilles and Havelberg programs that bracket it chronologically. In her important article on choir screen sculpture, Annette Weber described the Naumburg Jews as displaying "petulant faces framed by unkempt hair and beards, with sharp profiles and emphatically crooked noses," "small, dark, close-set eyes beneath deeply furrowed brows," and "devilish" grimaces.[38] Such features are certainly to be found on the Jewish captor who grasps Christ's tunic in the Naumburg Arrest scene (discussed below)—but what is remarkable for the whole program, especially in light of then-widespread visual conventions, is the fact that the remaining reliefs not only minimize physical differences among Jews, Romans, and Apostles but even reinforce the likenesses among them. At Naumburg, the Jews formed but one group among several whose members, through their personal decisions and actions,

[38] Annette Weber, "Die Entwicklung des Judenbildes im 13. Jahrhundert und sein Platz in der Lettner- und Tympanonskulptur: Fragen zum Verhältnis von Ikonographie und Stil," *Städel-Jahrbuch* 14 (1993): 35–54 at 35. Interestingly, German art historians of the 1920s and 1930s thought the figures looked not like Jews but like the Slavs who populated the eastern frontier region; see Jung, "West Choir Screen," 292, n. 35.

brought about the death of Christ. The first was a man from Christ's own inner circle—Judas.

The Naumburg West Choir Screen: Jews, Apostles, and the Dispersed Responsibility for Christ's Death

The scene of Judas's receipt of silver from the High Priest Caiaphas in return for his promised delivery of Christ—the second image in the Naumburg sequence (see fig. 8)—was rarely depicted in monumental sculpture of the Middle Ages.[39] When it was shown, the location of the treacherous act in a specific social setting, "the court of the high priest" (Matt. 26:3), tilted the scene toward sharp and varied anti-Jewish polemicizing. Most surviving examples employ compositional and iconographic devices designed to cast the Jewish high priests as the initiators and Judas as a passive, if not unwilling, participant in the exchange—a reversal of the Gospel accounts, where Judas approaches the chief priests, themselves uncertain how to apprehend Jesus without causing a ruckus, with his offer to turn Christ over to them.[40] At St-Gilles, an attendant shoves Judas toward Caiaphas, who waits with outstretched arm to pass off the coins (see fig. 3). In a console relief from the choir screen at Modena Cathedral (ca. 1180), which displays the tense moment just before the money changes hands, Judas likewise appears as a reluctant partner in crime (fig. 7).[41] Indeed, the prominent halo behind his head, whose form is echoed in the *empty* purse at Judas's side, suggests that he is still without malice, in contrast to the behatted Caiaphas and the hook-nosed *camerarius* who stands at the ready, weighing in his hands a bulging sack of coins. The *jubé* at Bourges Cathedral (ca. 1260) rendered the episode as a cool financial

---

[39] For other examples, Schiller, *Ikonographie*, 2: 34–35.

[40] Mt. 26:14–15; Mk. 14:10–11; Lk. 22:3–6. Cf. the comments on this scene by Schwarz, "Retelling the Passion," 63–65.

[41] For details of this early screen ensemble, *Il Duomo di Modena Atlante fotografico*, ed. Marina Armandi, photos by Cesare Leonardi (Modena, 1985), 858–85. For a color view of this relief, see *Il Duomo di Modena/The Cathedral of Modena: Atlante fotografico*, ed. Chiara Frugoni, photos by Ghigo Roli, 3 vols. (Modena, 1999), 2: 678, plate 1322. For the iconography of this screen, see Erika Doberer, "Il ciclo della passione sul pontile di Modena," in *Romanico padano, Romanico europeo* (Parma, 1982), 391–98. The comparison between Naumburg and Modena is also drawn by Schulze, *Westlettner*, 45–46.

transaction between equal partners.[42] A large rectangular purse dangles from one figure's fingertips, a familiar sign of his association with the new, and still threatening, cash economy.[43]

At Naumburg, by contrast, Judas appears as the active initiator of the exchange (fig. 8); he rushes in from the side, his face anxious and hurried, thrusting the bundled edge of his cloak into Caiaphas's lap.[44] Whereas the sculptors at Modena and St-Gilles drew upon the conventions of seals to portray the High Priest as a man of authority[45]—with frontal, open body, firmly planted feet, splayed knees, and angled elbows—the body of Caiaphas at Naumburg swivels toward one side and is largely obscured by Judas. Moreover, rather than turning his head to confront Judas actively, the High Priest turns *away* from him and toward beholders. Together, the two figures form what Stephen Kern—writing of a formula widely employed in nineteenth-century painting, in which a male figure in profile gazes at a thoughtful, frontally oriented female—calls a "proposal composition."[46] Kern emphasizes the "greater depth perception of binocular vision as well as a wider horizon of visual interests, a broader range of purposes, and more profound, if not more intense, emotions" implied in the frontal faces of the women in such pictures.[47] Although, obviously, the nature of the Passion narrative precludes an interpretation of the High Priest as a sympathetic character, the frontality of the Naumburg figure's head, his ocular engagement of beholders, and his ambiguous demeanor, suggestive of exhaustion or worry—an expression, in fact, resembling nothing so much as that of the Virgin Mary who weeps over her crucified Son in the portal below[48]—make this Caiaphas a character of

---

[42] See Fabienne Joubert, *Le jubé de Bourges* (Paris, 1994), 54 and fig. 31.

[43] See Lester K. Little, *Religious Poverty and the Profit Economy in Medieval Europe* (Ithaca, 1978); Jacques LeGoff, *Your Money or Your Life: Economy and Religion in the Middle Ages*, trans. Patricia Ranum (New York, 1990); also see Anne Harris's contribution in this volume.

[44] Cf. Schwarz, "Retelling the Passion," who interprets Judas's expression as "horrified" (65) and one of "despair" (68).

[45] For royal and imperial seals employing the same bodily configuration, see *Die Zeit der Staufer: Geschichte, Kunst, Kultur*, ed. Reiner Haussherr and Christian Väterlein, 5 vols. (Stuttgart, 1977), 3: plates 1–30.

[46] Stephen Kern, *Eyes of Love: The Gaze in English and French Culture, 1840–1900* (New York, 1996).

[47] Kern, *Eyes of Love*, 7.

[48] See Schubert and Stekovics, *Naumburger Dom*, 168–69.

considerable psychological complexity, complicating any impression of him as a thuggish instigator of a nefarious plot.

If the designers of this relief (and the clerical patrons who gave their approval) wished to highlight the depravity of Christ's Jewish antagonists, it is surprising that they included none of the usual signs that marked the Jews as servile, hostile, ignorant, or blind. The Chief Priest can be said to be stereotyped only in that he wears a beard without a mustache;[49] his nose is slightly larger than those of his attendants, but the strict frontality of his face makes its forward extension impossible to apprehend from a standpoint on the ground. The courtiers who frame the transaction are clean-shaven, and their physiognomies—with large, wide-set eyes, broad foreheads, square jaws, and full lips—make them more closely resemble the Apostle John in the Last Supper relief (see fig. 2), as well as several of the male donor figures in the west choir proper, than the High Priest.[50] Their noses are thin and straight; and if their hair appears "stringy and unkempt," it is no more so than that of Christ and the Apostles. Their costumes and mannerisms are designed to give the courtiers an air of nobility; they wear ankle-length, belted tunics under broad-collared cloaks, and the figure at the far right-hand side pulls his cloak around his back in a gesture often associated in Gothic sculpture with aristocratic refinement.[51]

Especially noteworthy here is the omission of a moneybag or purse, the attribute of Judas and emblem of Jewish greed in much thirteenth-century imagery.[52] Rather, Caiaphas lets the coins slip loosely through active hands, his gesture echoing, but inverting, that with which Christ fed Judas in the preceding relief (see fig. 2). Taking these pairs of hands as the conceptual as well as formal center of each image, we can recognize that the two reliefs are structurally analogous. Each features a transaction in which a bearded, frontally oriented man bestows one or

---

[49] On the beard as signifier of Jewish piety, see Lipton, *Images of Intolerance*, 20–21.

[50] Cf. the faces of Hermann of Meissen, Eckehard of Meissen, and Wilhelm of Camburg, in Schubert and Stekovics, *Naumburger Dom*, 82, 88, and 107.

[51] The margrave Hermann in the Naumburg west choir, and an Apostle on a lintel from Metz Cathedral, a work associated with the "Naumburg Master," handle their cloaks this way. On the formulaic quality of the gesture, Willibald Sauerländer, "Die Naumburger Stifterfiguren: Rückblick und Fragen," in Haussherr and Väterlein, eds., *Zeit der Staufer* (Stuttgart, 1979), 5: 169–245 at 192. On Metz, Richard H. L. Hamann, "Das Apostelrelief vom Liebfrauenportal am Metzer Dom um 1250," *Deutsche Kunst* 10, no. 6 (1943): 63–64.

[52] On this motif, see Strickland, *Saracens*, 140–43. On the stereotype of the cash-obsessed Jew, Trachtenberg, *Devil and the Jews*, 188–94.

more disk-shaped objects upon a beardless recipient in profile. Each exchange is framed by four figures who demonstrate group cohesion: whereas the Apostles of the Last Supper are united by gestures of consumption, the Jews at the High Priest's court are conjoined through both their hats and their gestures of intrigue.[53] The decisive difference between the two scenes is the manner in which Judas accepts the disk-shaped object(s) from his partner. Whereas Judas's reception of bread from the hand of Christ was audacious in its flippancy—accompanied as it was by his simultaneous groping in the sop-bowl[54]—his receipt of the coins from Caiaphas is reverent, even if rushed. These he treats as holy objects, scooping them up with veiled hands.

Although this Caiaphas is not overtly demonized the way his counterparts in other sculptural monuments were, his structural analogy with Jesus at the Last Supper invites viewers to recognize him as Christ's anti-type, distributing coins directly from his body as if in a perverted Eucharistic ritual. At the same time, by showing Judas actively approaching the High Priest and by eschewing overt signs of Jewish alterity, the designers of this image complicate the anti-Jewish message, for these choices call attention back to the errant Apostle, the loner who cherishes coins more than hosts.

In contrast to much contemporaneous pictorial imagery, which endowed Judas with the distorted features of stereotyped Jews,[55] the Naumburg Judas is tall, well-proportioned, and as handsome as any of the other Apostles. His deviance is conveyed rather through his gestures and behavior, which viewers know to be ill-intentioned, and through his social and psychological alienation from the surrounding figures.[56] Although fixed in the center of the scene, Judas is excluded from the chain of touching and whispering gestures that links the other men; his action thus appears self-motivated, and, to judge by the expressions

---

[53] Although the motif of close talking recalls the whispering Jews at St-Gilles, the Naumburg figures neither count anything nor display stereotyped facial features; their communication thus appears a more generalized instance of court intrigue. Medieval critics complained of secrecy and gossip-mongering as constant features of both secular and episcopal court life; see C. Stephen Jaeger, *The Origins of Courtliness: Civilizing Trends and the Formation of Courtly Ideals, 939–1210* (Philadelphia, 1985), 61–64.

[54] See Jung, "Peasant Meal," 51–52; cf. Schulze, *Westlettner*, 46–48

[55] On the increasing ugliness of Judas in later medieval art, Mellinkoff, *Outcasts*, 1: 134–35; and Peter Dinzelbacher, *Judastraditionen* (Vienna, 1977), 22–26

[56] Isolation, both spatial and social, was one of the most important defining features of Judas in visual representations before the later Middle Ages; see Dinzelbacher, *Judastraditionen*, 27–28.

of the courtiers' faces, it is unsettling. Costume details reinforce the impression of Judas's "otherness" at the High Priest's court. In a relief that places unusual emphasis on feet—pressing against the base of the throne, dangling from a crossed leg, twisting to follow the curve of a stooped body—Judas's bare feet and ankles signal his continued identity as an Apostle despite his appearance in a dressy milieu. In contrast to the other figures, Judas is also shown hatless, his hair flowing in undulating waves across his shoulder. Within the behatted crowd, it is now a bare head that signals outsider status.

From a frontal standpoint on the ground, however, this is not readily apparent; for Judas's body occludes another attendant figure on the back plane, whose funnel-cap is aligned directly with the top of Judas's head. Only by moving toward the right (toward the center of the screen) and thus changing the angle of view can a beholder discern the spatial distance between the heads of Judas and this other figure, which now peeks out from behind Judas's back (fig. 9). In a subtle but brilliant artistic maneuver, the sculptor has thus exploited the peculiar ability of his medium to shift appearances in conjunction with the viewer's movement in order to enhance the psychological content of the scene. Judas may be shown to be a dangerous outsider through the conventional iconography of his isolation—but his treachery, his shiftiness, his neither-nor status are rendered visible through the tricks his sculpted form plays on the eyes. If, sliding barefoot into the scene, he *seems* to adopt the Jewish hat that would make him an insider, the movements of viewers reveal him to be an imposter. The apparently troubled responses of the courtiers make it clear that, for all their own conspiratorial whispering, it is not Jewishness *per se* that makes one dangerous; it is, rather, the insinuating behavior of the renegade who moves betwixt and between social groups.

Although some medieval writers posited Judas's eventual despair of salvation, rather than his betrayal of Christ, as his greatest crime,[57] the Gospel narratives portrayed Judas's treason as contemptible—inspired, according to John 13, by Satan himself. This point would surely have resonated strongly among thirteenth-century upper-class laypeople and clerics alike, for whom loyalty to one's lord was paramount in the

---

[57] As discussed in Michael Viktor Schwarz, "Kathedralen verstehen (St. Veit in Prag als räumlich organisiertes Medienensemble)," in *Virtuelle Räume. Raumwahrnehmung und Raumvorstellung im Mittelalter*, Akten des 10. Symposiums des Mediävistenverbandes, Krems, 24.–26. März 2003, ed. Elisabeth Vavra (Berlin, 2005), 47–68, at 64–65.

maintenance of social stability.[58] By cloaking the Passion narrative in the guise of contemporary secular interactions, the Naumburg sculptors, more than any of their peers, invited—indeed, demanded—viewers to understand that story in terms of their own legal and social relations. Seen through that lens, the third relief in the series, showing Judas performing the action that leads to his lord's capture (fig. 10), would have carried all the more weight. In contrast to most depictions of the Betrayal, Judas here stands taller than Christ, so that he must stoop down slightly to plant the kiss on his lips. The male *osculum*, of course, was loaded with social significance in thirteenth-century legal culture, having long comprised the central moment of the rites of entry into vassalage.[59] Immediately following the *immixtio manum*, which expressed the "more or less marked subordination of the vassal to the lord,"[60] the mouth-to-mouth kiss reconfigured the relationship as one of equality and good faith; only after this was the final step of investiture, the establishment of a "reciprocal contract," possible.[61] Significantly, this—the one moment in the relief series where Judas engages in direct physical contact with another person, and the single instance in which he appears to act in accordance with social rules—leads not to solidarity with his lord but to radical alienation from him. Henceforth Judas disappears from view, and his leading role in the Naumburg Passion is taken over by the cathedral's co-patron, the Apostle Peter.

Dominating the frontal plane of this relief as he swings his broadsword down upon a crouching figure in a funnel-cap, Peter forms a visual and iconographic counterpart both to Judas, whose body he

---

[58] Throughout the Old Saxon *Heliand*, a vernacular translation of the Gospels written for an audience of newly converted warriors, Judas's betrayal of Christ is presented explicitly as a breach of a man's loyalty to his superior; see *The Heliand: The Saxon Gospel*, trans. and commentary by G. Ronald Murphy, S.J. (New York, 1992), 152, 158–59.

[59] The most influential discussion of the kiss in rites of fealty remains Jacques Le Goff, "The Symbolic Ritual of Vassalage," in *Time, Work, and Culture in the Middle Ages*, trans. Arthur Goldhammer (Chicago, 1980), 237–87. It has been reviewed and, in some details, revised by Yannick Carré, *Le baiser sur la bouche au moyen âge: Rites, symbols, mentalités, à travers les textes et les images, XIe–XVe siècles* (Paris, 1992). On the social nuances of the kiss, see also Klaus Schreiner, "'Er küsse mich mit dem Kuß seines Mundes' (*Osculetur me osculo oris sui*, Cant. 1,1): Metaphorik, kommunikative und herrschaftliche Funktionen einer symbolischer Handlung," in *Höfische Repräsentation: Das Zeremoniell und das Zeichen*, ed. Hedda Ragotzky and Horst Wenzel (Tübingen, 1990), 89–132; and Michael Camille, "Gothic Signs and the Surplus: The Kiss on the Cathedral," in *Contexts: Style and Values in Medieval Art and Literature*, special issue of *Yale French Studies*, ed. Daniel Poirion and Nancy Freeman Regalado (New Haven, 1991), 151–70.

[60] Le Goff, "Symbolic Ritual," 250.

[61] Le Goff, "Symbolic Ritual," 253.

abuts from behind, and to the Jewish captor on the opposite side of the panel. Peter and the captor, both wielding large swords, bracket the entire group, their expansive bodies lunging from the middle-ground to the frontal plane and their bearded heads positioned toward the center at a three-quarters angle. But Peter's smooth face and calm demeanor strike a contrast with the angular, agitated features of his counterpart. In the latter figure, for the first and only time on the Naumburg choir screen, we find the characteristic distortions of anti-Jewish pictorial polemic: the furrowed brows and narrowed eyes, the stretched, leering mouth, the oversized beak (fig. 11).[62] The physiognomic difference between these two dominating figures reinforces their differing actions toward Christ: at the same moment Peter defends the lord that Judas betrays, he also protects the lord that the Jew attacks.

Yet the word "attacks" does not quite describe what the captor—or any of the Jews who inhabit this scene—is doing here. Whereas the Gospel account read on Good Friday specifies that the "band of soldiers and servants from the chief priests and the Pharisees" apprehended Christ on the Mount of Olives bearing "lanterns and torches and weapons" (John 18:3),[63] the relief is curiously devoid of instruments of war. It does include the instruments of illumination mentioned in the Gospel: against the back plane, a behatted attendant raises aloft a flickering torch, its cluster of flames curling around the smooth circle of Christ's halo as if forming the material counterpart to Christ's immaterial radiance. But the armaments that feature so prominently both in the biblical text and in medieval renditions of the scene—on the Modena choir screen, for example, where Judas and Christ are framed by the strong vertical lines of a battle-axe and spear (fig. 12); at St-Gilles, where the clubs and swords brandished by stocky servile types punctuate the scene (see fig. 4); and in a relief from the destroyed choir screen at Amiens Cathedral (ca. 1260), where the chief captor, grasping Christ's collar with the same backhanded gesture as his counterpart at Naumburg, wears the chain mail, tunic, helmet and girdle of a Christian knight (fig. 13)[64]—are entirely absent. The captor's sword in the Naumburg

---

[62] For a closer view, Schubert and Stekovics, *Naumburger Dom*, 147. This is the figure to which Weber's description in "Entwicklung," 35 best applies.

[63] *Missale secundum rubricam Numburgensis* (Nuremberg, 1501), fols. lxxxiii verso–lxxxv verso. The Gospel reading comprised all of John 18–19. The quoted passage is from the Douay-Rheims translation of the Bible.

[64] See Dorothy Gillerman, "The *Arrest of Christ*: A Gothic Relief in the Metropolitan Museum of Art," *Metropolitan Museum of Art Journal* 15 (1981): 67–90; Charles T. Little,

Arrest, balanced upright against his shoulder, its blade bound in thick strips of leather, would have been recognizable to contemporary viewers not as a useable weapon, which both local and imperial law forbade Jews to bear, but as an emblem of judicial authority, which, in certain instances, it accorded them.[65] One did not need to turn to illustrated legal handbooks such as the *Sachsenspiegel* to see this manner of bearing the sword;[66] the bearded donor figure of the Thuringian count Sizzo in the west choir apse carries his sword in precisely this manner (fig. 14). So too does the figure of St. Sebastian in a stained glass window nearby, who, departing from traditional iconography, likewise wears a beard and peaked cap.[67] If the distorted facial features of the captor signaled his "otherness," then, his sword-bearing pose emphasized his dangerous *likeness* to modern representatives of worldly authority.

What we see here is not, therefore, what Debra Strickland has called an "iconography of rejection"[68]—though, to be sure, it is hardly an iconography of warm toleration either. The tendency in modern scholarship to regard any pictorial denigration of a Jewish figure as evidence *primarily* of cultural anti-Judaism (let alone anti-Semitism) flattens out the complexity both of medieval pictorial languages and of the relationships with and attitudes toward Jews such languages expressed.[69] At Naumburg, the figure most clearly portrayed as perfidous

"Monumental Gothic Sculpture from Amiens in American Collections," in *Pierre, lumière, coleur: Études d'histoire de l'art du Moyen Age en l'honneur d'Anne Prache*, ed. Fabienne Joubert and Dany Sandron (Paris, 1999), 243–53; Jung, "Beyond the Barrier," 638–39 and 640, fig. 18.

[65] On the sword as a symbol of judicial power, see Joachim Bumke, *Höfische Kultur: Literatur und Gesellschaft im hohen Mittelalter* (Munich, 1986), 226. For this gesture, Ruth Schmidt-Wiegand, "Gebärdensprache im mittelalterlichen Recht," *Frühmittelalterliche Studien* 16 (1982), 363–79. On Jewish rights in medieval Germany, including their right to present cases against Christians, Friedrich Lotter, "The Scope and Effectiveness of Imperial Jewry Law in the High Middle Ages," *Jewish History* 4 (1989): 31–58.

[66] See Walter Koschorreck, *Der Sachsenspiegel in Bildern* (Frankfurt am Main, 1976), figs. 21, 35, 36.

[67] See Christa Schmidt, *Glasfenster im Naumburger Dom* (Berlin, 1975), 8; Schubert and Stekovics, *Naumburger Dom*, 122–27.

[68] Debra Hassig, "The Iconography of Rejection: Jews and Other Monstrous Races," in *Image and Belief: Studies in Celebration of the Eightieth Anniversary of the Index of Christian Art*, ed. Colum Hourihane (Princeton, 1999), 25–46, an idea developed further in her *Saracens*.

[69] On the problem of historicizing Christian (or secular) attitudes toward Jews, see Johannes Heil, "'Antijudaismus' und 'Antisemitismus': Begriffe als Bedeutungsträger," *Jahrbuch für Antisemitismusforschung* 6 (1997): 93–114; and Zygmunt Bauman, "Allosemitism: Premodern, Modern, Postmodern," in *Modernity, Culture and "the Jew,"* ed. Bryan

seems to be targeted not for his Jewishness but for his motivated action as a representative of a legal system—a legal system under which the patrons, the makers, and the intended beholders of the choir screen also lived. The points of likeness that link the Jewish antagonist on the screen to noble Christian figures in the choir make plain that the line between good and bad social behavior was understood to be a fine one. It is in this sense that the captor's caricatured physiognomy becomes important. Precisely in its radical *contrast* to the faces of the other Jewish men in these reliefs—including his companions in this scene, and the character who accuses Christ before Pilate in a subsequent relief (discussed below)—it suggests a displacement of culpability from the Jews as a collective; the pairing of the ugly face with a gesture of active aggression against a peaceable subject—the violent grasping at Christ's chest, the hate-filled facial expression—posits a continuity between inner malevolence, manifested in an ugly exterior, and unjust *acts*. To put it another way: the absence of demonizing features in the other Jewish men in these reliefs suggests that the captor's ugliness arises less from the socio-religious identity he shares with them than from his vicious (even if legally sanctioned) behavior. The anti-Jewish features of this image are thus made to serve a message that includes but also transcends anti-Judaism: namely, that culpability rests on the deeds and motivations of individual agents acting within a highly structured world.

The problem of individual agency arises again in the representation of St. Peter, who wields the only proper weapon to be included in this scene. Here, too, we find a tension between the scriptural texts, in which Peter is immediately chastised by Christ for his aggression against the servant Malchus,[70] and the image, in which Peter forms a swashbuckling, heroic figure as he lunges across the frontal plane, expertly handling a huge broadsword. The depiction of Malchus as an able-bodied adult in fashionable knightly garb,[71] straining with his upper body against the

---

Cheyette and Laura Marcus (Stanford, 1998), 143–56. I thank Mitchell Merback for bringing these studies to my attention.

[70] See Mt. 26:51–54, Lk. 22:49–53, and Jn. 18:10–11. Each account renders Jesus's response to the attack differently; but in each, it is less Peter's violence that Jesus condemns than the underlying presumptions that he was in need of human defensive actions ("Thinkest thou that I cannot ask my Father, and he will give me... more than twelve legions of angels?") and that the ensuing redemptive process could or should be avoided through such actions ("The chalice which my Father hath given me, shall I not drink it?").

[71] Malchus's garb is nearly identical to that of the noble warrior Saint Pancratus in the stained glass of the choir; see Schmidt, *Glasfenster*, 7.

sword-blade in a vigorous crouching contrapposto, adds to the sense of adventure created by Peter's gesture. This was a highly unusual representational choice for the time. Typically, Malchus appeared as a buffoonish character: short, ugly, poorly dressed—hardly a worthy opponent for the Prince of Apostles. At St-Gilles, Peter ambushes Malchus from behind, grasping his neck with one hand and sawing at his ear with the other while the servant, with bulging eyes and lolling tongue, stumbles awkwardly and struggles for breath (see fig. 4).[72] His dwarfish counterpart at Modena yanks Christ's elbow as Peter, clutching a handful of the servant's close-shorn hair, calmly clips his ear (see fig. 12).[73] The Amienois Malchus sits plopped on the ground as Christ heals his ear from behind the back of Judas, his degradation revealed not only through the natural signs of his body—its scrawny limbs and dumb, slack-jawed face—but also through the conventional signs of clothing and haircut: as at St-Gilles and Modena, he wears the knee-length tunic and cropped hair of the socially low (see fig. 13).[74] As Peter, garbed in a voluminous mantle, sheathes his (now missing) sword with a grand flourish of the arm, his pride in victory appears misplaced; the disparity both in bodily stature and armaments (a little dagger, still sheathed, dangles at Malchus's side) suggests that there cannot have been much of a contest. A similar scene plays out at Havelberg, where Christ himself appears less to be healing the ear of the diminutive servant, who crawls on the ground clutching his phallic cap between his thighs, than pulling the latter's beard and thereby adding to his degradation.[75]

The parity of the Naumburg figures and the force with which Peter strikes Malchus imbues the episode with a dramatic seriousness absent in other renditions, lending it the flavor of the vernacular epics then being composed in secular (as well as ecclesiastical) courts.[76]

---

[72] See Hamann, *Abteikirche*, 1: 84–86; and Stoddard, *Façade*, 95.

[73] See Frugoni and Roli, *Il Duomo di Modena*, 2: 669, plate 1311; and Doberer, "Ciclo della passione," 391–98.

[74] On the association of short hair and garments with servile status, Jung, "Peasant Meal," 48–49.

[75] Lichte, *Inszenierung*, 53, fig. 35.

[76] The courts of the margrave of Meissen and the landgraves of Thuringia were hotbeds of literary production in the thirteenth century; see Joachim Bumke, *Mäzene im Mittelalter: Die Gönner und Auftraggeber der höfischen Literatur in Deutschland, 1150–1300* (Munich, 1979). For pictorial depictions of similar swordplay, Joan A. Holladay, *Illuminating the Epic: The Kassel* Willehalm *Codex and the Landgraves of Hesse in the Early Fourteenth Century* (Seattle, 1996), esp. 171–73, pls. 11–13; and Rita Lejeune and Jacques Stiennon, *The Legend of Roland in the Middle Ages*, 2 vols. (London, 1971), 1: 235, plate 26. In the

Yet contemporary viewers would have known that the apparent heroism of the Naumburg Peter was compromised by his victim's legal status. The local and imperial prohibitions of Jews and clergy from bearing arms meant that members of both groups, being unable to defend themselves adequately, were legally immune from armed attack.[77] The *Sachsenspiegel* warned that members of either group who did "carry arms in transgression of the law" forfeited that automatic protection.[78] But, as noted above, the Jews in the Naumburg relief act in a way consonant with Saxon law in their absence of visible weaponry. Thus Peter's attack, though partially legitimized (in terms of feudal relations) by being performed against an adult enemy in defense of a threatened lord, also conflicted with both chivalric injunctions against attacking any unarmed foes[79] and legal prohibitions against attacking Jews. If Christians guilty of the former might lose honor, those guilty of the latter might lose their heads; injury to persons under imperial protection was punishable by death.[80]

The little funnel-cap balanced atop Malchus's head would not have offered much protection against Peter's broadsword—a devastating instrument designed for hacking and crushing bones, not slicing off delicate appendages.[81] The relief makes plain that the precision with which the blade falls on the victim's ear cannot be credited to Peter's excellent marksmanship; rather, it is Christ's right hand, pressing forward with palm turned inward, that has gently deflected the blade from what must have been the intended target, Malchus's skull.[82] Here, too,

---

Heliand, Peter's violent defense of Christ was likewise legitimated through the transformation of the Jewish servant into "the first man of the enemy"; see *Heliand*, 160; and the commentary by G. Ronald Murphy, S.J., *The Saxon Savior: The Transformation of the Gospel in the Ninth-Century Heliand* (New York, 1989), 106–8.

[77] *The Saxon Mirror: A* Sachsenspiegel *of the Fourteenth Century*, trans. Maria Dobozy (Philadelphia, 1999), book 3, par. 2, p. 119. On the extent to which the imperial laws were applied throughout Germany, Lotter, "Scope and Effectiveness."

[78] *Saxon Mirror*, 119.

[79] On the ethics of knightly combat, Constance Brittain Bouchard, *Strong of Body, Brave and Noble: Chivalry and Society in Medieval France* (Ithaca, N.Y., 1998), 112–18; and Richard W. Kaeuper, *Chivalry and Violence in Medieval Europe* (Oxford, 1999), esp. 129–88.

[80] *Saxon Mirror*, book 3, par. 7, p. 118. The accompanying image shows a henchman casually wiping his sword-blade clean as the decapitated body of the Christian perpetrator falls to the ground; see Koschorrek, *Sachsenspiegel*, fig. 32.

[81] John France, *Western Warfare in the Age of the Crusades, 1000–1300* (Ithaca, NY, 1999), 22–23.

[82] Cf. Gillerman, "Arrest of Christ," 80, who does not seem to notice Christ's gesture. Likewise Schwarz, "Retelling the Passion," disregards this intervention in his discussion at 68.

the image presents an alternative interpretation to the Gospel texts; rather than admonishing Peter for his violence on the grounds that it will prove ineffective and healing the servant *post facto*, Christ is shown *controlling* Peter's violence behind the scenes, guiding the sword blade so as to inflict a comparatively minor injury rather than a grisly death.[83] This allows Peter's attack to retain its appearance of (ambivalent) heroism while also saving *two* lives: that of Malchus, whose head is not split in two; and that of Peter himself, who, by killing an unarmed Jew, would have been guilty of a capital offense under Saxon law. Peter thus functions as the dynamic opposite of the Jewish captor in ethical as well as formal terms: if the latter was contemptible for his malicious behavior despite the fact that his action itself was legally sanctioned, Peter appears admirable for his protective behavior despite the fact that his action broke the law.

The presentation of Peter's violence at Gethsemane as a valiant defense of his lord against outside threats—a defense simultaneously controlled and checked by the lord himself—also makes sense in light of the ongoing conflict between the Naumburg bishop and chapter, who, like the Jews, were prohibited from bearing arms, and Margrave Henry the Illustrious of Meissen, whose military prowess and resources were well known and widely feared.[84] A chastising letter written to the margrave by Innocent IV in 1247—as the choir screen was being planned, if not executed—suggests that Bishop Dietrich perceived his own situation to be like that of Christ on the Mount of Olives, surrounded on all sides by dangerous persecutors. Responding to Dietrich's complaints about the "injuries and offenses" the margrave had inflicted upon "the [Naumburg] church and the persons belonging to it," the pope warned Henry that "through such grievances to them our Lord Jesus Christ is vexed and seems himself to be persecuted."[85] Seen through the lens of

---

[83] Cf. Paulus Hinz, *Der Naumburger Meister: Ein protestantischer Mensch des XIII. Jahrhunderts* (Berlin, 1951), 52, who bizarrely claims that Christ's motion represents the artist's protest against the "kriegerischen Gewaltmethoden der mittelalterlichen Kirche."

[84] Wolf Rudolf Lutz, *Heinrich der Erlauchte (1218–88), Markgraf von Meißen und der Ostmark (1221–88), Landgraf von Thüringen und Pfalzgraf von Sachsen (1247–63)*, Erlanger Studien 17 (Erlangen, 1977), 227–320.

[85] See *Urkundenbuch des Hochstifts Naumburg, Teil 2 (1207–1304)*, ed. Hans K. Schulze (Cologne, 2000), no. 213, entry for January 22, 1247 (Lyon), pp. 238–39 at 238: "Quanto maiores creduntur potentie tue vires, tanto amplius te decet et convenit, ut ab ecclesiarum et personarum ecclesiasticarum abstineas iniuriis et offensis, cum in ipsarum molestiis offendatur et persequi videatur ipse dominus Iesus Christus."

such circumstances, the image of Peter's violence may have reminded local laymen of their duties to protect Christ, in the person of their bishop, against *any* outside encroachments—even as Christ's salutary intervention in the attack highlights the need to keep violence under control. The absence of demonizing devices in the portrayal of Malchus suggests that it was not specifically the Jews who were targeted, but anyone, including well-dressed nobles, who posed a threat.

This idea comes to the fore even more sharply in the depiction of Christ's trial before Pilate (fig. 15). Although Pilate's identity as a Roman prefect was well-known from the Gospel texts, and although the same texts stressed that it not malice but spinelessness that caused him to capitulate to calls for Jesus's blood, medieval artists tended to invest him with the same monstrous qualities—and sometimes the same attributes—as they did the Jews themselves. At St-Gilles and Modena, this likeness is conveyed through the clothing and body language of both Pilate and Caiaphas. At St-Gilles, each man sits frontally with splayed knees, his left arm extended and his right hand planted on his thigh, the elbow jutting outward from beneath a cloak fastened at shoulder.[86] Pilate and Caiaphas resemble each other even more closely on the *pontile* at Modena; not only do they wear identical clothing and echo one another in their angular arm positions, but they also display matching beards, prominent noses, and distinctive headdresses (a peaked cap for Caiaphas, a turban for Pilate).[87] Nearly two hundred years later the sculptors at Havelberg highlighted the depravity of the Roman prefect by giving him the costume, beard, and beaked nose of the Jewish Elders depicted elsewhere in the series (see figs. 5 and 6).

At Naumburg, Pilate appears as a contemporary Saxon count. Seated with his ankles crossed in the conventional pose of judicial authority, he wears a richly ornamented cyclas and cloak, along with the fur-lined flapped hat of a high-level judicial arbitrator.[88] His wavy bobbed

[86] See Stoddard, *Façade*, 82, figs. 111–112.

[87] See Frugoni and Roli, *Il Duomo di Modena*, 2: 670, plate 1312.

[88] The donor figures Dietmar and Sizzo, both visible through the screen's central portal, wear elements of this garb—the former the flapped cap, the latter the sleeveless tunic; see Schubert and Stekovics, *Naumburger Dom*, 92 (Dietmar), 97–99 (Sizzo). On crossed ankles or legs as a sign of authority, see H. Bächtold-Stäubli, "Beine kreuzen oder verschränken," *Schweizerisches Archiv für Volkskunde* 26 (1925–26): 47–54. In the *Sachsenspiegel* illustrations, the flapped cap is worn exclusively by upper-level judges (counts); see Koschorreck, *Sachsenspiegel*, 74.

hairstyle and his facial features, with a narrow nose, clean-shaven cheeks, robust jaw, and firm chin, echo those of John in the Last Supper and other Apostles in the Arrest scene. This physiognomy forms a marked contrast to that of Christ's bearded accuser, who, with mouth open in speech and finger pressed emphatically against his own chest, confronts Pilate from across the frontal plane. Yet despite his physiognomic difference from the Roman prefect, the Jewish figure cannot be said to be "demonized" in the way that his counterpart in the Arrest scene had been. The agitation conveyed by his furrowed brows and slightly opened mouth—a similar expression, again, to that of the donor Sizzo in the choir (see fig. 14)—acquires meaning and motivation through the figure's conventional gestures of legal complaint; with his right hand turning inward against the chest to assert the speaker's own agency, he grasps Christ's wrist with his left, not in a spontaneous motion of brutality or disrespect but in a formalized gesture that, according to the illustrations in Saxon law codes, was used when bringing an untried prisoner before a judicial authority.[89]

Despite the contrasting physical appearances of the Jewish plaintiff and the Roman judge, the sculptor has asserted continuity between them through the introduction of auxiliary figures in the background. Inverting the usual practice of applying to Pilate the distorted features of Jews, the Naumburg sculptor has flanked Christ with two identical attendants; wearing the funnel-caps that align them with Christ's accuser but displaying facial features and expressions identical to those of Pilate, they forge a visual link between plaintiff and judge. This absence of physical difference not only corresponds more closely to contemporary social reality than the sharp distinctions typically drawn between Jews and Gentiles in thirteenth-century art; it also enables the sculptor to shift the responsibility for the impending execution from either a single individual (Pilate) or a single group (the Jews) to the larger judicial *system* in which they all played a part.

Taken together, the Naumburg Passion reliefs thus convey a twofold message, one fraught with ambiguity and tension. One the one hand, the images emphasize the dangers posed by renegade actions within a rigorous social order (witness Judas's behavior both at the Last Supper and at Caiaphas's court). On the other, they pin responsibility for the unjust

[89] Koschorreck, *Sachsenspiegel*, fig. 63. The corresponding textual passage does not describe this gesture; see *Saxon Mirror*, Book 3, par. 60, p. 131.

treatment of an innocent man on a social order—envisioned in terms of the contemporary legal system—that subsumes everyone, regardless of religious identity (Pilate and the Jewish accusers alike). The Jews play their role here, to be sure; and the caricatured depiction of the captor in the Arrest scene proves that the screen's designer was hardly averse to employing well-worn pictorial methods of disparagement where the narrative called for the depiction of overtly malevolent behavior. But the images' simultaneous insistence on his and other figures' outward conformity to long-established codes of law, combined with the neutral or ambiguous portrayals of Jews in the remaining reliefs, suggests that the sculptor's and patron's concern was not primarily (if at all) to feed the flames of anti-Jewish sentiment. If, in general, the depiction of biblical Jews wearing modern clothes represented the medieval church's effort to pile "the sins of Jesus' contemporaries... upon the collective head of medieval Jewry,"[90] it must be admitted that at Naumburg, unlike at Modena, Havelberg, and elsewhere, the heads of judicial officials and other secular nobles were also made to bear a good deal of weight. Yet within this system of discrete, though also interlocking and overlapping, social communities and jurisdictions—the courtly nobles represented by Christ and his friends, well-to-do Jews, and judicial administrators—it was individual, self-motivated decisions and actions that propelled the narrative onward to its awful, bloody end.

Art as Mediator: Social Ethics and Local Politics in Medieval Naumburg

The thirteenth-century clergy of Naumburg Cathedral and the laypeople who attended Mass there on feast days were certainly aware of the anti-Jewish attitudes that undergird the Passion narrative; the Gospel writers themselves worked to enkindle bitterness toward Christ's Jewish persecutors.[91] Nor would they have been ignorant of the anti-Jewish ramifications of the heightened attention to Christ's suffering humanity characteristic of high medieval theological currents[92] and

---

[90] See the quotation by Trachtenberg above.

[91] See Trachtenberg, *Devil and the Jews*, 20. For anti-Jewish sentiments in the centuries just before and just after Christ, see Kurt Schubert, "Gottesvolk—Teufelsvolk—Gottesvolk," in Jüdisches Museum, ed., *Macht der Bilder*, 30–52.

[92] On the correlation between the rise of anti-Judaism and the "new humanism" of the so-called Twelfth-Century Renaissance, see Robert Chazan, "The Deteriorating Image of the Jews—Twelfth and Thirteenth Centuries," in *Christendom and Its Discontents:*

embodied, with unprecedented naturalism and emotional force, in the great Crucifixion group in their screen's central portal (see fig. 1).[93] The placement of the corpus in the doorway itself, rather than in its usual location atop the screen,[94] aimed to stimulate a new intensity in affective response. No longer aloof and triumphal, presiding over activity in the nave from on high, the broken body of Christ at Naumburg was made physically accessible and psychologically immediate, implicating each beholder who approached or passed through the doorway in the spectacle and drama of violent death.[95]

Through the stunning physical presence of the life-sized crucifix in the door, the engagement of viewers by the weeping Mary and John in the jambs, and the private nature of the confrontation between Christ and each individual traversing the portal, the culminating moment of the Passion was pulled from the distant biblical past into the here-and-now of the thirteenth-century Saxon cathedral.[96] In light of the fact that this Crucifixion scene itself was continually animated by the bodies of real people moving through it, it makes sense that the preceding narrative moments pictured in the reliefs above would show Christ surrounded by characters drawn from that same modern (i.e., mid-thirteenth-century) world. The nature and extent of identification between living subjects and the subjects of representation would have varied according to the viewer's social station, rank, gender, and so forth; what is clear, however, is that the program as a whole demonstrates a deep interest in contemporary questions of noble comportment and conduct within a rigidly structured social order.

As I have suggested, the concern with exploring the (largely negative) consequences of individual agency in the Naumburg Passion overrode

---

Exclusion, Persecution, and Rebellion, 1000–1500, ed. Scott L. Waugh and Peter D. Diehl (Cambridge, 1996), 220–33, esp. 226; Anna Abulafia, "Twelfth-Century Renaissance Theology and the Jews," in Cohen, ed., *From Witness to Witchcraft*, 125–39. For the state of the question of the Jews' guilt for Christ's death in the mid-thirteenth century, see Hood, *Aquinas*, 62–76.

[93] See Gerhard Lutz, *Das Bild des Gekreuzigten im Wandel: Die sächsischen und westfälischen Kruzifixe der ersten Hälfte des 13. Jahrhunderts* (Petersberg, 2004), esp. 46–47; Jung, "West Choir Screen," 112–229; and Michael Viktor Schwarz, "Mittelbarkeit und Unmittelbarkeit medial: Der Gekreuzigte am Naumburger Westchor," in *Visuelle Medien im christlichen Kult: Fallstudien aus dem 13. bis 16. Jahrhundert* (Vienna, 2002), 25–64.

[94] See Reiner Haussherr, "Triumphkreuzgruppen der Stauferzeit," in Haussherr and Väterlein, eds., *Zeit der Staufer*, 5: 131–68.

[95] See also Schwarz, "Mittelbarkeit und Unmittelbarkeit."

[96] On the spatial and optical dynamics of the portal group, Jung, "Seeing through Screens."

any concern with displaying the (supposedly negative) traits of any one group. Although included in large numbers, the Jewish characters at Naumburg comprise one group among several whose members propel the narrative forward. By eschewing the usual demonizing devices, and thereby downplaying any systematic Jewish antagonism, the program runs counter to the heightened vilification of the Jews evident in so many other areas of mid-thirteenth-century social life and representational practices.[97] In this sense, the reliefs served to mediate two overlapping yet seemingly contradictory sets of concerns: one the one hand, large-scale changes in ethics, manifested in a new attention to individual intentionality in various cultural domains,[98] and, on the other, old-fashioned small-scale political interests—in this case, the episcopal patron's concern to protect "his" Jews from local hostility, which, he knew, could easily escalate into violence.[99]

Although written documents do not attest the presence of Jewish residents in Naumburg until the fourteenth century, the location of the *Judengasse* in a central location, just next to the marketplace, suggests that they had settled in the town at a considerably earlier date.[100] They were

[97] For social manifestations of anti-Judaism in this period, Trachtenberg, *Devil and the Jews*; R.I. Moore, *The Formation of a Persecuting Society: Power and Deviance in Western Europe, 950–1250* (London, 1987); and Gavin I. Langmuir, *Toward a Definition of Anti-Semitism* (Berkeley, 1990). For their intellectual underpinnings, Amos Funkenstein, "Basic Types of Christian Anti-Jewish Polemics in the Later Middle Ages," *Viator* 2 (1971): 373–82; and Jeremy Cohen, "The Jews as the Killers of Christ in the Latin Tradition, from Augustine to the Friars," *Traditio* 39 (1983): 1–27. For manifestations in devotional writings, Thomas H. Bestul, *Texts of the Passion: Latin Devotional Literature in Medieval Society* (Philadelphia, 1996), 68–110; and Gavin I. Langmuir, "The Tortures of the Body of Christ," in Waugh and Diehl, eds., *Christendom and Its Discontents*, 287–309; in vernacular literature, see Winfried Frey, "Gottesmörder und Menschenfeinde: Zum Judenbild in der deutschen Literatur der Mittelalters," in Ebenbauer and Zatloukal, eds., *Juden in ihrer mittelalterlichen Umwelt*, 35–51; and in visual images, Stefan Rohrbacher, "The Charge of Deicide: An Anti-Jewish Motif in Medieval Christian Art," *Journal of Medieval History* 17 (1991): 297–321.

[98] See note 12 above.

[99] On the easy slippage from anti-Jewish rhetoric to actual violence and back again, see Miri Rubin, *Gentile Tales: The Narrative Assault on Late Medieval Jews* (New Haven, 1999); and Mitchell B. Merback, "Fount of Mercy, City of Blood: Cultic Anti-Judaism and the Pulkau Passion Altarpiece," *Art Bulletin* 87, no. 4 (Dec. 2005): 589–642, which appeared as this essay neared completion. As David Nirenberg, *Communities of Violence: Persecution of Minorities in the Middle Ages* (Princeton, 1996) reminds us, such violence was often motivated by social and political factors unrelated to religious identity *per se*.

[100] Dorothea Quien, "Zur Geschichte der Juden in Naumburg während des Mittelalters, 1302–1426," Kirchengeschichtliche Seminararbeit, Naumburg 1984 (Stadtarchiv Naumburg, photocopy), 19. On the significance of the location of Jewish quarters generally, see Haverkamp, "Jewish Quarters."

well established in the diocese by 1302, when they were mentioned in a charter as moneylenders in Pforte, five kilometers from Naumburg.[101] During his tenure, Bishop Dietrich seems to have taken advantage of the moneylenders in his midst—to the ultimate detriment of his diocese. In 1282, ten years after his death, his successor Ludolph complained of the impoverished state of the Naumburg church, as he sold off dozens of episcopal properties in order to begin clearing the debts accrued during Dietrich's reign.[102] Some of the borrowed money must have been spent defending the church's interests against the margrave of Meissen, as Heinz Wiessner and Irene Crusius have recently argued.[103] But if we take seriously Dietrich's insistence that he was indeed eager to "finish what has been begun" of the west choir—as a funding plea circulated in 1249 states[104]—it is reasonable to suppose that the money he had borrowed at precisely this time, possibly from Jews, was put into that endeavor. Cash-strapped as he was, Dietrich may not have wanted the images in his church to kindle hostility toward those providing him with substantial financial resources.

He did have good reason to worry about the safety of local Jews, given the well-known events of the previous decade. In late 1235, five Christian boys had perished in a fire that consumed their father's mill in Fulda. Fingers were immediately pointed at two Jewish men, who admitted that they had indeed killed the boys in order to collect their blood.[105]

---

[101] Quien, "Geschichte der Juden," 19.

[102] Schulze, ed., *Urkundenbuch*, Charter 497, entry for September 15, 1282 (Merseburg), 536–38 at 536: "Nam alicubi apud iudeos absorbebamur usurarum voragine, alicubi bona ecclesie nostre... obligata erant tytulo pignoris, alicubi vero fideiussores nostri a creditoribus nostris moniti secundum formam promissionis eorum iacere cogebantur more fideiussorio cum magno nostro et ecclesie nostre dispendio sive dampno."

[103] Heinz Wiessner and Irene Crusius, "Adeliges Burgstift und Reichskirche: Zu den historischen Voraussetzungen des Naumburger Westchores und seiner Stifterfiguren," in *Studien zum weltlichen Kollegiatstift in Deutschland*, ed. Irene Crusius (Göttingen, 1995), 232–58 at 246–48.

[104] The funding plea, issued in 1249 by Bishop Dietrich and the cathedral chapter and directed toward "all the faithful of every rank" (*omnis conditionis fidelibus*) is our most important source for dating the west choir. It names the church's twelve most important early (lay) patrons, many of whom were represented in the donor figures of the choir, and urges the living to join their ranks by contributing money to complete the building project (*consummationem totius operis*); see Schulze, ed., *Urkundenbuch*, 257–58 (Charter 236); for translation and further discussion, Jung, "West Choir Screen," 16–21.

[105] On Fulda case, see Langmuir, *Toward a Definition*, 263–81; and Friedrich Lotter, "Aufkommen und Verbreitung von Ritualmord- und Hostienfrevelanklagen gegen Juden," in Jüdisches Museum, ed., *Macht der Bilder*, 60–78 at 66–67. On the blood libel, see Trachtenberg, *Devil and the Jews*, 140–55.

The Christian townspeople, perhaps spurred on directly by the abbot of Fulda and certainly filled with fantasies of the bloody heretical rituals uncovered by the inquisitor Conrad of Marburg, killed the thirty-four Jews who then lived in Fulda before carrying the bodies of the boys to Emperor Frederick II in Haguenau. Despite Frederick's dismissal of the boys' sanctity, they were buried "with honor, as if they were martyrs." "There followed," the chronicler adds, "great persecutions against the Jews" throughout the region.[106] If the presentation of the bodies to the emperor was meant to urge him to sanction violence against the Jews (or to legitimate the cult in the absence of papal authorization), the plan backfired. For Jewish citizens, feeling the impending threats against them, had already appealed to Frederick for help.[107] He called together an assembly of converted Jews from England and France to comb the writings of the Talmud and the Hebrew scriptures for any demands for Christian blood, and came up empty. Thereafter, Frederick intensified measures to protect "his" Jews not only in Fulda but throughout the Empire, forbidding not only violence against them but even any accusations that they were out for blood and placing all the Empire's Jews under his immediate protection and legal jurisdiction.[108]

Nonetheless, virulent anti-Judaism reemerged in 1247, when many Jews in the town of Valréas, at the westernmost border of the Empire, were tortured and killed for purportedly having crucified a young child.[109] This time, it was Pope Innocent IV who leapt to their defense, condemning the persecutions, proclaiming the accusations false and forbidding similar ones in the future, and confirming his protection of Jews in a series of bulls issued during the same year.[110] During this period of tension between Jews and Christians, aggravated by crusading

[106] Johannes Trithemius, *Chronicum Monasterium Hirsaugenses* (written 1509–1514), quoted in *Varia insonderheit zur Witterungs-Geschichte, Band II, 1201–1400* (Naumburg Stadtarchiv, manuscript Sa 37): "Eodem anno [1236], ante expeditionem Imperatoris praescriptam in Italiam Judaei in oppido Fuldensi com(mem)orantes, quosdam pueros Christianorum ut sanguinem eoru(m) reciperent, in quodam molendino etiam occiderunt. Quo comperto facinore, multi ex eius combusti sunt. Corpora autem puerorum Imperatori conspicienda ad Hagenaum praesentata sunt, et ibidem quasi martyrum cum honore sepulta, et subsecuta est magna in Judaeos persecutio."

[107] I rely on Lotter, "Aufkommen und Verbreitung," 66 for the following information.

[108] Lotter, "Scope and Effectiveness," argues that German bishops consistently supported the repeated imperial injunctions against Jewish persecutions.

[109] Langmuir, *Toward a Definition*, 265.

[110] For the original bull of May 28, 1247, see Grayzel, *Church and the Jews*, 264–67. Further protection was granted the Jews of Germany in a bull of July 5, 1247; see ibid., 268–71.

fervor abroad and searches for heretics at home, the protection of Jews was one of very few points on which emperor and pope agreed. And while on cathedral façades and screens elsewhere Jewish degradation was visualized in figures of blind, helpless Synagoga[111] or hook-nosed villains gleefully battering Christ, the creators of the Naumburg Passion program took care to assure that no more malice could be ascribed to the Jewish characters than was required by the Gospel narrative—and that even this would be mitigated by an emphasis on enemies closer to home (the hatless Judas, the Saxon count Pilate).

While we do not have written documentation of special protection offered by Dietrich toward the Jews in his diocese, we also have no records of violence against them during or after his tenure. Events recorded in subsequent centuries indicate a close, persistent connection between episcopal authorities and the local Jewish community. During the Black Death in 1348–49, the Naumburg Jews were accused of plotting to set fire to the town, and the margrave of Meissen, Frederick, swiftly ordered their destruction.[112] This measure was opposed by the citizenry, however, and in the following year Jews were still living within the city walls. The arson accusation was later acknowledged to have arisen from the margrave's political hostility *toward the Naumburg bishop*.[113] Thus we have a clear case in which actions undertaken against Jews were calculated to harm an ecclesiastical leader who both relied on their financial support and was legally bound to protect them.[114] Yet the intimate association of Naumburg clerics with high-placed Jews continued unabated. In 1372, the bishop Gerhard was reprimanded by the pope for maintaining too close contact with a Jewish man named Marquard, who seems to have participated often in official church business.[115]

Although the twenty-two Jewish families still living in Naumburg by 1411 would be subjected to extortion at the hand of magistrates, no drastic measures were taken against this community until later in

---

[111] See the contribution by Nina Rowe in this volume.

[112] Quien, "Geschichte der Juden," 20–21.

[113] Ibid., 20, citing the chronicler Sixtus Braun, who claims that the accusation was made, in part, "weil der Bischof um diese Zeit einen Feind gehabt."

[114] For the political uses of anti-Jewish violence in Spain, see Nirenberg, *Communities of Violence*. Much of this had to do with the Jews' legal status as private property of the local ecclesiastical or secular lord; see James Parkes, *The Jew in the Medieval Community*, 2nd rev. edn. (New York, 1976), 101–54.

[115] Martin Onnasch, "Naumburg," in *Wegweiser durch das jüdische Sachsen-Anhalt*, ed. Jutta Dick and Marina Sassenberg (Potsdam, 1998), 143; and Wiessner, *Bistum Naumburg*, 858–59.

the century. In 1454, concurrent with the establishment of a Corpus Christi fraternity, came a mandate requiring the Naumburg Jews to wear distinguishing hats.[116] Forty years later, the city council, with the encouragement of the Saxon duke and imperial elector Frederick the Wise, expelled the Jews from the town "for all eternity."[117] This was considered a major blow to the bishop, who received for his loss a yearly fee of sixty Gulden, which the city continued to pay until 1803. In 1496, the synagogue, located near the center of town, was demolished and its stones used for new constructions. Today, more than five hundred years after the expulsion, the only Jews to be found in Naumburg reside in the cathedral, in the Passion reliefs of the west choir screen.[118]

---

[116] Onnasch, "Naumburg," 144. Onnasch connects this mandate with the intensified interest in Christian self-definition manifested in the fraternity, in a lecture given in the Naumburg Marienkirche, May 14, 1994, titled "Die Ausweisung der Juden aus Naumburg vor 500 Jahren" (manuscript in Naumburg Stadtarchiv), 2.

[117] An unsigned relief commemorating the event, made in 1994, is installed in the wall along the Judengasse in present-day Naumburg. On the expulsion and its repercussions, see Onnasch, "Naumburg," 144–45.

[118] Onnasch, "Ausweisung der Juden," 20. To my knowledge, no Jewish families have moved to Naumburg since Onnasch cited this statistic in 1998.

CHAPTER SIX

IDEALIZATION AND SUBJECTION AT THE SOUTH FAÇADE OF STRASBOURG CATHEDRAL*

Nina Rowe

The figures of Ecclesia and Synagoga adorning the south façade of Strasbourg cathedral are perhaps the most celebrated exemplars of their genre (figs. 1–6). For over a century, tourist guide books, introductory art history texts and specialized studies alike have lavished praise on these female personifications of Church and Synagogue because the figures are so lifelike, dramatic and beautiful.[1] While there is a wealth of scholarship on the style and iconography of these figures, both divorced from and in conjunction with their larger decorative context on Strasbourg south, there has been almost no consideration of the figures in relation to prevailing notions concerning Jews. Further, there has been only limited work on the political and social valences of the figures at the time of their creation.

The south porch at Strasbourg cathedral was completed during the reign of Bishop Berthold von Teck (r. 1223–1244). It seems that Berthold's predecessor, Heinrich von Veringen (1202–1223), in conjunction with the cathedral chapter, had ordered the construction of a new southern transept arm and southern portal to be built on to an already-standing twelfth-century structure as part of a campaign to enhance the eastern end of the cathedral.[2] Over the course of the thirteenth

* Research for this project was funded by the Leo Baeck Institute, the Deutscher Akademischer Austauschdienst, the Memorial Foundation for Jewish Culture, and Northwestern University. Thanks also to Fordham University for offsetting the cost of photographs. I am grateful to Sandra Hindman, O. K. Werckmeister and Larry Silver for advising me as I wrote the dissertation from which this study draws (Northwestern University, 2002). I am particularly indebted to Mitchell Merback who helped me see this material with fresh eyes. For their inspiration and support, I thank Janine Mileaf and Glenn Hendler.

[1] See for example, James Snyder, *Art of the Middle Ages*, 2nd edn. (Upper Saddle River, NJ, 2006), 441–443.

[2] On the building history, see the principal scholarly monograph on the cathedral, Hans Reinhardt, *La Cathédrale de Strasbourg* (Paris, 1972), 17–18 and 52–56; as well

century, Strasbourg cathedral's Romanesque nave and west façade were replaced with the Gothic structure still standing today. The south portal was defaced during the French Revolution but an engraving of c. 1617 by Isaac Brunn records its pre-modern appearance (fig. 7).[3]

In its original disposition the south façade of Strasbourg and the sculpture immediately inside it harnessed the theatrical power of stylistic realism to offer a vivid display of ecclesiastical might. On the south façade, at the left extreme is Ecclesia, the figure of the Church (figs. 1 and 3). Legs oriented outward and upper body turned to the right, she has just noticed Synagoga at the other end of the porch. The triumphant Queen Ecclesia thrusts her shoulders back and twists around to confront her predecessor. But she remains stable, the folds of her robe falling heavily, echoing the fluting of a column. Ecclesia's upper body is sturdy as well. Her royal mantle unifies her torso, shoulders and arms into a coherent unit. With her right hand she grasps the staff of a *labarum* and with her left she cradles a chalice.[4] Crown planted firmly on her head, Ecclesia extends her neck slightly outward so as to better her view across the portal complex. Her eyes are wide open and her lips are parted as if she has just called out.

Synagoga across the way is the subject of this direct address (figs. 2 and 4). Physically, she is the antithesis of the Church. While Ecclesia's luxuriant robe provides stability, Synagoga's diaphanous drapery falls in a tangle around her ankles. While Ecclesia's mantle unifies her upper

---

as Louis Grodecki and Roland Recht, "Le bras sud du transept de la cathédrale: architecture et sculpture," *Bulletin monumental* 129, no. 1 (1971): 7–38; and Hartmut Krohm, "Das Südquerhaus des Straßburger Münsters—Architecktur und Bildwerke," in *Meisterwerke mittelalterlicher Skulptur*, ed. Hartmut Krohm (Berlin, 1996), 185–203; and Jean-Philippe Meyer, "La Construction du portail sud du transept à la Cathédrale de Strasbourg," *Bulletin de la Société des amis de la Cathédrale de Strasbourg* 26 (2004): 93–110, all with further references. On the cathedral chapter, see Adam Vétulani, *Le Grand chapitre de Strasbourg* (Strasbourg, 1927). For discussion of the canons' role in the cathedral construction (though the evidence post-dates the south portal) see, Aloys Schulte, "Aus dem Leben des Straßburger Domkapitels 1150–1332," *Elsaß-Lothringisches Jahrbuch* 6 (1927): 34–40.

[3] This engraving was created for Oseas Schadaeus, *Summum Argentoratensium Templum, das ist Aussfürliche und Eigentliche Beschreibung des viel künstlichen, sehr kostbaren und in aller Welt berühmten Münsters zu Straßburg* (Strasbourg, 1617), pl. 6.

[4] At some point Ecclesia's round-cupped chalice was replaced with a fluted cup, as seen in figure 1, an archival image. I have found no source recording this alteration, but it is mentioned in the catalogue entry in Hartmut Krohm, ed., *Meisterwerke mittelalterlicher Skulptur* (Berlin, 1996), 503 n. 1. Now both the original sculpture, housed along with other cathedral sculptures in Strasbourg's Musée de l'Œuvre de Notre-Dame, as well as the copy that now adorns Strasbourg south, hold round-cupped chalices.

body, arms and attributes, Synagoga has no mantle and her arms jut out to either side. Her spear is broken and tangled in a banner, and she holds the tablets of the law tentatively, hiding them behind her body. The Brunn engraving indicates that originally a crown lay at her feet.

Blindfolded, the weakened Synagoga submits to her successor. But in her debased state, she is also beautiful. Though thirteenth-century artists had forged conventions for representing outsider status through deformed faces and anatomies,[5] the figure of Synagoga at Strasbourg (and consistently at other similar contemporary sites) follows the conventions for female pulchritude evident in representations of the Virgin, female saints and, indeed, Ecclesia, herself.[6] Synagoga is broken, but her beauty marks her as an essential component within the ecclesiological scheme at Strasbourg south.

Directly between Ecclesia and Synagoga is another figure, also carved in the round, an enthroned ruler with a sword, typically identified as Solomon (see fig. 5). Behind him, Christ raises an orb, alluding to the divine regulation of heaven and earth.[7] The Brunn engraving and archaeological fragments indicate that originally twelve Apostles adorned the jambs, standing as delegates to the divinely sanctioned king.[8] Of the corbels originally on the pillars beneath Ecclesia, Synagoga and Solomon, only Synagoga's can be identified. It presented two children fighting, perhaps Cain's murder of Abel, hence the first violent consequence of human sin.[9] Hovering above the double portal are reliefs in the tympana and lintels. To the left is the Virgin's dormition, deeply carved to enhance a sense of pathos and instability (fig. 10). Apostles

[5] See Ruth Mellinkoff, *Outcasts: Signs of Otherness in Northern European Art of the Late Middle Ages* (Berkeley, 1993); and Debra Higgs Strickland, *Saracens, Demons and Jews: Making Monsters in Medieval Art* (Princeton, 2003).

[6] See Annette Weber, "Glaube und Wissen—Ecclesia et Synagoga," in *Wissenspopularisierung: Konzepte der Wissensverbreitung im Wandel*, ed. Carsten Kretschmann (Berlin, 2003), 89–26, at 91. Thanks to Achim Timmermann for help locating this article.

[7] It is worth noting that already in the seventeenth or eighteenth century the Solomon and the bust of Christ had been replaced by copies. Mutilated fragments of the replicas survive, but no trace remains of the original figures; see Reinhardt, *La Cathédrale de Strasbourg*, 108 and 223, n. 1.

[8] It is impossible to offer a useful visual analysis of these figures because only fragments of the originals exist.

[9] The Brunn engraving shows that originally single figures were on the corbels beneath Ecclesia and Solomon, though these remain unidentified. The modern corbel beneath the ruler today depicts two mothers fighting over a child, a reference to the Judgment of Solomon.

making gestures of sorrow surround Mary and a woman sits on the floor, staring up in sadness, while Christ stands above his mother, holding her soul in the form of a child.[10] The story culminates in the right tympanum where Mary is crowned by her son as Queen of Heaven. In visual terms the chaos and drama of the left tympanum here give way to simplicity and order.

Entering the south portal, one gains a vision of heavenly splendor and divine justice on the eighteen-meter-high Pillar of Angels (figs. 8 and 9).[11] On the bottom tier are the four evangelists, each one twisting his body and gazing outward to engage the viewer. The second tier of the pillar features four angels who raise trumpets to their lips, sounding the Last Judgment, and at the summit are three more angels bearing the instruments of the Passion along with Christ, The Judge, who sits upon a corbel, displaying his wounds. Underneath him the dead emerge from their graves.

In this article I explore how the figures of Strasbourg south, with their dramatic poses and gestures and lifelike forms, collectively constituted a divine audience for the performance of ecclesiastical power. Some of the figures provided models for subjection to this order; while collectively the whole sculpted ensemble held out the promise of the rewards of participation within the divine plan of salvation. As figures that mediated between the realities of the lived world and an ideal celestial realm, the sculptures naturalized power structures by acting out authority and submission in familiar, lifelike forms.[12] In the early thirteenth century these power structures were both contested and, in part, played out through control over Jews. Berthold von Teck, the bishop who oversaw the completion of Strasbourg south, was an avowed enemy of Emperor Frederick II (1194–1250), and exercised this enmity on the battlefield, in clashes with the imperial army. During Berthold's reign, Frederick instituted new legal and tax codes, both protecting and restricting Jews. For the emperor as well as the bishop keeping the Jews in their place was a central component of keeping order more generally. In pictorial terms, I argue, the representation of

[10] The drama continues in the lintel where apostles carry the Virgin's bier and then she ascends to heaven. The surviving lintels are replicas unfaithful to their lost exemplars.

[11] See Valeria Schulte-Fischedick, "Der Straßburger Engelspfeiler," in *Meisterwerke mittelalterlicher Skulptur*, 167–183, with further references.

[12] On the concept of mediation, see Raymond Williams, *Marxism and Literature* (Oxford, 1977), 95–100.

a Christian milieu in which a beautiful yet restrained Synagoga is a principal member offered a conceptual template for the ideal ordering of the Christian realm more generally. As a means to investigate the function of Ecclesia and Synagoga within the network of political, social and ecclesiological ideals prevailing at Strasbourg in the 1230s, I will invoke Louis Althusser's theorization of the mechanics of ideology. Althusser's notion of ideology as that which interpellates—calls out to—subjects, subjects who in turn recognize themselves as the figures beckoned, will help demonstrate how the lifelike, beautiful, yet docile Synagoga, mediated between the social world and the idealized world of ecclesiological order, functioning as both promise and threat.

The Scholars, the Bishop and the Emperor

The Ecclesia-Synagoga motif in its various manifestations has been the subject of a wealth of scholarship. The figures appeared first in late Carolingian and Ottonian carved ivory panels incorporated into luxury book bindings. In the Ottonian era, illuminations of Ecclesia and Synagoga also began to adorn manuscript pages and by the twelfth century the figures appeared occasionally within stained glass and relief sculpture programs. It was in the second quarter of the thirteenth century that the motif enjoyed a veritable vogue when, as we find at Strasbourg, it became a principal component in sculpted decorative programs on church façades across northern Europe.[13] Iconographic compendia and surveys of the theme tend to review instances of the motif that appear in a variety of media and manifest a range of theological ideas.[14]

---

[13] Thirteenth and fourteenth-century examples include the cathedrals at Reims, south façade (c. 1220–35) and Chartres, north porch, now destroyed (c. 1220); the church of Saint Madeleine at Besançon, also destroyed (c. 1220–30); the cathedrals at Bamberg, north façade (c. 1225) and Magdeburg, north façade (c. 1250); the Liebfrauenkirche at Trier, west façade (c. 1250); Lincoln cathedral, south side, where the figures are now headless (c. 1260–1270); the church of Saint Seurin at Bordeaux, south façade (c. 1270); the castle chapel at Marienburg (Malbork), upper portal (c. 1270–80); the cathedrals at Minden, western narthex, now severely damaged (c. 1275), Freiburg im Breisgau, west porch (c. 1290–95) and Worms, south façade (c. 1300); the church of Saint Peter at Wimpfen im Tal, south façade (c. 1300); and the cathedrals of Béziers, west façade (fourteenth century) and Erfurt, west façade (c. 1335).

[14] The classic study of the theme is Paul Weber, *Geistliches Schauspiel und kirchliche Kunst in ihrem Verhältnis erläutert an einer Ikonographie der Kirche und Synagoge* (Stuttgart, 1894). Weber's insight that images of the Ecclesia-Synagoga motif may correspond to attitudes toward Jews was ground-breaking, if at times unsubtle. Reassessments, all of which

In such studies, scholars have observed that the figures either convey the ecclesiological notion of the harmony of the Old and New Testaments or allude to the triumph of the Age of Grace over the Age of Law. And, depending on context, this quite elastic motif could convey more nuanced theological and soteriological ideas.[15] Iconographic analyses of Ecclesia and Synagoga also typically attempt to coordinate the discussion of theology with observations on the social, economic and legal status of Jews. These discussions, however, tend not to theorize the relationship between representations and real-world conditions and therefore fail to probe the disjunction between the beautiful renderings of Synagoga on the public space of the cathedral façade and the often ugly anti-Jewish polemic and restrictive policy of the early thirteenth century.[16]

Some scholars have focused exclusively on a body of texts that present the figures of Ecclesia and Synagoga as characters within a legal debate. The *Altercatio Ecclesiae et Synagogae*, a fifth-century text, is an early exemplar that was widely disseminated throughout the Middle Ages because it was wrongly attributed to Augustine.[17] And the late thirteenth-century vernacular poem, *La Desputoison de la Sinagogue et de Sainte Eglise*, evidently composed by a street jongleur, attests to the currency of the genre in the era around the creation of the Strasbourg south portal.[18] In these texts Ecclesia is an elegant and proud queen who claims jurisdiction over the earth. Synagoga is an obsolete sovereign

---

attempt to refine Weber's fundamental proposition are: Wolfgang Seiferth, *Synagogue and Church in the Middle Ages: Two Symbols in Art and Literature*, trans. Lee Chadeayne and Paul Gottwald (New York, 1970); and Herbert Jochum, *Ecclesia und Synagoga: Das Judentum in der christlichen Kunst: Austellungskatalog* (Essen and Saarbrücken, 1993). For iconographic encyclopedias, see Adolf Weis, "Ekklesia und Synagoge," in *Reallexikon zur deutschen Kunstgeschichte*, ed. E. Gall and L. H. Heydenreich (Stuttgart, 1958), 1189–1215; Wolfgang Greisenegger, "Ecclesia und Synagoge," in *Lexikon der christlichen Ikonographie*, ed. E. Kirschbaum (Rome, 1968), 1:569–578; and Gertrud Schiller, *Ikonographie der christlichen Kunst*, 5 vols. (Gütersloh, 1976), 4, pt. 1:45–68.

[15] See the chapter by Elizabeth Monroe in this volume.

[16] See my article "Synagoga Tumbles, a Rider Triumphs: Clerical Spectatorship and the Fürstenportal of Bamberg Cathedral," *Gesta* 45, no. 1 (2006): 15–42.

[17] *Altercatio Ecclesiae et Synagogae*, ed. J. N. Hillgarth. Corpus Christianorum Series Latina 69 A (Turnhout, 1999).

[18] Hiram Pflaum, *Die Religiöse Disputation in der europaïschen Dichtung des Mittelalters* (Geneva, 1935), 31–40 and 92–100; Margaret Schlauch, "The Allegory of Church and Synagogue," *Speculum* 14 (1939): 448–464, esp. 452–455; and Arié Serper, "Le débat entre Synagogue et Église au XIIIe siècle," *Revue des études juives*, 4th ser., 3, no. 123 (1964): 307–333. For a brief overview of the genre with further references, see Gilbert Dahan, *The Christian Polemic Against the Jews in the Middle Ages*, trans. Jody Gladding (Notre Dame, IN, 1998), 69–70.

who ultimately cedes her title to her younger successor. Those who have studied these literary works recognize their influence on visual formulations of Ecclesia and Synagoga (and in the case of the *Desputoison*, the reverse influence of high medieval images on texts), but scholars have yet to explore the ways the development of a conception of Ecclesia and Synagoga as characters within a narrative bore upon conceptions of real-world Jews.[19]

The scholarship on the Ecclesia and Synagoga figures at Strasbourg in particular has likewise avoided analysis of both contemporary politics and the local conditions of Jews in the city and region.[20] Much early work on the Strasbourg figures focused on questions of form, aiming to discern the portal's position within the larger story of the development of naturalistic styles in early thirteenth-century France and Germany.[21] Other work examined content, aiming to decode the portal's iconography, particularly the integration of the Ecclesia-Synagoga motif with the central image of Solomon and the scenes of the Virgin's dormition and coronation. In 1972 Otto von Simson offered what has become a standard iconographic interpretation of the decorative complex.[22] Building

---

[19] This is an issue I only touch upon in the discussion below, but one which I will explore further in subsequent publications.

[20] Recent articles that address Ecclesia and Synagoga at Strasbourg are: Helga Sciurie, "Ecclesia und Synagoge an den Domen zu Straßburg, Bamberg, Magdeburg und Erfurt: körpersprachliche Wandlungen im gestalterischen Kontext," *Wiener Jahrbuch für Kunstgeschichte* 46–47 (1993–1994): 679–687 and 871–874; and Weber, "Glaube und Wissen." Sciurie takes particular note of the physical qualities of the sculptures and relates them broadly to contemporary lay, juridical and theological themes. Weber has argued that, in the years following the Fourth Lateran Council (1215), for lay viewers, Ecclesia and Synagoga likely were intended to connote salvation and damnation in general terms, through reference to the Eucharist. I have arrived at a similar conclusion, though I follow a different route than Weber.

[21] Classic studies are Karl Franck-Oberaspach, *Der Meister der Ecclesia und Synagoge am Straßburger Münster* (Dusseldorf, 1903); Erwin Panofsky, "Zur künstlerischen Abkunft des Straßburger 'Ecclesiameisters'," *Oberrheinische Kunst* 4 (1930): 124–129; Pierre Quarré, "Les sculptures du transept de la cathédrale de Strasbourg et celles de Notre-Dame de Dijon," in *Actes du quatre-vingt-douzième congrès national des sociétés savants: Strasbourg et Colmar, 1967* (Paris, 1970), 171–180; and Willibald Sauerländer, *Von Sens bis Straßburg. Ein Beitrag zur kunstgeschichtlichen Stellung der Straßburger Querhausskulpturen* (Berlin, 1966). An important recent discussion is found in Manfred Schuller et al., *Das Fürstenportal des Bamberger Domes* (Bamberg, 1993), 97–98.

[22] Otto von Simson, "Le programme sculptural du transept méridional de la cathédrale de Strasbourg," *Bulletin de la Société des amis de la Cathédrale de Strasbourg* 10 (1972): 33–50; reprinted and translated as "Ecclesia und Synagoge am südlichen Querhausportal des Straßburger Münsters," in *Wenn der Messias kommt: Das jüdisch-christliche Verhältnis im Spiegel mittelalterlicher Kunst*, ed. Lieselotte Kötzsche and Peter von der Osten-Sacken (Berlin, 1984), 104–125. Subsequent references to pages are from the German text.

on the earlier analyses of Adolf Weis and Adalbert Erler, von Simson explicated the program of the south façade and the Pillar of Angels as a manifestation of high medieval exegesis on the Song of Songs. In this conception Solomon is a type for Christ and here functions as both bridegroom and righteous judge.[23] Ecclesia and Synagoga serve as types for the beloved of Christ and for the scorned bride respectively; they also evoke the just and the unjust, separated by the Lord at the end of time. For Von Simson, this eschatological theme also refers to the exegetic hope that with Christ's return, the Jews will convert, allowing Christ ultimately to wed himself to all peoples.[24]

A recent discussion by Bernd Nicolai extends von Simson's assessments, tracing some of the pictorial sources for the Strasbourg sculptures and suggesting some of the social implications of the program.[25] Nicolai stresses the function of the south porch and interior south transept arm as sites of judical courts, an argument first advanced by Erler. Archaeological and pictorial evidence makes plain that originally the south façade was fitted with a graded roof so that the whole structure had the appearance of a loggia.[26] This porch seems to have opened on to a courtyard that was bounded by episcopal buildings. While the bishop held his episcopal court within his palace, he and twelve lay assessors oversaw a municipal court that met either outside, on the steps, in front of the south porch, or inside, beneath the Pillar of Angels (in inclement weather). Civic oaths were taken at the site and legal hearings were carried out there as well. Given these circumstances, Nicolai argues that the patently ecclesiological motifs that make up the program also would have been understood as a statement about earthly justice. He

---

[23] Cf. Adolf Weis, "Zur Symbolik der Bildwerke am Südportal des Münsters von Straßburg" (Ph.D. dissertation, Freiburg im Breisgau, 1946); idem, "Die 'Synagoge' am Münster zu Straßburg. Ein Beitrag zur historischen Betrachtung mittelalterlicher Kunst," *Das Münster* 1, no. 3/4 (1947): 65–80; and Adalbert Erler, *Das Straßburger Münster im Rechtsleben des Mittelalters* (Frankfurt, 1954).

[24] Though they deal with issues beyond the scope of the present discussion, two recent articles probe further the relevance of Song of Songs exegesis to high medieval representations of Synagoga as well as the Coronation of the Virgin: Jeremy Cohen, "Honorius Augustodunensis, the Song of Songs, and Christianity's 'Eschatological Jew'," *Speculum* 79, no. 2 (2004): 309–340; and T. A. Heslop, "The English Origins of the Coronation of the Virgin," *Burlington Magazine* 147 (December 2005): 790–797. I thank Isabel Falkenberg for bringing the latter article to my attention.

[25] Bernd Nicolai, "Orders in Stone: Social Reality and Artistic Approach: The Case of the Strasbourg South Portal," *Gesta* 40, no. 2 (2002): 111–128.

[26] A sixteenth-century print records the original appearance of the porch; see Erler, *Das Straßburger Münster im Rechtsleben*, 19–20 and fig. 8.

further observes that among the audiences for such displays of power were local heretics, and he suggests that in the eyes of the spiritually transgressive, Ecclesia and Synagoga would have embodied the power of the Church to quell enemies.[27] Nicolai, however, does not consider how Synagoga, a figure referring to the Old Testament and Judaic history, might also have signified heterodoxy in more general terms.[28] Moreover, both Nicolai and Von Simson conclude that the figure of a defeated Synagoga could have little relation to contemporary (official or popular) notions of Jews because the Jewish community of Strasbourg was relatively prosperous and there are no reports of attacks on the population during the first half of the thirteenth century.[29]

But the program of Strasbourg south pertains to Jews and Judaism in a manner that is less literal than some scholars might have it. Jeremy Cohen has coined the term the "hermeneutical Jew" to describe conceptions of Jews formulated by high medieval theologians to fit neatly into a Christian narrative of historical progression and sacred order.[30] Similar idealized notions functioned within the secular realm as magnates kept Jews in check as one element within larger programs aimed at maintaining social stability. Monumental public renderings of Synagoga on cathedral façades projected visually such a politicized notion of the hermeneutical Jew.[31] Though both Von Simson and Nicolai gesture toward a political reading of the Strasbourg ensemble when they suggest that the portal program manifests a spirit of peace propagated by Frederick II,[32] until now there has been no sustained

---

[27] Nicolai, "Orders in Stone," 122–124. In the early thirteenth century Strasbourg was the center for Cathars, Waldensians and Ortliebians in the lower Rhineland and these populations were pursued by both Bishop Heinrich von Veringen and Berthold von Teck; see Luzian Pfleger, *Kirchengeschichte der Stadt Straßburg im Mittelalter* (Colmar, 1941), 99–101; and idem, "Les 'hérétiques' strasbourgeois aux XIIIe et XIVe siècles," *Cahiers d'études cathares* 29, no. 79 (1978): 57–60.

[28] There is a wealth of recent scholarship on the elision of heretic and Jew in the Middle Ages; see Raoul Manselli, "La Polémique contre les juifs dans la polémique antihérétique," in *Juifs et judaïsme de Languedoc* (Toulouse, 1977), 251–267; Sara Lipton, *Images of Intolerance: The Representation of Jews and Judaism in the Bible moralisée* (Berkeley, 1999), 82–111; and Alexander Patschovsky, "Feindbilder der Kirche: Juden und Ketzer im Vergleich (11.–13. Jahrhundert)," in *Juden und Christen zur Zeit der Kreuzzüge*, ed. Alfred Haverkamp (Sigmaringen, 1999), 327–357, all with further references.

[29] Von Simson, "Ecclesia und Synagoge," 110; Nicolai, "Orders in Stone," 122.

[30] This term is explored in Cohen's introduction to *Living Letters of the Law: Ideas of the Jew in Medieval Christianity* (Berkeley, 1999), 1–17.

[31] For exploration of this issue at another site, see Rowe, "Synagoga Tumbles."

[32] See Von Simson, "Ecclesia und Synagoge," 109; and Nicolai, "Orders in Stone," 123.

analysis of the relationship between contemporary political contingencies and the south porch.[33] Published archives and several historical analyses make plain the vexed relationship between the city of Strasbourg and the imperial crown during the reign of Bishop Berthold, and suggest new ways to understand the adornment of the cathedral's south transept arm.[34]

In the second quarter of the thirteenth century rival claims over territories within Alsace repeatedly ignited hostilities between the Staufen house and the Strasbourg bishops.[35] Frederick II had inherited the kingdom of Sicily from his mother and much of his reign was spent at court in the south. When he came north, he resided for long periods at the Hagenau castle in Alsace (about 28 km north of Strasbourg), built at the order of his grandfather Frederick Barbarossa.[36] In 1237 Frederick II wrote that Alsace was "among all others of our

---

[33] Perhaps this is because there exists no recent, comprehensive, narrative civic history of medieval Strasbourg. Useful, albeit brief, discussions of medieval Strasbourg are found in Gustave Woytt, "L'administration épiscopale de Strasbourg au Moyen Age," *Révue historique* 61, no. 178 (1936): 177–197; Philippe Dollinger, "Origines et essor de la ville épiscopale," and "L'émancipation de la ville et la domination du patriciat (1200–1349)," in *Histoire de Strasbourg des origines à nos jours*, ed. Georges Livet and Francis Rapp (Strasbourg, 1981), 2:3–36 and 37–94; Francis Rapp, *Histoire des diocèses de France*, vol. 14, *Le diocèse de Strasbourg* (Paris, 1982), 35–63; and Georges Livet and Francis Rapp, *Histoire de Strasbourg* (Toulouse, 1987), 87–124.

[34] For archival sources, see Alfred Hessel and Manfred Krebs, *Regesten der Bischöfe von Straßburg*, 2 vols. (Innsbruck, 1928); on Bishop Berthold's reign, 2:34–91. Hessel and Krebs summarize and extrapolate from other published sources, the principal ones for Strasbourg during Bishop Berthold's reign being: *Annales Marbacenses*, ed. Hermann Bloch, MGH, *Scriptores rerum germanicarum* (Hannover, 1907), 90–92, 116–117 and 127; and Wilhelm Wiegand, ed., *Urkundenbuch der Stadt Straßburg*, vol. 1, *Urkunden und Stadtrechte bis zum Jahr 1266* (Strasbourg, 1879). For analyses see Alfred Hessel, "Die Beziehungen der Straßburger Bischöfe zum Kaisertum und zur Stadtgemeinde in der ersten Hälfte des 13. Jahrhunderts," *Archiv für Urkundenforschung* 6 (1918): 266–275; and Yuko Egawa, "Stadtherrschaft und Gemeinde in Straßburg vom Beginn des 13. Jahrhunderts bis zum Schwarzen Tod (1349)" (Doctoral dissertation, Universität Trier, 2001).

[35] The following discussion relies on Hessel, "Die Beziehungen der Straßburger Bischöfe." See also Aloys Meister, *Die Hohenstaufen im Elsaß, mit besonderer Berücksichtigung des Reichenbesitz und des Familiengutes derselben im Elsaß, 1079–1255* (Mainz, 1890), esp. 1–19, 84–85 and 91–94. I have been unable to consult Hella Fein, *Die Staufischen Städtgründungen im Elsaß*. Schriften des Wissenschaftlichen Instituts der Elsaß-Lothringer im Reich an der Universität Frankfurt, N. F. 23 (Frankfurt, 1939).

[36] On Frederick II, the best general discussion in English is Thomas Curtis Van Cleve, *The Emperor Frederick II of Hohenstaufen, Immutator Mundi* (Oxford, 1972). On earlier history of the Staufen and Alsace, Thomas Seiler, *Die Frühstaufische Territorialpolitik im Elsaß* (Hamburg, 1995).

rightful patrimony, [the land] we hold most dear."[37] Moreover, during the years when Frederick II's son, Henry (VII) was king of Germany (r. 1220–1235), Henry celebrated Christmas and Easter at the Hagenau palace and convened meetings with princes there.[38] Though after 1231 Henry infamously sided with various factions hostile to his father, his presence in Alsace in the 1230s remained an expression of Staufen authority in the region. This expression of authority was further bolstered by a local governor, Schultheiß Wolfhelm von Hagenau, installed by Frederick II in 1217 (r. 1217–1237).

Bishop Berthold, who stemmed from one of the most illustrious families in the empire, a cadet branch of the powerful house of Zähringen, did not hesitate to challenge imperial encroachment in his own backyard.[39] Between 1226 and 1227, Berthold asserted claims to lands formerly in the hands of the counts of Dagsburg.[40] In response, Henry (VII) forged an anti-episcopal coalition; ultimately, in June 1228, the bishop's army united with the Strasbourg civic militia and clashed with the forces under the emperor's son at the Battle of Blodelsheim.[41] The forces from Strasbourg overpowered the imperial confederacy, slaughtered hoards of enemies, cast their bodies into the Rhine and took numerous prisoners and booty. Though a treaty favorable to the bishop was settled the following month, hostilities quickly resumed.[42] Among the various sackings and commercial blockages on the bishop's lands, it also appears that in autumn of 1229 King Henry launched an attack upon Strasbourg itself—though the parameters of this campaign are unclear, and it is unknown whether the bishop and king themselves came to arms.[43] A truce between bishop and king was bolstered in 1235–1237 when Frederick II came to Alsace. There the emperor ratified a new

---

[37] "Alsatiam tamen, a vice hereditatis nostre funiculum quem inter alia jura nostra patrimonialia cariorem habemus;" *Historia diplomatica Friderici Secundi*, vol. 5, pt. 1, ed. Jean-Louis-Alphonse Huillard-Bréholles (Paris, 1857; repr. Turin, 1963), 60–61.

[38] Van Cleve, *Emperor Frederick II*, 365. Frederick II's son conventionally is designated as "King Henry (VII)" because, though King of the Romans, he was stripped of his title and never became emperor; the title distinguishes him from the later Luxembourg emperor, Henry VII.

[39] On Berthold von Teck, see Manfred Krebs, "Berthold I. von Teck," in *Neue deutsche Biographie* (Berlin, 1955), 2:158.

[40] Hessel and Krebs, *Regesten*, 2:43–46 (nos. 917–918, 921, 923–925 and 928). For discussion of the episcopal grab for territory, see Fritz Kiener, *Studien zur Verfassung des Territoriums der Bischöfe von Straßburg* (Leipzig, 1912), 22–53 and 93–127.

[41] Hessel and Krebs, *Regesten*, 2:48–49 (no. 933).

[42] Hessel and Krebs, *Regesten*, 2:49–51 and 52–53 (nos. 934 and 944).

[43] Hessel and Krebs, *Regesten*, 2:54–55 (no. 952).

treaty with Bishop Berthold, confirming outstanding questions of the bishop's juridical and fiscal authority.[44]

Beyond his personal clashes with Staufen forces, throughout the late 1220s and 1230s Berthold continually sided with Frederick II's enemies. For example, in 1229, when Pope Gregory IX wrote to the German secular and ecclesiastical princes entreating their support in his struggle against the emperor (excommunicated at the time), though most of the German bishops sided with Frederick, Berthold supported the pope.[45] Again, in 1240, during the emperor's second excommunication, Bishop Berthold remained loyal to Gregory IX.[46]

Ideals and Realities: Ecclesia, Synagoga and the Jews

So the climate in which the south portal at Strasbourg was created was not one of harmony and conciliation, as some scholars would have it, but one of conflict over questions of authority. And indeed, authority is one of the themes of the portal's iconography. At base, the image of Solomon enthroned and the bust of Christ behind him refer to prevailing ideals for temporal rule—with divine approbation, the terrestrial ruler brings heavenly order to the earth. But the figures of Ecclesia and Synagoga enhance this message by demonstrating the means through which terrestrial order is effected.

As mentioned previously, while Ecclesia and Synagoga are abstractions, personifications embodying transcendent notions concerning history and scripture, medieval audiences would have also understood them as concrete personages. As such, they convey figuratively the historical progression from the Age of Law to the Age of Grace: Synagoga was a queen, representative of God's original "chosen," but her time has passed. She has handed her crown over to Ecclesia who rules now in expectation of Christ's return at the Second Coming. The figures also convey the theological notion of the harmony between the Old and New Testaments. Synagoga represents the veiled Hebrew Bible, foreshadowing clear-sighted Ecclesia, who embodies the truth revealed in

[44] Hessel and Krebs, *Regesten*, 2:70–74 (nos. 1043, 1044, 1045 and 1052).

[45] Hessel and Krebs, *Regesten*, 2:53–54 (no. 948); for Gregory IX's reciprocal support of Strasbourg, 51 (nos. 936, 937, 938 and 939), among many possible examples; and Krebs, "Berthold I."

[46] Hessel and Krebs, *Regesten*, vol. 2, 81 (no. 1088).

Christian scripture. And those schooled in the hermeneutic explored by Von Simson and Nicolai would have seen the sculptures also as references to the beloved of Christ and the scorned bride, figures that anticipate the redemption at the end of days. Ecclesia and Synagoga are personifications who together act out a Christian notion of history.

But the figures on Strasbourg south could refer to micro- as well as macro-historical processes. I contend that in their public, monumental form they also proclaimed the rectitude of Jewish containment within a well-ordered society and, more broadly, the incapacity of all non-Christians in the face of the Church. Our evidence concerning the medieval reception of public images is limited.[47] But even the most circumspect of scholars concur that thirteenth-century viewers likely understood images, like texts, to signify on multiple levels—the literal, the moral, the allegorical and the anagogical (though probably only the literate would distinguished so neatly between these). It seems safe to presume then, that clerical and lay viewers alike would have recognized the official, standardized meanings of Ecclesia and Synagoga, but also would have considered the figures in more immediate terms. Style, I suggest, contributed to this recognition. Previously sculpture in the region around Strasbourg tended to be limited to low reliefs and diminutive ornamental figures, exhibiting varying degrees of stylization.[48] The south portal and the Pillar of Angels introduced sculptures carved in the round, handled with an unprecedented degree of realism. Moreover, the portal's tympana and lintels, Ecclesia, Synagoga, Solomon and the figures on the Pillar of Angels, originally were polychromed, though only the latter figures retain any coloration.[49] The direct gazes, lively gestures and vivid color, along with the installation of some of the figures on low pedestals, close to eye level, invited audiences to perceive the celestial realm represented in stone vividly and immediately—an

[47] For useful explorations of the problem see Robert Nelson, "Introduction: Descartes's Cow and Other Domestications of the Visual," and Michael Camille, "Before the Gaze: the Internal Senses and Late Medieval Practices of Seeing," in *Visuality Before and Beyond the Renaissance: Seeing as Others Saw*, ed. R. Nelson (Cambridge, 2000), 1–21 and 197–223 respectively.

[48] See Jean-Philippe Meyer, "Worms et les sculpteurs romans de l'Alsace," in *Burg und Kirche zur Stauferzeit: Akten der 1. Landauer Staufertagung 1997*, ed. Volker Herzner and Jürgen Krüger (Regensburg, 2001), 20–30; and Joseph Walter, "Le Pilier du Jugement, dit le Pilier des Anges," *Bulletin de la Société des amis de la Cathédrale de Strasbourg* 2, no. 1 (1925): 8–9.

[49] J. F., H. Z. and J. P. R., "Étude des sculptures de la Cathédrale de Strasbourg," in *Laboratoire de recherche des musées de France* (Aumales, 1978), 7–12.

ideal realm that was nonetheless in dialogue with the contingencies of earthly existence.

The earthly contingencies relevant to the Strasbourg sculpture concerned the status of Jews within the urban milieu and the surrounding region. Before the mid-twelfth century, the city of Strasbourg had no substantial Jewish population. But in the closing decades of that century large numbers of Jews migrated to the Rhineland, and within Alsace communities established themselves at four key sites: Oberehnheim, Rosheim, Hagenau and Strasbourg. Of these four places, Strasbourg appears to have had the largest community, and it became the intellectual and mercantile center for Jews of the region.[50] In Strasbourg, the street of the Jews (now *rue des juifs*), nestled between the streets of the parchment makers and weapons makers as well as the meat and fish markets, lay in the shadow of the cathedral and therefore at the spiritual and economic epicenter of the city. Though there is scant information pertaining to the daily lives of Jews in Strasbourg, the recent discovery of a wall inscription and wax tablets in the city's Jewish neighborhood suggests the wealth and sophistication of the community.[51] The city's rabbis were the prevailing authorities among Alsatian Jews, and by the end of the thirteenth century they had a synagogue, a ritual bath (*mikveh*) and their own cemetery.[52] Over the course of the thirteenth century, it appears that other buildings, including a *boucherie*, were added.[53]

---

[50] Principal studies of the Jews in Strasbourg, though of varying quality, are Carl Theodor Weiss, *Geschichte und rechtliche Stellung der Juden im Fürstbistum Straßburg* (Bonn, 1896); Alfred Glaser, *Geschichte der Juden in Straßburg* (Strasbourg, 1924); Gerd Mentgen, *Studien zur Geschichte der Juden im mittelalterlichen Elsaß* (Hannover, 1995), esp. 29–33 and 125–136, with further references; I. Elbogen, A. Freimann and H. Tykocinski eds., *Germania Judaica*, vol. 1, *Von den ältesten Zeiten bis 1238* (Breslau, 1934; repr. Tübingen, 1963), 367–372; and Zvi Avneri, ed., *Germania Judaica*, vol. 2, *Von 1238 bis zur Mitte des 14. Jahrhunderts*, pt. 2 (Tübingen, 1968), 798–806. On Jews in the Rhineland in general see Konrad Schilling, *Monumenta Judaica: 2000 Jahre Geschichte und Kultur der Juden am Rhein*, exhibition catalogue (Cologne, 1963).

[51] Robert Weyl and Marie-Dominique Waton, "Découverte de deux inscriptions hébraïques, Rue des juifs à Strasbourg," *Cahiers Alsaciens d'archéologie, d'art et d'histoire* 30 (1987): 145–147.

[52] The Strasbourg synagogue is first mentioned in 1292, but an inscription from the second half of the twelfth century indicates that synagogue already existed at that time. See Weiss, *Geschichte und rechtliche Stellung der Juden*, 2–3; Freddy Raphaël and Robert Weyl, *Juifs en Alsace: Culture, société, histoire* (Toulouse, 1977), 77–79 and 89–92; and Mentgen, *Juden im mittelalterlichen Elsaß*, 134–135. On the ritual bath, see Marie-Dominique Waton, "Des bains juifs à Strasbourg," *Cahiers Alsaciens d'archéologie, d'art et d'histoire* 29 (1986): 53–59.

[53] Bernhard Blumenkranz, *Art et archéologie des juifs en France médiévale* (Toulouse, 1980), 379–380. On recent discoveries—including fifteenth-century murals—see B. Parent and Marie-Dominique Waton, "Decouverte de peintures dans une maison gothique,"

Following trends across northern Europe, the Jews of Strasbourg were likely active in commerce. In particular, they may have worked in linen manufacture or trade in luxury fabrics, given their apparent charge as keepers of the city banner. The so-called Second Municipal Charter of Strasbourg (c. 1214) stipulates that, while the local monasteries were responsible for outfitting the civic militia with horses to pull the war chariot, it is the Jews who were to provide the banner, which was adorned with an image of the Virgin and Child.[54] More certain, of course, is local Jewish involvement in pawnbrokering and moneylending. In 1215 the nearby Benedictine abbey of Saint Leonhard pawned a golden cross, other liturgical objects and vestments as well as manuscripts to the Jews of Rosheim and Oberehnheim.[55] A source from 1228 tells of the abbot of Ebersheim who left his post, moved to Strasbourg and indebted himself to the Jews in order to support his life of luxury.[56] And throughout the thirteenth and fourteenth centuries prelates and nobles in the area continued to rely upon Jewish creditors.[57]

As was customary for bishops throughout Europe, in exchange for special levies Bishop Berthold protected the local Jews and saw to it that their presence within the city did not precipitate disorder. The bishop profited from Jewish economic activity, exacting taxes on Jewish pawnbrokering, moneylending and trade and enjoying payments paid to the episcopal coffers while, in return his forces threatened to punish those who would do the community harm.[58] But while Jews within

---

Archeologia 229 (November, 1987): 16–21; and Jean-Pierre Rieb et al., "Un ensemble medieval urbain exceptionnel, rue des juifs à Strasbourg," *Archéologie médiévale en Alsace* 3, no. 806 (1987): 149–169.

[54] "Hec sunt claustra, que in exitu civitatis ministrabunt equos ad plaustrum vexilli: Ebersheim, Marpach, Morsmunstre, Nuwilre, Swarzach, Gegenbach, Schutere. ministrabit autem prepositus sancti Arbogasti palafredum unum, quod scultetus cum plaustro equitabit. judei facient vexillum." Wiegand, *Urkundenbuch*, 481 (no. 617); for commentary, Mentgen, *Juden im mittelalterlichen Elsaß*, 125, with further references. On the banner itself, Paul Martin, "Das große Strasburger Stadtbanner," *Zeitschrift für historische Waffen- und Kostümkunde* 7 (1942): 185–189.

[55] Mentgen, *Juden im mittelalterlichen Elsaß*, 31.

[56] Julius Aronius, ed., with Albert Dresdner and Ludwig Lewinski, *Regesten zur Geschichte der Juden im fränkischen und deutschen Reiche bis zum Jahre 1273* (Berlin, 1902; repr. Hildesheim, 1970), 196 (no. 444); and Mentgen, *Juden im mittelalterlichen Elsaß*, 494–495.

[57] Mentgen, *Juden im mittelalterlichen Elsaß*, 495–501.

[58] There are no records for Jewish protection payments in Strasbourg, but scholars presume that such were standard across the empire. See Herbert Fischer, *Die verfassungsrechtliche Stellung der Juden in den deutschen Städten während des 13. Jahrhunderts* (1931; repr. Aalen, 1969), 34–36; and Mentgen, *Juden im mittelalterlichen Elsaß*, 126–127; and Isert Rösel, "Die Reichssteuern der deutschen Judengemeinden von ihren Anfängen bis

Strasbourg seem to have fared well under Bishop Berthold, times were more difficult across the empire, particularly in the mid–1230s. In the year spanning from winter 1235 to winter 1236 there were deadly riots at Wolfhagen (near Kassel), at Lauda and Tauberbischofsheim (both in Baden) and another at Fulda (in Hessen).[59] At these centers, Christian mobs got word that Jews had slain Christian children and used the blood for ritual purposes. In retaliation for these alleged crimes, enraged Christians plundered Jewish houses, violated Jewish bodies and tortured scores of Jews to death. The attack at Fulda is the best documented.[60] Here, following the discovery of five slain youths in a burned-down mill on the outskirts of town, locals raided the Jewish neighborhood and slaughtered thirty-four people.

Imperial intervention brought a reprieve to the violence ignited by the blood libel.[61] In the opening months of 1236, groups of both Jews and Christians complained to Emperor Frederick II, who at the time was residing at the imperial palace at Hagenau. The emperor launched an investigation and, when the baselessness of the charges was revealed, issued a new legal code denouncing the blood libel and outlawing attacks on Jews, the "Privilege and Judgment in Favor of the Jews" (*Privilegium et Sententia in Favorem Iudaeorum*).[62] A year earlier, the emperor had insti-

zur Mitte des 14. Jahrhunderts." *Monatsschrift für Geschichte und Wissenschaft des Judentums* 53 (1909): 697–708; and 54 (1910): 55–69, 206–223, 333–347 and 462–473.

[59] Aronius, *Regesten*, 206–209 (nos. 469, 472, 473 and 474). For a commentary on previous scholarship that erroneously places some of these attacks near Strasbourg, see Mentgen, *Juden im mittelalterlichen Elsaß*, 424–425, esp. n. 413.

[60] For thorough discussions, see Bernhard Diestelkamp, "Der Vorwurf des Ritualmordes gegen Juden vor dem Hofgericht Kaiser Friedrichs II. im Jahr 1236," in *Religiöse Devianz: Untersuchungen zu sozialen, rechtlichen und theologischen Reaktionen auf religiöse Abweichung im westlichen und östlichen Mittelalter*, ed. Dieter Simon (Frankfurt, 1990), 19–39; and Gavin Langmuir, "Ritual Cannibalism," in *Toward a Definition of Antisemitism* (Berkeley, 1990), 263–281.

[61] The accusations and violence continued into the twentieth century. See Alan Dundes, ed., *The Blood Libel Legend: A Casebook in Anti-Semitic Folklore* (Madison, WI, 1991); Rainer Erb, ed., *Die Legende vom Ritualmord: Zur Geschichte der Blutbeschuldigungen gegen Juden* (Berlin, 1993); and Robert C. Stacey, "From Ritual Crucifixion to Host Desecration: Jews and the Body of Christ," *Jewish History* 12, no. 1 (1998): 11–28. For late medieval and early modern accusations of Jewish ritual murder, R. Po-chia Hsia, *The Myth of Ritual Murder: Jews and Magic in Reformation Germany* (New Haven, 1988); and idem, *Trent 1475: Stories of a Ritual Murder Trial* (New Haven, 1992).

[62] *Constitutiones et Acta Publica Imperatorum et Regum*, ed. Ludwig Weiland, MGH, Legum sectio 4, vol. 2 (Hannover, 1896), 274–276 (no. 204); English translation in Robert Chazan, ed., *Church, State and Jew in the Middle Ages* (New York, 1980), 123–126; also see Klaus van Eickels and Tania Brüsch, eds., *Kaiser Friedrich II: Leben und Persönlichkeit in Quellen des Mittelalters* (Düsseldorf, 2000), 317–321.

tuted a new legal code for the whole German kingdom in the Peace of Mainz (*Mainzer Landfried* or *Constitutio Pacis*).[63] The imperial decrees represent a larger program that drew upon both theological and imperial precedents and ultimately cast Jews as special members of a Christian world, but also as feeble underlings. From Augustine on, theologians conceived of Jews as integral members of the Christian order.[64] Jews were the Lord's original "chosen" people and also were witnesses to Christ's Passion and the early Church. Because they rejected Jesus' status as messiah and, in the Christian understanding, orchestrated his torture and murder, at best Jews were seen as blind and stubborn adherents to an outmoded legal code. At worst they were murderous enemies of the faith.[65] Following Augustine, throughout the Middle Ages, theologians and Church leaders generally subscribed to the notion that, because of their special status, Jews were to be preserved as a relic of the origins of the Church, and their ultimate conversion would herald the end of time foretold in Revelation.

Building upon papal precedents, imperial policy concerning Jews translated these patently theological justifications for both Jewish protection and Jewish submission into a plan for Christian world order and imperial ascendancy.[66] From the Carolingian period through the eleventh

---

[63] For details, see Van Cleve, *Emperor Frederick II*, 382–386. The code details legal restrictions for members of multiple classes of subjects and was intended as a comprehensive guide to regulating earthly society according to divine will. The Privilege and Judgment in Favor of the Jews, then, was one ordinance within a larger program of social control.

[64] Paula Fredriksen, "Divine Justice and Human Freedom: Augustine on Jews and Judaism, 392–398," in *From Witness to Witchcraft: Jews and Judaism in Medieval Christian Thought*, ed. Jeremy Cohen (Wiesbaden, 1996), 29–54. High medieval developments of this theology are discussed in Amos Funkenstein, "Basic Types of Christian Anti-Jewish Polemics in the Later Middle Ages," *Viator* 2 (1971): 373–382; and John Y. B. Hood, *Aquinas and the Jews* (Philadelphia, 1995).

[65] Principal studies of this complex state of affairs include Cohen, *Living Letters of the Law*; Gavin Langmuir, *Toward a Definition of Antisemitism* (Berkeley, 1990); Robert I. Moore, *The Formation of a Persecuting Society: Power and Deviance in Western Europe, 950–1250* (Oxford, 1987); idem, "Anti-Semitism and the Birth of Europe," in *Christianity and Judaism*, ed. Diana Wood, Studies in Church History 29 (Oxford, 1992), 33–57; and Robert Chazan, *Medieval Stereotypes and Modern Antisemitism* (Berkeley, 1997). Recent publications which include trenchant case studies are: Christoph Cluse, ed., *Europas Juden im Mittelalter: Beiträge des internationalen Symposiums in Speyer vom 20.–25. Oktober 2002* (Trier, 2004); and Birk, Karin, Werner Transier and Markus Wener, eds., *Europas Juden im Mittelalter* exhib. cat. (Speyer, 2004).

[66] On papal policy, see Kenneth R. Stow, "Hatred of the Jews or Love of the Church: Papal Policy toward the Jews in the Middle Ages," in *Antisemitism Through the Ages*, ed. Shmuel Almog, trans. Nathan H. Reisner (Oxford, 1988), 71–89.

century, there was no standard, empire-wide code for the treatment of Jews. This changed in 1157 when Frederick I instituted a charter that, in keeping with norms established under Henry IV, outlawed the taking of Jewish property and ensured Jewish trade and safe travel, among other protections.[67] In another charter, the Rhenish-Frankish land peace of 1179, Barbarossa went further, stating that Jews were the concern of the imperial treasury (*ad fiscum imperatoris pertinent*)—special protectees, but implicitly special property as well. In his 1236 ruling, Frederick II renewed the notion that Jews were directly servile to the emperor and went further to insist upon Jewish accountability to the empire in exchange for these privileges. The 1236 charter in favor of the Jews includes new language deeming Jews to be serfs of the royal chamber (*servi camere nostre* or *Kammerknechte*).[68] Although Jews were not literal servants of any imperial court, they were required to pay new taxes to the emperor as a form of protection payment, underscoring their dependence on and submission to the crown.[69] In practice and in theory, then, Frederick's 1236 Privilege and Judgment in Favor of the Jews underscored a notion long prevailing in theology—that under the Christian world order, Jews are underlings, relics of a previous age and servile to Christian power.

[67] Chazan, *Church, State and Jew*, 63–66. For a broad discussion of Jewish legal status in the empire in the high Middle Ages, see Guido Kisch, *The Jews in Medieval Germany: A Study of their Legal and Social Status*, 2nd edn. (New York, 1970), esp. 129–168.

[68] See Salo Wittmayer Baron, *A Social and Religious History of the Jews*, vol. 9, *Under Church and Empire*, 2nd edn. (New York, 1965), 135–192; Fischer, *Die verfassungsrechtliche Stellung der Juden*, 3–7; J. Friedrich Battenberg, "Des Kaisers Kammerknechte: Gedanken zur rechtlich-sozialen Situation der Juden in Spätmittelalter und früher Neuzeit," *Historische Zeitschrift* 245, no. 3 (1987): 545–599; Dietmar Willoweit, "Vom Königsschutz zur Kammerknechtschaft: Anmerkungen zum Rechtsstatus der Juden im Hochmittelalter," in *Geschichte und Kultur des Judentums: Eine Vorlesungsreihe an der Julius-Maximilians-Universität Würzburg*, ed. Karlheinz Müller and Klaus Wittstadt (Würzburg, 1988), 71–89; Friedrich Lotter, "Geltungsbereich und Wirksamkeit des Rechts der kaiserlichen Judenprivilegien im Hochmittelalter," *Aschkenas* 1 (1991): 23–64, esp. 36–37; and Alexander Patschovsky, "Das Rechtsverhältnis der Juden zum deutschen König (9.–14. Jahrhundert)," *Zeitschrift der Savigny-Stiftung für Rechtsgeschichte* 110 (1993): 355–366. On the situation in the French kingdom, see Langmuir, "'Judei Nostri' and the Beginning of Capetian Legislation," and "'Tanquam Servi': The Change in Jewish Status in French Law about 1200," in *Toward a Definition of Antisemitism*, 137–166 and 167–194.

[69] Rösel, "Die Reichssteuern der deutschen Judengemeinden."

Ecclesia, Synagoga and the Real Conditions of Existence

The south façade of Strasbourg cathedral projects an ideal of order that echoes prevailing theological and legal codes pertaining to Jews. The earthly King Solomon at the center of the composition is endorsed by Christ behind him. Scenes of the Virgin's dormition and coronation in the tympana and lintels attest to the mystery and power of the Church to offer salvation after death. And Ecclesia and Synagoga together present the opposition between confident Christian might and debased Jewish weakness. Synagoga's presence is crucial. Like the Jews in the Christian empire, she is a servile yet integral member of the Christian milieu. Her beauty marks her as an insider within the ideal Christian system. Her decrepitude ensures her submission. It is a mistake, however, to look for a simple one-to-one equation between Synagoga and a real-world Jewish population. Synagoga is an abstraction, not an ideal Jew. Rather, she conveys the virtue of a Judaism that maintains a docile presence within the Christian domain.

This visualization of a Christian system at Strasbourg south was available to many classes of viewers within the city—the obedient cathedral canon, the burgher assessor working in conjunction with the bishop, the heretic who scowled at the luxurious excess of the cathedral every time she passed by, the Jewish child who feared the south façade's imposing sculptures and was taught that they exemplify Christian idolatry. All such viewers were addressed by the ensemble and, whether they accepted or rejected its message, were subject to it. For it represented the dominant ideology of their milieu. To explore this issue I turn to Louis Althusser, who considers the processes of subject formation through analysis of the mechanics of ideology:

> [I]deology "acts" or "functions" in such a way that it "recruits" subjects among the individuals (it recruits them all), or "transforms" the individuals into subjects (it transforms them all) by that very precise operation which I have called *interpellation* or hailing, and which can be imagined along the lines of the most commonplace everyday police (or other) hailing: "Hey, you there!"[70]

---

[70] Louis Althusser, "Ideology and Ideological State Apparatuses: Notes Towards an Investigation," in *Lenin and Philosophy and other Essays*, trans. Ben Brewster (New York, 2001), 85–126, at 118.

Althusser focuses on the role of institutions in the formation and replication of ideologies and indeed recalls the role of the medieval Church as an ideological organ, one that asserted itself through a persistent direct address: "I address myself to you, a human individual... in order to tell you that God exists and that you are answerable to Him."[71] The constellation of figures at Strasbourg south collectively interpellated or called out to urban viewers and recruited them as subjects. They could accept or reject the portal's message of Christian hegemony, but they were still subject to it by living under the power structures it represented.

The figures within the Strasbourg ensemble themselves present a remarkable visualization of the very mechanics of ideology Althusser analyzes. Ecclesia is the medieval cop who calls out, "Hey, you there!" Synagoga is the subject who recognizes she is being addressed, a process that completes the mechanism of interpellation (figs. 1–4). The call-out—from a policeman, from the church—"hardly ever miss[es]" its mark.[72] Synagoga's twisted posture suggests either that she is turning away from or, perhaps, turning back toward the call of Ecclesia. Both responses would be a recognition that it is indeed she who has been hailed, and either response implicates her within the Christian system. The Strasbourg program, then, offers a model for the act of being hailed, of being addressed by, and subject to, the Church, and it promises salvation to those who heed the call.

The call of the Church was amplified in the season of Lent and at other Rogation Days when penitential rituals were performed on the ecclesiastical stage outside and inside Strasbourg south. In a recent article Sabine Bengel has explored the relationship between the Strasbourg program and such rituals.[73] Building upon the argument of Gérard Cames, Bengel argues that the female figure kneeling before the Virgin's deathbed in the left tympanum is Mary Magdalene, whose cult had gained particular popularity in Strasbourg and the surrounding region in the 1220s (figs. 5 and 10).[74] The Magdalene functioned as an ideal penitent, a sinner who had renounced her past in favor of a

---

[71] Althusser, "Ideology," 120.

[72] Althusser, "Ideology," 118.

[73] Sabine Bengel, "Der Marientod am Südquerhausportal des Straßburger Münsters," in Krohm, ed., *Meisterwerke mittelalterlicher Skulptur*, 151–165.

[74] Cf. Gérard Cames, "Qui est la servante de la Dormition au portail sud de la cathédrale de Strasbourg?," *Bulletin de la Société des amis de la Cathédrale de Strasbourg* 10 (1972): 51–56.

future with Christ. On the Strasbourg tympanum, the Magdalene figure is the one carved in the highest relief and is closest to the viewer. Her emotional gesture and modish dress mark her as a bridge between the world of the biblical past and the domain of the present. Bengal takes note of the band around the Magdalene's head and, again, following Cames, observes the similarity between this headband and Synagoga's blindfold. Mary Magdalene, sitting at the deathbed of the Virgin, is the formerly sinful Synagogue who has removed the band from her eyes—pushed it up to her forehead—and recognized Christian truth.

Peter Cornelius Claussen's analysis of penitential performances on Ash Wednesday and other occasions at Strasbourg south and elsewhere allows us to reconstruct the experience of the repentant sinner surrounded by the portal's figurative ensemble.[75] On a day of atonement, penitents would gather barefoot at the cathedral's new south porch. There, at the bishop's order, they fell on their faces, praying and singing. As they made this ritual fall, they could look up and view Ecclesia, turning and hailing the subjected Synagoga (figs. 1–4). As the bishop then led the group into the cathedral, penitents would find themselves caught between the dramatic confrontation of Church and Synagogue, recognizing themselves as interpellated subjects of Queen Ecclesia. Looking up as they passed into the cathedral they could view an idealized model for overcoming their own sinful state: Mary Magdalene, bowing before the bed of the Virgin. Once inside the south transept, the penitents would be hailed yet again, this time by the piercing gazes of the Apostles at the lowest level of the Pillar of Angels (figs. 8–9). On this site they would then be ritually cleansed with holy water and sprinkled with ash by the bishop and his clerics, becoming new incarnations of the Magdalene, members of a remorseful flock under the watch of the pillar's evangelists, angels and judging Christ. Finally, the bishop would lead the penitents back out to the porch and deliver a parting admonition.[76]

[75] Peter Cornelius Claussen, *Chartres-Studien zu Vorgeschichte, Funktion und Skulptur der Vorhallen* (Wiesbaden, 1975), 11–12; see also Mary C. Mansfield, *The Humiliation of Sinners: Public Penance in Thirteenth-Century France* (Ithaca, 1995), 92–114 and 209–218; and Weber, "Glaube und Wissen," 97.

[76] Weber examines Strasbourg south in relation to another set of rituals, those surrounding the Ascension of the Virgin—the key feast at Strasbourg ("Glaube und Wissen," 95).

Already in 1972, O. K. Werckmeister had discerned a relationship be-tween portal programs and public penitential ritual.[77] His analysis showed that the lintel fragment representing Eve at Autun was part of a larger program presenting Adam, Eve and the serpent engaged in the Fall, set in opposition to the resurrected Lazarus. The early twelfth-century configuration, offering the promise of triumph over death through the triumph over concupiscence, hovered high in the tympanum and lintel of Autun's north façade, and were therefore remote from the penitents below, who at Lenten celebrations prostrated themselves on elbows and knees within the cathedral as part of a ritual reenactment of the Expulsion from Paradise.[78] Whereas the Autun Eve was contained within the frame of the portal's lintel, absorbed in an internal drama of sin and remorse, the Strasbourg figures, carved in the round or in high relief, many installed on pedestals, engaged viewers directly through gazes and gestures. Created roughly one century apart, the programs at Autun and Strasbourg exemplify a shift in modes of portal adornment, manifesting the church's quickening drive to use realism and theatricality in sculpture to implicate viewers directly in the drama of sin and its remission.

A parallel shift from internal deliberation toward theatrical campaign is evident in twelfth and thirteenth-century debates—both real and imagined—concerning the relationship of Judaism to Christianity. In the twelfth century theologians penned dialogues between Christians and Jews over questions of dogma. While the aim of these encounters always was to show the superiority of the Christian faith, they do suggest, at least theoretically, a spirit of open intellectual inquiry.[79] In the same era, however, there were also theologians developing new strains of vehemently anti-Jewish polemic, a polemic that gained ascendancy

[77] O. K. Werckmeister, "The Lintel Fragment Representing Eve from Saint-Lazare, Autun," *Journal of the Warburg and Courtauld Institutes* 35 (1972): 1–30. For related arguments about penitents, episcopal authority and mediating decorative programs, see Barbara Abou-El-Haj, "The Urban Setting for Late Medieval Church Building: Reims and its Cathedral between 1210 and 1240," *Art History* 11, no. 1 (1988): 17–41; and Gerald B. Guest, "The Prodigal's Journey: Ideologies of Self and the City in the Gothic Cathedral," *Speculum* 81, no. 1 (2006): 35–75.

[78] Werckmeister, "Lintel Fragment," 17–21.

[79] See Schlauch, "The Allegory of Church and Synagogue": 455–462; Aryeh Grabois, "The *Hebraica Veritas* and Jewish-Christian Intellectual Relations in the Twelfth Century," *Speculum* 50, no. 4 (1975): 613–634; and Beryl Smalley, *The Study of the Bible in the Middle Ages* (Notre Dame, IN, 1978), esp. 149–172.

by the second quarter of the thirteenth century.[80] A change in attitudes toward Jews came in part through the discovery of the Talmud—that body of post-biblical Jewish scholarship that became the authoritative source on ritual, custom and history. Jews, it turned out, were not relics of the pre-history of the Church, witnessing the authority of Old Testament scripture—the Augustinian justification for their survival. From this perspective Christian authorities enacted programs to try to reconfigure the Jew to fit the Christian mold. Pope Gregory IX's 1239 call to the leaders of Europe to condemn the Talmud, the subsequent "Talmud Trial" of Paris, and the incineration of thousands of Talmud manuscripts were displays aimed in part at humiliating and punishing Jews for frustrating Christian expectations.[81] These public defamatory acts, a departure from the philosophical exchanges of the previous century, are analogous to the equally emphatic projection of Christian authority over Jewish tradition visualized at Strasbourg south. Here Ecclesia calls out to her Jewish predecessor, but dialogue is impossible. Synagoga is already defeated and thus, kept in her place, serving as witness to Christian authority through her subjection to it.

Ideology—and by extension ideological projections such as those at Strasbourg south—Althusser observes, "represents the imaginary relationship of individuals to their real conditions of existence."[82] Ecclesia calling out to the defeated Synagoga projects an image of Christian containment of the Jewish tradition at a time when clerics increasingly recognized that they had no such control. The constellation of figures at Strasbourg south further proclaims the righteousness of a political order in which Jews were to be protected—because of their essential role in the developing market economy, because anti-Jewish riots threatened to disrupt social harmony—but also contained. The portal's visualization

[80] Anna Sapir Abulafia, *Christians and Jews in the Twelfth-Century Renaissance* (New York, 1995); and Dahan, *The Christian Polemic Against the Jews*.

[81] The scholarship on this episode is vast. Key studies are: Solomon Grayzel, "The Talmud and the Medieval Papacy," in *Essays in Honor of Solomon B. Freehof*, ed. Walter Jacob et al. (Pittsburgh, 1964), 220–245; Jeremy Cohen, *The Friars and the Jews: the Evolution of Medieval Anti-Judaism* (Ithaca, 1982), 51–99; Joel Rembaum, "The Talmud and the Popes: Reflections on the Talmud Trials of the 1240s," *Viator* 13 (1982): 203–223; Robert Chazan, "The Condemnation of the Talmud Reconsidered (1239–1248)," *Proceedings of the American Academy for Jewish Research* 55 (1988): 11–30; Shlomo Simonsohn, *The Apostolic See and the Jews*, (Toronto, 1991), 300–342; and William Chester Jordan, "Marian Devotion and the Talmud Trial of 1240," in *Religionsgespräche im Mittelalter*, ed. Bernard Lewis and Friedrich Niewöhner (Wiesbaden, 1992), 61–76.

[82] Althusser, "Ideology," 109–112.

of order had broader resonances as well. Penitential rituals activated the sculpted ensemble at Strasbourg south, investing penitents' real conditions of existence with sacrality, beauty and significance within a divine system. The sculptures at Strasbourg south visualize an ideal mechanism, then, in which earthly rulers govern according to divine mandate; in which Judaism is kept in check, impotent and blind under the watch of the Church; and in which faithful Christians, cleansed of sin, are promised the rewards of heaven at the feet of a regal Christ and Virgin.[83]

Synagoga's beauty is essential to these mechanisms. For thirteenth-century audiences, and for viewers still today, she stands as an idealization of subjection to Christian hegemony. Post-medieval viewers, seduced by her comeliness, sometimes have been tempted to read a conciliatory message in her form—as if her sympathetic artistic treatment was an expression of Christian tolerance toward Judaism, or at least of hopes for Jewish conversion. But examination of the fraught political, social and theological conditions in which Strasbourg south was created and used make it plain that Synagoga stood in the service of an ideology that often was anything but pretty.

[83] Sara Lipton has discovered a sermon by an abbott at Saint-Victor in Paris that admonishes canons not to be "like Synagoga." This evidence suggests that, in multiple contexts, the figure of Synagoga could stand in for all those who stray from the Christian fold. I thank Professor Lipton for sharing with me her unpublished insights.

CHAPTER SEVEN

THE JEWS, LEVITICUS, AND THE UNCLEAN IN MEDIEVAL ENGLISH BESTIARIES

Debra Higgs Strickland

Medieval bestiaries are well-known and admired by both popular audiences and historians of medieval art chiefly for their lively illustrations of various beasts, birds, fishes, reptiles, and other subjects from the natural and imaginary worlds.[1] Although the bestiary texts purport to describe the natural habits of the creatures pictured, more emphasis is placed on the spiritual significance of God's creation through Christian allegorical interpretations of these habits. In effect, the bestiarists described animal behavior in ways that were contrived to yield specific moral lessons that would encourage both lay and religious readers to look to Nature to learn how to lead good Christian lives as well as to understand the mysteries of salvation history. For example, the father lion's resuscitation of his stillborn cubs by breathing on them is compared to the resurrection of Christ. The flying fish's loss of motivation to race against ships—and its subsequent sinking into the deep—is compared to those hard-working Christians who give up too soon and are dragged down to the depths by the devil. The tender care of their aging parents by hoopoe chicks demonstrates the fulfilment of the Scriptural mandate to "honor your father and mother" (Exod. 20:12).[2]

Besides dispensing Christian morals, the bestiarists promoted a wide range of important theological ideas that informed contemporary social attitudes towards women, friends, enemies, marriage, and ecclesiastical and secular authorities, as I have discussed at length in my previous study of the English bestiaries.[3] In that book I noted just a few of the

---

[1] From a scholarly perspective, the two widely available English translations of Latin prose bestiaries are both unsatisfactory: T. H. White, *Book of Beasts* (London, 1954), a colloquial translation of the Cambridge Bestiary, and Richard Barber, *Bestiary* (Woodbridge [Suffolk], 1992), an abridged translation of Bodley MS. 764 (The Bodleian Library, University of Oxford).

[2] White, *Book of Beasts*, 8–9 (*leo*), 199 (*serra*), 31–32 (*epopus*).

[3] Debra Hassig, *Medieval Bestiaries: Text, Image, Ideology* (Cambridge, 1995).

ways, both verbal and visual, that the Christian bestiarists expressed negative attitudes towards Jews. It is to this aspect of the bestiary tradition that I return in the present essay, in order to examine in greater detail the key means by which Jews are evoked in the bestiaries, and how these characterizations fit into the wider arena of contemporary anti-Jewish polemic.[4] I shall argue that the bestiaries, as well as the early Christian text of the *Physiologus* on which they were based, should be ranked among the most popular and widely-disseminated of Christian polemical texts directed against Jews. This is a function of the bestiaries that to date has been overlooked. In the space of this essay I am only able to provide a preliminary investigation of this thesis, which I hope will encourage a re-examination of the genre as an important witness to the changing Christian theological and social attitudes towards Jews that are corroborated in other contemporary theological, literary, and pictorial contexts.[5]

As a key part of my argument for an essentially anti-Jewish character of the bestiaries, I shall explore the various ways that Christian ideas about Hebrew law informed their conception and formal structure. Most visible in this role is the Book of Leviticus, which is referred to both directly and indirectly in the bestiary texts. After noting some of the more general ways that Jews are described in the bestiaries, I shall devote the second part of this essay to an examination of selected references to Leviticus in both text and image in order to show how the Jews' own laws were used against them. More precisely, I shall examine the Christian bestiarists' use of the dietary system outlined in Leviticus 11

[4] Anti-Jewish aspects of selected bestiary images have been examined in Suzanne Lewis, "*Tractatus adversus Judaeos* in the Gulbenkian Apocalypse," *Art Bulletin* 68 (1986): 543–66; Michael Camille, *The Gothic Idol: Ideology and Image-Making in Medieval Art* (Cambridge, 1989), 165–66; Ruth Mellinkoff, *Outcasts: Signs of Otherness in Northern European Art of the Late Middle Ages*, 2 vols. (Berkeley, 1993) 1:92, 102–103; and Danièle Sansy, "Bestiaire des juifs, bestiaire du diable," *Micrologus: natura, scienza, e società medievali* 8 (2000): 561–79. I would like to thank Sam Cohn for bringing Sansy's article to my attention.

[5] On changing Christian images of Jews in works of later medieval art and literature, see William Chester Jordan, "The Last Tormentor of Christ: An Image of the Jew in Ancient and Medieval Exegesis, Art, and Drama," *Jewish Quarterly Review* 78 (1987): 21–47; Heinz Schreckenberg, *The Jews in Christian Art: An Illustrated History* (London, 1996); and Debra Higgs Strickland, *Saracens, Demons, and Jews: Making Monsters in Medieval Art* (Princeton, 2003). On changing Christian attitudes towards Jews, see especially R. I. Moore, *The Formation of a Persecuting Society: Power and Deviance in Western Europe, 950–1250* (Oxford, 1987); and Jeremy Cohen, *Living Letters of the Law: Ideas of the Jew in Medieval Christianity* (Berkeley, 1999).

as a strategy to assert the supersession of the Old Law by the New, and ultimately, the redundancy of Judaism itself. The persistent references to Leviticus in both the core *Physiologus* text and the later text additions to the bestiaries also necessitate their inclusion in the corpus of both early Christian and later medieval commentaries on Leviticus, which has formerly been considered a scriptural text that held little interest for Christian exegetes.[6]

As in my earlier studies, I shall focus my discussion on the English bestiaries, primarily because it was in England during the twelfth and thirteenth centuries that the genre reached its apogee.[7] Most important to note is the fact that this same period witnessed the greatest degree of Christian-Jewish tensions experienced in English history, tensions which culminated in the expulsion of the Jews in 1290. It has been recently observed that the Jewish experience in England is highly representative of medieval Ashkenazic life in general, and may be the best case study of Christian-Jewish relations for this period.[8] It is for this reason that a study of representations of the Jews in the English bestiaries might be expected to reveal something of general Christian attitudes towards Jews that may be linked to social reality both in England and elsewhere.

The Bestiaries as Anti-Jewish Polemic

Bestiaries as an illustrated genre apparently did not emerge until the twelfth century. By the thirteenth century, they were composed of varying

[6] Robert L. Wilken, "Origen's Homilies on Leviticus and Vayikra Rabbah," in *Origeniana Sexta: Origène et la Bible/Origen and the Bible*, ed. Gilles Dorival and Alain le Coulluec (Louvain, 1995), 81–91.

[7] Most of the evidence presented in this essay was drawn from a small selection of English bestiaries representative of different types and periods: Oxford, Bodleian Library, MS. Laud Misc. 247 (hereafter Laud Misc. 247), c. 1120 (the first extant illustrated bestiary); New York, Pierpont Morgan Library, MS. M. 81 (hereafter Morgan Bestiary), c. 1185; Cambridge, University Library, MS. Ii.4.26 (hereafter Cambridge Bestiary), c. 1200–10; London, British Library, MS. Harley 4751 (hereafter Harley 4751), c. 1230–40; Oxford, Bodleian Library, MS. Bodley 764 (hereafter Bodley 764), c. 1240–50; London, British Library, MS. Harley 3244 (hereafter Harley 3244), after 1255; Paris, Bibliothèque Nationale, MS. fr. 14969 (hereafter French 14969), c. 1265–70; London, Westminster Abbey Library, MS. 22 (hereafter Westminster Abbey Bestiary), c. 1270–90. I discuss all of these manuscripts at greater length in Hassig, *Medieval Bestiaries*.

[8] Robert Stacey, "Jews and Christians in Twelfth-Century England," in *Jews and Christians in Twelfth-Century Europe*, ed. Michael A. Signer and John Van Engen (Notre Dame, 2001), 340.

interpolations of different texts that range in date from the early Christian period to the twelfth and thirteenth centuries. However, the core text that provides the basic allegorical approach retained across the centuries is the *Physiologus*, thought to have been composed between the second and fourth centuries in Alexandria.[9] This is significant because during this period Alexandria was a prominent center of production of the earliest Christian *adversus Judaeos* literature, including the *Epistle of Barnabus* and Justin Martyr's *Dialogue with Trypho*, both dated to the second century.[10] Like other early Christian works produced here, the *Physiologus* incorporates a consistently anti-Jewish stance based on an opposition of the literal (Jewish) as opposed to spiritual (Christian) interpretation of Scriptures. True to the interests of Christians seeking to discredit Judaism, it reiterates the key themes of Jewish blindness, idolatry, perversity and deicide.[11] I suggest, therefore, that the *Physiologus* was an important contribution to early Christian anti-Jewish polemic, and as the foundational text of the bestiaries, can serve as a guide to this genre's initial conception and function in the context of the twelfth-century Jewish-Christian debate.[12]

A brief look at a few bestiary entries in which anti-Jewish themes are prominent will expose the method by which Christian bestiarists turned Nature against the Jews. One such entry concerns the bird known as the caladrius, whose story was included in the *Physiologus* and incorporated

---

[9] The version of the *Physiologus* favored in the English bestiaries is known as *versio B*. Text references in this essay are to *Physiologus Latinus (versio B)*, ed. Francis J. Carmody (Paris, 1939); and the English translation of the combined B- and Y versions: *Physiologus*, trans. Michael J. Curley (Austin, 1979); on dating, see xvi–xx. The attribution of the *Physiologus* to Alexandria is based on its allegorical structure, characteristic of the early Christian Alexandrian school. See Helen Woodruff, "The Physiologus of Bern: A Survival of Alexandrian Style in a Ninth Century Manuscript," *Art Bulletin* 12 (1930): 226–53; and Carmody, *Physiologus*, 16. On allegorical method, see also Henri de Lubac, *Medieval Exegesis*, trans. E. M. Macierowski (Edinburgh, 2000), 2:1–9; and Beryl Smalley, *The Study of the Bible in the Middle Ages* (Notre Dame, 1964), 1–36.

[10] Guy G. Stroumsa, "From Anti-Judaism to Antisemitism in Early Christianity?" in *Contra Iudaeos: Ancient and Medieval Polemics between Christians and Jews*, ed. Ora Limor and Guy G. Stroumsa (Tübingen, 1996), 1–26.

[11] These themes are examined in *Antisemitism and the Foundations of Christianity*, ed. Alan T. Davies (New York, 1979).

[12] On the genre of Jewish-Christian debate, see A. Lukyn Williams, *Adversus Judaeos: A Bird's-Eye View of Christian Apologiae until the Renaissance* (Cambridge, 1935); Anna Sapir Abulafia, *Christians and Jews in the Twelfth Century Renaissance* (London, 1995); and idem., *Christians and Jews in Dispute: Disputational Literature and the Rise of Anti-Judaism in the West (1000–1150)* (Aldershot, 1998). For a succinct overview, see Amos Funkenstein, "Basic Types of Christian Anti-Jewish Polemics in the Later Middle Ages," *Viator* 2 (1971): 373–82.

into the later bestiaries. According to the *Physiologus*, the caladrius is an entirely white bird which, if placed on the end of a sick man's bed, will turn away from the man if the illness is to be fatal but stares straight at him if he is to recover. The caladrius is subsequently identified as Christ, who, when he came down from heaven, turned towards the Gentiles and took away their infirmities, but turned away from the Jews owing to their refusal to believe in him.[13] The caladrius entry thereby incorporates the popular Christian theme of Jewish "blindness", the claim that the Jews failed to recognize Christ as the fulfillment of their own prophecy, rejected him, and so were abandoned by him.

Not all of the bestiary images corroborate the negative component of this interpretation; some of them picture its more positive aspect by showing the caladrius/Christ facing the sick man/Gentile, with whom the Christian reader would presumably identify.[14] It is possible, however, in light of the options presented by the text, that viewers of the caladrius-facing-man image identified the sick man not with the Gentiles, but with the Jews. If so, this type of image may be seen to override the written moral by implying that in spite of the sins of their ancestors, contemporary Jews are still eligible for salvation, an optimistic stance perhaps favored by mendicant bestiary owners charged with the conversion of English Jews.[15]

But other caladrius images clearly emphasize the negative side of the moral lesson. A representative of this type may be found in Harley 3244, in an image executed after 1255 (fig. 1). Medieval viewers would have recognized the peaked hat worn by the sick man as that of a Jew,

---

[13] *Physiologus*, ed. Carmody, 15 16.

[14] The caladrius looks towards the sick man in Laud Misc. 247 (fol. 142r) and the Cambridge Bestiary (fol. 33v). The images in French 14969 (fol. 10r) and the Westminster Abbey Bestiary (fol. 36v) show the bird twice, first flying away while looking back at the man, and then facing the man; while in Harley 3244 (see my fig. 1) the caladrius turns away (discussed below). The images in Bodley 764 (fol. 63v) and Harley 4751 (fol. 40r, reproduced in Ann Payne, *Medieval Beasts* [New York, 1990], 97) are especially interesting because in both, although the caladrius faces the sick man (depicted as a crowned king), it is the man who is turning away.

[15] On the problem of conversion, see Kenneth R. Stow, "Hatred of Jews or Love of the Church: Papal Policy Toward the Jews in the Middle Ages," in *Antisemitism through the Ages*, ed. Shmuel Almog, trans. Nathan H. Reisner (New York, 1988), 71–89. On the conversion of English Jews, see Robert C. Stacey, "The Conversion of Jews to Christianity in Thirteenth-Century England," *Speculum* 67 (1992): 263–83; and Reva Berman Brown and Sean McCartney, "Living in Limbo: The Experience of Jewish Converts in Medieval England," in *Christianizing Peoples and Converting Individuals*, ed. Guyda Armstrong and Ian N. Wood (Turnhout, 2000), 169–91.

and the figure's closed eyes may be interpreted as a sign of impending death but also as emblematic of Jewish blindness. The emphatic manner in which the caladrius/Christ is turning away from the sick man/Jew underscores rather than contradicts the text's anti-Jewish moral.

The metrical *Bestiaire* composed around 1210 by Guillaume le Clerc is an important witness to expanding anti-Jewish sentiment in thirteenth-century England, where we know the work circulated, owing to its emphasis on anti-Jewish themes which are also manifest in its accompanying illustrations.[16] In the manuscript French 14969, a richly illustrated copy of Guillaume's text produced in London or Oxford around 1270, the animal and the moral commentary receive separate illustrations. The commentary images, which regularly incorporate figures of contemporary clerics and Jews, are usually positioned before their associated text entries and are larger and more detailed than the animal representations, positioned at the end of each entry. By giving visual pride of place to the allegorical interpretations, this arrangement effectively foregrounds the links between the bestiary lessons and contemporary English social and theological concerns.

The artistic treatment of Guillaume's caladrius verse in French 14969 illustrates this very well. The theme of Christ's rejection of the Jews is expanded in the text through reference to the "sickness" of Jewish unbelief, which subsequently generates malice, stubbornness, an evil heart and sloth.[17] The accompanying commentary image provides a narrative context for these themes (fig. 2). On the left, Christ hangs on a cross surmounted by a dragon. Given the presence of Moses directly opposite, the dragon probably represents the brazen serpent (Num. 21:6–9), a well-known typological figure of the Crucifixion; or possibly the sins of humanity that Christ was said to have taken onto

[16] For the text and what little it reveals about the author, see *Le Bestiaire*, ed. Robert Reinsch (Weisbaden, 1967); and the English translation, *The Bestiary of Guillaume le Clerc*, trans. George Druce (Ashford, 1936). Subsequent text references are to these editions.

[17] "I cest uerrai caladrius/E ist nostre sauueur Iesus,/Ki uint de sa grant maieste,/Pur esgarder l'enfermete/Des Gius, ke il ot taunt amez/Tant guarnis e amonestez,/Tante forz peuz e guariz,/Tant honurez e encheriz,/E quant il uit ke il morreient/E la noufei, ou il esteient,/Uit lur malice uit lur duresce/E lur mal quer e lur peresce,/De lur esgard turna sa face;/Par (s)a beningne e seinte grace/Se turna dunc uer nos genz..." (from French 14969, fols. 9v–10r); see *Le Bestiaire*, ed. Reinsch, 241–42 (lines 491–505). In this and subsequent transcriptions from manuscripts, I have added punctuation and capitalization but have not corrected grammar or normalized spelling.

himself.[18] Kneeling onlookers on the far left include a hooded mendicant towards whom Christ inclines his head. Facing Christ on the right is a horned, bearded Moses who points towards him in recognition. But emerging from behind Moses, as if from his physical body and shown in varying degrees of visibility, are three hatted Jews. The one most fully visible has his back turned towards Christ, and, mirroring Moses's pointing gesture, faces a flaming hellmouth full of hatted, grotesquely grinning Jews stuffed into the maw by a bestial blue demon. In addition to translating Guillaume's moralization into a visual narrative, this image incorporates the contemporary association between Jews and demons, as well as the dual view of Jews as positive witnesses to the faith (represented by Moses) yet eternally damned (represented by the hellmouth inhabitants).[19]

Besides blindness, another anti-Jewish theme emphasized in the bestiaries is idolatry.[20] This subject is highlighted in the *Physiologus* entry for the hyena, which was incorporated into the bestiaries, including Guillaume's.[21] The hyena is described as a filthy beast who feeds on dead human bodies, and so the animal is typically pictured violating a sepulcher to feed on a corpse. The hyena also changes sex: sometimes it is male, and sometimes it is female. It is this characteristic of sexual perversity that provides Guillaume with a link between the hyena and the "duplicitous Jews," who first worshipped the true God—as shown in the upper register in the hyena commentary image in French 14969—but were later given over to idolatry, as depicted in the image's lower register (fig. 3). Guillaume goes ever further. Like the hyena, who is neither male nor female, the Jew is double-minded and weak and lying: he desires to serve both you and me, but will not keep faith with any.[22] And so we see, in the lower register of the French 14969

[18] Guillaume mentions both in the accompanying text; see *Le Bestiaire*, ed. Reinsch, 242–43 (lines 510–518).

[19] On the dual Christian view of Jews and demonic themes in medieval representations of Jews, see Strickland, *Saracens, Demons, and Jews*, 77–79, 97–102, 122–30; see also Joshua Trachtenberg, *The Devil and the Jews: The Medieval Conception of the Jew and Its Relation to Modern Anti-Semitism* (1943; repr. Philadelphia, 1983), 11–53. On the doctrine of witness as formulated by Augustine of Hippo, see John Y. B. Hood, *Aquinas and the Jews* (Philadelphia, 1995), 5–15; and Paula Fredriksen, "Divine Justice and Human Freedom: Augustine on Jews and Judaism, 392–398," in *From Witness to Witchcraft: Jews and Judaism in Medieval Christian Thought*, ed. Jeremy Cohen (Wiesbaden, 1996), 29–54.

[20] On the theme of "Jewish idolatry," see Camille, *Gothic Idol*, 165–94.

[21] *Physiologus*, ed. Carmody, 34.

[22] Reinsch, *Bestiaire*, lines 1596–1634, (291–93).

image, Jews worshipping the Golden Calf while the consequences of this action—execution by the sword—are graphically depicted behind their backs. In contemporary anti-Jewish polemical writing, the Old Testament episode of the back-sliding Israelites' worship of the Golden Calf (Exod. 32:4) was held out as "evidence" of a supposedly ongoing practice, a wicked desire on the part of contemporary Jews incapable of understanding their own laws. In the French 14969 image, this wicked practice is contrasted with that of the pious Jews depicted in the upper register, kneeling alongside Moses before the burning bush (Exod. 3:2–3). It is significant that the face of God appearing in the bush wears the cruciform halo that identifies him as Christ, as this would have allowed the image to function as a reference to contemporary efforts at conversion. If so, then the scene of execution in the lower register would have illustrated the price of not converting, a fate experienced by some Jews who chose to retain their faith in twelfth- and thirteenth-century England.[23]

At least one bestiary artist chose to link the charge of Jewish sexual perversity to a specific contemporary anxiety, by depicting the hyena violating not a male corpse—the choice of every other artist whose hyena images I have observed—but a female one (fig. 4). Showing a beast that represents the Jews in the act of molesting a naked (albeit dead) woman surely alludes to contemporary Christian fear of Jewish "violation" in social, sexual, and intellectual realms. It also calls to mind the Fourth Lateran Council's mandate that Jews distinguish themselves from Christians by their dress, for the stated reason of avoiding sexual intercourse between Jews (or Muslims) and Christian women, a transgression considered tantamount to bestiality.[24] In the bestiaries, the linking of idolatry to sexual perversity also demonstrates the contemporary Christian interest in constructing chains of sin. Another example of this technique may be observed in the thirteenth-century *Bibles moralisées*, in which the Jews' involvement in money-lending was

[23] I have discussed the reference to forced conversion in the lower register of this image in more detail in Strickland, *Saracens, Demons, and Jews*, 147–48.

[24] Hassig, *Medieval Bestiaries*, 152. For the text of the decree issued by Innocent III, see *The Church and the Jews in the XIIIth Century*, ed. Solomon Grayzel (Philadelphia, 1933), 308; for an English translation, Jacob R. Marcus, *The Jew in the Medieval World, A Source Book: 315–1791* (1983; repr. Cincinnati, 1990), 138.

presented as evidence that Jews idolatrously worshipped money, a sin ultimately linked to the Jewish allegiance to Antichrist.[25]

The bestiarists also endorsed the powerful Christian claim that the Jews murdered God, a "horrendous novelty" first described in detail in the second century by Melito of Sardis.[26] The myth of deicide especially fueled accusations of ritual murder made against Jews in England and elsewhere during the twelfth and thirteenth centuries.[27]

The early thirteenth-century Cambridge Bestiary image of the elephant provides an exceptionally gratuitous way into the Christ-killer theme (fig. 5). Its accompanying text, based on the *Physiologus*, is a lengthy allegory that identifies the elephant as Christ as well as a model for Christian marriage.[28] There is nothing here about the Crucifixion, much less about the Jews' supposed involvement in that event: it is the accompanying image that provides such extra-textual commentary. Once the viewer understands from the text that the fearful, grimacing elephant is a figure of Christ, the meaning of the wicked driver (manhout) wearing the pointed hat and threatening the elephant with a flail becomes clear. The manhout is a Jew, standing in for all contemporary Jews whose ancestors were accused of torturing and murdering Christ. I have suggested elsewhere that the contemporary knights riding inside the elephant's howdah in this and other bestiary elephant images represent Christian crusaders, a reference which in this context suggests another function of the deicide charge, that of justification for the ongoing Christian aggression in the Holy Land.[29] This spectacular case of text-image contradiction suggests that an anti-Jewish agenda in the bestiaries was not just the inevitable result of its dependence upon an

[25] Sara Lipton, *Images of Intolerance: The Representation of Jews and Judaism in the Bible moralisée* (Berkeley, 1999), 31–53; Strickland, *Saracens, Demons, and Jews*, 140–42.

[26] Stephen G. Wilson, "Melito and Israel," in *Anti-Judaism in Early Christianity, vol. 2: Separation and Polemic*, ed. Stephen G. Wilson (Waterloo, 1986), 99. Melito's *Peri Pascha* includes a shockingly graphic account of the Crucifixion, which is characterized explicitly as the murder of God by the Jews. For the parallel Greek/English text, see Melito of Sardis, *On Pascha and Other Fragments*, ed. and trans. Stuart George Hall (Oxford, 1979), 2–61; also Jeremy Cohen, "The Jews as Killers of Christ in the Latin Tradition, from St. Augustine to the Friars," *Traditio* 39 (1983): 1–27.

[27] See Trachtenberg, *The Devil and the Jews*, 124–39; and Gavin Langmuir, "Thomas of Monmouth, Detector of Ritual Murder," *Speculum* 59 (1984): 820–46. On deicide in the visual arts, Stefan Rohrbacher, "The Charge of Deicide: An Anti-Jewish Motif in Medieval Christian Art," *Journal of Medieval History* 17 (1991): 297–321.

[28] *Physiologus*, ed. Carmody, 57–58. For discussion, see Hassig, *Medieval Bestiaries*, 129–35.

[29] Hassig, *Medieval Bestiaries*, 135–41.

earlier, anti-Jewish text, but is indicative of an ongoing and developing concern promoted in the bestiaries by both authors and artists.[30]

Like the Cambridge Bestiary elephant image, the panther image from the Morgan Bestiary provides a stark contrast to the tenor of the text it accompanies (fig. 6). In this case, however, the image's effect is that of camouflage. We understand from the text that the delightful blue panther is emerging from his cave after three days of heavy digestion, belching in such a way to produce a sweet odor. This odor attracts all other animals except for the dragon, who shuns the panther's sweetness and flees underground. According to the *Physiologus*, Christ is the true panther, loved by all except the Devil, who is the dragon. So far, so good. But there is more:

> Just as the panther, having eaten and been filled, immediately lay down and slept, so also our Lord Jesus Christ, after he was satiated by Jewish illusions, that is, by whips, blows, injuries, reproaches, thorns, and spit, was hung on the cross by his hands, pierced with nails, his thirst quenched with vinegar and gall, and in addition his side was pierced with a spear. Satiated with all these great Jewish rewards, Christ slept and rested in the tomb and descended into hell and there bound the great dragon, our enemy...[31]

While it does corroborate the narrative as well as the allegorical links between the dragon and the Devil, and the panther and Christ, the Morgan Bestiary image—which is iconographically typical of the English bestiaries—makes no reference to Jewish tortures. Instead, it focuses on the power of Christ, allegorically represented by the wavy red lines of the panther's belch (!). It is undoubtedly visual contradictions such as this one that have made it easier for previous analysts to overlook the relentlessly anti-Jewish character of the bestiaries.

It is important to note that the anti-Jewish content of the bestiary texts is not confined to those entries based on the *Physiologus*. Later texts added during the twelfth and thirteenth centuries expand this theme, and the bestiarists also modified the earlier texts. Curiously, given the negative trend emphasized so far, these textual modifications sometimes

---

[30] Interestingly, the bestiary story of the elephant was appropriated for anti-*Christian* purposes by Rabbi Berechiah HaNakdan, an English Jew also writing in the thirteenth century; see Marc Michael Epstein, "The Elephant and the Law: The Medieval Jewish Minority Adapts a Christian Motif," *Art Bulletin* 76 (1994): 470; and idem, *Dreams of Subversion in Medieval Jewish Art and Literature* (University Park, 1997), 39–69.

[31] *Physiologus*, trans. Curley, 44; ed. Carmody, 41.

reduce rather than augment the anti-Jewish tenor of some of the especially negative *Physiologus* entries.[32] The reasons for these changes are unknown, and may have to do with the independent transmission of some of the texts. However, the fact that passages pertaining to the Jews seem to be the *only* part of the texts subject to such alteration strengthens the claim that the matter of the Jews remained a central one to bestiary patrons throughout the later Middle Ages.

An example of a post-*Physiologus*, anti-Jewish addition is the barnacle geese entry, adapted from the description given by Gerald of Wales in his twelfth-century *Topographia Hibernia*, dedicated to Henry II.[33] The text in Bodley 764, a bestiary probably produced in Salisbury around 1250, explains that these birds, found in Ireland, reproduce without copulation. They are instead generated by the logs from which they hang by their beaks. They continue to hang there, protected by shells, until they grow feathers and are able to fly away. The Bodley 764 image thus shows a group of limp, motionless geese suspended by their beaks from branches of a tree, like ripening fruit. A similar image and text entry may also be found in the closely related bestiary, Harley 4751, which is thought to have been produced about a decade earlier.[34]

Because they are not born of the flesh, the bestiarist explains, the barnacle geese are sinless and a sign of the reality of the virgin birth of Christ placed in Nature by God. Adopting the rhetoric of the twelfth-century Jewish-Christian debates, the bestiarist then addresses the Jews directly:

> Pause, O unhappy Jews, pause before it is too late. You do not dare to deny, because you respect the Old Law, that the first man was born of clay, without a male and female, and that the second was born of the male without the female. Only the third, born in the usual way from male and female, can you in your stiff-necked thinking approve and affirm. But the fourth generation, in which salvation was born of a woman

[32] Entries subject to this treatment in the present group of bestiaries are the phoenix (Laud Misc. 247, fols. 144v–145r; Harley 3244, fols. 53v–54r; Bodley 764, fol. 66r), panther (Harley 3244, fol. 37v; Bodley 764, fols. 7v–9r); and vulture (Bodley 764, fols. 61r–62r). In addition, the Westminster Abbey Bestiary contains modified versions of the entries for the pig (fol. 8v), hyena (fols. 24v–25r), and caladrius (fol. 36v).

[33] Gerald of Wales, *The History and Topography of Ireland*, rev. edn., trans. John J. O'Meara (New York, 1982), 41–42.

[34] Bodley 764, fol. 58v; Harley 4751, fol. 36r. On the relationship between Harley 4751 and Bodley 764, see Hassig, *Medieval Bestiaries*, 3–4.

> alone, without a man, you hate, to your own downfall, because you are obstinate in your malice.[35]

To contemporary Christians, Jewish denial of Mary's virginity *in et post partum* was just another sign of Jewish moral depravity. Not surprisingly, the virgin birth was one of the key points of Christian doctrine to which Jewish religious authorities did take issue, and against which they provided powerful and logical arguments that prompted energetic rebuttals by Christian apologists.[36] The inclusion of the barnacle geese in the bestiaries signals an obvious need on the part of Christians to use faith as the only available defense of the irrational concept of virgin birth, perhaps in response to the Jewish challenge. As well, the vehicle of the barnacle geese helped to convey this difficult point of doctrine to a popular audience, which may be why these entries were included in these two bestiaries in particular, books that were probably owned by lay, as opposed to monastic, patrons.[37]

The Bestiaries, Leviticus and the Abrogation of the Old Law

Besides Jewish blindness, idolatry, sexual perversity, denial of the virgin birth, and deicide, there is still another prominent anti-Jewish theme in the bestiaries that is also a favored theme in the contemporary *adversus Judaeos* literature. This theme is the redundancy of Hebrew Law. To demonstrate this redundancy, the bestiarists often used as their point of departure the dietary laws recorded in Leviticus 11. Although Leviticus was never a central text in the medieval Christian liturgy and, the *Physiologus* notwithstanding, received relatively little attention from the early

---

[35] *Bestiary*, trans. Barber, 121, with my corrections. "Respice, infelix Iudee, respisce, uel sero. Primam hominis generationem ex limo sine mare et femina. Secundam ex mare sine femina ob legis uenerationem diffiteri non audes. Terciam solam ex mare scilicet et femina crustialis est dura ceruice approbas et affirmas. Quartam ubo, in qua sola salus est ex femina scilicet, sine mare, obstinata malicia, in propriam perniciem, detestaris..." (from Bodley 764, fol. 59r).

[36] For Jewish arguments against the virgin birth and other points of Christian doctrine as presented in the thirteenth-century *Nizzahon Vetus* (Old Book of Polemic), see David Berger, trans., *The Jewish-Christian Debate in the High Middle Ages* (Philadelphia, 1979).

[37] I have argued elsewhere that both Bodley 764 and Harley 4751 were made for noblewomen (Hassig, *Medieval Bestiaries*, 126–27). This barnacle geese entry does not appear in any of the other bestiaries examined in this study.

Church Fathers,[38] it did enjoy a revival of interest during the twelfth century with the composition of a new, thirty-volume commentary by Ralph of Flaix (flourished c. 1157). Ralph, a Benedictine, dedicated his work to the young clerics of his monastery, who, as he observed in his prologue, were showing signs of wavering in their faith following confrontations with learned Jews who refuted key points of Christian doctrine.[39] In spite of its massive length, Ralph's commentary survives in many copies, which suggests a certain popularity at least among monastic audiences, who were also patrons of the bestiaries.[40] Given the prevalence of direct and indirect references to Leviticus contained therein, I suggest that the contemporary bestiaries also bear witness to revived interest in this book.

But before looking at bestiary references to Leviticus, it is important to understand their presence in this context as representative of two broader concerns of Christian scholars and churchmen. These were (1) to justify the continued use of the Old Testament in Christian worship and exegesis and (2) to discredit Judaism entirely by asserting the abrogation of the Old Law and its replacement by the New Law of the Gospels.[41] That the Laws of Moses were superseded by those of Christ had been expressed in relation to Levitican law in other early Christian contexts. During the third century, the anonymous author of the *Didascalia Apostolorum* asserted that the so-called Second Legislation, laws handed down to Moses subsequent to the Ten Commandments as punishment for the Israelites, was no longer binding on Christians because Christ had replaced them with the sacrament of baptism.[42]

---

[38] Gerard Rouwhorst, "Leviticus 12–15 in Early Christianity," in *Purity and Holiness: The Heritage of Leviticus*, ed. M. J. H. M. Poorthus and J. Schwartz (Leiden, 2000), 181–93.

[39] Beryl Smalley, "Ralph of Flaix on Leviticus," *Recherches de theologie ancienne et médiévale* (1968): 52–53. See also John van Engen, "Ralph of Flaix: The Book of Leviticus Interpreted as Christian Community," in Signer and Van Engen, eds., *Jews and Christians*, 150–70.

[40] On monastic patronage of bestiaries, see Willene B. Clark, "The Illustrated Medieval Aviary and the Lay-Brotherhood," *Gesta* 21 (1982): 68–74; and Hassig, *Medieval Bestiaries*, 170–71.

[41] An early articulation of the redundancy of the Old Law may be found in the second-century *Epistle* spuriously attributed to the apostle Barnabus. See *The Epistle of Barnabus*, ed. T. W. Crafer (New York, 1920); and *An English Translation of the Epistle of Barnabus*, trans. Secretary of the S.P.C.K. (New York, 1923).

[42] *The Didascalia Apostolorum in Syriac*, trans. Arthur Vööbus, Corpus Scriptorum Christianorum Orientalium 180 (Louvain, 1979), 226–27. A similar assertion was made in the second century by Justin Martyr, *Dialogue with Trypho, A Jew*, chap. 15; in

Taking a somewhat different line, Novatian attempted to debunk the dietary laws of Leviticus 11 in his short tract on *Jewish Foods*, also composed during the third century, by asserting that the Jews were ignorant of the Laws' true spiritual meanings, which were understood only by Christians.[43] I shall argue that through references to Leviticus and to Hebrew law, the later medieval bestiarists were likewise attempting to replace a "literal" Jewish hermeneutic with a "spiritual" Christian one, in order to support the claim that Judaism itself was defunct.

By the time the first twelfth-century English bestiaries were produced, Christian exegetes had long used the term "judaizing" to describe anyone who insisted on adhering to the letter rather than to the spirit of Scriptures.[44] In the bestiaries, the entry for the ant provides an effective way into the theme of Jewish literalism. The text, based on the *Physiologus*, explains that when the ant stores grain in its nest it divides the store in two, in order to guard against winter rains, which would soak it and make it germinate, thus causing the ant to die of starvation. The moral then proclaims:

> In the same way you, O men, should keep the word of the Old and New Testaments separate, that is, distinguish between the carnal and the spiritual, lest the letter kill you: for the Law is spiritual, as the Apostle says. "For the letter killeth, but the spirit giveth life." For the Jews paid attention only to the letter of the Law and ignored its spiritual meaning; therefore they perished of hunger and became murderers of the prophets and of God...[45]

In his *Bestiaire*, Guillaume le Clerc adds that by adhering to the letter of the Law and refusing to see its spiritual meanings, the Jews have far less sense than that of the ant.[46] And so, to accompany this text, the

The Writings of Justin Martyr and Athenagoras, trans. Marcus Dods et al., Ante-Nicene Christian Library 2 (Edinburgh, 1867), 104.

[43] See the English translation in *Novatian*, trans. Russell J. DeSimone (Washington, D.C., 1974), 137–56. This approach to the Levitican laws was adopted subsequently by Augustine of Hippo; see Cohen, *Living Letters*, 44–51.

[44] For example, according to Peter Abelard, "If you knew how to read Scripture in a prophetic spirit rather than in a Judaizing manner, and if you knew how to understand what is said of God under corporeal forms, not literally and in a material sense but mystically through allegory, you would not accept what is said as an unlettered person does" (*Dialogus inter Philosophum, Judaeum et Christianum*, ed. Rudolf Thomas [Stuttgart, 1970], 146, lines 2792–2795; trans. from Cohen, *Living Letters*, 143).

[45] *Physiologus*, trans. Curley, 21–22; *Physiologus Latinus* ed. Carmody, 23.

[46] *Bestiaire*, lines 950–960 (ed. Reinsch, 263–64; trans. Druce, 34); French 14969, fol. 18v.

French 14969 artist rendered an image of a bishop preaching before a crowd, including three Jews who turn their backs to him as a sign of their refusal to see the spiritual truth.[47] Whereas the bestiary entries on the caladrius and the hyena, which bluntly characterize Jews as blind and perverted, might be viewed as appealing to a more popular anti-Jewish mindset, this second approach, as exemplified by the ant entry, is more intellectual. As well, Christian viewers would have had to possess an understanding of the textual moral before they could see themselves in the benign bestiary images of tiny, orderly ants in serried ranks, gathering grain and congregating on anthills.[48]

In the bestiaries references to "the Law" and to "Leviticus" are often used interchangeably. It is the law expounded in Leviticus 11 that is typically referred to in both cases, because this is the chapter that preserves a record of law believed transmitted to Moses directly from God concerning Israel's use of animals as food and for sacrifice.[49] The law indicates which animals are clean and which are unclean; only the clean ones are acceptable for sacrifice and for food, and they are to be killed and offered to God in specified ways. Among the quadrupeds, the clean beasts are the ruminants with split hooves, which means that any beast without split hooves that chews the cud, such as the camel and the hare, is unclean; and the one animal with split hooves that does not ruminate—the pig—is also unclean (Lev. 11:1–8). Among the aquatic creatures, those with fins and scales are clean, but those without fins and scales, such as shellfish, are unclean (Lev. 11:9–12). Among the unclean reptiles are those that go on their bellies or creep upon the earth, such as serpents and lizards (Lev. 11:30–31, 41–44). The birds are more difficult to identify because we do not have modern equivalents for most of the Hebrew bird names, but among the unclean ones are the carrion-eaters, such as the eagle and the raven (Lev. 11:13–19). Four-legged, flying creatures are also unclean, but certain insects, such as locusts, are clean and therefore edible (Lev. 11:20–23).

Modern scholars have analyzed these dietary laws as the means by which the ancient Israelites preserved their special relationship with

---

[47] French 14969, fol. 17r.

[48] Morgan Bestiary, fol. 31v; Harley 3244, fol. 50r; Harley 4751, fol. 32r; Bodley 764, fol. 53v (reproduced in Barber, *Bestiary*, 114); Westminster Abbey Bestiary, fol. 29v.

[49] The laws of Leviticus 11 are summarized and recapitulated in Deuteronomy 14. The bestiarists therefore occasionally refer to "Deuteronomy" rather than to "Leviticus."

God; along with circumcision, they were the visible means by which they set themselves apart from neighboring, pagan tribes. Further, the laws relating to killing animals and not eating their blood were meant to ensure that Israel retained reverence for life across God's creation.[50] Medieval Hebrew commentators interpreted Leviticus in different ways. Moses Maimonides (1135–1204) viewed the dietary laws as arbitrary tests of obedience grounded in physiological principles,[51] but earlier Jewish philosophers, such as Philo of Alexandria (c. 20 B.C.E.–50 C.E.), gave them allegorical interpretations. For example, according to Philo, split hooves signify the two possible paths in life, one leading to virtue, and the other to vice.[52] The compilers of the widely consulted *Rabbah Leviticus* (mid-fifth century) interpreted the specifically named unclean animals as symbols of different nations: Babylonia (camel), Media (rock badger), Greece (hare), and Rome (pig).[53] Other important Hebrew commentators and exegetes, such as Rashi (Solomon ben Isaac, 1040–1105) and Ramban (Moses Nahmanides, 1194–1270) maintained the type of literal interpretation of the Levitican laws to which Christians continued to object.[54] As already noted, early Christian commentators on Leviticus were relatively few. Some of them, such as Origen, stressed the redundancy of the dietary laws and others pertaining to ritual purity, and warned Christians against continuing to follow them. Most emphasized that the laws were not to be taken literally, but rather that they carried spiritual meanings available only to Christians.[55]

---

[50] Jacob Milgrom, *Leviticus 1–16* (The Anchor Bible) (New York, 1991), 42–47, 733–35. There is a large literature on the interpretation of Leviticus from theological, symbolic, literary, historical, archaeological, and anthropological perspectives. See especially Mary Douglas, *Purity and Danger* (London, 1966); and idem, *Leviticus as Literature* (Oxford, 1999). See also Walter Houston, *Purity and Monotheism: Clean and Unclean Animals in Biblical Law* (Sheffield, 1993).

[51] Moses Maimonides, *Guide for the Perplexed*, chap. 48; see *The Guide for the Perplexed by Moses Maimonides*, trans. M. Friedländer, rev. edn. (New York, 1956), 370–71.

[52] See *Philo*, ed. and trans. F. H. Colson (Cambridge, 1939), 8:75 (chap. 18).

[53] Jacob Neusner, *Judaism and the Interpretation of Scripture: Introduction to the Rabbinic Midrash* (Peabody, Mass., 2004), 79–83.

[54] See Rashi, *Pentateuch with Rashi's Commentary*, 5 vols., ed. M. Rosenbaum and A. M. Silbermann (New York, 1946), 3:42–49 (on Lev. 11); and Ramban, *Commentary on the Torah*, 5 vols., ed. Charles Ber Chavel (New York, 1960), vol. 3.

[55] *Didascalia Apostolorum*, 236–37. Origen's homily on the clean and unclean animals of Leviticus 11 contains the allegorical interpretations repeated by most other early Christian exegetes. See Origen, *Homilia VII*, in Origène, *Homélies sur le Lévitique 1–11*, ed. Marcel Borret (Paris, 1981), 1:298–353 (parallel Latin/French text). On spiritual versus literal interpretation of Levitican law, see also Rob Meens, "'A Relic of Supersti-

The Jews' continued adherence to these laws was held up by Christians as evidence of Jewish literalism, "proof" that Jews were incapable of grasping the true meaning of their own laws because they remained mired in carnal concerns. In the twelfth century Christian exegetes such as Odo of Tournai (d. 1113) and Peter the Venerable (1092 or 1094–1156) suggested that this was so because Jews were incapable of reason and had to negotiate only with their senses; they therefore missed the point of the dietary laws entirely, which did not pertain to animals, but to the avoidance of sin.[56] In parallel fashion, Ralph of Flaix criticized the judaizing tendencies of clerics who were, in his view, overly dependent on the historical sense of Scripture, and called for a "liberation" of the primary meaning of the Old Testament from the "control" of the Jews.[57] It was towards such perceived liberation, I suggest, that the bestiarists interpreted the Levitican dietary laws. By identifying the Jews themselves as the unclean element in contemporary Christian society, the bestiarists asserted the triumph of Christianity over Judaism.

Although the allegorical understanding of Levitican law is consistently put forth by the bestiarists, they could only provide such an understanding after first connecting the dietary laws (literally) to animals through images. They thus used images to mark the hermeneutical shift from the literal to the spiritual. The Westminster Abbey Bestiary, probably produced for the Franciscans of York around the time of the 1290 expulsion, was in fact guided by Leviticus in its very arrangement of the animal entries. This book opens with the image of Adam naming the animals (Gen. 2:19–20), which serves here, as in other bestiaries, as a visual sign of the bestiary's function as a prolonged commentary on the Genesis creation story (fig. 7). Such images also remind the viewer that, like Leviticus 11, the bestiaries present the further implications of God's command that humans will have dominion over animals (Gen.

tion': Bodily Impurity and the Church from Gregory the Great to the Twelfth Century Decretists," in Poorthus and Schwartz, *Purity and Holiness*, 281–93.

[56] Odo of Tournai, *Disputatio contra Judaeum Leonem nomine de adventu Christi filii Dei*, in J.-P. Migne, ed., *Patrologiae cursus completus, Series Latina*, 221 vols. (Paris, 1844–55), 160:1111B [hereafter cited as PL]; trans. Irven M. Resnick in *On Original Sin and A Disputation with A Jew, Leo, Concerning the Advent of Christ, the Son of God* (Philadelphia, 1994), 96; see also Anna Sapir Abulafia, "Twelfth-Century Humanism and the Jews," in Limor and Stroumsa, *Contra Iudaeos*, 165.

[57] Cohen, *Living Letters*, 272–73.

1:26–28).[58] Here, as in the bible as well as in other bestiaries, naming is presented as the first act of establishing dominion.[59]

But what is unusual in the Westminster Abbey Bestiary image is that all but one of the animals receiving their names fall into the clean and unclean camps either specifically listed or following upon the principles set forth in Leviticus 11. The ox, goat, sheep, stag, and doe rank among the clean beasts, while the horse, hare, and lizards are unclean. Only the ape, shown riding the doe, does not fit into the Levitican classification scheme, having neither cloven hooves nor ruminating abilities. Rather, with his gesture, he mimics Adam, a role true to his ape-ness, as mimicry was a function of apes in many other medieval pictorial contexts.[60] Adam wears a Jewish hat, and the accompanying text points out that the original animal names were not given in Latin or Greek, but in Hebrew, the language spoken by everyone prior to the Flood.[61]

But what is even more significant is the fact that the subsequent animal entries in the Westminster Abbey Bestiary begin not with the customary lion, the king of beasts, and not in the order of the beasts specified by the *Physiologus*, which some bestiaries continued to follow. Nor does it exhibit the popular sequential presentation of four-legged beasts, followed by birds, then reptiles and fish.[62] Rather, this bestiary begins with the ox entry, and subsequent animals described in this first section all fall into the Levitican camp of clean, sacrificial beasts.

[58] On this point in relation to Leviticus, see Douglas, *Leviticus and Literature*, 135.

[59] Bestiary images of Adam naming the animals exhibit a good deal of iconographical variety even though they accompany the same text. See for example the c. 1200 Ashmole Bestiary (Oxford, Bodleian Library, MS. Ashmole 1511, fol. 9r) reproduced in Debra Hassig, "Beauty in the Beasts: A Study of Medieval Aesthetics," *Res* 19/20 (1990/1991), fig. 16; the c. 1230 Rochester Bestiary (London, British Library, MS. Royal 12.F.xiii, fol. 34v) reproduced in Payne, *Medieval Beasts*, as the frontispiece; the c. 1250 Northumberland Bestiary, fol. 5v (private collection) reproduced in Hassig, *Medieval Bestiaries*, fig. 10; and Harley 3244, fol. 46r.

[60] On ape antics, see H. W. Janson, *Apes and Ape Lore in the Middle Ages and Renaissance* (London, 1952); and Lilian Randall, *Images in the Margins of Gothic Manuscripts* (Berkeley, 1966), plates III–XIV. Mary Douglas (*Leviticus as Literature*, 139) proposes that Levitican law makes provision for all creatures, but to me it would appear to exclude the simians.

[61] "Nec secundam latinum linguam, aut grecam, aut quarumlibet gentium barbararum nomina illa imposuit Adam, sed illa lingua quod ante diluvium omnium una fuit, quae Hebrea nuncupatur" (from Westminster Abbey Bestiary, fol. 4r). The text is based on Isidore of Seville, *Etymologiae* 12.1 (PL 82: 424D).

[62] For example, Laud Misc. 247 and French 14969 follow the *Physiologus* order; while the Morgan Bestiary, Cambridge Bestiary, Harley 3244, Harley 4751, and Bodley 764 follow the classified arrangement.

Following the ox, these are the buffalo, cow, bull, bullock, ram, sheep, lamb, and goat. These are immediately followed by a section of entries devoted to beasts classed in Leviticus as unclean: the pig, ass, wild ass, horse, mule, camel, and dromedary.[63] However, as if to dispel any fears of "judaizing," the bestiarist provided anti-Jewish commentary in the opening entry on the ox. The ox, an animal not included in the *Physiologus*, is claimed by the bestiarist to represent the Jewish people, who will destroy (Christians) in the same way that the ox grazes grass to the roots.[64]

The Westminster Abbey Bestiary is unusual in its organizational reliance on the Levitican classification system; I know of no other bestiary for which the groups of animals were arranged according to the principle of clean/unclean. It should be noted, however, that following the section of unclean beasts just described, the remaining sequence of beasts, birds, and reptiles in this book is an arbitrary one, and so Leviticus may be seen as the guiding principle of arrangement only in its first two sections. More typically, concepts from Leviticus are evoked in this and other bestiaries either through direct quotation or indirectly through references to "the Law" or uncleanness.

For example, the Harley 3244 caladrius entry discussed above asserts that the caladrius is unclean "according to the Law."[65] Similarly, the ibis—one of the birds named in Levicitus—is also described as unclean "according to the Law." The ibis text, based on the *Physiologus*, draws a further connection between the ibis's uncleanness and its own diet, said to consist of carrion and other putrid and decayed matter.[66] In other words, it is the bird's feeding habits that render it unclean, just as the ingestion of unclean animals will render a Jew unclean. But the ibis's unclean diet is not to be taken literally. The carrion and unclean little fishes on which the ibis feed are identified allegorically as the works of the flesh, including adultery, fornication, lust, idolatry, and drunkenness. The text's moral thus guides the viewer past the literal dimension of the accompanying images—which consistently depict a generic bird of prey eating carrion—to their true Christian meaning.

---

63 Westminster Abby Bestiary, fols. 7r–8v (clean beasts), 8v–11v (unclean beasts).

64 "Bos specialis populus Iudaicus, unde sic delebit nos hic populus quomodo solet bos herbas usque ad radices carpere" (from the Westminster Abbey Bestiary, fol. 7r).

65 "...Sed dices quia caladrius secundum legem inmundus est..." (Harley 3244, fol. 52r).

66 *Physiologus*, ed. Carmody, 27–29.

The entry for one of the goats (*hircus*) in Bodley 764 refers to the ancient Hebrew expiation ritual of the scapegoat described in Leviticus 16.[67] It is notable that the goat entry is another post-*Physiologus* bestiary addition. The bestiary text states that under "the Law," the goat offered in atonement for sins signifies the sinner, who, in pouring out his blood in tears of penitence, dissolves the hardness of his sins. There is no negative commentary about the Jews here, only an additional statement that the two goats required for the Levitican rite are the two peoples, the Jews and the Gentiles, both coming from the vine-branch of sin.[68] The accompanying image is devoid of any overtly Jewish references (fig. 8). However, given that the text identifies one of the two goats as the Jews, the goat's beard and long, demonic horns may function as a negative, anti-Jewish sign, recognizable to viewers from many other contemporary pictorial contexts in which goats were used as derisory attributes of Jews.[69] At the same time, however, through his Christian redefinition of the scapegoat rite, the bestiarist sought to move the viewer from a literal to a spiritual reading of the pictured goat, and thus to see it as a figure of the *Christian* sinner.[70]

Another type of legal reference in the bestiaries is to animal sacrifice. In Bodley 764, the animals selected for this theme were taken directly from the Levitican roster of clean beasts specified as acceptable for sacrificial purposes. In the entry for the sheep, for example, the sacrificial rituals of the Israelites are compared to the sacrifice of Christ,[71] an exegetical technique that parallels the repeated equation in contemporary polemical literature between Christ and the Paschal Lamb.[72] Similarly, in this same bestiary, the calf is identified first as a sweet sacrifice on the holy altars, but then as Christ, who offered

[67] On the possible meanings of this rite, see Mary Douglas, "The Go-Away Goat," in *The Book of Leviticus: Composition and Reception*, ed. Rolf Rendtorff and Robert A. Kugler (Leiden, 2003), 121–41; also Milgrom, *Leviticus 1–16*, 1009–1084.

[68] "Duo hirci utique populus Iudeorum scilicet et gentium ex radice peccati uenientes in Leuitico" (Bodley 764, fol. 37r). According to Leviticus 16, two goats are required for the expiation ritual: one is to be sacrificed, and the other is to be set free.

[69] Strickland, *Saracens, Demons, and Jews*, 78, 134–37.

[70] Cyril of Alexandria (d. 444) and others interpreted both of the Levitican goats as Christ on the grounds that Christ took on the sins of humanity and was also sacrificed; see *Glaphyorum in Leviticum*, in J.-P. Migne, ed., *Patrologiae Cursus Completus, Series Graeca*, 161 vols. in 166 parts (Paris, 1857–66), 69:582B–583A and 586C–590B.

[71] Bodley 764, fols. 34r–34v.

[72] This parallel forms the gruesome focus of Melito's *Peri Pascha* (as above, n. 26). See also the virulent image of the Paschal Lamb assaulted by contemporary Jews in the early fourteenth-century Gradual of Gisela of Kerseenbruck, also known as the

himself as a sacrifice for humanity's salvation. The bestiarist then adds a third level of identification: "They are calves because they grow in the holy faith and their necks are free of the yoke of the Law. Calves also represent the lascivious Jews, as in the Psalm [21:12]: 'Many calves have surrounded me, the fat bulls have attacked me'."[73] To accompany this text, the Bodley 764 bestiary artist has rendered two calves: a subdued red one partly visible behind an exuberant brown one (fig. 9). The viewer is thus able to distinguish between the sacrificial red calf of the Old Law, representative of the Jews and made redundant by Christ, and the brown Christ-calf of the New Law, shown joyously bounding in the foreground.[74] It is an image that demands knowledge of the text before the semiotic significance of color and number can be fully understood. Without this knowledge, it might be mistaken for a neutral animal portrait.

The bestiarists also evoked Levitican principles by focusing closely on the proposed significance of a given beast's "uncleanness." As already noted, the hyena's uncleanness was said to have stemmed from its sexual perversity but ultimately referred to Jewish idolatry. Using this method, the bestiarist transferred the concept of uncleanness from the animal world to the Jews themselves. Other displays of this technique are found in the bestiary entries for the various owls, birds that are specified as unclean in Leviticus (11:16–17). For example, two types of owls are described in successive entries in Harley 4751: the *noctua* and the *bubo*.[75] According to the *Physiologus*, the owl (*nycticorax*) loves the night and shuns the light of day, just as the Jews rejected Christ and thus preferred darkness to light.[76] In Harley 4751 this and other excerpts from the *Physiologus* description of the *nycticorax* are included

Codex Gisle (Osnabrück, Archiv des Bischöflichen Generalvikariat, MS. 101, p. 141) discussed and reproduced in Strickland, *Saracens, Demons, and Jews*, 120 and pl. 11.

[73] "Uituli sancti fide crescentes et attigo legis libera colla habentes. Uituli Iudei lasciuientes ut in psalmo: 'Circumdedent me uituli multi, tauri pingues obsederunt me'" (Bodley 764, fol. 42v).

[74] The sacrifice of the two calves is given a New Testament interpretation in the *Epistle of Barnabus* (Secretary of the S.P.C.K., *English Translation*, 16).

[75] Harley 4751, fols. 46v–47v. In the bestiaries, the texts and images that describe the various owls (*bubo, nycticorax, noctua, ulula*) are interchangeable and there is no consensus on how to translate them into English. The *bubo* and *noctua* are named among the unclean birds in Jerome's translation of Leviticus, and the *nycticorax* is named in the Deuteronomy recapitulation (Deut. 14:17). The *Physiologus* only discusses the *nycticorax*, but the description of this particular owl clearly informed the later texts of the others.

[76] *Physiologus*, ed. Carmody, 18.

in the *noctua* entry, which is accompanied by a portrait image of two owls, one clutching a rodent in his talons. The next entry, devoted to the *bubo*, states that this particular owl numbers among the unclean beasts in Leviticus owing to the fact that he yields to the darkness of sin and flees the light of justice. He is therefore a sign of *all* sinners.[77] Jews are not singled out. However, the accompanying *bubo* image depicts the popular subject, also described in the text, of the owl attacked by other birds who know he is nearly sightless and therefore virtually defenseless by day (fig. 10). Given the consistent association between the owl and the Jews in the bestiaries as well as in other artistic contexts, the image was likely read as a legitimate Christian attack on the hated Jews.[78] It may have also functioned as an allegorical reference to actual physical assaults on Jews taking place during the thirteenth century. It is notable that the story of the owl's attack by other birds is yet another post-*Physiologus* alteration, and therefore constitutes a later expansion on the anti-Jewish theme in the owl entries. Given this context, even the non-narrative bestiary images of owls, with their forward-facing eyes and long beaks, may have suggested Jewish physiognomy to viewers familiar with stereotypical portraits of Jews with long, hooked noses.[79] While many other bestiary owls are rendered more naturalistically, the Harley 4751 *bubo* has a strangely humanoid appearance. As well, the accompanying description of the *bubo* as an "unhappy owl" (*infelix bubo*) recalls the rhetoric of the Christian-Jewish debates, in which the Christian is made to address his interlocutor as "unhappy Jew," a derogatory form of direct address similar to that quoted above from the Bodley 764 barnacle geese entry.

In Guillaume le Clerc's *Bestiaire* the *nycticorax* text provides an extended parallel between the owl's preference for darkness and the spiritual

---

[77] "Bubo tenebris peccorum deditos et lucem iusticie fugientes significat unde inter inmunda animalis in Leuitico deputatur. Unde per bubonem intelligere possumum quemlibet peccatorem" (Harley 4751, fol. 47r).

[78] Mariko Miyazaki, "Misericord Owls and Medieval Anti-Semitism," in *The Mark of the Beast: The Medieval Bestiary in Art, Life, and Literature*, ed. Debra Hassig (New York, 1999), 28. The attack on the owl by other birds and the owl's filthiness are referred to repeatedly in the late thirteenth-century Middle English poem, *The Owl and the Nightingale*, but there are no references to Jews. See *The Owl and the Nightingale: Text and Translation*, ed. Neil Cartlidge (Exeter, 2001).

[79] See for example the owl portraits in the Cambridge Bestiary, fol. 85v (reproduced in White, *Book of Beasts*, 133); and the Westminster Abbey Bestiary, fol. 40r (reproduced in Hassig, *Medieval Bestiaries*, fig. 104). On "Jewish noses" in medieval art, see Mellinkoff, *Outcasts*, 1:127–29; and Strickland, *Saracens, Demons, and Jews*, 77–78.

blindness of the Jews.[80] In the commentary image, the French 14969 artist provided a New Testament narrative context for this theme by juxtaposing figures of Jews with a scene of the Annunciation taking place before saints Peter and Paul. Both saints are haloed, and Paul is holding a large sword by the blade. The bearded, blindfolded Jew wearing an inverted funnel cap and accompanied by a small, grinning demon turns away from the Annunciation towards five other grotesque, bearded, hatted Jews arranged in a close, conspiratorial huddle.[81] Besides visualizing Jewish blindness and implying that, owing to demonic influence, contemporary Jews continue to reject the reality of Christ's incarnation; the image may also refer to contemporary slurs against the Virgin that Jews at this time were increasingly accused of making.[82]

During the thirteenth century, anti-Jewish polemic developed in an important new direction which was to some extent paralleled in the bestiaries. The newer tendency was to label Jews as heretics, a reconception related to Christian claims that the Talmud was heretical because it had nothing to do with God's law but was composed later out of accumulated lies and perversions.[83] This accusation led to the public burning of Talmud manuscripts in Paris in 1240.[84] Pictorially, the association of Jews with pagans, heretics, Saracens, and other non-Christian enemies of the Church was developed most fully in the great *Bibles moralisées* patronized by the Capetian court in Paris, but also found expression in many other artistic contexts.[85] Such imagery encouraged Christians to categorize Jews alongside other non-Christian groups, thus

[80] *Bestiaire*, lines 615–655 (ed. Reinsch, 247–49).

[81] French 14969, fol. 12r; reproduced in Sansy, "Bestiaires des juif," fig. 1.

[82] See William Chester Jordan, "Marian Devotion and the Talmud Trial of 1240," *Wolfenbütteler Mittelalter-Studien* 4 (1992): 61–76; reprinted in *Ideology and Royal Power in Medieval France: Kingship, Crusades and the Jews* (Aldershot, 2001).

[83] Jeremy Cohen, *The Friars and the Jews: The Evolution of Medieval Anti-Judaism* (Ithaca, 1982), 60–76; and idem, *Living Letters*, 157–59.

[84] Judah M. Rosenthal, "The Talmud on Trial: The Disputation at Paris in the Year 1240," *Jewish Quarterly Review* 47 (1956/1957): 58–76 (pt. 1), 145–69 (pt. 2); Hyam Maccoby, *Judaism on Trial: Jewish-Christian Disputations in the Middle Ages* (Rutherford, 1982), 1–38, 163–67; William Chester Jordan, *The French Monarchy and the Jews: From Philip Augustus to the Last Capetians* (Philadelphia, 1989), 137–41; idem, "Marian Devotion"; also see Kara Ann Marrow's chapter in this volume.

[85] Lipton, *Images of Intolerance*, 83–90; Elizabeth Carson Pastan, "*Tam haereticos quam Iudaeos*: Shifting Symbols in the Glazing of Troyes Cathedral," *Word & Image* 10 (1994): 66–83. The conceptual and pictorial similarities between representations of Jews and the other so-called enemies of Christendom are a major focus in Strickland, *Saracens, Demons, and Jews*.

strengthening the Church's polarized stance against the rest of humanity by collapsing the distinctions between its individual enemies.

In line with this trend, some of the thirteenth-century bestiarists lumped Jews in with other enemies of the Church, and sometimes they did so in the context of Levitican law. The Bodley 764 text entry for the sow (*sus*) reads in part:

> Swine signify sinners and unclean persons or heretics, about which it is laid down in the Law: because they divide the hoof and do not chew the cud let not their flesh be touched by true believers. Though these men take upon themselves each Testament of the Law and of the Gospel yet because they do not ruminate upon spiritual food, they are unclean... Swine's flesh belongs to polluted things, which, among other precepts of the Old Testament, are prescribed as unclean. They have, moreover, passed on the remains of their sins to their children when they cried out, "His blood be on us and on our children [Matt. 27:25]."[86]

Although the text does not mention Jews by name, the references to "the Law" and to the well-known condemnatory line from the Gospels account of Christ's Passion clearly refer to them. In this same entry, however, the concept of the unclean has been appropriated from Levitican law to describe *all* sinners, which has the effect of positioning the Jews within a much larger, impious group.

The Bodley 764 image that accompanies this text is a portrait of a standing brown sow nursing five piglets (fig. 11). In the first instance, such activity visually distinguishes this animal from the wild boar (*aper*) of the next entry, shown gored by hunters and described, like the sow, as unclean to the Jews.[87] Iconographically, the Bodley 764 sow compares uncomfortably to the notorious anti-Jewish figure of the *Judensau*,

---

[86] "Sues peccatores significant, et inmundos uel hereticos, de quibus in lege precipitur, ob hoc, quod ungulam findunt et non ruminant, ne a fidelibus eorum carnes contingantur. Hii licet utrumque testamentum legis et euangelii suscipiant, sed quia spiritalem cibum non ruminant, inmundi sunt.... Porcina ad polluta respicit, quae inter cetera Ueteris Testamenti precepta inmunda prenotantur. Transmiserunt autem reliquias peccatorum filiis suis, quando clamabant, 'Sanguis eius super nos et super filios nostros'" (from Bodley 764, fols. 37v–38v; trans. Isaiah Shachar, *The Judensau: A Medieval Anti-Jewish Motif and Its History* [London, 1974], 4–5). The same text, derived from Rabanus Maurus's *De universo* 7.8 (PL 111:206C–207A), is included in Harley 4751, fols. 20r–21r. Its accompanying image (fol. 20r), similar to that in Bodley 764 (except that four rather than five piglets are suckling), is reproduced in Shachar, *Judensau*, pl. 1; on the text, see p. 7.

[87] "Pro hoc autem nomen significatur Iudeis suis se contrarium, qui hoc animal inter cetera habere uidebantur inmundum (Bodley 764, fol. 39r). The image (fol. 38v) is reproduced in Barber, *Bestiary*, 86.

popular in Germany from the thirteenth through sixteenth centuries and among the most degrading of medieval anti-Jewish images precisely because it draws its pejorative power from the Jews' own dietary prohibition. In these images caricatured, hatted Jews in the place of piglets are shown being suckled by a sow, recalling in a mocking and derisory way the Roman imperial iconography of Romulus and Remus suckled by the she-wolf. To medieval Jews, the image may have evoked Rome in a rather different way because, as noted above, Rome is the allegorical interpretation of the pig given in the *Rabbah Leviticus*. The *Judensau* images also implied that contemporary Jews harbored a secret desire to violate the swine ban. In a famous fifteenth-century woodcut produced in Briesach, the legends accompanying the image of an enormous sow suckling four Jews and engaging three others in various ways before two Jewish witnesses suggest that this desire transcends merely eating the pig to interacting with it sexually (fig. 12).[88]

The resemblance between the *Judensau* and the English bestiary sow images points to a more disturbing aspect of the image of the Jews in the bestiaries: the Christian belief that certain undesirable animals are appropriate symbols of Jews because they all share irrational, bestial natures. Negative animal comparisons abound in other contemporary polemical contexts. According to Peter the Venerable, the extreme ignorance of the Jews invites comparison to the ass, the most stupid of beasts.[89] Alan of Lille in his twelfth-century theological encyclopedia defined a number of different animals as negative figures of the Jews, including the bee, the ass, the camel, and the bull.[90] In order to claim that contemporary Jewish observance of the Law had little relation to the ancient precepts of Moses, the Dominican, Raymond Martin, in his 1267 *Capistrum Iudeorum* (The Muzzle of the Jews), combined the themes of Levitican law and bestiality in a most shockingly derisory passage.[91] Such poisonous attitudes doubtless informed popular anti-Jewish animal

---

[88] On this image, see Shachar, *Judensau*, 34–35; Mellinkoff, *Outcasts*, 1:108. On the *Judensau*, see also Jay Geller, "It's 'Alimentary': Feuerbach and the Dietetics of Antisemitism," in *Cultures of the Abdomen: Diet, Digestion, and Fat in the Modern World*, ed. Christopher E. Forth and Ana Carden-Coyne (New York, 2005), 130–33.

[89] Peter the Venerable, *Adversus Iudaeorum inveteratam duritiem*, cap. 5, ed. Yvonne Friedman, Corpus Christianorum Continuatio Medievalis 58 (Turnhout, 1985), 125.

[90] Alan of Lille, *Liber in distinctionibus dictionum theologicalium* (PL 210:685–1012). I owe thanks to Joseph Pearson for alerting me to the anti-Jewish nature of this work.

[91] The relevant passage is cited and translated in Cohen, *Living Letters*, 351–52.

motifs such as the *Judensau*, whose conception and iconographical origins may well lie in the bestiaries.

Conclusions

The reliance of the *Physiologus* on Leviticus demonstrates the early Christian desire to appropriate and to reinterpret the Old Testament by replacing its literal Jewish meanings with christological ones. The twelfth- and thirteenth-century bestiaries that referred to Leviticus continued this effort. They also exhibit a diachronic change in their approach to anti-Jewish polemic that parallels the shift observable in other contexts from viewing Jews as Christ-killers to regarding them as heretics on a par with other non-Christian enemies of the Church. Far from mollifying the earlier condemnations of Jews, however, this last habit of mind served to compound Christian perceptions of Jewish sin by implying that the Jews not only rejected and killed Christ, but also failed to follow their own laws, relying instead on their "heretical" Talmud.

The medieval bestiaries represent a brand of Christian polemic that sought to validate traditional, negative views of Judaism by citing the "evidence" present in the natural world. Towards this goal the *Physiologus* author, and later the bestiarists and other contemporary Christian exegetes, assigned anti-Jewish significance to animals mentioned in Scriptures and used this as a basis for their negative commentaries. Thirteenth-century bestiaries continue to exhibit a special concern with the image of the Jews, evidenced by the fact that the only significant changes to the texts had to do with this subject. In some cases, as in the Westminster Abbey Bestiary, the most virulent passages have been omitted, but in others the anti-Jewish theme has been expanded through the introduction of new entries, such as those dedicated to the sow and the barnacle geese in Bodley 764 and Harley 4751.

Why were these changes made? Surely the reasons must have to do with the patronage of these books, about which we have little information.[92] However, there is at least indirect evidence of a varied readership even for the small group of bestiaries examined in this essay. For

[92] On changing patronage patterns of the bestiaries, see Hassig, *Medieval Bestiaries*, 167–81.

example, a monastic readership of Laud Misc. 247, which adheres closely to the *Physiologus* text and arrangement of beast entries, is almost certain. The same is true of the Morgan Bestiary, which has a lengthy inscription indicating that it was given to the Augustinian priory of Radford (now Worksop) in 1187.[93] Although the evidence is inconclusive, the Cambridge Bestiary, which contains the anti-Jewish elephant image (see fig. 5), has been linked to the Cistercians of Lincolnshire.[94] However, it is not possible to say more about the particular contents of these three bestiaries in relation to the specific concerns of their patrons, except to note that the negative characterizations of the Jews and themes of Jewish literalism prominent in all three are consistent with contemporary monastic beliefs and interests.

I have already hypothesized that both Bodley 764 and Harley 4751 were commissioned by lay patrons, who must have approved of their updated and expanded anti-Jewish contents. It is also true that both of these books were produced during the mid-thirteenth century, when Jewish-Christian social tensions in England were running especially high. In addition to the basic sense of religious conflict, these tensions included concerns about the economic activities of Jews and the king's protection of them.[95] By contrast, a different type of patronage for the Westminster Abbey Bestiary, whose later inscription connects it to the Franciscans of York,[96] may explain its more intellectual approach, oriented around the Levitican classification scheme rather than verbal or visual polemic. It is also possible that this choice of approach was somehow related to the fact that the book was produced close to, or perhaps during, the very year of the expulsion of the Jews from England (1290).[97]

---

[93] Morgan Bestiary, fol. 1v. The inscription is translated in Xenia Muratova, "Bestiaries: An Aspect of Medieval Patronage," in *Art and Patronage in the English Romanesque*, ed. Sarah Macready and F. H. Thompson (London, 1986), 118–19.

[94] The mostly illegible sixteenth-century inscription has been interpreted as evidence of ownership by Revesby Abbey near Lincoln, and the drawing style has been connected to Cistercian patronage. See J. Morson, "The English Cistercians and the Bestiary," *Bulletin of the John Rylands Library* 39 (1956–57): 146–70.

[95] For a succinct overview of this situation, see P. Hyams, "The Jews in Medieval England, 1066–1290," in *England and Germany in the High Middle Ages*, ed. Alfred Haverkamp and Hannah Vollrath, (Oxford, 1996), 173–92.

[96] The fourteenth-century ownership inscription reads: "Iste liber est de communitate fratrum minorum Ebor" (from Westminster Abbey Bestiary, fol. 64v).

[97] On the expulsion, see especially Robin R. Mundill, *England's Jewish Solution, 1262–1290* (Cambridge, 1998); and Sophia Menache, "The King, the Church and

Questions of patronage for Harley 3244 and French 14969 are especially intriguing. Many of the images in Harley 3244 are apparently unique and exceptionally inventive, and, as already noted, several of its entries have either excised or toned-down Jewish references. But beyond assuming a high degree of patron involvement in its contents, it is impossible to say more about the patron's identity. The combination of anti-Jewish and pro-mendicant themes in French 14969 supports the hypothesis that this book was made for a Franciscan, presumably one sympathetic to Guillaume's exceptionally anti-Jewish text.[98] Given the increased emphasis on the Christian mission during this period, in which Franciscans played a major role, the subject of the conversion of the Jews addressed in several of the commentary texts and images would have been especially apt for such a reader.[99]

In the bestiaries, deployment of the Levitican concept of the unclean serves its traditional Christian purpose of contrasting the supposed carnality and literalness of Judaism with the so-called spiritual truth of Christianity.[100] Whereas early Christian polemicists interpreted the Levitican laws "spiritually" rather than "literally" by assigning them christological meanings, the *Physiologus* author and bestiarists restored the Levitican connection to the animal world, which lent added justification for interpreting all of nature as a gigantic arena for God's revelation of hidden truths, and incidentally aided the Christian appropriation of Genesis. In other Christian contexts, the theme of "cleanness," in the sense of holiness, remained important throughout the later Middle Ages, culminating in the work of the Pearl poet, who, in addition to *The Pearl*

---

the Jews: Some Considerations on the Expulsions from England and France," *Journal of Medieval History* 13 (1987): 223–36.

[98] Xenia Muratova, "Les miniatures du manuscrit fr. 14969 de la Bibliothèque Nationale de Paris (Le Bestiaire de Guillaume le Clerc) et la tradition iconographique franciscaine," *Marche romane* 28 (1978): 141–48.

[99] The conversion references in the hyena commentary image (see my fig. 3) are discussed above. See also French 14969, fols. 26r (unicorn), 34v (wild ass), and 51r (stag). Conversion is also the subject of the eagle (fols. 14r–14v) and dove (fols. 54r–55r) moral interpretations, although not of their accompanying images (fols. 13r and 54r, respectively). On mendicant missionizing, see Cohen, *The Friars and the Jews*, 33–50.

[100] For a recent discussion of this theme, Sara Lipton, "The Temple is My Body: Gender, Carnality, and Synagoga in the *Bible moralisée*," in *Imagining the Self, Imagining the Other: Visual Representation and Jewish-Christian Dynamics in the Middle Ages and Early Modern Period*, ed. Eva Frojmovic (Leiden, 2002), 129–63.

composed a text on *Cleanness*.[101] This Middle English metrical work, which survives in a single fourteenth-century manuscript, transforms four Old Testament episodes—the Flood, the Destruction of Sodom, the Destruction of Jerusalem, and Beltassar's Feast—into contemporary courtly tales with distinctly Christian interpretations. It is an intellectual achievement that owes much to the bestiarists, who developed the theme of cleanness directly from Hebrew law, thus representing an earlier stage in the process of appropriating this concept for Christian consumption. It was a process designed to distance Christians from Jews, yet it paradoxically demonstrates the foundational role of Judaism in the formation of Christian thought. It is for this reason I suggest that the bestiaries are not only monuments to anti-Judaism, they are also monuments to Judaism itself.

Finally, this brief study of the Jews in the bestiaries has highlighted two important characteristics of the imagery created for these books. The first is its multivalence, which, like the Book of Leviticus, could be read on both literal and allegorical levels. The pictorial signs point the way to ideas beyond what is literally represented, and for this reason the bestiary illustrations should no longer be considered simple narrative images or repetitive zoological portraits, although literal narrative and portraiture do constitute one level of meaning. The second characteristic of the bestiary imagery revealed here is its close relationship to its accompanying text, the precise contents of which may vary widely from manuscript to manuscript. This dependent relationship, combined with the semiotic complexity of the images, seriously calls into question their supposed mnemonic function.[102] As demonstrated above, without knowledge of the particular texts they accompany, the viewer cannot understand the semiotic richness of the images: it is only when they are viewed in relation to their anti-Jewish texts that their allegorical nature becomes clear and gains its pejorative power. However, some bestiary images do generate anti-Jewish meanings independently from their texts, sometimes even in contradiction to them, often through the incorporation of negative motifs drawn from other pictorial contexts.

---

[101] *The Owl and the Nightingale/Cleanness, St. Erkenwald*, trans. Brian Stone, 2d edn. (London, 1988).

[102] On which, see Mary Carruthers, *The Book of Memory: A Study of Memory in Medieval Culture* (Cambridge, 1990), 126–27.

It is clear that the medieval bestiary is a genre in which text and image are inextricably linked, and also one that is itself linked to other important aspects of Christian thought and intellectual history. Our understanding of the bestiaries would benefit from a reevaluation of the genre from these perspectives in subsequent art historical analyses.

CHAPTER EIGHT

CONSTRUCTING THE INIMICAL JEW IN THE *CANTIGAS DE SANTA MARIA*: THEOPHILUS'S MAGICIAN IN TEXT AND IMAGE

Pamela A. Patton

The emergence of a distinct vocabulary of anti-Jewish imagery in the medieval art of northern Europe has been richly documented and analyzed by art historians, who often present it in the context of a general deterioration in Christian attitudes toward Jews from the twelfth century onward.[1] Less attention, however, has been paid to the question of how and when this phenomenon occurred in the visual culture of medieval Christian Spain. On the surface, medieval Iberian art of the twelfth and thirteenth centuries offers few parallels to the overtly derogatory images of Jews and Judaism that emerged with such force in northern Europe during that same period. Nonetheless, it can be argued that by the later years of that span, such imagery did begin to emerge in Christian Iberia, in tandem with other social transformations.

One focal point for this phenomenon was the reign of Alfonso X, king of Castile from 1252 to 1284. Although Jewish-Christian relations under Alfonso are less well documented in general than those in neighboring Aragon,[2] a largely favorable view of Jews has been attributed to the king on the basis of what is, in fact, a *mélange* of contradictory

---

1 Beyond the pioneering work of Bernhard Blumenkranz's *Le juif médiéval au miroir de l'art chrétien* (Paris, 1966), several more recent studies have addressed visual representations of Jews, almost exclusively in northern Europe. These include Michael Camille, *The Gothic Idol: Ideology and Image-Making in Medieval Art* (Cambridge, 1989); Ruth Mellinkoff, *Outcasts: Signs of Otherness in Northern European Art of the Late Middle Ages*, 2 vols. (Berkeley, 1993); Heinz Schreckenberg, *The Jews in Christian Art: An Illustrated History* (London, 1996); Sara Lipton, *Images of Intolerance: The Representation of Jews and Judaism in the Bible Moralisée* (Berkeley, 1999); and Debra Higgs Strickland, *Saracens, Demons, and Jews: Making Monsters in Medieval Art* (Princeton, 2003).

2 For an overview of the abundant documentation for Aragon, see Yitzhak Baer, *A History of the Jews in Christian Spain, Vol. I: From the Age of Reconquest to the Fourteenth Century*, trans. Louis Schoffman, 2nd edn. (Philadelphia, 1992), 138–185; on Aragon's Jewish communities, see Yom Tov Assis, *The Golden Age of Aragonese Jewry: Community and Society in the Crown of Aragon, 1213–1327* (London, 1997).

evidence. Some of the king's recorded actions did measurably benefit Jews, although they probably were motivated not so much by idealism as by the desire to take advantage of Jewish expertise in science, philosophy and the administration of newly conquered Andalusian cities. These actions include the king's donation of mosques to Jewish communities in recently captured Seville,[3] his ongoing employment of Jews as physicians and high-ranking administrators (at times in flagrant disregard of canon law) and his engagement of Jews in many of the spectacular scholarly undertakings for which his reign is famous. Contradicting these deeds, however, are the embedded elements of anti-Judaism found in many of the king's legal and literary projects and, as will be discussed below, the persecution of Jewish communities that marked the king's final years. In most historical accounts, nonetheless, the king's positive actions toward the Jews win out.[4]

A peculiarity of past inquiry on this topic is that it has centered so magnetically around the words and actions of Alfonso himself, the extraordinary scholar-king whose political idealism and literary and scientific ambition have earned the attention and affection of so many modern scholars. To credit the bulk of Castilian social development to such a compelling figure is indeed tempting, and probably not entirely inaccurate. However, in the present essay, which considers the visual imagery that was produced to accompany Alfonso's famous collection of Marian songs, the *Cantigas de Santa Maria*, I propose to move slightly away from the person of the king, examining this imagery not, as has been done before, in terms of the Alfonso's own ideas about Jews, but as at least partially separate from them—as a reflection of the increasingly

---

[3] These may have provided a loophole in laws forbidding construction of new synagogues; see Heather Ecker, "The Conversion of Mosques to Synagogues in Seville: the Case of the Mezquita de la Judería," *Gesta* 36, no. 2 (1997): 190–207.

[4] See, e.g., Baer, *History*, 1:111–130; Américo Castro, *The Structure of Spanish History*, trans. Edmund L. King (Princeton, NJ, 1954), 474–491; David Romano, "Los judíos y Alfonso X," *Revista de Occidente* 43 (1984): 203–217; José María Monsalvo Antón, *Teoría y evolución de un conflicto social. El antisemitismo en la Corona de Castilla en la Baja Edad Media* (Madrid, 1985), esp. 207–211; Dwayne Carpenter, *Alfonso X and the Jews: An Edition and Commentary on the Siete Partidas* 7.24 (Berkeley, 1986); Joseph F. O'Callaghan, *The Learned King: The Reign of Alfonso X of Castile* (Philadelphia, 1993), 96–113; Julio Valdeón Baruque, *Judíos y conversos en la Castilla medieval* (Valladolid, 2000), 27–46; and idem, *Alfonso el Sabio: La forja de la España moderna* (Madrid, 2003), 198–207. Specific information about Jews employed at court also is found throughout Antonio Ballesteros-Beretta's classic biography, *Alfonso X el Sabio* (Madrid, 1963).

hostile view of Jews emerging in a multilayered Castilian society where ideas and experience could and did differ from the king's own.

It may seem paradoxical to turn to a court product in order to investigate the culture that lies beyond the court, but there are good reasons to do this. One is that no other Christian work of art so rich in images of Jews survives from this period in Castilian history. The illustrations of the *Cantigas de Santa Maria* stand among the first works of art from Christian Iberia in which a fully developed vocabulary of visual signifiers specifically for representing Jews can be found.[5] Another is that the chronological disjunction between the composition of many *Cantigas* texts, particularly those concerning Jews, and the production of the illustrations raises questions about the extent of Alfonso's direct involvement in developing this imagery. I wish to show that the miniatures produced for the *Cantigas de Santa Maria*, despite their courtly origins, represent less Alfonso's "official" attitude toward Jews than ideological points of intersection between the king's presumed tolerance toward Jews and the increasingly hostile outlook of the society that surrounded him.

The collection of over 400 Marian songs known as the *Cantigas de Santa Maria* was composed in Galician-Portuguese at Alfonso's court, beginning around 1260. The majority of the songs are thought to have been composed at the instigation of Alfonso himself in the 1270s, but compositions continued to be added up to at least 1284, the year of the king's death.[6] The collection intersperses narrative songs about miracles performed by the Virgin with *loores*, or songs of praise, which appear at every tenth interval. In overall conception as well in many of its plots, the work emulates earlier Marian collections initiated and disseminated throughout Europe by figures such as Gautier de Coincy

[5] For a rare additional example, see the Bible dated 1273 (London, British Library, MS. 50.003); see Blumenkranz, *Le juif*, figs. 20–21.

[6] On the chronology of the *Cantigas* texts, see esp. Evelyn S. Procter, *Alfonso of Castile, Patron of Literature and Learning* (Oxford, 1951), 34–46; Manuel Pedro Ferreira, "The Stemma of the Marian *Cantigas*: Philological and Musical Evidence," *Cantigueiros* 6 (1994): 58–98, María Victoria Chico Picaza, "Cronología de la miniatura Alfonsí: estado de la cuestión," *Anales de la Historia del Arte* 4 (1993–1994): 569–576; Joseph O'Callaghan, *Alfonso X and the Cantigas de Santa Maria: A Poetic Biography* (Leiden, 1998), 8–13; and David Wulstan, "The Compilation of the *Cantigas* of Alfonso el Sabio," in *Cobras e Son: Papers on the Text, Music, and Manuscripts of the Cantigas de Santa Maria*, ed. Stephen Parkinson (Oxford, 2000), 154–185.

(d. 1236), whose *Miracles de Nostre Dame* often is cited as a model for Alfonso's project.[7]

The *Cantigas* are preserved today in four thirteenth-century codices.[8] Two of these volumes, now divided between the Escorial (Biblioteca del Escorial, MS. T.I.1; hereafter Escorial T.I.1) and Florence (Biblioteca Nazionale, MS. Banco Rari 20; hereafter Florence B.R. 20), originally formed a deluxe, heavily illustrated compilation of the songs that was begun in the late 1270s, well after much of the texts and music had been produced, but then abandoned, only partly finished, upon Alfonso's death.[9] The Escorial codex stands essentially complete: designed to contain 200 *cantigas*, it still preserves 192, with their complete musical notation and full-page illustrations. The Florence codex, the apparent continuation of Escorial T.I.1, remains unfinished, containing only 133 of the remaining 200 songs, lacking musical notation, and with miniatures in various stages of completion.[10] Both books share the same

[7] On the earliest Marian collections, see Richard Southern, "The English Origins of the 'Miracles of the Virgin'," *Medieval and Renaissance Studies* 4 (1958): 176–216. For the thirteenth century, see Beverly Boyd, *The Middle English Miracles of the Virgin* (San Marino, CA, 1964); Evelyn Faye Wilson, *The Stella Maris of John of Garland* (Cambridge, MA, 1946); and Gautier de Coincy, *Les Miracles de Nostre Dame*, ed. V. Frederic Koenig (Geneva, 1961–1970). The standard critical edition of the *Cantigas de Santa Maria* is by Walter Mettmann, *Cantigas de Santa Maria* (Coimbra, 1959–1972); my numbering of the *cantigas* follows his conventions. See also the English translation by Kathleen Kulp-Hill, *Songs of Holy Mary of Alfonso the Wise* (Tempe, AZ, 2000). The specific affiliation with Gautier has been analyzed by many authors; it was first considered in depth by Elise Forsyth Dexter, "Sources of the Cantigas of Alfonso el Sabio" (Ph.D. Diss., Univ. of Wisconsin, 1926), and Teresa Marullo, "Osservazioni sulle Cantigas de Alfonso e sui *Miracles* de Coincy," *Archivum Romanum* 18 (1934): 495–539.

[8] Madrid, Biblioteca Nacional MS 10069 was held until 1869 in Toledo Cathedral; it contains 127 *cantigas* with skeletal musical notation and is considered to reflect the earliest redaction of the collection. The latest, Biblioteca del Escorial, MS. J.B.2., is thought to have been produced at the very end of Alfonso's life, and contains 401 songs and musical notation, with depictions of musicians; see Mettmann, *Cantigas*, 1: vii–xxiv.

[9] Most scholars date the illustrated codices toward the end of Alfonso's life: e.g. Wulstan, "The Compilation," 170–172, dates Escorial T.I.1 to 1276–78 and that of Florence B.R. 20 to 1279 at the earliest, and a similar chronology is suggested by Chico Picaza ("Cronología," 572) and Ámparo García Cuadrado, *Las Cantigas: El códice de Florencia* (Murcia, 1993), 29–31. Ferreira, "The Stemma," 72, differs in placing both books slightly later, with the Escorial codex completed in the early 1280s and the Florence volume a posthumous work.

[10] On the Escorial Codex, see esp. José Guerrero Lovillo, *Las Cántigas: Estudio arqueológico de las miniatures* (Madrid, 1949) and José Filgueira Valverde, *Alfonso X, El Sabio: Cantigas de Santa Maria* (Madrid, 1985). For the Florence codex, see García Cuadrado, *Las Cantigas*, 25–31. Both manuscripts have been published in facsimile, with commentary: Alfonso X El Sabio, *Las Cantigas de Santa Maria: Edición facsimil, El Códice Rico del*

fundamental scheme in which each *cantiga*, accompanied by musical notation, is followed by either six- or twelve-paneled illustrations of the relevant story or *loor*.

Lauded for their robust characterizations of the tales, for their vivid evocation of the everyday trappings of Castilian life, and for their visual and material richness, the *Cantigas* manuscripts offer a wellspring of evidence for those concerned with the society of Alfonso's day. In this sense, they have attracted particular interest from literary historians, whose studies naturally tend to emphasize the contributions of the texts over that of the imagery, while published studies of the miniatures as an enterprise in their own right have remained comparatively limited.[11] As a result, in most studies concerned with how the *Cantigas* reflect Alfonsine society, the imagery of the codices functions as little more than an illustrative prop for self-sufficient historical arguments, an approach which underestimates both the autonomy and the complexity of the miniatures themselves. This has hampered study of the *Cantigas* imagery exactly where it might become most meaningful. In too quickly accepting the images as passive analogues to the verbal text, we miss what the visual narrative might add in its own right—its potential to

Escorial (Manuscrito escurialense T.j.1) (Madrid, 1979) and Alfonso X El Sabio, Cantigas de Santa Maria, *I: Edición facsímil del códice B.R. 20 de la Biblioteca Nazionale Centrale de Florencia, Siglo XIII; II: El códice de Florencia de las* Cantigas *de Alfonso X el Sabio; Volúmen complementario de la edición facsímil del ms. B.R. 20 de la Biblioteca Nazionale Centrale de Florencia* (Madrid, 1989).

[11] In addition to Guerrero Lovillo, *Las Cantigas*, Ana Domínguez Rodríguez has published several articles concerned with the manuscripts' stylistic roots and iconographic sources; see esp. her "Iconografía Evangélica en las *Cantigas de Santa Maria*," in *Studies on the Cantigas de Santa Maria: Proceedings of the First International Symposium on the Cantigas de Santa Maria of Alfonso X El Sabio (1221–1284)*, ed. Israel Katz and John Esten Keller (Madison, WI, 1987), and idem, "En torno al Árbol de Jesé (siglos XI–XIII): Tres ejemplos en las *Cantigas de Santa Maria*," in *Cobras e Son*, 72–92. María Victoria Chico Picaza considers the nature of the Alfonsine scriptorium and the impact of such external forces as Byzantine narrative themes and medieval music theory; see, e.g., "Cronología," 569–576; idem, "Hagiografía en las *Cantigas de Santa Maria*: Byzantinismos y otros criterios de selección," *Anales de la Historia del Arte* 9 (1999): 35–54; and idem, "La teoría medieval de la música y la miniatura de las *Cantigas*," *Anales de la Historia del Arte* 13 (2003): 83–95. See also Ellen Kosmer and James F. Powers, "Manuscript Illustration: The *Cantigas* in their Contemporary Art Context," in *Emperor of Culture: Alfonso X the Learned and His Thirteenth-Century Renaissance*, ed. Robert I. Burns (Philadelphia, 1990), 46–71. In addition, two dissertations on the illustrated *Cantigas* were completed in 2002: Francisco Prado-Vilar, "In the Shadow of the Gothic Idol: The 'Cantigas de Santa Maria' and the Imagery of Love and Conversion" (Harvard University, 2002) and Deirdre E. Jackson, "Saint and Simulacra: Images of the Virgin in the *Cantigas de Santa Maria* of Alfonso X of Castile (1252–1284)" (University of London, 2002).

embellish, inflect or even contradict the textual one in ways that reveal meaningful contrasts between redactor and artist.[12]

Jews in the Cantigas de Santa Maria

This contrast between image and text is strong in the *cantigas* representing Jews, who play major roles in fifteen of the narratives.[13] As in other medieval Marian collections, Jewish protagonists here appear most often as inimical figures whose anti-Christian acts swiftly earn them divine retribution. For example, in Cantiga 34 of the Escorial codex (Escorial T.I.1, fol. 50r), one of the oldest tales in the Marian tradition, a Jew who throws a stolen image of the Virgin and Child into a latrine is seized and killed by demons (fig. 1). Other, more benign tales describe the Virgin's power to convert Jews, as in the local legend of Marisaltos (Escorial T.I.1, fol. 154r), a Jewess in Segovia who is thrown off a cliff for a crime, then redeemed by Mary's intervention (fig. 2). With the exception of this and a very few others, the *cantigas* concerning Jews are not invented but imported tales, already widely disseminated by European miracle collections of the preceding century. They furthermore seem to have been among the earliest included in the Alfonsine

[12] An exception is the short article by Chico Picaza, "La relación texto-imágen en las *Cantigas de Santa Maria*, de Alfonso el Sabio," *Reales Sitios* 28, no. 87 (1986): 61–72; here, the author calls for the visual narratives to be considered on an equal footing with the textual ones, although in contrast to what I shall argue, she assumes the two to have developed in close concert. Some literary scholars also have analyzed the relationship between text and imagery; see below, note 23.

[13] Those in which Jews play more than an incidental role include Cantigas 2, 3, 4, 6, 12, 25, 27, 34, 85, 89, 107, 108, 109, and 286. My parameters are more exclusive than those employed by Dwayne Carpenter in "The Portrayal of the Jew in Alfonso the Learned's *Cantigas de Santa Maria*," in *In Iberia and Beyond: Hispanic Jews Between Cultures*, ed. Bernard Dov Cooperman (Newark, 1998): 15–42; and idem, "Social Perception and Literary Portrayal: Jews and Muslims in Medieval Spanish Literature," in *Convivencia: Jews, Muslims, and Christians in Medieval Spain*, ed. Vivian Mann et al. (New York, 1992), 61–81. Also on the portrayal of Jews in the *Cantigas*, see Albert Bagby, "The Jew in the *Cantigas* of Alfonso X, el Sabio," *Speculum* 46 no. 4 (1971): 670–688; idem, "The Figure of the Jew in the *Cantigas* of Alfonso X," in *Studies on the Cantigas*, ed. Katz and Keller, 235–245, and Angus Hatton and Vikki McKay, "Anti-Semitism in the *Cantigas de Santa Maria*," *Bulletin of Hispanic Studies* 61 (1983): 189–199. O'Callaghan comments only briefly on this question in *Alfonso X and the Cantigas*, 162–165.

group, nearly all appearing in the initial compilation of one hundred songs completed at Alfonso's court in the 1260s.[14]

The visual depiction of Jews in the *Cantigas* likewise echoes foreign examples, specifically in adopting a cluster of "Jewish" visual signifiers that already had gained currency elsewhere in Europe. Male Jews, the great majority of Jewish protagonists in these stories, typically wear long hoods or pointed hats, long robes, and exotic shoes (fig. 3).[15] Their abundant black hair curls wildly, and their unruly beards, beetling brows, and huge, hooked noses, almost always seen in profile, congeal into a physiognomic stereotype reminiscent of contemporary and slightly earlier English and French representations.[16] In contrast to the apparent flexibility with which such features were employed in earlier European works such as the Parisian Moralized Bibles, Jewish physiognomies in the *Cantigas* possess a formulaic consistency that admits little interpretive ambiguity.[17]

The intrinsic power of this facial stereotype can be measured by its deployment as an indicator of its wearer's spiritual status. For example, in Cantiga 4, a widely known conversion tale (Escorial T.I.1, fol. 9v), a Jewish boy who takes communion with his Christian friends is depicted initially with an oversized, beaky nose, a miniature version of the one worn by his father, who later attempts to kill the lad by putting him in a furnace (fig. 4). In the panels following the communion scene, the boy's Jewish nose becomes instantly smaller and straighter, as if reflecting his purified condition. Unaccounted for in the text and possibly unconscious on the part of the illuminator, this miraculous rhinoplasty

---

[14] Of the *cantigas* listed in the previous note, Dexter (*passim*) identifies European sources for all except 107, 108, 109, and 286.

[15] The predominance of male Jewish villains, as well as the tendency to stereotype these figures more heavily than female Jews, is consistent with the European tendency as a whole; see, Miri Rubin, *Gentile Tales: The Narrative Assault on Late Medieval Jews* (New Haven, 1999), 71–73.

[16] See, e.g., Mellinkoff, *Outcasts*, 2: III.24 and VI.26; Strickland, *Saracens*, 77–78 and 95–155, and Peter K. Klein, "'Jud, dir kuckt der Spitzbub aus dem Gesicht!' Traditionen antisemitischer Bildstereotype oder die Physiognomie der 'Juden' als Construct," in *Abgestempelt: Judenfeindliche Postkarten*, ed. Helmut Gold et al. (Heidelberg, 1999), 43–78. On the stereotype in the *Cantigas*, see Bagby, "Jew in the *Cantigas*," 676–677 and *passim*.

[17] As also observed by Klein, "Antisemitischer Bildstereotype," 45–47. On the comparative flexibility of such features in the Moralized Bibles, see Lipton, *Images of Intolerance*, 20–21, and Annette Weber, "'...Maria die ist des juden veind': Antijudische Mariendarstellungen in der Kunst des 13.–15. Jahrhunderts," in *Maria—Tochter Sion? Mariologie, Marienfrömmigkeit und Judenfeindschaft*, ed. Johannes Heil und Rainer Kampling (Paderborn, 2001), 69–119, esp. 87.

sharply distinguishes the redeemed child from his father, who retains his own exaggerated features as the boy is rescued unharmed from the flames (the father is incinerated in his place).[18]

Other markers of Jewish identity are deployed side by side with this facial stereotype, offering their own implicit subtexts about the Jews in each narrative. In some representations, elaborate interiors with expensive furniture, or even exotic magical emblems such as six-pointed stars and swastikas (neither of which had, at this date, acquired their modern symbolic meanings)[19] mark out the Jews' distance from the Christian norm by associating them simultaneously with money and black magic, conceptions that already had extensive roots in European cultural lore.[20] In the two-page illustration to Cantiga 25 (Escorial T.I.1, fols. 38v–39r), for example, a deceptive Jewish moneylender hides his riches away beneath a luxuriantly draped bedroom decorated with two six-pointed stars (fig. 5). A more culture-specific marker is the small panel of pseudo-Arabic inscription that appears on one of the curtains, a detail doubtless inflected by the increasingly common Christian conflation of Jews with Muslims as enemies of the faith.[21]

[18] On textual and visual permutations of this story in medieval Europe, see Rubin, *Gentile Tales*, 8–27. The association of Jewish physiognomy and dress with "bad" Jews and their absence in depictions of "good" ones has been discussed by many, including Mellinkoff, *Outcasts*, vol. 1, 128–130; for an Iberian example, see Pamela A. Patton, "The Cloister as Cultural Mirror: Anti-Jewish Imagery at Santa María la Mayor in Tudela," in *Der mittelalterliche Kreuzgang: Architektur, Funktion und Programm*, ed. Peter K. Klein (Regensburg, 2003), 317–332. The first to acknowledge this tendency in the *Cantigas* was Albert Bagby ("Jew in the *Cantigas*," 683 and 687).

[19] Both the swastika and the hexagram appear in multiple contexts in the *Cantigas*: in several miniatures: for example, repeated swastikas adorn the Virgin's altar cloth in several instances, and in Cantiga 187 hexagrams decorate the shield of a Muslim warrior. On the shifting associations of the hexagram toward the end of the Middle Ages, see Marc Michael Epstein, "The Elephant and the Law: The Medieval Jewish Minority Adapts a Christian Motif," *Art Bulletin* 76 no. 3 (September 1994), 465–478, esp. 472–473.

[20] On Jews and magic, see esp. Joshua Trachtenberg, *The Devil and the Jews: The Medieval Conception of the Jew and Its Relation to Modern Anti-Semitism* (1943; repr. Philadelphia 1993), esp. 88–96, and idem, *Jewish Magic and Superstition* (New York, 1939). See also Ronnie Po-Chia Hsia, "Witchcraft, Magic, and the Jews in Late Medieval Germany," in *From Witness to Witchcraft: Jews and Judaism in Medieval Christian Thought*, ed. Jeremy Cohen (Wiesbaden, 1996), 419–433. On Jews and money, see esp. Lipton, *Images of Intolerance*, 30–53.

[21] For northern Europe, see Jeremy Cohen, "The Muslim Connection: On the Changing Role of the Jew in High Medieval Theology," in *Witness to Witchcraft*, 141–162. For Iberia, see Kenneth Scholberg, "Minorities in Medieval Castilian Literature," *Hispania* 37 (1954): 203–209.

The complexity of the visual language used to depict Jews in these narratives has been acknowledged, but by no means fully analyzed, in previous literature on the *Cantigas*, and the topic merits far more extensive study.[22] The present essay contributes to this by focusing on one aspect of the *Cantigas* miniatures that speaks revealingly of the intensity and complexity of Castilian Christian views of Jews: the frequent discrepancies between the construction of Jews in the *Cantigas* illustrations and those in the adjacent text.

It might seem natural to assume that the illuminators of the *Cantigas* depended directly upon the content of the verbal narratives, that their overriding intent was to visually replicate, as faithfully as possible, the textual narrative. That this was not always the case has been shown by John Keller and Connie Scarborough, among others, in analyzing the distinction between the "verbalization" and "visualization" of certain tales.[23] What has not yet been fully acknowledged is the gap—not just creative but also linguistic, temporal, and social—between the activity of the text's author—whether Alfonso or a collaborator—and the subsequent work of its illuminators, which took place up to fifteen years later. This gap is particularly evident in several *cantigas* concerning Jews in which image and text sometimes represent versions of the story so different from, if not actually in conflict with, one another that they require us to recognize their separate creative contexts. A signal example is Cantiga 3, which represents the story of Theophilus.

[22] In addition to the works by Carpenter, Bagby, and Hatton and McKay, cited above, publications concerning Jews in the *Cantigas* include: Mary Louise Trivison, S.N.D., "Prayer and Prejudice in the *Cantigas de Santa Maria*," *Cantigueiros* 1 no. 2 (1988): 119–127; Olga Walmisley Santiago, "Alfonso el Sabio's Attitude Toward Moors and Jews as Revealed in Two of His Works," *Cantigueiros* 6 (1994): 30–41; Deirdre E. Jackson, "Marian Antisemitism in Medieval Life and Legend: A Study Based on Alfonso X's *Cantigas de Santa Maria* (Spain)" (M.A. Thesis, Univ. of Victoria, Canada, 1997); and José L. Freire, "The *Cantigas de Santa Maria*: Social Perception and Literary Portrayal of Jews and Muslims, and Historical Reality," in *Models in Medieval Iberian Literature and Their Modern Reflections: Convivencia as a Structural, Cultural, and Sexual Ideal*, ed. Judy B. McInnis (Neward, DE, 2002), 9–38.

[23] John E. Keller, "Some Remarks on Visualization in the *Cantigas de Santa Maria*," *Ariel* (April, 1974): 7–12; idem, "Verbalization and Visualization in the *Cantigas de Santa Maria*," *Oelschläger Festschrift*, Estudios de la Hispanófila, 36 (1976): 221–226; Connie S. Scarborough, "Verbalization and Visualization in MS T.j.I of the *Cantigas de Santa Maria*" (Ph.D. Diss., Univ. of Kentucky, 1983); and idem, "Verbalization and Visualization in MS T.I.1 of the *Cantigas de Santa Maria*: The Theme of the Runaway Nun," in Katz and Keller, eds., *Studies on the Cantigas*, 135–154.

Text and Image in the Miracle of Theophilus

Like most of the *cantigas* that feature Jewish characters, Cantiga 3 has deep extra-peninsular roots. Recorded earliest in Greek in the seventh or eighth century C.E., it was translated into Latin by Paul the Deacon in the ninth century and became a fundamental component of medieval European miracle collections.[24] The tale appears in many variations, but the essential elements are these: the vicar Theophilus, having declined the position of bishop, falls into misfortune and despair. Regretting his decision, he consults a Jewish magician who assists him in making a pact with the Devil, to whom Theophilus forswears Christ and the Virgin in exchange for wealth and power. Theophilus soon realizes his error and begs forgiveness of the Virgin, who retrieves and returns the letter, annulling the pact.

In many miracle collections, the story of Theophilus is among the lengthiest tales.[25] In the *Cantigas*, however, it is told with surprising concision:

> [refrain] *Holy Mary beseeches Her Son to pardon greater sins than we in our folly commit through default and error.*
>
> This is how Holy Mary made Theophilus recover the letter which he had signed with the devil, promising to become his vassal.
>
> Through her intercession God pardoned Adam, who sinned in tasting the apple and therefore suffered great travail and went to Hell. She of Good Will so pleaded with Her Son that He brought him out again.
>
> Likewise, She caused a servant of Hers called Theophilus to be pardoned. On the advice of a Jew, he had signed a letter with the devil in order to gain power and had given the letter into the devil's keeping. The devil made him disbelieve in God and to deny her.
>
> After Theophilus committed this treason, as I learned, he served the devil for some time. Then, so I heard, he repented and sought pardon there where a sinner is wont to find it.
>
> Weeping sorely, he asked pardon where he saw the statue of the Mother of God. In all sincerity he told Her: "My sins are so great, I confess that except by your prayers, I can never be pardoned."

---

[24] The history and sources of the tale are summarized by Boyd, *Miracles*, 127–129. See also Karl Plenzat, *Die Theophiluslegenden in den Dichtungen des Mittelalters* (Berlin, 1926); and Moshe Lazar, "Theophilus: Servant of Two Masters. The Pre-Faustian Theme of Despair and Revolt," *Modern Language Notes* 87, no. 6 (Nov. 1972), 31–50. On visual depictions of the legend, see below.

[25] For example, Koenig's edition of Gautier de Coincy's Theophilus tale in *Les Miracles de Nostre Dame* (1:50–176) is 2092 lines long.

> Then Theophilus wept without ceasing until She who exceeds all other ladies in worth made the pitch-black devil bring Her the letter from the infernal fires and She returned it to Theophilus before her altar.[26]

The brevity of this text may be attributed to many things, above all the necessity of simplifying it in order to set it to music. However, it seems significant that one of the most abbreviated elements in the narrative is the character of the Jew, whose minimal role in the written tale stands in sharp contrast to the accompanying miniatures. In the verbal narrative, the Jewish magician appears only once—off-stage, as it were—as the advisor who counsels Theophilus to enter into his pact. He then disappears from the narrative, leaving the Virgin and Theophilus as the primary agents in the latter's salvation. Indeed, his role in the story as written is so incidental that the phrase, "On the advice of a Jew" could be omitted from the *cantiga* entirely without noticeably affecting the progress of the narrative.[27]

By contrast, in the illustration (Escorial T.I.1, fol. 8r) the Jew gains considerable narrative prominence, playing a central role in two of the six panels in which the story is told (fig. 6). In the first panel, the hook-nosed, thickly bearded figure offers Theophilus his advice, while a stableboy waits with the vicar's horse. His stereotyped features and hooded robe distinguish him clearly from the Christian Theophilus, with his tidy *birrete* and neatly trimmed beard. The Jew, his face and

---

[26] English translation from Kulp-Hill, *Songs of Holy Mary*, 5–6. The Galician-Portuguese below is from Mettmann, *Cantigas*, I:9–10 (with refrain in italics and line endings indicated with slash marks):

Mais nos faz Santa Maria/seu Fillo perdõar, que nós per nossa folia/ll' imos falir e errar.

Por ela nos perdoóu/Deus o pecado d'Adam/da maçãa que gostou,/por que soffréu muit' affan/e no inferno entrou;/mais a do mui bon talan/tant' a seu Filio rogou,/que o foi end' el sacar.

Pois ar fez perdon aver/a Theophilo, un seu/servo, que fora fazer/per conssello dun judeu/carta por gãar poder/cono demo, e lla deu;/e fez-ll' en Deus descreer,/des i a ela negar.

Pois Theóphilo assi/fez aquesta trayçon,/per quant' end eu aprendi,/foy do demo gran sazon;/mas depoys, segund' oy/repentíu-ss' e foy perdon/pedir logo, ben aly/u peccador sol achar.

Chorando dos ollos seus/muito, foy perdon pedir,/u vyu da Madre de Deus/a omagen; sen falir/lle diss': "Os peccados meus/son tan muitos, sen mentir/que, se non per rogos teus,/non poss' eu perdon gãar."

Theophilo dessa vez/chorou tant' e non fez al,/trões u a que de prez/todas outras donas val,/ao demo mais ca pez/negro do fog' infernal/a carta trager-lle fez,/e deu-lla ant' o altar.

[27] Hatton and McKay, "Anti-Semitism", 192, suggest that this brevity reflects what they see as the relatively tolerant attitude toward Jews in thirteenth-century Castile.

body turned toward his listener, raises both hands and points aggressively, while Theophilus's open right hand and quiescent posture suggest a receptive state. Above, the caption reads: "How Theophilus sought counsel of the Jewish sorcerer."[28] The panel and caption together thus contribute several details not accounted for in the adjacent narrative: the boy holding the horse reveals that Theophilus has traveled to see the Jew; the caption identifies the Jew as a magician; and the position and gesture of both figures set the tone for each figure's role in the drama: the Jew takes a directive stance, Theophilus a submissive one.

The second panel is even richer in narrative detail, and remarkably so, since it represents an episode barely alluded to in the text: the actual making of the pact (fig. 7). Here, the vicar kneels obediently before a towering, shaggy Devil, who sits enthroned before a tent filled with grinning demons. Theophilus proffers his clasped hands toward the Devil, preparing to place them between his new lord's own in a traditional gesture of vassalage, the *inmixtio manum*.[29] Behind Theophilus stands the Jew, who points toward his protégé with his right hand as his left opens toward the letter, already clutched in the Devil's right hand. The Jew's discursive gestures are gleefully aped by a winged demon behind him, whose enormously hooked nose asserts a visual kinship that must have spoken volumes to a medieval viewer already well-steeped in the notion of the Jews as Satan's accomplices.[30] Above, the caption reads, "How Theophilus denied Jesus Christ and Saint Mary and signed a pact with the Devil."[31]

This panel adds much to the story that is absent from the written narrative. Whereas the text reports simply that Theophilus had signed a letter and given it to the Devil, the illustration introduces new details: the elaborate setting of tent and throne, the horde of gleeful demons, and

[28] "Como Teofilo demandou consello ao judeu encantador." Translation from Kathleen Kulp-Hill, "The Captions to the Cantigas de Santa Maria," *Cantigueiros* 7 (1995): 3–64, esp. 7.

[29] Peter K. Klein, "Kunst und Feudalismus zur Zeit Alfonse des Weisen von Kastilien und León," in *Bauwerk und Bildwerk im Hochmittelalter. Anschauliche Beiträge zur Kultur- und Sozialgeschichte*, ed. Karl Clausberg et al. (Giessen, 1981), 169–212, esp. 191–192.

[30] Strickland, *Saracens*, 122–130, describes similar "physiognomic" and "associative" references to the devil in northern European representations of Jews. See also Robert Bonfil, "The Devil and the Jews in the Christian Consciousness of the Middle Ages," in *Antisemitism Through the Ages*, ed. Shmuel Almog, trans. Nathan H. Reissner (Oxford, 1988), 91–98, esp. 95.

[31] "Como Teofilo negou Iesu Christo e Santa Maria e deu en carta ao demo." Translation from Kulp-Hill, "Captions," 7.

the active participation of the Jew. Moreover, it significantly develops the Jew's dramatic role: no longer an incidental advisor, he is now the broker of the vicar's misguided compact and the most active figure in the episode. It is the Jew, not the cringing Theophilus, who addresses the Devil directly; it is he who appears to negotiate the terms of the letter; and it is he toward whom Satan directs his gaze as he considers the deal.

The Jew's role in the narrative ends, nonetheless, at this pivotal moment. In the remaining four panels of the story, the Virgin Mary succeeds to the central role, sending angels to retrieve the contract from a horned demon (panel 3), then personally returning it to the sleeping Theophilus as he lies penitent before her altar (panel 4). Her statue presides over the final two panels, in which Theophilus displays his letter to the bishop, then settles beneath the altar as the miracle is announced to the people.

The Jew's differing roles in the textual and visual narratives bear commensurately different implications. In the text, the Jew's virtual absence places Theophilus's moral error and redemption at the center of the drama; the reader/listener is invited to empathize with his despair and humble repentance; his salvation by the Virgin is compared with that of the primordial penitent, Adam. In the pictorial narrative, by contrast, the Jew takes center stage in the planning and making of the pact: his active sponsorship of the ill-fated agreement highlights his responsibility for Theophilus's downfall. The Jew's promotion from off-stage advisor to demonic intermediary lightens Theophilus's implicit moral burden, casting the vicar, in a sense, as a victim of both Jew and Devil, and thus as all the more deserving of the Virgin's aid.

While other discrepancies between text and image in this particular *cantiga* have been acknowledged previously, the differing treatments of the Jewish magician has earned surprisingly little scholarly attention.[32] How and why did this figure come to play such a powerful role in the manuscript's visual drama when he did not do so in the text? If the text itself did not serve as a source for its own illustrations, then to what outside inspiration, either visual or verbal, might the artists have

[32] Keller, "Verbalization and Visualization," 222–226; Klein, "Feudalismus," 182–195; Scarborough, "Verbalization and Visualization," 37–40; Anthony J. Cárdenas-Rotunno, "The Theophilus Legend in Prose, Poetry, and Miniatures of the *Códice Rico* of Alfonso X: Compacting with Hell and Closing the Devil's Gate," in McInnis, ed., *Models in Medieval Iberian Literature*, 39–86.

turned, and what led them to prefer these to the written texts already at hand?

The question about sources must be answered first. Although contemporaneous pictorial depictions of the Theophilus legend in medieval Iberia are quite rare, in northern Europe the tale was the most widely represented of all Marian miracle stories, appearing as both extended cycles and single images in sculpture, stained glass and manuscripts from the twelfth century onward.[33] To some extent, the format of the *Cantigas* illustration seems allied with this tradition. For example, a depiction of Theophilus's pact in the early thirteenth-century north choir lancet in the cathedral of Laon compares generally with the *Cantigas* scene. It depicts a kneeling Theophilus proffering his clasped hands in a gesture of homage while the Jew, identified by a pointed hat, places his hand on the vicar's shoulder and extends the letter toward the enthroned Devil (fig. 8).[34]

These similarities, however, are balanced by significant differences: the scene at Laon is simpler overall; neither tent nor demons appear; and the Devil reaches forward to enclose Theophilus's hands in his own. The adjacent depiction of Theophilus consulting the Jew is likewise spare, showing simply two figures standing under an arcade, without the horse, stable-boy, or abbreviated townscape seen in the manuscript. Many of these contrasts must be attributed to the difference in medium and the extensiveness of the story at Laon, where most of the eighteen roundels relate Theophilus' actions before and after the signing of the pact. What comparisons may be drawn between this cycle and the *cantiga*, then, are too generic to be attributed to more than a shared broad tradition of imagery.

Perhaps more directly influential in the creation of the *Cantigas* miniatures was the artists' exposure to other illuminated manuscripts, especially those brought to Castile as a result of the king's own collecting

---

[33] A well-known early depiction, which lacks a Jewish intermediary, is the Romanesque relief at Souillac, treated by Meyer Schapiro in "The Sculptures of Souillac," *Medieval Studies in Memory of A. Kingsley Porter* (Cambridge, MA, 1939), 2:359–387. On Theophilus imagery in general, see Alfred C. Fryer, "Theophilus the Penitent as Represented in Art," *Archaeological Journal* 92 (1935): 287–333; and Michael Cothren, "The Iconography of Theophilus Windows in the First Half of the Thirteenth Century," *Speculum* 59, no. 2 (1984): 308–341; see also Klein, "Feudalismus," 190–191; and Weber, "Antijüdische Mariendarstellungen", 74–87. On Theophilus as a penitential model in the *Cantigas*, see the essay by Deirdre E. Jackson in *The Concept of Influence and the Study of Illuminated Manuscripts*, ed. Alix Bovey and John Lowden (Turnhout, forthcoming).

[34] See Lucien Broche, *La catedrale de Laon* (Paris, 1961), 56–59.

activity. It is known, for example, that Alfonso was given an elaborately illustrated Moralized Bible by his second cousin, Louis IX of France, probably in the 1260s.[35] Given Alfonso's own enthusiasm for lavish manuscripts, it is easy to surmise that he also might have owned other French works, perhaps even an illustrated copy of Gautier de Coincy's *Miracles de Nostre Dame*.[36] Most surviving thirteenth-century manuscripts of Gautier's work, when illustrated, contain fewer and less elaborate visual narratives than the *Cantigas*.[37] However, compositional coincidences between some of their imagery and that of the Castilian codices raises the possibility that such a manuscript could have served as a source for Alfonso's artists.

An example is the pact scene in MS. 551 of the Municipal Library of Besançon. The most lavishly illustrated of surviving thirteenth-century Gautier manuscripts, this codex was produced in the late thirteenth century and thus is approximately contemporary with the Alfonsine manuscript (fig. 9).[38] Its pact scene appears within an initial T, one of twenty-six initials dedicated to Theophilus's story. It compares with that in the *Cantigas* image not only in its depiction of Theophilus's submissive position and the active role of the Jew, who again holds the letter, but also in the inclusion of a cluster of demons looking on gleefully from behind Satan's throne. The possibility that a manuscript like this one inspired at least the broad outlines of the Alfonsine miniature seems strong.[39]

Other details of the *cantiga* illustration, however, are lacking from surviving monumental and manuscript examples. These must be sought not in verbal but in textual accounts of the miracle known from two

[35] John Lowden, *The Making of the Bibles Moralisées*, 2 vols. (University Park, PA, 2000), 1:132–134.

[36] Leopoldo Augusto de Cueto, Marqués de Valmar, and Julián Ribera, *Cantigas de Santa Maria, de Don Alfonso el Sabio*, 2 vols. (Madrid, 1889), 1:101–105; also Marullo, passim.

[37] As observed by Klein, "Feudalismus," 180–181 and 204 n. 62; see also Anna Russakoff, "The Role of the Image in an Illustrated Manuscript of *Les Miracles de Notre-Dame* by Gautier de Coinci: Besançon, Bib. Mun. 551," *Manuscripta* 47/48 (2003/2004): 135–144, at 135–136.

[38] Russakoff, "Role of Image," 140.

[39] Comparison also can be made with a manuscript of the *Miracles de Nostre Dame* in St. Petersburg (National Library of Russia, MS. Fr. XIV.9). As I will show in a forthcoming study, the small multi-episodic panels prefacing each miracle in this manuscript sometimes resemble the corresponding *Cantigas* illustrations. See I.P. Mokretsova and V.I. Romanova, *Les manuscrits enluminés français du XIIIe siècles dans les collections soviètiques, 1270–1300* (Moscow, 1984), 102–147.

locally circulated Marian collections: the *Liber Mariae* by Juan Gil de Zamora (d. 1318) and the *Milagros de Nuestra Señora* by Gonzalo de Berceo (c. 1198–after 1252). Unlike the *Cantigas*, these collections were not designed for a courtly context but for clerical and popular use. As such, they provide a contrasting voice to that of the Alfonsine songs.[40]

The Franciscan Juan Gil de Zamora became affiliated with Alfonso's court circa 1278, shortly after completing his studies in Paris. His Latin prose miracle collection is thought to have been composed at about this time, albeit for a clerical audience rather than a courtly one.[41] As the product of an author nonetheless affiliated with Alfonso's court, the *Liber Mariae* does much to indicate what variants of the Theophilus tale, oral as well as written, might have been available to the king's artists as they planned and produced their work.

As a prose composition, Gil de Zamora's version of the Theophilus legend is lengthier than the *cantiga*, allowing the introduction of many details that, although absent from the *Cantigas* text, present close parallels with the Alfonsine imagery. The Jew's role extends to a long paragraph, in which the pact scene is described in some detail.[42] Theophilus seeks out the Jew at night and describes his misfortunes. The Jew then instructs the vicar to return the next night to meet his "patron" (*patronum meum*), who, he promises, will give the vicar what he desires. The following night, he leads Theophilus to the outskirts of the city, cautioning him, regardless of what he sees, not to make the sign of the cross. The Devil then appears, seated among his "ministers" (*ministri*). Addressing the Devil as "my Lord" (*Domine mi*), the Jew presents the silent Theophilus and explains his troubles. The Devil responds that he is willing to accept Theophilus as a vassal and restore his wealth and power, while the Jew continues his intermediary role:

> The subverted [*conversus*] Hebrew said to wretched Theophilus: "Did you hear what he told you?" He responded: "I heard, and whatever he said to me I will do, so long as he helps." And he kissed the feet of the

[40] The possibility that alternative texts were known to the *Cantigas* artists has been raised by Keller, "Verbalization and Visualization," 226; Scarborough, "Verbalization and Visualization," 38; Hatton and McKay, "Anti-Semitism," 190; and Klein, "Feudalismus," 190, but none has analyzed Gil de Zamora's work in this regard.

[41] Manuel de Castro y Castro, *Preconiis Hispaniae. Estudio preliminary y edición crítica* (Madrid, 1955), lviii–lxxxii.

[42] *Liber Mariae*, trac. XVI, cap. 5, mir. 14; see Fidel Fita, "Cincuenta leyendas por Juan Gil de Zamora combinadas con las *Cantigas* de Alfonso el Sabio," *Boletín de la Real Academia de la Historia* 7 (1885): 54–144 (at 59–86 for Theophilus).

> prince and bound himself to him. Then the devil told the Hebrew: "He shall deny the son of Mary and herself, who are odious to me; and he shall confirm in writing before all that he denies them, and thereafter, whatever he wishes of me will come to pass." Then Satan entered into the vicar and he answered, "I deny Christ and his mother," and signing his name, he sealed it with his own ring. And with great rejoicing they departed to perdition.[43]

This variant of the story corresponds closely with the Alfonsine miniatures, particularly in its fleshing out of the Jew's role in both the consultation and the pact scene. Just as the manuscript's imagery portrays the Jew as speaking in place of Theophilus, Gil de Zamora allots him nearly all of the direct exchange with the Devil. This text also accounts for the exuberance of the grinning "ministers" who surround the Devil as the pact is signed.

Beyond these concrete similarities, Gil de Zamora's tale expresses an active negativity toward the Jew that is absent from the Alfonsine text, yet clearly implicit in the miniatures. While the *cantiga* text scarcely mentions the Jew at all, Gil de Zamora misses few opportunities to emphasize the magician's maleficent character. He is introduced as a practitioner of diabolical arts who already has led many others to perdition, and each subsequent reference to him is preceded by unflattering adjectives: he is "execrable" (*execrabilis*), "unspeakable" (*neffandus*), "unhappy" (*infelix*), and "evil" (*maligno*). Such terms suggest apt parallels to the visual deformation of his face and figure in the *cantiga* imagery. Moreover, Gil de Zamora's use of the epithet *conversus*, apparently in reference to the Jew's own conversion to the Devil's service, adds a suggestive parallel to the "Jewish" physiognomy worn by the Devil's followers in the *cantiga* illustration.

Gil de Zamora's hostility toward the Jew is not of his invention: virtually the same phrases and epithets already appeared in Paul the

---

[43] "Conversus hebreus dixit misero Theophilo: *Audisti quid tibi dixit?* Respondit: *Audivi, et quecumque dixerit mihi faciam, tantum ut subveniat.* Et cepit osculari pedes ipsius principis et rogare eum. Tunc diabolus ad hebreum: *Abneget*, inquit, *filium Mariae et ipsam, quia odiosi sunt michi; firmetque scripto per omnia se eum eamque abnegare; et postea, quecumque volouerit a me impetrabit.* Tunc introivit in vicedominum Sathanas, et respondit, *Abnego Christum et eius genitricem;* faciensque cirographum, imposita signavit anulo proprio. Et abscesserunt com nimio perditionis gaudio." Fita, "Cincuenta leyendas", 62. I have found no entirely satisfactory English equivalent for the word *conversus* in this context; I use "subverted" to preserve the implication that the Jew has been turned to evil (whereas "converted" could have misleadingly positive implications). I thank Elizabeth Haluska-Rausch for her assistance with this translation; errors or omissions are mine alone.

Deacon's ninth-century redaction of the legend, and a similarly antipathetic tone characterizes most of the other medieval European versions of the story, including that of Gautier de Coincy.[44] It thus is much more typical of the genre than the restrained Alfonsine text, with which it must have coexisted at just the time when the *Cantigas* themselves were being illustrated. Whether Alfonso's artists were easily able to read or hear Gil de Zamora's Latin text at court cannot be known. However, they very likely would have known the vernacular variant of the same tale from the *Milagros de Nuestra Señora* by the Benedictine Gonzalo de Berceo.[45] Composed in Castilian around the middle of the century, Berceo's vernacular poems are thought to have been intended primarily for popular listeners,[46] and his robust accounts enliven all the miracles with exceptional descriptive force. This extends to his characterization of Theophilus's Jewish magician.

Berceo's "Miracle of Theophilus" is a substantial tale, comprising 263 stanzas.[47] In it he magnifies the dark character of the Jew even more dramatically than Gil de Zamora.[48] Even before encountering Theophilus, the Jew is excoriated for six full stanzas as a "false trickster" (*trufán falsso*), a "traitor" (*traïdor*), and a vassal of the Devil; he knows magic and many "bad machinations" (*maleficios*). Indeed, the Devil is the very source of his power: "People thought that he cured by knowledge:/They did not understand that Satan guided it all."[49] Berceo's account of the consultation heavily emphasizes the Jew's agency in the pact with the

---

[44] For Paul's text see Robert Pletsch, *Theophilus: Mittelniederdeutsches Drama in drei Fassungen herausgegeben* (Heidelberg, 1908), 1–10. On Gautier's anti-Judaism, see Gilbert Dahan, "Les juifs dan les *Miracles* de Gautier de Coincy," *Archives Juives* 16 (1980): 41–48, 59–68.

[45] Gonzalo de Berceo, *Miracles of Our Lady*, trans. Richard Terry Mount and Annett Grant Cash (Lexington, KY, 1997). For the Castilian, see Brian Dutton, ed., *Gonzalo de Berceo, Obras Completas. II. Los Milagros de Nuestra Señora* (London, 1971).

[46] Michael Gerli, "Poet and Pilgrim: Discourse, Language, Imagery, and Audience in Berceo's *Milagros de Nuestra Señora*," in *Hispanic Medieval Studies in Honor of Samual G. Armistead*, ed. Michael Gerli and Harvey L. Sharrer (Madison, WI, 1992), 140–151; David A. Flory, "Berceo's *Milagros* and the *Cantigas de Santa Maria*: The Question of Intended Audience," *Cantigueiros* 8 (1996): 15–28; and Annette Grant Cash, "Holy Mary Intervenes for the Clergy in the *Cantigas* of Alfonso X and in the *Milagros* of Berceo: Observations Concerning the Implicit Audience," in *Cantigueiros* 8 (1996): 3–13.

[47] Mount and Cash, *Miracles*, 129–147; Dutton, *Gonzalo de Berceo*, 211–232.

[48] See Jesús Montoya Martínez, "El Milagro de Teófilo en Coinci, Berceo y Alfonso X el Sabio," *Berceo* 87 (1974): 152–185. On Berceo's anti-Judaism, see Paul Saugnieux, *Berceo y las culturas del siglo XIII* (Logroño, 1982), 73–119.

[49] "Cuidávanse los omnes que con seso qebrava/non entendién qe todo Satanás lo guïava...." Dutton, *Gonzalo de Berceo*, 213–214.

devil. He speaks soothingly to the compliant Theophilus, who responds "like someone drugged" (*como embellinado*), and he leads the vicar by the hand to the Devil's camp, where the entire verbal negotiation occurs between the Devil and the Jew. Throughout this exchange, Theophilus remains silent; his only evident action is the writing and sealing of the letter.[50] Thus, both in its magnification of the Jew's role in the plot and in his strongly negative treatment of the figure overall, Berceo's text parallels the story depicted in the *cantiga* illustration.

Berceo's treatment of the tale, moreover, explains some visual details that cannot be traced to other sources. For example, he specifies that the magician lives in the city's Jewish quarter; this justifies the presence in the first panel of Theophilus' horse, a sign of his journey through the city.[51] Berceo also offers more details about the setting where the pact takes place, describing the waiting Devil specifically as seated before a tent (*tienda*)—the only other occurrence of this detail, textual or pictorial, of which I am aware.[52] Coincidences such as these support the conclusion that a text very much like Berceo's, if not this text itself, played a role in the conception of the Alfonsine Theophilus miniatures.

No single work of art or text mentioned here accounts for every detail of the *cantiga* illustration. Whereas some of its fundamental visual elements, such as the gesture of *inmixtio manum* and the gathering of demons, are shared with French pictorial examples that may well have been known in Castile, other details, such as the Devil's tent and the evident visual kinship between the Jew and the Devil's followers, imply familiarity either with the texts of Gil de Zamora and Berceo or with oral versions of the story that must have been very much like them.[53] The evident availability of so many potential sources, both verbal and visual, in turn implies something even more important—that in crafting their own visual narrative, the Alfonsine illuminators must have

[50] Mount and Cash, *Miracles*, 132–133; Dutton, *Gonzalo de Berceo*, 213–216.

[51] "Do morava Teófilo, en essa bispalía,/avié y un judío en essa judería...." Dutton, *Gonzalo de Berceo*, 213.

[52] "Prisolo por la mano el trufán traïdor,/levólo a la tienda do sedié el sennor;..." Dutton, *Gonzalo de Berceo*, 215. Klein likewise identifies Berceo as the source of this detail ("Feudalismus," 186).

[53] The availability of still other alternative texts is illustrated by the Castilian prose account of the story that was copied on the lower margin of the miniature shortly after its completion. See Carmen Benito-Vessels, "Las prosificaciones de las *Cantigas* como traducciones exegéticas," *La corónica* 32, no. 1 (Fall 2003): 205–30.

preferred to refer to these sources, rather than to the text their work was intended to illustrate.

Why did they do this? Here we must consider more closely the gulf that separated the production of the texts for the *Cantigas*, which began in the 1260s, from the much later creation of illustrations for the Escorial and Florence codices around 1280. This gap must have been most influential in the case of the Jewish *cantigas*, which were among the first composed.

The Production and Social Context of the Cantigas *Miniatures*

Almost nothing is known about the actual mechanics of production for Alfonso's illustrated *Cantigas*. Clearly, however, Alfonso's painters did not work at the same time, nor under the same direction, as had the composers of the original texts. By the time the Escorial and Florence codices were undertaken, most of the songs, including nearly all of those concerning Jews, already had taken final form, some as much as fifteen years earlier.[54] The artists assigned to illustrate these texts probably had little contact with the itinerant Alfonso, who traveled almost constantly between 1277 and 1284 in an effort to cope with a series of political and personal crises, including invasions by the Marinids of North Africa, a rapidly weakening economy, a succession dispute following the death of crown prince Fernando de la Cerda, the rebellion of Fernando's brother Sancho, and the king's own worsening illness.[55] Given these preoccupations, the scriptorium seems unlikely to have received much direction from the king and his immediate circle. Moreover, although the project's unknown supervisor and at least some members of the scriptorium must have been sufficiently competent in Galician-Portuguese to compose the brief captions that were added

[54] Wulstan ("The Compilation," 168) and others date the compilation of the first 100 *cantigas* to the mid-1260s, although Ferreira ("The Stemma") would place their completion c. 1270. This early redaction, as reflected in the so-called "Toledo codex" (Madrid, Biblioteca Nacional MS. 10069), included ten of the fourteen songs concerning Jews, lacking only Cantigas 85, 107, 109 and 286 (see Wulstan, "The Compilation," Table 2, pp. 160–161). Once composed, the earliest *cantigas* seem to have undergone little alteration in subsequent manuscripts.

[55] O'Callaghan, *Learned King*, 234–269.

to each miniature,[56] it should not be assumed that the main texts would have been consistently accessible to the Castilian-speaking, and not necessarily literate, painters. Especially in the illustration of tales which, like that of Theophilus, were well known from outside sources, it would not be surprising to find that the artists might have drawn their inspiration from more familiar variants of the story.

The elements that the artists selected from these variants are telling: both in overall narrative structure and in specific iconographic motifs, they present a far more hostile view of the Jewish magician than is suggested in the Alfonsine text. This visual anti-Judaism may seem inconsistent with what has been seen by many scholars as the comparatively moderate social policies of Alfonso, as well as with the restraint often found in the *Cantigas* texts.[57] Instead, its parallels with the texts of Gil de Zamora and Berceo link it with a repertoire of anti-Jewish narratives well known beyond Alfonso's court. It therefore offers valuable insight into the views of those who stood outside this rarefied sphere, and who might have been more susceptible to the rising tide of anti-Judaism that had emerged throughout Castile in the last years of Alfonso's reign.

In Castile, in the second half of the thirteenth century, expressions and acts of hostility toward Jews increased significantly within the social circles just outside Alfonso's court, especially the lesser nobility and clergy. For the nobles, this seems to have been provoked particularly by the increasing financial power accorded to Jews as the economy declined. Castilian Jews had not played a predominant role in moneylending until the mid-thirteenth century, when canon laws against Christian usury began to be enforced in earnest, drawing significant numbers of Jews into the vacuum left by former Christian lenders. The ensuing resentment of Christian debtors, already burdened by increasing taxes and devaluations of the coinage, is discernible in repeated demands at the *Cortes* of Castile that Alfonso reduce the level of interest that Jewish

[56] Since the captions correspond more closely to the imagery than to the text, and because many captions have been adjusted to fit the spaces left for them in the borders, they must have been added following the completion of the relevant miniatures. See Kulp-Hill, "Captions," 4–5. The same practice is reflected in the unfinished Florence codex, where captions are lacking even for completed imagery. This provides further evidence of the artists' autonomy as designers.

[57] As most strongly argued by Hatton and McKay, "Anti-Semitism," 189–199; but see also Carpenter, "Portrayal of the Jew," 15–42.

lenders were permitted to charge.[58] Such tensions were compounded by the king's effort, in 1275, to replenish the dwindling royal coffers by directing his Jewish tax collectors to demand all arrears on taxes owed from 1261 onward.[59] The resultant hostility sometimes found expression in direct attacks upon wealthy Jews, as when rebellious nobles attempted to claim the property of several Jewish courtiers, even kidnapping and holding at ransom the king's Jewish astronomer.[60]

Ecclesiastical antagonism toward Jews in Castile likewise increased during this period, an outgrowth of papal efforts to counter the perceived threat posed by Judaism to Christians throughout the West.[61] One symptom of this was more stringent efforts to enforce canon laws designed to restrict Jewish contact with Christians, which traditionally had been handled rather casually by Iberian rulers. Alfonso's legal code, the *Siete Partidas*, demonstrates his own awareness of such regulations, although the fact that the code was never promulgated during his lifetime opens to question how seriously he took them.[62] Another new pressure on the Jews was the introduction into Castile of the Franciscan and Dominican Orders over the course of the thirteenth century. Although these missionaries' best known activity during this period occurred in the Crown of Aragon, their Castilian impact can be traced not only in the foundation of new Franciscan and Dominican houses throughout the realm, but in their prominence both at court and in the ecclesiastical hierarchy. Alfonso's trusted courtier Juan Gil de Zamora is the best-known Franciscan of his circle, while Dominicans held the Castilian bishoprics of Seville, Badajoz, Cádiz, and Cartagena.[63] Perhaps no clearer sign of this predominance was the concurrent emergence in Castile of new polemical treatises against the Jews, written by local authors.[64]

---

[58] Alfonso acceded to this demand in 1268, dropping the original rate of 33 1/3% to 25%. See Monsalvo Antón, *Teoría y evolución*, 209; Valdeón, *Alfonso X*, 200–201, and idem, *Los judíos de Castilla y la revolución Trastámara* (Valladolid, 1968), 17–18.

[59] Joseph O'Callaghan, "The *Cortes* and Royal Taxation During the Reign of Alfonso X of Castile," *Traditio* 27 (1971): 379–398, esp. 390–391.

[60] Baer, *History*, 1:117–136.

[61] Valdeón, *Judíos y conversos*, 42–43.

[62] Carpenter, *Alfonso X and the Jews*, esp. 103–105.

[63] Valdeón, *Alfonso X*, 103–105.

[64] Such as the *Tractatus contra caecitatem iudeorum* of Bernardo Oliver; see Monsalvo Antón, *Teoría y evolución*, 216, and Valdeón, *Trastámara*, 16–17. See also Baer, *History*, 1:128–129. For an overview of missionizing in thirteenth-century Spain, heavily weighted toward Aragon, see Jeremy Cohen, *The Friars and Jews: The Evolution of Medieval*

Even Alfonso's relative leniency toward his court Jews seems to have diminished in the final years of his reign, which are marked by unprecedented harshness toward Jewish individuals and communities at large. The most notorious case is the execution of the king's chief tax collector, Zag de la Maleha (Isaac Ibn Zadok), who in September 1280 was accused of having turned over to the king's rebellious son Sancho money that he had been transporting on Alfonso's behalf. After hanging his courtier, Alfonso imprisoned his other Jewish tax collectors and then, in 1281, ordered mass Jewish arrests in an effort to extract a ransom of 4,380,000 *maravedíes*, double the normal annual tribute.[65]

Clearly, whatever tolerance Castilian Jews might have enjoyed during Alfonso's reign was in decline by the time the illuminated *Cantigas* codices were under way. This alone may go far to explain why the miniatures begun in the late 1270s so supersede the texts in their vilification of Jews. The artists' reliance on strongly anti-Jewish miracle accounts like those of Gil de Zamora and Berceo suggests a receptivity fully in keeping with the growing hostility toward Jews evident in many levels of Castilian society during these years. Whether Alfonso himself had come to be equally receptive to such views is difficult to say: the eccentric, often violent behavior of his final years, attributed by some scholars to an advancing brain tumor,[66] render his personal motivations in this period obscure. It seems safe to suggest, however, that the ambitious young ruler under whom the *Cantigas* first took verbal form would not have foreseen such visual vitriol.

Anti-Judaism (Ithaca: Cornell University, 1982), 103–169; Robert Chazan, *Barcelona and Beyond: The Disputation of 1263 and its Aftermath* (Berkeley, 1992); and the informative, if rather apologetic, treatment of the Franciscans by Jill R. Webster, *Els Menorets: The Franciscans in the Realms of Aragon from Saint Francis to the Black Death* (Toronto, 1993).

[65] On this affair, see Baer, *History*, 129–130; O'Callaghan, *Learned King*, 248–250; and Valdeón, *Alfonso X*, 201–202. Ballesteros-Beretta, *Alfonso X*, 917–920, presents a sharply contrasting interpretation of Zag de la Maleha's culpability.

[66] O'Callaghan, *Learned King*, 279–80; see also Maricel Presilla, "The Image of Death and Political Ideology in the *Cantigas de Santa Maria*," in Katz and Keller, eds., *Studies on the Cantigas*, 432–440, and Juan Delgado Roig, "Examen médico-legal de unos restos históricos: Los cadáveres de Alfonso X y Beatriz de Suabia," *Archivo Hispalense* 9 (1948):135–153.

Conclusion

The apparent independence of redactors and artists that is evident in the Theophilus tale reveals the impracticability of any attempt to explicate the *Cantigas* imagery solely in light of the king's personal ideology. More important, it throws into high relief the distinction between Alfonso's "official" view of Jews, which was at least complex enough to permit significant modern debate over its degree and character, and the more broadly rooted anti-Judaism from which the *Cantigas* imagery emerged. Liberated from modern expectations about the miniatures' dependence on the Alfonsine texts, we can better appreciate what they might reveal about the ideals and attitudes of those who lived and worked beyond Alfonso's court, populations already on the verge of dramatic social and spiritual change. If this recognition draws more sharply the social and chronological boundaries of Alfonso's vaunted "tolerance," then it also leaves us better prepared to understand the contradictory world of which he was a part.

CHAPTER NINE

IMAGES OF 'JUD SÜSS' OPPENHEIMER, AN EARLY MODERN JEW*

Vivian B. Mann

> *Portraiture and narrative are almost the only means [whereby one can preserve the fame of great men]... The History that I have undertaken is made up of these two parts: the pen and the etcher's needle are engaged in noble combat as to which will be the better at representing the objects being treated.*
>
> —François Mézeray (b. 1610)[1]

At the dawn of the early modern period in Jewish history, in the year 1738, the only Court Jew to have attained political power was executed following the sudden death of his patron, Carl Alexander, the Duke of Württemberg (r. 1733–7). Joseph Oppenheimer (1698/9–1738) had spent most of his life in relative obscurity, but during the final years of his career he was the extraordinarily wealthy and powerful Privy Financial Adviser and Cabinet Fiscal Officer to the duke.[2] This ruler's death allowed the opposition to arrest and charge Oppenheimer with various "crimes," none of which could be substantiated. Nevertheless,

* I want to express my gratitude to Ralf Busch of Hamburg whose enthusiasm for an exhibition on the Court Jews was an important factor in its realization, and to Richard I. Cohen of the Hebrew University with whom I collaborated on *From Court Jews to the Rothschilds 1600–1800. Art, Patronage, Power* (Munich and New York, 1996). I would also like to acknowledge the Institute for Advanced Study of the Hebrew University for welcoming me as a Fellow in the Spring of 1996, and my colleagues there who commented on an early version of this text.

[1] Quoted in Francis Haskell, *History and its Images: Art and the Interpretation of the Past* (New Haven and London, 1993), 72. According to Haskell, Mézeray's *History* was one of the earliest erudite histories to appear with illustrations.

[2] On Jud Süss Oppenheimer and the prints, see Barbara Gerber, *Jud Süss. Aufsteig und Fall im frühen 18. Jahrhundert. Ein Beitrag zur historischen Antisemitismus- und Rezeptionsforschung* (Hamburg, 1990), 151–269, and there the older literature; also Hellmut G. Haasis, *Beilage zu in Salomon Schächter, Relation von dem Tod des Joseph Süss seel. Gedächtnis* (1738) (Reutlingen-Betzingen, 1994).

in what one contemporary termed a "judgment in opposition to the laws of Germany and Württemberg,"[3] Oppenheimer was hung from the gallows on February 4, 1738. His biography, his arrest, trial, and execution were treated as media events in the modern sense of the term. A total of fifty-five prints informed the public about his life and fall from grace. Their production began soon after his arrest, with the earliest examples marketed at the Easter fairs held in 1737 in Frankfurt and Leipzig. The greatest number were produced in 1738, the year of the hanging, with some additional prints appearing in 1739 and later. Most were issued by presses in Stuttgart and other German cities such as Augsburg, Breslau, Esslingen, Frankfurt, Offenbach, Leipzig, Nuremberg, Regensburg and Tübingen, while additional examples appeared in foreign cities: Amsterdam, Basel, Bologna, and Prague.

The geographical spread of the prints and the magnitude of the corpus are extraordinary, and give rise to a number of questions: What attitudes toward the subject are expressed in the prints and their texts? What does the large number of compositions devoted to Jud Süss signify? Who was the audience for these prints? To understand the historical and art historical context of the large print corpus devoted to Oppenheimer is the purpose of this chapter.

Joseph Oppenheimer, born in Heidelberg in 1698/9, succeeded in emancipating himself from Jewish life as it was commonly lived in German lands during the first half of the eighteenth century. At the age of twenty-five, he became a *Hoffaktor* at the court in Mannheim; there Count Metternich dubbed him Jud Süss, a name that was used for the remainder of his life. In 1732, he met Carl Alexander of Württemberg, and became his agent. When the reigning duke of Württemberg died shortly thereafter, Jud Süss came to Stuttgart to serve the new regime. Like other Jews in similar positions, Oppenheimer financed his ruler's lifestyle, supplied his army, minted coins, procured jewelry and works of art for the court, and taxed the people.[4] The phenomenon of the Court Jew filled the need for new sources of economic power in the

[3] Selma Stern, *Der Hofjude im Zeitalter des Absolutismus. Ein Beitrag zur europäischen Geschichte im 17. und 18. Jahrhundert*, commentary, trans. and ed., Marina Sassenberg (Tübingen, 2001), 245.

[4] On the Court Jews, see Heinrich Schnee, *Die Hoffinanz und der moderne Staat. Geschichte und System der Hoffaktoren an deutschen Fürstenhöfen im Zeitalter des Absolutismus*, 6 vols. (Berlin-Munich, 1953–1967); Selma Stern, *The Court Jew: A Contribution to the History of the Period of Absolutism in Central Europe.* trans. Ralph Weiman (Philadelphia, 1980); and Jonathan I. Israel, *European Jewry in the Age of Mercantilism 1550–1750* (Oxford and New York,

duchies, principalities, and empires into which the German lands were subdivided in the seventeenth and eighteenth centuries.

Throughout the period of Oppenheimer's activities as a Court Jew, most other Jews lived marginally, eking out an existence as beggars, at a time when one-third to one-half of the general population belonged to the underclass.[5] Like many of his fellow Court Jews, however, Jud Süss had an affluent lifestyle. He amassed a substantial collection of paintings and prints, a very large wardrobe made of sumptuous materials (including 166 wigs), jewelry, furniture, and four carriages,[6] and a mansion in the capital at a time when no other Jew was allowed to live in Stuttgart. To this ostentatious lifestyle Oppenheimer added numerous Christian mistresses, which increased the animosity of his fellow courtiers and countrymen.

Of all the hundreds of Jews who served at German courts,[7] Jud Süss was the only one to achieve a position of official political power. In January 1734 he became the Cabinet Fiscal Officer and Privy Financial Adviser to the Duke of Württemberg. As Barbara Gerber has written, he was "the most significant Jewish politician prior to the Emancipation."[8] In effect, Jud Süss emancipated himself a century before the

---

1989). For an account of Jud Süss's creative service to Duke Carl Alexander and his reform of the duchy's finances, see Stern, *The Court Jew*, 115–27.

[5] Gerber, *Jud Süss*, 62 and 82–84; Otto Ulbricht, "Criminality and Punishment of the Jews in the Early Modern Period," in *In and Out of the Ghetto: Jewish-Gentile Relations in Late Medieval and Early Modern Germany*. ed. R. Po-chia Hsia and Hartmut Lehmann (Washington D.C., 1995), 65.

[6] The fine arts and other possessions of Jud Süss are detailed in inventories recorded after his arrest. The generalized nature of most of these documents, however, rarely allows a precise identification of works, an assessment of their quality, or an analysis of Oppenheimer's taste in art. An occasional entry lists both subject and artist, for example, "'Portrait of the Widowed Duchess of Württemberg' with gilt frame by von Groth," referring to an artist and inspector of galleries in Stuttgart. Much more common are brief citations such as "two Hunting Scenes" or those recording print copies of paintings, for example, "two small framed pieces after Ostade." The sum of the prints (4,256 works) suggests that Oppenheimer was dealing in art in addition to collecting for his own uses. (*Süss-Oppenheimerische Inventar-Deputation zu Stuttgart*, Stuttgart 1737–51 [Stuttgart, Württembergische Landesbibliothek, Cod. hist. 2° 1022]). This copy contains details not included in other publications; see Mann and Cohen, *From Court Jews to the Rothschilds*, cat. no. 49, there the older literature; and Selma Stern, *Jud Süss: Ein Beitrag zur deutschen und zur jüdischen Geschichte* (Munich, 1973), 288–303, for a partial listing of the inventory in modern German; and Cornelia Foerster, "Inventar der Wohnung Joseph Süss Oppenheimers... in Frankfurt, in *Siehe der Stein schreit aus der Mauer: Geschichte und Kultur der Juden in Bayern*, ed. B. Deneke (Nuremberg, 1988), 285.

[7] For a listing of Court Jews, see Schnee, *Die Hoffinanz und der moderne Staat*, passim.

[8] Gerber, *Jud Süss*, 21.

majority of German Jewry were empowered with civil rights through legislation. Like other Court Jews, he functioned outside the normal Jewish social order.[9] But his roles as financier, politician, and collector of taxes, and his association with a Catholic duke who ruled a largely Protestant duchy seriously weakened his position. Oppenheimer was an outsider as a Jew, and the Catholic ruler on whom he depended was an outsider to the population of Württemberg. Although no malfeasance in office could be proved after the duke's death, Jud Süss was condemned to hang for his "crimes."

The Print Culture of the German Lands in the Seventeenth and Eighteenth Centuries

The earliest prints to appear in the German lands were playing cards and woodcuts. By the 1490's, they were followed by *Andachtsbilder*, devotional images intended to afford their viewer access to a supernatural being, and to serve their owners as expressions of personal piety.[10] Geiler von Keysersberg, a famed preacher in fifteenth-century Strasbourg, recommended printed images to his congregants:

> If you cannot read, then take one of those paper images on which the meeting of Mary and Elizabeth is painted. You can buy one for a penny. Look at it, and think how happy they were and full of hope, and come to know that in your faith! Then show your extreme reverence for them; kiss the picture on the piece of paper, bow down before it, kneel in front of it![11]

In the course of the sixteenth century, individual prints were created on a wide variety of subjects (religious, historical, and secular), and were hung on the walls of homes and inns for decoration and instruction.[12] A major development was the addition of texts that elaborated on the representational aims of the composition. This combination within one composition of two types of information, the pictorial and the literary, is known as a broadsheet or broadside. Peter Wagner has

---

[9] Gerber, *Jud Süss*, 73.

[10] For an example see, Rainer Schoch, "A Century of Nuremberg Printmaking," in *Gothic and Renaissance Nuremberg* (New York, 1986), fig. 103.

[11] Quoted in Schoch, "Nuremberg Printmaking," 93.

[12] For examples, see Keith Moxey, *Peasants, Warriors and Wives: Popular Imagery in the Reformation* (Chicago, 1989), 51, and fig. 3.7.

termed the broadside an "iconotext," a composition whose text channels the viewer's understanding of its image to that intended by the artist, rather than leaving open the viewer's interpretation of the visual.[13] The accompanying texts reinforced the believability of the image and established a unity between the artist/publisher and his audience, both of whom shared the same visual language.[14] Sometimes, as in the case of the later Jud Süss prints, the meaning of illustrations was transformed by the accompanying texts,[15] as if the coupling of words and prints arose from a sense that images were inadequate to convey the specific message of the artist or patron.[16] The change in format to image plus text in the sixteenth century also had consequences for the audience of prints. The illiterate became dependent on those who could read for a full understanding of the composition.

The cost of prints further defined their buying public. In the sixteenth century an illustrated woodcut broadsheet, generally produced in editions of one thousand, cost between four and eight pfennig in an economy where two pfennig bought six eggs or three herrings, and a master mason (i.e. a skilled worker who supervised helpers) earned twenty-eight pfennig per day.[17] In this context the groups who could afford to buy broadsides were the upper middle class, wealthy merchants, professionals, and artisans. Still, in the seventeenth and eighteenth centuries, broadsides were the cheapest form of art.

After the Reformation and through the eighteenth century, a favorite subject of broadsheets was the topical event, one of the means by which the general population learned of new happenings. Sometimes these were extraordinary natural occurrences such as the appearance of comets or landslides, which were viewed as signs of God's anger, or abnormal births, which were interpreted as signs of spiritual corruption.[18] Another subject of German woodcuts through the first half of

[13] Peter Wagner, *Reading Iconotexts: From Swift to the French Revolution* (London, 1995), 9.

[14] Dietmar Peil, "Das Sprichwort im illustrierten Flugblatt," *Mikrokosmos* 50 (1998): 33.

[15] Wagner, *Reading Iconotexts*, 168.

[16] David Freedberg makes a similar point about Flemish prints in "Prints and the Status of Images in Flanders," in *Le Stampe e la Diffusione delle Immagine e degli Stili, Atti del XXIV Congresso Internazionale di Storia dell'Arte*, ed. Henri Zerner (Bologna, 1979), 47.

[17] Moxey, *Peasants, Warriors and Wives*, 23.

[18] For example, Jacob Sing's *Warhafftige und gründliche beschreibung/Von dem grossen Cometen... Erfurt*, and *Eine rechte warhaffte Abcontrofaktur eines wunderbarlichen Geschöpfes*, discussed in Ingeborg Lehmann-Haupt, "German Woodcut Broadsides in the Seventeenth Century," in Hellmut Lehmann-Haupt, *An Introduction to the Woodcut of the Seventeenth Century*

the eighteenth century was the "World Upside Down," whose various types expressed the inversion of the social order.[19] These works gave expression to the social contract of the German states by depicting its opposites: men ridden by women in the place of the customary male dominance, or animals riding in carriages drawn by humans. Scenes of the "World Upside Down" appealed to political dissidents who wished the overthrow of the wealthy and powerful, and to those who liked fantasy.[20]

A popular type of print depicted the ceremonial events of baroque culture: court festivities such as tournaments or fireworks, ceremonies including coronations, and life-cycle events of the ruling family.[21] Festival books were first produced in the later sixteenth century and were still popular in the nineteenth century. Representative subjects are images of tournaments and processions in honor of the ruler, for example the *Procession of the Jews of Prague on the occasion of the birth of Joseph II, 1741.*[22] Similar compositions depicting Roman imperial triumphs were first popularized during the Renaissance by Italian printmakers. By adopting their conventional composition of a densely populated procession weaving from side to side, German printmakers appropriated the values associated with Roman military victories: triumph and immortality. The festivities themselves and the prints that recorded them conveyed political messages, signaling claims to dynastic and political authority and leadership.[23] The prints were designed to impress subjects with their ruler's power, and to remind enemies of the force opposing them. Funerary prints and books commemorating the deceased were likewise examples of political propaganda.[24]

(New York, 1977), figs. 186–87. On the link to spiritual corruption, see Christiane Andersson, "Polemical Prints in Reformation Nuremberg" in *New Perspectives on the Art of Renaissance Nuremberg*, ed. Jeffrey Chipps Smith (Austin, 1985), 44.

[19] For a discussion of this genre, see Moxey, *Peasants, Warriors and Wives*, 101–26.

[20] David Kunzle, "World Upside Down: The Iconography of a European Broadsheet Type," in *The Reversible World*, ed. Barbara Babcock (Ithaca, 1978), 89.

[21] See, for example, the illustrations in Rainer Koch and Patricia Stahl, *Wahl und Krönung in Frankfurt am Main. Kaiser Karl VII 1742–1745*, 2 vols. (Frankfurt am Main, 1986).

[22] Mann and Cohen, *From Court Jews to the Rothschilds*, cat. no. 233; cf. Koch and Stahl, *Wahl und Krönung*, figs. 5.31 and 6.3.

[23] Jill Bepler, "German Funeral Books and the Genre of the Festival Description: A Parallel Development," in *The German Book 1450–1750*, ed. John L. Flood and William A. Kelly (London,1995), 146.

[24] It is estimated that there are 220,000 copies of early modern printed funerary books in German libraries and that even more were produced (Bepler, "German Funeral Books," 145.)

Disruptions of the social order like criminal activity were also a significant theme of early modern prints. Depictions of criminals, their crimes and punishments fed an appetite for sensationalism, but they also reinforced the moral order and restored the world damaged by crime. As Richard van Dülmen has written: "The nature of the punishment indicated the crime and annihilated it symbolically."[25] These prints bore the reassuring message that society was preserved through the elimination of dangerous elements. A grisly example of a criminal subject is the print by Jacob Sing titled, *News of Heinrich Rosenzweig who Murdered his Wife and Six Children in Quedlinburg on January 6, 1621.* Portraits of Jewish criminals and narrative scenes of their incarcerations and executions are part of this genre. It is estimated that, at the beginning of the eighteenth century, an unusually large proportion of Jews were robbers and bandits, while another large group lacked a regular income and worked as beggars.[26] Mause David (Johann David Wagner) and Jonas Meyer were two Jewish criminals made famous by prints depicting their evil deeds and executions.[27] Special modes of execution, such as being hung upside down together with dogs, were used for Jewish miscreants,[28] emphasizing their double-exclusion from society: first by their religion and second by their having violated societal norms.

All the events depicted on early modern broadsides, the natural, as well as the unusual and the immoral, were made credible by their publication. As Charles Talbot has written, "To put something in black and white suggests in itself a permanent statement subject to public verification,"[29] while the addition of an accompanying text in the vernacular interpreted the events with ideological overtones that reflected the beliefs, superstitions and fears of the public.[30] All of these printed

---

[25] Richard van Dülmen, *Theater of Horror: Crime and Punishment in Early Modern Germany*, trans. Elisabeth Neu (Cambridge, 1990), 4.

[26] Ulbricht, "Criminality and Punishment of the Jews," 49–50; and Gerber, *Jud Süss*, 62–63.

[27] For Jonas Meier, see Georg Liebe, *Das Judentum in der deutschen Vergangenheit* (Leipzig, 1903), fig. 86; for Mause David, see the frontispiece of *Historische Relation von dem Leben und Ubelthaten eines verstockten Diebes und Kirchen-Raubers, Johann David Wagners, sonst Mause David genannt* (Leipzig, 1721).

[28] Heinz Schreckenberg, *The Jews in Christian Art: An Illustrated History* (New York, 1996), 360.

[29] Charles Talbot, "Prints and Illustrated Books," in *From a Mighty Fortress: Prints, Drawings and Books in the Age of Luther 1483–1546*, ed. Christiane Andersson and Charles Talbot (Detroit, 1983), 175.

[30] Jean Michael Messing, "German Illustrated Broadsheets," *The Print Quarterly* 8 (1991): 84.

works would not have been effective in communicating information by pictorial and textual means, unless the artists and printers shared with their public a common artistic heritage, a common bank of symbols, and a similar way of viewing social issues. Phrased another way, the broadsides were not merely the personal expressions of their makers' artistry, but constructions embodying social meanings held in common by artists/printers and their viewers. The distribution of woodcuts, produced in large editions and sold as individual works, or as parts of books, or by printers to their colleagues in other countries, assured the widespread dissemination of their contents.

The Prints of Jud Süss: Portraits

The fifty-five extant prints of Jud Süss may be divided into three categories: portraits, narrative accounts of his life and execution, and allegorical compositions.

Only one portrait image on a broadside of Jud Süss is completely neutral (fig. 1). It was published in 1738 as the frontispiece to *Sicherer Bericht von dem Juden Joseph Süss Oppenheimer* by Elias Beck of Augsburg (1681–1747).[31] Oppenheimer is shown as a bewigged, paunchy man in three-quarter pose, with his head turned to face the viewer. He is dressed in a richly embroidered waistcoat and jacket, a mark of the high office that Jud Süss had assumed even before he was entitled to do so.[32] His clothes were similar to those of the highest officials at court, which was considered an affront to established norms.[33] Jud Süss's pose and his dignified expression also signify an exalted position in society. The similarity of this portrait to others of Oppenheimer suggests they are all based on an official portrait, like those painted for courtiers and their rulers.[34] A man of Oppenheimer's stature and interest in art

[31] Alfred Rubens published a list of thirteen compositions on the subject of Jud Süss; see his *A Jewish Iconography* (London, 1954), nos. 2164–2178; and idem, *Jewish Iconography. A Supplementary Volume* (London, 1982), no. 1957.

[32] According to the trial records, Oppenheimer spent more than 551 gulden in the last four months of 1736 on clothes from France, the center of European fashion.

[33] The dress regulations in force from the late Middle Ages until the mid-eighteenth century expressed the wearer's position in the social order. Court Jews like Jud Süss broke the system; see Gerber, *Jud Süss*, 86.

[34] I want to thank Professor Walter Cahn for this suggestion.

could be expected to commission such a work, and two are listed in the inventory compiled after his arrest.[35]

The other portraits of Jud Süss are accompanied by derogatory texts that reverse the positive impression conveyed by the likeness. The pictorial representation is neutral; the accompanying text transforms the benign sitter into a heinous criminal, a seducer of Christian women, or an enemy of the Protestant State. An example is a portrait by Matthäus Deisch of Augsburg (1718–ca. 1789; fig. 2) to which the engraver added a cartouche with gallows in the space usually occupied by a coat-of-arms. The following text replaces the customary list of titles:

> Wer grosser Herr'n Gunst misbraucht mit bösen Rath
> Wie dieser freche Jud Süss Oppenheimer that
> Wen Geitz und Übermuth auch Wollust eingenommen
> Der muss wie Haman dort zuletzt an Galgen kommen.
>
> ("The great lord who misused favor through evil advice,
> This criminal Jud Süss Oppenheimer,
> Whose spirit and arrogance appear together with debauchery.
> He must, like Haman, go to the gallows at last.")

The text inverts both the image and biblical history. The Jew, Jud Süss, is identified with the wicked Persian vizier Haman, emphasizing his role as oppressor of the Protestant people of Württemberg, who are equated with the persecuted Children of Israel in the biblical Book of Esther. Martin Luther's emphasis on the identification of Protestants with the Israelites of the Hebrew Bible provided the intellectual basis of this inversion.[36] The conceit that Jud Süss was Haman was applied to all Jews in the contemporaneous treatises on Judaism by Johann Jacob Schudt (1716) and Johann Andreas Eisenmenger (1741).[37] The important role of the text in the interpretation of the Oppenheimer portrait demands that both be viewed as a unit, an iconotext.

In this portrait, as in other examples, the setting reinforces the negative tone of the text. The shape of the frame becomes an aperture or

[35] One is described as a state portrait in a plain frame without gilding and the other is said to have been similar; Stern, *The Court Jew*, 293.

[36] Luther's 1543 translation of the complete Bible included the story of Esther for the first time and made it available to the German-reading public.

[37] Johann Jacob Schudt, *Jüdisches Ceremonial* (Nuremberg, 1716); Johann Andreas Eisenmenger, *Entdecktes Judenthum* (Frankfurt, 1741); on Eisenmenger, see Mitchell Merback's chapter in this volume.

window from whose apex hangs an iron chain.[38] The looping chain is an ironic reminder of the swags of drapery often used in portraits to convey a sense of luxurious, palatial surroundings. Its presence in the Oppenheimer portrait transforms the neutral ground of the print into a prison. This popular composition was printed as a broadsheet in Stuttgart, then reversed and used as the frontispiece for two books published in Frankfurt and Leipzig in the same year: *Curieuser Nachrichten aus dem Reich der Beschnittenen zwischen Sabathai Sevi und dem Fameusen Würtembergisch Avanturier Jud Joseph Süss Oppenheimer*, and the *Leben und Tod des Beruchtigen Juden Joseph Süss Oppenheimers*... The same images accompany pamphlets about Jud Süss that borrow from the literature on criminals.[39] In the most elaborate of these prison portraits, traditionally titled *Wer Grossen Herrn gunst missbraucht durch bösen Rath*, 1738 (fig. 3), symbols of Oppenheimer's activities as a Court Jew and of his imprisonment—a powder horn, boots, arms, sacks of money, irons, a ladder, padlocks—fill two framing panels at right and left. Two devils in the middle space taunt Jud Süss. Above are six rabbis in contemporary dress who gesticulate and comment on the image below in the manner of a Greek chorus.[40] Ancillary texts are added to the standard Haman stanza condemning the sitter. Although the framing of a portrait of a man of affairs by objects symbolizing his activities was common in the seventeenth century,[41] the portraits of Jud Süss draw on multiple artistic motifs to form an elaborate image of condemnation. This image was deconstructed on the frontispiece of a four-page pamphlet printed in Bologna, *Distinta Relazione dell'infame Vita et obbrobriosa Morte della scellerator Ebreo Gioseffo Suss nella cita' de Stutgard* (c. 1738).[42] Here

---

[38] There are four other portraits in which the chain appears. The prison setting is even more explicit in a composition whose background is articulated as the masonry of a cell; see Rubens, *Jewish Iconography*, nos. 1946–9; and Mann and Cohen, *From Court Jews to the Rothschilds*, pl. 80.

[39] Gerber, *Jud Süss*, 60.

[40] The same compositional device was used on the frontispiece of Luther's German translation of the third part of the Hebrew Bible, published in 1524. In that print, Moses and other Jews comment on a scene of the Passion; see Heimo Reinitzer, *Biblia Deutsch. Luthers Bibelübersetzung und ihre Tradition* (Wolfenbüttel, 1983), no. 81, fig. 76. The motif appeared again in early eighteenth-century books describing Jewish mores for Christian audiences. An example is the frontispiece of *Neue Franckfurter jüdischer Kleiderordnung*, published in Schudt, *Jüdisches Ceremonial*, Bk. 3, pt. 4, 74; for an illustration, see Liebe, *Das Judentum in der deutschen Vergangenheit*, fig. 88; see also Mann and Cohen, *From Court Jews to the Rothschilds*, 100.

[41] Mann and Cohen, *From Court Jews to the Rothschilds*, pl. 67.

[42] Mann and Cohen, *From Court Jews to the Rothschilds*, cat.no. 220.

the elements appear in separate frames: a neutral likeness in an oval; an enlarged image of the hanging; and the coat of arms. The same elements appear individually on the three lead medals created to commemorate the hanging.[43]

It must be emphasized that Jud Süss is always depicted naturalistically in these portraits. Neither his features, nor his body, are distorted. There are no traces of an anti-Jewish characterization, just as there are very few in portrayals of Jews throughout the eighteenth century. Rather, Oppenheimer is condemned by the accompanying texts and symbols that surround him. Comparable images are a 1654 print with a portrait of the criminal Melchior Nedeloff who was not Jewish, and the eighteenth-century engraving of the thief Jonas Meyer, who was.[44] Only the texts indicate the criminality of these subjects.

Prints of Jud Süss: Narratives

More than thirty prints of the Jud Süss corpus depict narrative subjects such as Openheimer's life, trial, imprisonment, and hanging; many include multiple scenes. The most inclusive cycle is the set of watercolors in seven mocking "Screw Medals" (*Spott-Medaillen* or *Schraubtalers*) of 1738 (fig. 4). These comic book-like narratives were encased in split medals or coins;[45] a Jud Süss *Schraubtaler* was fitted into one of the lead medals struck to commemorate his hanging.[46] It was the metal case and the subjects, rather than the art form, which gave the Süss narrative a negative slant. Each contains nineteen scenes beginning with his birth in Heidelberg and ending with his death on the gallows.[47] A few of

[43] Mann and Cohen, *From Court Jews to the Rothschilds*, cat. nos. 15–17.

[44] For Nedeloff, see Lehmann-Haupt, "German Woodcut Broadsides," fig. 185; and Alexander and Strauss, *The German Single-Leaf Woodcut*, 432; for Jonas Meier, see Liebe, *Das Judentum in der deutschen Vergangenheit*, fig. 86.

[45] The subjects of *Schraubtaler* varied from religious subjects to the lives of rulers, to contemporary fashions, to depictions of wedding guests. The form itself was neutral. See, for example, a series of religious subjects by Hans Sebald (1500–1550) in F. W. H. Hollstein, *German Engravings, Etchings, and Woodcuts, ca. 1400–1700* (Amsterdam, 1955), 2:217.

[46] For a listing of extant examples and sample illustrations, see Mann and Cohen, *From Court Jews to the Rothschilds*, cat. nos. 15–18.

[47] The number of scenes is no greater than the number of broadsheets concerning non-Jews, such as a print on the appearance of a devil in Augsburg, which includes nineteen scenes; see Lehmann-Haupt, "German Woodcut Broadsides," 242.

the roundels bear images of Oppenheimer's relationships with women, a subject also treated in independent prints. These are unusual depictions in an age when popular images of male-female relations were usually satirical, as seen in broadsheets of the topsy-turvy world. An image of Jud Süss in a garden with a beautiful woman represents the height of his achievement of courtly life. Some individual prints were devoted to related scenes of the Finance Minister and his mistresses, for example, *Iud Ioseph Süs Oppenheiemer, gewester Finanzien Rath*, a double portrait with Henrietta Luciane Fischer, the favorite who was installed in Oppenheimer's Stuttgart palace.[48] Another, entitled the *Lamentirende Frauenzimmer* (Mourning Women) shows Fischer in an oval frame above a row of Süss's principal mistresses, with throngs of other women waiting outside the door.[49] A scene of Oppenheimer in prison has him exclaiming, "*Oy vey*" to the crowd of women out of reach beyond his cell door.[50] The interest in Jud Süss's women evidenced in these prints reflects both voyeurism and the widespread revulsion that his intimate relations with Christian women inspired in Stuttgart society, in an era when intercourse between a Christian and a Jew was a capital offense.[51] Unable to convict Oppenheimer of malfeasance in office, the tribunal spent days exploring his relations with women. But the necessity of punishing the women (many of them aristocrats) as well as Süss forced the judges to abandon this avenue of conviction.

Various broadsheets depict Oppenheimer's downfall as a series of episodes: 1) Jud Süss flees after the duke's death, but is returned to Stuttgart; 2) he is judged by a tribunal; 3) in prison; 4) at a hearing; and 5) hung on the gallows. Some depictions of these subjects are very detailed, resembling other eighteenth-century prints of criminals in this regard.[52] An example is the scene of Jud Süss in prison in *Wahrhaffte und grundliche Relation*, an engraving by Elias Baeck published in 1738 by Romanus Held and Johann Baumgartner of Augsburg (fig. 5). Objects such as Jud Süss's last meal, Hebrew books, even the toilet are numbered in the illustration and explained in a label. Jud Süss is depicted

---

[48] Mann and Cohen, *From Court Jews to the Rothschilds*, cat. no. 206.

[49] For a reproduction, see Mann and Cohen, *From Court Jews to the Rothschilds*, pl. 76.

[50] Haasis, *Beilage*, 119.

[51] Haasis, *Beilage*, 91.

[52] For a comparable print, see the frontispiece to the *Historische Relation von dem Leben und Ubelthaten einer verstockten Diebes und Kirchen-Raubers, Johann David Wagners/sonst Mause David genannt*, published in Leipzig in 1722.

as thinner than in earlier portraits. According to all written records, Oppenheimer lost weight in jail due to repeated fasts and his refusal to eat non-kosher food. His eyes are darker and deeper set than earlier; he is bearded and no longer wears a courtier's wig. Like other Jewish criminals, Oppenheimer was shown being visited by Christian pastors eager to convert him. But most Jewish prisoners demanded their life in return for abjuring Judaism.[53] When this wish was not granted, they died affirming their Jewishness, as would Jud Süss. At the end of his career, then, the former Finance Minister of Württemberg was portrayed as a Jew, the perennial outsider in Christian society.

In comparison with other prints based on the lives of criminals, in which their death is but one of a series of similarly-sized scenes that appears in its correct narrative sequence, the broadsheets of Oppenheimer's execution are striking for the emphasis given to the gallows by their central placement and enlargement within the print. Some prints bear *tituli* detailing the history of the gallows, noting, for example, that they were built in 1596 and used the following year for the execution of Jorg Honauer, who had deceived Prince Friedrich by promising to turn iron into gold. The Stuttgart gallows stood thirty-five feet tall and were made of 1800 kilograms of iron. On one Oppenheimer print, bust portraits of Honauer and Jud Süss float above the multitudes gathered for Jud Suss's hanging in a composition similar to one depicting an execution following the 1614 Fettmilch riots in Frankfurt.[54] The size of the gallows, their use as a coat-of arms for Jud Süss and as a symbol of his life, reflect the effort and expense expended on the hanging and its symbolism. The Court Jew was placed in a metal bird's cage that was especially commissioned for this execution to express the magistrates' condemnation of his sexual exploits. On the gallows, he became a "bird," an image equated with the sexual act in both popular and artistic culture to symbolize his promiscuity.[55] Unable to convict Oppenheimer on his relationships with Christian women, the government of Stuttgart had its revenge by transforming his execution into a symbol

[53] Ulbricht, "Criminality and Punishment of the Jews," 54.

[54] Haasis, *Beilage*, 164–65; for the Fettmilch image, see Robert Brandt, Olaf Cunitz, Jan Ermel and Michael Graf, *Der Fettmilch-Aufstand. Bürgerunruhen and Judenfeindschaft in Frankfurt am Main 1612–1616* (Frankfurt am Main, 1996), 37.

[55] E. De Jongh, "Erotica in Vogelperspectief. De dubbelzinnigheid van een reeks 17de eeuwse genrevoorstellingen," in *19de euuwse Nederlandse Schilderkunst*, ed. P. Heck, P. Hifling, E. De Jongh (Haarlem, 1973), 22–74. I am indebted to Sharon Assaf for this reference.

of his heinous sexuality. The gallows became the primary symbol of the history of Jud Süss and was often the single image depicted on prints, as in a singular calligram.[56] As Christiane Andersson has noted, "Polemical attacks always required the simplification and vulgarization of issues and an arbitrary accentuation of certain characteristics over all others."[57]

Another striking feature of the prints depicting the final events of Jud Süss's life is the inclusion of representations of the multitudes witnessing Oppenheimer's exit from Stuttgart to his hanging outside the city. The crowd is set within a realistic cityscape (fig. 6). The presence of a mass audience recalls another genre of baroque print, the court festival, a type that also included life-cycle moments in the history of the ruler and his family. In scenes of execution the crowds remind the modern viewer that during the Middle Ages, and later, executions were a form of mass entertainment and a community ritual.[58]

Prints of Jud Süss: Allegory

Jud Süss was also shown in allegorical scenes: as the Other; on the Wheel of Fortune, a popular subject in eighteenth-century literature; in a Harrowing of Hell; and as a martyr mourned by his followers.

Despite the animosity and contempt for Jud Süss evident in his sentence and hanging, and the numerous references to him as a Jew in the printed texts, only one image depicts Oppenheimer in the guise of the Other (fig. 8). In this print he is shown as an Indian wearing conch shells, a type that appeared in early descriptions of the Americas,[59] whose tribes were interpreted as the Lost Tribes of Israel. In this

---

[56] For example, Liebe, *Das Judentum in der deutschen Vergangenheit*, fig. 70 (whereabouts unknown). Although calligrams appear in Carolingian, Arabic, Hebrew and Bohemian manuscripts, one of the first printed pre-modern use of words arranged in the shape of images appeared in a German publication dated ca. 1645, Sigmund von Birken's *Fortsetzung der Pegnitz Schaferey*, a more immediate model for the lost Jud Süss print; see Jeremy Adler, "Arcadian Semiotics: The Visual Poetry of Sigmund von Birken (1626–1681)," in Flood and Kelly, eds., *The German Book 1450–1750*, 213–32. The print of the Stuttgart gallows also includes micrographic elements.

[57] Andersson, "Polemical Prints in Reformation Nuremberg," 60.

[58] Richard J. Evans, *Rituals of Retribution: Capital Punishment in Germany* (Oxford, 1996), 3.

[59] The same figure type appears in eighteenth-century Hebrew books of blessings; for an example, Kurt Schubert, "Die Österreichischen Hofjuden und ihre Zeit," *Studia Judaica Austriaca* 12 (1991), fig. 23.

version Jud Süss's skin is singed and his hair short and curly, as if he had just returned from Hell.

The changing fortune of Jud Süss is symbolized by a globe ruled by the goddess Fortuna on a print appearing in the pseudonymous work, Arnoldo Liberio's *Volkommene Historie und Lebens Beschreibung des fameusen und berüchtigen Würtembergischen Avanturier, Jud Joseph Süss Oppenheimer*, published in Frankfurt and Leipzig in 1738 (fig. 9). Female figures and animals representing vices surround the base of the globe. Fortuna separates the rising figure of Oppenheimer from his falling counter-image. On this print, the accompanying text reinforces the image rather than contradicting it, as was the case with some portraits.[60] Another composition with the same theme relies on bust-length figures of Oppenheimer to convey the theme of changing fortune.[61] On the left side, he wears richly embroidered court dress and a wig; on the right, Jud Süss is a bound, bearded prisoner in plain clothes. The rubric describes him as "a poor Jew from Württemberg."[62] These prints of Jud Suss's world turned upside down signify the courtier's removal from his previous position in society and public disapproval of his perceived misbehavior.[63]

The most richly developed allegorical theme concerned with Jud Süss was the Harrowing of Hell. In a full-length comedy of 1738, *Das Justificierten Juden, Joseph Süss Oppenheimers Geist/In den Elisäischen Feldern*, the hero appears at the River Styx and is ferried by Charon to the underworld where he meets Jewish souls suffering in hell, among them Shabbetai Sevi (1626–1676), the false messiah, widely known in the seventeenth century even by Christians (fig. 10).[64] Oppenheimer is contrasted with the hero of the play, a lowly Christian who rises to become a lord of the realm. In another work, *Die Curieuser Nachrichten aus dem Reich der Beschnittenen*, Jud Süss again meets Shabbetai Sevi in hell.[65] Sevi listens while Oppenheimer describes the cost of his lifestyle at the Württemberg court. Both Jews are depicted naturalistically; only

---

60 Gerber, *Jud Süss*, 55.

61 Haasis, *Beilage*, 198–99.

62 Other examples of the same motif appear in the roundels of fig. 6 and in Gerber, *Jud Süss*, 6.

63 Matthias Lenz, "Schmähbriefe und Schandbilder: Realität und Visualität spätmittelalterliche Normenkonflikte," in *Bilder, Texte, Rituale: Wirklichkeitsbezug und Wirklichkeitskonstruktion politisch-rechtlicher Kommunikationsmedien in Stadt- und Adelgesellschaften des späten Mittelalters*, ed. Klaus Schreiner and Gabriela Signori (Berlin, 2000), 52.

64 Lenz, "Schmähbriefe und Schandbilder," fig. 5a–b.

65 Lenz, "Schmähbriefe und Schandbilder," 267.

the text indicates their wrongdoings, as when Jud Süss is described as vermin on the body of Württemberg. Another text on the same theme is *Merckwürdige Staats-Assemblé in Dem Reiche derer Todten... Dem Duc de Ripperda, Dem Grafen von Hoymb, Und dem Juden Süss-Oppenheimer...*[66] The three named were all statesmen who met unnatural deaths. Count von Hoymb hung himself in the fortress of Königstein during the reign of Augustus II of Poland (r. 1709–33); Johann Wilhelm Graf von Ripperda, an adventurer who served the sultan of Morocco and converted to Islam, was killed in Tetuan in 1737; while Oppenheimer was hung on the gallows. Although the title singles out Jud Süss as a Jew, and his shadow is in the outline of a monkey or ape (a symbol of bestial behavior beyond the norms of society),[67] these negative elements are offset by his inclusion in the same treatise as two Christian nobles.

The Harrowing of Hell was probably chosen as a theme because it allowed artists and writers to link Oppenheimer with infamous Jews of the past, Jews like Shabbetai Sevi who misled his followers, just as Jud Süss misled the people of Württemberg. Just as he was linked to figures of the past, Oppenheimer would be associated for many years to come with Jews accused of criminal misdeeds. In 1740 the Court Jew of Ansbach, Isaac Nathan Ischerlein, had a terrifying nightmare in prison in which he saw Jud Süss on the gallows.[68] In the *Grossen vollständing Universals-Lexikons Aller Wissensschaften und Künste*, published from 1732 to 1754, Jud Süss was given as much space as Charles V, and more words than Galileo.[69]

A striking association with Christian iconography is found in the work titled *Les Regrets du Serail du Juif Süss, Suite de la relation curieuses des choses les plus remarquable arrivées en Europe* (fig. 10). At the center of the composition is a mistress riding the Devil's pitchfork to deliver a *billet-doux* to Oppenheimer, who is encaged on the gallows, a reference to the popular belief that prostitutes are transformed into witches. From a Christian viewpoint, the hanging was a type of Purim ritual, in which the Haman of Württemberg (Jud Süss) received his due punishment. In the foreground are seven other mistresses in various grief-stricken poses. One of the mistresses, labeled no. 4, is dressed in the dark

[66] Mann and Cohen, *From Court Jews to the Rothschilds*, pl.79.

[67] On the symbolism of monkeys, Horst W. Janson, *Apes and Ape Lore in the Middle Ages and the Renaissance* (London, 1952).

[68] Liebe, *Das Judentum in der deutschen Vergangenheit*, fig. 72.

[69] Gerber, *Jud Süss*, 28.

robe and wimple worn by Mary in scenes of the Crucifixion. Similar female mourners appear in Renaissance images of the Deposition in varied poses that symbolize stages of grief. By utilizing familiar Christian iconography for the execution of a Jewish courtier, the engraver mocked the court of the Catholic Duke Wilhelm and, at the same time, transformed Oppenheimer into a Christ-like figure, albeit one dying for his own sins.

Significance of the Corpus

The depictions of Jud Süss had a widespread audience that stretched beyond the borders of Stuttgart to nine other German cities and four foreign countries. This fact, together with the number of compositions produced, indicates that the history of the former Finance Minister of Württemberg captured the imagination of the public of several countries. That public was broad-based, since not only were broadsides printed—whose audience could have included the illiterate—but so were pamphlets and books meant for educated readers.

The corpus of Jud Süss material was created and circulated by and for Christians. This fact distinguishes the Oppenheimer material from all other portrayals of Court Jews, which were commissioned by the subjects themselves, or by close followers.[70] As a result, many of the prints are based on well-known Christian iconography, but inverted. The gallows are an inversion of the cross; his adoring mistresses mock portrayals of the Holy Women at the Crucifixion and Deposition. These Christian images draw on a traditional bank of pictorial types. The basic compositions are not in themselves negative, nor do the depictions of Jud Süss encompass the distortions of physiognomy that characterize modern antisemitica. Only in their subtle alteration through the addition of accusatory texts, symbols, or settings were the types transformed into messages of public outrage.

One Jewish account of Oppenheimer's last days has been published. Known from an early Yiddish translation, the text was written in Hebrew by a relative, Solomon Schächter, in 1738 and published by Chaim ben Zvi Hirsch in Fürth.[71] Schächter confirms Christian

---

[70] See Mann and Cohen, *From Court Jews to the Rothschilds*, pl. 66.
[71] Haasis, *Beilage*, 3–11.

descriptions of Oppenheimer's fasting and his refusal to eat non- kosher food in his cell, and notes that the prisoner read various Hebrew books that were brought to him by members of the Jewish community. In his last days Jud Süss wrote a will in which he remembered his relatives. Schächter refers repeatedly to Oppenheimer as a holy man who died with correct faith, uttering the phrase "God is the only God" as he mounted each step of the gallow's ladder and the prayer *Shema Yisra'el* (Hear O Israel) in the cage at top.

What did the prints surveyed here mean to their buyers? Their interest may have prurient, captivated by accounts of a thirty-eight-year-old single man with many mistresses and many possessions, or their interest may haven been aroused by a Court Jew who vastly overstepped the bounds defining Jewish life in early eighteenth-century Germany. As the texts accompanying Jud Süss's images make clear, this Jew's rise was an anomaly and a sore on the body politic of Württemberg. He achieved too much too fast, and his downfall was as justified as that of Haman, whose latter-day equivalent he had become. The prints, which could be executed quickly in abundant numbers, were produced as Jud Süss's last days unfolded, heightening his contemporaries' reactions to the events before their eyes both in reality, and in print. At the same time, the representations were a means of framing the deeds of the Court Jew within the values of society, and excising the evil of Jud Süss from the state, as if he were a criminal.

No other Court Jew, indeed no other Jew before the modern period, was the subject of so many literary and graphic works that allow the viewer and reader to recreate his appearance and the varied stages of his career. It has been said of Jud Süss Oppenheimer and his fellow *Hoffuden* that they were the first modern Jews, attempting to straddle two worlds: the worlds of the Jew and that of the Court, the world of tradition and the world outside.[72] In various stages of Jud Süss's life and career, he achieved that synthesis and a greater position than any of his colleagues. Oppenheimer went the furthest, leaving Jewish life and the Jewish community behind for most of his brief and meteoric career. But all was overshadowed by an infamous death.

---

[72] This point appears in Mann and Cohen, *From Court Jews to the Rothschilds*, 123.

PART III

"THE HEBREW TRUTH"

CHAPTER TEN

OLD TESTAMENT HEROES IN VENETIAN HIGH RENAISSANCE ART

Paul H. D. Kaplan

On the first of June, 1509, about two weeks after the Venetian military catastrophe at Agnadello and only a few days before the troops of the Holy Roman Emperor were to occupy Padua, Venice's most prized mainland possession, the Paduan walls suddenly broke out in graffiti: a thousand repetitions of the words *Lux horta est in tenebris* (Light rises in the darkness). The phrase is David's from the 112th Psalm, a celebration of the Lord's bestowal of earthly power on the righteous, and in this context unmistakably anti-Venetian.[1] When, on June 6, the Venetian doge's troops had finally fled, one of the many pro-imperial members of the city's old ruling class wrote that the city, like Moses and his people, had thrown off Pharaoh's yoke.[2] Even those loyal to the Venetian state, like the merchant Martino Merlini, wrote a few months later that Padua (which by then had been reconquered by Venice) and the other rebellious mainland cities were still eagerly awaiting the Holy Roman Emperor as if they were the Jews and he was the Messiah.[3]

Given the anti-Judaic attitudes and acts that pervaded Christian European culture throughout the medieval and early modern periods, it may seem odd that the rebellious Paduans likened themselves to the people of David and Moses. But this identification with the Hebrews of the heroic age was widespread among Christian Italians of the early

---

[1] Psalms 112 (111): 4; Leonardo Amaseo and Gregorio Amaseo, *Diarii udinesi dall'anno 1508 al 1541 di Leonardo e Gregorio Amaseo e Giovanni Antonio Azio*, Monumenti storici pubblicati dalla R. Deputazione Veneta di storia patria, serie 3, Cronache e diarii (Venice, 1884), 2:86; discussed in Angelo Ventura, *Nobiltà e popolo nella società veneta del '400 e '500* (Bari, 1964), 177. Another version of this graffito appeared the next day: Marino Sanuto, *I diarii*, ed. Rinaldo Fulin et al., 58 vols. (Venice, 1897–1903), 8:496.

[2] Jacopo Bruto, "[C]ivitas Padue exeverat de jugo et servitute Faraonis," quoted in Andrea Gloria, *Di Padova dopo la lega stretta in Cambrai dal maggio all'ottobre 1509. Cenni storici con documenti* (Padua, 1863), 54, and also 32, 53.

[3] Giuseppe Dalla Santa, *La lega di Cambrai e gli avvenimenti dell'anno 1509 descritti da un mercante veneziano contemporaneo* (Venice, 1903), 18.

modern period. Its most famous manifestation is the attachment of the Florentines to the figure of David. From Donatello to Michelangelo, public representations of David expressed the Florentine sense of being a "chosen people" blessed with divine courage and righteousness even in the face of fearsome opponents.[4] But David was not the only biblical Jew admired in Florence. Machiavelli, for example, at the end of *The Prince*, calls for a "reborn Moses" to act as a messianic agent in the reunification of Italy.[5] A generation earlier, Pope Sixtus IV's decision to include an extensive narrative cycle dedicated to the exploits of Moses on the walls of the Sistine Chapel had already expressed a similar concept.

Less well known is the fact that the Venetians, during the period of desperate crisis accompanying the middle of the Italian wars (1494–1527), were deeply drawn to the protagonists of the Old Testament. On the eve of and especially during the War of the League of Cambrai (1509–1517), Venetian artists and patrons demonstrated an unusual and often explicitly politicized affection for David, Moses, Solomon, and Judith, among other Old Testament characters. The restive Paduans, during that brief five-week period of independence from Venetian rule, may have projected themselves verbally as the reincarnations of Moses, David and other ancient Israelites. But as the present chapter will show, it was Venetian artists such as Giorgione, Titian, Sebastiano del Piombo, Catena and Cariani, prompted above all by their private patrons, who left behind a more permanent and moving expression of homage to the heroism of the Hebrews their countrymen hoped to emulate.[6]

In a strange counterpoint to this valorizing trend in the visual arts, the fairly large community of Jews in Venice and its hinterland experienced

[4] Frederick Hartt, "Art and Freedom in Quattrocento Florence," in *Essays in Memory of Karl Lehmann*, ed. Lucy Freeman Sandler (New York, 1964), 114–131; Sarah Blake McHam, "Donatello's Bronze *David* and *Judith* as Metaphors of Medici Rule in Florence," *Art Bulletin* 83 (2001): 32–47.

[5] Niccolò Machiavelli, *Machiavelli. The Chief Works and Others*, ed. Allan Gilbert, 3 vols. (Durham, 1965), 1: 93–94.

[6] No doubt the politically motivated papal interdict imposed on Venice on April 27, 1509 raised the ideological stakes. The interdict was Pope Julius II's attempt to loosen the loyalty of Venetian subjects on the *terraferma*, especially those of the formerly papal cites of the Romagna, and had no theological motivation; but this kind of ecclesiastical challenge made the lagoon city's claim of divine favor all the more important as a means of sustaining Venetian morale. See Maurizio Bonicatti, *Aspetti dell'umanesimo nella pittura veneta dal 1455 al 1515* (Rome, 1964), 122.

a tumultuous and sometimes encouraging series of shifts in their fortunes.[7] In 1502, as a vast European alliance aimed at reversing Venice's strategic successes began to form, the legal status of the relatively few Jews living in Venice was at a nadir. While there were longstanding and even prosperous Jewish communities on the *terraferma*, since 1397 Jews had been barred from permanent residence in the lagoon city. In 1496, as a result of a xenophobia directed at those Jews recently expelled from the kingdoms of Iberia, Venetian restrictions tightened, requiring a full year's interval between permitted visits of only fifteen days at a time. In 1503, however, the Jewish moneylenders of Mestre obtained a contract which permitted them to take refuge in Venice in time of war, a measure designed to safeguard the pledges of Christian Venetian borrowers. The Venetian collapse at Agnadello in May of 1509 brought many refugees to the metropolis, among whom were hundreds of Jews. Though anti-Judaism flared up—there were rumors of Jews in the emperor's army desecrating mainland churches, and Jewish homes and businesses in Padua were sacked once the Venetians recovered the city—Jewish refugees were allowed to remain in Venice itself.[8] As the war dragged on these refugees proved useful both to the urban poor (to whom they made small loans) and to the government (who taxed them heavily); occasional initiatives to expel them did not succeed; and moneylending by Jews residing in Venice was legally endorsed in 1513.

The Venetians were never exactly welcoming. The patrician diarist Marino Sanuto was fairly typical in his pious resentment of a Jewish presence in the city. Easter week was a time of the year in which anti-Jewish sentiment always came to a head, and on Good Friday (April 6)

---

[7] Benjamin Ravid, "The Religious, Economic and Social Background and Context of the Establishment of the Ghetti of Venice," in *Gli Ebrei e Venezia secoli XIV–XVIII*, ed. Gaetano Cozzi (Milan, 1987), 211–259; and Robert Finlay, "The Foundation of the Ghetto: Venice, the Jews, and the War of the League of Cambrai," *Proceedings of the American Philosophical Society* 126 (1982): 140–154.

[8] Girolamo Priuli, *I diarii* (L. A. Muratori, *Rerum italicarum scriptores*, Raccolta degli storici italiani dal cinquecento al millecinquecento, vol. 24, parte III, fasc. 1–14, 4 vols.), ed. Roberto Cessi (Bologna, 1938–1940), 4: 253–254, claims there were 500 to 1000 Jews in the imperial army, who delighted in defecating in Christian places of worship. There is also a mass of viciously anti-Judaic material in the letter of G. M. Girardo, in the Biblioteca Nazionale Marciana, Venice, MS. Lat. XI, 142 (= 3943), fols. 38r–47r, and 46v–47r. The version of this letter copied by Sanuto (*Diarii*, 9:220) includes a passage to the effect that the other Italian powers betrayed the Italian nation (by allying against Venice) just as the Jews betrayed Christ. On the looting of the property of Paduan Jews in July of 1509, see Sanuto, *Diarii*, 8:523, 527.

of 1515 Sanuto complained that the Jews who lived in the zones near Rialto were failing to keep out of sight as they previously had during the holy season. "Now till yesterday they were going about and it is a very bad thing, and no one says anything to them, since because of the wars, one has need of them, and thus they do what they want."[9] At this very moment Franciscan preachers were also publicly attacking the Venetian Jews, and just two weeks after Sanuto's comment the Collegio, an executive committee of the Senate, took up a proposal to confine the Jews to a separate quarter so as to reduce their contamination of the Christian body politic. But the proposal failed to gather electoral support.

The following Eastertide, by contrast, witnessed the rapid passage of an ordinance which brought about the creation of the Ghetto, not the first but the most famous of all legally mandated exclusively Jewish quarters. Robert Finlay has persuasively argued that this act, which the Venetian Jews resisted, was precipitated by Venetian disappointment in the recent course of the war, and that their confinement was an attempt to secure divine favor in the conflict.[10] I would also describe it as part of a Christian attempt to replace the first "chosen people" in the Lord's affection. From April 10, 1516 onward the Venetian Jews were forced to live with a severely restricted status, but developments such as the increase of the population of the Ghetto and the construction of a synagogue by the end of the 1520s testify to the positive aspects of the situation. In the end, the Ghetto proved a remarkably stable institution, persisting through various crises until the end of the Republic. And while the Venetian Christian Francesco Sansovino, writing in 1581, less than a decade after another threat of expulsion, surely exaggerated when he stated that the Ghetto's Jews "repose[d] in most singular peace, enjoying this nation almost like a true promised land,"[11] the Ghetto did create an enduring community that forged a sustainable coexistence with Christian Venice and created a distinctive culture as well.

At the end of this chapter I will return to the events surrounding the creation of the Ghetto, and also consider a set of Jewish-Venetian images from the 1520s that embodies one aspect of this cultural

[9] Sanuto, *Diarii*, 20:98.

[10] Finlay, "Foundation of the Ghetto," 151–154.

[11] *Venetia città nobilissima*, Venice, 149r: "...riposandosi in singolarissima pace, godono questa patria quasi come vera terra di promissione."

coexistence. However, the principal goal of this chapter is to examine Venetian Christian images of Old Testament protagonists in light of Jewish experience, especially during the era of the High Renaissance. Toward this end, I will next consider the medieval and early Renaissance origins of the Venetian focus on Old Testament figures, and then move to a more extended analysis of visual representations from the 1490s to the 1520s, with special emphasis on the subjects of David, Judith and Moses.

Early Examples: Trecento and Quattrocento

As is so often the case in iconographical studies of Venetian art, our starting point must be the city's churches, especially San Marco. Its narthex contains a prominent and extensive cycle of medieval narrative mosaics dating to the thirteenth century, dedicated to the events of Genesis and Exodus.[12] These spectacular and easily legible stories provided a thorough presentation of the major themes of the first part of the Pentateuch—it is hard to think of another church which provided such a clear account of early sacred history. Although the cycle is emphatically narrative rather than typological, the viewer entering the church would proceed from the narthex, with its Old Testament focus, into the church itself, whose mosaic subjects were dominated by events from the Gospels and the life of St. Mark. For the Venetians, it must be emphasized, San Marco was not merely a sacred space: it was the state church, which, along with the adjoining ducal palace, articulated how divine supervision and preferment inevitably led to the Republic's perfection and dominance. Old Testament imagery also had an unusually strong ecclesiastical presence elsewhere in Venice, in the form of churches dedicated not to Christian saints but rather to the Hebrew patriarchs and prophets Moses, Job, Samuel, Jeremiah and Daniel. While little is known about their early figurative embellishment,

[12] Otto Demus, *The Mosaic Decoration of San Marco, Venice*, ed. Herbert Kessler (Chicago, 1988), 127–178. Sicilian or Roman narrative cycles may have had an influence at San Marco, but imagery from the Byzantine Empire itself was not a factor; on the Jews in Byzantine art (mostly in manuscript illumination), see Elisabeth Revel-Neher, *The Image of the Jew in Byzantine Art*, trans. David Maizel (Oxford, 1992).

these Venetian churches mark the city as having long had a special relationship with figures from the Old Testament.[13]

I begin with the figure of David, despite the fact that he was not the subject of special ecclesiastical veneration in Venice, nor was his story highlighted in the mosaics of San Marco. Nevertheless, the young shepherd and warrior David—as opposed to his other guises as psalmist, king and lover—later came to be a notable feature of Venetian art. In medieval art from other European regions the confrontation with Goliath was often depicted in manuscript illuminations, with a diminutive David dressed in simple rustic garments.[14] However, one of the first monumental images of David as warrior is actually to be found in Venice. This David appears in one of a set of reliefs located not in a sacred but rather in a secular context, the Grand Canal façade of the Palazzo Corner-Piscopia (now called the Palazzo Loredan, and part of Venice's city hall complex), and dated to c. 1363–1365. At the right corner of the *piano nobile* is an armored Goliath, while across the façade at the left corner is a youthful David, dressed in cloth but holding, along with his slingshot, a shield (fig. 1). These reliefs, along with several others between them representing an enthroned woman with a lion-crowned column (personifying Fortitude and apparently the city of Venice as well) and a second enthroned woman (personifying Justice), were produced to commemorate the visit of King Pierre de Lusignan of Cyprus and his knighting of Federico Corner, the palace's owner.[15] The story of David was presumably chosen to allude to Lusignan's struggle against Islamic forces in the Levant, which then occupied the lands of Goliath's people, the Philistines. But the effect in Venice was to create a public expression of a heroic David linked to images of the state itself, one which was highly visible thanks to its central location near

[13] Flaminio Corner, *Notizie storiche delle chiese e monasteri di Venezia e di Torcello* (orig. edn. Padua, 1758; repr. Sala Bolognese, 1990), 100–106, 204–205, 209–210, 249–252, 283–288.

[14] As in the famous miniature by Master Honoré in the *Breviary of Philip the Fair*, Paris, Bibliothèque Nationale, MS. lat. 1023, fol. 7v. David appears, with crown, sword, and the head of Goliath, in damaged wall-paintings from the Emmaus cloister in Prague (c. 1370); see Joseph Neuwirth, *Die Wandgemälde in Kreuzgange des Emausklosters in Prag* (Prague, 1898), 27, pl. 5.

[15] 130 cm high, Istrian stone, originally polychromed; Wolfgang Wolters, *La scultura veneziana gotica, 1300–1460*, 2 vols. (Venice, 1976), 1: 196, cat. 98; 2: figs. 282–285; Alberto Rizzi, *Scultura esterna a Venezia* (Venice, 1987), 139–140 (cat. San Marco 277).

the Rialto.[16] With this work, the warrior David became a conspicuous presence in Venice well before his debut in Florence.

In the late Trecento and early Quattrocento large sculptures of Old Testament protagonists were erected at each of the three corners of the Ducal Palace. As at San Marco, anyone approaching and entering this central building of the Venetian state had to pass through a zone dominated by renderings of early sacred history. At the corner near San Marco, for example, one finds Solomon demonstrating his famously shrewd judgment, thus serving as a model for the wisdom and justice of the Venetian state; at the other two corners, the drunken Noah and irresponsible Ham, and the transgressing Adam and Eve showed that human sin has long required the laws, courts, and punishments that the state must provide.[17] A very different use of Old Testament stories appears in a painted and carved wooden altar frontal from the church of the Corpus Domini, dating from around 1400. In this work made for Dominican nuns six Old Testament narratives (including the Gathering of Manna, Abraham and Isaac, and Daniel in the Lions' Den), serve as types for Christian manifestations of miraculous nourishment.[18] If on the Ducal Palace characters from the Jewish Bible were alternately to be emulated and used as object lessons, on the Corpus Domini frontal Old Testament events supply a template that is both emulated and surpassed by Jesus and his followers.

During the Quattrocento, even as Venetian painting prospered both in terms of quantity and quality, Old Testament subjects were apparently quite uncommon. The most notable exception to this trend was a set of eight painted narratives treating David, Moses, Abraham and Noah produced for the *sala capitolare* (members' meeting room) of the Scuola Grande di San Marco. Each image in this group of eight—begun around 1463 but destroyed by fire just as the cycle was

---

[16] In light of later developments, it is worth stressing the fact that this work, for all its patriotic sentiment, was a private commission displayed on a private patrician palace.

[17] On the *Judgment*, see Wolters, *La scultura veneziana gotica*, 1:120–122, 287–288, cat. 245; 2: pl. 813. In the historiated capital beneath the statue of Solomon there are two vignettes of Moses as lawgiver; see Staale Sinding-Larsen, *Christ in the Council Hall: Studies in the Religious Iconography of the Venetian Republic*, vol. 5 of *Acta ad archaeologiam et artium historiam pertinentia* (Rome, 1974), 167–170, pl. 11a. See also David Rosand, *Myths of Venice: The Figuration of a State* (Chapel Hill, 2001), 97–100.

[18] Paul Kaplan, "The Paliotto of the Corpus Domini: A Eucharistic Sculpture for a Venetian Nunnery," *Studies in Iconography* 26 (2005): 121–74.

nearing completion in 1485[19]—may have included more than a single narrative moment, and is to some degree reminiscent of the set of ten Old Testament bronze reliefs completed by Lorenzo Ghiberti for the east doors of the Florentine Baptistry in 1452. Alas, virtually nothing is known of what these Venetian paintings looked like, but we do know that the cycle included at least eight Old Testament subjects matched with at least two scenes from the Passion (the latter by Jacopo Bellini). Gentile Bellini was responsible for two compositions with Moses (Exodus/Crossing of the Red Sea, and Israelites in the Desert); Andrea da Murano and Bartolomeo Vivarini were to produce two compositions treating the life of Abraham; and Lazzaro Bastiani was to produce two compositions with the Life of David. Giovanni Bellini was at first (in 1470) commissioned to make the two images from the life of Noah (including the ark and the flood), but in 1483 Bartolomeo Montagna was asked to make an image of the Deluge as well as another creation scene from Genesis, apparently in lieu of the earlier Giovanni Bellini project. (A trace of Montagna's ideas for this project may survive in a drawing of the *Drunkenness of Noah* now in the Pierpont Morgan Library).[20] Collectively these images would have constituted an imposing sequence of sacred histories celebrating God's selection of Noah and then the three Hebrew leaders as his chosen instruments, and the culmination of this plan in Christ's sacrifice. There may have been a deliberate attempt to echo the Old Testament mosaics from the narthex of San Marco; at any rate, this program was not imitated by the other *scuole*. When the Scuola Grande di San Marco was rebuilt after 1485, no attempt was made to replace the Old Testament images.[21] While in Florence and in Mantua there seems to have been a significant demand by private patrons for images of Old Testament heroes and

---

[19] Patricia Fortini Brown, *Venetian Narrative Painting in the Age of Carpaccio* (New Haven, 1988), 269–270, cat. 10.

[20] N. I, 56; Lionello Puppi, *Bartolomeo Montagna* (Venice, 1962), 30, 42, 76, 149, fig. 26; Brown, *Venetian Narrative Painting*, 270.

[21] Philip Sohm, *The Scuola Grande di San Marco 1437–1550; The Architecture of a Venetian Lay Confraternity* (New York, 1982). Some idea of the lost cycle may perhaps be given by the bronze reliefs of Old Testament subjects (including Cain and Abel, Abraham and Isaac, the Selling of Joseph, the Crossing of the Red Sea, the Golden Calf, the Brazen Serpent, Jonah, Samson, David and Goliath, Judgment of Solomon, and Judith) made by Bartolomeo Bellano for the choir of the Santo in Padua around 1483–1487; Volker Krahn, *Bartolomeo Bellano* (Munich, 1988), 116–156. Artists such as Carpaccio, whose career was largely driven by confraternity commissions, apparently had no opportunity to paint Old Testament subjects.

heroines during the second half of the 1400s—Judiths by Donatello, Botticelli and Mantegna, Davids by Andrea del Castagno, Verrocchio, Ghirlandaio and Mantegna[22]—private commissions of this kind are scarce in Venice. It is true that Jacopo Bellini's sketchbooks contain a number of drawings of Judith and David, but there is no evidence that these designs were converted into finished works of art for individual patrons.[23] A small relief of Judith is part of Tullio Lombardo's huge tomb for Doge Andrea Vendramin, originally in the church of the Servi; this monument was nearly complete in 1493.[24]

The Cinquecento

With the onset of the Italian wars in 1494, the explicitly patriotic connotations of Old Testament heroes such as David took on new life in Italian culture. Though Michelangelo's *David* (begun in 1501) is the best known example of this trend, by 1495 David was already being claimed as a patriotic model in Venice. A Venetian civic celebration

---

[22] In addition to McHam, "*David* and *Judith*," see also Jaynie Anderson, *Judith* (Paris, 1997); idem, "The Head-hunter and Head-huntress in Italian Religious Portraiture," in *Vernacular Christianity. Essays in the Social Anthropology of Religion Presented to Godfrey Lienhardt*, ed. Wendy James and Douglas Johnson (Oxford, 1988), 60–69; Volker Herzner, "Die 'Judith' der Medici," *Zeitschrift für Kunstgeschichte* 43 (1980): 139–80; Doris Karl, *Il David del Verrocchio/Verrocchio's David* (Florence, 1987); Christine Sperling, "Donatello's Bronze *David* and the Demands of Medici Politics," *Burlington Magazine* 134 (1992): 218–224. For Mantegna images, see Paul Kaplan, "Isabella d'Este and Black African Women," in *Black Africans in the Renaissance*, ed. K. J. P. Lowe and T. F. Earle (Cambridge, 2005), 125–154 (multiple images of Judith); Ronald Lightbown, *Mantegna* (Berkeley, 1986), 470, cat. 141, pl. 171 (David). On Mantegna's image of Samson, see Lightbown, 449, cat. 50, fig. 139. On the Paduan artist Bellano's figurines of David and Judith with links to Mantegna and Donatello, see Susan Smith, "A Nude *Judith* from Padua and the Reception of Donatello's Bronze *David*," *Comitatus. A Journal of Medieval and Renaissance Studies* 25 (1994): 59–80; Terisio Pignatti, "La *Giuditta* diversa di Giorgione," in *Giorgione. Atti del convegno internazionale di studio per il 5° centenario della nascita, 29–31 Maggio 1978* (Castelfranco Veneto, 1979), 269–271, 270, fig. 196.

[23] Colin Eisler, *The Genius of Jacopo Bellini. The Complete Paintings and Drawings* (New York, 1989): David: pl. 145 (London, British Museum, fol. 46r), pl. 146 (London, British Museum, fol. 45r), pl. 147 (Paris, Louvre, fol. 82v) (identification as David tentative), and possibly pl. 150 (London, British Museum, fol. 61v); Judith: pl. 149 (British Museum, fol. 35r). Eisler (282, pl. 17) notes that Bellini may have drawn a second Judith in the margin of his Louvre sketchbook (fol. 77r). See also Gigetta dalli Regoli, "David trionfante: una ipotesi e un disegno poco noto," *Antologia di Belle Arti* 3, nos. 9–12 (1979): 34–42.

[24] Now SS. Giovanni e Paolo; Serena Romano, *Tullio Lombardo: il monumento al doge Andrea Vendramin* (Hermia, 2) (Venice, 1985), especially 16–19, 23, fig. 11.

of the recently assembled anti-French League on 12 April of that year included a float with enthroned figures of David and Abigail.[25] And more permanent visual representations expressing the revival of heroic Old Testament themes in the city appeared shortly after Michelangelo's Florentine project was finished in 1504. In 1505, just two years after the Mestre Jews had improved their status, Alessandro Leopardi included a personification of Venetian Justice with the attributes of the victorious Judith on one of his bronze flagpoles (commissioned by Doge Leonardo Loredan) for Piazza San Marco.[26] This composite female Venice/Justice grasps a severed head, which alludes to Judith's defeat and decapitation of Holofernes. But this insertion of an Old Testament reference into the art of the state did not establish a pattern of official civic imagery. The ensuing wave of Venetian depictions of Old Testament characters was largely generated by private patrons, most of whom were probably members of the patriciate.

Probably around 1505 (and no later than 1508), Giorgione began to emerge as the most inventive and distinguished producer of depictions of Old Testament heroes and heroines. A few art historians—most recently Augusto Gentili—have argued that Giorgione's penchant for Old Testament subjects can be accounted for by the artist's purported Jewish or crypto-Jewish identity; but there is no real evidence for that claim and, as we will see, many other Venetian artists were also attracted to such subjects in the early 1500s.[27] Two smaller works now in the Uffizi Gallery depict the *Judgment of Solomon* (fig. 2) and the much rarer subject of the *Trial of the Infant Moses* (fig. 3), in which the young Hebrew protagonist is obliged to choose a painful burning coal over an offering of gold to divert Pharaoh's suspicions that Moses will one

[25] A "caro portato da fachini sora (era vestiti da Davit propheta) et Abigail con una navicella, bellissima et di gran valor, di crestallo, piena di formento, davanti," followed by another float with symbols of Italy and Venice; Michele Jacoviello, *Venezia e Napoli nel Quattrocento. Rapporti fra i due stati e altri saggi* (Naples, 1992), document VIII (a passage from Marino Sanuto's *La spedizione di Carlo VIII in Italia*), 395–401, 396. The grain alludes to the food that Abigail generously brought to David (1 Samuel 25).

[26] David Rosand, "Venetia Figurata: The Iconography of a Myth," in *Interpretazioni veneziane. Studi di storia dell'arte in onore di Michelangelo Muraro*, ed. David Rosand (Venice, 1984), 177–196, 194, n. 11.

[27] See entry on "Giorgio da Castelfranco" in the *Dizionario Biografico degli Italiani*, (Rome, 1960-), and now "Traces of Giorgione. Jewish Culture and Astrological Science," in *Giorgione: Myth and Enigma*, ed. Sylvia Ferino Pagden and Giovanna Nepi Scirè (Vienna, 2004), 57–69. Gentili is, however, one of the few who has noticed the concentration of Old Testament subjects.

day challenge him.[28] This little-known tale, in which the hero's choice contradicts the widespread contemporary stereotype of the avaricious Jew, is not related in the Old Testament itself; it first appears in the writings of Josephus, but became familiar in Christian sources during the Middle Ages. The story does appear in the narthex mosaics of San Marco, but is uncommon in Renaissance art; and no other surviving examples pair it with Solomon's Judgment.[29]

Several elements connect the two stories—rulers setting up ingenious tests, children who escape execution—but the primary thematic link is the wise judgment of both Solomon and Moses. This suggests that the panels, too small for public display, were a private commission for a proud magistrate or a patrician office-holder, and the Gothic balcony on the large structure in the background of the *Solomon*, which resembles those on the ducal palace, points in the same direction.[30] One might note the similarities between the subject of the *Moses* and northern European "justice" pictures such as Dirc Bouts the Elder's *Judgment of Otto III* (c. 1470–75), which includes an ordeal with a red-hot iron; however, Bouts's diptych is much larger and was made for a public judicial setting in Louvain.

The dress worn by the protagonists and observers in the *Moses* and *Solomon* panels ranges from ancient robes to contemporary Venetian and Levantine (Ottoman and Greek) fashion. The Levantine clothing, when combined with long beards, might have suggested a Jewish identity for some figures, but it is in fact hard to ascertain exactly what Italians believed to be typically Jewish appearance or dress in this era. Jews in Italy generally strove to be unremarkable in dress, because clear identification as being Jewish exposed them to violence and insult. Indeed, the laws requiring badges of infamy would have been unnecessary had Jews willingly worn distinctive clothing. In 1496 Venetian law specified that Jews staying in Venice were to wear yellow hats rather than the yellow circular insignia on robes that had previously been required; the

[28] Both works measure 89 × 72 cm; estimated dates vary from before 1504 to 1507; see Terisio Pignatti, *Giorgione* (New York, 1971), 98–99, cat. 8, and Jaynie Anderson, *Giorgione: The Painter of 'Poetic Brevity'* (Paris, 1997), 291.

[29] Demus, *Mosaic Decoration of San Marco*, 151, 158, 175, fig. 85, pl. 61A; Louis Réau, *Iconographie de l'art chrétien* (Paris, 1956), 2, part 1:182–183. A rather weak claim that Giorgione must have known Jewish sources concerning the tale is made by Dalia Haitovsky, "Giorgione's *Trial of Moses*, a New Look," *Jewish Art* 16–17 (1990–1991): 20–29.

[30] Anderson, *Giorgione*, 291.

yellow hat rule was confirmed and made more rigorous in 1517, after the foundation of the Ghetto.[31] In the *Solomon* and *Moses* panels, the only figure with a yellow hat is—ironically—Pharaoh. Neither here nor elsewhere in the images I am discussing are there unmistakable markers in dress of contemporary Jewish identity. It is generally uncommon in this era for an Italian depiction of any Hebrew protagonist from the Old Testament to exhibit legally mandated Jewish insignia, though Michelangelo did include a ring-like circle of yellow fabric (a common form of such insignia) on the figure of Aminadab, one of the ancestors of Christ in the lunettes of the Sistine Chapel (finished 1512).[32]

Solomon's Judgment is also the subject of a much larger work usually dated to about 1506–1509, once regarded as a work by Giorgione but now (according to most scholars) as largely or entirely the work of Sebastiano del Piombo.[33] Here the royal court is presented by means of partly classicized and partly modern dress and setting. It is tempting to see this vast canvas (208 × 315 cm) as intended for some public space, and several of the very few surviving documents attesting to the work of Giorgione concern a canvas executed in 1507–1508 for one of the rooms of the Council of Ten, a powerful state committee with judicial powers.[34] However, the radically unfinished state of the work (the infants at the center of the dispute are lacking) proves that it cannot have been the picture made for the Council of Ten, and if it was commissioned for display in some other state office, it can never

[31] David Jacoby, "Les juifs à Venise du XIVe au milieu du XVIe siècle," in *Venezia centro di mediazione tra Oriente e Occidente (secoli xv–xvi): aspetti e problemi*, ed. Hans-Georg Beck, Manoussos Manoussacas, Agostino Pertusi, 2 vols. (Florence, 1977), 1:163–216, 175–177; Ariel Toaff, "The Jewish Badge in Italy during the Fifteenth Century," in *Die Juden in ihrer mittelalterlichen Umwelt*, ed. Alfred Ebenbauer and Klaus Zatloukal (Vienna, 1991), 275–280, 277–278.

[32] Barbara Wisch, "Vested Interest: Redressing Jews on Michelangelo's Sistine Ceiling," *Artibus et Historiae* 48 (2003): 143–172, who points out (157, 159, fig. 14) that the artist's sources for this motif include a woodcut from a Venetian bible of the early 1490s of Jews being warned by the prophet Malachi; for a pictorial instance of the badge on specific contemporary Italian Jews, see Dana Katz, "Painting and the Politics of Persecution: Representing the Jew in Fifteenth-Century Mantua," *Art History* 23 (2000): 475–495, fig. 3.

[33] Kingston Lacy, National Trust; see entry by Michael Hirst in *The Genius of Venice, 1500–1600* ed. Jane Martineau and Charles Hope (London, 1983), 210–211, cat. 97; Keith Laing and Michael Hirst, "The Kingston Lacy *Judgment of Solomon*," *Burlington Magazine* 128 (1986): 273–282; *Le siècle de Titien* (Paris, 1993), 348, cat. 33.

[34] Archivio di Stato di Venezia, Provveditori al Sal, Notatorio, b. 60 (formerly n. 3), fs. 114v (14 Aug. 1507), 119r (24 Jan. 1508), 121r (23 May 1508); reprinted in Anderson, *Giorgione*, 363.

have been installed. The earliest surviving notice of the Kingston Lacy work is in the 1648 writings of Carlo Ridolfi, who saw it in the Palazzo Vendramin-Calerghi, the great Grand Canal residence built just after 1500 by the powerful patrician Andrea Loredan.[35] Loredan is said to have employed Giorgione and Titian, and he apparently owned a large canvas of the *Flight into Egypt* by Titian. While Loredan, who held many important offices, may have acquired a state commission that remained unfinished, it is just as likely that he ordered the *Solomon* privately. The details of dress are mostly incomplete in this painting, but it is clear that the artist did not use dress, Levantine or otherwise, to suggest any link between Solomon and his court and contemporary Jews.

Solomon may have been an appealing role model for members of the Venetian elite, especially when those elites felt themselves to be in relatively confident control of their political destiny. The two examples we have been examining probably date to before Venice's first major military crisis during the Italian wars in 1509. During the War of the League of Cambrai, from 1509 to 1517, Solomon seems to have been less attractive a character, though in the more stable 1520s and 1530s at least three images of the *Judgment* were deployed in public venues within the Venetian Republic, including a new mosaic of the story in the narthex of San Marco (1538).[36] Just before and during the Cambrai wars, however, Venetian artists and patrons were more drawn to Old Testament figures like Judith, David, and the Moses of the Red Sea drama, underdogs who bravely challenged the oppression of their people by powerful foreign enemies.

The courageous widow Judith's beheading of the Assyrian general Holofernes, alluded to in the Venice/Justice personification on Alessandro Leopardi's 1505 flagpole in Piazza San Marco, appears more explicitly in Giorgione's famous painting of c. 1507, acquired by another shrewd and ruthless widow, Catherine the Great of Russia, and now in the Hermitage (fig. 4).[37] The heroine's discreet but slightly kinky sensuality has blinded some critics to the artist's forceful evocation of female

[35] For Ridolfi, see Pignatti, *Giorgione*, 178; on Andrea Loredan, see Massimo Gemin and Filippo Pedrocco, *Ca' Vendramin Calergi* (Venice, 1990), 29–30.

[36] On this work, Titian's lost image for the Palazzo della Curia in Vicenza (c. 1521), a Bonifazio de' Pitati picture for the Magistrato del Sale at Rialto (1533, now Accademia), and also a lost work by Palma Vecchio whose patronage is not known, see Michael Hirst, *Sebastiano del Piombo* (Oxford, 1981), 18.

[37] 144 × 67 cm, panel now transferred to canvas; Anderson, *Giorgione*, 292.

valor.[38] The image, smaller than life size, once decorated the door to some sort of cupboard, probably in a private dwelling rather than a public building. A year or two later, in 1508 or 1509, Giorgione's large project for the exterior fresco decoration of the Fondaco dei Tedeschi included a colossal *Judith as Justice*.[39] This work survives in faded original form, and somewhat more legibly in later reproductive prints by Jacopo Piccini (fig. 5) and Antonio Maria Zanetti. A powerful woman, partly disrobed, grinds a severed male head under one foot while she tilts a hefty sword in warning at a man with a dagger behind his armored back; this treacherous soldier is probably an imperial enemy of Venice's—so thought Vasari, at any rate—though he is not represented in the costume of a German mercenary or *Landsknecht*. It is to Giorgione's junior partner in the Fondaco project, Titian, that the execution of this work is most often ascribed, though the senior painter may have laid out the composition. Soon after the completion of the fresco the German merchants of the Fondaco were obliged to leave the city as total war erupted between Emperor Maximilian and Venice, and as a kind of punishment the great structure was used to house refugees from the devastated *terraferma*.[40] Some of these may have been Jewish, and one wonders how they might have reacted to the presence of this familiar figure—whose name simply means "Jewish woman"—as they entered the Fondaco through the doorway below the fresco.

Giorgione may have painted a third version of Judith in half-length, now known through a presumed copy by Vincenzo Catena, an older artist who is identified as Giorgione's "colega" in the inscription on Giorgione's 1506 painting of *Laura*, and through an engraving in David Teniers's *Theatrum Pictorium* of 1658, reproducing the now lost original

[38] Jan Bialostocki, "La gamba sinistra della Giuditta: il quadro di Giorgione nella storia del tema," in *Giorgione e l'umanesimo*, ed. Rodolfo Pallucchini, 2 vols. (Florence, 1981), 1:193–226; for a more balanced view, see Wilhelm Steinböck, "Giorgiones 'Judith' in Leningrad," *Jahrbuch des Kunsthistorischen Instituts der Universität Graz* 7 (1972): 51–60.

[39] Now Accademia, on deposit at Galleria Giorgio Franchetti at the Ca' d'Oro. See Michelangelo Muraro, "The Political Interpretation of Giorgione's Frescoes on the Fondaco dei Tedeschi," *Gazette des Beaux-Arts* 86 (1975): 177–184; Michelangelo Muraro, "Titien: iconographie et politique," in *Symboles de la Renaissance* (Paris, 1976), 31–39; Paul Kaplan, "Giorgione's *Assault*: War and Rape in Renaissance Venice," in *Early Modern Visual Allegory: Embodying Meaning*, ed. Cristelle Baskins and Lisa Rosenthal (Aldershot, forthcoming 2007), on gender and politics in this and other images by Giorgione.

[40] Muraro, "Iconographie e politique," thinks the fresco may not have been begun until after the beginning of the Cambrai hostilities. On refugees, see Sanuto, *Diarii*, 9:161, 164.

(fig. 6).[41] This sort of composition was clearly destined for private consumption, and toward the close of the Cambrai wars the Giorgionesque painter Giovanni Cariani produced two further variants of this type. One of these bears the inscription "PRO LIBERANDA/PATRIA," which makes the patriotic and military import of these images of Judith explicit.[42]

While none of the foregoing images of Judith specifically articulates a link to modern Jews, a curious picture of c. 1515–1520 by Bartolomeo Veneto suggests a certain connection between modern Jewry and another Old Testament heroine (fig. 7). The subject of this work is a charming and rather flirtatious young woman who holds a small hammer of the kind used by jewelers.[43] Her cuff bears the inscription *sfoza dela ebra* ("dress of the Jewish woman"). The presence of the hammer, in conjunction with the inscription, recalls Jael, the Jewish woman who killed Sisera by hammering a tent-peg through his skull. Bartolomeo's work is significant here in that it implies that there is characteristically Jewish contemporary costume, although (paradoxically) such costume apparently requires a textual label to be evident. The young woman holds a ring and wears jewelry herself, and it has been noted that Jews in Italy did work as metalsmiths and jewelers in this era.[44] The particular forms of her costume are, however, not closely paralleled in the depictions of Judith previously cited.

Just as common as Judith as a subject for privately commissioned pictures in the wartime era was David, who is nearly always shown—as

[41] Catena: Querini-Stampalia Gallery, Venice; Giles Robertson, *Vincenzo Catena* (Edinburgh, 1954), 67, cat. 47 (dated c. 1530). On the *Laura*, see Anderson, *Giorgione*, 299–300. On the print, engraved by Lucas Vorsterman, see Anderson, *Giorgione*, 206–207, 318, and Anderson, "The Head-hunter and Head-huntress," 62, defending Giorgione's authorship.

[42] The work with the inscription is in a Milanese private collection; Rodolfo Pallucchini and Francesco Rossi, *Giovanni Cariani* (Bergamo, 1983), 132, cat. 57, fig. 18, dated c. 1516–1517; the other work was formerly at Grittleton House (Wilts), collection of Sir Audley Neeld; Pallucchini and Rossi, 120, cat. 36. Another work of this sort, once attributed to Giorgione (Rasini Collection, Milan), is discussed in Pignatti, *Giorgione*, 127, cat. A29, pl. 150; and see also Vittorio Sgarbi and Mauro Lucco, eds., *Le ceneri violette di Giorgione. Natura e Maniera tra Tiziano e Caravaggio* (Milan, 2004), 108–111, cat. 14.

[43] Milan, Private Collection; Laura Pagnotta, *The Portraits of Bartolomeo Veneto* (Timken Museum of Art, San Diego) (Seattle, 2002), 26; Laura Pagnotta, *Bartolomeo Veneto: L'opera completa* (Florence, 1997), 101, 216–217, cat. 28, col. pl. XVI.

[44] Pagnotta, *Portraits* (2002); see also Paul Kaplan, "Jewish Artists and Images of Black Africans in Renaissance Venice," in *Multicultural Europe and Cultural Exchange in the Middle Ages and Renaissance*, ed. James Helfers, Arizona Studies in the Middle Ages and the Renaissance 12 (Turnhout, 2005), 67–90.

in previously cited instances—as the victor over Goliath rather than in one of his other known roles. Probably the first example of this trend is a complicated image, again by Giorgione, which shows the artist himself in the role of David, posing with his enemy's severed head. A surviving painted fragment of the original, now in Braunschweig, lacks Goliath's head, but a good sixteenth-century engraving by Wenzel Hollar provides the missing information (fig. 8).[45] This is one of the first Italian independent self-portraits, as well as one of the first cases where an Italian artist assumed for himself the role of a famous character from the past; Albrecht Dürer's 1500 *Self-Portrait* in Munich, with its deliberate reference to Christ (another Jew) comes to mind as one of the immediate precedents for Giorgione's picture. The modern metal breastplate, most scholars agree, fixes the work's date around 1508–1510.[46] These last two years of the artist's short life witnessed the first desperate battles of the Cambrai wars, and this painting seems to have created a fashion amongst patricians for having themselves shown in the accoutrements of combat.[47] We do not know for sure whether the Braunschweig painting was made by Giorgione for his own purposes or whether it was commissioned; by 1528 it was in the hands of the patrician prelate Marino Grimani, who was just old enough to have ordered it from the artist in 1509 or 1510. Marino's uncle, Cardinal Domenico Grimani, owned another Old Testament subject, a picture of *Jonah and the Whale* by Hieronymous Bosch.[48] More significantly, his venerable grandfather Antonio Grimani was one of the few Venetian patricians to publicly state his support for the Jews. In 1519 this noble

---

[45] 52 × 43 cm, Herzog Anton Ulrich-Museum; Anderson, *Giorgione*, 306–307; Cornelius Müller Hofstede, "Untersuchungen über Giorgiones Selbstbildnis in Braunschweig," *Mitteilungen des Kunsthistorischen Institutes in Florenz* 8 (1957): 13–34.

[46] Müller Hofstede, "Untersuchungen über Giorgiones Selbstbildnis," 34 (1508); Jaynie Anderson, "La contribution de Giorgione au gènie de Venise," *Revue de l'art* 66 (1984): 59–68, 67 (after 1508); Alessandro Ballarin, "Giorgione: per un nuovo catalogo e una nuova cronologia," in *Giorgione e la cultura veneta tra '400 e '500. Mito, allegoria, analisi iconologica* (Atti del Convegno, Roma—Novembre 1978) (Rome, 1981), 26–30, 29–30 (1509–1510).

[47] Marcantonio Michiel described portraits by Giorgione in the collections of the patricians Girolamo Marcello and Giovanni Antonio Venier; *Marco Antonio Michiel, Notizia d'opere del disegno*, ed. Theodor Frimmel (Florence, 2000), 53, 55; Giorgio Padoan, "Giorgione e la cultura umanistica," in *Giorgione. Atti del convegno internazionale di studio per il 5° centenario della nascita, 29–31 Maggio 1978* (Castelfranco Veneto, 1979), 25–36, 33. One of these paintings may be the portrait of an armed man attributed to Giorgione in the Kunsthistorisches Museum in Vienna.

[48] Michiel, *Notizia*, 56, along with a *Tower of Babel* by the Antwerp painter Joachim Patinir.

procurator, soon to be elected Doge (1521), argued against the foundation of a Christian loan-bank (called a Monte di Pietà), which would have made Jewish moneylending unnecessary in Venice. Grimani's naval campaigns in 1499 had been made possible by Jewish loans to the state, and this may have affected his attitude twenty years later. Far from considering it unlucky to harbor this people within Christian society, Grimani affirmed that good fortune and material help could be derived from a Jewish presence in Venice: "Whilst [the Jews] were at Mestre," Grimani argued, "Mestre was burned by the enemy, but when they came to this city we recovered our dominions. And in this war they have assisted us with large sums of money."[49] As in Giorgione's painting, Antonio Grimani's words suggest a fusion rather than an opposition between Christians and Jews, let alone the supersession of one "chosen people" over another.

Giorgione's followers, apparently responding to the demands of eager patrons, created as many as five other half-length versions of the victorious David, but the original circumstances under which these works (some now lost and known only through rough sketched copies or from inventory entries) are difficult to establish. In 1510 Cima da Conegliano produced a little picture of *David and Jonathan* with a landscape setting, less fierce than Giorgione's *Self-Portrait* but still martial in emphasis.[50] David and Judith as a pair of valorous Jewish heroes also began to appear in several churches on the Venetian *terraferma*; one of the earliest of these, painted in all likelihood during the Cambrai wars, is found in the cathedral of the fortress town of Montagnana, southwest of Padua.[51] This set of images, like those made around 1520 and later in Bergamo, Friuli, and the Scuola di San Rocco in Venice, is perhaps indebted to the first truly famous pairing of David and Judith, Michelangelo's placement of them in the corner spandrels of the Sistine Chapel ceiling (completed 1512).[52] Virtually all of the Sistine ceiling, it

---

[49] Sanuto, *Diarii*, 28:62–63; cited in Brian Pullan, *Rich and Poor in Renaissance Venice* (Oxford, 1971), 493–494.

[50] London, National Gallery, 40.5 × 39.5 cm; Peter Humfrey, *Cima da Conegliano* (Cambridge, 1983), 111–112, cat. 67.

[51] Probably by Giovanni Buonconsiglio (il Marescalco); Zereich Princivalle, *Il Duomo di Montagnana* (Montagnana, 1981), 88–90, fig. 29; also, with a dubious attribution to Giorgione, Enrico Maria Dal Pozzolo, "Giorgione a Montagnana," *Critica d'Arte* 6th ser., 58 (1991): no. 8, 23–42, figs. 1–2.

[52] Earlier, less conspicuous pairings include works in the Emmaus Monastery in Prague (1360s), at Or San Michele (c. 1400), and paintings by Botticelli and Pinturicchio; Neuwirth, *Wandgemälde*, 27, pls. IV–V; Werner Cohn, "Franco Sacchetti und das

should be noted, is dedicated to Old Testament narratives and Hebrew prophets and ancestors of Christ, and by 1512 it was Rome, rather than Florence or Venice, that had become the epicenter of Italian images of Old Testament protagonists. It still remains to be determined to what extent the choice of these subjects from the Hebrew Bible is connected either to contemporary ideas about the Jews or to the political requirements of papal policy and ideology during the middle years of the Italian wars.[53] For the moment it is enough to point out that in the first years of the Cinquecento it was not only the elites of Republican Florence and Venice but also the Pope who laid claim to the heroism of David and Judith.[54]

The Old Testament story with the most direct relevance to Venice's political and military challenges during the Cambrai wars was undoubtedly the Drowning of Pharaoh and His Army in the Red Sea. Venetian political thinkers, at least by the later Cinquecento, were generally prepared to make analogies between Moses' forceful but consultative leadership with that of the doge, and to see a reflection of Venice's mixed form of political authority (in which the doge shared authority with powerful elected state councils) operating at that moment of sacred history.[55] But it was the story itself, the drama of the Red Sea parting for the Israelites and destroying their enemies, that truly fascinated the residents of a city built upon water, especially since it resonated with the legend of Venice's own foundation by refugees seeking safety in the marshes from the depredations of Attila the Hun. And Moses himself had been fated from the first to preside over such a miraculous rescue, since as an infant he had floated to safety on a basket of bulrushes

ikonographische Programm der Gewölbemalereien von Orsanmichele," *Mitteilungen des Kunsthistorischen Institutes in Florenz* 8 (1957): 65–77; Ronald Lightbown, *Sandro Botticelli*, 2 vols. (Berkeley, 1978), 1:141–145, pl. 55, 2:101–106, cat. B91; N. Randolph Parks, "On the Meaning of Pinturicchio's *Sala dei Santi*," *Art History* 2 (1979): 291–317, 298. For a later pairing with explicit patriotic meaning by Pellegrino da San Daniele in the Cathedral (Duomo) of Udine (1519–1521 or later), see Massimo Bonelli and Rossella Fabiani, *Pellegrino a San Daniele del Friuli* (Milan, 1988), 92–95, figs. 111–112. Lorenzo Lotto's *intarsie* choir parapet at S. Maria Maggiore in Bergamo (1525–1527) includes a *David* and a *Judith*, matched with *The Flood* and *The Crossing of the Red Sea*; Giordana Mariani Canova with Rodolfo Pallucchini, *L'opera completa di Lotto* (Milan, 1975), 102. David and Judith also appear as sculpture on the mid-Cinquecento staircase in the Scuola Grande di San Rocco in Venice.

[53] But see Wisch, "Vested Interest."

[54] Isabella d'Este had a more personal identification with Judith; see Kaplan, "Isabella d'Este."

[55] Sinding-Larsen, *Christ in the Council Hall*, 141, n. 2, 151.

carried by the Nile. There were other available sacred evocations of God's power to use the sea to punish the wicked, but one supposes that the story of Noah and the universal deluge was too frightening for most Renaissance inhabitants of flood-prone Venice to set before themselves. The Deluge, unlike the story of the Red Sea, spared no nation but only a single human family. Michelangelo, in 1508–1510, was busy painting this ghastly event in a prominent spot on the ceiling of the Sistine Chapel, and one can imagine Pope Julius fantasizing that he had the power to call down such liquid destruction upon his vulnerable Venetian enemies.

The Venetians had their own favorite fantasy, and it decisively cast their opponents as Pharaoh and his minions.[56] At least one Venetian patrician polemicist, Giovanni Matteo Girardo, quoted the story in his defense of Venice against a papal critique in 1509,[57] and the Red Sea story was depicted at least three times on a large scale by artists working in Venice during or just after the war. The earliest of these is a big canvas of c. 1509–1512 by Andrea Previtali (fig. 9).[58] Because its original destination is unknown, there is no guarantee it was made for display in a sacred space; it may in fact have first adorned a civic office. By the early 1600s, however, it was installed in a chapel (built in the late Cinquecento) in the Palazzo Ducale; and in 1771 it was moved to an adjoining chamber. In Previtali's painting Moses wears a turban, which may refer to contemporary Jewish dress, since Jews arriving in Venice from the Ottoman Empire often wore such headgear. However, Moses's Hebrew followers are fitted out like Renaissance soldiers and Italian peasants, as if to associate the poor Christian refugees from the *terraferma* with the ancient Hebrews. Lightning licks the water, probably a reference to the pillar of flame which guided the Israelites in their flight (Exodus 13) but also an allusion to a common analogy between

[56] See William Barcham, *The Religious Paintings of Giovanni Battista Tiepolo* (Oxford, 1989), 23–25. On the Cambrai period, see Loredana Olivato, "La submersione di Pharaone," in *Tiziano e Venezia*, Convegno internazionale di studi, Venezia, 1976, (Vicenza, 1980), 529–537.

[57] See above, n. 8, esp. fol. 42r.

[58] Measuring 130 × 210 cm, and now in the Accademia in Venice; see Sandra Moschini Marconi, *Gallerie dell'Accademia di Venezia. Opere d'arte del secolo XVI* (Rome, 1962), 179–180, cat. 298, fig. 299. David Rosand and Michelangelo Muraro, *Titian and the Venetian Woodcut* (Washington DC, 1976), 72–73, link the work to contemporary events.

thunderstorms and war most famously articulated in Giorgione's *Tempesta* of 1509.[59]

Links to the ongoing war are even more apparent in Titian's monumental woodcut, the *Crossing of the Red Sea* (fig. 10). Nearly the same size as Previtali's canvas, its twelve constituent blocks together measure 123 × 222 cm! Despite the similarity in scale and format, however, the composition is quite different, with much more space given over to the Egyptians and their distant city. The woodcut has a perplexing history: it appears to have been prepared by February 1515, but—except for one small fragment—all surviving copies date from a second edition of 1549.[60]

Like Previtali's work, it is not part of a Moses cycle, and it is even more dramatic. A huge Red Sea dominates the woodcut, bearing down on the wedge of Egyptian soldiers (dressed in a mixture of ancient and modern armor) at the left; a skyline with Gothic towers is threatened by turbulent clouds behind the doomed army. At the right Moses gathers the mostly unarmed and roughly dressed Israelites, including two conspicuous mothers with children, on the slim stretch of the farther shore; here the weather is serene. Just in front of Moses, a dog awkwardly defecates, its rear end obscenely pointed toward the drowning Egyptians. Many of these details have been used to sustain a persuasive reading of the print as a piece of patriotic propaganda: the Gothic towers merge Pharaoh's identity with that of the Emperor Maximilian; the Red Sea resembles the Venetian lagoon; the Renaissance armor brings the event into the present; the modern rustic dress of many of the Israelites echoes the Venetian sympathy for *terraferma* peasantry; the dog's behavior mirrors that of Venetian partisans taunting their enemies during the war; and the nursing Jewish mother appears to be a symbol of patriotic charity.[61] As Loredana Olivato points out, the

[59] Paul Kaplan, "The Storm of War: The Paduan Key to Giorgione's *Tempesta*," *Art History* 9 (1986): 405–427.

[60] Rosand and Muraro, *Titian and the Venetian Woodcut*, 17, 70–87, cat. 4; Olivato, "La submersione"; Loredana Olivato, entry on Titian's woodcut of the *Crossing of the Red Sea*, in *Titian: Prince of Painters*, exhib. cat. (Venice, 1990), 166–167, cat. 10.

[61] On the mother as charity, see Kaplan, "The Storm of War," 411. For further political readings, see Michelangelo Muraro and David Rosand, with Feliciano Benvenuti, *Tiziano e la silografia veneziana del Cinquecento* (Vicenza, 1976), 82, and also Benvenuti's remarks on 17–20, especially 19; Muraro, "Titien: iconographie et politique," 33; Philip Sohm, "Palma Vecchio's *Sea Storm*: A Political Allegory," *Revue d'art canadienne/Canadian Art Review* 6, no. 2 (1979–1980): 85–96, 93–94; Robert Finlay, *Politics in Renaissance Venice* (New Brunswick, NJ, 1980), 224; Mario Universo, entry on Titian's *Red Sea*, in *I tempi*

woodcut, unlike most paintings, potentially reveals something of Titian's individual political views, or at least a conscious decision on the artist's part to appeal to patriotic sentiment, and can thus be associated with Titian's 1513 offer to paint a large canvas of *The Battle of Spoleto* for the Ducal Palace. For Olivato, the decline of Venice's martial fortunes in 1513—enemy troops even reached the edge of the lagoon—was the spur which prompted Titian to carry out both large projects.

The large-scale images of Previtali and Titian were not, of course, the first depictions of the Crossing of the Red Sea in Venetian art. A thirteenth-century mosaic in San Marco (now lost) depicted the story within the Moses cycle in the north aisle of the narthex, and there was also Gentile Bellini's *Red Sea* at the Scuola Grande di San Marco (discussed above); as this latter work was destroyed by fire in 1485, however, neither Titian nor Previtali would have known it. Early in the first decade of the sixteenth century a *Crossing of the Red Sea* by a certain "Jan de Brugia" (possibly Jan van Eyck) was in the Venetian collection of the citizen Michele Vianello, but in 1506 Isabella d'Este purchased it and brought it to Mantua.[62]

After 1515, however, we find increasing instances of the subject's presentation (or collection) in Venice. On May 15, 1516, as the Cambrai war was moving toward its close, a Brescian friar asked the Venetian authorities for a privilege to publish a print of *Pharaoh Pursuing the Jews*, which was perhaps also a Red Sea image.[63] In Marcantonio Michiel's 1521 list of the works owned by the Venetian citizen Francesco Zio there appears a *Crossing of the Red Sea* on canvas by Jan van Scorel; this

di Giorgione, ed. Ruggero Maschio (Rome, 1994), 27–28; Monika Schmitter, "'Virtuous Riches': The Bricolage of *Cittadini* Identities in Early-Sixteenth-Century Venice," *Renaissance Quarterly* 57 (2004): 908–969, 928–931. During the siege of Padua in 1509 Venetian troops famously taunted their enemies with a cat suspended just out of reach, its rear end pointed mockingly at the besiegers; Sanuto, *Diarii*, 9:194; Polibio Zanetti, "L'assedio di Padova del 1509," *Nuovo Archivio Veneto* 2 (1891): 5–168, at 113.

62 The work was seen by Isabella in 1502, but she only obtained it after Vianello's death, after it had been bought by the Doge's brother Andrea Loredan. The picture was on canvas, making Van Eyck's authorship less likely; it may possibly correspond to a "French-style" rendition of the same subject in the 1492 Medici inventories. See Clifford Brown with Anna Maria Lorenzoni, "An Art Auction in Venice in 1506," *L'Arte* n.s. 5, nos. 18–19/20 (1972): 121–136, 123–131. Mantua, surrounded by its own lagoon, is another city with reason to find the Red Sea story appealing; the 1627 Gonzaga inventory lists two versions of the subject, one by Giulio Romano, and the other anonymous.

63 See below, pp. 299–300 and n. 73; Olivato, "La submersione," 531, also refers to a print by Agostino Veneziano that I have not been able to find.

was probably not an import, since van Scorel is believed to have been in Venice around 1518–1520. A painting of the *Crossing of the Red Sea* by Van Scorel, recently rediscovered in a Milanese private collection, may be the same work owned by Zio, though this rather large picture (54 × 134 cm) is on panel.[64] As befits a work made just after peace had been reestablished between Venice and its opponents, this painting stresses the happiness of the Jews in a lush landscape, rather than the violent destruction of the Egyptian army.[65] Of the collectors visited by Michiel, Zio was the only one with a significant number of Old Testament subjects: in addition to the Scorel, he possessed an *Adam and Eve* by Palma Vecchio as well as a curious crystal cup with unspecified stories from the Jewish Bible by Cristoforo Romano.[66] Two further Venetian images of the *Red Sea* survive from later in the 1500s, and there are also two surviving references to possibly lost pictures, including one mentioned in the posthumous 1569 inventory of Gabriele Vendramin, the first known owner of the *Tempesta*.[67]

Though Previtali's and Van Scorel's paintings are hardly negligible works, Titian's woodcut would have been the better known representation of the theme during this period; however, we know virtually nothing about how it was received or displayed. Its huge size was not an anomaly: there were several other such colossal woodcuts produced in Venice during the war, and about half of them focus on Old Testament subjects. Also from 1515 are a *Susanna and the Elders* by Girolamo da Treviso and Titian's *Abraham and Isaac*. There may have been some concern that these subjects might be taken as too favorable to the Jews,

---

[64] Bert Meijer, "Over Jan van Scorel in Venetië en het vroege werk van Lambert Sustris," *Oud Holland* 106 (1992): 1–19, 1–6, figs. 1–4; *Renaissance Venice and the North: Crosscurrents in the Time of Bellini, Dürer, and Titian*, ed. Bernard Aikema and Beverley Louise Brown (New York, 2000), 462–463, cat. 125; *Fiamminghi a Roma 1508/1608. Artistes des Pays-Bas et de la principauté de Liège à Rome à la Renaissance* (Brussels, 1995), 319–321; Molly Faries and Martha Wolff, "Landscape in the Early Painting of Jan van Scorel," *Burlington Magazine* 138 (1996): 724–733, 727.

[65] Schmitter, "'Virtuous Riches'," 931.

[66] Michiel, *Notizie*, 55; on Zio's collection, much of which passed to another *cittadino* visited by Michiel, Andrea Odoni, see Schmitter, "'Virtuous Riches.'"

[67] "Un quadro de un sumercion de faraon"; Aldo Ravà, "Il 'Camerino delle Anticaglie' di Gabriele Vendramin," *Nuovo Archivio Veneto* 39 (1920): 155–81, 179; possibly to be identified with the Jan van Scorel painting now in Milan (see above). Barcham (discussing politicized Red Sea and Judith imagery in Venice in 1716, see pp. 14–27, 94) cites a Palma Giovane picture in the old sacristy of S. Giacomo dall'Orio, and an anonymous work from the mid-1500s in the sacristy of S. Sebastiano; *The Religious Paintings*, 23–24. Olivato, "La submersione," 531, mentions a painting by Lambert Sustris recorded by Ridolfi.

since an inscription on a now lost impression of the *Abraham and Isaac* indicated it had been made "in the most Christian city of Venice."[68] These woodcuts were costly endeavors, and the publishers often asked the Venetian government for ten-year copyrights on their work to ensure a profit. On February 9, 1515, Bernardino Benalio asked the Collegio for copyright on all three of the prints just discussed; evidently it was granted.[69] This occurred two months before the concerted but unsuccessful attempt to confine the Jews during Easter of 1515. Local publishers may have even been emboldened by the failure of this anti-Jewish initiative, as the next copyright application, dated April 23, concerning a Christian-backed plan to publish Hebrew holy books and a Hebrew grammar, suggests. This application was not only granted but included a provision which allowed four Jewish advisors to the project to be relieved of the requirement of wearing the stigmatizing yellow hat for four months. Two of the Hebrew texts were published later in 1515.[70]

The successful creation of a Ghetto during the following Easter seems to have had a different effect on publishers. The first copyright application following the enclosure of the Jews on April 10, 1516, was Gregorio de' Gregoriis's April 23 request involving a printed Office of the Virgin (identified as Venice's "queen") and sacred prints including Titian's *Triumph of Christ* (also called the *Triumph of Faith*) (fig. 11).[71] No Old Testament subjects were listed. On an application dated May 6 Benalio similarly asked for rights to a *Last Judgement*, a *Triumph of Mary*, and a *Procession of the Savior* probably very similar to Titian's work for de' Gregoriis; again no Old Testament themes were listed.[72] On May 15, however, one Fra Hippolito de Pregnachi of Brescia asked for and received a privilege to publish images of "the story of Sodom and

[68] Rosand and Muraro, *Titian and the Venetian Woodcut*, 55. A Dugento relief represents Abraham and Isaac on the façade of San Marco; Otto Demus with Lorenzo Lazzanni, Mario Piana, and Guido Tigler, *Le sculture esterne di San Marco* (Milan, 1995), 59, cat. 64. On a Cariani painting depicting Susanna and Daniel, see Sgarbi and Lucco, *Le ceneri violette*, 214–215, cat. 61.

[69] Rosand and Muraro, *Titian and the Venetian Woodcut*, 19, 32, 35, n. 5, 55, cat. 3A, 88, cat. 5; Rinaldo Fulin, "Documenti per servire alla storia della tipografia veneziana," *Archivio Veneto* 33 (1882): 84–212, 181, no. 196.

[70] Fulin, "Documenti," 181–183, no. 197.

[71] Fulin, "Documenti," 188, no. 207; Rosand and Muraro, *Titian and the Venetian Woodcut*, 35, n. 3.

[72] Fulin, "Documenti," 188–189, no. 208; Rosand and Muraro, *Titian and the Venetian Woodcut*, 35, n. 5.

Gomorrah with that of Pharaoh persecuting the people of Israel" which he had already prepared.[73] These works are not known today, but the emphasis on the corruption and punishment of the cities, and on the suffering (rather than the revenge) of the Israelites, indicates a more ambiguous approach to Old Testament stories and protagonists than that of the previous year.

Another index of changed circumstances can be found within Titian's *Triumph of Christ*. There are serious disputes about the original date of this nearly three-meter-wide woodcut. It may have been laid out as early as 1508, though a recent analysis argues that the earliest surviving impression, issued by de' Gregoriis in 1517, is in fact the "original."[74] At the front of Christ's parade is a conspicuous delegation of Old Testament protagonists, including (in rough order from right to left): Eve, Adam, Abel, Noah, Moses, Joshua, Jonah, Isaac, Abraham and David (portrayed in a Levantine turban). Behind an intervening group of pagan sibyls are several additional Hebrew prophets.[75] This is reminiscent of the Sistine Chapel, but ultimately descends from medieval cycles, including one from the 1200s on the third archivolt of the central portal of San Marco. Here and in other such cycles one of the important textual sources is the Pseudo-Augustine's *De Symbolo contra Judaeos, Paganos et Arianos*, which articulated a message of hostility toward contemporary Jews as being blind to the visions of their forbears.[76] In this light these Old Testament figures may have formed an implicit reproach rather than compliment to any Venetian Jew. All the Old Testament figures in Titian's woodcut are literally Christ's forerunners, and play a major role in the print, but they are also carefully "confined" to two of the five blocks, and separated from Christ and his followers by the large cross located in front of the triumphal car. The marked sense of Christian control and compartmentalization here forms an eerie parallel to the new Venice which emerged in 1516: a city in which the physical

[73] Rosand and Muraro, *Titian and the Venetian Woodcut*, 73.

[74] Michael Bury, "The *Triumph of Christ*, after Titian," *Burlington Magazine* 131 (1989): 188–197, who suggests a date of 1516–1517, especially for the blocks at the right which include all the Old Testament figures; Rosand and Muraro, *Titian and the Venetian Woodcut*, 37–44, cat. 1 (dated sometime between 1508 and 1511), with bibliography of earlier sources; Konrad Oberhuber, entry in *Siècle de Titien*, 526–527, thinks the print was begun in 1510 but finished only in 1516.

[75] Images of Hebrew prophets, divorced from narrative, have not been emphasized in this essay; less consistently connected to patriotic themes, they merit a separate investigation; see, for example, Wisch, "'Vested Interest'."

[76] Guido Tigler, *Il portale maggiore di San Marco a Venezia* (Venice, 1995), 324–338.

intermixing of Christians and Jews was now carefully regulated, but at the same time a city distinguished by an important and potentially permanent Jewish community. If just before and during the first phases of the War of the League of Cambrai the rise in Venetian images of Old Testament heroes had accompanied and perhaps encouraged the Venetian elite's acceptance of the Jewish presence in the city, the final phase of the war and the return of peace gave rise to more restrictive policies and representational strategies.

This does not mean, however, that we should expect to find Venetian narrative images of Old Testament protagonists from this period explicitly manifesting Christian hostility to or disparagement of contemporary Jewry. This would, of course, have been an odd choice and an ineffective strategy: why select such relatively unusual subjects only to undermine them? If there is any work which leans in this direction, it would be Giovanni Bellini's *Drunkenness of Noah* (c. 1513–1515), which gives the unfilial Ham a central position, and seems to eroticize the patriarch's strangely youthful body.[77] (The closest parallels to Bellini's drunk and dozing Noah are the sleeping nymph in Bellini's own *Feast of the Gods* and the slumbering, self-stimulating goddess of Giorgione's *Dresden Venus*.) There is no iconographic scheme which connects Noah's lapse to a larger plan of redemption, as in Michelangelo's version of the story on the Sistine ceiling. Though one scholarly attempt has been made to situate Bellini's painting in the context of the intermittent anxiety about the Jews during the wartime period, it is not easy to imagine how such fears would have shaped this picture, which for now remains resistant to a clear historicizing interpretation.[78] One can find more unmistakable visual traces of anti-Judaic feeling in this era, but (as usual) one has to look outside the realm of Old Testament subjects; an excellent example would be Vittore Carpaccio's 1511 *Preaching of St. Stephen* for the Scuola di S. Stefano.[79]

No examination of Old Testament subjects in Venetian High Renaissance art may conclude without touching on a cycle of narratives which in its breadth, and perhaps also in its accessibility to a wider audience,

---

[77] Besançon, Museum; 103 × 157 cm.

[78] Stefano Coltelacci, "*Obedite praepositis vestris, et subiacete illis*. Fonti letterarie e contesto storico della *Derisione di Noè* di Giovanni Bellini," *Venezia Cinquecento* 1 (1991): 119–156; see also Daniel Arasse with Orsola Sveva Barberis, "Giovanni Bellini et la mythologie de Noé," *Venezia Cinquecento* 1 (1991): 157–183.

[79] Augusto Gentili, *Le storie di Carpaccio. Venezia, i Turchi, gli Ebrei*, (Venice, 1996), 137–138.

is comparable only to the Dugento mosaics of the narthex of San Marco. I refer to the so-called "picture-Pentateuch," a cycle of woodcut illustrations with brief captions, produced by the Jewish artist Moisè dal Castellazzo and his daughters. This ambitious project was endorsed and awarded a ten year copyright by the powerful Council of Ten on July 27, 1521.[80] Long thought to have vanished without a trace (or perhaps never to have been actually produced), Moisè's masterwork is now known through a surviving photograph of one untraceable woodcut and, more importantly, a complete watercolor copy of the prints, made around 1550.[81] Despite the publication of a facsimile of the latter set of images more than two decades ago, few scholars of Venetian art are as yet familiar with this cycle, whose 211 compositions are mostly derived from late medieval manuscript sources but also influenced by Venetian art of the Middle Ages and Renaissance.

Although Moisè vowed to continue his project and illustrate the entire Old Testament, he appears not have gone much beyond the Pentateuch. Consequently he did not depict David, Solomon or Judith; but Noah, Abraham, and Moses are repeatedly represented. *The Crossing of the Red Sea* (fig. 12) is broken into three narrative sections, as if in imitation of the grandiose conception found in Titian's woodcut and the paintings of Previtali and Van Scorel.[82] Each of the images was evidently equipped with matching Hebrew and Italian captions; Moisè explicitly strove to appeal to both a Jewish and a Christian Venetian audience. While very much a resident of the Ghetto in the early 1520s and a participant in the internal events of Jewish life there, Moisè was equally adept at dealing with Christian rulers and intellectuals. At various points during his career (b. c. 1466, d. 1526), he lived in Mantua, Milan, Ferrara, Mestre and Venice, producing objects for the humanist patrician Pietro Bembo and his mistress Maria Savorgnan, and receiving privileges not only from the Council of Ten but also

[80] Fulin, "Documenti," 196–197, no. 226 (Archivio di Stato di Venezia, Capi del Consiglio X, Notatorio, no. 5, carte 120f); also given in Kaplan, "Jewish Artists," 71–72, n. 11.

[81] Formerly Warsaw, Library of the Jewish Historical Institute, cod. 1164; Kaplan, "Jewish Artists"; Moses dal Castellazzo, *Bilder-Pentateuch von Moses dal Castellazzo: Venedig 1521: Völlständige Faksimile-Ausgabe im Originalformat des Codex 1164 aus dem Besitz des Jüdischen Historischen Instituts Warschau*, ed. Kurt Schubert and Ursula Schubert, 2 vols. (Vienna, 1983–1986). Sadly, the manuscript was stolen in the 1980s and has not been traced.

[82] Nos. 87–89.

the Duke of Milan and the Marquis of Mantua.[83] The 1521 request and granting of copyright by the Council of Ten occurred only three weeks after the installation of the pro-Jewish doge Antonio Grimani (discussed above), which suggests that Moisè may have been calling in a favor, or at least that he was responding to a particularly auspicious moment as far the Jews of the Ghetto were concerned.[84] Although, as I have tried to show, the Christian Venetian images of Old Testament heroes and heroines were shaped partly by the political events of the early Cinquecento—and in particular by the fluctuating position of the Jews in Venetian society and political discourse—it was ultimately the images made by Moisè and his daughters that most concretely connected the protagonists of the Jewish Bible to the world of contemporary Jews during the Venetian High Renaissance.

---

[83] Maria Savorgnan and Pietro Bembo, *Carteggio d'amore 1500–1501*, ed. Carlo Dionisotti (Florence, 1950), xx–xxi, 36–37, 40–41, 129–131; on the Milanese and Mantuan privileges, see Kaplan, "Jewish Artists," 70, n. 7 (1515), 71 (1519 and 1521); also Moses dal Castellazzo, *Bilder-Pentateuch*, 2:132–133.

[84] Kaplan, "Jewish Artists," 71; Pullan, *Rich and Poor*, 493–494, 496.

CHAPTER ELEVEN

CLEANSING THE TEMPLE: THE MUNICH GRUFTKIRCHE AS CONVERTED SYNAGOGUE[1]

Mitchell B. Merback

One block north of the famed neo-Gothic townhall on Marienplatz, the epicenter of Munich's bustling tourist industry, lies an open green known as the Marienhof. Once as densely crowded with buildings as the blocks surrounding it across Weinstrasse to the west, across Schrammergasse to the north, and across Dienergasse to the east, the Marienhof was devastated by Allied air-bombing during the Second World War.[2] Blasted into oblivion were not only the buildings that occupied the site but the east-west street that divided it, called Gruftstrasse.[3] This street took its name from a church which once stood there, facing south, known in its late medieval incarnation as the Neustifts-Kirche and later, at the height of its fame as a Counter-Reformation pilgrimage shrine to "Our Lady of the Crypt" (*Unser Lieben Frauen in der Grufft*),

[1] Research for this article was funded at various stages by the Leo Baeck Institute, Deutscher Akademischer Austauschdienst, DePauw University, the Norman and Irma Braman Foundation, Robert Weingarten and Joseph and Tema Merback—thanks go to all of them. I am also indebted to Wolfgang Augustyn, Johannes Heil, Rupert Karbacher, Helmuth Stahleder and Keith Nightenhelser for their kind assistance and many helpful suggestions. Special gratitude is reserved for Jacqueline Jung, who offered spot-on criticisms of a penultimate draft, and helped me redefine the meaning of sanctuary. And I should mention the anonymous readers at two preeminent scholarly journals, whose impatience with an earlier version of this essay prompted me to make many improvements. Unless otherwise noted, all translations are my own. Throughout the abbreviation BHStA = Bayerisches Hauptstaatsarchiv, Munich.

[2] By 1948 the last remaining buildings had been removed from the site; for published photographs, see Richard Bauer, *Ruinen-Jahre. Bilder aus dem zerstörten München 1945–1949* (n.p. [Munich], 1983), 136–7. For the archaeological report, Heike Fastje, "Die Ausgrabungen auf dem Geläude des Marienhofs in München," *Jahrbuch der Bayerischen Denkmalpflege. Forschungen und Berichte* 43 (1994): 20–32.

[3] Also known as "Gruftgasse," though other designations appear in the records; see *Haus- und Straßennamen der Münchener Altstadt*, ed. Helmuth Stahleder (Munich, 1992), 144; also *Häuserbuch der Stadt München, vol. 1: Graggenauer Viertel* (Munich, 1958), 80f.

simply as the Gruftkirche (fig. 1).[4] Administered by the Benedictines of nearby Andechs monastery, the Gruftkirche attracted pious visitors from shortly after its founding until its forced closure and liquidation by the Kurfürstliche Landesdirektion, part of the Bavarian royal government's secularization of monasteries, in 1803.[5] Prior to the church's consecration, however—between 1380 and 1442, to be exact—the two-story townhouse that it occupied served as the Munich Jewish community's synagogue,[6] while the street which later became Gruftstrasse, running

[4] The historiography on the Gruftkirche is sodden with pious repetition, the only critical re-examination being Helmuth Stahleder, "Die Münchener Juden im Mittelalter und ihre Kultstätten," in *Synagogen und jüdische Friedhöfe in München*, ed. Wolfram Selig (Munich, 1988), 11–33, esp. 16–23 and 30–1. I have found only two brief notices on the church prior to 1799: Caroli Strengelii, *Hodoeporicum Mariano-Benedictum* (1659), ch. 12 (unpaginated); and Johann Pezzl, *Reise durch den Baierischen Kreis*, Faksimileausgabe der 2. erweiterten Auflage von 1784, ed. Josef Pfennigmann (München, 1973), 127–8 and 192–3. The foundational source for all nineteenth-century historiography is the memoir of circa 1799 by the Andechs abbot P. Placidus Scharl, *Geschichte der Kruft zu München* (Andechs Klosterarchiv, Sign. 69); from Scharl's account came many of the facts and anecdotes of P. Magnus Sattler, "Die ehemalige Gruftkirche am Gruftgäßchen in München," *Kalender für katholische Christen* 27 (Sulzbach, 1867), 41–5; a fuller account is given in idem, *Chronik von Andechs* (Donauwörth, 1877), 206–13 and 615–19; see also Jakob Gufler, "Ergänzungen und Berichtigung. 'Die ehemalige Gruftkirche und Gruftgäßchen zu München'," *Kalender für katholische Christen* 28 (Sulzbach, 1868), 120–22; J. M. Forster, *Das gottselige München* (Munich, 1895), 366–78; Fridolin Solleder, *München im Mittelalter* (1938; repr. Aalen, 1962), 522–3; Peter Steiner, "Die Gruftkirche," in *Altmünchener Gnadenstätten. Wallfahrt und Volksfrömmigkeit im Kurfürstlichen München*, exhib. cat. (Munich, 1977), 28–30; Willibald P. Mathäser OSB, *Andechser Chronik. Die Geschichte des Heiligen Berges nach alten Dokumentaten und aus neueren Quellen* (Munich, 1979), 47–9 and 135–7; Norbert Lieb, "Klosterhäuser im alten München," *Studien und Mitteilungen zur Geschichte des Benediktiner-Ordens und seiner Zweige* 9, nos. 11–12 (1980): 154–6, 167, and 178–81; and Alexander Rauch, "Münchens jüdische Denkmäler," in *Denkmäler jüdischer Kultur in Bayern*, Bayerisches Landesamt für Denkmalpflege, Arbeitsheft 43 (Munich, 1994), 10–11.

[5] Following the dissolution of the Andechs monastery on November 4, 1803, the entire compound at Gruftgasse 1 was closed off and put up for auction; it sold for 10,100 Gulden to the bookbinder Johann Georg Jaud, who converted it into a residence and workshop; see *Häuserbuch*, 1: 80; and Lieb, "Klosterhäuser," 156, n. 79, for documentary sources and further references. The property passed through the hands of several private owners before finally being purchased in 1865 by the royal government. In 1867 Gruftgasse 1 and 2 were torn down to make way for the new city courthouse; cf. also Rauch, "Münchens jüdische Denkmäler," 11; and Fastje, "Ausgrabungen," 24. It was this complex of buildings that the Allied bombers reduced to rubble by the war's end.

[6] Stahleder, *Chronik*, 164–5; also idem, "Die Münchener Juden," 17, 31. References to an earlier (1210) synagogue abound in the literature on the history of Munich's medieval Jewish community (see esp. Rauch, "Münchens jüdische Denkmäler," 10), but neither unambiguous textual nor archaeological evidence supports the claim.

through the heart of the old walled city, was known by another name: it was the Judengässel.[7]

The present chapter examines the Gruftkirche's 350-year career through a set of three historical vignettes, each of them revealing a different aspect of a long-term process I call, borrowing a term, *cultic anti-Judaism*. At the historical beginning of this process we find an expulsion decree, a transfer of valuable real-estate, and plans for the conversion of a synagogue into a church.

Converted Synagogues and Cult Images in Imperial South Germany

In early 1442 the Wittelsbach duke of Upper Bavaria-Munich, Albrecht III (r. 1438–60),[8] expelled the Jews from his territories, and presided over their removal from Munich, Straubing and close to forty other locales in Upper Bavaria.[9] Decreed only four years into his reign, the duke's expulsion appears as a dramatic reversal of the *Judenpolitik* of his father Ernst (r. 1373–1438). Under Duke Ernst the Jews, whose presence in the city can be dated back to the late twelfth century,[10] had secured

---

[7] The name "Judengässel" appears for the first time in 1380, most likely prompted by the foundation of the synagogue and the fact that Judengasse 2 was owned by Master Jakob from Landshut, Jewish *Leibarzt* to the rival Wittelsbach duke of Bavaria-Ingolstadt, Stephan III; the street-name remained in use until about 1524, when it was largely replaced by the name "Neustiftgässel" (*Haus- und Straßennamen*, 169, 236).

[8] On Albrecht III, named *der Fromme* ("the Pious"), see *Neue Deutsche Biographie*, ed. Historischen Kommission bei der Bayerischen Akademie der Wissenschaften, multiple volumes (Berlin, c. 1953–) [henceforth cited as NDB], 1:156–7; Sigmund von Riezler, *Geschichte Baiern*, 8 vols. (Gotha, 1878–1914; repr. Aalen, 1964), 3:314; *Handbuch der bayerischen Geschichte*, ed. Max Spindler (Munich, 1966), 2:190, 226–7, 244, 257, 266–7, 288; also Sattler, *Chronik von Andechs*, 123–34.

[9] Doubts remain about the exact date of expulsion, since the last record of a Jewish presence in Munich is the confirmation of receipt, dated July 4, 1439, of a new tax of 2,000 Rhenish Gulden; see Stahleder, *Chronik*, 319 and 324 for references and commentary.

[10] Jewish settlement in Munich may have begun only a short time after the founding of the city by Henry the Lion in 1158 (Leo Baerwald, "Juden und jüdische Gemeinde in München vom 12. bis 20. Jahrhundert," in *Vergangene Tage. Jüdische Kultur in München*, ed. Hans Lamm [Munich, 1982], 19–30, at 19); but reports concerning Jews in Munich prior to 1229 can not be supported with sources; see *Jüdisches Lexikon* (Berlin, 1930), 4:332. Some scholars put the earliest settlements around the time following the expulsion of the Jews from France by King Philip Augustus in 1182, and therefore regard the early Munich community as a colony of former French Jews; see *Germania Judaica*, vol. 2, pt. 2, ed. Zvi Avineri (Tübingen, 1968), 556–59, which documents the arrival of one prominent French Jew, and argues that Munich possessed an attractive power for displaced French Jews. More likely, however, the settlers in Munich came

permission to establish not only a synagogue but also a cemetery.[11] Already as a prince Albrecht's anti-Jewish attitudes were on display.[12] In 1432, for example, following on the heels of the last failed anti-Hussite crusade led by the Munich Wittelsbachs, Albrecht attempted to exact a special tax in order to settle his war debts.[13] In 1435, under the pretext that Jewish men had allegedly been cultivating sexual relationships with Christian women, he imprisoned the Jews of Straubing and attempted to seize their assets; Ernst himself had to step in to thwart the plan.[14] Albrecht's indebtedness to Jewish lenders probably continued up to the time of the 1442 expulsion and very likely provided the underlying motive for the territorial ban. With this initiative, the duke succeeded in—among other things—expropriating valuable real estate that had passed into Jewish hands during the reign of his father.

In legal terms the expulsion represented little more than a formal end to a corporate franchise held temporarily by a community of *Schutzjuden* whose taxes and monetary services had once filled important gaps in the ducal finances; and since it was accomplished without violence, historians refer to it and others like it as a "peaceful expulsion."[15] Nor was the fate of Munich's Jews unusual for this time and place. Here as

---

from Regensburg, the leading city in the Oberpfalz region, whose Jewish population formed the root of all Jewish communities in Bavaria; see Stahleder, "Die Münchener Juden," 11.

[11] A document of March 29, 1416 grants them a portion of land "upon the hill between Moosach and the Rennweg," a privilege they paid for with a new yearly tax; BHStA, Kurbaiern U 16332, cited and summarized in Stahleder, *Chronik*, 243; also discussed in Solleder, *München*, 131 and Rauch, "Münchens jüdische Denkmäler," 11, with further references. Before this time the existence of a synagogue in Munich is debatable: despite documentary evidence that, in 1210, Duke Ludwig der Kelheimer granted the fledgling community permission to build an underground synagogue "in die Stadtmauer am Judengäßl," we can not be sure that Ludwig's clients ever redeemed the promise and actually completed a building; Rauch (at 10) offers the strongest argument in favor of the existence of a thirteenth-century synagogue.

[12] Solleder, *München*, 523.

[13] Rauch, "Münchens jüdische Denkmäler," 8; for Bavarian involvement in the Hussite Wars, *Handbuch der bayerischen Geschichte*, 2:252–4. The last campaign involving the Munich house appears to be the failure of 1431; for references to key documents, see Stahleder, *Chronik*, 282 and 285. On the matter of Albrecht's debts, *Jüdisches Lexikon*, 4:332.

[14] Josef Kirmeier, "Aufnahme, Verfolgung und Vertreibung. Zur Judenpolitik bayerischer Herzöge im Mittelalter," in *Geschichte und Kultur der Juden in Bayern*, ed. Manfred Treml and Josef Kirmeier (Munich, 1988), 101–02.

[15] Albrecht's territorial expulsion led the way to a similar action by Duke Ludwig der Reiche of Bavaria-Landshut in 1450; this trend among Bavaria's territorial princes culminated in the *Landesordnung* of Albrecht V in 1553; see Stefan Schwarz, *Die Juden in Bayern im Wandel der Zeiten* (Munich, 1963), 51–60, esp. 54.

elsewhere in the German empire, late medieval Jewish communities were caught in the crossfire of social and political conflicts even when they were not themselves the targets of ideological persecution.[16] Ernst's reign had offered the Munich Jews considerable respite from an otherwise deteriorating legal and social situation, one which saw them, from the later thirteenth century onward, subjected to incendiary accusations (at least one ritual murder charge), persecutions (at least one pogrom), several dispossessions, and finally their official expulsion.[17]

In the century preceding the expulsion from Upper Bavaria-Munich, synagogues in Würzburg, Nuremberg, Amberg, Heidelberg, Bamberg, Rothenburg, Ingolstadt—in short, some of the most prominent episcopal, imperial and princely cities in southern Germany—had been expropriated from their Jewish communities and converted into Christian churches in the wake of expulsions. By the onset of the Reformation, a similar drama would play out in numerous other cities, the case of the chapel and pilgrimage to the "Fair Virgin" (*Schöne Maria*) of Regensburg (1519) being only the most widely studied.[18] Throughout

[16] See Phillip N. Bebb, "Jewish Policy in Sixteenth Century Nuremberg," *Occasional Papers of the American Society for Reformation Research* 1 (1977): 125–36, who has counted ninety expulsions in German-speaking territories from 1388 to 1520. The authoritative survey of the imperial cities is Markus J. Wenninger, *Man bedarf keiner Juden mehr. Ursachen und Hintergrunde ihrer Vertreibung aus den deutschen Reichsstädten im 15. Jahrhundert* (Vienna, 1981), where the Bavarian expulsions are only mentioned briefly on 251; see also Alfred Haverkamp, "Judenvertreibungen in Mittelalter und Frühneuzeit—Erscheinungsformen und Zusammenhänge, Betrachtungsweisen und Erkenntnischancen. Zur Orientierung," in *Judenvertreibungen in Mittelalter und früher Neuzeit*, ed. Friedhelm Burgard, Alfred Haverkamp and Gerd Mentgen (Hannover, 1999), 1–21.

[17] A comprehensive survey of Jewish communities in Munich has never been written. In addition to the sources cited above in note 10, see Eduard Schöpflich, "Zur Geschichte der Juden in München," *Das Bayerland* 37, no. 20 (October 2, 1926): 613–18; and very useful, despite the author's antisemitic attitudes, is Solleder, *München*, 130–4, 226–31, 495–7, 522–3, 532–4. For general works on the Jewish communities of Bavaria, see Johann Christian Freiherr von Aretin, *Geschichte der Juden in Bayern* (Landshut, 1803); Schwarz, *Juden in Bayern*; and Klaus Geissler, *Die Juden in Deutschland und Bayern bis zur Mitte des 14. Jahrhunderts* (Munich, 1976); Manfred Treml and Josef Kirmeier, eds., *Geschichte und Kultur der Juden in Bayern: Aufsätze* (Munich, 1988).

[18] The best overall accounts remain Gerlinde Stahl, "Die Wallfahrt zur Schönen Maria in Regensburg," *Beiträge zur Geschichte des Bistums Regensburg*, ed. Georg Schwaiger and Joseph Staber, vol. 2 (Regensburg, 1968), 35–281; and Achim Hubel, "'Die Schöne Maria' von Regensburg. Wallfahrten—Gnadenbilder—Ikonographie," in *850 Jahre Kollegiatstift zu den heiligen Johannes Baptist und Johannes Evangelist in Regensburg 1127–1977*, ed. Paul Mai (Munich, 1977), 199–231. Insightful is the more recent study by Allyson F. Creasman, "The Virgin Mary Against the Jews: Anti-Jewish Polemic in the Pilgrimage to the Schöne Maria of Regensburg, 1519–25," *Sixteenth Century Journal* 33, no. 4 (2002): 963–80.

this same region and period—two centuries widely acknowledged as nadir of Ashkenazic Jewish life in western Europe prior to the twentieth century—synagogues and other community buildings were expropriated or destroyed also in the wake of host-desecration charges. In these cases, where expulsions were more likely to be accompanied by pogroms, synagogues and community houses were converted into—or destroyed and replaced by—pilgrimage chapels consecrated to the miraculous bleeding host (*Heilig Blut*), or to Christ as the Holy Savior (*Sankt Salvator*).[19]

Of the scholars who have treated the broad phenomenon of the "converted synagogue" critically, Hedwig Röckelein has produced the most reliable data; she counts sixteen places in imperial south Germany where synagogues were converted into Marian chapels between 1349 and 1520 (recent research has raised the number only by a few).[20]

[19] For example, the Church of the Holy Savior (Salvatorkirche) in Passau, founded in 1479 on the site of a community house that served as a synagogue after the community's expulsion; analysed in Mitchell B. Merback, "The Vanquished Synagogue, the Risen Host, and the Grateful Dead at the Salvatorkirche in Passau," *Peregrinations* 1, no. 4 (Autumn 2005) [http://peregrinations.kenyon.edu/welcome.html]. For a discussion of legend-motifs that supported the identification of synagogue sites with host-desecrations and subsequent chapels, see idem, "Fount of Mercy, City of Blood: Cultic Anti-Judaism and the Pulkau Passion Altarpiece," *Art Bulletin* 87, no. 4 (Dec. 2005): 588–641.

[20] See Hedwig Röckelein, "Marienverehrung und Judenfeindlichkeit in Mittelalter und früher Neuzeit," in *Maria in der Welt: Marienverehrung im Kontext der Sozialgeschichte 10.–18. Jahrhundert* (Zurich, 1993), 279–307, whose list of sixteen *places* actually includes seventeen *cases* (two conversions occurred in Rothenburg on the Tauber in 1404 and 1520 respectively). The work of J. M. Minty, "Judengasse to Christian Quarter: The Phenomenon of the Converted Synagogue in the Late Medieval and Early Modern Holy Roman Empire," in *Popular Religion in Germany and Central Europe, 1400–1800*, ed. Bob Scribner and T. Johnson (New York, 1996), 58–86, raises the total count to thirty two by including synagogue conversion cases that did not result in Marian shrines, but her documentation is less reliable in a few cases; in my view only two cases of Marian shrines from her list, Deutz (date unknown) and Mainz (1441), can be used to supplement Röckelein's list, for a total of nineteen cases. Though published after the two works just cited, Wolfgang Glüber, "'Die Judengaßen thet man zerstören/der hymelkünigen zu eren.' Synagogenzerstörung und Marienkirchenbau," in *Maria Tochter Sion? Mariologie, Marienfrömmigkeit und Judenfeindschaft*, ed. Johannes Heil and Rainer Kampling (Paderborn, 2001), 163–86, is based on research discontinued in 1987 and, though useful, documents only eleven cases, all listed by Röckelein and Minty. Still valuable (though only eight cases are discussed) is Wilhelm Volkert, "Die Juden in der Oberpfalz im 14. Jahrhundert," *Zeitschrift für bayerische Landesgeschichte* 30, no. 1 (1967): 161–200; and the earliest scholarly treatment of the phenomena I have found is Alfred Grotte, *Synagogenspuren in schlesischen Kirchen* (Breslau, 1937), 4–8, with some inaccuracies. Official Church policy, as reflected in papal documents, is reviewed in Schlomo Simonsohn, ed. *The Apostolic See and the Jews: Documents, 492–1404* (Toronto, 1988), 122–30.

Virtually all of these conversions occurred in the wake of regional or municipal expulsions, though only the incident at Würzburg in 1349, so far as sources reveal, was directly associated with an outbreak of popular violence.[21] Those episodes for which we have the best information appear to have been thinly disguised power plays by local elites, intent on expanding key economic resources in the city, in particular the central market square (*Marktplatz*), which Jewish settlements often adjoined or directly overlapped. That expropriated synagogues were to become churches was, therefore, not always a foregone conclusion. A different course would have seen the property "secularized" and converted into a private residence; this happened in several other cases where former synagogues were handed over or pawned by local lords to wealthy burghers.[22] What has misleadingly come to be called "Marian antisemitism" (i.e., the connections between Christian anti-Judaism and Marian devotionalism) is therefore only one aspect of the converted synagogue phenomenon overall, and not always the most important.[23] This critical insight prepares us to understand why, in terms of their cult environment, the Marian "synagogue-churches" of imperial south Germany exhibit few peculiar traits, that is, no distinctive image-types or symbols that betray their origins in anti-Jewish actions or ideas.[24] This presents a challenge to interpretation.

---

[21] Röckelein, "Marienverehrung," 200, Gluber, "Synagogenzerstörung," 184. In Nuremberg a massacre which claimed 562 victims did take place in the same year as the city's decision to raze the synagogue and build in its place a Marian chapel, but the massacre followed rather than preceded the conversion.

[22] Such a conversion took place in 1404 in not-too-distant Rothenburg ob der Tauber through he initiative of the burgher Peter Krelinger; see Hedwig Röckelein, "'Die grabstain, so vil ta^e^usent gulden wer sein': Vom Umgang der Christen mit Synagogen und jüdischen Friedhofen im Mittelalter und am Beginn der Neuzeit," *Aschkenas. Zeitschrift für Geschichte und Kultur der Judentum* 5 (1995): 19–22; for the resulting chapel, see *Die Kunstdenkmäler von Mittelfranken 8: Stadt Rothenburg ob der Tauber, Kirchliche Bauten*, ed. Anton Ress (Munich, 1959), 528–33.

[23] I will not take space here to explore the special antagonism towards Mary attributed to the Jews; on this subject, William Chester Jordan, "Marian Devotion and the Talmud Trial of 1240," in *Religionsgespräche im Mittelalter*, ed. Bernard Lewis and Friedrich Niewöhner (Wiesbaden, 1992), 61–76; Denise L. Despres, "Immaculate Flesh and the Social Body: Mary and the Jews," *Jewish History* 12, no. 1 (Spring 1998): 47–69; Annette Weber, "'...Maria die ist juden veind': Antijüdische Mariendarstellungen in der Kunst des 13.–15. Jahrhunderts," in Heil and Kampling, eds., *Maria Tochter Sion?* 69–91; and Creasman, "The Virgin Mary."

[24] After 1490, however, the imperial cult of the Immaculate Conception, with its militant, crusading piety, ensured it would be the apocalyptic image of the "Fair Virgin" (*Schöne Maria*) that presided over expulsions, pogroms and the destruction of synagogues;

Another challenge is the general paucity of artefactual evidence: few of the converted synagogues survive, and fewer bear any resemblance to their medieval incarnations.[25] Also no printed miracle books of the kind produced for other Marian shrines in Bavaria—places such as Tuntenhausen, Altötting and Regensburg—have come down to us for Munich.[26] Thus we have no contemporary corroboration about the scale and character of the pilgrimage otherwise well-attested in later sources, nor any knowledge of the Gruftkirche's medieval foundation legend, if there ever was one (discussed below). That a pilgrimage of some kind was initiated in the wake of the chapel's foundation can, however, be shown by a series of papal and episcopal indulgences issued between 1443 and 1451 (also discussed below).[27]

Also generally difficult to trace in the case of the Marian synagogue-churches are cult images of demonstrable medieval provenance.[28]

---

see esp. Lionel Rothkrug, "Holy Shrines, Religious Dissonance and Satan in the Origins of the German Reformation," *Historical Reflections* 14 (1987): 143–286, at 228.

[25] And even less can be known about the Gruftkirche's late medieval career, in part because the last excavations performed in the area did not include the entire area of the two houses on Gruftgasse 1 and 2; see Fastje, "Ausgrabungen," 24–6.

[26] Of the many known sites, only the three mentioned here have surviving books; see Philip M. Soergel, *Wondrous in His Saints: Counter-Reformation Propaganda in Bavaria* (Berkeley, 1993), 31; for comprehensive overview, see Dieter Harmening, "Fränkische Mirakelbücher. Quellen und Untersuchung zur historischen Volkskunde und Geschichte der Volksfrömmigkeit," *Würzburger Diözesangeschichtsblätter* 28 (1966): 25–144; on the saints' shrines from this region, Steven D. Sargent, "Miracle Books and Pilgrimage Shrines in Late Medieval Bavaria," *Historical Reflections/Réflexions Historique* 13, no. 2 & 3 (1986): 455–71; and Gabriela Signori, "The Miracle Kitchen and its Ingredients: A Methodical and Critical Approach to Marian Shrine Wonders (10th to 13th century)," *Hagiographica* 3 (1996): 277–303.

[27] Recent research on other Bavarian shrines founded in converted synagogues, and involving anti-Jewish legends, has shown the need for a healthy skepticism when it comes to assigning medieval origins to pilgrimages, foundation legends, and cult-images; see, for example, Marianne Stößl, "Maria Schutter—'Schuttermutter.' Zur Genese eines Ingolstädter Kult," Inaugural dissertation, Ludwig-Maximilians-Universität (Munich, 1995), a critical study of the Ingolstadt chapel to the so-called "Schuttermutter," founded in 1397 in a converted synagogue (and destroyed in the Second World War). Stößl shows the development of the pilgrimage and its associated "image-desecration" (*Bildfrevel*) legend to be products of the seventeenth century.

[28] Apart from the two surviving sculptures associated with the Gruftkirche (discussed below), I know of only one other medieval image that can, with reasonably certainty, be connected with a Marian chapel built on the site of a synagogue, the "Schuttermutter" of Ingolstadt, a polychromed wood statue dateable to the fourteenth century, now in the city's Franciscan church. Its cult home was the "Capellan unnser lieben Frawen der Schütter," although when it arrived there is an open question; see Stößl, "Maria Schutter," 113; Minty, "Judengasse to Christian Quarter," 222, n. 16; Röckelein, "Marienverehrung," 286; *Germania Judaica*, vol. 3, pt. 1, ed. Arye Maimon (Tübingen, 1987), 582; and Israel Schwierz, *Steinerne Zeugnisse jüdischen Lebens in Bayern.*

In this respect, at least, the Gruftkirche has yielded an embarassment of riches: not only are post-Reformation sources plentiful, corroborating the existence a sculpted figure-group "in der Grufft,"[29] but there survive today two sculptures traceable in some way to the shrine. In his *Geschichte der Kruft zu München* (c. 1799), the church's last clerical administrator, Abbott P. Placidus Scharl of the nearby Andechs monastery, speaks of an "old Pietà" (*altes Vesperbild*) that, he speculated, came from the "thirteenth or fourteenth century."[30] In the roughly contemporary travelogue by Johann Pezzl, *Reise durch den Baierischen Kreis* (1784), the author refers to "a Pietà worthy of devotion" (*ein andächtiges Vesperbild*), and claims that it had been offered in thanksgiving for the expulsion of the Jews.[31] Neither source, however, offers enough information to suggest a match to a specific type of the Pietà or to an existing object. Once modern scholarship tried to do this, opinion divided into two opposing camps, each ready to identify one of two surviving Pietàs as the "original" wonder-working image. The more impressive of the two is a monumental poplar-wood group of circa 1340, carved in a severe style that has made it, in the eyes of numerous commentators, emblematic of the pathetic realism of German late Gothic art; since 1893 it has been housed in the village church in Salmdorf, a neighborhood of present-day Munich (fig. 2).[32] The other work, now residing in the pilgrimage church of St. Rasso in Grafrath, Upper Bavaria, is a more

Eine Dokumentation, 2nd edn. (Munich, 1992), 313. Although widely assumed by art historians, it is unlikely that Albrecht Altdorfer's painting of the *Schöne Maria* in Regensburg (Kunstsammlung des Bistums Regenburg, Diözesansmuseum) served as the actual *Kultbild* in the pilgrimage chapel of 1519 in that city.

[29] Strengelii, *Hodoeporicum*, ch. 12. The book also includes the first known engraving of the "alte Vesperbild" on its altar, signed by G. A. Wolfgang; for a reproduction, see Hans Ramisch, "Das Vesperbild aus der ehem. Gruftkirche München, ein Spätwerk Erasmus Grasser," *Jahrbuch der Bayerische Landesamt für Denkmalpflege* 26 (1967), fig. 4; also the account in Wilhelm Gumppenberg, *Marianischer Atlas*, pt. 2 (Munich, 1673), 71; quoted in Stahleder, "Die Münchener Juden," 31.

[30] Scharl, *Geschichte der Kruft*, 18; for a summary, see Lieb, "Klosterhäuser," 179; Sattler (*Chronik von Andechs*, 208) reinforces this notion by stating that a Pietà was the object of special honor in the chapel "from the start"; although he readily admits that "authentic reports about the image are not to be found." More recent writers take for granted that, for example, "In 1442 it [the Pietà] was set out for veneration in the chapel newly built by the doctor Johann Hartlieb"; from Peter Steiner, "Die Gruftkirche," in *Altmünchener Gnadenstätten. Wallfahrt und Volksfrömmigkeit im Kürfurstlichen München*, exhib. cat. (Munich, 1977), 28–30, at 30.

[31] Pezzl, *Reise*, 192.

[32] *Ausstellung 1000 Jahre christliche Kunst im Zeichen der Passion*, exhib. cat., ed. Karl Feuchtmayer (Munich, 1950), cat. 60; *Bayerische Frömmigkeit. 1400 Jahre christliches Bayern*, exhib. cat. Munich, Stadtmuseum, ed. Erwin Schalkhausser (Munich, 1960), cat. 204;

lyrical work of circa 1510 by the Munich woodcarver Erasmus Grasser (fig. 3).[33] This is not the place, however, to adjudicate their rivalry. In devotional engravings such as Johann Baptist Klauber's sheet from c. 1760 (fig. 4), which purports to convey the Gruftbild's public face, few specific features are discernible because all but the faces remains hidden under the sumptuous *Ehrenkleider* typically given to German pilgrimage images.[34] Early conservation reports support a tentative identification of the Salmdorf group with the Gruftkapelle,[35] but any convincing reconstruction of image and shrine will require a clearer understanding of the character of the lower chapel where the figure was displayed. For now our concerns must lie elsewhere.

Cultic Anti-Judaism and the Logic of Appropriation

In this essay I distinguish three key phases in the Gruftkirche's 350-year history, and here I will outline them. The first phase concerns the transformation of synagogue into a Marian chapel in the wake of the expulsion of 1442, a process that entailed the retrofitting of the building, the consecration of altars, the procurement of indulgences, the (presumed) installation of a cult-image and, later in the century, the promotion of a pilgrimage. Behind these processes, I argue, we can discern an attitude toward the Jewish legacy of the building in which positive and negative perceptions mingled. The second phase concerns the renewal of the shrine and its pilgrimage in the first half of the seventeenth century, a typical Counter-Reformation rehabilitation effort, here catalyzed by a visionary miracle and the (re)discovery of a wonder-working cult-image. These events unfolded in the apparent

Stabat Mater. Maria unter dem Kreuz in der Kunst um 1400, exhib. cat. (Salzburg, 1970), cat. 3.

33 Ramisch, "Das Versperbild"; on Grafrath, see *Die Kunstdenkmäler von Bayern, vol. 1: Oberbayern* (1892), 461; Sigfried Grän, *Wallfahrts- und Klosterkirche Grafrath/Amper*, Kunstführer no. 519, 4th edn. (Regensburg, 1995), 14–15; also Bauerreiss, *Pie Jesu*, 33.

34 On the baroque outfitting of medieval cult-images, Hannes Etzlstorfer, "Gotisches—im barocken Kleid: Stil- und Kultbildadaptationen im 17. und 18. Jahrhundert," in *Gotik Schätze Oberösterreich*, exhib. cat., Oberösterreichisches Landesmuseums, ed. Lothar Schultes and Bernhard Prokisch (Weitra, 2002), 459–68.

35 Rupert Karbacher, "Die Salmdorf Pietà. Ein monumentales Vesperbild aus dem frühen 14. Jahrhundert. Erst Untersuchungsergebnisse" (unpublished report, Bayerische Landesamt für Denkmalpflege, 1998). I am deeply grateful to the author for sharing his research with me.

absence of any negative myths about the former Jewish inhabitants, but again we can discern an ambivalent interest in the Jewish pre-history of the site, evidenced in the appropriation of the site's underground water supply—connected to what was once, in all probability, a Jewish ritual bath (*mikveh*)—to create a well with healing waters sacred to Mary. During the third stage, concentrated around the Gruftkirche's tricentennial in the mid-eighteenth century, anti-Jewish myths made their dramatic reappearance in the form of revived ritual murder tales; in this process local myths of long-standing notoriety were retrospectively linked to the old synagogue, leading to the shrine's redefinition—and historicization—as a species of "atonement chapel" (*Sühnekapelle*). These notions, I will show, were informed directly by pious archaeology conducted at the site, and indirectly by the tendentious Christian "exegesis" of Judaism undertaken by Hebraist scholars such as Andreas Eisenmenger, a professor of Oriental languages at the University of Heidelberg.

Each of these stages in the Gruftkirche's career were characteristic of a key stage in the medieval and post-medieval development of what I am calling *cultic anti-Judaism*.[36] As I use it, the term describes a set of functionally interdependent cultural processes: conflict-driven discourses (myth-making, accusations, polemics, repressive decrees, and so on) and/or coercive actions (pogroms, synagogue or cemetery desecrations, trials, expulsions, and so on), aimed at Judaism and particular Jewish communities, unfold in a fluid connection to otherwise normative aspects of Christian cult-formation. These include: the financing, building and consecration of chapels and churches; the translation of relics and cult-images; the procurement of indulgences and the mobilization of pilgrims; the dissemination of legends and the promotion of miracles; the orchestration of pious donations and further improvements to the church—all procedures that routinely occurred in connection with the establishment, renewal and promotion of sacred shrines. One of my contentions is that the meanings deposited by each of these procedures accumulate over the course of the shrine's history, whether or not they become embedded visually in the cultic environment itself. In

[36] To my knowledge, the term was coined by Denise Despres, "Mary of the Eucharist: Cultic Anti-Judaism in Some Fourteenth-Century English Devotional Manuscripts," in *From Witness to Witchcraft: Jews and Judaism in Medieval Christian Thought*, ed. Jeremy Cohen (Wiesbaden, 1996), 375–401; also see idem, "Immaculate Flesh." For my earlier applications, see Merback, "Vanquished Synagogue"; and idem, "Fount of Mercy," esp. 593, 625.

this model local memory, always absorptive and malleable, becomes the key renewable resource, especially when it comes time to arouse popular interest in the shrine, and to generate public acclaim for its role in the salvific economy.

But what was the nature of this interest, what were the sources of this acclaim, and how can we trace them? Because it has been mostly clerical writers who have narrated the Gruftkirche's story, the nature of the Christian interest in the site's Jewish legacy has never been critically examined. Yet it should be of interest to us, aware as we now are of the *ambivalences* that marked Christian perceptions of Jews, Judaism, Jewish customs and ritual, and the Hebrew language.[37] Far from representing merely another chapter in the history of European antisemitism, Christian attitudes towards Jews in the period between the fifteenth and eighteenth centuries were marked by a changing combination of antagonism and admiration, fear and fascination, "judeophobia" and "judeophilia," and it was this ambivalence, I will argue, through which the long-term transformations of the buildings at Judengasse/Gruftstrasse must be understood.

My goal, then, is to revisit the church's public history with an eye to the peculiar constellation of myths and memories that formed around the synagogue site during its long career as a Christian sanctuary. I ask whether there once existed, behind the scenes of the Jews' expulsion and the takeoever of the building, a kind of exotic fascination with the idea of "Jewish sacred space."[38] In particular I will argue that, at various points in its history, the Gruftkirche was promoted and recognized as a special locus of the Virgin's mercy and grace (*Gnadenstätte*) precisely because it has been rescued from the "idolatry," "superstition," "blasphemy" and "magic" imputed to Jewish ritual and belief. Not only had Ecclesia triumphed ideologically over Synagoga once more; through the routine practices constituitive of Christian cult, a characteristically "Jewish" form of demonic pollution had been eliminated, and the site delivered into Christian hands as a new locus of sanctity.

---

[37] Zygmunt Baumann places *ambivalence* centrally in his broad redefinition of terms for the study of historical antisemitism; see his "Allosemitism: Premodern, Modern, Postmodern," in *Modernity, Culture and 'the Jew,'* ed. Bryan Cheyette and Laura Marius (Stanford, 1998), 143–56.

[38] I should emphasize that my references to Jewish "sacred" space throughout this essay are ironical, since it is only within the *Christian* understanding of the religious sanctuary that synagogues were conceived as sacred, that is, liturgically consecrated. Medieval Jews held distinct conceptions of the sanctity of space.

At the heart of this process lies a dynamic of *appropriation*, and at the heart of this dynamic lies a paradox that runs through the long history of Christian anti-Judaism. In the Christian theological interpretation of Judaism and its role in the divine plan of salvation, the Hebrew Scriptures were regarded as an authentic source of truth. Yet only Christian exegesis, with its superior method for apprehending the "spiritual" meanings of God's law and the utterances of the prophets, had succeeded in illuminating the logic of Israel's salvation through Christ. Despite the keen awareness that, in Paul's words, "unto them [the Jews] were committed the oracles of God" (Romans 3:2), theologians believed that the post-biblical Jews had, in their willful "blindness" to the proper christological interpretation of their own sacred texts, turned away from the essential truth that would lead to their salvation. Paradoxically, this primeval truth embedded in Hebrew Scripture, once realized, would foreclose the very possibility of a Jewish religion; and this was why, churchmen reasoned, Jewish leaders (who from the patristic period onward were cast in the mold of the biblical Pharisees) actively sought to hide the truth both from their own people, and from Christians. What meanings Christian exegesis had not been able to unlock were therefore accessible only to those with a knowledge of the Jews' "secret language," and from the twelfth century onward scholars pursued this "Hebrew Truth" (*Hebraica veritas*) both with the help of living Jewish interlocutors and, in rarer instances, by learning Hebrew themselves. In the mid-fifteenth century German humanists, like their Italian counterparts, reinvested themselves in this old scholastic project of Christian Hebraism—the attempt to discover in "original" Hebrew sources truths capable of, among other things, refuting Judaism as a living religion.[39]

This attribution to the Jews of a "secret language"—inaccessible to Gentiles but necessary for illuminating God's plan—and a "secret

[39] The expression *Hebraica veritas* has been attributed to Stephen Harding, Abbott of Cîteaux, who created the order's official bible based on the study of Hebrew sources; see Aryeh Grabois, "The *Hebraica Veritas* and Jewish-Christian Intellectual Relations in the Twelfth Century," *Speculum* 50, no. 4 (Oct. 1975): 613–34; and Michael A. Signer, "Polemic and Exegesis: The Varieties of Twelfth-Century Hebraism," in *Hebraica Veritas? Christian Hebraists and the Study of Judaism in Early Modern Europe*, ed. Allison P. Coudert and Jeffrey S. Shoulson (Philadelphia, 2004), 21–32. For the late medieval and humanist context, Heiko A. Obermann, "Discovery of Hebrew and Discrimination against the Jews: The *Veritas Hebraica* as Double-Edged Sword in Renaissance and Reformation," in *Germania Illustrata: Essays on Early Modern Germany Presented to Gerald Strauss*, ed. Andrew C. Fix and Susan C. Karant-Nunn (Kirksville, 1992), 19–34.

knowledge" of sacred things that would ultimately be delivered into Christian hands was grounded in Augustine of Hippo's (354–430) doctrine of Jewish "witness." According to Augustine, the survival of the Jews after the Crucifixion formed a necessary part of God's right ordering of the world: Jewish exile and dispossession testified to their punishment for rejecting Christ, and their continued adherence to the Mosaic law corroborated the authenticity of the Scriptures from which Christianity derived its ancient legitimacy.[40] Such ideas about the power of a theologically-constructed Judaism to negatively authenticate Christian claims also had a conceptual analogy in medieval ideas about sacred space, in particular, the belief that Christian propriety over the sacred places once occupied by infidels—Jews and, in later variations, Muslims—would invariably be "restored" by God through miraculous means. Symbolic appropriation of sacred space is a prevalent theme in a variety of ancient legends, and many of these made their way into medieval miracle collections in the thirteenth century. From his analysis of the early legends, Ora Limor has gone so far as to conclude that "The Jew is to be found at the heart of the Christian sacred space."[41]

I concur, and part of my aim here is to provide additional testing of this claim, though in a very different context. Recognizing that the Christian logic of appropriation and conversion of what was once Jewish had temporal *and* spatial dimensions will better prepare us to understand the phenomenon of adaptive reuse in the case of late medieval synagogues. It may also lead to insights about the symbolic dialogue between church and synagogue architecture in the Middle Ages, a dialogue rooted in late antiquity, in competing Christian and Jewish claims to the inheritance of the Jerusalem Temple, in particular its distinctive construction of sanctity.[42] In the end mythmaking and memory, if not temporality itself, became spatialized at the Gruftkirche

---

[40] These are only the essential components of the Augustinian doctrine; for a detailed explication, Jeremy Cohen, *Living Letters of the Law: Ideas of the Jew in Medieval Christianity* (Berkeley, 1999), with extensive bibliography and sources.

[41] Ora Limor, "Christian Sacred Space and the Jew," in Cohen, ed., *From Witness to Witchcraft*, 55–77, at 76; and, more recently, the excellent study by Amy G. Remensnyder, "The Colonization of Sacred Architecture: The Virgin Mary, Mosques, and Temples in Medieval Spain and Early Sixteenth-Century Mexico," in *Monks, Nuns, Saints & Outcasts: Religion in Medieval Society. Essays in Honor of Lester K. Little*, ed. Sharon Farmer and Barbara H. Rosenwein (Ithaca, 2000), 189–219.

[42] That both early synagogues and early churches encoded an idealized "Temple space" in the disposition of their interior spaces is brilliantly demonstrated by Joan R. Branham, "Sacred Space under Erasure in Ancient Synagogues and Early Churches,"

through a kind of allegorical reading of the site, a Christian exegesis of the building's artefactual history. Throughout the unfolding of this long process, we will see why the former presence of Jews in the heart of Munich's Christian polity was not seen by the majority as an unfortunate accident better soon forgotten. Rather, the revelation of sanctity through the dialectic of Jewish presence and absence on the site formed a necessary stage in the inauguration of a new cult to the Sorrowing Mother, one that retrospectively validated Christian claims to ownership of the site.

From Judenschule to Gruftkapelle

On September 14, 1442, Duke Albrecht III and his second wife, Anna of Braunschweig, presented the property at Judengasse 1, and several adjoining rear buildings, to the physician, humanist author and occultist Johann Hartlieb (d. 1468) as a gift.[43] Mentioned in the deed as "our highly learned, beloved and trusted doctor, Master Johann Hartlieb, professor of medicine," Hartlieb would go on to write important treatises on mnemotechnics, chiromancy and witchcraft among other things, and would eventually serve Albrecht as court physician, spiritual confessor, and a trusted political advisor.[44] Furthermore, by 1442 Hartlieb was also engaged—possibly already married—to the duke's daughter, Sibylla.[45] Given this special favor and access, and the gain that came

Art Bulletin 74, no. 3 (Sept. 1992): 375–94. Provocative as it is for the phenomenon at hand, I will not explore this theme in the present chapter.

[43] Sattler, "Die ehemalige Gruftkirche," 42; idem, *Chronik von Andechs*, 207–08; Forster, *Das gottselige München*, 370; Karl Drescher, "Johann Hartlieb. Über sein Leben und seine schriftstellerische Tätigkeit," *Eurphorion: Zeitschrift für Literaturgeschichte* 25 (1924): 224–41, 354–70 and 569–90, here 228, 234; Solleder, *München*, 346–7; Lieb, "Klosterhäuser," 154; Stahleder, "Die Münchener Juden," 30–1; Mathäser, *Andechser Chronik*, 47–8; Rauch, "Münchens jüdische Denkmäler," 10; also see Stahleder, *Chronik*, 324.

[44] "*hochgelehrten unserm Arzt und lieben getreuen Meister Johann Hartlieb, Lehrer der Arznei*"; quoted in Solleder, *München*, 346. For Hartlieb's life and career, see Sigmund von Riezler, *Geschichte Baierns*, 8 vols. (1878–1914; repr. Aalen, 1964), 3: 867f.; NDB 7:722–3; on his service to Albrecht, see Drescher, "Johann Hartlieb," 227–31; on his interests in occult philosophy and science, see ibid., 354–7; and Sattler, *Chronik von Andechs*, 618–19. For Hartlieb's place in the early discourse of witchcraft, Wolfgang Behringer, *Witchcraft Persecutions in Bavaria: Popular Magic, Religious Zealotry and Reason of State in Early Modern Europe*, trans. J. C. Grayson and David Lederer (New York, 1997), 71.

[45] Sibylla first appears in relation to Hartlieb in a document of May 18, 1444, where she is mentioned as "seiner 'hawsfrau' Sibilla" (BHStA Andechs, Urk. Fasz. 2, Nr. 14; reproduced in Drescher, "Johann Hartlieb," 229), but Hartlieb is not designated as

to him, it seems all but a foregone conclusion that Hartlieb advised the duke closely in the decision to expel the Jews.[46] Given his interest in the occult and witchcraft, which among other things involved him in the Christian Hebraism of his Italian and German colleagues, the Jewish prehistory of the building on Judengasse 1 must have been of keen interest to Hartlieb. How did this interest translate into plans for the founding and dedication of a Marian chapel?

Once in possession of the place, Hartlieb's first move was to create a small prayer chapel (*oratorium*) in honor of the Virgin in the cellar level, or *Gruft*.[47] This seems to have been accomplished swiftly. By April 1443 he had already secured an indulgence for the new chapel, or "Neustift," from the papal legate for Germany at the Council of Basel, Cardinal Alexander, the Patriarch of Aquileja.[48] This was the first of four indulgences granted in the first decade of the chapel's career—documents that confirmed the legitimacy of the place as the site of miracles and authorized the veneration of its cult objects by the faithful.[49] A second indulgence came in the following year, expressly identifying the chapel as "located in the former synagogue."[50] In the newly converted upper chapel an altar was dedicated to the honor of the Immaculate Conception and the holy martyrs Cosmas and Damian. While the choice of Mary as principal patron reflects both the general practices of synagogue conversion in imperial south Germany and her traditional role as a civic *Schutzpatron*,[51] the dedication to Cosmas and Damian, two patron saints of medicine, reflect Hartlieb's intention to

Albrecht's son-in-law until the indulgence letter of November 20, 1447 for the new chapel (BHStA, KU Andechs Nr. 21).

[46] Drescher, "Johann Hartlieb," 234, and NDB 3:157, both make this assertion unequivocally; other writers have refrained from comment.

[47] Lieb, "Klosterhäuser," 154; Rauch, "Münchens jüdische Denkmäler," 10.

[48] Stahleder, *Chronik*, 324; idem, "Die Münchener Juden," 31; cf. Solleder, *München*, 523.

[49] For more direct documentary evidence of a pilgrimage during this period, see the indulgence letter of November 20, 1447, discussed below with sources cited in note 55.

[50] Solleder, *München*, 523; Stahleder, *Chronik*, 327, attributes it to Cardinal and Bishop of Freising, Johannes Gründwalder. The occasion for this may have been renovations which also saw the separation of the synagogue property from the two houses behind it on Schrammerstraße 11, which once served as its rear-buildings; according to Stahleder, "Die Münchener Juden," 31, the work is documented for May 18, 1444.

[51] See Klaus Schreiner, *Maria. Jungfrau, Mutter, Herrscherin* (Munich, 1994), esp. 333–73.

create a family memorial.[52] Contrary to what is often asserted, Hartlieb never used Judengasse 1 as a private residence; he had other houses in Munich for this purpose. The ultimate goal appears to have been the elaboration of the chapel into an endowed Franciscan convent, a type of pious endowment then quite popular among the city's wealthy burghers.[53] The terms and plans for such a family *Stift* would surely have been known and sanctioned by Albrecht himself, since his heirs would have been involved. This lends some weight to the theory that the building made up part of a Wittelsbach dowry, though no records exist to confirm it.

Between 1444 and 1447, prompted by rumors of miracles, the new chapel attracted increasing numbers of pious visitors and donations, some of them, at least, cognizant of the chapel's Jewish legacy. A record of donations made by several wealthy Munich burghers—in 1447 and again in 1469—for perpetual Saturday masses suggests an interest in "commemorating" a key aspect of Jewish religious observance, namely, the sabbath.[54] On November 20, 1447 the church received its third indulgence, this one from Cardinal Johann of Bavaria (who was also the Bishop of Freising), a grant that appears to be the culmination of a rebuilding effort, and the occasion to elevate the shrine from a private chapel (*capellum*) to the status of a church offering public masses (*ecclesia*).[55] Involved in this rebuilding was the vaulting of the Gruft. This served the dual purpose of emphasizing the ecclesiastical character of the space and preparing for major renovations of the upper church. Upon completion, the new, brighter space created from the mezzanine level of the former synagogue was furnished with three new altars,

---

[52] Scharl, *Geschichte der Kruft*, 17 (summarized in Lieb, "Klosterhäuser," 178); cf. Sattler, "Die ehemalige Gruftkirche," 42.

[53] Stahleder, "Die Münchener Juden," 31; cf. documents in Drescher, "Johann Hartlieb," 229–30. For the older views, see Aretin, *Geschichte*, 32; and Gufler, "Ergänzungen ,"122.

[54] Lieb, "Klosterhäuser," 154; cf. Rauch, "Münchens jüdische Denkmäler," 11 (with second date given incorrectly as 1464).

[55] BHStA KU Andechs Nr. 21, where the building is acknowledged as having been recently converted from the former synagogue, and the site exalted as a place where the faithful gathered in pious expectation of Mary's heavenly grace (*novissime ex quadam Judeorum sinagoga constructa congruis frequentetur honoribus fidelesque ipsi eo libentius devotionis causa confluant ad eandam, quo ibidem dono celestis gracie uberius conspexerint se refectos*); text reproduced in full in Drescher, "Johann Hartlieb," 234–5; see also Stahleder, "Die Münchener Juden," 31; idem, *Chronik*, 331; Solleder, *München*, 523. This change of ecclesiastical status may not have been formalized until 1450; cf. Gufler, "Ergänzungen," 122; also Sattler, *Chronik von Andechs*, 209.

the central one dedicated to the Immaculate Conception. Another document from the same year distinguishes between this part of the building, calling it "der newen stifft," and the lower chapel, called "Unser lieben Frawen Kapellen."[56] The process of transformation probably reached completion by about 1450. Upper church and lower chapels together received another indulgence on March 24, 1451, this one by Nicholas V and underwritten by the Cardinal Legate to Germany, Nicholas of Cusa, who several days earlier had preached in Munich and arranged for indulgences for several other sanctuaries, notably the "holy mountain" (*heilige Berg*) pilgrimage church at Andechs, which housed the famed "Three Holy Hosts."[57] Buoyed by the success of his foundation, Hartlieb petitioned Rome for permission to found a Franciscan priory on the site (though this plan ultimately came to naught).[58] Already in 1452 the Judengasse, now cleared of Jews, was being referred to in some sources as the "Neustiftgässel."[59] The first stage of the Gruftkirche's career had reached its culmination.

Twelve years after the death of their father in 1468, two of Hartlieb's children, Gotthard and Dorothea, sold the building at Gruftgasse 1 for an unknown sum.[60] The purchaser was one Thomas Piperl, a man who served Albrecht IV (r. 1465–1508) in a variety of official capacities between 1476 and 1492 and maintained close ties to the Benedictines of Andechs.[61] In 1494 Piperl's second wife and then-widow, Beatrix, transferred ownership of the Neustifts-Kirche to the monastery.[62] With the transfer to Andechs the Munich "Grufthaus," as it then became

[56] BHStA, KU Andechs, Nr. 20. Recorded in for January 29, 1447 is the donation of a house on Residenzstraße, "zu der newen stifft und Unser lieben Frawen Kapellen"; quoted in Stahleder, "Die Münchener Juden," 31.

[57] Scharl, *Geschichte der Kruft*, 22, quoted in Lieb, "Klosterhäuser," 179; Sattler, *Chronik von Andechs*, 209; Drescher, "Johann Hartlieb," 590; the other indulgence letters are discussed in Stahleder, *Chronik*, 338, with further references. On Cusa's grant to Andechs, Gerda Möhler, "Wallfahrten zum Heiligen Berg," in *Andechs: Der Heilige Berg. Von der Frühzeit bis zur Gegenwart*, ed. Karl Bosl et al. (Munich, 1993), 119–33, at 124.

[58] For the document and brief exposition, Franz Martin, "Zur Geschichte der Gruftkirche in München," in *Altbayerische Monatsschrift* 13 (1915/16): 22.

[59] See *Haus- und Straßennamen*, 236, for this and related names.

[60] Lieb, "Klosterhäuser," 154; cf. Sattler, *Chronik von Andechs*, 209–10.

[61] Mathäser, *Andechser Chronik*, 48; on Piperl's ownership of Gruftgasse 5, Stahleder, "Die Münchener Juden," 30.

[62] The deed of gift survives in BHStA, KU Andechs, Nr. 67; quoted by Lieb, "Klosterhäuser," 155, n. 66. The donation, received under the abbacy of Johannes von Schrattenbach, was confirmed on April 12, 1494 by Bishop Sixtus of Freising; in 1501 it received special apostolic confirmation from the Papal Legate, Cardinal Raimund Peraudi; and on May 14, 1511, a special eighty-day indulgence was granted by the

known, began a new career as an urban-based sister church for the monastery (*Klosterhaus*).[63] Ironically, then, it appears that the renovations undertaken by Hartlieb in 1447–50 spelled the beginning of the end of the medieval history of the lower chapel itself, which under the Andechs administrators became a subsidiary chapel to the larger Neustifts-Kirche. In the sixteenth century, perhaps under pressure from reformers, the Gruft fell into neglect and its cult-image, evidently, into oblivion.[64]

From Judenbad to Gruftbrunnen

A groundplan dated 1696 conveys the essentials of the old synagogue layout, despite the renovations that separate the seventeenth-century church from its late medieval precursor (fig. 5). Two principal spaces are recognizable: a main chapel above ground, and a long, narrow room at the cellar level, which later became the "lower crypt chapel." Completely underground and invisible from the street, the lower chapel (identified on the plan by the altar, indicated by a cross) extended laterally underneath the two side-by-side houses of Judengasse 1 and 2. What gave this space its gloomy, sepulchral character was its enclosure by the hulking remains of an old city wall consisting of an inner and outer ring. Rather than lying directly over the lower chapel, the upper space was sited towards the front (south) part of the complex, so the greater part of it laid under the roof of Judengasse 2. Given that the upper space was larger and more commodious, it is safe to assume that it once served as the men's prayer hall in the synagogue.[65]

Recall that when Johann Hartlieb planned his first chapel in the building in 1442–3, it was not the better-lit upper space which he converted for use, but the gloomier lower chapel. What accounts for this rather unpragmatic choice? Having already dispensed with the

Bishop of Freising; see also Sattler, *Chronik von Andechs*, 210; and Mathäser, *Andechser Chronik*, 47.

[63] At its inception in 1494, the Andechser Klosterhaus was one of ten similar institutions founded for Benedictine houses in the duchy, but one of only three in the city that had publicly accessible chapels; for an overview, Lieb, "Klosterhäuser," 139f.

[64] Cf. Mathäser, *Andechser Chronik*, 48; Sattler, *Chronik von Andechs*, 209.

[65] Rauch, "Münchens jüdische Denkmäler," 11, explains that the upper chapel would have been expanded toward the north; evidently this necessitated some demolition of the rear buildings that were formerly part of the synagogue complex; cf. Sattler, *Chronik von Andechs*, 209, and Stahleder, "Die Münchener Juden," 31.

notion that Hartlieb sacralized the Gruft as a private chapel in order to reserve the rest of the building for residential purposes, we should ask whether there was some *positive* feature of the Gruft, something about the space and perhaps also its legacy, real or imagined, which attracted, inspired or compelled him to locate the new shrine there. What about the cellar space might have interested this wide-ranging humanist-occultist scholar and physician?[66]

From the Middle Ages to the twentieth century, interested parties from clerics to archaeologists have mis-identified the vaulted cellar spaces and staircased shafts found underneath the remains of medieval synagogues as "catacombs," places of Jewish burial. Better-informed researchers have identified them as ritual purification baths (*mikvot*).[67] Numerous medieval *mikvot* survive in north and south Germany, some having escaped the destruction of the synagogues under which they were built. These were of two types. One was constructed as a rectangular shaft accessed by flights of stairs built into the walls; in this type, the bath itself, fed by groundwater and often no larger than needed for one person to immerse completely, lay at the bottom of the shaft. A second type was characterized by a simpler staircase leading down to a more open space with the bath sunken into the floor; these open spaces around the bath served in effect as a changing room.[68] Both types perforce met the two ancient requirements governing the ritual dipping or cleansing (*mikveh*, meaning a "gathering of water" [cf. Lev. 11:36]) of a menstruating woman (*niddah*), namely, that the bath's source be running ground water or naturally collected rainwater, and that it

---

[66] Stahleder asked the question already in 1988 ("Die Münchener Juden," 21), and proposed that the choice had something to do with contemporary Christian ideas about a space that was formerly used for Jewish cultic purposes, though he did not follow up on the idea.

[67] This was the case, for example, in Heilbronn and Friedberg (in Hessen); see Stahleder, "Die Münchener Juden," with further references; also Schwierz, *Steinerne Zeugnisse*, 25, 52, 53. On medieval *mikvot* in Germany and Spain, see Richard Krautheimer, *Mittelalterliche Synagogen* (Berlin, 1927), 138–9; Hannelore Künzel, "Die Architektur der mittelalterlichen Synagogen und rituellen Bäder," in *Judentum im Mittelalter*, exhib. cat., ed. Kurt Schubert (Eisenstadt, 1978), 44–9; idem, "A Recently Discovered MIQWEH in Rothenburg ob der Tauber: Preliminary Report," *Jewish Art* 14 (1988): 28–34; and Ursula Mandel, "Zeugnisse jüdischer Geschichte in Rothenburg ob der Tauber," in *Denkmäler Jüdischer Kultur in Bayern* (Munich, 1994), 47–51. For general information on *mikvot* and purification practices, Jakob Pinchas Kohn, "Mikvaoth" and "Mikveh," in *The Universal Jewish Encyclopedia*, ed. Isaac Landman (New York, 1948), 7:557; and Max Grunwald, "Bathing," in 2:108.

[68] Künzel, "Die Architektur," 45.

be provided in sufficient quantity to cover an entire body, immersed upright and crouching.[69]

Had the lower cellar space beneath the houses of Judengasse 1 and 2 housed a mikveh? As has been documented for the synagogue at Ingolstadt, which was also converted into a Marian chapel (in 1397), the proximity of the Munich synagogue to two separate fresh water sources strongly suggests the possibility.[70] One of these, an open stream, once flowed along the outside (the north side) of the old city wall; the second, a well, or *Brunnen*, was located in an open court between Judengasse and Schrammergasse, and can be seen on the plan of 1696 (cf. fig. 5). Either one of these might have been tapped to meet the mikweh's ritual requirements. Looking again at the groundplan, we see niche-like recesses between the masonry buttresses that run along the Gruft's northern wall; these are characteristic features of the second mikveh type, mentioned above, and suggest that the cellar at Judengasse housed not only a mikveh proper (the "gathering" basin for immersion), but also a surrounding dressing room. In this context such niches would have served to store clothing. Recesses with similar functions have been found at the mikvot in Speyer, Worms, and Offenburg in Baden.

If the existence of a mikveh in the cellar of Judengasse 1 and 2 can be accepted hypothetically, two related questions concerning the relationship between Hartlieb's early Gruftkapelle and this former ritual function arise: Did Hartlieb comprehend this former function, and was the early chapel designed to interface with it symbolically? In what capacity might the mikveh area, or the hydraulics that supplied its waters, have been appropriated in the cultic programming of the lower chapel? And should we see this adaptive reuse of the cellar as a positive or negative moment in the Christian reception of this "sacred" Jewish space?

Some light might be shed on the reception of the mikveh area by looking backwards from the well located between Gruftgasse and Schrammergasse, known after 1600 as the "Gruftbrunnen." P. Placidus Scharl, the Andechs abbot whose memoirs of 1799 I cited earlier,

---

69 See Rahel R. Wasserfall, "Introduction: Menstrual Blood into Jewish Blood," in *Women and Water: Menstruation in Jewish Life and Law*, ed. Rahel R. Wasserfall (Hanover, NH, 1999), 1–12, esp. 4–6.

70 Stahleder, "Die Münchener Juden," 23; for Ingolstadt, Stößl, "Maria Schutter," 4. Recovered mikvot may have played parallel roles in the configuration of cult spaces when host-desecration charges prompted expulsions and expropriations; see Merback, "Fount of Mercy," 624–25, for one likely case.

reports that in earlier times "the *Gruftbrunnen* provided almost the entire neighborhood with fresh, healthy water."[71] For this reason, a publicly accessible alley to the church, running along the eastern shared wall of the property at Gruftgasse 1 (and visible in the 1696 plan), was created between Schrammergasse and Gruftgasse.[72] Already by this time the spring must have been associated with the curative powers of the Virgin and became part of the pious visitor's itinerary. Among the faithful who arrived to venerate Our Lady in the Gruft on the heels of a miraculous vision reported for 1612 (discussed below), one could find, according to Sattler, illustrious women "in their time of expectation [visiting] the sorrowing Mother of God almost daily, in order to pray to God for protection from all dangers."[73] Such a preponderance of pregnant women suggests that the miracle of 1612 boosted the sagging fortunes of the Gruftkirche precisely by reviving its reputation as a healing shrine; certainly the waters from the Gruftbrunnen played a key role in this salvific economy, as they did at Marian shrines elsewhere.[74] More tantalizing yet is the possibility that the old hydraulic system of the mikveh was reused to supply the Gruft itself with healing waters from the well.[75] Such creative cultic programming, which entailed a controlled distribution of healing reserves throughout the shrine, would have closed the symbolic circle of the mikveh's Christian appropriation—a transformation from *Judenbrunnen* to *Gruftbrunnen*.

Pilgrimage stations associated with holy springs were plentiful in early modern Catholic Bavaria; springs could be associated with a variety of saints (especially martyrs), or with Christ (through eucharistic miracles),

---

[71] Scharl, *Geschichte der Kruft*, 54, as quoted in Rauch, "Münchens jüdische Denkmäler," 10.

[72] Fastje, "Ausgrabungen," 25.

[73] From material quoted in Sattler, *Chronik von Andechs*, 213.

[74] Pregnant women, and mothers seeking cures for sick, dying, or even dead children, appear to have formed a pervasive group among the visitors to medieval Marian shrines. At Chartres Cathedral, for example, an ancient well, accessible through the crypt, served as a popular site for women seeking the Virgin's intercession; see Laura Spitzer, "The Cult of the Virgin and Gothic Sculpture: Evaluating Opposition in the Chartres West Facade Capital Frieze," *Gesta* 33, no. 2 (1994): 142.

[75] Early modern *Brunnenkapelle* in Bavaria were often furnished with cult-images fitted with interior plumbing, which allowed them to dispense water from the *heilige Quelle*. At the church of the Holy Blood in Rosenheim (Upper Bavaria), for example, Christ appears as the *fons pietatis* inside the exterior *Brunnenkapelle* and spouts water from the stigmata; for a comparable Marian image from Upper Austria (seventeenth century), preserved in the collection of the Bavarian National Museum, see Lenz Kriss-Rettenbeck, *Bilder und Zeichen religiösen Volksglaubens* (Munich, 1963), no. 299.

but the majority were sacred to Mary.[76] Clerical promoters of *Quellenkulte* were often eager to link their sites to pagan cults overcome by true religion, and drew upon the authenticating power of legend. Typical of the European narratives linking churches and pilgrimages to holy springs is the Spanish Shepherd's Cycle (*El ciclo de los pastores*), a collection of Marian miracle tales so called because rustic characters—shepherds, cowherds, farmers—play the role of the visions' humble recipients.[77] From the twelfth century onward, the histories of most Marian pilgrimage stations attributed their origins to a miraculous discovery of an image; in some of these legends images are found nearby springs, at the place where a spring erupts, or in the water itself.[78] By narrating the revelation (and activation) of a new terrestrial channel for the Virgin's intercessionary grace, image-discovery and spring-formation legends operated as powerful engines for the sanctification of place.

Not only do the legends explain the salvific efficacy of a particular geographical site, then, they also reconfirm Christian claims to it. Tales from diverse historical contexts exhibit this same logic. The tales from the Shepherd's Cycle acquire the full breadth of their meaning only against the *Reconquista*, the military reconquest of Spain after centuries of Muslim control. Later medieval legends in northern Europe portrayed images protecting themselves against the iconoclastic fury of heretics and infidels, in particular the Hussites of Bohemia, but also Jews. During and after the Reformation, new variants employed the tropes of protective concealment and self-exile to show the power of images in resisting Protestantism; in Counter-Reformation Bavaria especially, legends fueled the progressive sanctification of the duchy against Protestant, heretical and "judaizing" influences, yielding in the process an expanded Catholic "territory of grace" delivered from alien occupation.[79]

---

[76] See the lists offered in Rudolf Kriss, *Die Volkskunde der altbayerischen Gnadenstätten*, 3 vols. (Munich-Pasing, 1956), 3: 58–61. For a more accessible survey, Heidemarie and Peter Strauss, *Heilige Quellen zwischen Donau, Lech und Salzach* (Munich, 1987).

[77] See Steven Sharborough, "El Ciclo de los Pastores," *History of Religions Newsletter* 3 (1975): 7–11; also discussed in Victor Turner and Edith L. B. Turner, *Image and Pilgrimage in Christian Culture: Anthropological Perspectives* (New York, 1978), 41–2, 47.

[78] Stephan Beissel, *Wallfahrten zu Unsere Lieben Frau in Legende und Geschichte* (Freiburg im Breisgau, 1913), 24.

[79] Turner, *Image and Pilgrimage*, 46–7. During the Counter-Reformation in the Netherlands, images allegedly concealed during the upheavals of iconoclasm "reappeared" to help foster new cults; see Beissel, *Wallfahrten*, 28, for examples.

Cleansing the Temple

Such tropes of cleansing and deliverance were clearly operative in the era of the Gruftkirche's post-Reformation renewal, but did they have any currency at the time of the shrine's foundation? In what sense might Hartlieb's program for the rededication of the shrine have been likewise aimed against the former *Jewish occupation of the site?* Recall first the long-standing purificatory and apotropaic function of cult-images, and the special role given to them in the rededication of pagan temples. In late antiquity newly installed Christian "temple-images" functioned in the displacement of pagan gods from their cult-sites—driving out demons, ridding a place of pollution, and the vestiges of *superstitio*, and redefining sanctity in terms of the triumphant religion.[80] Add to this the essential characteristic of consecration ceremony for churches: they were purification rituals. Standard consecration ceremonies therefore invoked the presence of Mary, whose maternal body represented a pure space of passage, transition and conversion, and who personified the Church as a mystical unity that superseded the Old Synagogue.[81] A legend that circulated widely in the thirteenth century tells of the miraculous appearance of a painted image of the Virgin in the very first church dedicated to her—a church that began as a synagogue purchased by the Apostles from the Jews. When the Jews renege and try to repossess the building, Mary proclaims her presence visually, driving out the Jews, who finally renounce their claims to the space.[82]

A special consecration liturgy used for medieval churches dedicated on the sites of defunct or destroyed synagogues condenses these themes of cleansing and vindication. Surviving in the *Liber Sacramentorum Romanae Ecclesiae*, the service book derived from the late eighth-century "Gelasian Sacramentary" (attributed to Pope Gelasius I), the prayer calls for the "expulsion of old Jewish error" (vetustate Iudaici erroris expulsa),

[80] Helen Saradi-Mendelovici, "Christian Attitudes toward Pagan Monuments in Late Antiquity and Their Legacy in Later Byzantine Centuries," *Dumbarton Oaks Papers* 44 (1990): 47–61, who quotes an imperial decree of 435, ordering that sanctuaries in which pagan cults were still active were to "be destroyed by the command of the magistrates, and shall be purified by the erection of the sign of the venerable Christian religion" (54); cf. Hans Belting, *Likeness and Presence: A History of the Image in the Era Before Art*, trans. Edmund Jephcott (Chicago, 1994), 31–41.

[81] Remensnyder, "The Colonization of Sacred Architecture," 197–99.

[82] Discussed in Remensnyder, "The Colonization of Sacred Architecture," 198–99, with a listing of medieval sources.

the "cleansing of hideous Jewish superstitions" (Judaicae superstitionis foeditate detersa), and so on.[83] Such language—borrowed in part, it seems, from the rhetoric of anti-pagan imperial legislation—suggests that the ritual cleansing of the spirit of Judaism from the site was regarded as a form of exorcism.[84] Likewise did expulsions of Jews from German towns assume the character of exorcisms. In the overcharged climate of 1519–20 in cities like Regensburg and Rothenburg ob der Tauber, for example, anti-Jewish preaching relied on exorcistic formulas and imagery.[85]

Add to this the fact that, as in other iconic religions, consecration of a Christian shrine or chapel is traditionally coterminous with the priestly "activation" of its wonder-working cult object; once consecrated the image becomes—like a relic—an efficacious channel for supernatural presence at the shrine.[86] Did the early Gruftkapelle's consecration ceremony serve as the touchstone for the cult-image's ability to work miracles, the same miracles that generated public acclaim for the shrine and paved the way for the conversion of Hartlieb's *oratorio* into a pilgrimage church? Given the confluence of tradition, discourse, mentality and practice we have traced here, it is difficult to imagine it otherwise. The parallel motifs of cleansing and banishment found in the *Liber Sacramentorum* suggest at the very least that images had a significant part to play in the ritual work of decontaminating "sacred" spaces associated with Judaism. The venerable Gruft, once under the occupation of a

[83] Reproduced in H. A. Wilson, ed., *The Gelasian Sacramentary* (Oxford, 1898), 141–2; for discussion, James Parkes, *The Conflict of the Church and the Synagogue: A Study in the Origins of Antisemitism* (London, 1934), 401; and Simonsohn, *The Apostolic See*, 124. Similar language was used for the consecration of churches from mosques; see Remensnyder, "The Colonization of Sacred Architecture," 194. Research is not sufficiently advanced to know whether this prayer was added to the liturgy for the consecration of converted synagogues in Germany.

[84] The demonological conception of the synagogue and its rituals held by the medieval Christian majority is well documented and requires no elaboration here; basic sources are Joshua Trachtenberg, *The Devil and the Jews: The Medieval Conception of the Jew and its Relation to Modern Antisemitism* (Philadelphia, 1983); Jean Delumeau, *La Peur en Occident (XIVe–XVIIIe siècles): Une cité assiégée* (Paris, 1978), 273–304; Robert Bonfil, "The Devil and the Jews in the Christian Consciousness of the Middle Ages," in *Antisemitism Through the Ages*, ed. Shmuel Almog, trans. Nathan H. Reisner (Oxford, 1988), 91–8.

[85] For example in the polemical tract by the Rothenburg preacher Johannes Teuschlein; see Röckelein, "Umgang der Christen," 42–3; idem, "Marienverehrung," 296, 304, n. 57. For Regensburg, see Creasman, "The Virgin Mary," 967, 970, 980.

[86] See David Freedberg, *The Power of Images: Studies in the History and Theory of Response* (Chicago, 1989), 82–96.

"foreign" religion mired in *superstitio*, had been forfeited by the Jews in order to be delivered into Christian hands and converted to become a "place of grace" (*Gnadenstätte*) for the true religion. Mediated first by the venerable, wonder-working image, and later also by the sanctified waters of the Gruftbrunnen, the purification of the edifice seems to have been an ongoing project—one that preserved key aspects of its Jewish prehistory at the same time it celebrated Judaism's negation and defeat.[87]

This process bespeaks an ambivalent, multi-layered attitude, an odd mixture of fear and exotic fascination, cultural anxiety and cultic allure, "judeophobia" and "judeophilia"—an attitude exemplified in the person of the chapel's founder, Johann Hartlieb. As an inspired occultist and early propagator of the inquisitorial definition of witchcraft—namely, that witchcraft was a crime akin to heresy—Hartlieb scarcely could have been indifferent to the residues of Jewish ritual and esotericism that haunted the Gruft.[88] At the same time, as a good Christian humanist and doctor, he may have been drawn to the mikveh for "enlightened" reasons as well: toward the end his life, during his seven year tenure as court physician to Albrecht III's son, Sigismund (r. 1460–67), Hartlieb accompanied his patron on therapeutic mineral bathing excursions, and even wrote a short balneological treatise (*Bäderbuch*).[89] We can not know if Hartlieb recognized the cellar space as a mikveh properly speaking, or a "Judenbad," or something else entirely. But if the preceding discussion has established anything, it is the compatibility of Hartlieb's attraction to the Gruft—as a space fretted with esoteric associations—with the capacity of Christian legend and ritual practice to master the alien,

---

[87] Not surprisingly, the Protestant critique of pilgrimage swiftly dismantled this fragile logic, arguing, for example, that the idolatrous excesses observed at shrines like the Schöne Maria Chapel in Regensburg were the result of a demonic influence attributable to the former occupation of the site by the Jews. As Creasman's analysis makes clear, whereas Catholics believed that the Jewish presence had called forth the power of the Virgin, Protestants believed it had called forth the Devil ("The Virgin Mary," 976–77).

[88] Under the influence of Nicholas of Cusa, from about 1450 onward Hartlieb began to turn away from his dabblings in the occult; his *Puch aller verpotten Kunst, Unglaubens und der Zauberey*, written in 1458 for the Markgraf Johann den Alchemisten von Brandenburg-Kulmbach, was apparently part of this effort; see NDB 7:323, and Stahleder, *Chronik*, 357, with further references. The book was also an attempt to make the newly defined crime of witchcraft better known in his home country; see Behringer, *Witchcraft Persecutions*, 70–71 (as in n. 44).

[89] Bayerische Staatsbibliothek, Cgm. 732 and 733; discussed in Hanns Fischer, "Zu Johannes Hartlieb's Bäderbuch," *Beiträge zur Geschichte der deutschen Sprache und Literatur* 84 (1962): 296–300.

demonic or polluted nature of non-Christian sacred sites. Like Mary's active grace appearing at a particular place and mediated by an image, sanctity itself could take root only once the Jews were expelled and their spirit cleansed from the site.

A Vision of the Sorrowing Mother

Marian shrines attracted pilgrims by virtue of their wonder-working images (*Gnadenbilder*) and the protective, salvific and curative powers attributed to them. As the shrine's "dominant symbol,"[90] the cult-image served as a vehicle for Mary's numinous presence at the site and the conduit of her celestial grace, actualized in the form of miracles. Until the thirteenth century it was generally the Romanesque sculpted groups of the enthroned Virgin and Child whose powers were enlisted at European shrines; later, especially after the Latin conquest of Constantinople in 1204, which brought an influx of Byzantine models into Europe, painted panels as well as carved statues were venerated. In Bavaria as elsewhere the range of themes grew to encompass both the seated and standing Virgin and Child types, and the Pietà, representing the sorrowing Mother of God holding her dead Son in her lap.[91] The earliest pilgrimages to the *schmerzenhafft Muttergottes* in south Germany are traceable back almost to 1200, and by the mid-fifteenth century they were widespread.[92]

While medieval evidence for such a wonder-working Marian image in the early Gruftkapelle is sparse, post-Reformation sources are plentiful,

---

[90] The term is from Turner, *Image and Pilgrimage*, esp. 245–9.

[91] On the early seated Virgin and Child tradition, see Ilene H. Forsyth, *The Throne of Wisdom: Wood Sculptures of the Madonna in Romanesque France* (Princeton, 1972); for Marian cult-images in medieval Bavaria, see Torsten Gebhard, "Die Marianischen Gnadenbilder in Bayern. Beobachtungen zur Chronologie und Typologie," in *Kultur und Volk. Beiträge zur Volkskunde aus Österreich, Bayern und der Schweiz. Festschrift für Gustav Gugitz*, ed. Leopold Schmidt (Vienna, 1954), 93–116. The literature on the Pietà is considerable; a well-balanced introduction is Peter Hawel, *Die Pietà. Eine Blüte der Kunst* (Würzburg, 1985).

[92] For the German phenomenon, the heydey of which was roughly 1300–1400, see Romuauld Bauerreiss, *Pie Jesu. Das Schmerzensmann-bild und sein Einfluss auf die mittelalterliche Frömmigkeit* (Munich, 1931), 108–16. Why the Pietà was chosen as a theme for cult-images at shrines associated with sacrileges is a theme I can not explore here; perhaps giving visible form to the suffering of Christ and Mary at a particular site served to explain the expulsion of the Jews in terms of their punishment due to them for the Crucifixion; on this point, see Glüber, "Synagogenzerstörung," 179.

and attest to the existence of a sculpted figure-group "in der Grufft."[93] Of great interest and decisive importance are the events half-hidden behind a story told about a Franciscan nun who lived not far from Gruftgasse in a convent known as the Püttrichkloster. One night in 1612 Sister Maria Franziska Kammerloherin, confined to bed with crippling pains in her feet, was visited by an apparition of Mary, who appeared in the form of a "life-sized figure" of the Pietà. This apparition, she later recounted, awakened in her the most powerful trust in the goodness of God and, after praying to Mary, she found herself miraculously healed. Getting to her feet, the nun declared:

> It was through the intercession of the sorrowing Mother of God in the Gruft that God's grace has healed me. Never before had I seen the [actual sculpted] image, but during the night I had a very vivid conception of it. If I could only seek out this image, and before it thank the Lord God for my regained health![94]

The search was on. Although the city swirled with rumors of a miracle, no one, the story goes, knew where to find the artefact glimpsed in the nun's vision. Maria and her cohort eventually journeyed to the Gruftkirche and there, in the "lower Gruft, among the array of old church implements," she recognized the neglected sculpture as the Pietà of her vision.[95] In celebration the object was resurrected from its place of dormition, brought for a time to the Pütrich convent, and finally returned to the Gruft, where it received new honors and veneration.

It would be pedantic to draw lines between fact, fiction and convention in this little tale of the cult-image's rediscovery. Clear enough is the operative value of the story in redeeming the Gruftkirche from neglect and recovering its patron's image from exile—a surge of popular devotion followed upon the story's circulation, the pilgrimage was reborn. According to reports, high- and lowborn mingled in pious solidarity in

---

[93] See discussion and note 29 above.

[94] Quoted in Sattler, *Chronik von Andechs*, 211; cf. Forster, *Das gottselige München*, 371; and the accounts in Pezzl, *Reise*, 192–3; Scharl, *Geschichte der Kruft*, 33–4; and Sattler, "Die ehemalgie Gruftkirche," 42–3. On the Pütrich convent, which like many female houses underwent claustration after the Council of Trent, and Sister Maria Franziska Kammerloherin, see Michael Hartig, "Die Heiligen, Seligen und Gottseligen in und aus München," in *Der Mönch im Wappen. Aus Geschichte und Gegenwart des katholischen München* (Munich, 1960), 181–207, here 192; and the excellent article by Ulrike Strasser, "Bones of Contention: Cloistered Nuns, Decorated Relics, and the Contest over Women's Place in the Public Sphere of Counter-Reformation Munich," *Archiv für Reformationsgeschichte* 90 (1990): 254–88.

[95] Sattler, "Die ehemalige Gruftkirche," 43; cf. Pezzl, *Reise*, 193.

the grace-filled gloom of the Gruft.[96] Members of the princely house left behind expensive tokens of their devotion; and even the duke himself, Maximilian I (r. 1598–1651, subsequently to become Elector in 1623), donated an "eternal light" in 1614.[97] According to a report of circa 1620, upwards of 4,000 masses were celebrated in the Gruftkapelle before the wonder-working Pietà, netting the church more than 2,000 Gulden.[98] Later in the century orthodox histories of Bavaria's Marian shrines extolled the glories of the Gruft and its Gnadenbild, though only one I have been able to find made much of the Jewish origins of the place. In the *Hodoeporicum Mariano-Benedictum* (1659) the author enfolds a clichéd account of Bavaria's emancipation from the Jews within his celebration of Mary's numinous presence at the site.[99] Undoubtedly the church was renovated in conjunction with the promotion of new miracles. One look at the engraved isometric city-plan made by Matthäus Merian the Elder for his *Topographia Bavariae*, first published in 1644, shows the most visible result of the rebuilding effort: a square tower, capped by *Spitzhelm* and *Gipfelkreuz* rising up above the "New Stifft Kirch" (fig. 6).[100]

Thus centuries after its founding, at a time of vigorous Catholic renewal of Bavaria's sacred landscape, Johann Hartlieb's dream of a spired church to the sorrowing Mother of God "in der Gruft" had finally been realized (though under very different sponsorship). In this project the wonder-working Pietà, heir to the early Christian "temple image" that drove away demonic pollution and pagan magic in the name of the true religion, had clearly played a pivotal role. Lost but not forgotten and resurrected from its hidden sepulchre, the shrine's Gnadenbild was vindicated against its putative enemies, but earned its reputation in the apparent absence of explicit anti-Jewish propaganda.

---

[96] Forster, *Das gottselige München*, 372.

[97] Maximilian's donation of 1614 to the altar of the Muttergottes "in der Gruft bei der neuen Stift" is recorded in BHStA, KU Andechs Nr. 42 (original parchment document of 1614, with signature); quoted and cited in Lieb, "Klosterhäuser," 155, n. 71. Subsequent to this he commissioned then-abbott of Andechs, Michael Einslin, to prepare an official report on the recent events in the Gruft, but I have not been able to determine if this report survives in any form.

[98] Pezzl, *Reise*, 193, cites a treatise by one "Magister Barth Schreckenfuß," entitled *Tractatu mariano ad annum 1620* as the source of this information.

[99] Strengelii, *Hodoeporicum*, ch. 12.

[100] The church is indicated with a number 13; see Matthäus Merian the Elder, *Topographia Bavariae*, 2nd edn. (1647), edited in facsimile by Lucas Heinrich Wüthrich (Kassel, 1962).

Bestowing grace here and in many other places in the Catholic duchy, the Virgin herself orchestrated the image's recovery once the danger of a "judaized' Protestant iconoclasm had passed.[101]

Cult Archaeology, Atonement and Communal Memory

If the seventeenth century can be called the era of the Gruftkirche's cultic renewal, the eighteenth century was the time of its historicization. A mere fifty years before its liquidation in 1803, the Gruftkirche served as the stage of its own tricentennial celebration. Planned in advance of the great *Klosterjubiläum* for Andechs in 1755, the event lasted for eight days in August 1750.[102] Pilgrims arrived to find a splendid triumphal arch erected along Gruftgasse, a lavish cycle of wall paintings (adorning both the upper and lower spaces) narrating the history of the church, daily high masses and sermons, and cult-images set out on a battery of altars. Principal among them was the shrine's Gnadenbild, the sorrowing Mother of the Pietà, who became the subject of several small devotional pictures printed for the occasion (see fig. 4). Benedict XIV granted a plenary indulgence for the entire eight days of the celebration, a spiritual reward sought after by "an extraordinary throng of people."[103] Church administrators were once again in a position to undertake improvements. But work got underway only in 1753, as both the upper and lower chapels received facelifts. Apparently no longer interested in preserving the somber mood in the Gruft, Abbott P. Josephus Hörl attempted to illuminate the lower chapel with new windows. To complement this new luminosity, the altar of the Gnadenbild was refurbished "entirely in marble and trimmed with silver ornamentations."[104] Exterior improvements to the church included a new facade

[101] It may be from this symbolic nexus that the shadowy legend of a cult-image *buried* beneath the floor of the old synagogue, and discovered in the aftermath of the expulsion, first began to take shape. It appears first in Sattler, "Die ehemalgie Gruftkirche," 42, who tells the story "according to legend"; see also idem, *Chronik von Andechs*, 208, where it is "the tradition of the image" that is cited.

[102] See Mathäser, *Andechser Chronik*, 111f.

[103] Scharl, *Geschichte der Kruft*, 42, as quoted in Lieb, "Klosterhäuser," 180; and Mathäser, *Andechser Chronik*, 133. According to Sattler, *Chronik von Andechs*, 615, the triumphal arch was adorned "with diverse historical and religious emblems, which described in concise terms the purpose of the celebration."

[104] Scharl, *Geschichte der Kruft*, 41, 48, as quoted in Lieb, "Klosterhäuser," 180; and Sattler, *Chronik von Andechs*, 616.

with voluted gabels and a small ridge turret, features visible in the pen drawing made by Johann Paul Stimmelmayr (c. 1800) for his inventory of Munich's houses and streets (see fig. 1).

With interest in the building's origins stimulated by such lavish visual propaganda, the Gruftkirche became the mis-en-scène of bizarre discoveries linked to its Christian founder and its former Jewish inhabitants. In July 1753 workers carrying out renovations in the Gruft began the demolition of two massive piers that once formed part of the old city walls. One of these piers enclosed a staircase that led to the upper church. From within a hollow underneath these stairs, the story goes, workers glimpsed a flickering light. Moving quickly to unearth its source, they discovered an old glass lamp filled with yellow liquid—and still burning! No sooner was it extracted from its hiding place, alas, a gust of wind extinguished the flame. Beckoned to the scene, Abbott Hörl arrived in time only to examine the mysterious lamp: he found the glass still warm and its wick still glowing.[105]

At first the relic was displayed in the upper church; later it was brought to the court of the Elector Maximilian Joseph, where his brother-in-law, the Kurprinz of Saxony, August the Strong, admired it and secured it for his collection of antiquities in Dresden.[106] Speculation ensued about the antiquity of this "eternal light," straining both the learning and imagination of local officials. Since the section of the building from which it was excavated had not been altered since Hartlieb's day, some sought for an explanation in the doctor's sojourn to Italy and his dabblings in the occult. Some considered that it might predate Hartlieb, and was of Roman origin. Another theory was that the Jews of medieval Munich had consecrated their place of worship with it, an interpretation that made it, in Christian eyes, a kind of "holy fire" (*heiliges Feuer*).[107] Perhaps the Jews had first sought out this place for

---

[105] Scharl, *Geschichte der Kruft*, 22, evidently believed the glass to have originated with Hartlieb (see summary in Lieb, "Klosterhäuser," 179); as a native Münchener, Scharl recalls that he and his childhood mates had seen mysterious glimmers beneath this staircase; cf. also Sattler, "Die ehemalige Gruftkirche," 44; for the fullest set of hypotheses, see idem, *Chronik von Andechs*, 616–19; also Forster, *Das gottselige München*, 374–5; and Rauch, "Münchens jüdische Denkmäler," 32.

[106] Forster, *Das gottselige München*, 373–74; and Sattler, *Chronik von Andechs*, 616–17, for more on the connection betwee the two courts. The glass object itself survives today in the Grünes Gewölbe Museum (Staatliche Kunstsammlungen Dresden). I thank Rupert Karbacher for this information.

[107] Forster, *Das gottselige München*, 375. This is a nineteenth-century idea; the use of hanging "eternal lights" in synagogues can not be traced back before the seventeenth

their synagogue precisely because of the existence of such an ancient relic, and Hartlieb, having learned of this, acquired the building in recognition of the same marvel! Topping this concoction of theories were allegations that, alongside the lamp, an unglazed earthenware jar was found containing fragments of human bone, one of which resembled the cranium of a child. According to Sattler, this discovery aroused speculation that the bones were "the remains of a sacrificial victim of Jewish cruelty," that is, a ritual murder victim. Before the relics could be preserved and examined further, however, the vessel broke during recovery, and the fragile remains disintegrated.[108]

Is the dubious tale of the bone-jar's exhumation simply a modern antisemitic fiction? Yes and no. Better to say, I think, that we are confronted here with a corrupted account of an attempted "discovery" of relics (*inventio*), that is, a clerical effort to add a new set of forensic marvels to the devotionalia already on display for a cult imbued by judeophobic memories. This interpretation prompts several questions. Were lurid notions about the city's former Jews central, or incidental, to the propaganda function these latest "discoveries" in the Gruft were calculated to serve? What was the relationship of these new artefacts—or the rumors about them—to the Catholic cult of the *schmerzenhaffte Muttergottes* whose locus was the enigmatic lower chapel? How did they merge into the ongoing development of cultic anti-Judaism around the Gruftkirche?

Ritual murder charges, and their circulation by chroniclers and hagiographers, frame the history of Munich Jewry from within a century of the earliest settlements in the ducal Altstadt, through the baroque period when Jews were physically absent, down to the reconstitution of the community preceding the Enlightenment. The foundational event of this history emerges from a group of near-contemporary reports on a pogrom that seems to have occurred on October 12, 1285, during the reign of Duke Ludwig der Strenge (r. 1253–1294), in apparent retaliation for the murder of a Christian boy.[109] Almost certainly the

century; see Louis Loeb-Laroqcque, "Ewig-Licht-Ampel", in *Reallexikon zur deutschen Kunstgeschichte* (Munich, 1973), 4:639–48. I thank Wolfgang Augustyn for bringing this information to my attention.

[108] Sattler, "Die ehemalige Gruftkirche," 617, 619; idem, *Chronik von Andechs*, 44; cf. Forster, *Das gottselige München*, 374.

[109] Veit Arnpeck, *Chronica Baioariorum* (1491–5), in *Sämtliche Chroniken*, ed. Georg Leidinger (Munich, 1915), 517. On the pogrom, *Germania Judaica*, 2/2: 556–8; Solleder, *München*, 495; Geissler, *Die Juden in Deutschland und Bayern*, 45, n. 9, and 222. None of

entire community—numbering more than sixty persons, according to the *Nürnberger Memorbuch*—was wiped out.[110] A second ritual murder charge is recorded in some sources for 1345: in this case the Jews were accused of the crime, and a massacre only narrowly averted, after the mutilated body of a boy known as "Heinrich" was discovered in a field between the Neuhauser Tor and the Schwabinger Tor.[111]

Whether or not either of these accusations—let alone the murders—actually happened, already in 1615 both crimes, that of 1285 and 1345, were being depicted in full-page captioned engravings made by Raphael Sadeler the Elder (d. 1632) for the hagiographical compilation, *Bavaria Sancta* (figs. 7 and 8).[112] Written by a Jesuit philologist and professor of rhetoric, Matthäus Rader, the book made its appearance at a pivotal moment in Bavaria's cultural history. Maximilian I., Wittelsbach Duke of Bavaria and later imperial Elector (1623), commissioned the book as part of a sweeping program of Catholic reform and consolidation which emphasized the providential role of Bavaria's ducal house in the defense of the Church and the sanctification of the land. Alongside the cult of the Virgin, the cults celebrating martyrs and their pilgrimages were actively promoted as a strategy of "confessional state building."[113] Originally published in Latin, *Bavaria Sancta* was later translated into German by another Jesuit, Maximilian Rassler, under

the contemporary reports are local, but come from chroniclers operating out of Freising, Augsburg and Salzburg; for a discussion of sources, Stahleder, "Die Münchener Juden," 12.

[110] See Stahleder, *Chronik*, 54 for additional references.

[111] Aretin, *Geschichte*, 35; Gufler, "Ergänzungen," 121; Sattler, *Chronik von Andechs*, 207; Forster, *Das gottselige München*, 368 n. 3; *Germania Judaica*, 2/2:557. Stahleder points out that the two sixteenth-century reports on which the modern accounts are based, written by the humanist historiographer Aventius (Johannes Turmair) in 1519/20 and 1533 respectively, do not mention Jews at all in connection with the corpse's discovery; for the detailed source criticism, Stahleder, *Chronik*, 125–7.

[112] For introduction and further references, Carsten-Peter Warncke, *Bavaria Sancta—Heiliges Bayern. Die altbayerischen Patrone aus der Heiligengeschichte des Matthaeus Rader* (Dortmund, 1981), 295–312; *Macht der Bilder. Antisemitische Vorurteile und Mythen*, exhib. cat., Jüdisches Museum der Stadt Wien (Vienna, 1995), cat. no. 44a–c; Heinz Schreckenberg, *The Jews in Christian Art: An Illustrated History*, trans. John Bowden (New York, 1996), 290; also *Siehe der Stein schreit aus der Mauer. Geschichte und Kultur der Juden in Bayern*, exhib. cat. (Nuremberg, 1988), cat. no. 4/39.

[113] The phrase is Ulrike Strasser's ("Bones of Contention," 261, 272). Propagation of martyrs went hand in hand with the cult of the Virgin, celestial patron of the dynasty, land and people, as cornerstones of the effort to make Catholic Bavaria a true "territory of faith"; see Georg Schwaiger, "Maria Patrona Bavariae," in *Bavaria Sancta. Zeugen christlichen Glaubens in Bayern*, ed. Georg Schwaiger, 3 vols. (Regensburg, 1970), 1:28–37.

the title *Heiliges Bayerland* and published in Augsburg (1714), Straubing (1840) and Munich (1861–82). Beneath the caption, "A boy martyred by the Jews in Munich" (fig. 7), Sadeler depicts a cabal of hooded Jews slicing and stabbing the naked child, laid out on a wooden table. With women watching from the steps and windows, the scene transpires in a darkened cellar space reminiscent of Gruftkirche's lower chapel. More striking in this regard is the depiction of a gloomy subterranean space—characterized by heavy groin vaults and massive columns with aniconic capitals—in the second scene, which purports to show the 1345 murder of Heinrich (fig. 8). Surrounded by a gang of fiends who immobilize him on a crude wooden table, the young martyr, already pierced, releases a double-stream of blood into a waiting basin.

Cult memorabilia and propaganda of the kind surrounding the boy-martyrs of Munich characterizes the penultimate stage of cultic anti-Judaism as I have been describing it. Once again we are witnessing a twin process of appropriation and historicization with the Gruftkirche as its fulcrum. What must be emphasized for the eighteenth-century context, however, is that now the keepers of the Gruftkirche's legacy saw the need not only to reconfirm the building's historic transformation from synagogue to church, but to do so specifically by enshrining there Jewish crimes of centuries past. The Gruftkirche's identity as a site of anti-Christian sacrilege was not to be denied but asserted, and this required a redefinition of the church's place in local, *communal* memory. To understand how this happened requires an additional analytical step.

Catholic tradition in Germany, carrying forward collective perceptions with ancient roots, offered a powerful method for overcoming pollution in a local context: the practice of erecting crucifixes, wayside shrines and memorials, specifically commemorative chapels, later called "atonement chapels" (*Sühnekapellen*), at sites where sacrileges or blood-crimes had been committed.[114] Like an unavenged murder, the desecration of sacred objects—relics, images, and the Eucharist in particular—was an event that aroused intense pollution fears, and had an especially galvanizing effect on communities for whom it represented a dangerous

[114] To my knowledge, no anatomy of the "atonement chapel" as a species of shrine *sui generis* has been written; although the term appears to be of nineteenth-century origin, the practices are far older. On the tradition of the "atonement cross" (*Sühnekreuz*), see Paul Werner and Richilde Werner, *Vom Marterl bis zum Gipfelkreuz. Flurdenkmal im Oberbayern* (Berechtesgaden, 1991), esp. 13–19.

breach in the relationship with a celestial patron.[115] Miracles forged the mediating link between the original sacrilegious act, its revelation to the community and, when called for, the punishment of evildoers. Shrines marking the site of such past events therefore arose from a communal need for an ecclesiastically-guided reconciliation with the celestial patron and an overcoming of taboo. Misfortunes visited upon the community could be reversed through a kind of collective votive offering, seen in theological terms as atonement for the sin of permitting the dishonor to occur.

Grafting the concept of atonement retrospectively onto cult-stations with presumed but uncertain medieval pedigrees was one strategy of renewal for Catholic pilgrimage culture in the early modern era. Quite a few of the so-called "host-desecration churches" (*Hostienfrevelkirchen*) visited by pilgrims between the sixteenth century and the time of secularization were in fact retrofitted with stereotyped sacrilege and atonement narratives through newly published legends. In 1753, as we have seen, the Gruftkirche was brimming with cultic, narrative, commemorative, devotional and propagandistic imagery connecting the old building at Gruftgasse 1 to a fabulous legacy of Jewish violence and sacrilege. Clerical planners seem to have been ready to exploit the Gruftkirche's tricentennial in order to reinvent the old place as an "atonement chapel," using Munich's legacy of ritual murder charges as a renewable resource capable of boosting the shrine's share in the local cult economy. But was this inflation of anti-Jewish lore driven solely by the existing, internal mythology of the building and the artefactual wonders it perennially coughed up? Or had other, external, factors come into play?

[115] Such dishonors could be visited on sacred things by enemies of the faith *or* by Christians, whether it was out of deviant intent, misguided piety or simple clumsiness; for an introduction to this family of legends, see Manfred Eder, "Eucharistische Kirchen und Wallfahrten im Bistum Regensburg," in *Wallfahrt im Bistum Regensburg*, ed. Georg Schwaig und Paul Mai [= *Beiträge zur Geschichte des Bistums Regensburg* 28] (Regensburg, 1994): 97–172; and Mitchell B. Merback, "Channels of Grace: Pilgrimage Architecture, Eucharistic Imagery, and Visions of Purgatory at the Host Miracle Churches of Late Medieval Germany" in *Art and Architecture of Late Medieval Pilgrimage in Northern Europe and the British Isles*, ed. Sarah Blick and Rita Tekippe (Leiden, 2005), 587–646, at 595–604.

Artefacts, Exegesis and Defamation

Relevant to this question is the early modern renewal of a Jewish presence in the Bavarian capital. As early as the 1570s and 1580s, with the rise of absolutist and mercantilist governmental policies, Jewish communities began reassembling themselves in German territories from which they previously had been expelled. During the Thirty-Years War the Jewish presence was markedly enhanced in most regions, since both the Austrian Hapsburgs and, after 1630, the occupying Protestant powers under Gustavus Adolphus, recognized the value of Jewish assets and trade connections, and geared their Jewish policy to accord with practical needs. Despite the partial reaction that accompanied the withdrawal of foreign occupation forces after 1648 (including some re-expulsions from several imperial cities), the gains to German Jewry in this, the era of the "Court Jew," were durable.[116] During the Austrian occupation (1704–14) a small number of Jews were allowed to settle in Munich; but with the resumption of power by the elector Maximilian II Emanuel (r. 1662–1726) came a swift end to this franchise. Jewish residents in Munich appear again in official lists from as early as 1728, then in greater numbers during the reign of Maximilian III. Joseph (1745–77), when twenty persons are recorded in 1750. Here as elsewhere it was Jewish families of relative prominence and privilege who were being settled by authorities.

This direct coincidence between the Gruftkirche's tricentennial jubilee and the reappearance of important Jewish families in the city is hard to ignore. Within a generation this number had almost tripled, and by the century's end there were thirty-five Jewish families, at least 220 persons, residing in the capital.[117] But in isolation these facts tell us little; they must be evaluated in light of contemporary attitudes.

Despite the slow bloom of Enlightenment rationalism, public opinion about the Jews in the first half of the eighteenth century was still largely beholden to a set of outmoded, theologically-inspired conceptions

[116] Jonathan I. Israel, "Central European Jewry during the Thirty Years War," *Central European History* 16 (1983): 3–30, at 6, 28–9; Selma Stern, *The Court Jew: A Contribution to the History of Absolutism in Europe*, trans. Ralph Weiman (New Brunswick, 1985).

[117] Arthur Cohen, "Die Münchener Judenschaft 1750–1861. Eine bevölkerungs- und wirtschaftsgeschichtliche Studie," *Zeitschrift für die Geschichte der Juden in Deutschland* 1 [new series] (1930): 262–83, with table on 263. See also Schöpflich, "Zur Geschichte der Juden," 616; and Rauch, "Münchens jüdische Denkmäler," 8, both of whom offer data for 1728 (seventeen persons) not given in Cohen.

about Jews and Judaism. Complicit in the perpetuation of traditional Christian anti-Judaic attitudes were a number of prominent university professors whose "research" propped up the old accusations. This brand of Christian anti-Judaism received an elaborate new scholarly gloss in 1741 with the landmark publication of the two-volume treatise, *Entdecktes Judenthum* (Judaism Revealed), a work whose author, Johann Andreas Eisenmenger (1654–1704), had been appointed by the Elector Johann Wilhelm as professor of Oriential languages in Heidelberg.[118] Training his considerable erudition on the task of proving Judaism's superstitiousness, its vulgar, anthropomorphic conception of God, its ingrained tribal viciousness and its deep-seated moral degeneracy, Eisenmenger believed his work to be aimed at a single purpose: to remove the Jews' spiritual blindfold, lift them out of their abject state of ignorance, and reveal the truth of Christianity—in short, to bring them to conversion where others had failed.[119]

Eisenmenger's method was rigorously scholarly and exegetical; he relied entirely on Jewish sources, and neither forged nor fabricated a single reference. By interpreting the often contradictory ethical precepts found in the Mishnaic and Talmudic traditions, he believed he had uncovered within Judaism a veritable canon of negative commandments, obeyed by all Jews, past and present. These included the obligation to defraud, rob, murder, and commit all manner of sacrileges against non-Jews, especially Christians. In accordance with this view, Eisenmenger seems to have taken literally the reports of Jewish ritual murder by chroniclers and hagiographers.[120] And so it must have been for many a lay reader of his work. Even if one did not believe the blood libel to begin with, lacking a basic familiarity with the Jewish texts Eisenmenger used, the reader could not but have been swayed by the exegete's "discovery" of a "religious" basis for Jewish bloodlust in their own sacred texts![121] Recognizing this danger, and to prevent the agitation of the German populace, the prominent financier and

[118] Johann Andreas Eisenmenger, *Entdecktes Judenthum* (Königsberg, printed with original publication date of 1711, issued in 1741; repr. Dresden, 1893).

[119] On Eisenmenger, Jacob Katz, *From Prejudice to Destruction: Anti-Semitism, 1700–1933* (Cambridge, Mass., 1980), 13–22.

[120] Katz, *From Prejudice to Destruction*, 20.

[121] Eisenmenger's work formed the basis for the notorious fabrications of the Roman Catholic theologian and professor at the University of Prague, August Rohling (1839–1931), who testified at the blood libel trial in Tisza-Eszlar, Hungary, in 1882, one of several high-profile trials in Eastern Europe before World War I.

rabbi Samson Wertheimer (1658–1724) appealed to emperor Leopold on July 12, 1700 to have the recently printed book suppressed. Only in 1741, less than a decade prior to the Gruftkirche's tricentennial, did Eisenmenger's heirs finally receive permission to publish the book.[122]

Were the clerical redactors of the Gruftkirche's propaganda aware, on the occasion of its tricentennial, of the support available to them in *Entdecktes Judenthum*? It seems it could scarcely have escaped their notice. Rather than positing a direct influence, however, it may be more useful to speak of an "Eisenmenger paradigm" filtering through the (mis)information that came out of the Gruftkirche around this time. For what are the discovery reports of an "antique" glass lamp burning with a mysterious *heiliges Feuer*, the relics of a boy-martyr in a broken ceramic jar, and the intense speculation all of this aroused—what are they if not ciphers of a kind of Christian "exegesis" of a Jewish artefactual past, a tendentious form of "research" into esoteric archaeological remains rather than texts? Like Eisenmenger's appropriation of actual Jewish texts against the historical legitimacy of Judaism itself, these propagandistic reports turn on an appropriation of fictional Jewish rites and objects whose locus was the synagogue. In this sense, mythmaking at the Gruftkirche became a kind of *allegorical reading of the site.* Outright pious fraud did the rest.

Ordinary Christian Müncheners, laboring under the learned illusions of Eisenmenger's tomes, or simply accepting the didactic displays outside and inside the Gruftkirche, must have looked with some foreboding upon the return of Jews to the capital in increasing numbers from 1750 onward. Were the Jews with their special privileges now getting ready to renew their claim to "sacred space" within the city's topography? Would the ancient torturers of Jesus and Mary resume their nefarious rites under the noses of upright Christians, as they had in the Middle Ages?

That the dark lower chapel of the Gruftkirche might itself be experienced as an imaginative surrogate for the dungeon beneath Caiaphas's palace in Jerusalem, where late medieval Passion tracts reconstructed the cruelties of Jesus' night in captivity, is shown by a devotional engraving sold to pilgrims around 1790 (fig. 9). Captioned "The Suffering Jesus, worshipped in the Gruft in Munich" (*Der leÿdente Jesus so in der Grufft zu München verehret wird*), the image portrays Christ heavily shackled to a

---

[122] Stern, *The Court Jew*, 200.

truncated column and seated upon a wedge-shaped bench, an image often used to illustrate printed tracts devoted to the "Secret Passion" (*Geheimen Leiden*) of Christ. In all likelihood the image indexes a gruesome, life-sized carved figure of the type, fitted with real iron chains—a type still seen in Bavarian churches—that was once part of the pious itinerary through the Gruftkirche.[123] Both the engraving and the multimedia spectacle in the Gruft, therefore, transformed the sacred gloom of the lower chapel into a kind of environmental palimpsest through which pilgrims might enter Caiaphas's prison or its medieval counterpart, the former synagogue on Gruftgasse.

Such devotional experiences, conditioned as they were by the clerical propaganda, fed anxieties about the readmission of Jews into Christian society and amplified the need to reassert the historic condemnation of the synagogue. That meant, as I have suggested, reaffirming the appropriation of "sacred space" from the Jews as an eternal Christian right and duty. As for the Jews of eighteenth-century Munich, once they began reappearing on the streets after their long banishment, in exchange for the privilege of physical coexistence with Gentiles they had to submit (once again) to a falsely "historical" reification of their importance to Christianity. Even at the height of German Jewish influence on the commerce, finance and politics of Central Europe, they were again forced to dwell in popular perception, as they had in the Middle Ages, as living witnesses of their own dispossession and exile.

Conclusion

As territorial and municipal expulsions progressively brought an end to an Ashkenazic presence in the southern Empire, Christian anti-Judaism mutated into a strange ideological admixture that no longer depended on the actual presence of Jews.[124] In fact, but for the last century of the Gruftkirche's 350-year history, Jews and Judaism had been actually or virtually absent from the scenes of public life in Munich. And

---

[123] Nina Gockerell, *Bilder und Zeichen der Frömmigkeit. Sammlung Rudolf Kriss* (Munich, 1995), 57, with further examples; on the early tradition of the "Secret Passion," see James H. Marrow, *Passion Iconography in Northern European Art of the Late Middle Ages and Early Renaissance* (Kortrijk, 1979), 95–170.

[124] R. Po-chia Hsia, "Christian Ethnographies of Jews in Early Modern Germany," in *Problems in the Historical Anthrpology of Early Modern Europe*, ed. R. Po-chia Hsia and R. W. Scribner (Wiesbaden, 1997), 35–47.

yet it would seem that hardly a single generation could have failed to witness some episode in the life of the edifice that did not evoke the Christian shrine's notorious—and fascinating—Jewish prehistory. While some chapters in the church's history seem to pass with minimal reference to its Jewish origins, at other times—when memories of past horrors were reactivated as cult propaganda—the shrine could once again became a lodestone of anti-Jewish myths. In the formation of collective perceptions among Christians, as I have argued, those factors that a scholarly focus on antisemitism tends to relagate to the background—in the present case, "ethnological" interests in Jewish ritual, Hebraist fascinations with the esoteric Jewish "secrets," affective devotions to the suffering Christ, the Sorrowing Virgin and boy-martyrs—may actually have been more decisive than the traditional libels. How positive and negative images of Jews cross-fertilized in the majority culture is something we find hard to grasp, in part because none of the descriptive and analytical terms at our disposal, neither "anti-Judaism," nor "antisemitism," nor "Judeophobia," all of which denote purely negative attitudes, can adequately encompass this disorderly constellation of perceptions and attitudes. Nor can they account for the modes of behavior arising from them.[125] Nor can any of them account for the different ways cultural anxiety, myths and persecutions sometimes *converge* with otherwise normative Christian cultic and devotional practices. The preceding analysis underscores the need to find a better way to describe and analyze those modalities of Christian religion that interlocked functionally with Christian society's anti-Jewish myths and its persecutory practices. This applies equally to those myths that are not explicable as crude expressions of prejudice or hatred, but display elements of "philosemitic" fascination with Jews and Judaism. I have called this process of convergence *cultic anti-Judaism*.

By taking the long-view, we have also demonstrated that, because cult environments designed for pilgrimage typically change throughout their histories, meanings are never fixed. Not only will churches periodically be renewed or rebuilt; new legends can often be grafted onto old ones; demographic shifts, political upheavals or ecological shocks might change the social constitution of the shrine's patrons and clients, create novel demands for celestial assistance, and so on. With

[125] Cf. the trenchant remarks by Johannes Heil, "'Antijudaismus' und 'Antisemitismus': Begriffe als Bedeutungsträger," *Jahrbuch für Antisemitismusforschung* 6 (1997): 92–114.

every internally or externally motivated change in the cultic programming of a shrine, certain ideological requirements might be met while new ones take shape. The process is only complete when the historical career of the cult itself comes to a close. But to say that the process of cultic anti-Judaism runs its course only once a pilgrimage is terminated is not to imply that cult-stations with Jewish legacies always conserve within them a kernel of antagonistic content, latent but recuperable by propagandists at any time. Against the outmoded assumption that antisemitism springs eternal, we must admit the possibility of a partial or complete withering away of anti-Jewish sentiments, motivations and myths at the local level. Memories which once centered on the shrine may become moribund once Jews have been banished beyond the life-world of the majority population, and their revival is hardly inevitable. Of course the withered root can always be unearthed and artificially invigorated. Under new pressures and in the right hands, anti-Jewish myths can be made into an instrument for fashioning group identity and clearing new spaces for its needs. Collective memory finds itself filled with a content it never knew it had.

CHAPTER TWELVE

NEW ATTITUDES TOWARDS THE JEWS IN THE ERA OF REFORMATION AND COUNTER-REFORMATION: THE PATRONAGE OF BISHOP ECHTER VON MESPELBRUNN

Annette Weber

Even today, Julius Echter von Mespelbrunn, who reigned as bishop of Würzburg for more than forty years (1573–1617), is remembered as one of the outstanding personalities in a long line of ecclesiastical sovereigns of that episcopality. Both older and more recent publications present his achievements in the most favorable terms. Among these were the re-catholicization of Würzburg and its territories in the early days of the Counter-Reformation, the reopening of the local university, and the foundation of the Julius-Hospital, a renowned institution of church-sponsored welfare.[1] But his reign was not a blessing for all of the residents in his territories. During his tenure, Bishop Echter openly declared his intolerance of any confession other than the Catholic (as was the case, for example, in Münnerstadt in 1586), and consequently he expelled or persecuted mercilessly those who did not fit the Catholic mold—notably Protestants, Jews, and women accused of sorcery.[2] The present essay examines one aspect of Bishop Echter's program of

---

1 Friedrich Merzbacher, *Julius Echter und seine Zeit* (Würzburg, 1973); *Julius Echter von Mespelbrunn 1573–1617, Fürstbischof von Würzburg, Begründer der Universität und des Juliusspitals*, exhibition catalogue, ed. Staatsarchiv Würzburg (Würzburg, 1973); Gottfried Mälzer, *Julius Echter von Mespelbrunn: Leben und Werk* (Würzburg, 1989). The author would like to thank Mitchell Merback for his interest in discussing the subject and his many useful suggestions. I also would like to thank Eva Frojmovic for her kind support.

2 Vitus Brander, *Julius Echter von Mespelbrunn, Fürstbischof von Würzburg* (Würzburg, 1917), 93; cf. his declaration to the burghers of Münnerstadt, 19 September 1586, when asked to tolerate two confessions, i.e. Catholicism and Protestantism: "Ihr habt mir weder Ziel noch Maß zu geben, wie ich mit Schulen und Kirchen gebaren soll; denn ich bin der Herr; so seid ihr mir nicht allein in weltlichen, sondern auch in geistlichen Dingen zu gehorsamen schuldig.... Ich kann unmöglich in meinem Lande zweierlei Religionen dulden.... Das Stift steht und fällt mit dem katholischen Glauben." (You aren't entitled to make any claims of how I should deal with schools and churches, as I am the lord. Thus you are obliged to obedience not only in secular but also in

church renewal, his patronage of churches and chapels dedicated to the miraculous bleeding host (*Heilig Blut*), especially those whose legends linked them to sacrileges committed by Jews against the eucharistic host; my purpose is to present a brief sketch of the treatment of the Jews in the episcopal territories of Würzburg during Echter's reign, and consider this treatment in relation to that of other minorities and outsiders, in order to gain a better understanding of the Jews' position amidst the social and political ferment preceding the Thirty Years War.

Between 1585 and 1587, after public interrogations, Protestants were expelled from every town and village in the episcopal territories. Those who still refused submission were forced to sell their immobile property within days, and were ordered to leave the territories together with their families. In March 1586 in Gerolzhofen, a district town, seventy-one burghers were forced to leave within four days. They took with them some 100,000 florins, which represented a considerable financial drain when compared to the 6,392 florins which were later needed for building the new town hall by order of the bishop.[3] In Würzburg itself all Protestant families, among them some of the most prominent and wealthy merchants, were forced to leave in March 1587, and here as well the municipal economy suffered.

Harsher still was the fate of those accused of witchcraft at the instigation of Echter's confessor, the Jesuit Gerard Phyen. So ruthless were Phyen's inquisitorial activities that he became legendary throughout the Franconian countryside and was widely despised as a devil in human form. Bishop Echter even tried to extend the persecution of alleged sorceresses beyond the borders of his territories. In 1611 Count Wolfgang zu Castell, sovereign of his territory and a neighbour of Bishop Echter, refused to turn over to the episcopal court several women accused of sorcery. In a letter he adduced the following reasons: while in principle not averse to executing persons truly guilty of sorcery, he could not countenance it in undisclosed cases (i.e. those tried in secret), especially where the guilty plea had been extracted under torture; the poorest of people were still God's creatures and vulnerable to injustice; and finally, he argued, he himself wouldn't be able to justify such a procedure when standing trial before God at the Last Judgment. Just as

ecclesiastical affairs.... In no way would I tolerate two confessions in my territories.... The episcopal territories stand and fall with Catholic faith).

[3] Brander, *Julius Echter*, 91–92 (on the expulsion of Protestants from episcopal territories), and 129 (on the building of the town hall in Gerolzhofen).

most jurists would reject any confession extracted by torture, so Castell himself knew how to protect his own subjects against such nonsense.[4] When Bishop Echter did not reply to this letter, the count took the trouble to send it a second time, affirming his position by asking not to be bothered again with such a matter. The bishop gave in eventually, but in his territories he continued to burn sorceresses with great fury. In 1617 alone, some 300 people in Würzburg and its territories suffered the cruellest tortures before being burnt at the stake on the bishop's orders.[5] Such fanatical intolerance towards anyone suspected of being an unbeliever, or who deviated from the Catholic faith, seems to be fairly typical not only of Mespelbrunn, but of other princely proponents of Catholic reaction. This fanaticism—specifically towards Protestants and people accused of sorcery—runs like a thread through Echter's reign and colored his treatment of Jews as well.

The Jews in Episcopal Würzburg

What of the Jews of episcopal Würzburg? They had settled there some time before the Second Crusade, between 1147 and 1148, when twenty-one martyrs were recorded in Hebrew necrologies after a pogrom provoked by the crusaders. In the late Middle Ages after a period of peace, their situation again became difficult. In 1298 the entire community was annihilated by the mob under the leadership of a local nobleman called Rintfleisch, after an alleged host desecration had been reported from the nearby district town of Röttingen on the Tauber. The reinstalled community of Würzburg was massacred again during the pogroms associated with the Black Death in 1349. Even after this event, some Jewish families returned to the city and lived there as moneylenders and pawnbrokers. After the Black Death imperial protections were growing weaker and weaker, and the bishop of Würzburg gained rights over the Jews in this territory. Subsequently the Jews were caught between canons, burghers and bishop, that is, all

[4] Elmar Weiss, "Die Hexenprozesse im Hochstift Würzburg," in *Unterfränkische Geschichte II*, ed. Peter Kolb and Ernst-Günter Krenig (Würzburg, 1992), 333–334.

[5] Weiss, "Die Hexenprozesse," 334 (recorded in the chronicle of Jakob Röder from Würzburg, entry of September 11, 1617).

those parties struggling for municipal power.[6] From the mid-fifteenth century onward, burghers and canons alike had been repeatedly calling for the expulsion of the Jews, whom they saw as unwanted rivals in commerce and local pawnbrokering, but the bishops were unwilling to forgo the Jews, whom they still considered an important source of revenue. In the early sixteenth century the economy was in a severe decline, and during the peasant upheavals—beginning in 1512 and ending in the Great Peasant's War of 1525–1526—the Jews were even invited to join with the rebels against the local nobility and ecclesiastical authorities.[7] This suggests that the peasants had finally understood how the authorities oppressed the Jews and exploited them as instruments of plunder against the peasants.

During the same period, however, the clamor in Würzburg against Jewish commercial activities was diminishing, suggesting that Jews no longer presented much of an economic threat to the burghers. Instead, new objections arose to their presence in Christian society: in 1543, for example, some Jews were accused of ritual murder, but the attempt was scotched by the emperor Charles V after the intervention of the eminent court Jew Josel of Rosheim.[8] A little later, in 1555, canons and burghers started complaining about the great number of Jews living in the city, a population they claimed would overwhelm Christian inhabitants. Some 300 Jews were allegedly residing in the city alongside more than eight thousand Christian burghers, though by the bishop's own count there were only sixty. A further complaint was that Jews would offer medical assistance and medications to Christians despite an episcopal order aimed at Jewish doctors and midwives, in

---

[6] For the history of the Jews in Würzburg see Julius Aronius, ed., *Regesten zur Geschichte der Juden im fränkischen und deutschen Reiche bis zum Jahr 1273* (Berlin, 1902), no. 245; Zvi Avneri, ed., *Germania Judaica*, vol. 2, part 2 (Tübingen 1968), 928–934; Arye Maimon, Mordechai Breuer, and Yacov Guggenheim, eds., *Germania Judaica*, vol. 3, pt. 2 (Tübingen 1995), 1468–1473; Peter Herde, "Probleme der christlich-jüdischen Beziehungen in Mainfranken im Mittelalter," *Würzburger Diözesangeschichtsblätter* 40 (1978): 79–94; Roland Flade, "Jene, einem rebenreichen Weinstock vergleichene Gemeinde. Zur Situation der Juden im mittelalterlichen Würzburg," in *Geschichte und Kultur der Juden in Bayern*, vol. 2: Aufsätze, ed. Manfred Treml and Josef Kirmeier (München, 1988), 173–180; Roland Flade, *Die Würzburger Juden. Ihre Geschichte vom Mittelalter bis zur Gegenwart*, 2nd edn. (Würzburg, 1996).

[7] Flade, *Die Würzburger Juden*, 47–49. The invitation was forwarded by the peasants of the village Bildhausen who were moving against the bishop of Würzburg in 1525.

[8] Selma Stern, *Josel von Rosheim* (Stuttgart, 1959), 158–161; Flade, *Die Würzburger Juden*, 50–51.

effect forbidding them to assist their Christian neighbours.[9] With the Jews' commercial and political powers on the wane, then, burghers and canons might also use them as death pledges against episcopal rule, and in the years after 1555 they were in a position to force the bishop's hand. Echter's predecessor, Bishop Friedrich von Wirsberg, had already given in to such demands. Having gained imperial consent for such an action three years earlier, Bishop Friedrich expelled the Jews from Würzburg in 1562.

Thus when Echter von Mespelbrunn came to power in 1573, there were in fact no longer any Jews living in the city. Some Jewish presence did remain in the form of small-scale commercial activities conducted with the rural population in the areas surrounding Würzburg. Therefore it was mainly in the villages in the vicinity of the capital, and also in the tiny territories of imperial knights intermingled among the episcopal territories (the so-called *Hochstift Würzburg*), that Jews based themselves; and it was in this context that they would peddle their goods from one village to the next, crossing the borders regularly as they did so. Nevertheless, a year after his election in November 1574, as one of his first political actions, the new bishop still felt compelled to banish all Jews still living within the Hochstift, and to mandate their financial deprivation as well. The following reasons were given in the official decree:

a) Jews bought on the cheap, in cash, the yearly obligations from poor people
b) Jews took usurious interest, such as one, two or even three hellers per florin a week
c) Jews advanced credit for wine, crops and other things
d) Jews dealt and bartered in horses, oxen, cows and other livestock

To resolve these problems, the episcopal bailiffs were ordered to acquire the obligations instead of the Jews, and to charge a special episcopal account for the purpose. Furthermore they should redeem all usurious debts without handing the proceeds over to the Jews. However, they should also graciously repay those Jewish debts related to the cattle trade, even if those debts would have fallen to the sovereign according

[9] Flade, *Die Würzburger Juden*, 51–53.

to older imperial regulations. The action, which was allegedly taken to stop Jewish usury in the countryside, helped to resolve the financial problems of the episcopality, which was almost bankrupt when Bishop Echter came to power.[10] Instead of ending usury, however, the measures allowed the bishop's government to effectively replace the Jews as the chief creditor in his territories, and later on he personally became the biggest moneylender to other German princes, as was noted by the duke of Bavaria in 1610.[11]

While this first step against the Jews followed an established pattern of medieval prohibitions against usury, and was obviously dictated by financial interests, Echter's second anti-Jewish measure was fuelled rather by a new kind of religious zeal. In 1575 the bishop forbade Jews living in other territories the right to cross the borders of his own. He thereby effectively confined Jews to the territories of local knights, thus immobilizing their commercial activities with threats to seize any Jewish property found in the episcopal territories. It seems that, in this respect, Bishop Echter was imitating the actions of his powerful neighbor, Duke Albrecht V of Bavaria, who had driven out the Jews in 1553 and the Protestants in 1571, despite the impending economic losses these moves caused. The Bavarian expulsion decree was equally strict in that it banned Jews from settling within the duchy for at least 200 years, and prohibited any crossing of its borders. Every transgression would entail the complete confiscation of goods. And yet, despite appearances it is clear that the expulsions ordered by both rulers were dictated less by financial motives, or the need to protect their subjects from usury, than by an ardent desire to foster the Catholic faith exclusively within their

[10] Brander, *Julius Echter*, 127–128, quote of the transliterated German text of the order to the episcopal bailiffs, November 3, 1574: "Weil die Juden von armen Leuten viele jährliche Zielfristen um eine geringe bare Summe an sich gebracht haben, ferner weil dieselben von Unterthanen einen wucherlichen Zins nehmen, nämlich 1, 2 oder 3 Heller wöchentlich von einem Gulden, auch auf Wein, Getreide und andere Dinge Geld borgen, endlich weil Juden mit Pferden, Ochsen, Kühen und anderem Vieh handeln und schachern, so sollen die Amtleute solche von den Juden erkaufte Zielfristen selbst einnehmen und unter einer besonderen Rubrik dem Fürsten in Rechnung bringen; ferner sollen sie alle jene Judenschulden, welche zu hohen Zins entrichten, auch einziehen und den Juden nicht aushändigen, dagegen die Judenschulden, welche von verkauftem Vieh herrühren, obwohl sie nach älteren kaiserlichen Verordnungen an den Fürsten verfallen wären, dennoch ihnen gnädigst auszahlen." The edict was repeated in a more general way in February 1575; see Hans Peter Baum, "Quellen der Judenverfolgungen von 1147–1938" in *Zeugnisse jüdischer Geschichte in Unterfranken*, ed. Hans Ulrich Wagner, Schriften des Stadtarchivs Würzburg 16 (Würzburg, 1987), 48.

[11] Brander, *Julius Echter*, 124.

princely jurisdictions—in effect, calling upon the principle of *cuius regio eius religio* proclaimed in the Treaty of Augsburg of 1555.[12] This new regulation entitled each ruler to define the religion of his territories and included the right to expel all dissenters.

The Franconian nobility protested Echter's anti-Jewish policies of 1575. In an extraordinary written petition addressed to the emperor in March 1575 they levied several related complaints: first they claimed that the bishop was, without warrant, cutting off an important source of revenue for them—tax payments from Jews. Moreover, it was asserted that he was impeding the imperial knights' right to establish new settlements within their territories, by preventing settlers from earning a living nearby. But the most surprising argument came last: the bishop's action would violate not only the imperial mandate over the Jews and public peace, as established by the civil imperial chamber court (the so-called *Reichskammergericht*), but would also contravene natural justice and the law of the nations—for it is unlawful, they maintained, to banish an innocent and upright person, to refuse him passage, or to seize his property and hamper him from gaining a livelihood.[13] This is significant as one of the earliest cases in modern European history in which Jews were portrayed not as serfs or indentured communities, but as subjects endowed with human dignity and entitled to legal protection according to Roman law. Even if this short paragraph in the nobles' petition was in fact dictated by the financial interests of the Franconian knights, it remains a remarkable text, embodying a new legal perception of their subjects, including the Jews, whose inclusion is most surprising.

This new attitude was based upon ideas which pertained to natural rights, Roman law and the idea of human dignity embracing all mankind. These ideas were gaining some ground in the era of the Renaissance due to the writings of humanists who attempted to define the duties and responsibilities of the ideal ruler. A seminal text in this

---

[12] Stefan Schwarz, *Die Juden in Bayern im Wandel der Zeiten* (Munich, 1963), 57–59, who presumes that the harsh order of Albrecht V of Bavaria, forbidding any Jewish presence in Bavaria, was dictated by the princely desire for religious unity. In 1581 Bishop Echter justified his actions against Protestants as in accordance with the Augsburg treaty; see Brander, *Julius Echter*, 103.

[13] Baum, "Quellen," 50, with the following quote: "(Dies laufe) auch aller volckher und Naturrecht zuwider, einen unverdampten menschen, also mit der that Anzugreiffen zu uerjagen, das seine zu nehmen, den Paß zu [ver]wehren, handlen und wandlen verbieten, unnd unser befreite Aigene Gütter zu kerckhern der Juden machen, unnß zum höchsten beschwerlich und nachteilig" (original in the municipal archive of Würzburg, Inv. no. Judensachen 10/101, fol. 43–46).

project was Erasmus of Rotterdam's *Institutio Principis Christiani* of 1516, a widely-read treatise which shaped political communication in the sixteenth century. It generated a multitude of similar writings, such as Jacob Omphalius's *De officis et potestate Principis* (Basel, 1550), which put a new emphasis on *jus naturale* and *jus gentium*.[14] A ruler, Omphalius stated, could only deal legally with a subject and his property if the latter was living in his territory, but he was not entitled to render any legal decisions affecting subjects beyond his borders.[15] These teachings, which put important limitations on princely powers, nevertheless persuaded many of the German knights that without these lessons no one was fit to rule or lead, because they offered relative security and mutual peace within the numerous tiny territories of the Holy Roman Empire, which was still lacking any kind of comprehensive legal system. Seen in this light, the objections made by the Franconian knights against Echter von Mespelbrunn concerning his treatment of Jews were directed against his very capacity as a ruler.

An attitude toward Jews similar to the one put forth by the Franconian knights was in evidence several generations earlier in 1511, when the humanist scholar Johannes Reuchlin defended the Jews and their literary traditions against the vehement accusations of Johannes Pfefferkorn, a convert, at the time of an emerging Catholic reaction to the humanism of the Renaissance.[16] Reuchlin, who was trained by Italian Renaissance teachers such as Pico della Mirandola, was the first to bring north a new respect for the "People of the Book," conveying this regard to a small group of humanist intellectuals consisting of learned burghers and municipal patricians, as well as some imperial knights such as Ulrich von Hutten. These erudite circles, it seems, while still devoted to the Catholic faith and the idea of the Holy Roman Empire, were willing to accept that any person was entitled to respect and legal protection regardless of religious, political or social association, if she or he was carrying a valuable heritage or executing a respectable profession or business which was of some public utility. Thus they came to perceive

[14] Ingmar Ahl, *Humanistische Politik zwischen Reformation und Gegenreformation. Der Fürstenspiegel des Jakob Omphalius* (Stuttgart, 2004), 21–23 and 295–301.

[15] Ahl, *Humanistische Politik*, 298; Jacobus Omphalius, *De officis et potestate Principis in re publica bene ac sancte gerenda, Basileia 1550*, 2:20, 98.

[16] Heiko A. Obermann, *Wurzeln des Antisemitismus* (Berlin, 1981), 38–39.

Jews as unjustly subordinated, and viewed them as "members of the Empire and imperial burghers."[17]

One should be cautious, of course, in attributing this attitude to a sort of premodern humanitarianism or even "philosemitism," and it is also not clear whether it was simply related to the medieval idea of preserving Jewish knowledge as a necessary source for advancing Christian study (which, ironically, would eventually lead to the conversion of all Jews). Instead, it appears that the humanist attitude of Reuchlin as well as the legal teachings of Erasmus of Rotterdam, which were taken further in later humanist writings, might have prepared the ground for a new legal perception which regarded the Jews as any other person living under the Roman law, that is, entitled to a proper life and legal protection—all this in order to secure social order and public utility.[18] This view is supported by the fact that the new teachings, while gaining some ground among the imperial knights touched by the humanist movement, applied not only to Jews but also to other minority groups, even women accused of sorcery, as is evident in the answer of Count Faber zu Castell to Bishop Echter in 1611, discussed earlier.

It seems, therefore, that the argument between Bishop Echter and the imperial Franconian knights concerning the Jews was not so much about financial interests but rather about the question of princely power and the application of legal principles as a sovereign ruler. This becomes evident in another statement the imperial knights directed against Bishop Echter somewhat later, in 1581. There the petitioners state that the bishop was not entitled to exercise absolute power over his subjects or to subordinate them in excess of his rights, since, as a prelate, he had been elected to his office, though as a prince he had not inherited the lands that made up the territories under his jurisdiction; therefore, the argument runs, the prince-bishop was in a position inferior to his secular counterparts, whose ancestors had acquired their land by themselves.[19] The imperial knights' preference for legal principles

[17] Friedrich Lotter, "Der Rechtsstatus der Juden in den Schriften Reuchlins zum Pfefferkornstreit," in *Reuchlin und die Juden*, ed. Arno Herzig and Julius Schoeps (Sigmaringen, 1993), 66–88, esp. 84.

[18] Lotter, "Der Rechtsstatus"; and Ahl, *Humanistische Politik*, 222–223, on the issue of public utility (*utilitas publica*), which Jacob Omphalius considers to be the goal of the princely virtue of *iustitia* in his *De officio et potestate Principis*.

[19] Brander, *Julius Echter*, 103, for the German text: "Zwischen den weltlichen und geistlichen Fürsten ist ein großer Unterschied, denn die weltlichen Fürsten sind Erbherren ihrer Land und Leute, die geistlichen Fürsten aber werden zu fürstlichen Hoheiten

limiting princely power was a slap in the face for Bishop Echter, who explicitly demanded total submission to his will.[20]

The latter's self-understanding as a sovereign ruler becomes all the clearer if we consider the next step he took against the Jews following the expulsion of 1574–1575. In order to consolidate his power, in 1576 Bishop Echter ordered the occupation and destruction of the old Jewish cemetery within the city of Würzburg. This provoked a letter from the emperor, who declared the action unlawful; but the bishop stood his ground, arguing in reply that, after the expulsion of Jews from the city, the cemetery would no longer be in use anyway. Never mind that the Jews had purchased it anew in 1446 and that it had been granted them as an eternal possession by one of Echter's predecessors: Echter took possession of the vast field, sold the Jewish tombstones to builders working on projects such as the nearby cloister of St. Marx, and used the available ground as the site of the new Julius-Hospital. He took it for granted that he could violate the contract of purchase and claimed to possess no copy of it anyway. In one action he thereby demonstrated his disrespect for Jewish mortuary custom and the emperor's guarantee of legal protection for the Jews. When the emperor threatened to set up an investigative committee, the bishop arrogantly advised him to stop allowing the Jews to bother him with their continuous and futile grievances.[21]

This harsh and cynical response shows the bishop to be supremely confident in his position—and indeed the emperor seems to have been powerless in this case to impose his will. Echter duly built the Julius-Hospital on the cemetery, and congratulated himself on converting infidel ground into a holy place.[22] The Julius-Hospital became one of the largest welfare institutions ever built in Würzburg. It was designed for the elderly, the ill and orphans, but also for new converts, though Echter strictly limited the access to the poor, men and women alike. All

---

gewählt und in ein Land gesetzt, da sie von ihren Eltern nicht einen Stecken haben; sondern es ist von andern erlangt und gewonnen worden; da vertraut man einem in Wahrheit nicht dergestalt an, dass er nach seinem freien Willen regieren soll oder die Inwohner des Landes, heute diesen, morgen einen andern nach seinem Gefallen in unbilliger Weise beschweren."

[20] See Bishop Echter's statment in Münnerstadt 1586, in Brander, *Julius Echter* (note 2 with the text and translation).

[21] Klaus Wittstadt, "Die Juden unter den Würzburger Fürstbischöfen vom Mittelalter bis in die Gegenwart," in *Geschichte und Kultur des Judentums*, ed. Karlheinz Müller (Würzburg, 1988), 151–173.

[22] Flade, *Juden*, 55.

persons admitted to the hospital were required to adhere to Catholicism and were ordered to pray for the souls of their earthly benefactors—especially the bishop's—several times daily. The first three Jews who converted to Christianity in the beginning of Echter's reign were in fact led to baptism in the newly built church of the Julius-Hospital, a ceremony orchestrated with great pomp by the proud bishop himself on the occasion of the church's dedication in 1580 (fig. 1).[23] The sheer dimensions of the hospital building and the magnificence of the architecture seemed to validate the bishop's claims of absolute power, which gained sublime expression in his stated goal of guarding the physical and spiritual welfare of his subjects.

The Revitalization of Pilgrimage

The building of the Julius-Hospital demonstrates the intimate linkage between Bishop Echter's zeal for strengthening the Catholic faith and his perception of himself as an absolute ruler. In order to ensure his position he not only set up a new, centralized administration which replaced the medieval system of knightly bailiffs, but took further steps to restore religious discipline in the episcopal territories. He initiated, for example, a new program of visitations of the parishes in order to impose celibacy among the clerics; he also reorganized preaching and the instruction of the young, especially with the help of the Jesuits. Most importantly, he rebuilt and redecorated more than 300 rural churches and reactivated many of the medieval pilgrimage sites that had been abandoned during the turmoil of the Reformation. Not only did he re-establish key pilgrimage sites but created new ones, and thereby set up a whole new network of pilgrimage shrines in Lower Franconia. Otherwise a parsimonious ruler, Echter spent the enormous amount of 300,000 florins on revitalizing or establishing churches, chapels and pilgrimage sites, and from this investment some fifty new pilgrimage sites were born in and around Würzburg itself.[24]

---

[23] Brander, *Julius Echter*, 117–119; Mälzer, *Julius Echter*, 42, reports another baptism of Jews in the church of the Julius-Hospital in 1611. The original painting depicting the baptism of 1580 was destroyed in 1943 during the air-strikes of the Second World War, but a black and white photograph still exists in the municipal archive of Würzburg.

[24] Brander, *Julius Echter*, 112.

Echter also took great care to bestow upon these sacred places appropriate images of the holy persons, images allegedly endowed with miraculous powers (*Gnadenbilder*). His favorite objects of veneration were the Eucharist, represented most prominently at the shrine at Walldürn (situated in the center of the Odenwald), and the Virgin Mary, whose principal shrines in the territory were Maria Buchen, Maria im Sande in Dettelbach, and St. Maria im Weinberg, near Volkach.[25] All three Marian pilgrimage sites were situated on the Main river within a day's journey from Würzburg and attracted pilgrims from far away (most of the other sites attracted visitors only from the vicinity). These shrines continue to attract pilgrims today.

The veneration of the Eucharist, which had gained momentum in the thirteenth century and become an exceptionally popular focus for worship in the end of the Middle Ages, is especially important for our purposes.[26] The religious fervor surrounding this form of piety was fuelled in large part by tales of miraculous hosts, legends which first sprang up in large numbers during the fourteenth century, and were propagated further at the end of the fifteenth century, sometimes in the aftermath of the preachings of wandering Franciscans such as Johannes Capistrano.[27] A good number of the pilgrimage sites that resulted were linked to anti-Jewish legends. It therefore comes as no surprise that the very existence of some of the pilgrimage sites revived by Bishop Echter were established through the promotion of medieval—or medievalizing—legends of alleged Jewish host desecrations. This is the case in places such as Lauda, Röttingen, Iphofen and Heiligenblut bei Spalt.[28] Another category of miraculous images whose

[25] Ibid. 112–114.

[26] Peter Browe, "Die Hostienschändungen der Juden im Mittelalter," *Römische Quartalsschrift für christliche Altertumskunde und Kirchengeschichte* 34 (1926): 167–197; Miri Rubin, *Corpus Christi: The Eucharist in Late Medieval Culture* (Cambridge, 1991), 83–129; Friedrich Lotter, "Hostienfrevelvorwurf und Blutwunderfälschungbei den Judenverfolgungen von 1298 (Rindfleisch) und 1336–1338 (Armleder)", in *Fälschungen im Mittelalter. Internationaler Kongreß der Monumenta Germaniae Historica-München 1986, Teil V: Fingierte Briefe, Frömmigkeit und Fälschung, Realienfälschung* (Hannover, 1988), 533–538.

[27] Friedrich Lotter, "Aufkommen und Verbreitung von Ritualmord- und Hostienfrevelanklagen gegen Juden" in *Die Macht der Bilder. Antisemitische Vorurteile und Mythen*, exhib. cat., ed. Jüdisches Museum Wien (Vienna, 1995), 60–78, at 70–71; and Miri Rubin, *Gentile Tales: The Narrative Assault on Late Medieval Jews* (New Haven, 1999), 21–39.

[28] Romuald Bauerreiss, *Pie Jesu: Das Schmerzensmannbild und sein Einfluss auf die mittelalterliche Frömmigkeit* (Munich, 1931), 46, for Iphofen, the legend of which started allegedly in 1294; also 46, for Heiligenblut bei Spalt, which started around 1444; 48, for the Röttingen legend from 1299; and 52, for Lauda, the legend of which is dated

sanctity arose in connection with anti-Jewish legends were representations of the Pietà, which depicts Mary holding her dead son on her lap. In the age of Counter-Reformation, Mary as the mother of Jesus became the predominant patron saint of Franconia, and many of her sites enshrined a miraculous image, or *Gnadenbild*, which offered to share her son's potential power with the faithful. Jews were alleged to have violated such images, as was reported for the small sculpted Pietà promoted at Maria-Buchen.[29]

In fostering the veneration of Mary and the Eucharist in the form of miraculous images, Bishop Echter was following good Counter-Reformation precepts—including the notion that following the Catholic faith was not just a matter of passive listening, sheer obedience and personal belief, but also a practical issue, requiring active communal worship and shared religious experiences, miracles included. This sense of a more popular faith led to a well-organised system of Marian and eucharistic confraternities and public pilgrimages, which involved burgher society and rural communities alike in an elaborate annual calendar of local peregrinations.[30] But the program for the revitalization of pilgrimages set in motion by Bishop Echter, who took every possible step to rid the episcopal territories of Jews, is distinctive in its emphasis on sites where Jewish infidelity had been overcome by a miracle revealing the true religion, that is, the Catholic faith. His activities in four of the towns just mentioned may now be considered in some detail.

after 1283. The pilgrimage church at Heiligenblut bei Spalt was shut down in 1803 during the secularization; see also Karl Kolb, *Vom heiligen Blut: Eine Bilddokumentation der Wallfahrt und Verehrung* (Würzburg, 1980), 146. The author, while adopting an attitude of popular Catholicism, offers nevertheless some very interesting insights as he provides a wealth of detailed information concerning religious practices. The book enumerates further sites where Jews allegedly had desecrated hosts such as Klein- and Großostheim, Königshofen, Rottenburg and Wörth. Most of the sites are in Lower Franconia, i.e., the dominions of Episcopal Würzburg.

[29] Wolfgang Brückner, *Maria-Buchen: Eine fränkische Wallfahrt* (Würzburg, 1979); Alfons Ruf, *600 Jahre Mariabuchen* (Lohr am Main, 1995), 8. A similar legend is reported from Dettelbach for a monument standing today in the churchyard of Maria im Sande. The baroque relief reports the story of the *Dettelbach Pièta* violated by Jews, which immediatedly reacted against the offenders by striking their ears.

[30] Hans Dünninger, "Processio Peregrinatoris: Volkskundliche Untersuchung zu einer Geschichte des Wallfahrtswesens im Gebiet der heutigen Diözese Würzburg," in *Wallfahrt und Bilderkult: Gesammelte Schriften von Hans Dünninger* (Würzburg, 1995), 38–50. For the importance of maintaining religious discipline through processions during the Counter-Reformation in Munich (especially with the help of the procession of the Eucharist at the occasion of the feast of Corpus Domini), see Philip M. Soergel, *Wondrous in His Saints: Counter-Reformation Propaganda in Bavaria* (Berkeley, 1993), 86–94.

First, the small town of Röttingen on the Tauber. In 1298 its Jewish community was massacred in full, following the rumor of a host desecration. However, the historical circumstances of what really happened remain unclear, as there exist several versions of the legend. One later version of the legend relates that a host stolen from the parish church of Röttingen on the eve of Good Friday was desecrated by Jews who threw it into the Tauber. There pious nuns of a nearby cloister discovered and rescued the host, which was emanating a miraculous light. The next day, the burghers went out to bring the host back, and with their return to town the house of the Jews miraculously started to burn, killing those who had allegedly pierced and martyred it.[31] In the aftermath, the town became the launching pad of anti-Jewish riots (the so-called "Rintfleisch pogroms") throughout Franconia, which touched many places, among them Lauda, Iphofen and Würzburg itself.[32]

More than three hundred years after these founding events, Bishop Echter took pains to reinforce the Catholic faith by authorizing new buildings and renovating the churches of Röttingen, especially the parish church, traditionally held to be the site from which the host allegedly had been stolen. To the present day there exists a local painting showing in the center the half-length figure of Christ as the *Salvator Mundi* surrounded by six scenes detailing the events (fig. 2). The two scenes on the left show a Christian stealing the host from the altar. On the right the Jews, wearing the typical late sixteenth-century habit, are shown violating the host; one of them throws it into the river. In the scene above the image of Christ, the nuns are depicted rescuing the host from the waters and beneath the Jews are shown being burnt on the stake. An inscription on top and at the bottom refers to the legend and dates the events erroneously to 1288. Stylistically the painting dates from the late eighteenth century, but its iconography and some contemporary details—in particular the Jewish costumes, which were worn also by the Jews of Frankfurt am Main and Fürth—point to an earlier original, probably of late sixteenth or early seventeenth-century origin.[33] In contrast to medieval paintings and illuminated manuscripts, which could present Jews wearing the Jewish hat or with distorted

[31] Friedrich Lotter, "Die Judenverfolgung des 'König Rintfleisch' in Franken um 1298," *Zeitschrift für Historische Forschung* 15, no. 4 (1988): 385–422, at 395.

[32] Baum, "Quellen zu Judenverfolgungen," 27–30; Lotter, "Judenverfolgung," with a list of Jewish communities destroyed during the Rintfleisch pogroms, 421–422.

[33] Israel Schwierz, *Steinerne Zeugnisse jüdischen Lebens in Bayern* (Munich, 1988), 109.

features, the eighteenth century painting shows no such stereotyped "signs of otherness."

As in Röttingen, so too in Lauda, a district town which was situated in the valley of the Tauber not far from Röttingen, from which the rumor of a host allegedly desecrated by Jews had spread in 1298. There we find another host desecration report from the end of the thirteenth century, but its exact date and historical circumstances are even more dubious than in Röttingen. After expelling from Lauda all those burghers who had participated in a peasants' upheaval, and decapitating their leaders, Bishop Echter made sure to recatholicize the parish church and dedicate its revenues to his newly built Julius-Hospital. And he apparently rebuilt the local chapel of the Holy Sepulchre, standing on the ground of a former Jewish home, where the host desecration had allegedly taken place in 1283. According to an inscription—once placed above the entrance—the chapel of 1683 was the result of a thorough renovation of an earlier building, already nearly a hundred years old; this indicates that it stemmed from the time of Bishop Echter.[34] The story of the host desecration is captured in a popular narrative painting, reworked in 1791 but probably originating considerably earlier (fig. 3). In four scenes it shows the Jew pestering a Christian women to steal a host; the theft of the host; the Jew's purchase of the host and his attempt to violate it; and the discovery of the buried host by miraculous signs.[35] The Jew is marked as such only by his outmoded costume, similar to the ones represented in Röttingen.

Now to the town of Iphofen. From 1605 to 1615 Bishop Echter renovated and extended the medieval church of the Holy Blood (sometimes called also the church of the Holy Sepulchre) that was a site of a host desecration alleged to have occurred in 1294. According to a document of 1690, it became a pilgrimage destination confirmed by papal authority in 1296. Recent examinations have concluded with good reason that the Jewish community of Iphofen fell victim to the pogroms spreading from Röttingen in 1298 and that the local legend of the host desecration was a later addition, of which several versions

[34] *Die Kunstdenkmäler des Großherzogtums Baden, Amt Tauberbischofsheim*, ed. Adolf von Oechselhaeuser (Tübingen, 1898), 108; for the reproduction of the inscription on the chapel in Lauda, see Kolb, *Vom heiligen Blut*, 123.

[35] Joachim Hahn, *Erinnerungen und Zeugnisse jüdischer Geschichte in Baden-Württemberg* (Stuttgart, 1988), 350.

exist.[36] After several rebuildings, the last in 1984, the monument once erected over the miraculous site in the center of the nave, has been relocated into the north chapel, which now features a curious mish-mash of furnishings: a late nineteenth-century altar decorated with four antisemitic legend scenes in quatrefoils (fig. 4), together with a statue of a Man of Sorrows, a late nineteenth-century copy after an original possibly from the time of Bishop Echter; and on the northern wall of the main sanctuary, an eighteenth-century wooden votive statue of Christ, portrayed as the "Source of Salvific Blood" with two putti receiving the blood pouring from his wounds (fig. 5). This sculptural ensemble once stood in the main apse of the church and served as the principal image of the baroque high altar, located over the site where the miraculous host had allegedly been found.[37]

Finally to the site of Maria Buchen; the pilgrimage is situated in the vicinity of a former medieval Jewish cemetery, which apparently was abandoned after the Jewish community of the nearby town of Lohr had been destroyed during the Rintfleisch pogrom in 1298.[38] There we find a small wooden Pietà of the late fourteenth century (fig. 6), allegedly violated by a Jew and venerated since at least 1406, the moment when the image was discovered, according to a late medieval inscription.[39] As in other places, Echter von Mespelbrunn zealously re-established the site. In 1613 he financed the renovation and partial rebuilding of the fifteenth-century chapel, the choir of which was subsequently incorporated in the church rebuilt in 1692–1694.[40] And he promoted pilgrimage by advertising the town's miraculous story in simple printed devotional images (fig. 7a). In the extant copies of these prints we can see the Jew, with dagger drawn, in the act of violating the statue of the Pietà,

---

[36] Lotter, "Judenverfolgung," 395; Harald Schwillus, "Hostienfrevellegende und Judenverfolgung in Iphofen. Ein Beitrag zur Entstehungsgeschichte der Kirche zum Hl. Blut im Gräberviertel," *Würzburger Diözesangeschichtsblätter* 58 (1996): 87–107; and Mitchell B. Merback, "Channels of Grace: Pilgrimage Architecture, Eucharistic Imagery and Visions of Purgatory at the Host Miracle Churches of Late Medieval Germany," in *Art and Architecture of Late Medieval Pilgrimage in Northern Europe and the British Isles* ed. Sarah Blick and Rita Tekippe (Leiden, 2005), 587–646, at 609–611.

[37] Andreas Brombierstäudl, *Iphofen, Die Kirche zum hl. Blut* (Regensburg, 1999), 20–26; Merback, "Channels of Grace," 621–22.

[38] Ruf, *600 Jahre Maria-Buchen*, 14–15.

[39] Ruf, *600 Jahre Maria-Buchen*, 19.

[40] Ruf, *600 Jahre Maria-Buchen*, 38–54; also see Annette Weber, "Maria die ist Juden veind"—Antijüdische Mariendarstellungen in der Kunst des 13.–15. Jahrhunderts," in *Maria Tochter Sion? Mariologie, Marienfrömmigkeit und Judenfeindschaft*, ed. Johannes Heil and Rainer Kampling (Paderborn, 2001), 90–91, fig. 14.

hidden in a tree. The newly built chapel is visible in the background. Again the Jew is represented unsensationally—he possesses an ordinary bearded face and wears a peasant's costume. There are none of the traditional markers favored by medieval illustrators—no pointed hat, physical distortions or the like. The only signs of his Jewishness are a sort of *tallith katan* (prayer shawl) worn over his long blouse and some pseudo-Hebrew letters on its hems.

This printed image seems to have proven highly successful: some hundred years later, it was still in use, slightly updated for rococo tastes by providing a more realistic appearance of a local Jewish peddler (fig. 7b). Recording the same story is the principal image in a panel painting that includes a long text with a lunette above (fig. 8). The painting, retouched in 1687, was originally shown in the chapel. It shows the very same moment as the prints, but depicts it in a more elaborate way. The Jew, though dressed again like a peddler, appears frenzied while attacking the Pietà. His entire attitude signifies the social misfit, but once more there are no traits of medieval anti-Jewish stereotyping.

These baroque representations reflect the long-standing tradition of anti-Jewish medieval legends about desecrated hosts and ritual murders, tales which had begun springing up at the end of the thirteenth century and whose numbers grew steadily until the sixteenth century. At first the tales would have been transmitted orally in gossip or local reports, but from the late thirteenth and early fourteenth century onward they were incorporated into the popular legends created by clerics to entertain the laity while preaching. By popularizing the image of the Jew as the demonic and vicious other, they contributed to increasing Christian suspicion towards living Jews. This process of alienation accelerated during the later fifteenth century, when the legends of alleged host desecration and ritual murder, reported initially by word of mouth, were also now propagated, very effectively, by printed single-leaf woodcuts (fig. 9). These primitive and simply cut images reinforced the voyeuristic appeal of the horrible stories, and probably succeeded in shaping collective memory more profoundly than any tale on its own could do.[41]

[41] Peter Browe, "Hostienschändungen," counted thirty-five charges of host-crimes directed against Jews which occurred in German-speaking regions between 1220–1566, whereas Romuald Bauerreiß, *Pie Jesu*, enumerates twenty-eight new pilgrimage sites which emerged between 1300 and 1350 due to alleged host desecrations by Jews. Regarding the impact of single-leaf woodcuts in spreading popular anti-Jewish beliefs, see Christine Mittlmeier, *Publizistik im Dienste antijüdischer Polemik* (Frankfurt am Main, 2000), esp. 39–41; also Miri Rubin, "Imagining the Jew: The Late Medieval Eucharistic

One prominent set of examples arose from the case of the alleged ritual murder of Simon of Trent in 1475, which gained a European-wide popularity and an almost iconic cultural status not just through preaching and writing but, even more dramatically, through a single woodcut by Michael Wolgemut, an image that appeared in Hartmann Schedel's famous *Nuremberg Chronicle* of 1493 and continued to shape Christian prejudices until the time of Goethe (fig. 10).[42] The woodcut, with its allusions to deep-rooted anxieties of castration and humiliation by infidels, became a kind of public image of Jewish perfidy and an alert to every Christian to be wary. In their folkish appearance and simple narrative manner the small scenes of the two late eighteenth-century paintings in Röttingen and Lauda still recall the structure of medieval print series that were produced to appeal a popular taste.

When considering the origin of all four sites, it seems that they all came into existence in context with the Rintfleisch-persecutions at the very end of the thirteenth century. Apparently, the rumour of the host desecration spreading from Röttingen generated further anti-Jewish legends at other places where Jewish communities had been wiped out as well. There are good reasons to consider these legends as *ex post facto* inventions, however, created in places like Röttingen and Iphofen in order to justify the massacres of these Lower Franconian Jewish communities.[43] Besides religious zeal, these persecutions were most certainly fuelled by other motivations, for example, the wish to get rid of burdensome debts, as was the case of the sovereign of Röttingen, Count Kraft von Hohenlohe-Weikersheim, who was heavily indebted to the Jews and apparently profited from the Rintfleisch persecutions.[44] Thus the spreading anti-Jewish legends in Franconia during the late Middle Ages seem to have followed a pattern of exculpation offered by the Catholic church in the aftermath of pogroms: the persecutions were sanctioned, as they were directed against the ones who allegedly

Discourse," in *In and Out of the Ghetto: Jewish Gentile Relations in Late Medieval and Early Modern Germany*, ed. Ronnie Po-chia Hsia and Hartmut Lehmann (Cambridge, 1995), 177–208.

[42] R. Po-chia Hsia, *Trient 1475: Geschichte eines Ritualmordprozesses* (Frankfurt, 1997), 86–90; Gabriela Schlick, "Was Johann Wolfgang Goethe hatte sehen können...Die Judengasse in Frankfurt am Main," in *"Außerdem waren sie ja auch Menschen": Goethes Begegnung mit Juden und Judentum*, ed. Annette Weber (Berlin, 1999), 47–48.

[43] Merback, "Channels of Grace," 610–611.

[44] Lotter, "Judenverfolgung," 401–403.

tried to re-enact the murder of the Savior by violating his body in form of the host.

The surviving pictorial decorations at all four sites demonstrate that Echter von Mespelbrunn dedicated himself to reorganizing these sites and, it seems, to emphasizing the alleged miraculous powers of their devotional images. In effect, then, when Bishop Echter resolved to revive the pilgrimage sites with miraculous relics and images, and thereby to "re-verify" the misdeeds of the Jews, he was following a mainstream public feeling that already existed. Sometimes this effect was working through the alleged miraculous powers of the cult-images themselves, as in the case of the Pietà of Maria Buchen, whereas in the cases of the veneration of the desecrated hosts the effect sometimes was enhanced by narrative images that were placed next to the site of devotion, as in Lauda and in Röttingen. The narrative paintings seem to have been crucial in supporting the veneration of the somewhat inconspicuous host. The other solution of visualization of the sacred consisted in presenting Christ *in corpore*, i.e. as the Holy Savior or as the *imago pietatis*, as in Iphofen, which Bishop Echter well might have established himself in reference to the latest developments of Eucharist imagery, especially at those sites with dubious wonderhosts.[45]

Echter von Mespelbrunn did choose those sites deliberately, and he did so almost certainly in the knowledge that the legends and the pilgrimages based upon them were of dubious origin, having been questioned by reform-minded theologians since the humanist era.[46] In fact, the Catholic church itself, as far back as the mid-fifteenth century, had taken some steps to keep the growing veneration of miraculous hosts at bay, and no less a prelate than Nicolas Cusanus was sent off to examine some of the pilgrimage sites suspected of making fraudulent use of a host, such as Wilsnack.[47] A particular topic of skeptical discussion was the veneration of alleged ritually murdered children, a fashion that surfaced repeatedly from the fourteenth to the later fifteenth century

[45] Merback, "Channels of Grace," 628–633, argues very convincingly that a new form of the *imago pietatis* prevailed since the end of the fifteenth century at many of the miraculous sites linked to the veneration of the Eucharist; see also idem, "Fount of Mercy, City of Blood: Cultic Anti-Judaism and the Pulkau Passion Altarpiece," *Art Bulletin* 87, no. 4 (Dec. 2005): 589–642.

[46] Ruf, *600 Jahre Mariabuchen*, 11.

[47] Kolb, *Vom Heiligen Blut*, 108–109.

in southern Germany.[48] In 1529 Andreas Osiander (1498–1552), a reform-minded humanist and a pupil of Reuchlin, published an essay in Nuremberg, *Ob es war und glaublich sey, daß die Juden der Christen kinder heymlich erwürgen und ir blut gebrauchen* (Whether it might be true that Jews would secretly murder Christian children and use their blood). In it he argued convincingly against such legends, even drawing on the testimony of the convert Johannes Pfefferkorn, who had also tried to show those stories up as Christian myths. Osiander regarded them solely as inventions of covetous and greedy nobles and burghers in debt to Jews, and also of impudent clerics eager to inaugurate a new miraculous pilgrimage site![49]

Osiander's attitude and the humanist perception of Jews as imperial burghers correspond somewhat to the changed pictorial depiction of Jews following the Renaissance. In the famous chronicle by Lorenz Fries, written anew and lavishly illustrated by order of Echter von Mespelbrunn (figs. 11a and 11b), the artists of all three existing copies decline to depict the Jews as they had been depicted in the Middle Ages—as outsiders wearing strange dress and pointed hats, or with distorted faces.[50] In all of the illustrations, Jews—with the notable exception of the so-called *Juden-Bischoff*, who is distinguished by his medieval garb—are represented as looking much like anyone else, in standard civil dress and distinguished only in the appearance of the yellow badge. And because they are depicted like normal persons, the cruelty against them appears all the more flagrant. It would therefore seem that the new legal perspective as developed by the humanist movement, which viewed Jews as citizens of the empire, prevailed not only among imperial knights but also within the educated entourage of Bishop Echter himself.

In sum, Echter von Mespelbrunn must have been aware of the changing attitudes regarding Jews, and also of the attempts to declare as

---

[48] Ronnie Po-chia Hsia, *The Myth of Ritual Murder: Jews and Magic in Reformation Germany* (New Haven, 1988).

[49] Obermann, *Wurzeln des Antisemitismus*, 44–45.

[50] Gottfried Mälzer, *Die Fries-Chronik des Fürstbischofs Julius Echter von Mespelbrunn* (Würzburg 1989). Jews are depicted several times in this illustrated chronicle, which exists in three copies. One of them was executed for Bishop Echter himself in 1574 and contains the most lavish illustrations. But also the copy in the municipal archive in Würzburg (Ratsbuch 417) depicts Jews wearing mostly sixteenth-century dress and shows them being killed by Christians following the preachings of a monk in 1147 during the second crusade (fol. 100v), and again in the illustrations of the Armleder-persecutions in 1336, and of the pogrom in 1349 (fols. 172r and 181v respectively).

groundless their alleged offences against the host and small children. It seems that he knowingly chose to ignore the views of his reform-minded colleagues and of earlier humanists, and to maintain the medieval legends for the sake of promoting his pilgrimage sites. In fairness, he could argue that he was only following the model set by the papal court in the case of Simon of Trent of 1475, which confirmed the legality of the trial of Jews for ritual murder, despite its patently questionable circumstances.[51]

Conclusion

It seems clear that Bishop Echter's declared mandate to maintain the Catholic faith and promote, at times ruthlessly, the Counter Reformation impeded him from tolerating any other religion. His cruel conduct towards the powerless Würzburg Jews, as in sweeping aside their chartered rights to the cemetery, was for him a virtuously orthodox course of action, as was the upkeep of all those spurious pilgrimage sites. We therefore must consider Bishop Echter's dealings with the Jews in conjunction with his religious zeal and his territorial politics alike. Since the beginning of his reign, he seems to have been preoccupied with two issues: imposing Catholicism and attaining absolute power in his territories. Both aims seem to be inseparably linked; the *cura religionis* became instrumental for ruling: the reorganisation of the civil and religious administration, his objections to the imperial knights' complaint about actions against Jews and Protestants, and the answers he gave to the burghers of Münnerstadt in 1586 all point in this direction.[52] Even the ruthless persecution of sorceresses could be regarded as a further attempt to stabilize his dominion by (once more) following the Bavarian model.[53] Obviously, he rejected the new legal perspective according to which any person, Jews and sorceresses included, should be entitled to treatment respectful of natural rights, because it would have meant a diminution of his power as a sovereign. In his claims for absolute rule

[51] Hsia, *Trient 1475*, esp. 155–69.

[52] Cf. Ahl, *Humanistische Politik*, 237; regarding the statement in Münnerstadt, cf. text of the original quotation in note 2.

[53] Stefan Kestler, "Frühneuzeitliche Hexenverfolgungen in Bayern und Franken. Bemerkungen zu einem historischen Problembereich," *Würzburger Diözesangeschichtsblätter* 58 (1996): 171–180, esp. 174.

he anticipated the era of Absolutism, and in that respect he was more a man of his time than his opponents, the imperial knights, who attempted to preserve the old order by inducing new legal perspectives.

In the same context, one might ask whether the assertion of medieval anti-Jewish legends at pilgrimage sites owed more to the retrograde character of Bishop Echter's piety than to traditional anti-Judaism; a shrewd calculation of how to reinforce his sovereignty by luring the masses back to Catholicism with the help of tales and legends that appealed to popular taste was also part of this strategy. If one accepts this account of Echter's political motivation, this would also suggest that the parameters of how Jews could be and were perceived might have shifted in the course of time. During the Middle Ages, the perception of Jews had been defined predominantly by religious ideas, as it is demonstrated by the *ex post facto* inventions of anti-Jewish legends of host desecration in order to sanction the violence of the Rintfleisch pogroms. Even the questions of usury and imperial protections were linked to it. In the era of the Renaissance this attitude apparently changed, due in part to the influence of the idea of natural rights—rights as pertaining to any person, regardless of religious confession. Moreover, the notion of treating Jews and non-Jews alike according to legal principles rather than religious categories points to a new interest in a constitutional order that was based upon reason. This new idea is evident from the argumentation of the imperial knights, when they insisted that dealing with Jews was a state affair and not just a personal matter or religious issue. Even if Bishop Echter rejected their point of view, his policy of foresaking the actual Jewish communities in his territories while retaining the medieval anti-Jewish legends in order to impose the will of the sovereign shows the influence of the new way of perceiving Jews within a political framework. One could say that dealing with religion politically became a principal issue of ruling. Thus, the anti-Jewish legends used to promote pilgrimage sites served to reinforce the allegiance of Bishop Echter's subjects, confirming their affiliation to true faith and a righteous rule.

History has proved that Bishop Echter von Mespelbrunn was highly successful in his unwavering commitment to supporting the orthodox Catholic faith and providing new state-run facilities for communicating it. These efforts, as we have seen, resulted in the creation of an absolutist reign in the territories of Würzburg and a population subordinated solely to the will of its ecclesiastical sovereign. But in his ruthlessly calculated intolerance he would also exert a powerful influence on the moral behavior of later generations. The pilgrimage sites that he established enjoyed a longstanding public reputation, and following his reign Franconia became a center for rigid Catholicism in later centuries. In Echter's time the numerically insignificant Jews were unlikely to be seen as the arch-enemy, or feared as an economic power, since they had to live mainly in the countryside and in neighboring territories, where they struggled to earn a living as beggars and peddlers. Yet they were still regarded with suspicion, as unreliable neighbors possibly endowed with supernatural powers akin to that of sorcerers.[54] This double perception is very clearly reflected in those tales of desecrated hosts and ritual murders—tales which continued to have an impact, especially on the rural population, for centuries beyond the Counter-Reformation. That impact was constantly reinforced by the pilgrimage sites, whose popular devotional images, even while depicting Jews as an almost ordinary element of rural folk life, at the same time revealed their alleged other, more sinister and demonic side, which was perceived no longer only as a religious but moreover as a social threat.

[54] According to Abraham Berliner (*Aus dem Leben der deutschen Juden im Mittelalter* [Berlin, 1900], 102), Jews were held thought of as magicians and sorcerers up to his own days, and especially in rural areas in Franconia and Swabia Christians went so far as to request from their Jewish neighbours amulets to protect their houses from fire; often these amulets consisted of the so-called "Judenmatz," a piece of the Passover *matzah* known as the *afikoman*, said to have magical powers.

CHAPTER THIRTEEN

BETWEEN CALVINISTS AND JEWS: HEBREW SCRIPT IN REMBRANDT'S ART*

Shalom Sabar

Israeli tourists who visit churches and museums in Europe are surprised anew every time they discover Hebrew letters in works of art of the Renaissance and baroque periods. The combination of the Hebrew alphabet with overtly Christian themes such as the Crucifixion, or its appearance in Tuscan and Flemish landscapes painted by Christian artists, seems at first bizarre and puzzling. Those tourists who make the effort and attempt to decipher the messages behind the familiar letters are usually disappointed. Often the letters are nothing but graphic designs imitating Hebrew script, and even when letters are correctly written they often do not make up words and sentences with any clear meaning. Moreover, even in those cases when the meaning of the Hebrew words is intelligible, the connection to the image remains obscure. The frustrated visitor is thus left wondering why such inscriptions were written in the first place, how they came about and whether the master painters of the past actually knew any Hebrew.

The phenomenon of Hebrew script in European Christian art is indeed complex and a full account of it has yet to be written.[1] While

---

* This essay is an expanded and updated version of my essay, "Hebrew Inscriptions in Rembrandt's Art," which appeared in Hebrew in the exhibition catalog for the Israel Museum, *Rembrandt's Holland*, ed. Martin Weyl and Rivka Weiss-Blok (Jerusalem, 1993), 169–187. I benefited from the remarks made by colleagues, and am especially grateful to Gary Schwartz for his close reading of the Hebrew essay, and to Mitchell Merback for his professional support.

[1] Some basic studies on the topic include: Moshe Barasch, "Hebrew Inscriptions in Renaissance Works of Art" [in Hebrew], in *Scritti in memoria di Leone Carpi: Saggi sull'Ebraismo Italiano*, ed. Daniel Carpi, Attilio Milano and Alexander Rofé (Jerusalem, 1967), 141–150 (with Italian summary on 319); Avraham Ronen, "Hebrew Script in European Art of the Fifteenth Century" [in Hebrew], in *Proceedings of the Tenth World Congress of Jewish Studies*, Division D, Vol. 2: *Art, Folklore and Music* (Jerusalem, 1990), 1–8; idem, "Iscrizioni ebraiche nell'arte italiana del Quattrocento," in *Studi di storia dell'arte sul medioevo e il rinascimento. Atti del Convegno internazionale Arezzo-Firenze 1989*, 2 vols. (Florence, 1992), 2: 601–624; and Ruth Mellinkoff, *Outcasts: Signs of Otherness in Northern*

in the Middle Ages artists showed little interest in inserting Hebrew letters in their works—and when they did, the script was commonly incorrect and often used, especially in Germany, to mock Judaism and contemporary Jews[2]—that approach changed gradually in the course of the fifteenth century, and the number of Hebrew inscriptions increased steadily in the subsequent centuries. This is one of the by-products of Renaissance humanism, when intellectuals in countries such as Italy, Germany and later also Holland and England, started to show interest in Judaism and its ancient tongue. The knowledge of the language was viewed as a key to understanding the Holy Scriptures, God's word, and even the culture of ancient Israel. Italian humanists in particular considered Hebrew, along with Latin and Greek, as one of the three languages of the cultural world of antiquity that they were obliged to comprehend and emulate. Christian Hebraism, as the new field came to be known, made enormous progress in the first decades of the sixteenth century, when chairs for the study of Hebrew were established in universities throughout Europe.[3] Eventually it included several "Jew-

European Art of the Late Middle Ages, 2 vols. (Berkeley, 1993), 1:97–108. The most comprehensive list of Western works of art containing Hebrew inscriptions, containing 362 items, was prepared not by an art historian but a Hebrew linguist, Gad B. Sarfatti, "Hebrew Script in Western Visual Arts," *Italia: Studi e ricerche sulla storia, la cultura e la letteratura degli Ebrei d'Italia*, 13–15 (2001): 451–547, and "Addenda," *Italia* 16 (2004): 135–156; Sarfatti also dedicated short essays to specific inscriptions (see my note 4).

[2] A prominent example is the popular German early fifteenth-century *Judensau* woodcut, depicting mock-Hebrew letters on the hems of a young Jew riding backwards on the sow, holding up her tail and sucking it, while his friend is about to lick the sow's behind; see Debra Strickland's chapter in this volume and her fig. 12; and Isaiah Shachar, *The Judensau: A Medieval Anti-Jewish Motif and its History* (London, 1974), 34–35 and pl. 30. Many additional examples are reproduced in Heinz Schreckenberg, *The Jews in Christian Art: An Illustrated History* (New York, 1996), for example, 250 (no. 3), 262–63, 277 (no. 6a), 278 (no. 6e), 308, etc. For an analysis of the pejorative connotations of Hebrew script in late medieval northern European art, see Mellinkoff's chapter, cited in the previous note.

[3] For a general survey of the phenomenon in the sixteenth century, Jerome Friedman, *The Most Ancient Testimony: Sixteenth-Century Christian-Hebraica in the Age of Renaissance Nostalgia* (Athens, Ohio, 1983). For some specific works by Christian Hebraists, see the exhibition catalog *Christian Hebraism: The Study of Jewish Culture by Christian Scholars in Medieval and Early Modern Times* (Cambridge, MA., 1988). For the negative (antisemitic) impact of Hebrew studies by Christians, see Heiko A. Oberman, "Discovery of Hebrew and Discrimination against the Jews: The *Veritas Hebraica* as Double-Edged Sword in Renaissance and Reformation," in *Germania Illustrata: Essays on Early Modern Germany Presented to Gerald Strauss*, ed. Andrew C. Fix and Susan C. Karant-Nunn (Kirksville, MO, 1984), 19–34. For Holland in this period, see Aaron L. Katchen, *Christian Hebraists and Dutch Rabbis: Seventeenth-Century Apologetics and the Study of Maimonides' "Mishneh Torah"* (Cambridge, MA., 1984). See also the recent selection of essays in *Hebraica Veritas?*

ish" disciplines (Bible, Talmud, rabbinic—*Midrashic*—literature, religious philosophy, Kabbalah, etc.), which increased the intellectual interest in Hebrew, the Bible and Judaism among Christian scholars. The visual arts are but one of the cultural areas that benefited from this growth from the early sixteenth century on. In this essay I will show not only that Rembrandt's work reflects the intellectual support provided by the Christian Hebraists of his time, but also that it furnishes us with substantial evidence for the artist's personal contacts with the Jews of Amsterdam.

On the Nature and Scope of Hebrew Script in Christian Art

Attempting to imbue their works with "historical authenticity," Italian artists in particular embedded in their images elements that pertain to the classical world, such as ancient-looking architectural elements, or actual monuments of classical provenance, plenty of which were still visible on Italian soil. The idea of complementing works depicting figures and stories from the Old and New Testaments with inscriptions that supposedly came from the time and place where the events took place attracted many Italian artists.[4] A little-known example that reflects this spirit is a miniature in a Missal illuminated by Giulio Clovio (1498–1578) ca. 1532 (fig. 1).[5] It is an initial decoration depicting St. John holding a scroll in which he begins to write his book. The evangelist is shown seated barefoot in an open landscape, while his

---

Christian Hebraists and the Study of Judaism in Early Modern Europe, ed. Allison P. Coudert and Jeffrey S. Shoulson (Philadelphia, 2004).

[4] As mentioned above, only a few studies have been dedicated to an analysis of the Hebrew and its meaning in such inscriptions; see Barasch, "Hebrew Inscriptions," 142–45. A series of short essays along these lines is in Gad B. Sarfatti, *In the Language of My People: Essays on Hebrew* [in Hebrew] (Jerusalem, 1997), 245–283 (the essays originally appeared in *Leshonenu la'Am: A Popular Journal for the Hebrew Language* 46–47 [1995/96]); idem, "Latin Inscriptions in Hebrew Letters on an Italian Statue from the Renaissance," *Italia: Studi e ricerche sulla storia e la cultura e la letteratura degli Ebrei d'Italia* 10 (1992/93): 137–41; see also Dalia Haitovsky, "A New Look at a Lost Painting: The Hebrew Inscription in Lorenzo Costa's 'Presentation in the Temple'," *Artibus et historiae* 29 (1994): 111–120; Giulio Busi, "Invenzione simbolica e tradizione ebraica nel rinascimento italiano. Alcuni esperimenti figurativi," *Henoch: Studi storicofilologici sull'ebraismo* 21, no. 1–2 (1999): 165–177. Other studies deal briefly with inscriptions in the general context of the work in question.

[5] Manchester, John Rylands Library, Latin Ms. 32, fol. 79; reproduced in color in Geron Sievernich and Hendrik Budde, eds. *Europa und der Orient, 800–1900*, exhib. cat. (Berlin, 1989), no. 1/9, pl. 1 p. 19.

surroundings and the frame of the page are filled with Egyptian and classical monuments (for example, Trajan's column juxtaposed with an obelisk), as well as mythological heroes (predominantly, Hercules fighting the giant Cacus).[6] Enhancing the "authentic" atmosphere is the open scroll of St. John, upon which are written two correctly-spelled Hebrew words: יוחנן שמו ("his name is John"). Just as the ancient monuments show the illuminator's close familiarity with the ancient world, so does the inscription in the ancient tongue. Moreover, it does not transliterate the Latin (Johannes) or even Italian (Giovanni) version of the evangelist's name, but provides the original Hebrew equivalent. Obviously the erudite artist had researched his topic, and either consulted with a Christian Hebraist or, more likely, employed the assistance of a local learned Jew.[7]

Not all artists, however, were as pedantic and diligent as Clovio. An examination of a considerable number of works with Hebrew inscriptions allows us to group them into six levels, or categories of competence with the language: 1) pseudo-Hebrew, in which imitation Hebrew letters at best only approximate the shapes of actual characters; 2) meaningless Hebrew script, that is, actual characters copied without any attempt to create meaningful words; 3) partially meaningful script, in which Hebrew letters form actual words but with varying mistakes in construction (often confusing letters of similar shape, such as ד and ר or ב and כ); 4) meaningful, correct inscriptions, where letters and words are copied from an authoritative source, based primarily on well known, usually printed, texts (chiefly the Old and New Testaments); 5) meaningful, correct translations, where authoritative texts, usually in Latin or Greek, are translated into (supposedly) ancient Hebrew (for example, the tri-lingual inscription on the *titulus* over the cross in Cru-

[6] For the full description of the scenes and figures, see Sievernich and Budde, *Europa*, 388–89.

[7] The phenomenon actually worked at "both ends"—Jewish patrons in Renaissance Italy often employed Christian artists (see, for example, Joseph Gutmann, *Hebrew Manuscript Painting* [New York, 1978], pls. 33, 35–37, 39), while Italian-Christian patrons at times commisioned local Jewish scribes to write for them biblical and other manuscripts in Hebrew; see Luisa Mortara-Ottolenghi, "Scribes, Patrons and Artists of Italian Illuminated Manuscripts in Hebrew," *Jewish Art* 19/20 (1993/94), 86–97, and Nurit Pasternak, "A Meeting Point of Hebrew and Latin Manuscript Production: A Fifteenth Century Florentine Hebrew Scribe, Isaac ben Ovadia of Forlì," *Scrittura e civilita* 25 (2001): 185–200.

cifixion scenes); and 6) original, meaningful inscriptions, which appear to be texts created especially for the work of art in question.[8]

Beyond the different categories in which Hebrew script had been used, and beyond its meaning from an art-historical point of view, the phenomenon sheds light on Jewish-Christian relations as well as Jewish history on European soil. When properly investigated, the inscriptions may provide insights into a number of questions: Do Hebrew inscriptions in works of Christian art testify to relationships between Christians and local Jews? And if so, what kind of Jews—rabbis and scholars, professional scribes, or converts? How did authorities on both sides react to such cultural interactions? Are there differences among the various Jewish communities of Europe involved in such exchanges (for example, were Italian Jews more inclined to collaborate with artists than their German brethren)? How did inscriptions relate to rabbinic texts, whether in manuscripts or, more probably, in printed Hebrew books? How did Jewish printers and Hebrew books influence non-Jewish audiences in the various capitals of European printing?

Such an investigation, I believe, can not only shed light on Jewish-Christian relationships but might also provide valuable insights into the way Jewish themes are treated in Christian works of art. A noteworthy example is the *Birth of the Virgin* by Vittore Carpaccio (1465?–1525), who employed Hebrew script in a number of works that still wait to be deciphered and studied (fig. 2).[9] As in other works, Carpaccio turns the sacred story into a local genre scene, which takes place in the interior of a patrician Venetian house. Striking is the uncovered plaque hung on the wall next to Anna's bed, which is inscribed in clear Hebrew words, provided with largely accurate vocalization marks: קדוש קדוש קדוש/במרום ברוך/הבא בשם יהוה ("Holy, holy, holy! in Heaven. May he who enters be blessed in the name of the Lord"). The words from the first part are from Isaiah (6:3) and were traditionally interpreted as alluding to Christ's birth (cf. Luke 2:11–14), whereas the quotation from Psalms in the second part (Psalms 118:26) refers to

[8] Cf. Ronen ("Hebrew Script," 2), who lists only three basic categories. Indeed, at times more than one category may appear in a given image; however, the materials I have examined definitely attest to a wider variety. And see Sarfatti ("Hebrew Script," 453), who follows Ronen, but adds two categories: "transcriptions of Latin in Hebrew letters" and "Hebrew words in Latin or Greek script." In my view the inclusion of the last two categories requires further examination.

[9] Cf. Barasch, "Hebrew Inscriptions," 142–143; Sarfatti, *Language of My People*, 276–83.

his symbolic entry into Jerusalem (cf. Mark 11:9). While the Christian message is clearly the one intended,[10] Carpaccio combined it with a close examination of the interior of a well-to-do Jewish home in the Veneto.[11] Inscribed plaques of this type were hung on the wall to protect newborn children from Lilith, the witch who kills babies at birth or during the first days of their lives.[12] However, no such Jewish plaques survive from sixteenth-century Italy, and Carpaccio's painting is the only visual source for the Jewish practice from this period. In the process of exploring this practice, the artist probably became aware that the words of Psalm 118:26 are recited at the first ceremony celebrating the birth of a Jewish baby, the circumcision. In so doing the artist reinstated a Jewish meaning over the traditional Christian interpretation. Thus, it would appear that contacts with local Jews and the use of Hebrew inscriptions enabled Carpaccio to enrich the familiar theme from a novel point of view.

Leiden University and the Young Rembrandt

During the seventeenth century, Rembrandt's town of birth, Leiden, was an important center for the study of what came to be called Oriental languages. Within the framework of Protestant theological studies in particular, the University of Leiden (established 1575) put great emphasis on the reading of Scripture in the original language.[13] Several of its professors taught Eastern languages, including Hebrew,

[10] Cf. Sarfatti, *Language of My People*, 283.

[11] The painting of Carpaccio is generally dated to 1504–08, while the permanent residence of the Jews in Venice itself started slightly later (the Ghetto was officially established in 1516); however, Jews resided in many other Venetian towns, including nearby locales such as Mestre and Padua. For a selection of essays on the history of the community, see Benjamin C.I. Ravid, *Studies on the Jews of Venice, 1382–1797* (Aldershot, 2003); also see Paul Kaplan's chapter in this volume.

[12] The display of written childbirth amulets on the walls of Jewish houses in Italy is recorded by the noted rabbi of Venice, Leone da Modena (1571–1648), in his *Historia de' Riti Hebraici: Vita & Osservanza degli Ebrei di questi tempi* (Modena, 1728 [first rev. edn. Venice, 1638]), 123. On the practice and art of Jewish childbirth amulets, including specimens from Italy (though of a later period and of a different kind), see Shalom Sabar, "Childbirth and Magic: Jewish Folklore and Material Culture," in *Cultures of the Jews: A New History*, ed. David Biale (New York, 2002), 670–722.

[13] Anthony Grafton, "Civic Humanism and Scientific Scholarship at Leiden," in *The University and the City: From Medieval Origins to the Present*, ed. Thomas Bender (New York, 1988), 59–78.

Syriac, Aramaic and Arabic, and manuscripts in these fields were assembled by the university's library. Thus, even before the foundation of a Hebrew press by Jews in the Netherlands, textbooks for the study of Hebrew were being printed in Leiden.[14] The noted humanist and printer Christophe Plantin of Antwerp (1514–1589) was officially invited to Leiden in 1583 to print Hebrew books for the academic needs of the new university.[15] Plantin, and other members of his family who remained in Leiden when he returned to Antwerp, printed textbooks, grammars, dictionaries, and Hebrew editions of the Bible. The Antwerp printer also issued—though not in Leiden itself—a polyglot bible and a bilingual bible in which the Latin translation of every word, running like the Hebrew from right to left, appeared between the Hebrew lines.[16] Such bibles and grammars, which were distributed and became popular throughout Europe, could serve artists who needed immediate and reliable sources for authoritative Hebrew passages, even if they did not have any competence in the language.

In his youth Rembrandt studied in the Latin school at Leiden. This school prepared students for higher studies in the local university. Indeed, in 1620 the fourteen-year-old Rembrandt enrolled in the university, though he apparently never attended, as his heart was not inclined towards academic studies. Despite the brevity of his stay at the university, scholars have entertained the possibility that he must have been exposed to Hebrew in this period.[17] Yet this assumption has no

[14] On Hebrew printing in Leiden and for a list of the books printed there, see Lajb Fuks and R. G. Fuks-Mansfeld, *Hebrew Typography in the Netherlands 1585–1815: Historical Evaluation and Descriptive Bibliography*, 2 vols. (Leiden, 1984–87), 1:11–64.

[15] For Plantin's involvement with Hebrew printing and a list of the books with Hebrew characters his firm printed in Leiden in the years 1583–1619, see Fuks and Fuks-Mansfeld, *Hebrew Typography*, 1:15–32; and cf. the exhib. cat. (Israel Museum), *Plantin of Antwerp: Books & Prints from the Collections of the Plantin-Moretus Museum, Antwerp* (Jerusalem, 1981).

[16] Plantin printed his Bible (*Biblia Hebraica—eorundem Latina interpretatio*) in Antwerp in 1584; the Latin translation is by the Italian Hebraist, Santes Pagnini. For a facsimile of the opening page of Exodus, printed on attractive green paper, see Brad Sabin Hill, *Hebraica (saec. X ad saec. XVI): Manuscripts and Early Printed Books from the Library of the Valmadonna Trust*, exhib. cat. (n.p. [London], 1989), no. 47. The author calls Plantin's *Biblia Regia* (Royal Polyglot—Antwerp, 1568–72) "the most complex typographical undertaking of the 16th century."

[17] This theory has been advanced in the past literature not only by Jewish scholars, who attempted to show Rembrandt's favorable relationships with the Jews, but also by noted authorities on the artist and his work. For example, Wilhelm Reinhold Valentiner, "Rembrandt at the Latin School," in *The Art of the Low Countries* (New York, 1914), 136. For a critical survey of the early studies of Rembrandt and the "Jewish problem,"

foundation, and the likelihood that the fourteen-year-old youth took Hebrew in the Latin school or the university, even at the elementary level, is inconceivable. Indeed, in Rembrandt's earliest known Old Testament painting, *The Angel and the Prophet Balaam*, of 1626, the letters appearing on the upper document in the prophet's saddlebag, though possibly intended to look like Hebrew,[18] clearly reveal a lack of familiarity with the language and its alphabet.

Franz Landsberger (1883–1964), the noted historian of Jewish art, attempted to show that Rembrandt had a basic knowledge of Hebrew at the beginning of his artistic career—namely, before moving to Amsterdam, while he was still in Leiden.[19] His assumption was based on one of Rembrandt's most important early works, the *Repentant Judas Returning the Thirty Pieces of Silver* (fig. 3). This painting, which the artist created while he was only twenty-three years old, depicts the dramatic moment in which the tormented and sorrowful Judas, convulsed by deep remorse, kneels before the chief priests and elders in the Temple; the thirty coins which he had received for betraying his master shine on the wooden floor in front of him (Matt. 27:3–5).[20] From a Jewish point of view, this early work already reveals Rembrandt's novel and humanistic approach to a figure that had for centuries been negatively associated with the Jews. Indeed, since the Middle Ages, Judas was often given

see Shelley K. Perlove, "Perceptions of Otherness: Critical Responses to the Jews in Rembrandt's Art and Milieu (1836–1945)," *Dutch Crossing: A Journal of Low Countries Studies* 25, no. 2 (2001): 243–290.

[18] As suggested by Mirjam Alexander-Knotter, "An Ingenious Device: Rembrandt's Use of Hebrew Inscriptions," *Studia Rosenthaliana* 33 (1999): 132. For analysis of the painting, see Josua Bruyn et al., *A Corpus of Rembrandt Paintings*, trans. D. Cook-Radmore, 3 vols. (The Hague, 1982–1989), 1:74–81 (no. A 2). Curiously, this painting was acquired from Rembrandt by the art collector Alfonso López, a Portuguese Jew who converted to Christianity; and although the theme would fit a convert (for the eyes of Balaam were opened to see the new vision, regarded as a prefiguration of the coming of Christ), López did not commission Rembrandt to create this image, as the two met for the first time in Leiden only in 1628; cf. Gary Schwartz, *Rembrandt: His Life, His Paintings* (New York, 1985), 41–42, 214. Doron Lurie has called my attention to another early Rembrandt painting, *The Rich Man from the Parable* of 1627, in which a pile of papers seen on the right evidently bear pseudo-Hebrew letters. Though it is hard to tell whether Hebrew is intended here, the authors of the *Corpus* support this thesis and even imply there is a possible connection between the theme of the painting (avarice) and the "Hebrew-like letters" (see Bruyn et al., *Corpus*, 1:137, 140, no. A 10).

[19] Franz Landsberger, *Rembrandt, the Jews and the Bible*, 2nd edn. (Philadelphia, 1961), 32.

[20] Bruyn et al., *Corpus*, 1:177–195 (no. A 15).

Jewish features, especially in German and other northern European art.[21] Artists generally highlighted the moment when he betrays Jesus, and even in Last Supper scenes his negative "Jewish" features were made apparent. Rembrandt, however, chose not to paint the familiar themes but rather to show Judas as a humble figure, deeply regretful of what he had done.

Some of the unique qualities of the painting, in particular the expression of human emotions, were noted as early as 1630 by Constantijn Huygens, who visited the studio in Leiden Rembrandt shared with Jan Lievens at the end of 1628 or early in 1629.[22] Despite his academic background and even rudimentary knowledge of Hebrew,[23] Huygens's praises of the *Repentant Judas* did not include the two Hebrew inscriptions noted by Landsberger: one on the upper mantle of the furious priest with the tall cap, shown standing behind the seated Caiaphas; the other inscribed in the large open book lying on the table before a seated scribe (left foreground) (fig. 4). The letters on the priest's mantle are too blurry and fragmentary to be deciphered. Those in the book, however, are more complete and written in orderly lines. When enlarged, they are revealed as meaningless scribble intended to suggest writing—not necessarily in a particular language.[24] Clearer Hebrew letters appear at the top of the left page, though these are partly hidden by the fold at the upper left corner. Landsberger suggested reading these words as לדע[ת מ]צותיך ("To know Your Law"), but did not mention the source for the inscription or its meaning in the context of the painting.[25] For

[21] On the image of Judas as the Jew in European culture in general, see Hyam Maccoby, *Judas Iscariot and the Myth of Jewish Evil* (New York, 1992); on his negative image in northern medieval art as well as his portrayal as a Jewish caricature, see Ruth Mellinkoff, "Judas's Red Hair and the Jews," *Journal of Jewish Art* 9 (1982): 31–46; and idem, *Outcasts*, 1:134–35, 150–54.

[22] For Huygens' account, see Bruyn et al., *Corpus*, 1:193–194.

[23] It appears that when Huygens was young, the noted Amsterdam Jew Leon Templo gave him "some instructions [...] in the Hebrew literature"; see Adri K. Offenberg, "Jacob Jehuda Leon (1602–1675) and his Model of the Temple," in *Jewish-Christian Relations in the Seventeenth Century: Studies and Documents*, ed. Johannes van den Berg and Ernestine G. E. van der Wall (Dordrecht, 1988), 99. Alexander-Knotter hypothesizes that the table and the book were completed only after Huygens' visit ("Ingenious Device," 158).

[24] An enlarged detail of the book is reproduced in Bruyn et al., *Corpus*, 1:191; Weyl and Weiss-Blok, *Rembrandt's Holland*, 170.

[25] Alexander-Knotter reads these words: לרעה שבך ("for evil/mesh of branches")—each taken from another verse (II Samuel 18:9 and 18:32), associated with the story of Absalom ("Ingenious Device," 156–57). However, this is a highly hypothetical reading

Landsberger, the appearance of these strange words strengthened the conjecture about Rembrandt's attraction to Hebrew and his meeting with Jews in Amsterdam a couple of years earlier.[26]

Indeed no Jewish community existed in Leiden at the time.[27] As for Amsterdam, a few Marrano Jews of Spanish and Portuguese origin began to settle in the city as early as the 1590s—though at first without disclosing their Judaism. The civic authorities, in contrast to the Reform Church, unofficially supported their presence and allowed them religious freedom. The community increased significantly during the first two decades of the seventeenth century; by 1620 Amsterdam's Jewish population numbered about 1,000 souls, mostly former Marranos and only some Ashkenazi Jews. The Sephardim were organized in three congregations, which were actively engaged in establishing benevolent societies, schools, synagogues, their own cemetery (in Ouderkerk), and other institutions that gave the community a growing prominence in the Sephardi Diaspora. The Ashkenazi community, comprised of German (*tudescos*) and Polish Jews (*polacos*), was much poorer, led a marginal life alongside the Sephardi congregations, and did not establish its own independent congregation until the mid-1630s.[28]

Support for Landsberger's hypothesis regarding a possible encounter between Rembrandt and Amsterdam's Jews may be traced by returning to the *Repentant Judas* (see fig. 3) and looking at one item of Jewish clothing in particular: the tall cap of the priest on the right, an article

---

of the two words, which seem rather sketchy and incidental. It attributes to Rembrandt the knowledge of Hebrew, which he could not conceivably have had at this stage in his life. Moreover, were he indeed knowledgeable in the meaning of these two words and interested in showing a connection between the story of Absalom and that of Judas, the reference to the former would certainly have not been hidden in two unrelated and obscure words, which are hardly legible and written in broken Hebrew letters.

[26] Landsberger, *Rembrandt, the Jews*, 30.

[27] There were Jewish students at Leiden University. Research has shown, however, that they were very much isolated and were not encouraged to interact with the local population. Moreover, before 1632 there were very few of them in Leiden, and as Prof. Yosef Kaplan has assured me, the likelihood that Rembrandt could have known or formed any relationships with them is extremely scarce; see Yosef Kaplan, "Sephardi Students at the University of Leiden," in Kaplan, *An Alternative Path to Modernity: The Sephardi Diaspora in Western Europe* (Leiden, 2000), 196–210.

[28] For the early history of the Jews in Amsterdam, especially the formation of the Sephardi (Portuguese) community, see Miriam Bodian, *Hebrews of the Portuguese Nation: Conversos and Community in Early Modern Amsterdam* (Bloomington, IN., 1997).

that could be interpreted as a *kolpak*,[29] the sable fur hat worn by Ashkenazi Jews from Poland.[30] Though it is unlikely that during the short period of six months in which the artist was apprenticed in the studio of Pieter Lastman in Amsterdam he either developed personal relationships with Jews or strengthened his knowledge of Hebrew (if he ever had any), he could have seen such caps in the streets of Amsterdam. Impressed by Jews' special costumes throughout his career, he may have even purchased an example of this unusual item. This kind of Jewish hat appears in another early portrait by Rembrandt (dated 1630), depicting an elderly man who definitely cannot, however, be identified as an Ashkenazi Jew.[31] Therefore, even if Rembrandt met Polish Jews in Amsterdam during his early sojourn the effects of such encounter could not have been more than superficial and external.

What, then, was Rembrandt's source for the Hebrew inscription in the *Repentant Judas*? Remarkably, Landsberger did not notice another clearly written Hebrew word, which in fact appears twice in the painting. This is the Tetragrammaton, יהוה (*YHVH*), written in square capitals at the top of the right page in the book, as well as on the cap of the priest at right in the pair ascending the stairs in the background. The letters here again help to identify the figure as a Jew. Assuming that Rembrandt had neither learned Hebrew nor befriended Jews at this stage in his life, we must conclude that he either consulted one of the theologians or Hebraists at Leiden University, or acquired one of the Hebrew textbooks or grammars printed and sold locally—readily accessible for someone who spent some time at the university—and copied the inscription

[29] Bruyn et al., *Corpus*, 1: 193.

[30] For the various traditional items in the male and female dress of Polish Jews and their aesthetic background, see Tamar Somogyi, *Die Schejnen und die Prosten: Untersuchungen zum Schönheitsideal der Ostjuden in Bezug auf Körper und Kleidung unter besonderer Berücksichtigung des Chassidismus* (Berlin, 1982). Comparative images from the nineteenth century appear in Alfred Rubens, *A History of Jewish Costume* (London, 1973), 104–113.

[31] In the earlier literature the sitter was identified as "Rembrandt's Father," an affirmation which the authors of the *Corpus* (1:285–292 [no. A 29]) correctly reject—inter alia because of the "Jewish *kolpak*"—and suggest instead that the portrait was "intended to be seen as a Jewish figure" (289). As proof they cite an etching of a Polish Jew in Sabbath attire, dated 1765 (!)—reproduced in the first edition of Rubens, *Jewish Costume* (New York, 1967), 111, fig. 154. The authors fail to consider where Rembrandt might have seen a Polish-Jewish hat, but Gary Schwartz suggests the artist could have purchased such a hat while he was in Amsterdam (Schwartz, *Rembrandt*, 61).

from this source.[32] The four-letter Hebrew name of God appears often in such books and even in standard theological Protestant books.[33]

Still more decisive proof that the artist consulted a contemporary intellectual or a university textbook comes from an unexpected source. In 1953 the Israeli linguist and authority on Syriac, Moshe Goshen-Gottstein, noticed that the Syriac word *Allaha*, which is the equivalent of God's name, appears in the painting at the center of the right page, inscribed in "quite an elegant Syriac hand."[34] In fact, the Syriac word appears on the left page as well. Obviously, the artist could have easily employed one of the Hebrew-Syriac textbooks or dictionaries printed for the university, or directly contacted one of the Hebraists who taught

[32] For example, the Hebrew and Chaldaic dictionary by the aforementioned Italian Hebraist Santes Pagnini (edited by Franciscus Raphelengius), first printed by Plantin in Antwerp in 1570; its third edition appeared in Leiden, 1609. For a bibliographic list of Hebrew dictionaries and grammars containing comparative materials in Syriac, Aramaic or Arabic, which appeared in Leiden during Rembrandt's youth, see Fuks and Fuks-Mansfeld, *Hebrew Typography*, 1:29–32 (the aforementioned dictionary is no. 24 on p. 29). It should be noted, that the frequent usage of these books is attested by the fact that some of them were published in as many as six editions within a few years (e.g., no. 26, p. 30).

[33] The Tetragrammaton had become a widely known element in the Dutch Christian society, especially following the iconoclastic outbreaks of last quarter of the sixteenth century. Under the influence of Calvinist teachings about the place of the graven image in Christian life, it became common to replace the name of God with the Tetragrammaton; see David Freedberg, "The Hidden God: Image and Interdiction in the Netherlands in the Sixteenth Century," *Art History* 5 (1982): 133–53, esp. 140 and figs. 14–15. A curious relevant incident concerns the noted Last Judgment triptych by Lucas van Leyden (Leiden, Lakenhal Museum), commissioned for Leiden's Pieterskerk in 1526/27. Following the iconoclastic controversies, the image of God the Father in the central panel was overpainted with the Tetragrammaton. Growing up in Leiden in these years, Rembrandt could have seen the panel in its "corrected" version—no longer visible today (in 1935 the panel was cleaned and restored to its original state). I am grateful to Peter Parshall for drawing my attention to the possible influence of this incident on the young Rembrandt. The popularity of the Tetragrammaton shown emerging from heaven is additionally attested on many title pages of Dutch bibles printed in this period, both in Leiden and Amsterdam, as well as in other Protestant bibles (for example, "The Holy Bible" printed in Cambridge, 1629). It is interesting to note that this feature was also imitated by some of the Jewish printers of Amsterdam, including Menasseh ben Israel, for example, in the Bible Menasseh printed in 1635, which is, significantly, the very bible held open at the title page by the Calvinist preacher Gualterus Boudaan in the portrait painted by Cornelis Janssens van Ceulen (preserved at the Joods Historisch Museum, Amsterdam); see Christian Tümpel et al., *Het Oude Testament in de Schilderkunst van de Goude Eeuw*, exhib. cat., Joods Historisch Museum (Amsterdam, 1991), 208–209 (no. 1).

[34] Goshen-Gottstein's brief note appeared as a letter to the editor of *Burlington Magazine* 95 (1953): 212. The Syriac inscription appears in addition to the Hebrew and not, as the authors of the *Corpus* (1:193) assume, in its stead. I'm grateful to my brother, Yona Sabar, for his assistance in checking the Syriac in the painting.

the subject there. God's Hebrew name appeared also in paintings and prints of past masters that Rembrandt cherished and acquired. Such was apparently the source for the most popular Hebrew inscription in Renaissance and baroque art, namely the *titulus* or trilingual inscription above the cross in Crucifixion scenes (cf. Luke 23:38; John 19:19–20).[35]

The Influence of the Artist's Encounter with Jews in Amsterdam

Once Rembrandt moved to Amsterdam in 1632, his use of Hebrew inscriptions changed dramatically. From the beginning of this period he lived in the vicinity of the Jewish neighborhood, and in 1639 he settled on Breestraat, known today as Jodenbreestraat, where he acquired the large house that became the center of his artistic activity until his insolvency in 1656. Living on the Jewish street, in close proximity to the community's rabbis, intellectuals, and the leading Sephardi families (e.g., Pinto, Belmonte, and Rodrigues), exerted a crucial influence on Rembrandt's use of Hebrew script, and in the course of years his approach became more original and meaningful. It is not surprising that he would turn to his neighbors for help when he wished to amplify biblical characters and stories by the usage of Hebrew script. In fact, it is through these usages that his relationships with the local community can be examined, providing solid and reliable evidence for his continuous contacts with its members.

Already in his first years on Breestraat, Rembrandt attempted to innovate in this field and included unusual Hebrew inscriptions in two paintings with New Testament themes: *Christ Before Pilate and the People* of 1634 (fig. 5) and *St. John the Baptist Preaching in the Desert*, dated 1634/45 (fig. 6).[36] Clearly in Rembrandt's eyes the addition of sharp and clear

---

[35] On Hebrew letters in early devotional and polemical Christian images, see Petra Schöner, *Judenbilder im Deutschen Einblattdruck der Renaissance: Ein Beitrag zur Imagologie* (Baden-Baden, 2002), 259–88. As Rembrandt scholars have shown, the young Rembrandt based his *Crucifixion* of 1631 on earlier versions (Rubens, Gortzius Geldorp). Moreover, Lievens created a strikingly similar painting in the same year; cf. Schwartz, *Rembrandt*, 86–89. Thus, although the *titulus* inscription in Rembrandt's image presents a slightly different version than that of Lievens or the other artists (see Alexander-Knotter, "Ingenious Device," 135–37), it still offers little evidence of his special approach to Hebrew and Jewish culture.

[36] See Bruyn et al., *Corpus*, 3:70–88 (*John the Baptist*).

Hebrew characters in events associated with Jesus was appropriate, imbuing his images with credibility and authenticity in the humanistic spirit of the time. The two paintings are nearly monochromatic, as they were apparently made in preparation for smaller etchings. Of these only the *Ecce Homo* etching is known—featuring reversed Hebrew letters, the result of a careless transfer from one medium to another.

In both paintings the Hebrew inscription does not occupy a central place in the composition. Rather, it is nearly hidden in the costume of one of the many figures that crowd each of the two images. In the *Ecce Homo* it is inscribed on the headgear that hangs loosely behind the back of the priest who kneels before Pilate, handing him the rod of justice. In the *John the Baptist* it appears on the left figure in the group of three, among the many who came to listen to John from many remote places, including the East (Turkish, African, American Indian, Japanese, etc.). The three, who represent the Jewish Pharisees and Sadducees, are shown animated in the midst of a heated discussion, apparently furious at the Baptist, who—notoriously—had just called them a "generation of vipers" (Matt 3:7). The "Jewishness" of the group is again hinted at by the headgear of the left figure, inscribed with crowded Hebrew letters.

Despite the clarity of the letters, they are fragmentary, and some are hidden, as Rembrandt followed the curves of the clothes. In the *Ecce Homo* one can read the following isolated letters and words יהוה אלה...כל ר...[[יך ("All...the Lord [your] God..."). In the *John the Baptist* more words are visible and thus the complete verse can be rather easily deciphered: ["ואהבת את] ה' אלהיך בכל לבבך ובכל [נפשך ובכל מאדך] ("[And you shall love] the Lord your God with all your heart and with all [your soul and with all your might]").[37] Taken from Deuteronomy (6:5), these words are recited by Orthodox Jews twice a day as part of the *Shema* prayer (*Keri'at Shema*). Moreover, because of its importance the verse is inscribed on Jewish ritual objects, such the parchments of the *tefillin* (phylacteries worn during prayer) or the *mezuzah* (the tiny scroll attached to doorposts).[38] In both images Rembrandt insisted on placing the Hebrew words on the same type of elongated textile that is

[37] Cf. Bruyn et al., *Corpus*, 3:70. The authors, however, don't seem to be aware of the meaning and physical reality from which this inscription has been taken (on which see below).

[38] For introductory surveys of these items, see the respective entries in *Encyclopaedia Judaica* (Jerusalem, 1971).

suspended from the heads of the figures. Could it therefore be interpreted as another kind of Jewish ritual object?

What Rembrandt scholars call "headgear" or a "shawl" is nothing but a *tallit*, or prayer shawl—and more specifically, the type of *tallit* customary among the Sephardim of Amsterdam. An etching by the Dutch engraver Jan Luyken (1649–1712), who depicted Jewish ceremonies and rituals in a most authentic manner, depicts a contemporary Sephardi Jew standing in front of the Esnoga—Amsterdam's well-known Portuguese synagogue—as he dons the *tefillin* and *tallit* (fig. 7).[39] The elongated prayer shawl placed above his wide hat falls from his shoulders down to his waist—exactly in the manner in which it appears in Rembrandt's two paintings. Though Luyken's *tallit* bears no visible inscription, selected verses are customarily either woven on the "collar" (known in Hebrew as *atarah*—"diadem") to mark the upper part that goes around the neck, or on the head; or else they are placed on the four corners and other parts of the *tallit*. Thus, Rembrandt may have observed Sephardi Jews in prayer, or perhaps a member of the community showed him how this item of liturgical clothing was used. The fact that the figures wearing the *tallit* in the two images are hostile to Jesus and his teachings may imply a negative approach to the ancient Jews (Pharisees and Sadducees).[40] At the same time it provides yet another example of the artist's attempt to imbue his figures with "authentic" paraphernalia. Just as in *John the Baptist* Rembrandt included various contemporary ethnic types—or, as Schama calls it, "Amsterdam turned

[39] The etching is labelled *Der Joden Biddekleed, en Gedenk-Gceedels aan Hoofd en Hand. Deut. 6:8,9* ("The Jew's Praying Shawl and Phylacteries worn on the Head and Hand"); the verses deal with phylacteries and the *mezuzah*, shown at the top of the page. The etching is taken from W. Goerce, *Mozaise Historie de Hebreeuwse Kerke* (Amsterdam, 1700), vol. 3, pl. 22; cf. Susan W. Morgenstein and Ruth E. Levine, *The Jews in the Age of Rembrandt*, exhib. cat., Judaic Museum (Rockville, MD, 1981), 61. Luyken illustrated a few other books on Jewish ceremonies—most prominently the Dutch edition of Rabbi Modena's aforementioned *Historia de Riti Hebraici*—the first guidebook of Jewish ceremonies written by a Jew for a Christian audience. In this work and the other books he illustrated Luyken shows close familiarity with and good knowledge of Jewish customs and rituals. For his other etchings of Jewish ceremonies, see Morgenstein and Levine, 63–64; also Alfred Rubens, *Jewish Iconography* (London, 1981), 28 nos. 251–54, 33 nos. 299–303 (the *tallit* print: 176, no. 1653).

[40] Michael Zell, *Reframing Rembrandt: Jews and the Christian Image in Seventeenth-Century Amsterdam* (Berkeley, 2002), 70–72, who points out that the Jewish figures in the *John the Baptist* are "strongly caricatured types." Alexander-Knotter ("Ingenious Device," 143) raises another interesting point: the words of Deut. 6:5 are the very words Christ uses when he rebukes the Pharisees elsewhere in Matthew (22:37).

Israel"[41]—so too in the *Ecce Homo* (the priest) and in the *John the Baptist* (the group of the Pharisees) the artist carefully observed the local Jewish scene and modelled his figures accordingly.

In the years that followed, Rembrandt's attempt to provide an authentic view of the Jewish past using information culled from the Jews in his immediate environment became more deliberate. It is best revealed in his important biblical painting of 1635, *Belshazzar's Feast* (fig. 8).[42] Unlike any of the previous examples, the Hebrew inscription here is neither hidden nor secondary to the event or figures depicted. On the contrary, it is the focus of attention—a crucial part in the dramatic narrative of the story. Moreover, the mystic light emanating from the mysterious letters—the main source of light in the painting—amazes all the characters, and their eyes, as well as those of the spectators, are irresistibly attracted to this section of the painting. As noted by Michael Zell and others, in previous works of art of the same theme by various artists, the inscription either does not appear or else is transliterated into Latin.[43]

Rembrandt's unique rendering of the four-word Aramaic inscription, *mene mene tekel u-farsin*—which Daniel interpreted for the Babylonian king as a prophecy about the fall and the destruction of his empire (Daniel 5:26–28)—raises a number of critical issues. First, although the artist could have found the words in a bilingual bible, the shape, order and calligraphy of the letters clearly imply that they were not copied from a printed source but from a manuscript, a process probably assisted by a professional Hebrew scribe. Moreover, as noted by Mirjam Alexander-Knotter, the calligraphy reveals a typical Sephardi hand of the time[44]—markedly different from the familiar Ashkenazic script appearing in contemporary German and Dutch manuscripts. We must also account for the order of the quoted words, which curiously appear from top to bottom rather than from right to left. The explanation for this order is found in the Babylonian Talmud, tractate *Sanhedrin* (21b–22a), hidden in a lengthy and illuminating discussion on the nature of the change from ancient Hebrew script to the square Aramaic script, which Jews use to

---

[41] Simon Schama, *Rembrandt's Eyes* (New York, 1999), 409.

[42] Bruyn et al., *Corpus*, 3: 124–33 (no. A 110).

[43] Zell, *Reframing Rembrandt*, 61. Note, however, the Hebrew in a Jewish work of art cited in note 50, below.

[44] Alexander-Knotter, "Ingenious Device," 145–46.

this day.[45] In the context of this discussion the Talmudic rabbis bring up the question why the wise men of Belshazzar could not interpret the seemingly simple Aramaic words (Aramaic being the language of ancient Babylonia), and the obvious answer in the eyes of some of them is that it is because the inscription appeared in the new script, which was unfamiliar to Belshazzar's magicians. Other rabbis of old, however, were of the opinion that this was not the reason, and suggested instead that the inscription on the wall was a form of cryptic writing, such as *gematria* or other codes common in rabbinic literature.[46] Thus, according to the leading Babylonian *amora* (Talmudic sage) Rav (third century C.E.), the ancient inscription read יטת יטת אדך פוגמחט—explaining that the words were "hidden" according to the Talmudic code called *atbash*, in which the first letter of the Hebrew alphabet, א, is substituted for the last—ת; the second, ב, for the penultimate, ש, etc.[47] The noted Palestinian *amora* Rabbi Johanan (bar Nappaha; c. 180–c. 279 C.E.) suggested the inscription was אנם אנם לקת ניסרפו—explaining that each of the four words appeared backwards on the wall; while in the formula offered by Rav Ashi (Babylonia, 335–427/28 C.E.), נמא נמא קתל פורסין, the first two letters in each word were transposed. The fourth and most puzzling opinion is attributed to the *amora* Samuel (late second—mid-third century C.E.): "And Samuel said [it was written] ממתוס ננקפי אאלרן MaMTOS NaNKaFI AaALRaN]." The Talmud does not elaborate further on the code Samuel used, but the great medieval Jewish exegete of France, Rashi (Solomon ben Isaac, 1040–1105), comments on this expression and explains that Samuel meant the four words Belshazzar saw turned into three words of five letters each, so that the first word in the new formula was comprised of the initial letters, the second word of the second letters, and so forth.[48] Thus, in

[45] For the development of the Hebrew script in antiquity, see Joseph Naveh, *Early History of the Alphabet* (Jerusalem, 1987). Naveh suggests we call the ancient Hebrew script "Hebrew," while the Aramaic script adopted by Second Temple Jews, still in use to this day, should be termed "Jewish" (see esp. 112–124).

[46] For *gematria* and some of the other rabbinic codes and their usage in Jewish (especially mystical) literature, see Gershom Scholem et al., "Gematria," in *Encyclopaedia Judaica*, 7:369–374.

[47] According to *atbash*, מ equals י; נ = ט; and א = ת—hence מנא cryptically appears as יטת, and so forth (note that in the standard Vilna editions of the Talmud the third word is mistakenly spelled אידך). Note that *atbash* appears already in the Bible, though not in the book of Daniel but rather Jeremiah (25:26; 51:1 and 41).

[48] The first three words (מנא מנא תקל) contain three letters each, while the fourth (ופרסין) has six; conveniently dividing it into two groups of three letters each allows the pattern of Samuel to work.

order to read the inscription properly, it must be arranged in three lines of five parallel columns, and read from top to bottom:

מ מ ת ו ס
נ נ ק פ י
א א ל ר ן

Rembrandt seems to have followed closely the code of the sage Samuel, as interpreted by Rashi. But how would Rembrandt have known such an obscure passage hidden in a page of the Talmud? Moreover, the topic of discussion there is not the Book of Daniel per se; the problem of the code behind the inscription is discussed only indirectly, in the associative manner typical of the Talmud.[49] The obscurity of the Talmudic discussion is further confirmed by its absence in works by Jewish artists, who were typically either unaware or else did not avail themselves of this passage when they illustrated the scene (fig. 9).[50]

The key to this mystery was provided by Reiner Haussherr, who in 1963 found that this very format of the inscription appears in a book published by the noted Sephardi rabbi of Amsterdam, Menasseh ben Israel (1604–1657).[51] In his Latin book *De termino vitae*—printed by Menasseh's own press in Amsterdam in 1639—the rabbi explained that Belshazzar and his sages could not have read the inscription on the wall because they attempted to read it from right to left (*linea recta*)

[49] The possibility that a Dutch Hebraist, well versed in the Talmud, helped the artist should be ruled out. As mentioned above, the Hebrew letters clearly betray the influence of a professional Sephardi scribe.

[50] A case in point is the Belshazzar scene in a Passover Haggadah produced in Copenhagen (1769) by the competent Jewish scribe-artist Judah Leib ha-Cohen (Darmstadt, Hessische Landes- und Hochschulbibliothek, Cod. Or. 7). Ha-Cohen depicted the scene with the writing on the wall in the simple manner that appears in the Bible; see *Pessach-Haggadah: Vollständige Faksimile-Ausgabe im Originalformat der Handschrift Codex Orientalis 7* (Graz, 1989). It should be noted, however, that the theme of Belshazzar's Feast is extremely rare in Jewish art, and the influence of Christian art in ha-Cohen's version is evident.

[51] Reiner Haussherr, "Zur Menetekel-Inschrift auf Rembrandts Belsazarbild," *Oud Holland* 78 (1963): 142–49. Note, however, that in a posthumous essay by Erwin Panofsky ("Rembrandt und das Judentum," *Jahrbuch der Hamburger Kunstsammlungen* 18 [1973]: 88, n. 11) the author pointed out that the passage in Sanhedrin had been associated with Rembrandt's inscription as early as 1904 (by Johs. Dyserinck, "Eene Hebreeuwsche inscriptie op eene schilderij van Rembrandt," *De Nederlandische Spectator* [1904]: 160). Moreover, Landsberger, who cites the Dyserinck essay in his bibliography (*Rembrandt, the Jews*, 185), did not employ this important evidence in his discussion of the Hebrew in the painting (see 151).

instead of from top to bottom (*linea longa*). Based on this evidence, Haussherr suggested dating the Belshazzar painting to 1639—a theory Rembrandt scholars reject, primarily on stylistic grounds.[52] As a matter of fact, Menasseh started to work on his book several years earlier at the request of Protestant theologians, who argued over the issue of life expectancy—whether it is incidental or determined by a higher power.[53] The various opinions appeared in a work entitled *Epistolica quaestio, de vitae termino, fatali an mobili?* printed in Dordrecht (1634); subsequently the editor—the noted Dordrecht professor of medicine, Jan van Beverwyck (Beverovicius, 1594–1647)—asked Menasseh to provide the Jewish point of view in that matter. No doubt Menasseh discussed his ideas with Christian colleagues before he published his own book on the topic five years later. As the painting shows, his neighbor Rembrandt must have been one of those who asked for Menasseh's advice before the book saw light.[54] Thus, the artist used the obscure disposition of the Aramaic inscription provided by the rabbi to enhance the enigmatic nature of the episode depicted in his painting—preferring Menasseh's explanation to that of Christian theologians.[55]

Much has also been written on the apparent mistake in the inscription's final letter—namely that it looks like a ז instead of a ן—while x-rays of the painting show that at an earlier stage it was correct. According to Zell, "Rembrandt... apparently was not supervised [by Menasseh] when he mistakenly changed the last letter."[56] However,

[52] Haussherr, "Menetekel-Inschrift," 149. For arguments for an earlier date for the painting, see Bruyn et al., *Corpus*, 132–33.

[53] On the circumstances leading to the publication of the book, see Cecil Roth, *A Life of Menasseh ben Israel: Rabbi, Printer, and Diplomat* (Philadelphia, 1934), 94–95; see also Zell, *Reframing Rembrandt*, 65–66.

[54] Alexander-Knotter noted that the design of the letters in the inscription was not taken from the book ("Ingenious Device," 145).

[55] As noted by Haussher, Calvin specifically rejected the Jewish explanations ("Menetekel-Inschrift," 148). Instead, Calvin offered that Belshazzar could not decipher the inscription "either because [of] his dullness or because God had stupefied all his senses and, as it were, weakened his eyes...And the same must be said of the magi and arioles. For they could have read had they not been blinded by God"; see John Calvin, *Daniel I (Chapters 1–6)*, trans. T. H. L. Parker (Grand Rapids, 1993), 233. Obviously Rembrandt did not select this commentary, which would have altered his composition. However, this does not necessarily imply that the artist preferred Menasseh's theological exposition as presented in *De termino vitae* over the competing ideas presented by the Protestant theologians. Zell rightly warns that "Rembrandt's consultation with Menasseh necessarily reflects the artist's tolerant ecumenism, or that he accepted Jews as Jews" (*Reframing Rembrandt*, 70).

[56] Zell, *Reframing Rembrandt*, 63–64.

there is really no need to offer this explanation and to assume that Rembrandt erred here. As the underpainting reveals, the position of the hand of God has been altered—evidently to make the event depicted more dramatic. The final version shows the inscription not as a finished product but in the very last stage of its formation—God is about to draw the last stroke of the descender of the *nun sofit*. The diagonal upper stroke of the letter is simply following the gesture of God's hand in creating the final letter, shocking all those present.[57] By showing the enigmatic words actively being composed by the hand of God, Rembrandt increases the theatrical element of the painting, "freezing" the highest moment in the drama. In fact the compositional device of a dramatic hand-gesture repeats the same motif in *The Sacrifice of Isaac* (St. Petersburg, Hermitage Museum), likewise painted in 1635, where the hand of the angel dramatically grasps the wrist of Abraham while the knife is suspended in mid-air.

One final aspect of Rembrandt's association with Menasseh that has escaped attention concerns the preference of both men for cryptic inscriptions rather than straightforward biblical words. The Sephardim of Amsterdam during this period were fascinated with what is generally known in Hebrew as *Kabbalah ma'asit* ("practical Kabbalah")—namely, sympathetic magical practices stemming from the desire to alter the course of events via various ritualistic techniques.[58] A defining aspect of this phenomenon is the preparation of amulets and talismans for protection against adversity in one's life. Drawn on one side of a rectangular piece of paper or an elongated parchment scroll, these objects are inscribed with carefully copied inscriptions in elegant Hebrew calligraphy.[59] The kabbalistic texts often contain mystical names of God (*shemoth*), and other selected passages that are comprised of groups of letters written in neatly arranged lines and set in geometrical designs.[60]

---

[57] Additionally, replacing the *nun* with a *zayyin* implies that Rembrandt was familiar with the Hebrew alphabet and just erred in picking the correct letter based on his memory of the text—which to me seems unlikely.

[58] For a succinct historical survey of this phenomenon, see Gershom Scholem, "Kabbalah," in *Encyclopaedia Judaica*, 10:632–38.

[59] Some examples from Holland are reproduced in the exhibition catalog, *Treasures from the Library Ets Haim/Livraria Montezinos of the Portuguees Israëlietisch Seminarium Ets Haim, Amsterdam*, Jewish National and University Library (Jerusalem, 1980), 26–27, 110.

[60] Cf. the chapter "Magical Triangles, Squares, Hexagrams and Pentacles," in T. Schrire, *Hebrew Amulets: Their Decipherment and Interpretation* (London, 1966), 59–68. Note that many of these geometric-form inscriptions appear in *Sefer Raziel ha-Malakh* ("Book of Raziel the Angel"), which was published for the first time in Amsterdam in

Like his contemporaries, Menasseh was deeply interested in Kabbalah and mystical formulations,[61] and the interest Protestants showed in these topics drove him to compose works aimed at non-Jews. In a recently discovered kabbalistic manuscript attributed to Menasseh, the auther explains in Latin to his Protestant readers what *gematria, temurah*[62] and other Talmudic codes mean.[63] Even the printer's device, which he selected for himself and used on the title pages of some of the non-Hebrew books he wrote, is designed as a rectangular form divided into nine boxes, and the letters in them form a biblical verse (Psalm. 85:12) that can be read horizontally (from right to left), as well as vertically, from top to bottom (fig. 10).[64] It is thus no surprise that in his *De termino vitae*, a book aimed at non-Jews, he favored the commentary of Rabbi Samuel and presented it in his book in a diagram strikingly similar to the shape and structure of his device: a rectangle divided into boxes, each containing a letter (or two) of a carefully selected biblical verse. That Rembrandt would follow such a mystical trend may seem at first unlikely. However, scholars have pointed out that the artist did show some interest in kabbalistic formulations—as is evidenced especially in his

1701 by the Sephardi printer Moses Mendes Coutinho. *Sefer Raziel* is one of the most popular collections of Hebrew mystical and magical works, and was widely circulated in manuscript for centuries before Mendes Coutinho printed it. On the angel Raziel and the book cf. the entries: Gershom Scholem et al., "Raziel" and "Raziel, Book of," in *Encyclopaedia Judaica*, 13:1592–93.

[61] Best expressed in his Hebrew work, *Nishmat Hayyim* [Spirit of Life] (Amsterdam, 1651). Cf. Moshe Idel, "Kabbalah, Platonism and Prisca Theologia: The Case of R. Menasseh ben Israel," in *Menasseh ben Israel and His World*, ed. Yosef Kaplan et al. (Leiden, 1989), 207–19.

[62] *Temurah* refers to substitution of letters by a given code in general; *atbash* is, in fact, a common form of *temurah.*

[63] The Latin manuscript, apparently copied by a Christian contemporary of Menasseh, was discovered by Richard Popkin in the Herzog August Bibliothek, Wolfenbüttel. See Richard H. Popkin and Jan van den Berg, "Menasseh ben Israel, *Compendium Kabbalae*," in *Jewish-Christian Relations* (as in note 23), 171–86, esp. 176–77.

[64] The verse reads, "Truth springs up from the earth" (Psalm 85:12); Menasseh used this device between 1635 and 1638. In his books the Latin translation of the verse, *Veritas e terra oritur*, is added beneath the square; see Abraham Ya'ari, *Hebrew Printers' Marks from the Beginning of Hebrew Printing to the End of the 19th Century* [in Hebrew] (Jerusalem, 1943), 36, 144, no. 57. The device appears, for example, in the book *De resurrectione mortuorum* (Amsterdam, 1636); see the title page of the Spanish edition, with the device as well, in Roth, *Life of Menasseh*, facing 166), in which Menasseh, in the words of Zell, "referred to the rewards awaiting those who conduct themselves with kindness toward the Jews" (Zell, *Reframing Rembrandt*, 85). This device rarely appears on the Hebrew books Menasseh printed (for example, Isaac Tyrnau, *Minhagim* [Amsterdam, 1635/36]; cf. Fuks and Fuks-Mansfeld, *Hebrew Typography*, 1:122, no. 164).

Dr. Faust etching.[65] Though not Hebrew, the inscription *AGLA* in the outer circle is reminiscent of אגלא, an abbreviation of אתה גבור לעולם אדני ("You are mighty for ever, O Lord"—recited daily in the *Amidah* prayer). Considered one of the most powerful magical names of God,[66] it appears on countless Hebrew amulets, as well as some Christian ones.[67] Setting aside the question of whether Rembrandt's purpose in using this device was, as Perlove suggests, "to convert Jews like Menasseh,"[68] the etching clearly alludes to the interest the artist shared with the Sephardi *hacham* (rabbi) in mystic or divine visions conveyed or revealed through anagrams and kabbalistic conjurations.

The *Belshazzar* painting is thus a key work for understanding the intellectual relationships between Rembrandt and Menasseh. Of all the explanations provided in the Talmud and other Jewish sources for the mysterious inscription, the *hacham* favored the one offered by the talmudic *amora* Samuel—totally disregarding in his book the commentaries of the other authorities. It was this explanation that accorded with Menasseh's interest in kabbalistic teachings and formations. He must have shared Samuel's explanation with Rembrandt, who had a similar fascination with such arcane formulations and readily adopted it in his painting.

---

[65] Shelly Perlove, "Awaiting the Messiah: Christians, Jews, and Muslims in the Late Work of Rembrandt," *Bulletin of the University of Michigan Museums of Art and Archaeology* 11 (1994–96): 91–96 (and see there, 108 n. 38 for the earlier studies by scholars who accept the kabbalistic interpretation of the etching).

[66] Cf. Henri van de Waal, "Rembrandt's Faust Etching: A Socinian Document, and the Iconography of the Inspired Scholar," *Oud Holland* 79 (1964): 7–47, at 9. Note that the *Amidah* is not the "eight hour prayer," as noted by van de Waal. The source for the mistake is apparently derived from the alternative name of the prayer, *Shemoneh-Esreh*, common especially among Ashkenazi Jews. *Shemoneh-Esreh* simply means "eighteen"—the original number of benedictions in the prayer (later changed to 19).

[67] For God's magical names in Hebrew amulets, including the *AGLA* name, see Joshua Trachtenberg, *Jewish Magic and Superstition: A Study in Folk Religion* (New York, 1939), 260–64; and Schrire, *Hebrew Amulets*, 91–135 (esp. 121). Note that in addition to the Christian amulets with Latin letters, which are generally cited in the context of Rembrandt's etching, there are contemporary Christian amulets also in Hebrew characters. Cf. Schrire, 71, 165 and pls. 42–43.

[68] Perlove, "Awaiting the Messiah," 95.

The Ten Commandments in Rembrandt's Art and the Portuguese Synagogue

Rembrandt's use of Hebrew culminated and found its most sophisticated artistic expression in his painting of 1659, *Moses Holding the Tablets of the Law* (fig. 11). Scholars generally agree that a number of his works in the preceding years provide evidence for the artist's continued, even deepening, interest in the Jews of Amsterdam—both Sephardi and Ashkenazi—though the nature of these relations is debatable.[69] However, the Hebrew inscriptions in the *Moses* painting show more than an interest in the language as a tool for authenticity, or collaboration with intellectuals, or even interest in mystical messages. Rather, it demonstrates Rembrandt's deep understanding of theological doctrines and a genuine attempt to employ Hebrew in order to create novel and influential religious concepts.

The large painting shows the prophet descending from Mt. Sinai, holding high above his head two black tablets upon which are painted, as if engraved, gilt Hebrew letters. The impressive tablets occupy more than one third of the painting (missing a strip at the bottom section, the painting was originally larger), and the glowing letters on them are inscribed in monumental and elegant square Hebrew letters. Obviously the artist made a great effort to make the letters clear, sharp and legible even from a distance. At the same time, the second tablet covers most of the first, and thus only the ends of the lines in the first group of commandments are actually visible. This issue might seem trivial

---

[69] In addition to the studies by Landsberger, Panofsky, Perlove, and Zell, cited in the previous notes, see Moshe Barasch, "Rembrandt's Representations of Jews" [in Hebrew], *Eretz-Israel: Archaeological, Historical and Geographical Studies* 6 (1960): 179–188 (English summary, 39*–40*); Richardson H. Fuchs, "The Jewish Community, the Bible, and Religion," in *Rembrandt in Amsterdam* (Greenwich, CT, 1969), 40–50; Henri van de Waal, "Rembrandt and the Feast of Purim," *Oud Holland* 84 (1969): 199–223; Jacob Leshem, "Rembrandt and Rabbi Menashe Ben Israel" [in Hebrew], *Tziyyur u-Pissul [Painting and Sculpture]* 12 (1976): 3–13; Shelly Perlove, "An Irenic Vision of Utopia: Rembrandt's *Triumph of Mordecai* and the New Jerusalem," *Zeitschrift für Kunstgeschichte* 1 (1993): 38–60; idem, "Templus Christianus: Rembrandt's 'Jeremiah Lamenting the Destruction of Jerusalem," *Gazette des Beaux-Arts* 126 (1995): 159–170; and most recently, Steven Nadler, *Rembrandt's Jews* (Chicago, 2003). It should be noted that the identification of "Jewish types," Jewish clothing, "Jewish themes" (notably "The Jewish Bride"), and even individual portraits—notably the famous etching of Menasseh—in the work of Rembrandt have been questioned in the literature (see the list of studies cited in Nadler, 238 n.15). For the disputable nature of the relationships between the artist and Menasseh (regarding the four etchings Rembrandt prepared for Menasseh's book *Piedra Gloriosa* [Amsterdam, 1655] as well as other relevant issues), see Zell, *Reframing Rembrandt*, 72–98 (and there the earlier literature).

at first, since the text of the commandments was well-known from the Bible and the manner in which it was shown familiar from numerous works of art, both Jewish and Christian. However, upon reading the visible text of the upper tablet it immediately becomes evident that Rembrandt did not find it sufficient to inscribe the first two words of each commandment—as is common in Jewish and many Christian works of art.[70] Rather, the last two commandments of the upper tablet are longer, and the same may be deduced for the covered tablet. As will be shown, Rembrandt chose to employ a version of the Ten Commandments that was unfamiliar before his time, whether in Christian or Jewish art.

The exact text of the commandments on the first, partly eclipsed, tablet can be deciphered by evidence provided by an earlier painting, Rembrandt's *Hannah and Samuel at the Temple*, dated circa 1650 (fig. 12). For many years *Hannah* was firmly attributed to Rembrandt, whose typical and apparently genuine signature actually graces it. However, scholars nowadays postulate that it was painted in the master's workshop by one of his students, and that Rembrandt only signed it.[71] The large tablets in the background, with the entwined Brazen Serpent in the center, are clearly and fully inscribed. Comparing the parallel inscriptions in both paintings—including the few letters of the first tablet that are visible in the *Moses*—reveals that they are nearly identical. Therefore, the inscriptions on the first (right) tablet in *Hannah* allows the reconstruction of the missing parts in Moses, thereby providing the

[70] On the Ten Commandments in Jewish and Christian art, see Israel Abrahams, "The Decalogue in Art," in *Studies in Jewish Literature Issued in Honor of Kaufmann Kohler* (Berlin, 1913), 39–55 (reprinted in *No Graven Images: Studies in Art and the Hebrew Bible*, ed. Joseph Gutmann [New York, 1971], 19–35); Gregor-Martin Lechner, "Zur Ikonographie der Zehn Gebote. Fresken in Nonnberg, Landkreis Altötting," *Ostbairische Grenzmarken* 11 (1969): 313–39; Ernst Murbach, "Die Zehn Gebote als Wandbild: Ein Beitrag zur Darstellung des Dekalogs im späten Mittelalter," *Unsere Kunstdenkmäler* 20 (1969): 145–50; Gad Ben Ami Sarfatti, "The Tablets of the Law as a Symbol of Judaism," in *The Ten Commandents in History and Tradition*, ed. Ben-Zion Segal and Gershon Levi (Jerusalem, 1990), 383–418; Bezalel Narkiss, "Illustrations of the Ten Commandments in the Thirteenth-Century Minute Mahzor," in Segal and Levi, *The Ten Commandments*, 419–440. There are in addition studies that deal with related issues—e.g., the Giving of the Law or the anti-Jewish symbolism of the Tablets' shape (for example, Ruth Mellinkoff, "The Round-Topped Tablets of the Law: Sacred Symbol and Emblem of Evil," *Journal of Jewish Art* 1 [1974]: 28–43).

[71] For the two paintings and the commandments on them, cf. Christopher Brown et al., *Rembrandt: The Master & his Workshop: Paintings* (New Haven, 1991), 272–74.

full version of the Ten Commandments as they must have crystallized in Rembrandt's workshop. They read:

First Tablet (*Hannah*)

I am the Lord your God (Ex. 20:2a)	אנכי ה' אלהיך
You shall have no other gods besides Me (20:3)	לא יהיה לך אלהים אחרים על פני
You shall not make for yourself a graven image (20:4a)	לא תעשה לך פסל
You shall not take in vain the name of the Lord your God (20:7a)	לא תשא את שם ה' אלהיך לשוא
Remember the Sabbath day and keep it holy (20:8)	זכור את יום השבת לקדשו
Honor your father and your mother (20:12a)	כבד את אביך ואת אמך

Second Tablet (*Moses*)

You shall not murder (20:13)	לא תרצח
You shall not commit adultery (20:13 [14])	לא תנאף
You shall not steal (20:13 [15])	לא תגנב
You shall not bear false witness against your neighbor (20:13 [16])	לא תענה [ב]רעך עד שקר
You shall not covet your neighbor's house; you shall not covet your neighbor's wife, or his male or female slave, or his ox or his ass, or anything that is your neighbor's (20:14 [17])	ל[א] תחמד בית רעך ל[א תחמד אשת רע]ך ועבדו ואמתו ושו[רו וחמורו וכל] אשר לרעך

Comparing this version with the standard manner in which the Ten Commandments were inscribed in synagogues and Jewish ceremonial objects reveals how much Rembrandt deviated from the standard Jewish formula. If there was a collaboration with Jews in this matter, it was therefore of a different nature, necessitating not only familiarity with the Hebrew lettering but also the creation of a formula that deviates from known earlier ones. First, if we consider where each commandment begins, it is clear there are not ten commandments but eleven! ("You shall have no other gods" is separated from "You shall not make a graven image"). Likewise puzzling is the fact the artist selected long passages rather than the traditional two (or three) opening words of each commandment, as is common in Jewish art as well as in most Christian images inscribed with Hebrew.[72]

Although the Bible several times calls the set of commandments given to Moses on Mt. Sinai עשרת הדברים ("ten words"—Exodus 34:28; Deut. 4:13, 10:4), nowhere does it specify how either of the two familiar versions of the Ten Commandments (Ex. 20:2–14 [17] and Deut. 5:6–18 [21]) should be divided into ten separate units. Moreover, in neither version is it clear where each commandment ends and where the following one begins. Another problematic issue is how the ten were actually divided on the biblical tablets. According to the most detailed physical description of the two tablets in Exodus, they were "inscribed on both their surfaces; they were inscribed on the one side and on the other...and the writing was God's writing, incised upon the tablets" (Ex. 32:15–16).

Jewish and Christian theologians who coped with this issue offered, according to their respective beliefs and religious inclinations, several methods of dividing the text.[73] Three major systems of division and enumeration developed over the ages:

1. The traditional rabbinic division, in which "I am the Lord your God" is the first commandment, while "You shall have no other gods...You shall not make graven image...You shall not bow down to them...," together make the second. In this tradition the rabbis explained that each tablet contained the same number of commandments, namely five.[74]

---

[72] The standard manner in which the Commandments appear in Jewish art is known from the thirteenth century, appearing in illuminated Hebrew bibles of Spain; see for example, a Bible from Perpignan, 1299 (Paris, Bibl. Nat. Ms. hébr. 7, fol. 12v), reproduced in Gutmann, *Hebrew Manuscript Painting*, pl. 6. Other examples are cited by Sarfatti, "Tablets of the Law," 383–90. For the later appearance of the Decalogue in synagogues, see below.

[73] The rabbinic enumeration appears in several Midrashic sources; see those gathered by Louis Ginzberg, *The Legends of the Jews*, 7 vols. (Philadlephia, 1909–38), 3: 98–106; and cf. Benno Jacob, "The Decalogue," *Jewish Quarterly Review* 14 (1923/24): 141–187.

[74] The rabbinic division is similar, though not completely identical with the division found in the writings of two early Jewish writers, Philo and Josephus.

2. The division of St. Augustine, in which "I am the Lord... You shall have no other gods... sculptured image... bow down to them" constitute the first commandment (Ex. 20:2–6); while the second begins with "You shall not take in vain the name of the Lord your God" (20:7). In order to maintain a total of ten, Augustine suggested that the commandment, "You shall not covet," be divided into two: "your neighbor's house" (as the ninth) and "your neighbor's wife..." (as the tenth). On the first tablet, according to this method, appear three commandments, while on the second (starting with "Remember the Sabbath"), seven. St. Augustine's method has been accepted by the Roman Catholic as well as Lutheran churches.[75]
3. John Calvin's method deviates from the other two. Calvin claimed that the assertion "I am the Lord..." is not a commandment but rather a "preface to the whole law."[76] This distinction actually harks back to Hellenistic-Jewish authors, notably Josephus and Philo, whose writings were highly valued by the Church Fathers of later generations. Calvin, therefore, defined the first commandment as "You shall have no other gods..."; the second is the commandment concerning graven images, while the two parts of "You shall not covet" constitute the tenth. In Calvin's enumeration, then, there are four commandments on the first tablet ("other gods" through "Remember the Sabbath"), and six on the second.[77]

Rembrandt's *Moses* does not follow any of the three systems. It is most distant from the Catholic-Lutheran system, for the covetousness verses appear as a single continuous commandment, and there are now seven commandments on the second (upper) tablet. It is closer

[75] Augustine's system is formulated in his *Quæstionum in Heptateuchum libri VII*, Book 2, Question 71. This system was officially adopted at the Council of Trent (1545–1564).

[76] John Calvin, *Institutes of the Christian Religion*, trans. Henry Beveridge, 2 vols. (London, 1953), 1:326.

[77] According to Calvin, the four commandments on the first tablet deal with "piety"—namely the relationships between God and man; while the six commandments in the second tablet are concerned with "justice" and "charity," or "how men ought to live with each other"; see John Calvin, *Commentaries on the Four Last Books of Moses Arranged in the Form of a Harmony*, trans. Charles W. Bingham, 4 vols. (Grand Rapids, MI, 1950), 3:6. For a table which sums up the different divisions, see E. Nielsen, *The Ten Commandments in New Perspective* (London, 1968), 10.

to the rabbinical division, since it opens with "I am the Lord" and contains five commandments on the second tablet. On the other hand, the aforementioned separation of "other gods" and "graven images" into two commandments does not follow the rabbinic system but rather Calvin's. As most of the Dutch Reformed churches accepted the theological principles formulated by Calvin and his followers, it would indeed be only logical that Rembrandt would follow the Swiss theologian's enumeration of the commandments. However, this does not solve the problem entirely, as the second tablet opens with "You shall not murder"—in accordance with the rabbinic division—and not with "Honor your father and mother" as required in Calvin's scheme. It should be emphasized that Calvin knew very well the Jewish division of the commandments, and cites Josephus in this matter, but also goes on to rebuke the ancient author, who "improperly attributes five Commandments to each Tablet, as if God had had regard to arithmetic rather than to instruct His people."[78] Why, then, did Rembrandt elect a method that strongly reflects Jewish and Calvinist ideas without strictly following either of them?

To answer this question one has to examine the place of the Decalogue in Protestant teachings, especially in Calvinist Holland. Both Luther and Calvin emphasized the importance of the Ten Commandments for the proper conduct of the Christian. However, while Luther followed the Catholic tradition and rejected the "practical commandments" such as observing the Sabbath or the prohibition against making graven images, Calvin went one step further and based his teachings on the interpretation of the commandments. In his writings he dedicated fifty-nine chapters comprising hundreds of pages to elucidating in great detail each and every commandment.[79] Calvin further maintains that the entire narrative, ideas and precepts contained in the "Last Four Books of Moses" relate to and stem from the Ten Commandments.

[78] Calvin, *Commentaries*, 3:6. In *Institutes*, 1:326, Calvin calls Josephus' division "repugnant to reason," but, toning down his criticism, he notes that the Jewish author merely followed "the general consent of his age." It should be noted that Calvin likewise sharply criticizes Augustine and the Catholic Church, for "foolishly" enumerating the commandments—such as the division of the covetousness section into two—a mistake which inevitably led to an erronous distribution of the commandments (*Commentaries*, 3:5–6; and cf. *Institutes*, 1:325).

[79] Calvin, *Commentaries*, 1:417–3:189. A précis of his approach to the Ten Commandments is contained in *Institutes*, 1:314–362.

Moreover, he did not avoid the practical-ceremonial meaning of this approach and dealt with its implications as well.[80]

The Decalogue had thus become a central concern in Protestant teachings, influencing the decoration of churches as well. The Anglican Canon issued by King James I in 1604 ordered that the Decalogue be "set upon the east end of every church and chapel where the people may best see and read the same."[81] In Holland Reformed churches were often decorated with a board showing Moses holding large tablets prominently inscribed with the Ten Commandments. At times, such pictures were the only decoration on the otherwise whitewashed walls of the churches—in accordance with Calvin's teachings.[82] Known in Dutch as *Tiengebodenbord*, such decorated boards survive from many churches, and the inscriptions on them, generally in Dutch, follow closely Calvin's aforementioned method of enumeration (fig. 13).[83]

Rembrandt, like any Dutch churchgoer at the time, must have seen such Decalogue boards, and it is not improbable that his initial idea (or that of his patrons) to paint Moses was inspired by such a view. However, it would appear that the traditional pedagogical and rather

[80] Most relevant is his detailed and lengthy discussion of the prohibition on images (*Commentaries*, 2:106–407), and the pragmatic injunctions deduced from its strict interpretation. Important in this context is also his struggle with the problematic Sabbath commandment and its practical meaning for contemporary Christians (*Commentaries*, 2:432–72).

[81] See G. W. O. Addleshaw and Frederick Etchells, *The Architectural Setting of Anglican Worship* (London 1948), 158; and cf. Abrahams, who cites an earlier order of 1564 stating that "the tables of the commandments may be comlye set or hung up in the east end of the chauncell, to be not only read for edification, but also to give some comelye ornament and demonstration that the same is a place of religion and prayer." ("*The Decalogue*," 49).

[82] See, for example, the painting of Pieter Saenredam, *Interior of the Buurkerk at Utrecht*, of 1644 (London, National Gallery), which clearly depicts the colorful picture of Moses holding the tablets as the most prominent decoration on the white walls of the church (see Gary Schwartz and Marten Jan Bok, *Pieter Saenredam: The Painter and his Time* [New York, 1989], 199, 200 and fig. 211). Moreover, below the *Moses* tablet appear two boys, one of whom is training a puppy—symbol of Christian aptitude (*leerzugtigheid*) and pedagogical discipline and obedience; cf. Simon Schama, *The Embarrassment of Riches: An Interpretation of Dutch Culture in the Golden Age* (Berkeley, 1988), 547–48. Note that the qualities of proper Protestant instruction are emphasized in some of the Tablets by framing the Commandments with the words of Deut. 12:28.

[83] For examples of *Tiengebodenbord* tablets in Reformed Dutch churches, see C. A. van Swigchem et al., *Een huis voor het woord. Het Protestante kerkinterieur in Nederland tot 1900* (The Hague, 1984), 66, 112, 154, 174, 274, 276, and 278–79. According to Schwartz and Bok, Pieter Saenredam's father, the artist Jan Saenredam, made a panel of the Ten Commandments for the Reformed church in his village of Assendelft (Schwartz and Bok, *Pieter Saenredam*, 19).

folkloristic mode of depicting *Moses Giving the Law* on these boards was not sufficient in his eyes. Rembrandt's personal and tragic understanding of the story, conveyed in the expression he gives Moses,[84] and his ability to employ authentic biblical sources, apparently led him to imbue the scene with new meanings, which mix and join together Calvinist doctrines with Judaism. The fact that the upper tablet contains carefully selected sections of the commandments, rather than full passages from the Bible, suggests he did not use a printed source. That his guide or collaborators were Jews becomes evident by the way some of the letters are written—for example, the final *bet* of לא תגנב ("You shall not steal") is considerably dilated in order to create an even left margin, exactly as a traditional Jewish scribe would do.[85] A further connection with Jewish culture arises from Landsberger's suggestion that the unusual way Moses holds the tablets above his head was influenced by the artist's visit to the synagogue, where he could see the customary Jewish ceremony of *hagbaha* (raising of the Torah scroll) done in a like manner.[86] Indeed, at least two graphic artists, the aforementioned Jan Luyken as well as Bernard Picart (1673–1733), who likewise observed closely the rituals of Amsterdam Jews, chose to depict the impressive manner in which the Portuguese community in particular celebrated the *hagbaha* (fig. 14).[87] Moreover, this ceremony is closely associated in the Jewish tradition with the Giving of the Law, and while the Torah scroll is raised the following words are recited: "This is the Torah that

[84] Cf. Joseph L. Koerner, "Rembrandt and the Epiphany of the Face," *RES* 12 (Autumn, 1986): 5–32.

[85] For a discussion of the designs and shapes of the letters on the tablets, see Alexander-Knotter, "Ingenious Device," 151–53 (and there the earlier literature on the topic).

[86] Landsberger, *Rembrandt, the Jews*, 168, 170.

[87] The Picart etching is entitled *Maniere d'exposer la loy au peuple, avant que de commencer a la lire* (unlike the Ashkenazim, the Sephardim and Jews of Islamic lands perform the *hagbaha* before the public reading of the Torah portion). Among the Sephardim of Amsterdam raising the Torah was considered a great ritual honor, for which they nominated a *levantador*—a specially selected member of the community—to perform the ritual (cf. Julie-Marthe Cohen, "From Rimmonim to Persian Rugs: Ceremonial Objects from the Collection of the Portuguese-Jewish Synagogue," in Judith C. E. Belifante et al., *The Esnoga: A Monument to Portuguese-Jewish Culture* [Amsterdam, 1991], 77). On Picart's depiction of Jewish ceremonies, see Richard I. Cohen, *Jewish Icons: Art and Society in Modern Europe* (Berkeley, 1998), 43–52; Naomi Feuchtwanger-Sarig, "Bernard Picart: Image, Text and Material Culture," in *Gifts from the Heart: Ceremonial Objects from the Jewish Historical Museum, Amsterdam*, ed. Julie-Marthe Cohen et al. (Amsterdam, 2004), 82–96.

Moses set before Israel" (Deut. 4:44); or, in a parallel formula: "This is the Torah given by God, through Moses."

While it is not known who commissioned the *Moses* painting, or under what circumstances, it is strongly connected to the Sephardi community by a curious piece of evidence that has thus far escaped the attention of scholars. On August 2, 1675, several years after Rembrandt passed away, the Esnoga, or Portuguese synagogue of Amsterdam, was inaugurated with much pomp and grandiose festivities, a celebration that lasted eight days and attracted many non-Jewish visitors.[88] Influenced by the architecture of the Reformed churches, the synagogue contained a highly unusual feature for its time—an engraved Decalogue placed over the costly wooden Torah ark (fig. 15).[89] Moreover, its two rectangular tablets are not engraved in the traditional Jewish manner known from other synagogues, whether earlier (i.e., the Italian) or later. Rather, the commandments on them are practically identical with the wording and division presented in Rembrandt's *Moses*, and as they are made of copper laid in wood, their coloring and appearance is also reminiscent of the painting.[90]

The Ten Commandments created by Rembrandt and his workshop suited well the cultural aspirations of the wealthy Sephardi families who financed the enormous building costs of the Esnoga.[91] Creating what Yosef Kaplan called "an alternative path to modernity," or in their own

[88] See the selection of essays in Belifante et al., *The Esnoga*.

[89] Cf. Rachel Wischnitzer, *The Architecture of the European Synagogue* (Philadelphia, 1964), 82–87, 90–97 (see especially 90, where Wischnitzer points to several Reformed churches in which the Tablets of the Law appear); cf. Abrahams, "The Decalogue," 52. Outside of Holland, it was only in Italy that Jews used the Ten Commandments in the decoration of their synagogues prior to the seventeenth century. However, the Tablets were not placed over the Torah ark but illustrated on the inner side of the doors. For an early extant example, from Urbino, ca. 1500, see Vivian Mann, "The Recovery of a Known Work," *Jewish Art* 12/13 (1986/87): 269–278. In contrast to what is widely believed, even in later times Ashkenazi rabbis in particular strongly objected to the practice of decorating the synagogue with the Tablets. See the opinions quoted in Isaac Ze'ev Kahana, "Synagogue Art in Halakhic Literature" [in Hebrew], in Kahana, *Studies in the Responsa Literature* (Jerusalem, 1973), 368–69; and cf. Shalom Sabar, "Synagogue Interior Decoration and the Halakhah," in Rivka and Ben-Zion Dorfman, eds., *Synagogues Without Jews and the Communities that Built and Used Them* (Philadelphia, 2000), 314–15.

[90] I am grateful to Julie-Marthe Cohen of the Jewish Museum, Amsterdam, for verifying this technical aspect of the Tablets at the Esnoga.

[91] See Belifante et al., *The Esnoga*, 46–47. The total costs of the construction, excluding the amount spent on the acquistion of the land, reached the sum of 164,365 guilders.

words *bom judesmo* ("worthy Judaism"),[92] they sought to achieve parity with the prosperity of their Gentile neighbors, integrating their riches, Jewish faith and ideals with the benefits of living in a prosperous Protestant society. The Amsterdam Sephardim became a model for other Sephardi communities in the Old and New Worlds, and their Esnoga was imitated in several towns, for example, Bevis Marks in London (1701) and Touro Synagogue in Newport, Rhode Island (1763), the oldest surviving synagogue in North America.[93] The architectural settings of the interiors in these synagogues and their impressive Torah arks are clearly modeled after that of the Esnoga, but with one major difference—in both London and Newport the inscribed Ten Commandments do not follow the disposition of the unique Amsterdam version, but the traditional rabbinic formula found in a countless synagogues throughout the Diaspora.[94] It seems that the fruitful cultural atmosphere that inspired Rembrandt to create an image expressing the integration of Jewish and Christian traditions—a phenomenon welcomed by the Amsterdam Sephardim when they erected their new synagogue—all but disappeared following the period of efflorescence Dutch society experienced in the seventeenth century.

Conclusion

Tracing Rembrandt's use of Hebrew inscriptions from the early years in Leiden to the mature paintings in the later phases of his life has shown how this theme attracted him throughout his artistic career. Going beyond the desire of many Renaissance and baroque artists to imbue their works with an historic-authentic dimension, Rembrandt kept developing and perfecting his use of Hebrew. From incidental and meaningless ornament in the early works, his inscriptions gradually

[92] Kaplan, *Alternative Path to Modernity*; and idem, "Bom Judesmo: The Western Sephardic Diaspora," in Biale, ed., *Cultures of the Jews*, 639–669.

[93] On these synagogues and the roots of the two communities in Amsterdam, see Richard D. Barnett and Abraham Levy, *The Bevis Marks Synagogue* (Plymouth, 1987); Theodore Lewis, "History of the Touro Synagogue," *Bulletin of the Newport Historical Society* 48, no. 3 (1975): 281–320. And cf. Rachel Wischnitzer, *Synagogue Architecture in the United States* (Philadelphia, 1955), 13–19. For the influece of the Esnoga on Sephardi synagogues, see also Belifante et al., *The Esnoga*, 58–61.

[94] For the image of the Decalogue in Bevis Marks, see Barnett and Levy, *Bevis Marks*, 7; in the Touro Synagogue, see Lewis, "History," 302 (designed by Benjamin Howland in 1828).

became more and more significant. While at the beginning of this project his sources were incidental Hebrew texts available to every artist, later on Rembrandt took advantage of the scholarly circle of Christian and Jewish intellectuals in Amsterdam and drew upon their knowledge and understanding of the Bible. Hebrew script in these later paintings became integral to their iconographic themes and essential as keys to their interpretation. This process culminated in *Moses Holding the Tablets*, where the carefully crafted Hebrew script points to ideas taken from both Jewish and Protestant teachings, creating a curious and short-lived harmony between the two cultures.

The integration of Hebrew in the work of Rembrandt epitomizes certain trends in Jewish-Christian relationships in seventeenth-century Holland. From the Jewish side, it points to the willingness of the Amsterdam Jews, especially the aristocratic Sephardi community, to present a positive image of their religion and culture and "gain the approbation and sympathy of their host society."[95] From the Christian point of view, Rembrandt and the Calvinist Hebraists of his time showed genuine interest in the language of the Bible as well as the Jews who lived around them. This phenomenon does not necessarily imply a harmonious confluence of Jewish-Christian ideas, or, as mentioned above, that the Dutch Christians fully accepted the Jews as Jews. At best it allowed for a better knowledge of the other, closer interaction and an exchange of ideas, all of which reflects a rather improved and tolerant approach to Jews and Judaism.[96] The Hebrew inscriptions in Rembrandt's work provide tangible and reliable evidence for these trends, and appear as

---

[95] See Yosef Kaplan, "For Whom Did Emanuel De Witte Paint His Three Pictures of the Sephardi Synagogue in Amsterdam?" in *Alternative Path to Modernity*, 29–50, esp. 30; and cf. idem, "The Self-Definition of the Sephardi Jews of Western Europe and Their Relation to the Alien and the Stranger," 51–77.

[96] David S. Katz calls this phenomenon "philo-semitism"; see his two studies: *Philo-Semitism and the Readmission of the Jews to England 1603–1655* (Oxford, 1982), and "The Phenomenon of Philo-Semitism," in *Christianity and Judaism: Papers Read at the 1991 Summer Meeting and the 1992 Winter Meeting of the Ecclesiastical History Society*, ed. Diane Wood (Oxford, 1992), 327–61. Though other scholars emphasize the antisemitic elements and polemical nature of the Hebraists' "project," their evidence is predominantly derived from Germany as well as from the writings of Hebraists of Jewish descent (i.e., converts to Christianity). These issues are addressed in the selection of essays in Coudert and Shoulson, eds., *Hebraica Veritas?* (as in note 3)—for example, Yaacov Deutsch, "Polemical Ethnographies: Descriptions of Yom Kippur in the Writings of Christian Hebraists and Jewish Converts to Christianity in Early Modern Europe," 202–33; and cf. Elisheva Carlebach, *Divided Souls: Converts from Judaism in Germany 1500–1750* (New Haven, 2001).

one important way in which the visual arts in general, and Rembrandt in particular, contributed to the cultural interactions between the two religions. Menasseh ben Israel, the most eloquent representative of the Jewish-Christian relationships in Rembrandt's Amsterdam, summed up these ideas with the following words:

> So at this day we see many [Christians] desirous to learn the Hebrew tongue of our men. Hence may be seen that God has not left us; for if one persecutes us, another receives us civilly and courteously.[97]

[97] Menasseh ben Israel, *The Hope of Israel*, ed. Henri Mechoulan and Gerard Nahon (Oxford, 1987), 155; cf. Katz, "The Phenomenon of Philo-Semitism," 361.

SELECTED BIBLIOGRAPHY

Abulafia, Anna Sapir. *Christians and Jews in Dispute: Disputational Literature and the Rise of Anti-Judaism in the West (1000–1150)*. Aldershot: Ashgate, 1998.

——. *Christians and Jews in the Twelfth Century Renaissance*. London: Routledge, 1995.

Almog, Shmuel, ed. *Antisemitism through the Ages*, trans. Nathan H. Reissner. Oxford and New York: Pergamon Press, 1988.

Arendt, Hannah. *Antisemitism* (part one of *The Origins of Totalitarianism*). San Diego: Harcourt, Brace & Co., 1979.

Aronius, Julius, ed., with Albert Dresdner and Ludwig Lewinski. *Regesten zur Geschichte der Juden im fränkischen und deutschen Reiche bis zum Jahre 1273*. Berlin, 1902; repr. Hildesheim: Georg Olms, 1970.

Assis, Yom Tov. *The Golden Age of Aragonese Jewry: Community and Social Change in the Crown of Aragon, 1213–1327*. London: Vallentin Mitchell, 1997.

Avneri, Zvi, ed. *Germania Judaica*, vol. 2: *Von 1238 bis zur Mitte des 14. Jahrhunderts*, pt. 2. Tübingen J. C. B. Mohr (Paul Siebeck), 1968.

Baer, Yitzhak. *A History of the Jews in Christian Spain*, 2nd edn., 2 vols., trans. Louis Schoffman. Philadelphia: Jewish Publication Society of America, 1961–66.

——. "On the Disputations of R. Yehiel of Paris and R. Moses ben Nahman." [in Hebrew] *Tarbiz* 2 (1930–31): 172–87.

Baerwald, Leo. "Juden und jüdische Gemeinde in München vom 12. bis 20. Jahrhundert." In *Vergangene Tage. Judische Kultur in München*, ed. Hans Lamm. Munich: Langen/Müller, 1982, pp. 19–30.

Bagby, Albert. "The Jew in the Cantigas de Alfonso X, el Sabio." *Speculum* 46, no. 4 (1971): 670–688.

——. "The Figure of the Jew in the Cantigas of Alfonso X." In *Studies on the Cantigas de Santa Maria: Proceedings of the First International Symposium on the Cantigas de Santa Maria of Alfonso X El Sabio (1221–1284)*, ed. Israel Katz and John Esten Keller. Madison, WI: Hispanic Seminary of Medieval Studies, 1987, pp. 235–45.

Barasch, Moshe. "Hebrew Inscriptions in Renaissance Works of Art" [in Hebrew]. In *Scritti in memoria di Leone Carpi: Saggi sull'Ebraismo Italiano*, ed. Daniel Carpi, Attilio Milano and Alexander Rofé. Jerusalem, 1967, pp. 141–150.

Baron, Salo. *A Social and Religious History of the Jews*, 2nd edn. 24 vols. New York: Columbia University Press, 1952–83.

Battenberg, J. Friedrich. "Des Kaisers Kammerknechte: Gedanken zur rechtlich-sozialen Situation der Juden in Spätmittelalter und früher Neuzeit." *Historische Zeitschrift* 245, no. 3 (1987): 545–599.

Bauerreiss, Romauld. *Pie Jesu. Das Schmerzensmannbild und sein Einfluss auf die mittelalterliche Frömmigkeit.* Munich: Widmann, 1931.

Baum, Hans-Peter. "Quellen der Judenverfolgungen von 1147 bis 1938." In *Zeugnisse jüdischer Geschichte in Unterfranken*, ed. Ulrich Wagner. Würzburg: Schöningh, 1987, pp. 19–58.

Bauman, Zygmunt. "Allosemitism: Premodern, Modern, Postmodern." In *Modernity, Culture and "the Jew,"* edited by Bryan Cheyette and Laura Marcus. Stanford, CA: Stanford University Press, 1998, pp. 143–56.

Bebb, Phillip N. "Jewish Policy in Sixteenth Century Nuremberg." *Occasional Papers of the American Society for Reformation Research* 1 (1977): 125–36.

Bell, Dean Phillip. *Sacred Communities: Jewish and Christian Identities in Fifteenth-Century Germany*. Boston and Leiden: Brill, 2001.

Belting, Hans. *Likeness and Presence: A History of the Image in the Era Before Art*, trans. Edmund Jephcott. Chicago: University of Chicago Press, 1994.
Berger, David. "The Attitude of St. Bernard of Clairvaux toward the Jews." *American Academy for Jewish Research* 40 (1972): 89–107.
——. "From Crusades to Blood Libels to Expulsions: Some New Approaches to Medieval Antisemitism." *Second Annual Lecture of the Victor J. Selmanowitz Chair of Jewish History*. New York: Touro College, Graduate School of Jewish Studies, 1997.
——, ed. and trans. *The Jewish-Christian Debate in the High Middle Ages: A Critical Edition of the Nizzahon Vetus.* Philadelphia: Jewish Publication Society of America, 1979.
——. "Mission to the Jews and Jewish-Christian Contacts in the Polemical Literature of the High Middle Ages." *American Historical Review* 91, no. 3 (1986): 576–91.
Bestul, Thomas H. *Texts of the Passion: Latin Devotional Literature in Medieval Society*. Philadelphia: University of Pennsylvania Press, 1996.
Birk, Karin, Werner Transier and Markus Wener, eds., *Europas Juden im Mittelalter*. Exhibition catalog, Historischen Museum der Pfalz Speyer. Ostfildern-Ruit: Hatje Cantz Verlag, 2004.
Blumenkranz, Bernhard. *Die Judenpredigt Augustins. Ein Beitrag zur Geschichte der jüdisch-christlichen Beziehungen in den ersten Jahrhunderten*. Basel: Helbing & Lichtenhahn, 1946.
——. *Juifs et chrétiens dans le monde occidental, 430–1096*. Paris: Mouton, 1960.
——. *Les auteurs chrétiens-latins du moyen âge sur les juifs et le judaïsme*. Paris: Mouton, 1963.
——. "Das Bilderevangelium des Hasses," in *Judenhass—Schuld der Christen?* ed. W. P. Eckert and E. L. Ehrlich. Essen: Hans Driewer, 1964, pp. 249–56.
——. *Juden und Judentum in der mittelalterlichen Kunst*. Stuttgart: Kohlhammer, 1965.
——. *Art et archéologie des juifs en France médiévale.* Toulouse: Private publisher, 1980.
Bodian, Miriam. *Hebrews of the Portuguese Nation: Conversos and Community in Early Modern Amsterdam.* Bloomington: Indiana University Press, 1997.
Browe, Peter. "Die Hostienschändungen der Juden im Mittelalter." *Römische Quartalschift für christliche Altertumskunde und Kirchengeschichte* 34 (1926): 167–97.
Burgard, Friedhelm, Alfred Haverkamp and Gerd Mentgen, eds. *Judenvertreibungen in Mittelalter und früher Neuzeit.* Hannover: Hahnsche Buchhandlung, 1999.
Camille, Michael. *The Gothic Idol: Ideology and Image-Making in Medieval Art*. Cambridge: Cambridge University Press, 1989.
Carlebach, Elisheva. *Divided Souls: Converts from Judaism in Germany 1500–1750*. New Haven: Yale University Press, 2001.
Carpenter, Dwayne. *Alfonso X and the Jews: An Edition and Commentary on the Siete Partidas 7.24.* Berkeley: University of California Press, 1986.
——. "Social Perception and Literary Portrayal: Jews and Muslims in Medieval Spanish Literature." In *Convivencia: Jews, Muslims, and Christians in Medieval Spain*, ed. Vivian B. Mann, Jerrilyn Dodds and Thomas F. Glick. New York: Braziller and Jewish Museum, 1992, pp. 61–81.
Chazan, Robert, ed. *Church, State and Jew in the Middle Ages*. New York: Behrman House, 1980.
——. *European Jewry and the First Crusade*. Berkeley: University of California Press, 1987.
——. "The Condemnation of the Talmud Reconsidered (1239–1248)." *Proceedings of the American Academy for Jewish Research* 55 (1988): 11–30.
——. *Barcelona and Beyond: The Disputation of 1263 and Its Aftermath*. Berkeley: University of California Press, 1992.
——. *Medieval Stereotypes and Modern Antisemitism*. Berkeley: University of California Press, 1997.
——. *Fashioning Jewish Identity in Medieval Western Christendom*. Cambridge: Cambridge University Press, 2004.
Christmann, Gérard. "L'image du juif dans la société chrétienne de la fin du moyen âge." *Saisons d'Alsace* 20 (1975): 55–56.

Cluse, Christoph, ed. *Europas Juden im Mittelalter: Beiträge des internationalen Symposiums in Speyer vom 20.–25. Oktober 2002*. Trier: Kliomedia, 2004.
——. "Jewish Elementary Education in Medieval Ashkenaz." In *Seriis Intendere: A Collection of Essays Celebrating the Twenty-Fifth Anniversary of the Centre for Medieval Studies*, ed. Sharon Abra Hanen. Leeds: privately published, 1994, pp. 7–14.
Cohen, Gerson D. "The Song of Songs and the Jewish Religious Mentality." In *Studies in the Variety of Rabbinic Cultures*, ed. Gerson D. Cohen. Philadelphia: Jewish Publication Society of America, 1991, pp. 3–17.
Cohen, Jeremy. *The Friars and the Jews: The Evolution of Medieval Anti-Judaism*. Ithaca: Cornell University Press, 1982.
——. "The Jews as the Killers of Christ in the Latin Tradition, from Augustine to the Friars." *Traditio* 39 (1983): 1–27.
——. "Scholarship and Intolerance in the Academy: The Study and Evaluation of Judaism in European Christendom." *American Historical Review* 91, no. 3 (1986): 592–613.
——, ed. *Essential Papers on Judaism and Christianity in Conflict: From Late Antiquity to the Reformation*. New York: University Press, 1991.
——, ed. *From Witness to Witchcraft: Jews and Judaism in Medieval Christian Thought*. Wolfenbütteler Mittelalter-Studien, vol. 11. Wiesbaden: Harrassowitz, 1996.
——. *Living Letters of the Law: Ideas of the Jew in Medieval Christianity*. Berkeley and Los Angeles: University of California Press, 1999.
——. "*Synagoga conversa*: Honorius Augustodunensis, the Song of Songs, and Christianity's 'Eschatological Jew'." *Speculum* 79, no. 2 (2004): 309–40.
Cohen, Richard I. *Jewish Icons: Art and Society in Modern Europe*. Berkeley: University of California Press, 1998.
Constable, Giles. *Three Studies in Medieval Religious and Social Thought*. Cambridge: Cambridge University Press, 1995.
Coudert, Allison P. and Jeffrey S. Shoulson, eds. *Hebraica Veritas? Christian Hebraists and the Study of Judaism in Early Modern Europe*. Philadelphia: University of Pennsylvania Press, 2004.
Creasman, Allyson F. "The Virgin Mary Against the Jews: Anti-Jewish Polemic in the Pilgrimage to the Schöne Maria of Regensburg, 1519–25." *Sixteenth Century Journal* 33, no. 4 (2002): 963–80.
Crossan, John Dominic. *Who Killed Jesus? Exposing the Roots of Anti-Semitism in the Gospel Story of the Death of Jesus*. New York: Harper Collins, 1995.
Cutler, Allan. "Innocent III and the Distinctive Clothing of Jews and Muslims." *Studies in Medieval Culture* 3 (1970): 92–116.
Dahan, Gilbert. *The Christian Polemic Against the Jews in the Middle Ages*, trans. Jody Gladding. Notre Dame: University of Notre Dame Press, 1998.
——. "Les juifs dan les *Miracles* de Gautier de Coincy." *Archives Juives* 16 (1980): 41–48 and 59–68.
Das, A. Andrew. *Paul and the Jews*. Peabody, MA: Hendrickson, 2003.
Davies, Alan T., ed. *Antisemitism and the Foundations of Christianity*. New York: Paulist Press, 1979.
Denkmäler Jüdischer Kultur in Bayern. Bayerisches Landesamt für Denkmalpflege Arbeitsheft 43. Munich: Bayerisches Landesamt für Denkmalpflege, 1994.
Despres, Denise L. "Immaculate Flesh and the Social Body: Mary and the Jews." *Jewish History* 12, no. 1 (Spring 1998): 47–69.
Dick, Jutta and Marina Sassenberg, eds. *Wegweiser durch das jüdische Sachsen-Anhalt*. Potsdam: Verlag für Berlin-Brandenburg, 1998.
Diestelkamp, Bernhard. "Der Vorwurf des Ritualmordes gegen Juden vor dem Hofgericht Kaiser Friedrichs II. im Jahr 1236." In *Religiöse Devianz: Untersuchungen zu sozialen, rechtlichen und theologischen Reaktionen auf religiöse Abweichung im westlichen und östlichen Mittelalter*, ed. Dieter Simon. Frankfurt: Klostermann, 1990, pp. 19–39.

Dinzelbacher, Peter. *Judastraditionen*. Vienna: Österreichisches Museum für Volkskunde, 1977.

Dundes, Alan, ed. *The Blood Libel Legend: A Casebook in Anti-Semitic Folklore*. Madison, WI: University of Wisconsin Press, 1991.

Ebenbauer, Alfred and Klaus Zatloukal, eds. *Die Juden in ihrer mittelalterlichen Umwelt*. Vienna: Böhlau, 1991.

Elbogen, I., A. Freimann and H. Tykocinski, eds. *Germania Judaica*, vol. 1: *Von den ältesten Zeiten bis 1238*. Breslau, 1934; repr. Tübingen: J. C. B. Mohr (Paul Siebeck), 1963.

Emmerson, Richard K. and Bernard McGinn, eds. *The Apocalypse in the Middle Ages*. Ithaca: Cornell University Press, 1992.

Epstein, Marc Michael. "The Elephant and the Law: The Medieval Jewish Minority Adapts a Christian Motif." *Art Bulletin* 76 (1994): 465–478.

——. *Dreams of Subversion in Medieval Jewish Art and Literature*. University Park, PA: Pennsylvania State University Press, 1997.

Erb, Rainer, ed. *Die Legende vom Ritualmord: Zur Geschichte der Blutbeschuldigungen gegen Juden*. Berlin: Metropol, 1993.

Finlay, Robert. "The Foundation of the Ghetto: Venice, the Jews, and the War of the League of Cambrai." *Proceedings of the American Philosophical Society* 126 (1982): 140–154.

Fishbane, Michael. *The Exegetical Imagination: On Jewish Thought and Theology*. Cambridge, MA: Harvard University Press, 1998.

Flade, Roland. *Die Würzburger Juden: Ihre Geschichte vom Mittelalter bis zur Gegenwart*, 2nd edn. Würzburg: Stürtz, 1996.

Freedberg, David. *The Power of Images: Studies in the History and Theory of Response*. Chicago: The University of Chicago Press, 1989.

Friedman, Jerome. *The Most Ancient Testimony: Sixteenth-Century Christian-Hebraica in the Age of Renaissance Nostalgia*. Athens, OH.: Ohio University Press, 1983.

Freire, José L. "The *Cantigas de Santa Maria*: Social Perception and Literary Portrayal of Jews and Muslims, and Historical Reality." In *Models in Medieval Iberian Literature and Their Modern Reflections: Convivencia as a Structural, Cultural, and Sexual Ideal*, ed. Judy B. McInnis. Newark, DE: University of Delaware Press, 2002, pp. 9–38.

Frey, Winfried. "Zur Rolle der Juden in mittelalterlichen deutschen Texten des Weihnachtsstoffkreises." In *Spannungen und Konflikte menschlichen Zusammenlebens in der deutschen Literatur des Mittelalters*. Bristoler Colloquium 1993, ed. Kurt Gärtner, Ingrid Kasten, and Frank Shaw. Tübingen: Niemeyer, 1996, pp. 125–41.

Fried, Johannes, ed. *Schulen und Studium im sozialen Wandel des hohen und späten Mittelalters*. Sigmaringen: Thorbecke, 1986.

Frizzell, Lawrence E. and J. Frank Henderson. "Jews and Judaism in the Medieval Latin Liturgy." In *The Liturgy of the Medieval Church*, ed. Thomas J. Heffernan and E. Ann Matter. Kalamazoo, MI: Medieval Institute Publications, 2001, pp. 187–214.

Frojmovic, Eva, ed. *Imagining the Self, Imagining the Other: Visual Representation and Jewish Christian Dynamics in the Middle Ages and Early Modern Period*. Leiden: Brill, 2002.

Fulton, Rachel. *From Judgment to Passion: Devotion to Christ and the Virgin Mary, 800–1200*. New York: Columbia University Press, 2002.

Funkenstein, Amos. "Basic Types of Christian Anti-Jewish Polemics in the Later Middle Ages." *Viator* 2 (1971): 373–82.

Geissler, Klaus. *Die Juden in Deutschland und Bayern bis zur Mitte des 14. Jahrhunderts*. Munich: Beck, 1976.

Gentili, Augusto. "Traces of Giorgione: Jewish Culture and Astrological Science." In *Giorgione: Myth and Enigma*. Exhibition catalogue, Kunsthistorisches Museum, Vienna, ed. Sylvia Ferino-Pagden and Giovanna Nepi Sciré. Milan: Skira, 2004, pp. 57–69.

Gerber, Barbara. *Jud Süss. Aufsteig und Fall im frühen 18. Jahrhundert: Ein Beitrag zur historischen Antisemitismus- und Rezeptionsforschung*. Hamburg: Hans Christians Verlag, 1990.

Gilman, Sander L. and Steven T. Katz, eds. *Anti-Semitism in Times of Crisis*. New York: New York University Press, 1991.
Ginzberg, Louis. *The Legends of the Jews*, 7 vols. Philadelphia: Jewish Publication Society of America, 1909–38; repr. (in 2 vols.) 2003.
Glaser, Alfred. *Geschichte der Juden in Straßburg*. Strasbourg: Imprimerie Française, 1924.
Gow, Andrew Colin. *The Red Jews: Antisemitism in an Apocalyptic Age, 1200–1600*. Leiden: Brill, 1995.
Graboïs, Aryeh. "Ecoles et structures sociales des communautés juives dans l'Occident aux IXe–XII siècles." In *Gli Ebrei nell'Alto Medioevo*. Settimane di Studio del Centro Italiano di Studi sull'Alto Medioevo, 26, 2 vols. Spoleto: Centro Italiano di Studi sull'Alto Medioevo, 1980, vol. 2, pp. 937–62.
Grabois, Aryeh. "Les juifs et les seigneurs dans la France septentrionale aux XIe et XIIe siècles." In *Les Juifs dans l'histoire de France*, ed. Myriam Yardeni. Leiden: E.J. Brill, 1980, pp. 11–23.
——. "The *Hebraica Veritas* and Jewish-Christian Intellectual Relations in the Twelfth Century." *Speculum* 50, no. 4 (Oct. 1975): 613–34.
Graus, Frantisek. *Pest—Geissler—Judenmorde. Das 14. Jahrhundert als Krisenzeit*. Göttingen: Vandenhoeck & Ruprecht, 1987.
Grayzel, Solomon. *The Church and the Jews in the XIIIth Century: A Study of Their Relations During the Years 1198–1254, Based on the Papal Letters and Conciliar Decrees of the Period*, 2nd rev. edn. New York: Hermon Press, 1966.
——. "The Talmud and the Medieval Papacy." In *Essays in Honor of Solomon B. Freehof*, ed. Walter Jacob, Frederick C. Schwartz and Vigdor W. Kavaler. Pittsburgh: Rodef Shalom Congregation, 1964, pp. 220–45.
Gregg, Joan Young. *Devils, Women, and Jews: Reflections of the Other in Medieval Sermon Stories*. Albany: State University of New York Press, 1997.
Güdemann, Moritz. *Geschichte des Erziehungswesens und der Kultur der abendländischen Juden während des Mittelalters und der neueren Zeit*, 3 vols. Vienna: Hölder, 1880–88.
Hahn, Joachim. *Erinnerungen und Zeugnisse jüdischer Geschichte in Baden-Württemberg*. Stuttgart: Konrad Theiss, 1988.
Haitovsky, Dalia. "Giorgione's *Trial of Moses*: A New Look." *Jewish Art* 16–17 (1990–1991): 20–29.
Hassig, Debra. *Medieval Bestiaries: Text, Image, Ideology*. Cambridge: Cambridge University Press, 1995.
——. "The Iconography of Rejection: Jews and Other Monstrous Races." In *Image and Belief: Studies in Celebration of the Eightieth Anniversary of the Index of Christian Art*, ed. Colum Hourihane. Princeton: Princeton University Press, 1999, pp. 25–46.
Hatton, Angus, and Vikki McKay. "Anti-Semitism in the *Cantigas de Santa Maria*." *Bulletin of Hispanic Studies* 61 (1983): 189–199.
Heil, Johannes. "'Antijudaismus' und 'Antisemitismus': Begriffe als Bedeutungsträger." *Jahrbuch für Antisemitismusforschung* 6 (1997): 93–114.
——, and Rainer Kampling, eds. *Maria Tochter Sion? Mariologie, Marienfrömmigkeit und Judenfeindschaft*. Paderborn: Ferdinand Schöningh, 2001.
——. *Gottesfeinde - Menschenfeinde. Die Vorstellung von jüdischer Weltverschwörung (13.–16. Jh.)*. Antisemitismus: Geschichte und Strukturen, vol. 3. Essen: Klartext, 2006.
Hood, John Y. B. *Aquinas and the Jews*. Philadelphia: University of Pennsylvania Press, 1995.
Hsia, R. Po-chia. *The Myth of Ritual Murder: Jews and Magic in Reformation Germany*. New Haven: Yale University Press, 1988.
——. *Trent 1475: Stories of a Ritual Murder Trial*. New Haven: Yale University Press, 1992.
——, and Hartmut Lehmann, eds. *In and Out of the Ghetto: Jewish-Gentile Relations in Late Medieval and Early Modern Germany*. Cambridge: Cambridge University Press, 1995.

——. "Christian Ethnographies of Jews in Early Modern Germany." In *Problems in the Historical Anthropology of Early Modern Europe*, ed. R. Po-chia Hsia and R. W. Scribner. Wiesbaden: Harrassowitz, 1997, pp. 35–47.

Hubel, Achim. "'Die Schöne Maria' von Regensburg. Wallfahrten—Gnadenbilder—Ikonographie." In *850 Jahre Kollegiatstift zu den heiligen Johannes Baptist und Johannes Evangelist in Regensburg 1127–1977*, ed. Paul Mai. Munich: Schnell & Steiner, 1977, pp. 199–231.

Hyams, P. "The Jews in Medieval England, 1066–1290." In *England and Germany in the High Middle Ages*, ed. Alfred Haverkamp and Hanna Vollrath. Oxford: Oxford University Press, 1996, pp. 173–92.

Israel, Jonathan I. "Central European Jewry during the Thirty Years War." *Central European History* 16 (1983): 3–30.

——. *European Jewry in the Age of Mercantilism, 1550–1750.* London: Littman Library of Jewish Civilisation, 1989.

Isaac, Jules. *Jesus and Israel*, ed. Claire Huchet Bishop, trans. Sally Gran. New York: Holt, Rinehart & Winston, 1971.

Jacobs, Irving. *The Midrashic Process: Tradition and Interpretation in Rabbinic Judaism.* Cambridge: Cambridge University Press, 1995.

Jacoby, David. "Les juifs à Venise du XIVe au milieu du XVIe siècle." In *Venezia centro di mediazione tra Oriente e Occidente (secoli xv–xvi); aspetti e problemi.* 2 vols., ed. Hans-Georg Beck, Manoussos Manoussacas and Agostino Pertusi. Florence: Olschki, 1977, vol. 1, pp. 163–216.

Jakob, Reinhard. "Judenschul und jüdische Schule. Zur Bildungsgeschichte der Juden in Schwaben vor Moses Mendelssohn." In *Geschichte und Kultur der Juden in Schwaben: Wissenschaftliche Tagung der Heimatpflege des Bezirks Schwaben in Zusammenarbeit mit der Schwabenakademie Irsee am 14./15. Oktober 1989 in Irsee*, ed. Peter Fassl. Sigmaringen: Thorbecke, 1994, pp. 45–61.

Jochum, Herbert. *Ecclesia und Synagoga: Das Judentum in der christlichen Kunst.* Exhibition catalogue. Essen: Alte Synagoge Essen, and Saarbrücken: Regionalgeschichtliches Museum Saarbrücken, 1993.

Jordan, William Chester. "The Last Tormentor of Christ: An Image of the Jews in Ancient and Medieval Exegesis, Art, and Drama." *Jewish Quarterly Review* 78 (1987): 21–47.

——. *The French Monarchy and the Jews: From Philip Augustus to the Last Capetians.* Philadelphia: University of Pennsylvania Press, 1989.

——. *Ideology and Royal Power in Medieval France: Kingship, Crusades and the Jews.* Aldershot: Ashgate, 2001.

Jung, Jacqueline E. "Beyond the Barrier: The Unifying Role of the Choir Screen in Gothic Churches." *Art Bulletin* 82 (2000): 622–57.

——. "Peasant Meal or Lord's Feast? The Social Iconography of the Naumburg Last Supper." *Gesta* 42 (2003): 39–61.

Kampling, Rainer. *Das Blut Christi und die Juden: Mt 27,25 bei den lateinischsprachigen christlichen Autoren bis zu Leo dem Grossen.* Münster: Aschendorff, 1984.

Kanarfogel, Ephraim. *Jewish Education and Society in the High Middle Ages.* Detroit: Wayne State University Press, 1992.

Kaplan, Paul. "Jewish Artists and Images of Black Africans in Renaissance Venice." In *Multicultural Europe and Cultural Exchange in the Middle Ages and Renaissance.* Arizona Studies in the Middle Ages and the Renaissance 12, ed. James Helfers. Turnhout, Belgium, 2005, pp. 67–90.

Kaplan, Yosef. *An Alternative Path to Modernity: The Sephardi Diaspora in Western Europe.* Leiden: Brill, 2000.

Katz, Dana. "Painting and the Politics of Persecution: Representing the Jew in Fifteenth-Century Mantua." *Art History* 23 (2000): 475–495.

Katz, David S. *Philo-Semitism and the Readmission of the Jews to England 1603–1655*. Oxford: Clarendon, 1982.
Kirmeier, Josef. "Aufnahme, Verfolgung und Vertreibung. Zur Judenpolitik bayerischer Herzöge im Mittelalter." In *Geschichte und Kultur der Juden in Bayern*, ed. Manfred Treml and Josef Kirmeier. Munich: K. G. Sauer, 1988, pp. 101–02.
Kisch, Guido. "The Yellow Badge in History." *Historia Judaica* 19, no. 2 (October 1957): 89–146.
——. *The Jews in Medieval Germany: A Study of their Legal and Social Status*, 2nd edn. New York: KTAV Publishing, 1970.
Klein, Peter K. "'Jud, Dir kuckt der Spitzbub aus dem Gesicht!' Traditionen Antisemitischer Bildstereotype oder die Physiognomie der 'Juden' als Construct." In *Abgestempelt: Judenfeindliche Postkarten*, ed. Helmut Gold and Georg Heuberger. Heidelberg: Umschau Braus, 1999, pp. 43–78.
Kolb, Karl. *Heilig Blut. Eine Bilddokumentation der Wallfahrt und Verehrung*. Würzburg: Echter, 1980.
Köllermann, Antje-Fee. "Die Darstellung der Passion Christi am Naumburger Westlettner." In *Meisterwerke mittelalterlicher Skulptur*, ed. Harmut Krohm. Berlin: Reimer, 1996, pp. 349–64.
Kraus, Henry. *The Living Theatre of Medieval Art*. Philadelphia: University of Pennsylvania Press, 1967.
Krauss, Samuel. *The Jewish-Christian Controversy from the Earliest Times to 1789*, ed. and rev. William Horbury. Tübingen: Mohr, 1995.
Krautheimer, Richard. *Mittelalterliche Synagogen*. Berlin: Frankfurter-Verlags, 1927.
Künzel, Hannelore. "Die Architektur der mittelalterlichen Synagogen und rituellen Bäder." In *Judentum im Mittelalter*, exhibition catalog, Schloß Halbturn, ed. Kurt Schubert. Eisenstadt: Schloß Halbturn, 1978, pp. 44–49.
Landsberger, Franz. *Rembrandt, the Jews and the Bible*, 2nd edn. Philadelphia: Jewish Publication Society of America, 1961.
Langmuir, Gavin I. *Toward a Definition of Anti-Semitism*. Berkeley: University of California Press, 1990.
——. *History, Religion and Antisemitism*. Berkeley: University of California Press, 1990.
Lavin, Marilyn Aronberg. "The Altar of Corpus Domini in Urbino: Paolo Uccello, Joos van Ghent, Piera della Francesca." *Art Bulletin* 49, no. 1 (March 1967): 1–24.
Le Goff, Jacques. *Your Money or Your Life: Economy and Religion in the Middle Ages*, trans. Patricia Ranum. New York: Zone, 1990.
Lenz, Matthias. "Schmähbriefe und Schandbilder. Realität und Visualität spätmittelalterlicher Normenkonflikte." In *Bilder, Texte, Rituale: Wirklichkeitsbezug und Wirklichkeitskonstruktion politisch-rechtlicher Kommunikationsmedien in Stadt- und Adelsgesellschaften des späten Mittelalters*, ed. Klaus Schreiner and Gabriela Signori. Berlin: Duncker und Humblot, 2000, pp. 34–67.
Lewis, Bernard, and Friedrich Niewöhner, eds. *Religionsgespräche im Mittelalter*. Wolfenbütteler Mittelalter-Studien, Vol. 4. Wiesbaden: Harrassowitz, 1992.
Lewis, Suzanne. "*Tractatus adversus Judaeos* and the Gulbenkian Apocalypse." *Art Bulletin* 68 (1986): 543–66.
Liebe, Georg. *Das Judentum in der deutschen Vergangenheit*. Leipzig: Eugen Diederichs, 1903.
Lillich, Meredith. "Gothic Glaziers: Monks, Jews, Taxpayers, Bretons, Women." *Journal of Stained Glass Studies* 27 (1985): 72–92.
Limor, Ora and Guy G. Stroumsa, eds. *Contra Iudaeos: Ancient and Medieval Polemics between Christians and Jews*. Tübingen: Mohr, 1996.
Lipton, Sara. *Images of Intolerance: Jews and Judaism in the* Bible Moralisée. Berkeley: University of California Press, 1999.
Little, Lester K. *Religious Poverty and the Profit Economy in Medieval Europe*. Ithaca: Cornell University Press, 1978.

Lotter, Friedrich. "Die Judenverfolgung des 'König Rintfleisch' in Franken um 1298." *Zeitschrift für historische Forschung* 15, no. 4 (1988): 385–422.

——. "Hostienfrevelvorwurf und Blutwunderfälschung bei den Judenverfolgungen von 1298 ('Rindfleisch') und 1336–1338 ('Armleder')." In *Fälschungen im Mittelalter. Internationaler Kongreß der Monumenta Germaniae Historica München, 16.–19. September 1986, Teil V: Fingierte Briefe, Frömmigkeit und Fälschung, Realienfälschung.* Hannover: Hahnsche Buchhandlung, 1988, pp. 533–83.

——. "The Scope and Effectiveness of Imperial Jewry Law in the High Middle Ages." *Jewish History* 4 (1989): 31–58.

——. "Geltungsbereich und Wirksamkeit des Rechts der kaiserlichen Judenprivilegien im Hochmittelalter." *Aschkenas* 1 (1991): 23–64.

——. "Der Rechtsstatus der Juden in den Schriften Reuchlins zum Pfefferkornstreit." In *Reuchlin und die Juden*, ed. Arno Herzig and Julius H. Schoeps. Sigmaringen: Thorbecke, 1993, pp. 66–88.

Lubac, Henri de. *Medieval Exegesis*, trans. E. M. Macierowski. 4 vols. Edinburgh: Clark and Grand Rapids, MI: Eerdmans, 2000.

Maccoby, Hyam. *A Pariah People: The Anthropology of Antisemitism.* London: Constable, 1996.

——, ed. and trans. *Judaism on Trial: Jewish-Christian Disputations in the Middle Ages.* Rutherford, NJ: Fairleigh Dickinson University Press, 1982.

Die Macht der Bilder. Antisemitische Vorurteile und Mythen. Exhibition catalogue, Jüdisches Museum der Stadt Wien. Vienna: Picus Verlag, 1995.

Maimon, Arye, Mordechai Breuer and Yacov Guggenheim, eds., *Germania Judaica*, vol. 3, pt. 2. Tübingen: J. C. B. Mohr (Paul Siebeck), 1995.

Mann, Vivian B. and Richard I. Cohen, eds. *From Court Jews to the Rothschilds: Art, Patronage, and Power.* Munich: Prestel, and New York: Jewish Museum, 1996.

Marcus, Ivan G. "Hierarchies, Religious Boundaries, and Jewish Spirituality in Medieval Germany." *Jewish History* 1, no. 2 (1986): 7–26.

——. "Medieval Jewish Studies: Toward an Anthropological History of the Jews." In *The State of Jewish Studies*, ed. Shaye J. D. Cohen and Edward L. Greenstein. Detroit: Wayne State University Press, 1990, 113–27.

——. "Jews and Christians Imagining the Other in Medieval Europe." *Prooftexts* 15, no. 3 (1995): 209–226.

——. *Rituals of Childhood: Jewish Acculturation in Medieval Europe.* New Haven: Yale University Press, 1996.

Marcus, Jacob R., ed. and trans. *The Jew in the Medieval World, A Source Book: 315–1791.* 1938; repr. Cincinnati: Hebrew Union College Press, 1990.

Marrow, James H. "*Circumdederunt me canes multi*: Christ's Tormentors in Northern European Art of the Late Middle Ages and Early Renaissance." *Art Bulletin* 59 (June 1977): 167–181.

——. *Passion Iconography in Northern European Art of the Late Middle Ages and Early Renaissance.* Kortrijk: Van Ghemmert, 1979.

McMichael, Steven J. and Susan E. Meyers, eds. *Friars and Jews in the Middle Ages and Renaissance.* Boston: Brill, 2004.

Mellinkoff, Ruth. *The Horned Moses in Medieval Art and Thought.* Berkeley: University of California Press, 1970.

——. "The Round-Topped Tablets of the Law: Sacred Symbol and Emblem of Evil." *Journal of Jewish Art* 1 (1974): 28–43.

——. *The Mark of Cain.* Berkeley: University of California Press, 1981.

——. *Outcasts: Signs of Otherness in Northern European Art of the Late Middle Ages*, 2 vols. Berkeley: University of California Press, 1993.

Menache, Sophia. "The King, the Church and the Jews: Some Considerations on the Expulsions from England and France." *Journal of Medieval History* 13 (1987): 223–36.

Mentgen, Gerd. *Studien zur Geschichte der Juden im mittelalterlichen Elsaß*. Hannover: Hahn, 1995.

Merback, Mitchell B. *The Thief, the Cross, and the Wheel: Pain and the Spectacle of Punishment in Medieval and Renaissance Europe*. Chicago: The University of Chicago Press, 1999.

——. "The Vanquished Synagogue, the Risen Host, and the Grateful Dead at the Salvatorkirche in Passau." *Peregrinations* 1, no. 4 (Autumn 2005) [http://peregrinations.kenyon.edu/welcome.html]

——. "Fount of Mercy, City of Blood: Cultic Anti-Judaism and the Pulkau Passion Altarpiece." *Art Bulletin* 87 (2005): 589–642.

Minty, J. M. "Judengasse to Christian Quarter: The Phenomenon of the Converted Synagogue in the Late Medieval and Early Modern Holy Roman Empire." In *Popular Religion in Germany and Central Europe, 1400–1800*, ed. Bob Scribner and T. Johnson. New York: St. Martin's, 1996, pp. 58–86.

Mittlmeier, Christine. *Publizistik im Dienste antijüdischer Polemik: Spätmittelalterliche und frühneuzeitliche Flugschriften und Flugblätter zu Hostienschändungen*. Frankfurt am Main: Peter Lang, 2000.

Miyazaki, Mariko. "Misericord Owls and Medieval Anti-Semitism." In *The Mark of the Beast: The Medieval Bestiary in Art, Life, and Literature*, ed. Debra Hassig. New York: Garland, 1999.

Moore, R. I. *The Formation of a Persecuting Society: Power and Deviance in Western Europe, 950–1250*. Oxford: Blackwell, 1987.

Moses dal Castellazzo. *Bilder-Pentateuch von Moses dal Castellazzo, Venedig 1521: Völlständige Faksimile-Ausgabe im Originalformat des Codex 1164 aus dem Besitz des Jüdischen Historischen Instituts Warschau*. 2 vols., ed. Kurt Schubert and Ursula Schubert. Vienna: Bernthaler & Windischgraetz, 1986.

Moxey, Keith. *Peasants, Warriors and Wives: Popular Imagery in the Reformation*. Chicago: The University of Chicago Press, 1989.

Mundill, Robin R. *England's Jewish Solution, 1262–1290*. Cambridge: Cambridge University Press, 1998.

Nadler, Steven. *Rembrandt's Jews*. Chicago: The University of Chicago Press, 2003.

Neusner, Jacob. *Judaism and the Interpretation of Scripture: Introduction to the Rabbinic Midrash*. Peabody, MA: Hendrickson, 2004.

Nicolai, Bernd. "Orders in Stone: Social Reality and Artistic Approach. The Case of Strasbourg South Portal." *Gesta* 41 (2002): 111–128.

Nirenberg, David. *Communities of Violence: Persecution of Minorities in the Middle Ages*. Princeton: Princeton University Press, 1996.

Obermann, Heiko A. *The Roots of Anti-Semitism in the Age of Renaissance and Reformation*, trans. James I. Porter. Philadelphia: Fortress, 1984.

——. "Discovery of Hebrew and Discrimination against the Jews: The *Veritas Hebraica* as Double-Edged Sword in Renaissance and Reformation." In *Germania Illustrata: Essays on Early Modern Germany Presented to Gerald Strauss*, ed. Andrew C. Fix and Susan C. Karant-Nunn. Kirksville, MO: Sixteenth Century Journal Publishers, 1992, pp. 19–34.

Onnasch, Martin. "Die Ausweisung der Juden aus Naumburg vor 500 Jahren." Paper presented in the Naumburg Marienkirche, May 14, 1994 (unpublished, Naumburg Stadtarchiv).

Parkes, James. *The Jew in the Medieval Community*, 2nd rev. edn. New York: Hermon Press, 1976.

Pastan, Elizabeth Carson. "*Tam haereticos quam Iudaeos*: Shifting Symbols in the Glazing of Troyes Cathedral." *Word & Image* 10 (1994): 66–83.

Patschovsky, Alexander. "Der 'Talmudjude' Vom mittelalterlichen Ursprung eines neuzeitlichen Themas." In *Juden in der christlicher Umwelt während des späten Mittelalters*, Zeitschrift für historische Forschung, Beiheft 13, ed. Alfred Haverkamp and Franz-Josef Ziwes. Berlin: Duncker und Humblot, 1992, pp. 13–27.

——. "Das Rechtsverhältnis der Juden zum deutschen König (9.–14. Jahrhundert)." *Zeitschrift der Savigny-Stiftung für Rechtsgeschichte* 110 (1993): 331–371.

——. "Feindbilder der Kirche: Juden und Ketzer im Vergleich (11.–13. Jahrhundert)." In *Juden und Christen zur Zeit der Kreuzzüge*, ed. Alfred Haverkamp. Sigmaringen: Thorbecke, 1999, pp. 327–57.

Patton, Pamela A. "The Cloister as Cultural Mirror: Anti-Jewish Imagery at Santa María la Mayor in Tudela." In *Der mittelalterliche Kreuzgang: Architektur, Funktion und Programm*, ed. Peter K. Klein. Regensburg: Schnell und Steiner, 2003, pp. 317–32.

Perlove, Shelley K. "Awaiting the Messiah: Christians, Jews, and Muslims in the Late Work of Rembrandt." *Bulletin of the University of Michigan Museums of Art and Archaeology* 11 (1994–96): 91–96.

——. "Perceptions of Otherness: Critical Responses to the Jews in Rembrandt's Art and Milieu (1836–1945)." *Dutch Crossing: A Journal of Low Countries Studies* 25, no. 2 (2001): 243–290.

Pflaum, Heinz. "Les scènes de juifs dans la littérature dramatique." *Revue des Études Juives* 89 (1930): 111–34.

——. *Die religiöse Disputation in der europaïschen Dichtung des Mittelalters*. Geneva: Olschki, 1935.

Poliakov, Léon. *The History of Antisemitism*. 3 vols. New York: Vanguard Press, 1965–75.

Poorthus, M. J. H. M., and J. Schwartz, eds. *Purity and Holiness: The Heritage of Leviticus*. Leiden: Brill, 2000.

Räisänen, Heikki. "Paul, God, and Israel: Romans 9–11 in Recent Research." In *The Social World of Formative Christianity and Judaism: Essays in Tribute to Howard Clark Kee*, ed. Jacob Neusner, Ernest S. Frerichs, Peder Borgen and Richard Horsley. Philadelphia: Fortress Press, 1988, pp. 178–206.

Raphaël, Freddy and Robert Weyl. *Juifs en Alsace: Culture, société, histoire*. Toulouse: Private publisher, 1977.

Ravid, Benjamin. "The Religious, Economic and Social Background and Context of the Establishment of the Ghetti of Venice." In *Gli Ebrei e Venezia secoli XIV–XVIII*, ed. Gaetano Cozzi. Milan: Edizioni Comunità, 1987, pp. 211–59.

Ravid, Benjamin C. I. *Studies on the Jews of Venice, 1382–1797*. Aldershot: Ashgate, 2003.

Reider, Joseph. "Jews in Medieval Art." In *Essays on Anti-Semitism*, ed. Koppel S. Pinson. New York: Conference on Jewish Relations, 1942, pp. 45–56.

Revel-Neher, Elisabeth. *The Image of the Jew in Byzantine Art*, trans. David Maizel. Oxford: Pergamon Press, 1992.

Riquet, Michel. "Saint Louis, roi de France et les Juifs." In *Septième centenaire de la mort de Saint Louis: Actes des colloques de Royaumont et de Paris, 21–27 mai 1970*. Paris: Les Belles Lettres, 1976, pp. 345–50.

Röckelein, Hedwig. "Marienverehrung und Judenfeindlichkeit in Mittelalter und früher Neuzeit." In *Maria in der Welt: Marienverehrung im Kontext der Sozialgeschichte 10.–18. Jahrhundert*. Clio Lucernensis 2, Veröffentlichung des Lehrstuhls für Allgemeine und Schweizer Geschichte Luzern. Zurich: Chronos, 1993, pp. 279–307.

——. "'Die grabstain, so vil taeusent gulden wer sein': Vom Umgang der Christen mit Synagogen und jüdischen Friedhofen im Mittelalter und am Beginn der Neuzeit." *Aschkenas. Zeitschrift für Geschichte und Kultur der Judentum* 5 (1995): 19–22.

Rohrbacher, Stefan. "The Charge of Deicide: An Anti-Jewish Motif in Medieval Christian Art." *Journal of Medieval History* 17 (1991): 297–321.

—— and Michael Schmidt. *Judenbilder: Kulturgeschichte antijüdischer Mythen und antisemitischer Vorurteile*. Reinbek bei Hamburg: Rowohlt, 1991.

Romano, David. "Los judíos y Alfonso X," *Revista de Occidente* 43 (1984): 203–217.

Rösel, Isert. "Die Reichssteuern der deutschen Judengemeinden von ihren Anfängen bis zur Mitte des 14. Jahrhunderts." *Monatsschrift für Geschichte und Wissenschaft des Judentums* 53 (1909): 697–708; and 54 (1910): 55–69, 206–223, 333–347 and 462–473.

Rosenthal, Judah M. "The Talmud on Trial: The Disputation at Paris in the Year 1240." *Jewish Quarterly Review* 47 (1956/1957): 58–76 (pt. 1) and 145–69 (pt. 2).
Roth, Cecil. A *Life of Menasseh ben Israel: Rabbi, Printer, and Diplomat.* Philadelphia: Jewish Publication Society of America, 1934.
Rothkrug, Lionel. "Holy Shrines, Religious Dissonance and Satan in the Origins of the German Reformation." *Historical Reflections/Reflexions historiques* 14 (1987): 143–286.
Rowe, Nina. "Synagoga Tumbles, a Rider Triumphs: Clerical Spectatorship and the Fürstenportal of Bamberg Cathedral." *Gesta* 45, no. 1 (2006): 15–42.
Rubens, Alfred. *A History of Jewish Costume.* New York: Crown, 1973.
——. *A Jewish Iconography*, rev. edn. London: Nonpareil, 1981.
Rubin, Miri. *Gentile Tales: The Narrative Assault on Late Medieval Jews.* New Haven: Yale University Press, 1999.
Ruether, Rosemary Radford. *Faith and Fratricide: The Theological Roots of Antisemitism.* New York: The Seabury Press, 1974.
Sabar, Shalom. "Childbirth and Magic: Jewish Folklore and Material Culture." in *Cultures of the Jews: A New History*, ed. David Biale. New York: Schocken, 2002, pp. 670–722.
Sansy, Danièle. "Bestiaire des juifs, bestiaire du diable." *Micrologus: Natura, scienza, e societé medievali* 8 (2000): 561–79.
Santiago, Olga Walmisley. "Alfonso el Sabio's Attitude Toward Moors and Jews as Revealed in Two of His Works." *Cantigueiros* 6 (1994): 30–41.
Sarfatti, Gad B[en Ami]. "Hebrew Script in Western Visual Arts." *Italia: Studi e ricerche sulla storia, la cultura e la letteratura degli Ebrei d'Italia* 13–15 (2001): 451–547.
——. "The Tablets of the Law as a Symbol of Judaism." In *The Ten Commandents in History and Tradition*, ed. Ben-Zion Segal and Gershon Levi. Jerusalem: Magnes Press (Hebrew University of Jerusalem), 1990, pp. 383–418.
Shachar, Isaiah. *The Judensau: A Medieval Anti-Jewish Motif and Its History.* London: Warburg Institute, 1974.
Schilling. Konrad, ed. *Monumenta Judaica: 2000 Jahre Geschichte und Kultur der Juden am Rhein.* Exhibition catalogue, Cologne: Kölnisches Stadtmuseum, 1963.
Schlauch, Margaret. "The Allegory of Church and Synagogue." *Speculum* 14 (1939): 448–464.
Schöner, Petra. *Judenbilder im deutschen Einblattdruck der Renaissance: Ein Beitrag zur Imagologie.* Baden-Baden: Valentin Koerner, 2002.
Schreckenberg, Heinz. *Die christlichen Adversus-Judaeos-Texte (11.–13. Jh.) mit einer Ikonographie des Judenthemas bis zum 4. Laterankonzil.* Frankfurt am Main: Lang, 1991.
——. *The Jews in Christian Art: An Illustrated History*, trans. John Bowden. New York: Continuum, 1996.
Schreiner, Klaus. "Antijudaismus in Bildern des späten Mittelalters." In *Das Medium Bild in historischen Ausstellungen. Beiträge zur Sektion 6 des 41. Deutschen Historikertags in München 1996*, ed. Manfred Treml and Evamaria Brockhoff. Materialien zur Bayerischen Geschichte und Kultur, 5/98. Augsburg: Haus der Bayerischen Geschichte, 1998, pp. 9–34.
Schubert, Kurt, ed. *Die Österreichischen Hofjuden und ihre Zeit*, Studia Judaica Austriaca 12. Exhibition catalogue, Eisenstadt: Österreichisches Jüdisches Museum, 1991.
Schuder, Rosemarie, and Rudolf Hirsch. *Der Gelbe Fleck. Wurzeln und Wirkungen des Judenhasses in der deutschen Geschichte: Essays.* Röderberg: Pahl-Rugenstein Verlag, 1988.
Schwarz, Michael Viktor. *Visuelle Medien im christlichen Kult: Fallstudien aus dem 13. bis 16. Jahrhundert.* Vienna: Böhlau, 2002.
——. "Retelling the Passion at Naumburg: The West-Screen and Its Audience." *Artibus et historiae* 51 (2005): 59–72.
Schwarz, Stefan. *Die Juden in Bayern im Wandel der Zeiten.* Munich: Günter Olzog, 1963.

Schwierz, Israel. *Steinerne Zeugnisse jüdischen Lebens in Bayern. Eine Dokumentation*, 2nd edn. Munich: Bayerische Landeszentrale für politische Bildungsarbeit, 1992.
Schwillus, Harald. "Hostienfrevellegende und Judenverfolgung in Iphofen. Ein Beitrag zur Entstehungsgeschichte der Kirche zum Hl. Blut im Gräberviertel." *Würzburger Diözesangeschichtsblätter* 58 (1996): 87–107.
Sciurie, Helga. "Ecclesia und Synagoge. Bilder von Sinnlichkeit und Gewalt am deutschen Kirchenportal des 13. Jahrhunderts." In *Blick-Wechsel: Konstruktionen von Männlichkeit und Weiblichkeit in Kunst und Kunstgeschichte*, ed. Ines Lindner et al. Berlin: Reimer, 1989, pp. 243–50.
——. "Ecclesia und Synagoge an den Domen zu Straßburg, Bamberg, Magdeburg und Erfurt: körpersprachliche Wandlungen im gestalterischen Kontext." *Wiener Jahrbuch für Kunstgeschichte* 46–47 (1993–1994): 679–687 and 871–874.
Sears, Elisabeth and Thelma K. Thomas, eds. *Reading Medieval Images: The Art Historian and the Object*. Ann Arbor: University of Michigan Press, 2002.
Seiferth, Wolfgang. *Synagogue and Church in the Middle Ages: Two Symbols in Art and Literature*, trans. Lee Chadeayne and Paul Gottwald. New York: Ungar, 1970.
Serper, Arié. "Le débat entre Synagogue et Église au XIIIe siècle." *Revue des études juives*, 4th ser., 3, no. 123 (1964): 307–333.
Siehe der Stein schreit aus der Mauer. Geschichte und Kultur der Juden in Bayern. Exhibition catalog, Nuremberg: Germanisches Nationalmuseum, 1988.
Signer, Michael A., and John Van Engen, eds. *Jews and Christians in Twelfth-Century Europe*. Notre Dame: University of Notre Dame Press, 2001.
Simon, Marcel. *Verus Israel. A Study of the Relations between Christians and Jews in the Roman Empire (135–425)*, trans. H. McKeating. Oxford: University Press, 1986.
Simonsohn, Shlomo, ed. *The Apostolic See and the Jews. Documents: 492–1404*. Toronto: Pontifical Institute of Medieval Studies, 1988.
——. *The Apostolic See and the Jews: History*. Toronto: Pontifical Institute of Medieval Studies, 1991.
Simson, Otto von. "Ecclesia und Synagoge am südlichen Querhausportal des Straßburger Münsters." In *Wenn der Messias kommt. Das jüdisch-christliche Verhältnis im Spiegel mittelalterlicher Kunst*, ed. Lieselotte Kötzsche and Peter von der Osten-Sacken. Berlin: Selbstverlag Institut Kirche und Judentum, 1984, pp. 104–25.
Smalley, Beryl. *The Study of the Bible in the Middle Ages*, 2nd edn. Oxford: Blackwell, 1952.
Stacey, Robert C. "The Conversion of Jews to Christianity in Thirteenth-Century England." *Speculum* 67 (1992): 263–83.
——. "From Ritual Crucifixion to Host Desecration: Jews and the Body of Christ." *Jewish History* 12, no. 1 (1998): 11–28.
Stahl, Gerlinde. "Die Wallfahrt zur Schönen Maria in Regensburg," *Beiträge zur Geschichte des Bistums Regensburg*, vol. 2, ed. Georg Schwaiger and Joseph Staber. Regensburg, 1968, pp. 35–281.
Stahleder, Helmuth. "Die Münchener Juden im Mittelalter und ihre Kultstätten." In *Synagogen und jüdische Friedhöfe in München*. Munich: Aries, 1988, pp. 11–33.
Stern, Selma. *Der preussische Staat und die Juden*, 7 vols. Tübingen: Leo Baeck Institut, 1962–71.
——. *Josel of Rosheim: Commander of Jewry in the Holy Roman Empire of the German Nation*, trans. Gertrude Hirschler. Philadelphia: Jewish Publication Society of America, 1965.
——. *Jud Süss: Ein Beitrag zur deutschen und zur jüdischen Geschichte*. Munich: G. Miller, 1973.
——. *The Court Jew: A Contribution to the History of the Period of Absolutism in Central Europe*, trans. Ralph Weiman. Philadelphia: Jewish Publication Society of America, 1980.
Stow, Kenneth R. "Papal and Royal Attitudes toward Jewish Lending in the Thirteenth Century." *Association for Jewish Studies* 6 (1981): 161–184.

——. *Alienated Minority: The Jews of Medieval Latin Europe*. Cambridge: Harvard University Press, 1992.
Strickland, Debra Higgs. *Saracens, Demons, and Jews: Making Monsters in Medieval Art*. Princeton: Princeton University Press, 2003.
Taylor, Miriam S. *Anti-Judaism and Early Christian Identity: A Critique of the Scholarly Consensus*. Leiden: Brill, 1995.
Thérel, Marie-Louise. "L'origine du thème de la 'Synagogue répudiée.'" *Scriptorium* 25 (1971): 285–89.
Timmerman, Achim. "The Avenging Crucifix: Some Observations on the Iconography of the Living Cross." *Gesta* 40 (2001): 141–60.
Torrell, Jean-Pierre. "Les Juifs dans l'oeuvre de Pierre le Vénérable." *Cahiers de civilisation médiévale* 30 (1987): 331–346.
Trachtenberg, Joshua. *Jewish Magic and Superstition: A Study in Folk Religion*. 1939; repr. New York: Atheneum, 1982.
——. *The Devil and the Jews: The Medieval Conception of the Jew and its Relation to Modern Anti-Semitism*. 1943; repr. Philadelphia: Jewish Publication Society of America, 1983.
Treml, Manfred, and Josef Kirmeier, eds. *Geschichte und Kultur der Juden in Bayern: Aufsätze*. Munich: K. G. Sauer, 1988.
Valdeón Baruque, Julio. *Judíos y conversos en la Castilla medieval*. Valladolid: Universidad de Valladolid, 2000.
Van den Berg, Jan, and Ernestine G. E. van der Wall, eds. *Jewish-Christian Relations in the Seventeenth Century: Studies and Documents*. Dordrecht: Kluwer Academic Publishers, 1988.
Waton, Marie-Dominique. "Des bains juifs à Strasbourg." *Cahiers Alsaciens d'archéologie, d'art et d'histoire* 29 (1986): 53–59.
Wasserfall, Rahel R., ed. *Women and Water: Menstruation in Jewish Life and Law*. Hanover: Brandeis University Press, 1999.
Waugh, Scott L. and Peter D. Diehl, eds. *Christendom and Its Discontents: Exclusion, Persecution, and Rebellion, 1000–1500*. Cambridge: Cambridge University Press, 1996.
Weber, Annette. "Die Entwicklung des Judenbildes im 13. Jahrhundert und sein Platz in der Lettner- und Tympanonskulptur: Fragen zum Verhältnis von Ikonographie und Stil." *Städel-Jahrbuch* 14 (1993): 35–54.
——. "Glaube und Wissen—Ecclesia et Synagoga." In *Wissenspopularisierung: Konzepte der Wissensverbreitung im Wandel*, ed. Carsten Kretschmann. Berlin: Akademie, 2003, pp. 89–126.
Weber, Paul. *Geistliches Schauspiel und kirchliche Kunst in ihrem Verhältnis erläutert an einer Ikonographie der Kirche und Synagoge*. Stuttgart: Ebner und Seubert, 1894.
Weis, Adolf. "Die 'Synagoge' am Münster zu Straßburg. Ein Beitrag zur historischen Betrachtung mittelalterlicher Kunst." *Das Münster* 1, no. 3/4 (1947): 65–80.
Weiss, Carl Theodor. *Geschichte und rechtliche Stellung der Juden im Fürstbistum Straßburg*. Bonn: Hanstein, 1896.
Wenninger, Markus J. *Man bedarf keiner Juden mehr. Ursachen und Hintergrunde ihrer Vertreibung aus den deutschen Reichsstädten im 15. Jahrhundert*. Vienna: Böhlau, 1981.
Weyl, Robert and Marie-Dominique Waton. "Découverte de deux inscriptions hébraïques, Rue des Juifs à Strasbourg." *Cahiers Alsaciens d'archéologie, d'art et d'histoire* 30 (1987): 145–147.
Williams, A. Lukyn. *Adversus Judaeos: A Bird's-Eye View of Christian Apologiae until the Renaissance*. Cambridge: Cambridge University Press, 1935.
Willoweit, Dietmar. "Vom Königsschutz zur Kammerknechtschaft: Anmerkungen zum Rechtsstatus der Juden im Hochmittelalter." In *Geschichte und Kultur des Judentums: Eine Vorlesungsreihe an der Julius-Maximilians-Universität Würzburg*, ed. Karlheinz Müller and Klaus Wittstadt. Würzburg: Schöningh, 1988, pp. 71–89.
Wilson, Stephen G., ed. *Anti-Judaism in Early Christianity*. 2 vols. Waterloo, Ontario: Wilfrid Laurier University Press, 1986.

Wisch, Barbara. "Vested Interest: Redressing Jews on Michelangelo's Sistine Ceiling," *Artibus et historiae* 48 (2003): 143–172.

Wischnitzer, Rachel. *The Architecture of the European Synagogue*. Philadelphia: Jewish Publication Society of America, 1964.

Wistrich, Robert S. *Demonizing the Other: Antisemitism, Racism, and Xenophobia.* Studies in Antisemitism, Vidal Sassoon International Center for the Study of Antisemitism, The Hebrew University of Jerusalem, vol. 4. Amsterdam: Overseas Publishers Association and Harwood Academic Publishers, 1999.

Wolfson, Elliot R. "Asceticism and Eroticism in Medieval Jewish Exegesis." In *With Reverence for the Word: Medieval Scriptural Exegesis in Judaism, Christianity and Islam*, ed. Jane Dammen McAuliffe, Barry Walfish and Joseph Ward Goering. New York: Oxford University Press, 2003, pp. 92–118.

Wood, Diana, ed. *Christianity and Judaism: Papers Read at the 1991 Summer Meeting and the 1992 Winter Meeting of the Ecclesiastical History Society*. Studies in Church History, vol. 29. Oxford: Blackwell (for the Ecclesiastical History Society), 1992.

Young, Karl. *The Drama of the Medieval Church*. 2 vols. Oxford: Clarendon Press, 1933.

Yuval, Israel Jacob. *Two Nations in Your Womb: Perceptions of Jews and Christians in Late Antiquity and the Middle Ages*, trans. Barbara Harshov and Jonathan Chipman. Berkeley: University of California Press, 2006.

Zafran, Eric M. "The Iconography of Antisemitism: A Study of the Representation of the Jews in the Visual Arts of Europe 1400–1600." Ph.D. dissertation, New York University; repr. Ann Arbor, 1973.

Zell, Michael. *Reframing Rembrandt: Jews and the Christian Image in Seventeenth Century Amsterdam*. Berkeley: University of California Press, 2002.

INDEX

PLATES SECTION

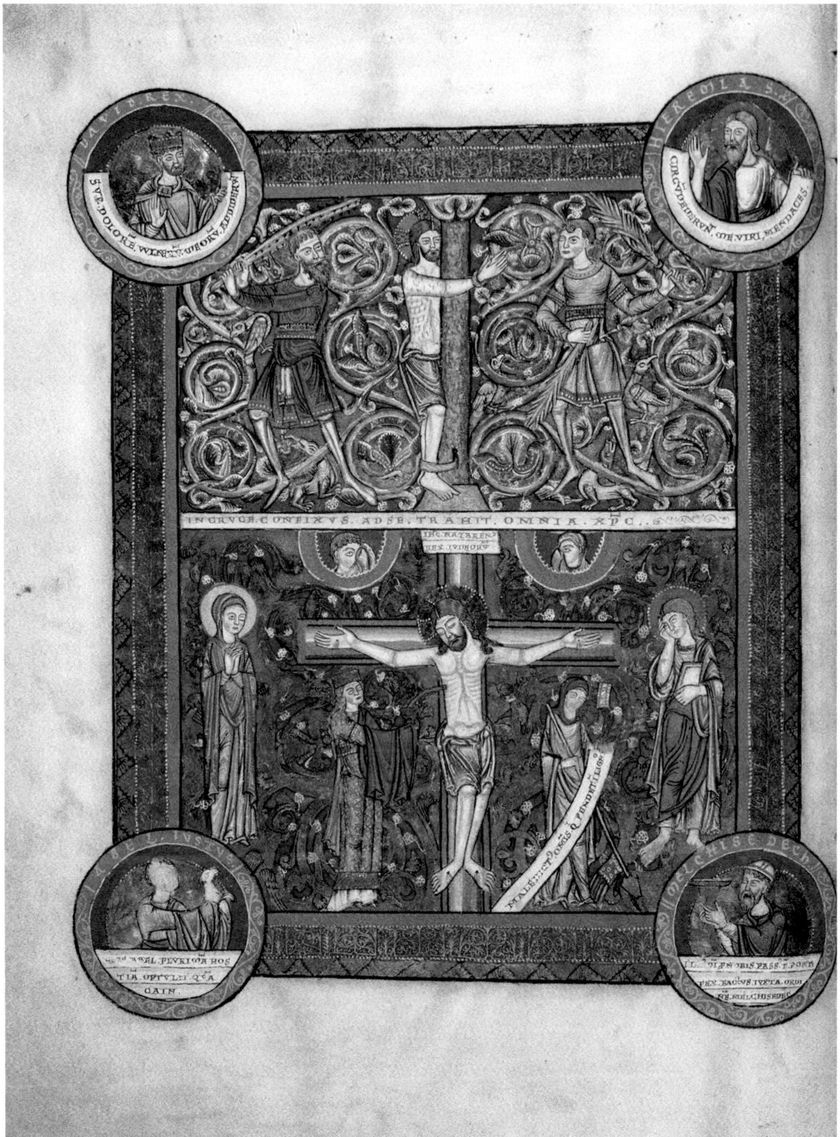

Figure 1. Ecclesia and Synagoga flanking the Crucifixion, illumination from the *Gospels of Henry the Lion*, c. 1175. Herzog August Bibliothek Wolfenbüttel, Cod. Guelf. 105 Noviss. 2°, fol. 170v.

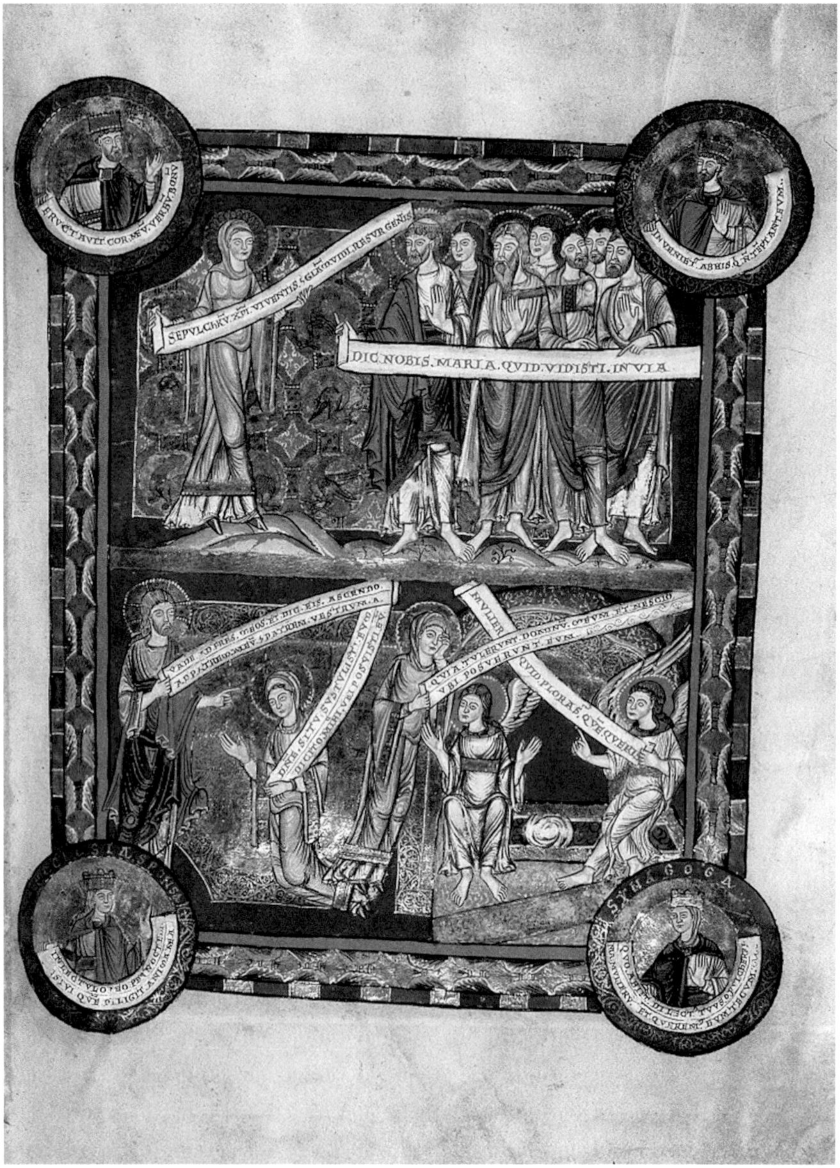

Figure 2. Lower roundels: Ecclesia and Synagoga as Christ's Brides, illumination from the *Gospels of Henry the Lion*, c. 1175. Herzog August Bibliothek Wolfenbüttel, Cod. Guelf. 105 Noviss. 2°, fol. 171r.

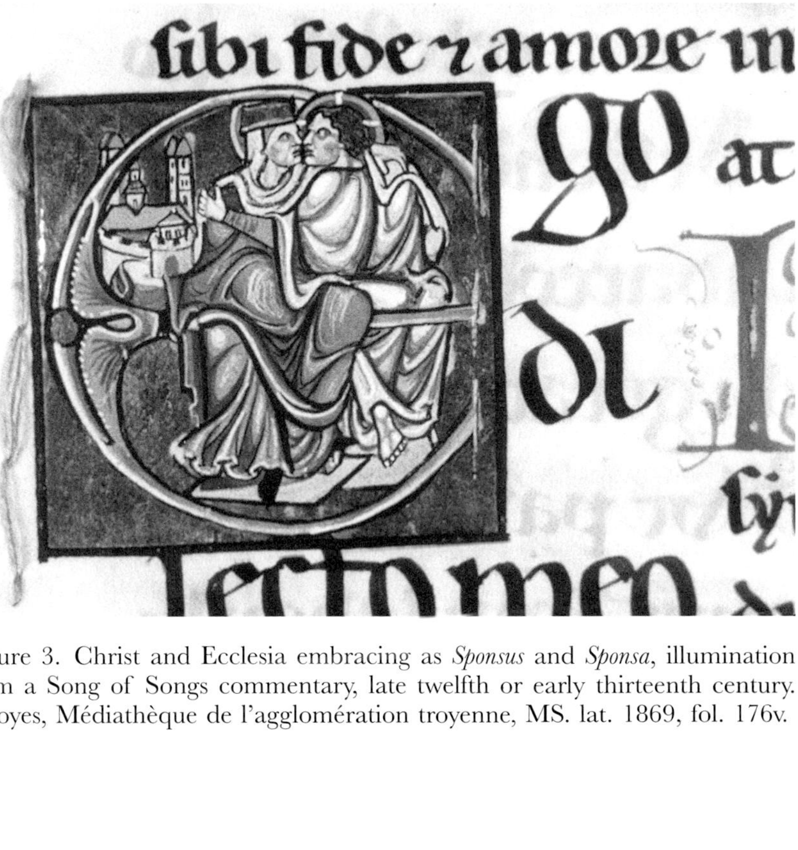

Figure 3. Christ and Ecclesia embracing as *Sponsus* and *Sponsa*, illumination from a Song of Songs commentary, late twelfth or early thirteenth century. Troyes, Médiathèque de l'agglomération troyenne, MS. lat. 1869, fol. 176v.

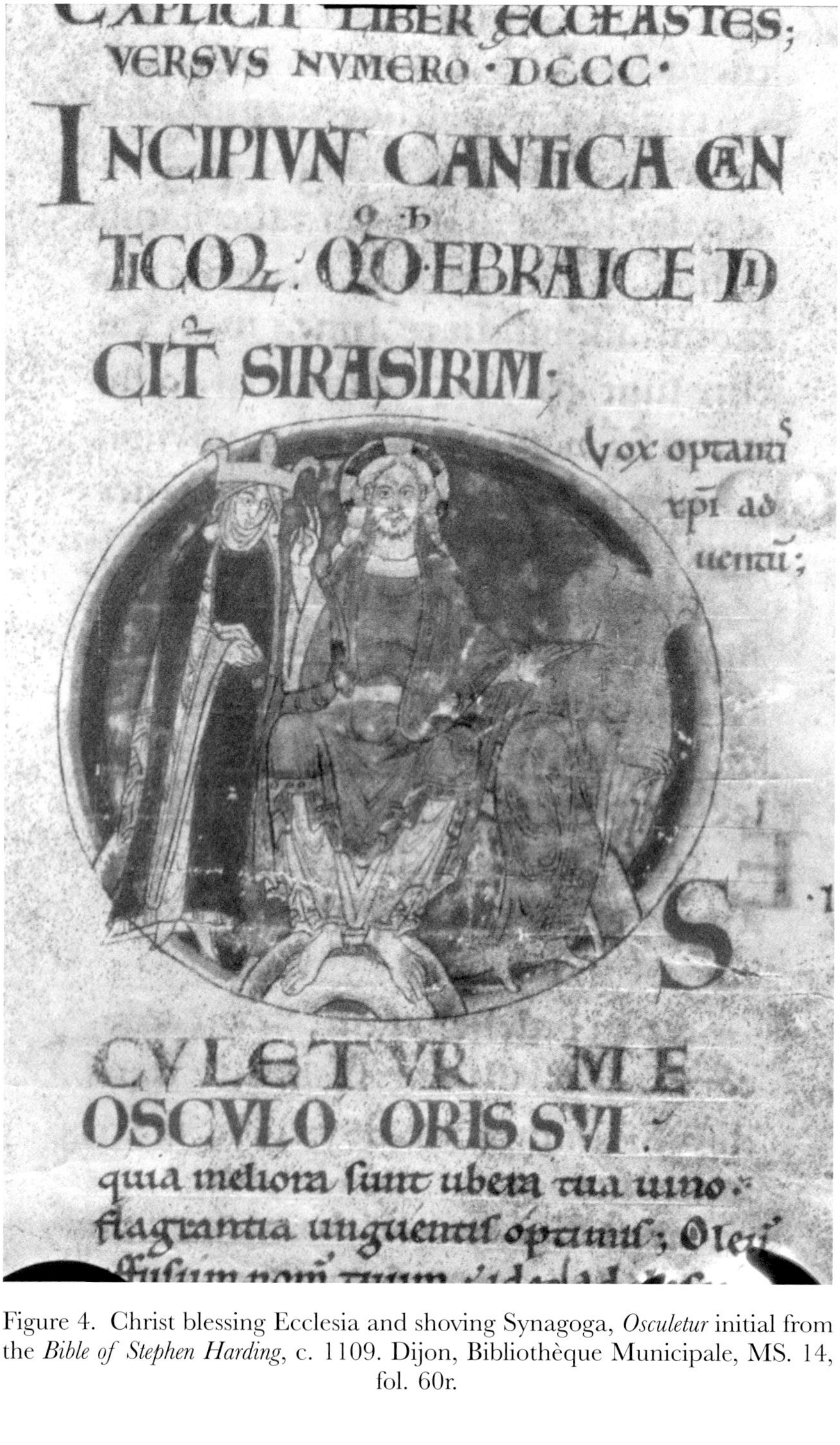

Figure 4. Christ blessing Ecclesia and shoving Synagoga, *Osculetur* initial from the *Bible of Stephen Harding*, c. 1109. Dijon, Bibliothèque Municipale, MS. 14, fol. 60r.

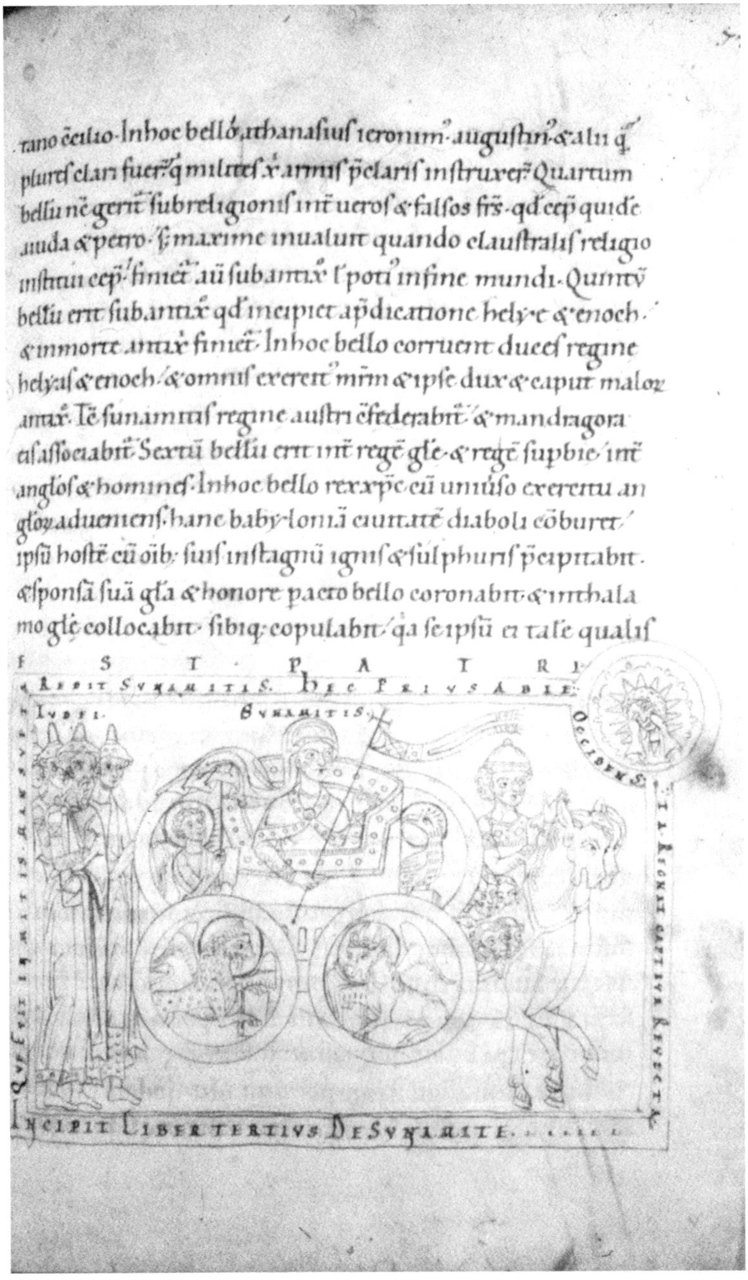

Figure 5. Synagoga as the Sunamite, illumination from a c. 1140 copy of Honorius Augustodunensis's *Expositio in Cantica canticorum*. Munich, Bayerische Staatsbibliothek, Cod. Lat. 4550, fol. 77r.

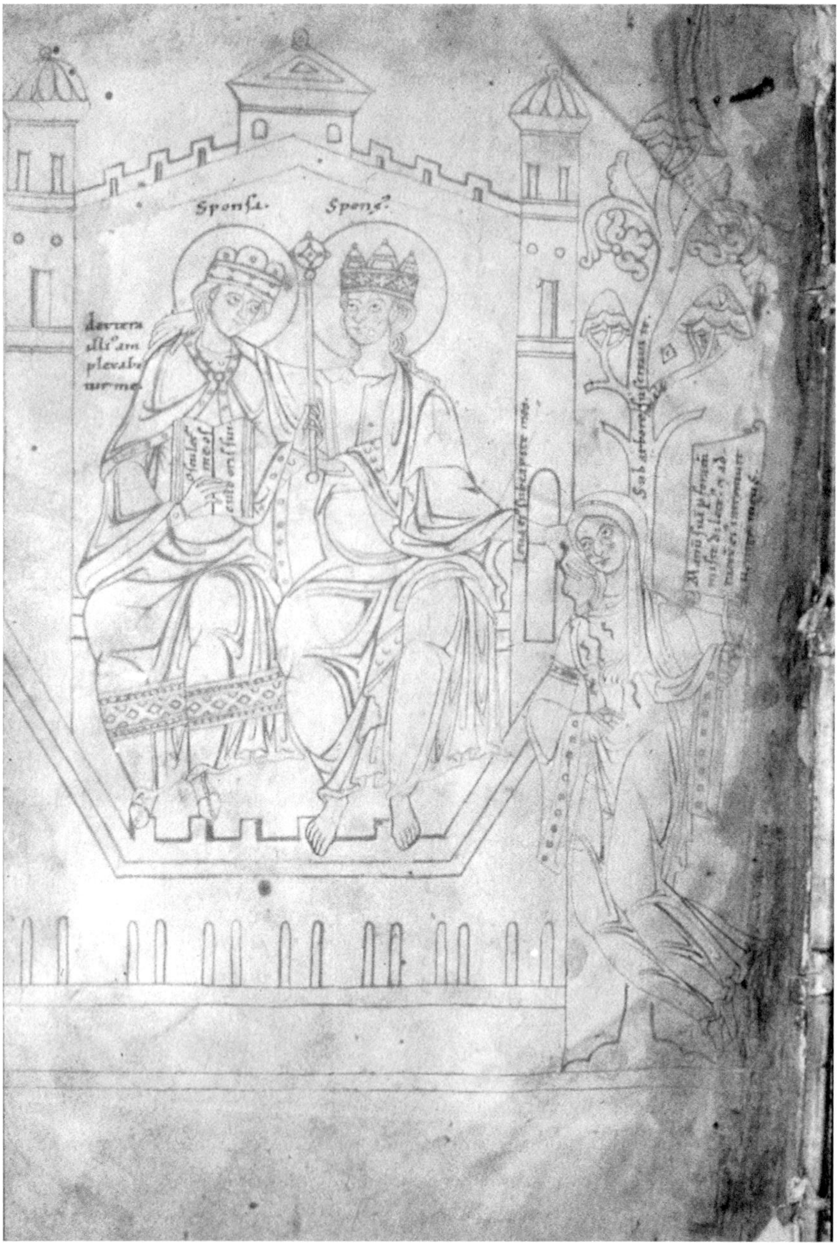

Figure 6. *Sponsus* embracing the *Sponsa* and reaching out to Synagoga as the Sunamite, frontispiece to a c. 1140 copy of Honorius Augustodunensis's *Sigillum beatae Mariae* and *Expositio in Cantica canticorum*. Munich, Bayerische Staatsbibliothek, Cod. Lat. 4550, fol. 1v.

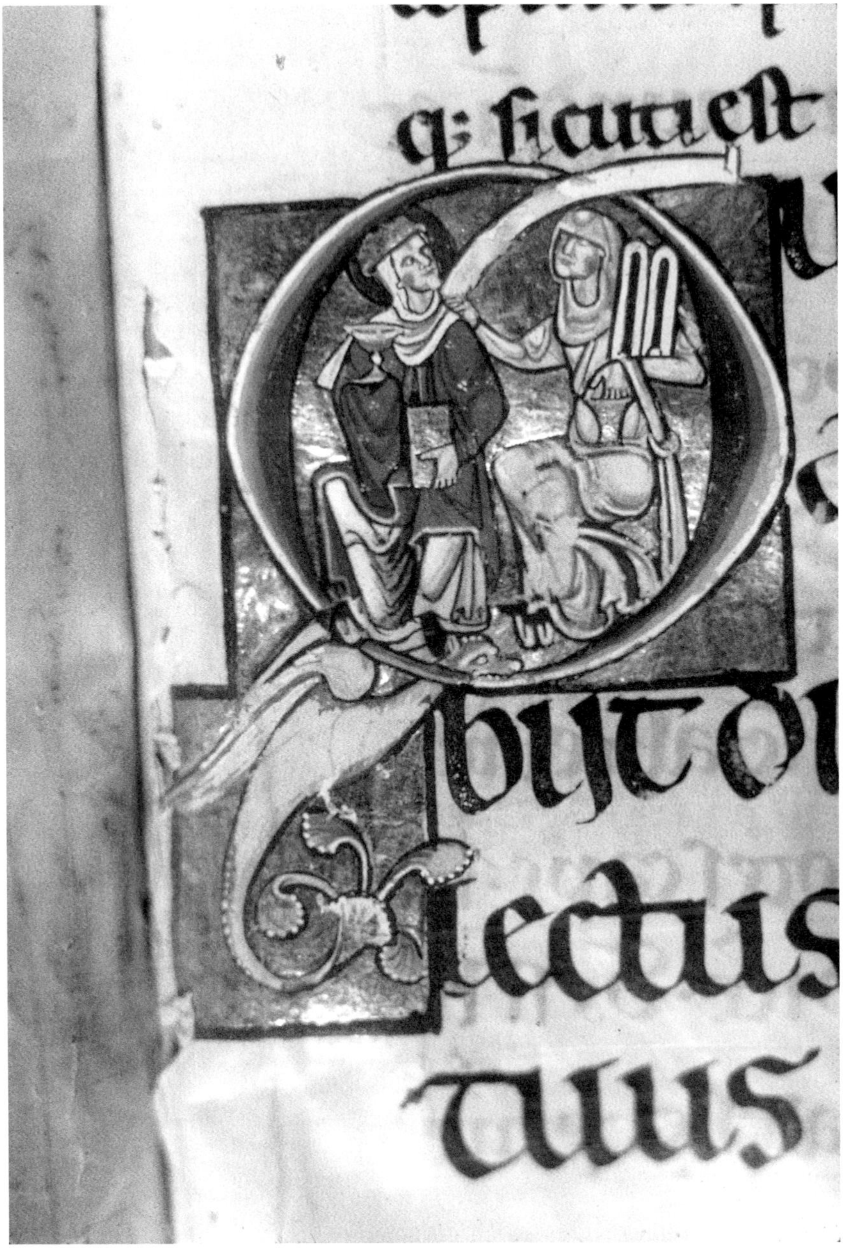

Figure 7. Synagoga rests her hand on Ecclesia's shoulder, illumination from a Song of Songs commentary, late twelfth or early thirteenth century. Troyes, Médiathèque de l'agglomération troyenne, MS. lat. 1869, fol. 173r.

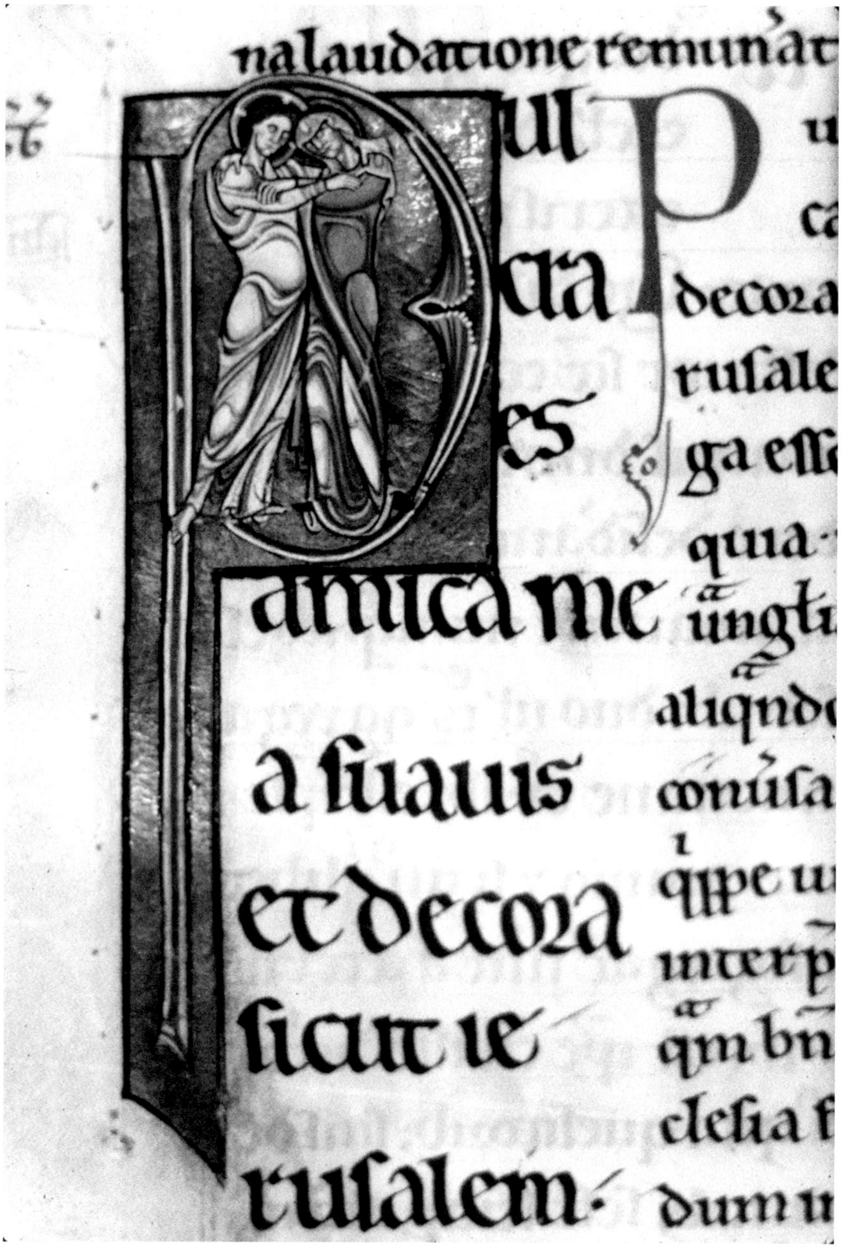

Figure 8. Christ and haloed Synagoga embracing as *Sponsus* and *Sponsa*, illumination from a Song of Songs commentary, late twelfth or early thirteenth century. Troyes, Médiathèque de l'agglomération troyenne, MS. lat. 1869, fol. 177v.

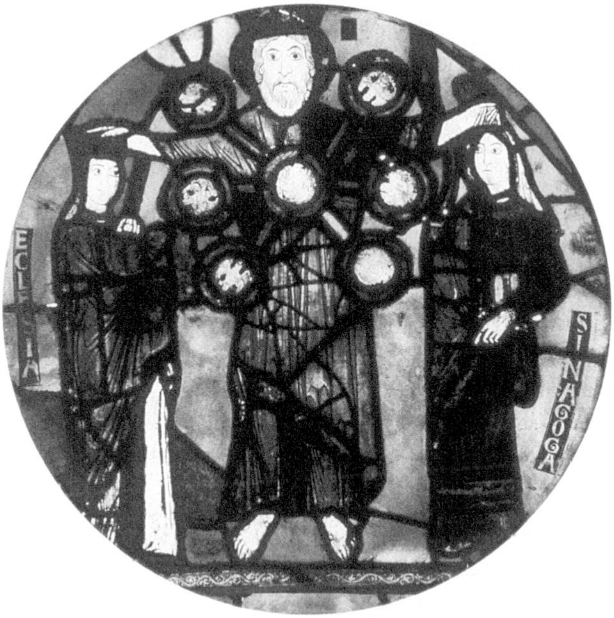

Figure 9. Christ crowning Ecclesia and unveiling Synagoga. Stained glass panel, Abbey Church of Saint-Denis, c. 1145.

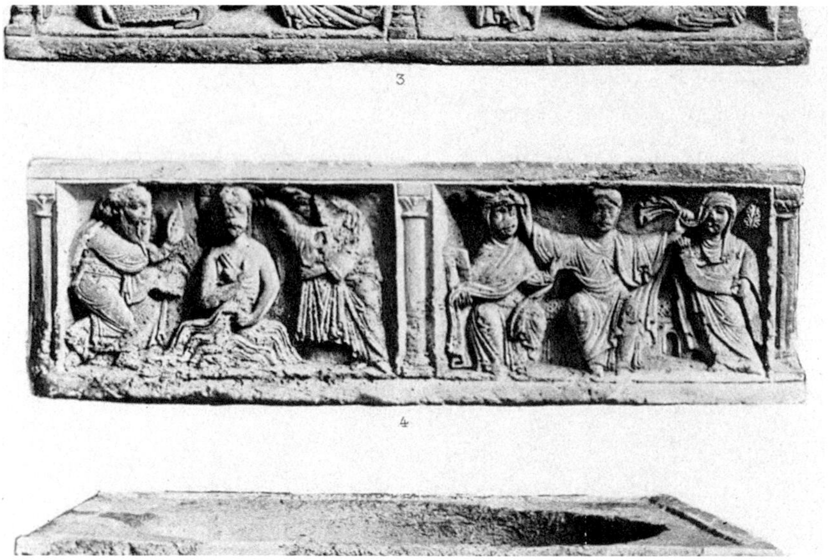

Figure 10. Christ crowning Ecclesia and unveiling Synagoga, detail of stone baptismal font from Sainte-Larme de Sélincourt, mid-twelfth century. Amiens, Musée de Picardie.

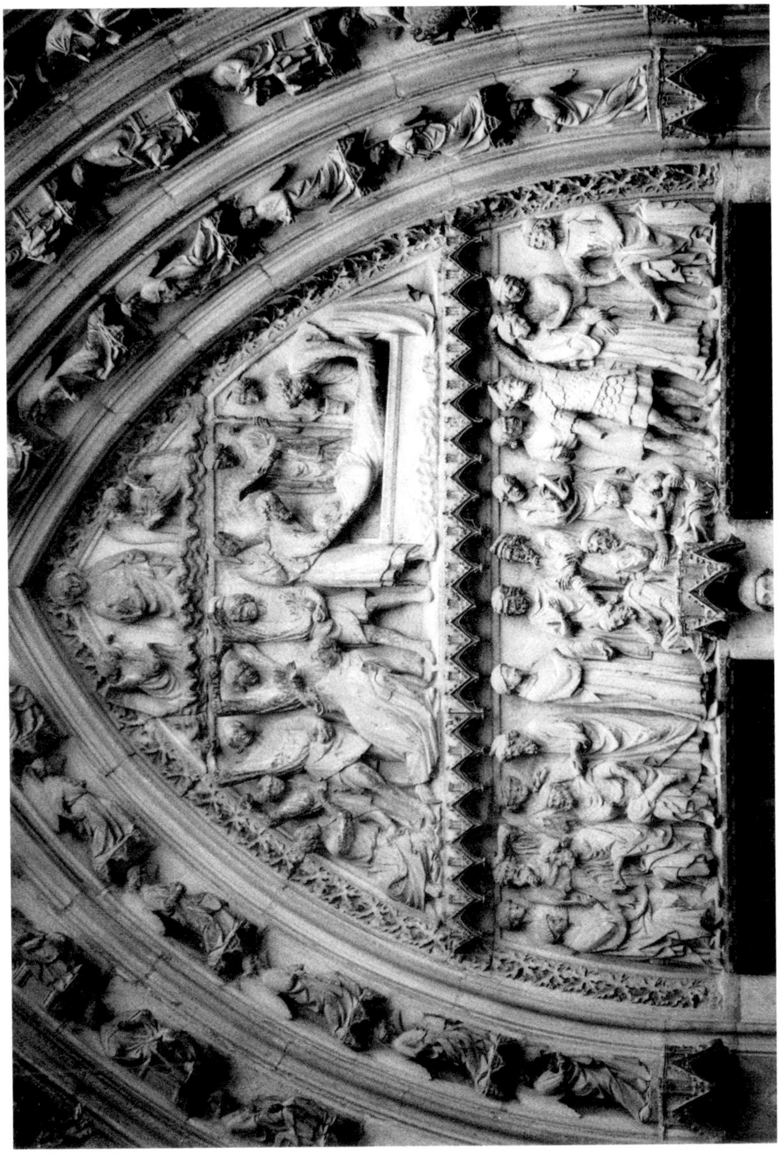

Figure 1. St. Stephen portal tympanum, south transept, Cathedral of Notre-Dame, Paris, 1258. Author's photo.

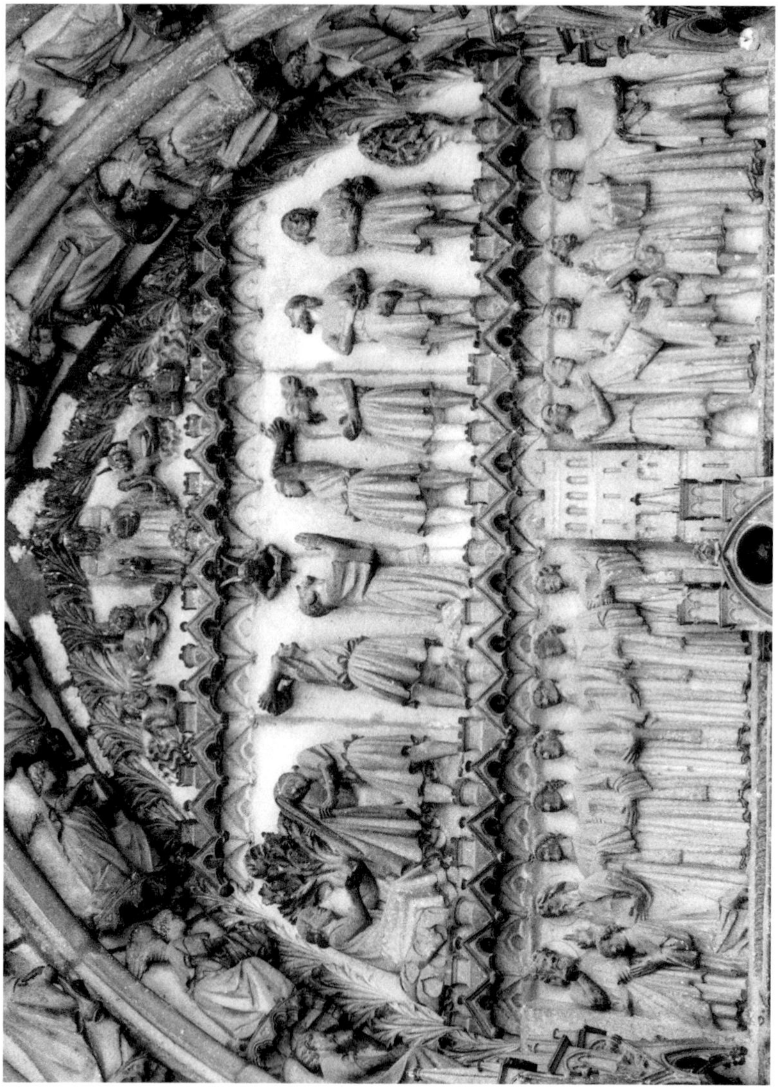

Figure 2. St. Stephen portal tympanum, west façade, Cathedral of St. Etienne, Bourges, mid-thirteenth century. Author's photo.

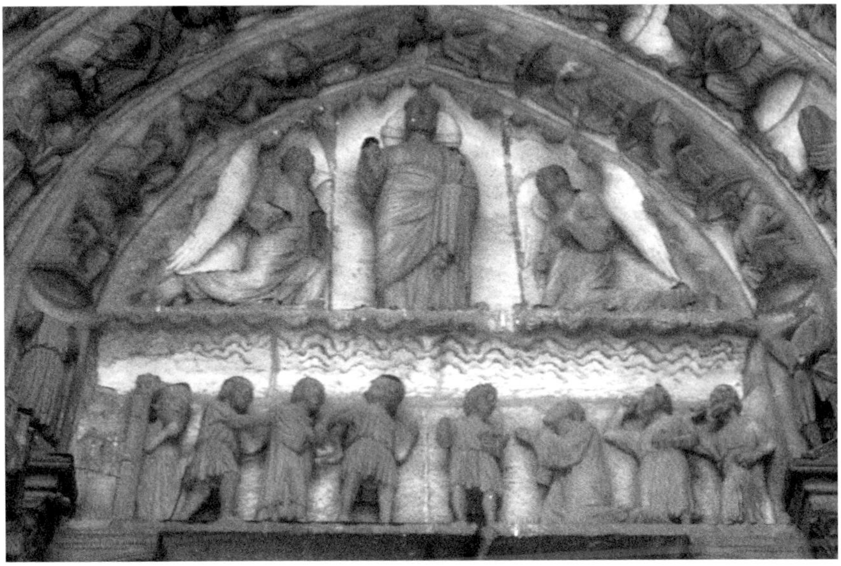

Figure 3. St. Stephen portal tympanum, south transept, Cathedral of Notre-Dame, Chartres, 1215. Author's photo.

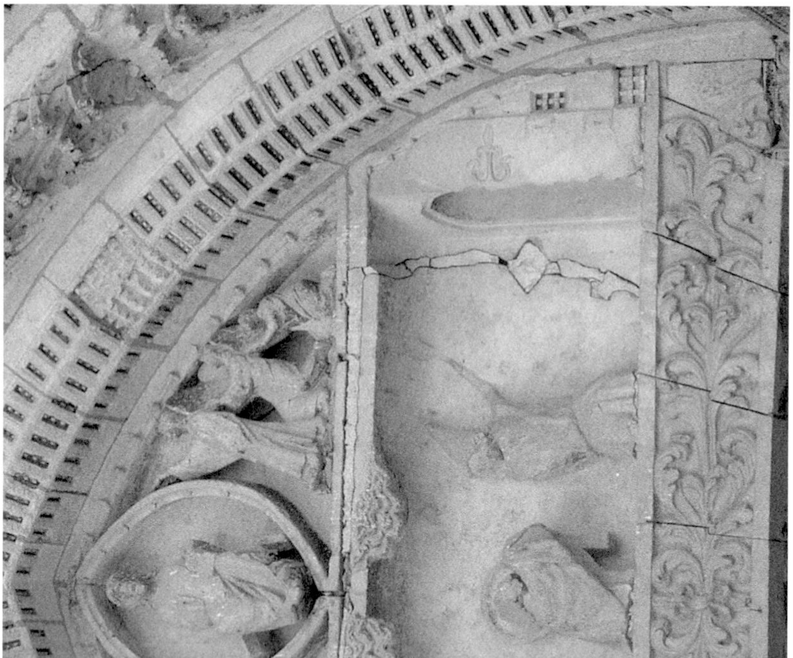

Figure 4. St. Stephen portal tympanum, west façade, Cathedral of Notre-Dame, Rouen, c. 1240. Author's photo.

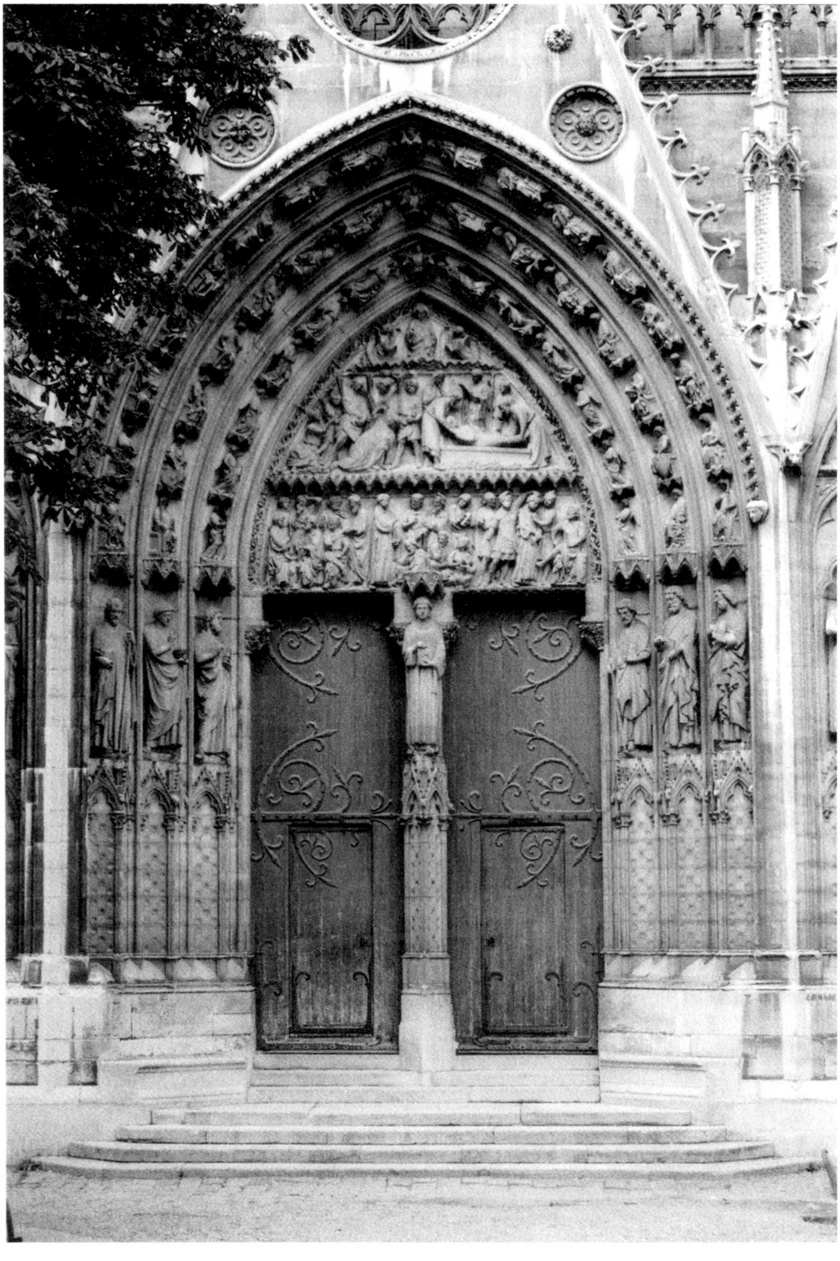

Figure 5. St. Stephen portal, south transept, Cathedral of Notre-Dame, Paris, 1258. Author's photo.

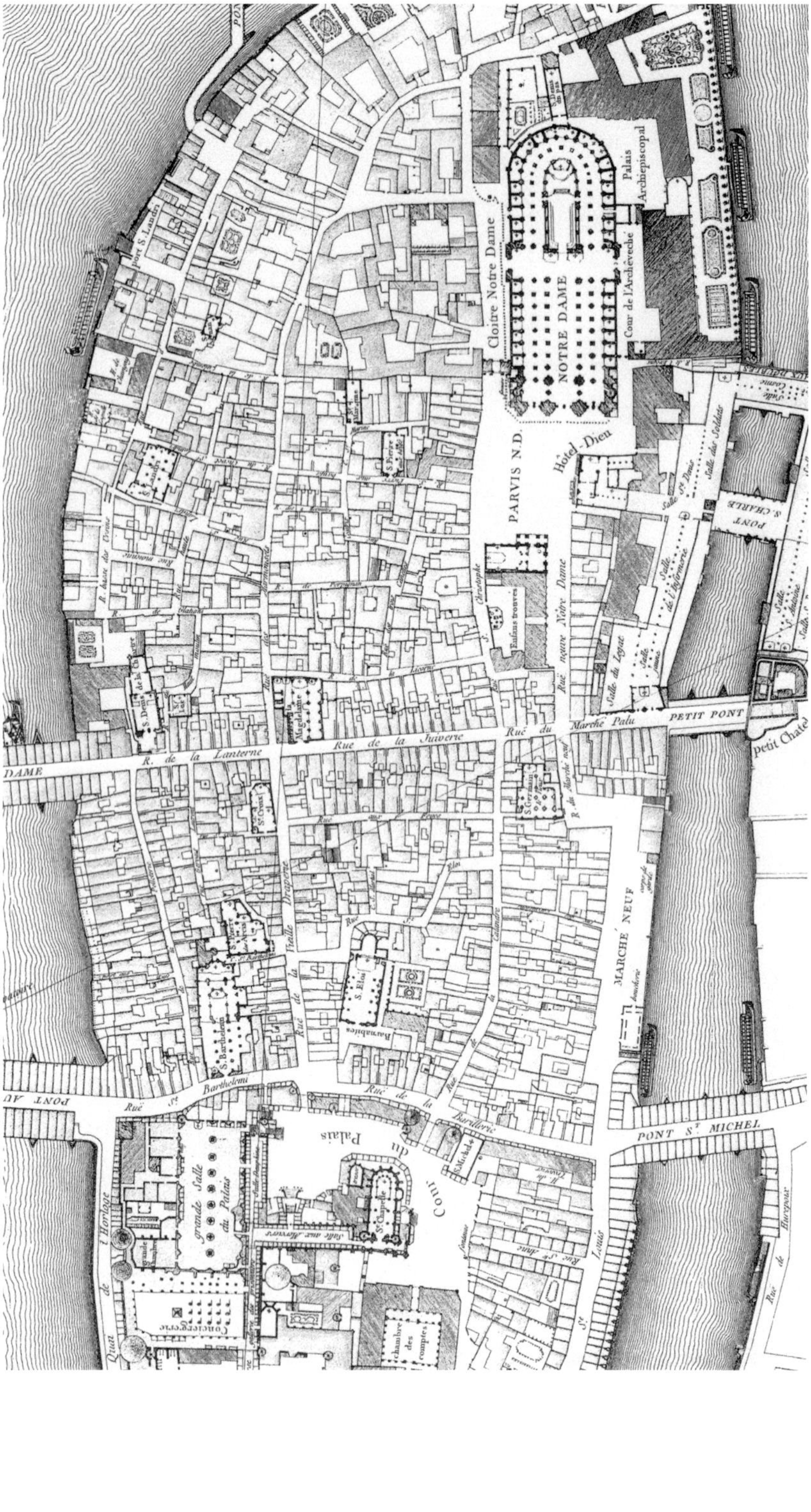

Figure 6. *Plan detaillé de la Cité* by M. l'Abbé Delagrive, 1754, showing the arrangement of the episcopal complex, which varied little from its late-medieval arrangement, and the location of the Sainte Chapelle to the left. Reproduction published by Historic Urban Plans, Inc., Ithaca, NY.

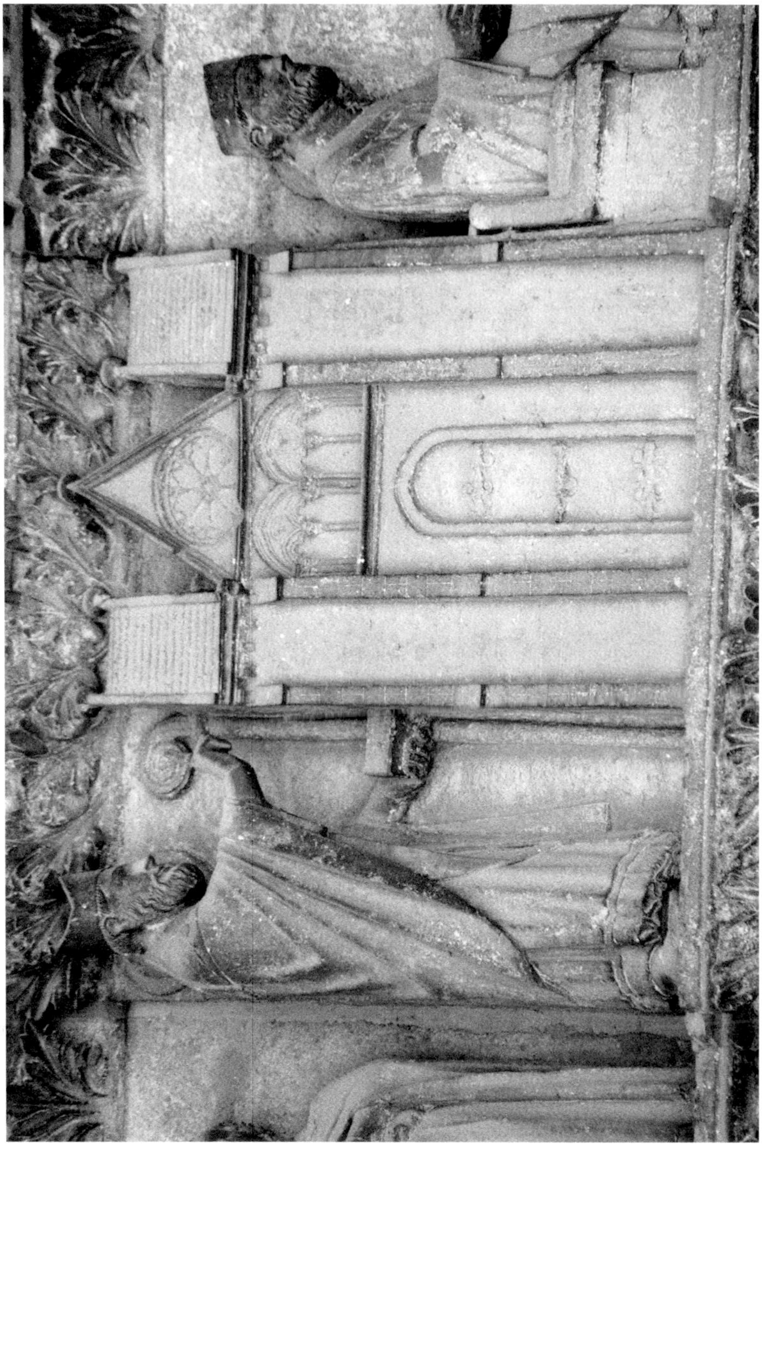

Figure 7. St. Ursin depositing the relics of Stephen into the church, St. Ursin portal tympanum, west façade, Cathedral of St. Etienne, Bourges, mid-thirteenth century. Author's photo.

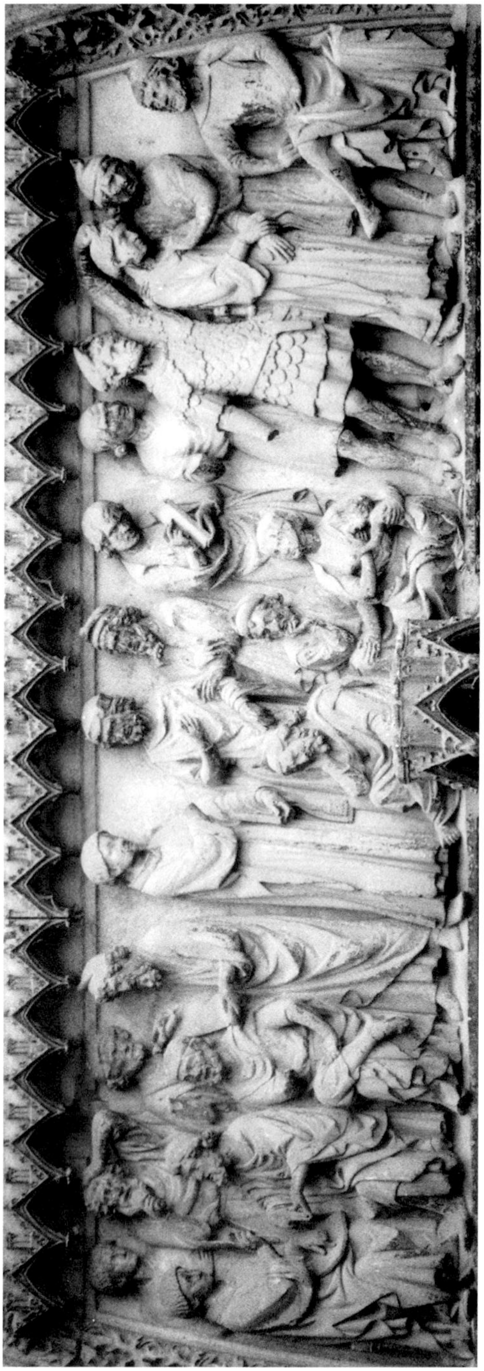

Figure 8. View of the lower register, St. Stephen portal tympanum, south transept, Cathedral of Notre-Dame, Paris, 1258. Author's photo.

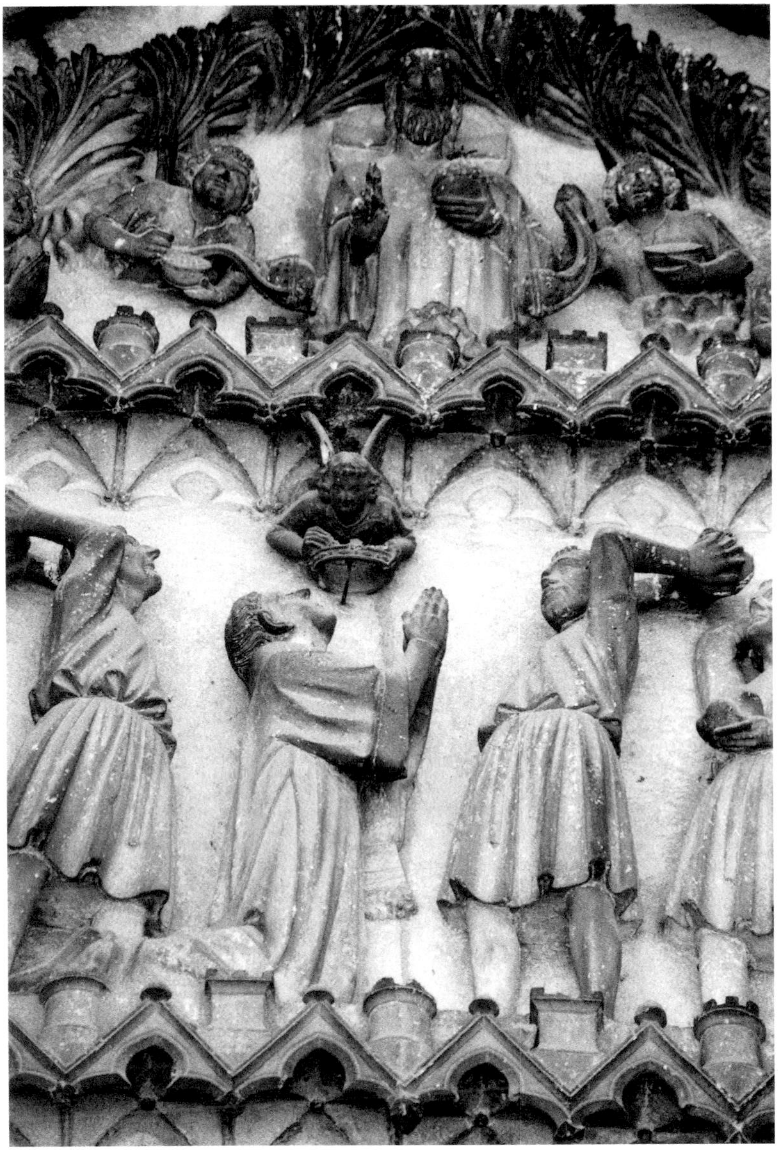

Figure 9. St. Stephen crowned by angels as he is stoned, St. Stephen portal tympanum, west façade, Cathedral of St. Etienne, Bourges, mid-thirteenth century. Author's photo.

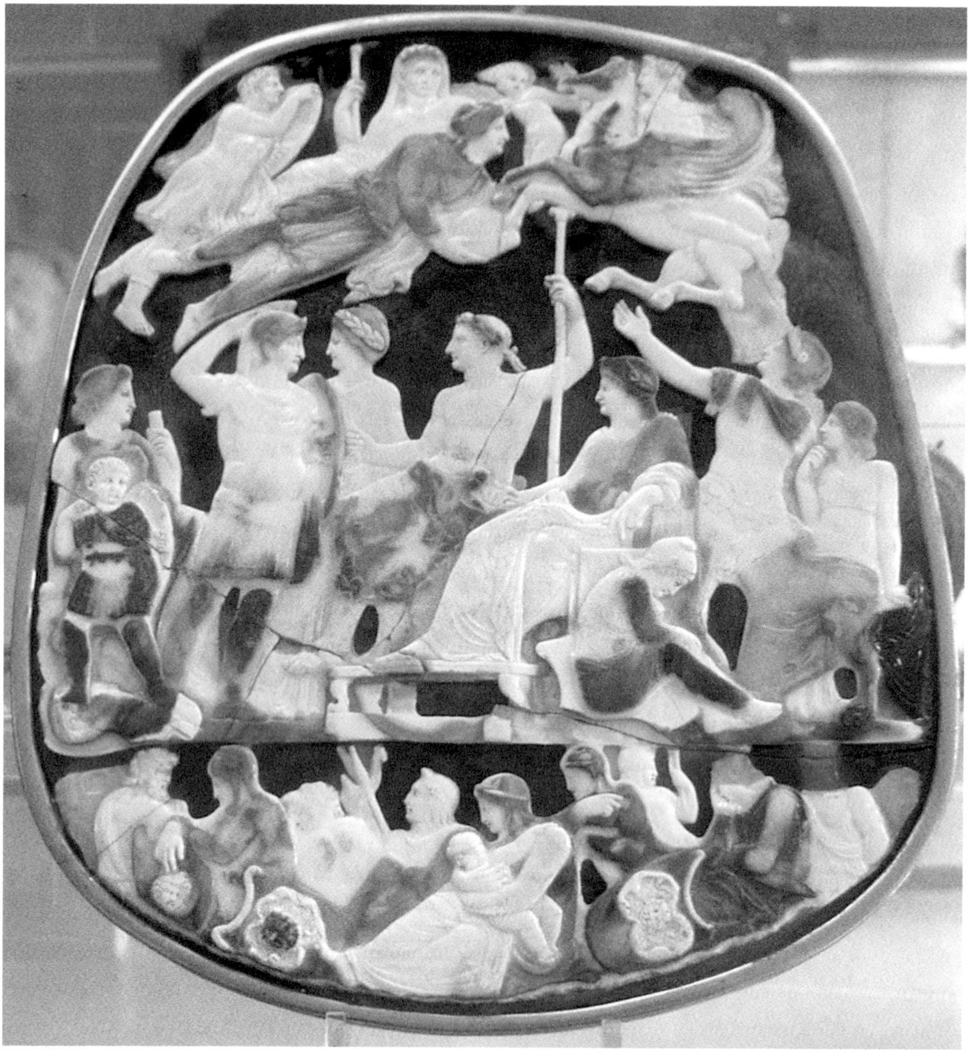

Figure 10. *Gemma Tiberiana*, also known as the Grand Camée de France, Cabinet des Estampes, Bab. 264, Bibliothèque Nationale de France.

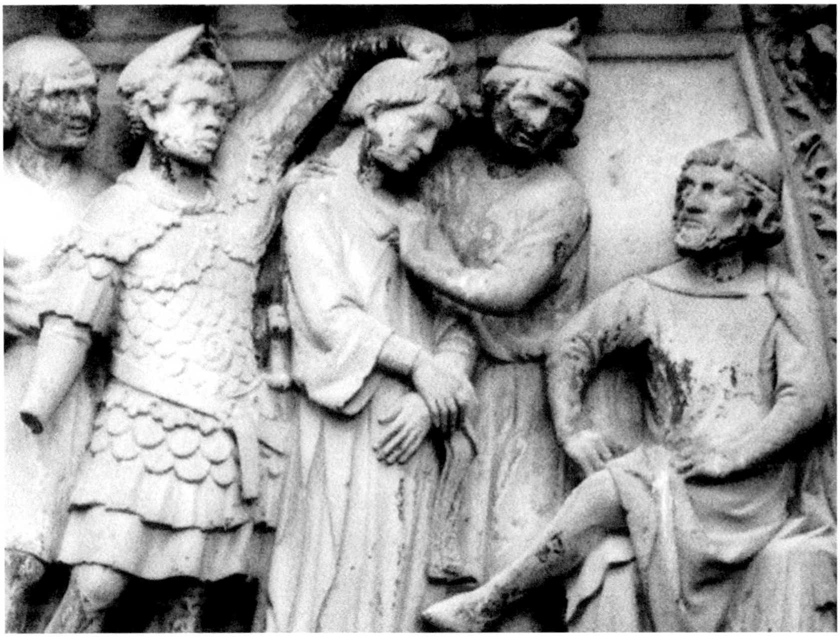

Figure 11. Arrest of Stephen, St. Stephen portal tympanum, south transept, Cathedral of Notre-Dame, Paris, 1258. Author's photo.

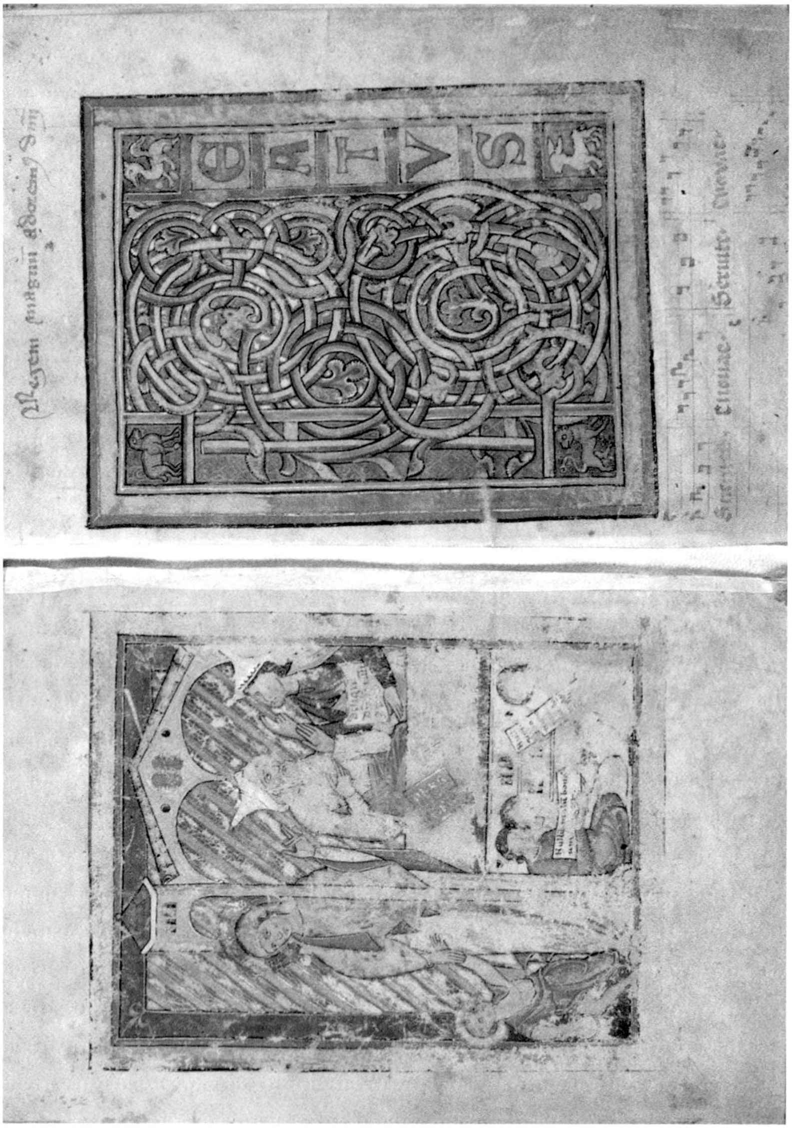

Figure 1. Mary taking Jesus to school, from the Waldkirch Psalter, thirteenth century. Stuttgart, Württembergische Landesbibliothek, Cod. Brev. 4° 125, fol. 10v.

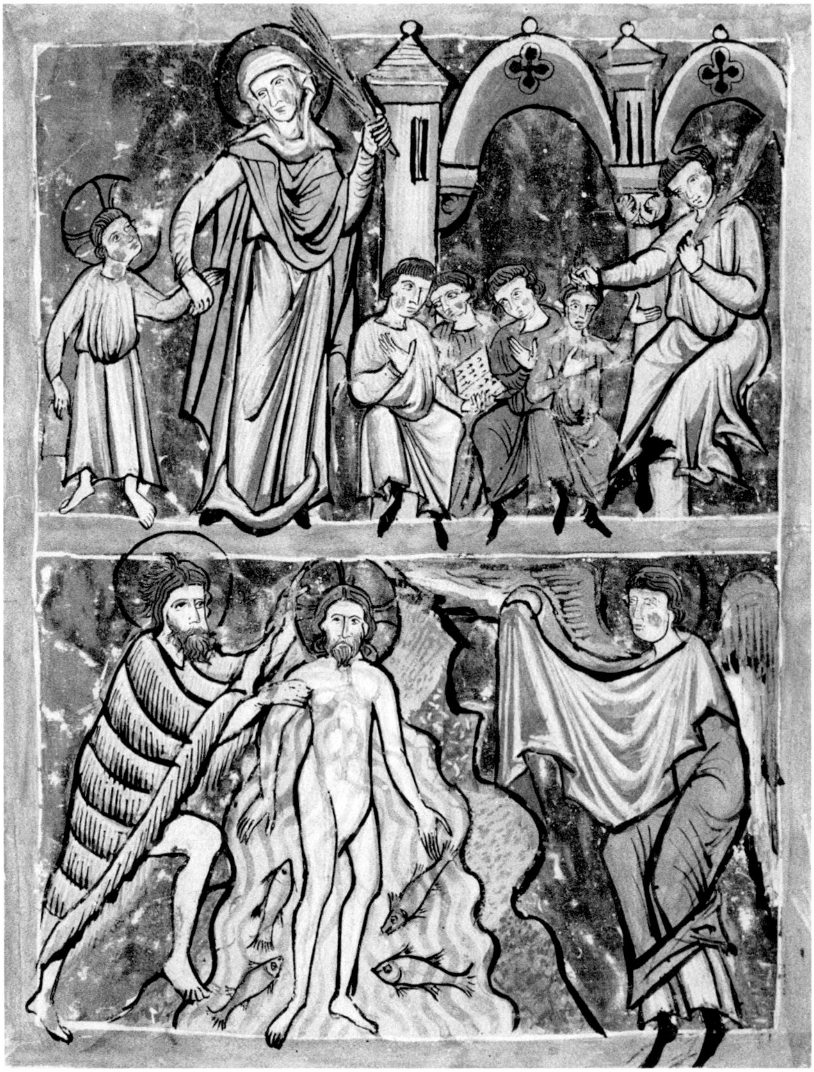

Figure 2. Mary taking Jesus to school and Baptism of Christ, from the Liverpool Psalter, thireenth century. Liverpool, Walker Art Gallery, Ms Mayer 12004, fol. 7r.

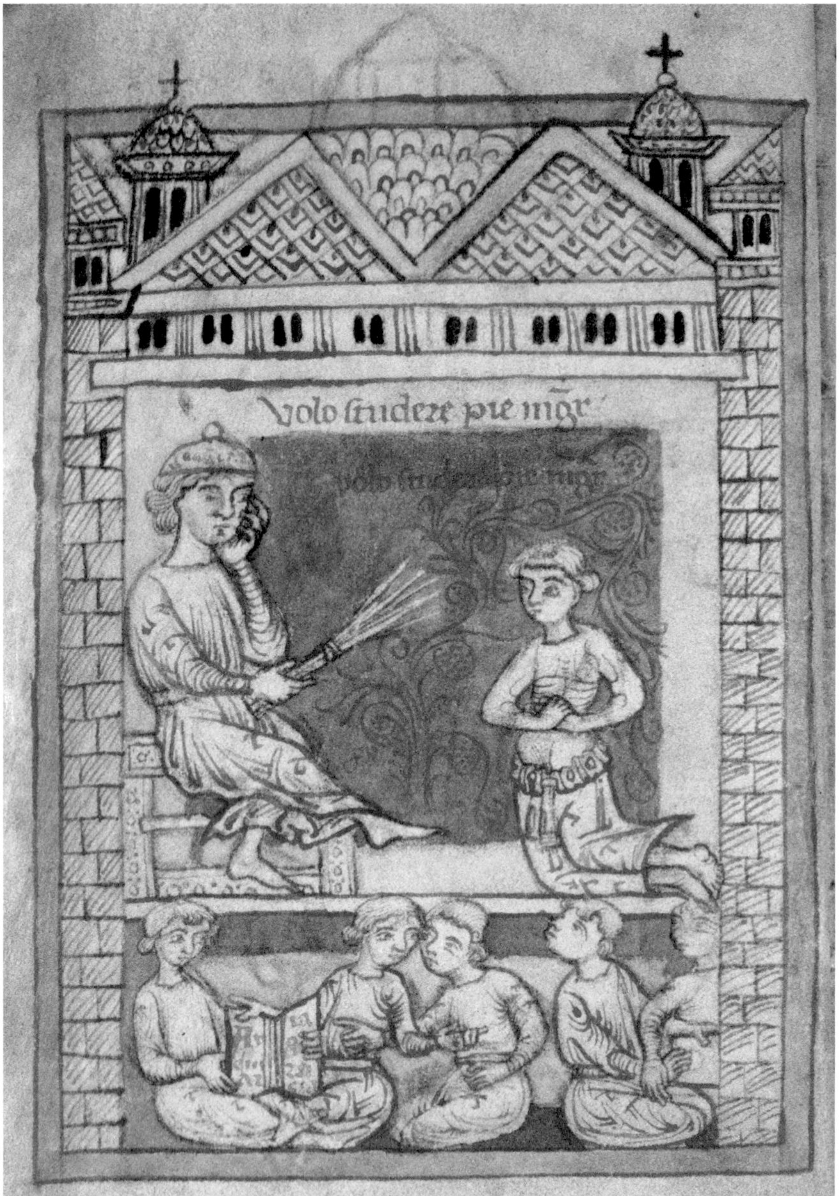

Figure 3. Scene in a Grammar school, frontispiece from a treatise on Grammar, c. 1210–20. Vienna, Österreichische Nationalbibliothek Cod. 2499 (Philol. 396), fol. 1v.

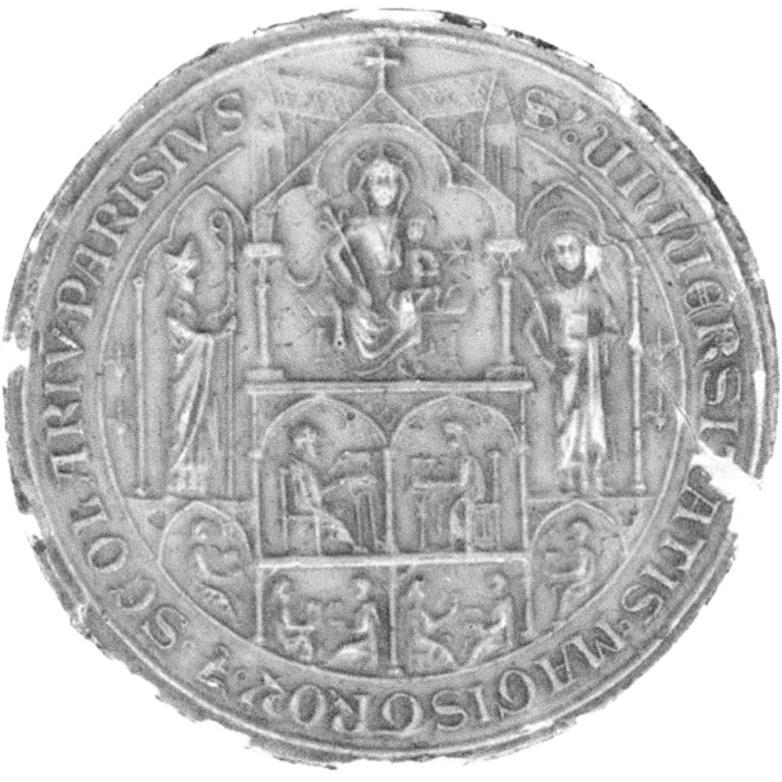

Figure 4. Great Seal of the University of Paris, thirteenth century. Photo source: Graven, "Die Hoheitszeichen der alten Kölner Universität," in *Festschrift zur Erinnerung an die Gründung der alten Universität Köln im Jahre 1388* (1938), p. 404. fig. 28.

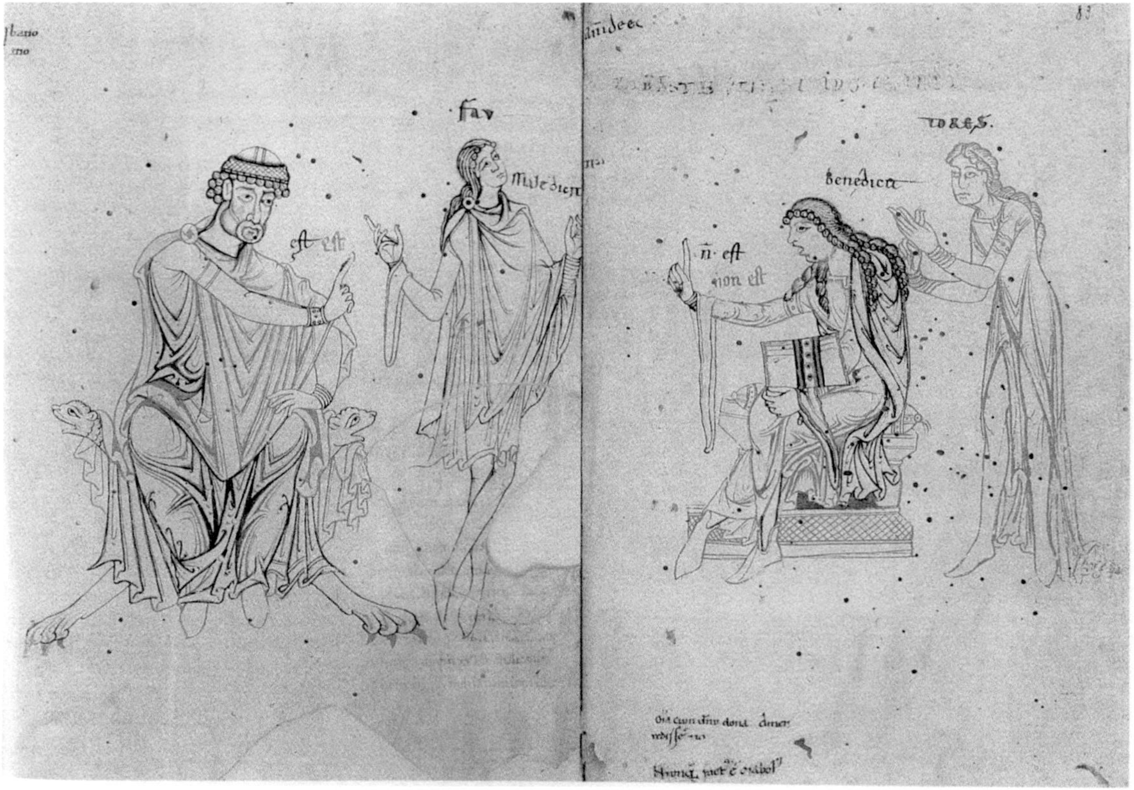

Figure 5. Disputation scene, double-page illustration from a manuscript of *De Sacramentis* by Hugo of St. Victor, two-tone drawing, twelfth-century. Klosterneuburg, Stiftsbibliothek Klosterneuburg, CCl 311, fols. 82v–83r.

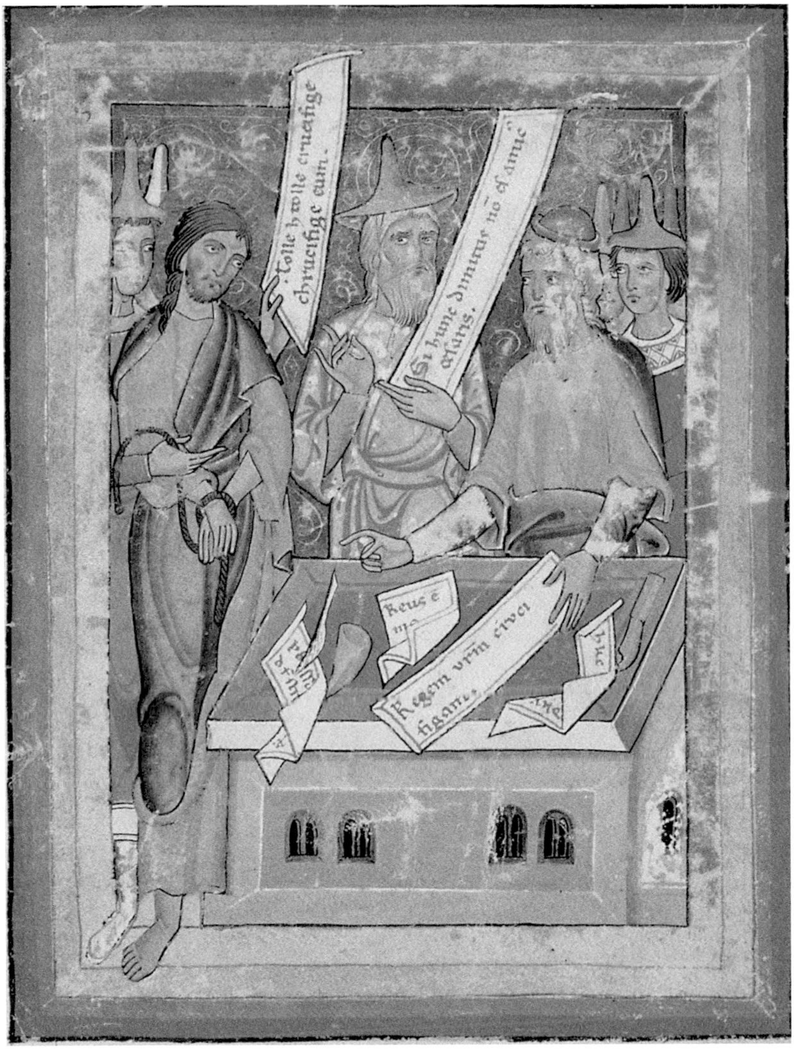

Figure 6. Jesus before Pilate, Stuttgart, from the Waldkirch Psalter, thirteenth century. Stuttgart, Württembergische Landesbibliothek, Cod. Brev. 4° 125, fol. 92.

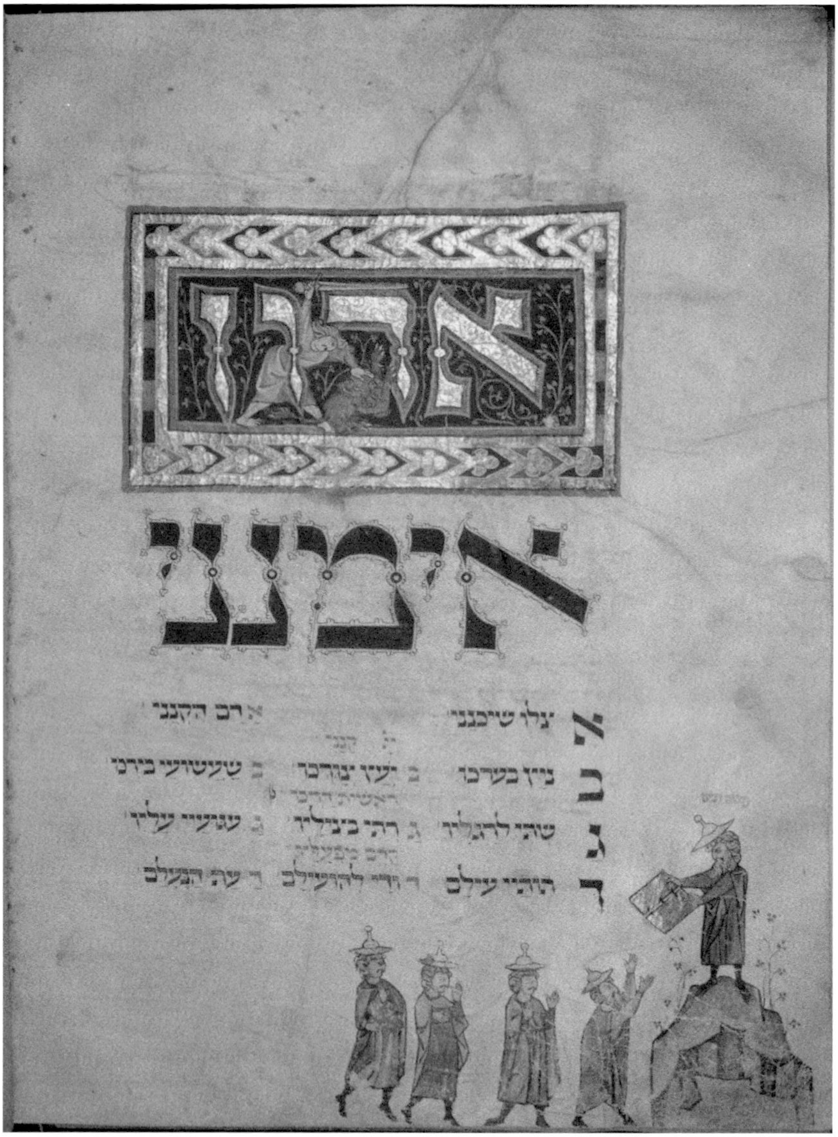

Figure 7. Moses transmitting the Torah from Sinai, from the Leipzig Mahzor (High Holiday Prayerbook). Leipzig, Universitätsbibliothek, Ms Vollers 1102, fol. 130v.

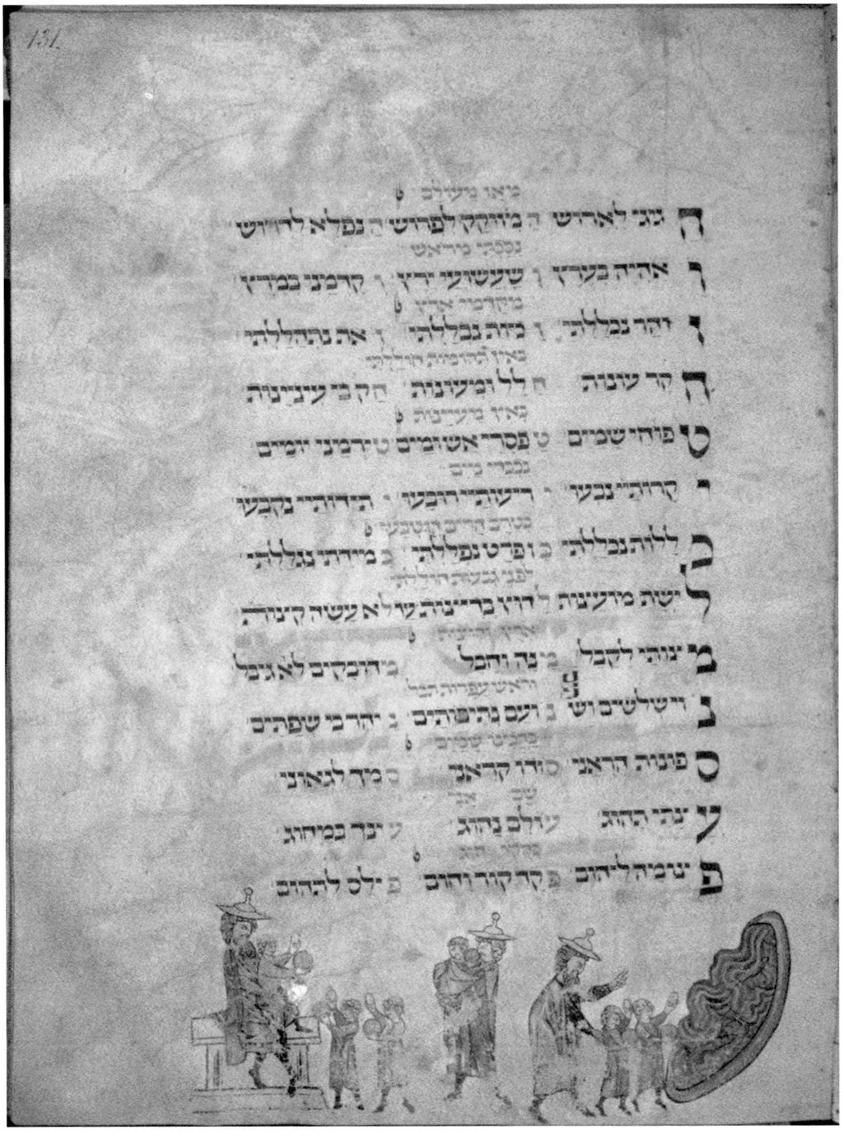

Figure 8. The first day of school, from the Leipzig Mahzor (High Holiday Prayerbook). Leipzig, Universitätsbibliothek, Ms Vollers 1102, fol. 131r.

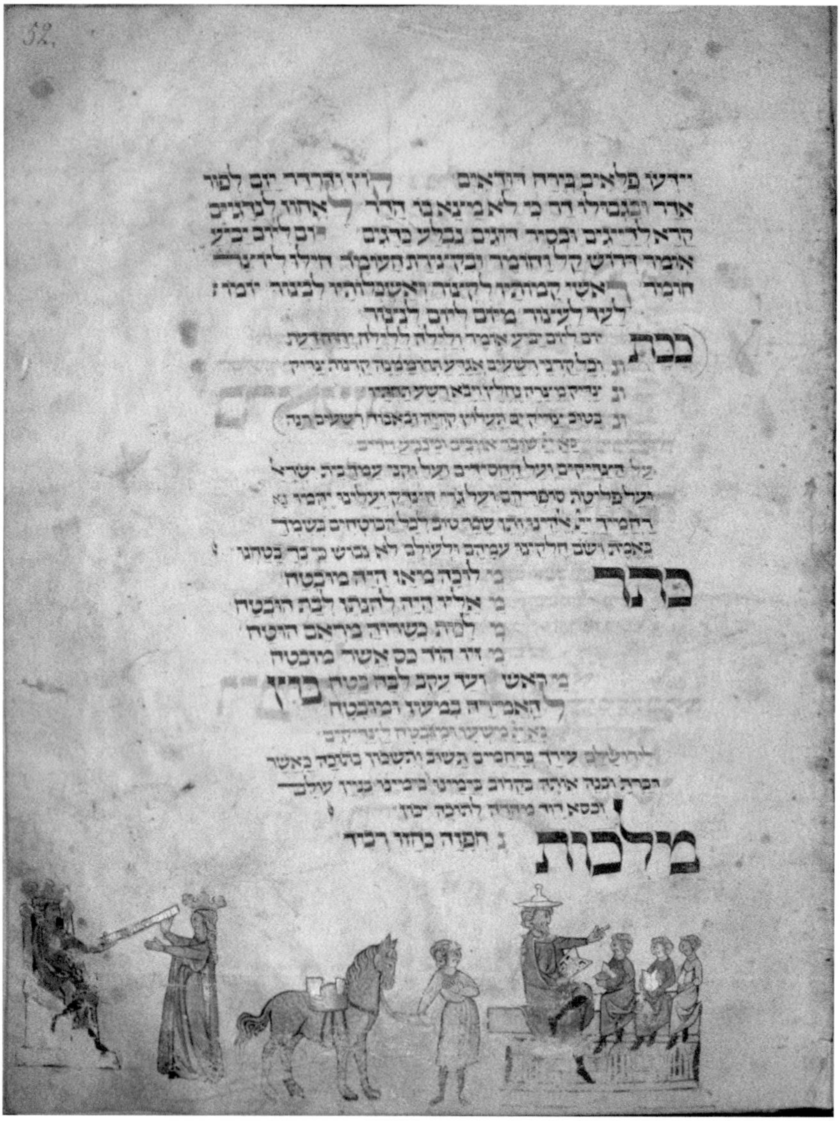

Figure 9. Mordechai teaching, from the Leipzig Mahzor (High Holiday Prayerbook). Leipzig, Universitätsbibliothek, Ms Vollers 1102, fol. 52r.

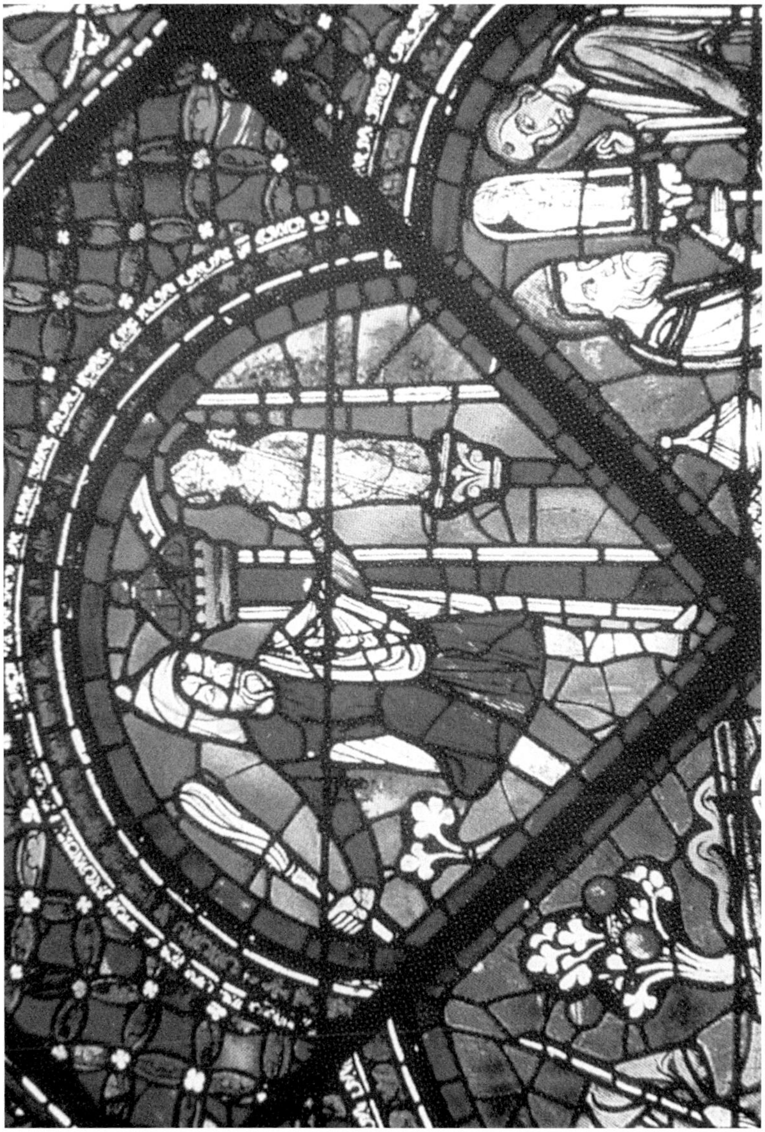

Figure 1. Scene from the *Iconia* Tale: A Jewish man beats a statue of Saint Nicholas, stained glass window in the nave, Chartres Cathedral, 1210–1235 (Corpus Vitrearum window no. 39, panel 26). Photo source: Colette Manhes Deremble, *Les vitraux de la Cathédrale de Chartres: Étude iconographique* (Paris: Comité du Corpus Vitrearum Français et Le Léopard d'Or, 1993).

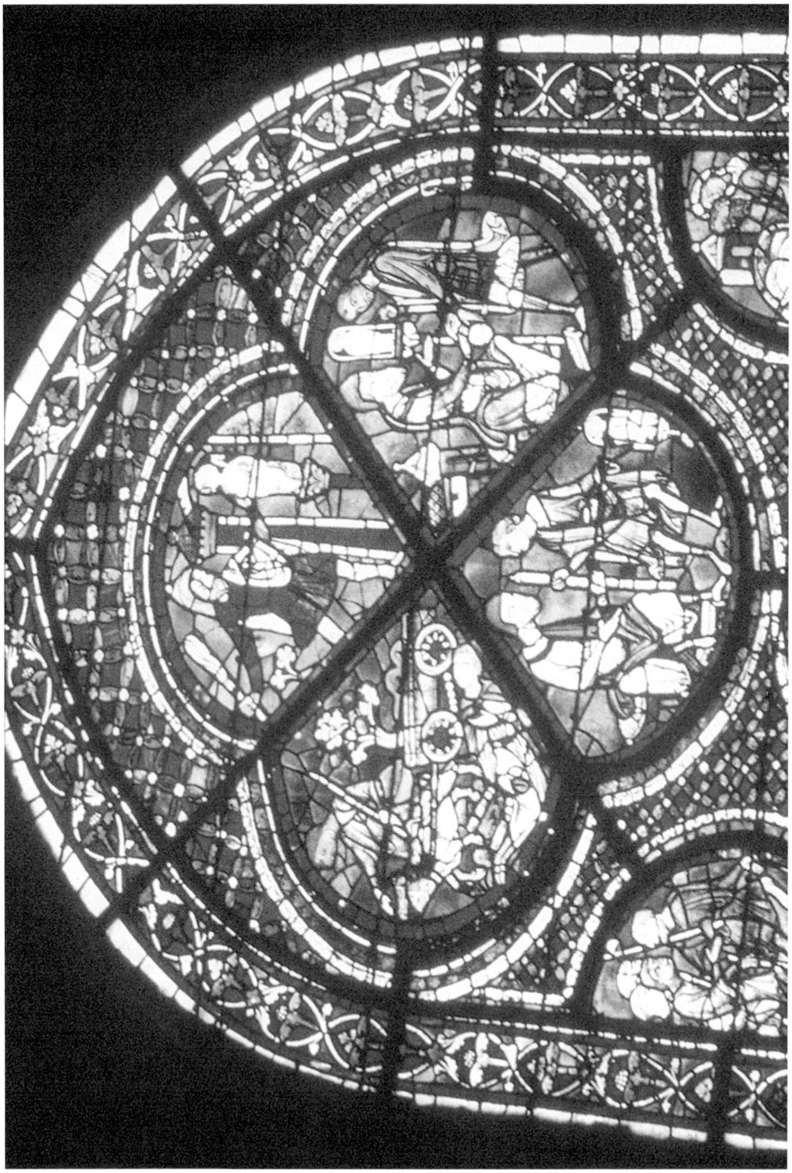

Figure 2. *Iconia* Tale and the Tale of the False Borrower, stained glass window in the nave, Chartres Cathedral, 1210–1235 (Corpus Vitrearum no. 39, panels 23–26). Author's photo.

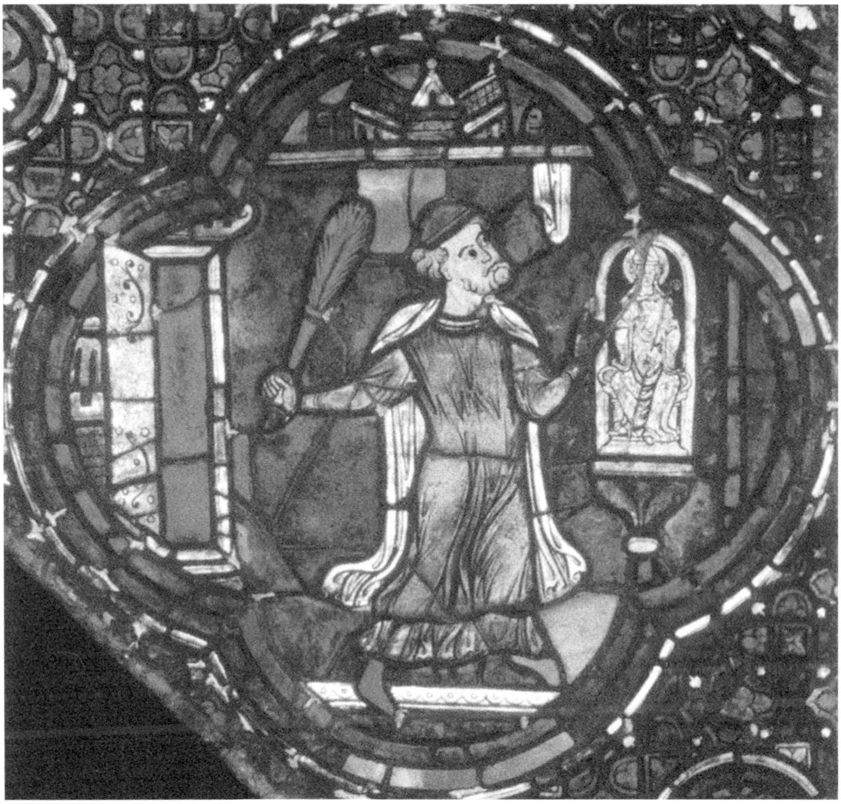

Figure 3. Scene from the *Iconia* Tale: Beating of an icon of Saint Nicholas, stained glass window in the ambulatory, Chartres Cathedral, 1210–1235. (Corpus Vitrearum no. 14, panel 20). Photo source: Colette Manhes Deremble, *Les vitraux de la Cathédrale de Chartres: Étude iconographique* (Paris: Comité du Corpus Vitrearum Français et Le Léopard d'Or, 1993).

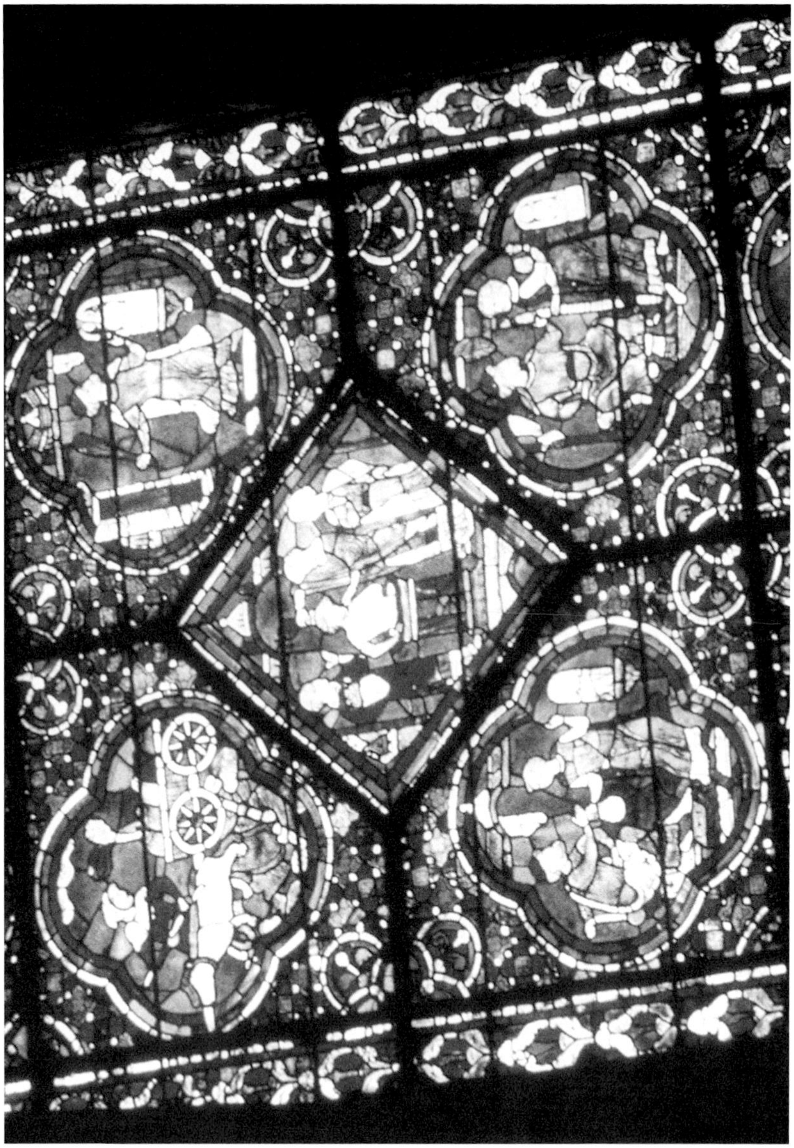

Figure 4. *Iconia* Tale and the Tale of the False Borrower, stained glass window in the ambulatory, Chartres Cathedral, 1210–1235 (Corpus Vitrearum no. 14, panels 16–20). Author's photo.

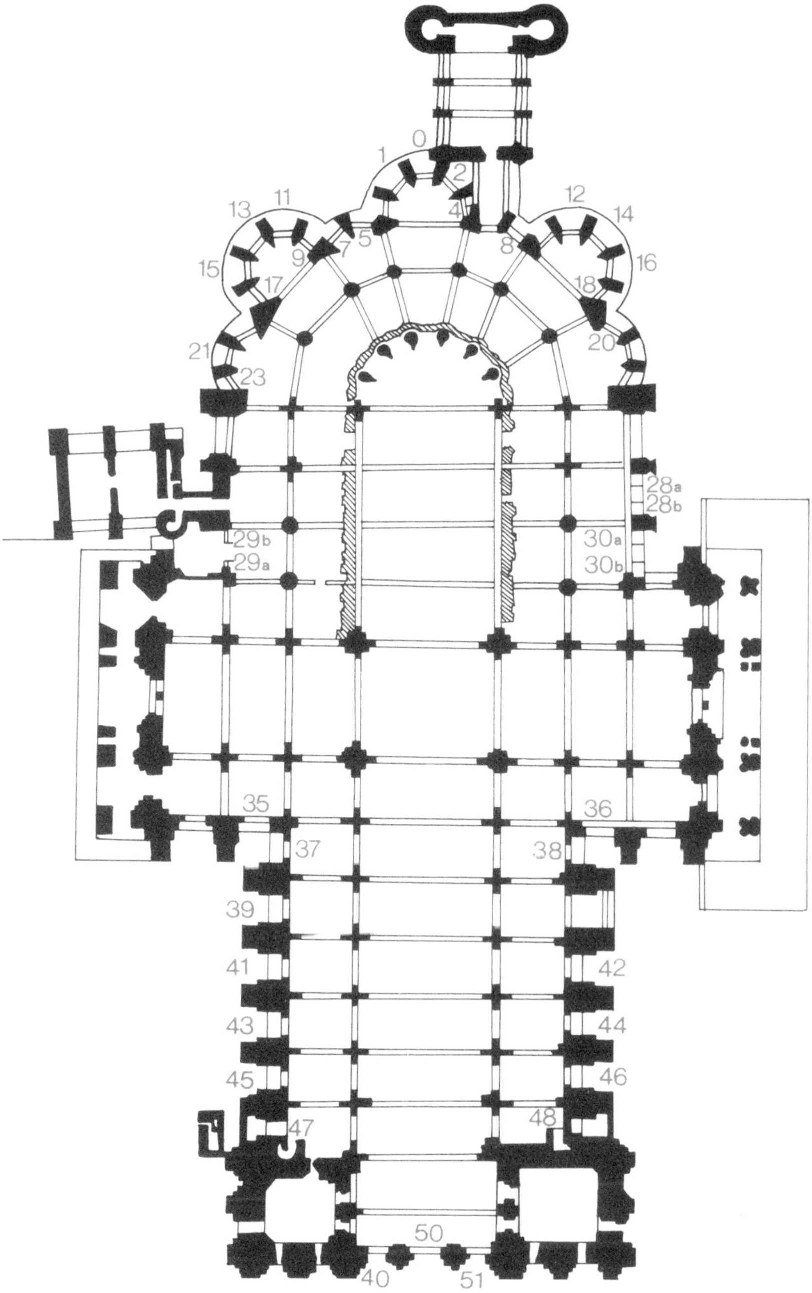

Figure 5. Plan of Chartres Cathedral. The Nicholas window in the nave is labelled no. 39; the Nicholas window in the ambulatory is no. 14.

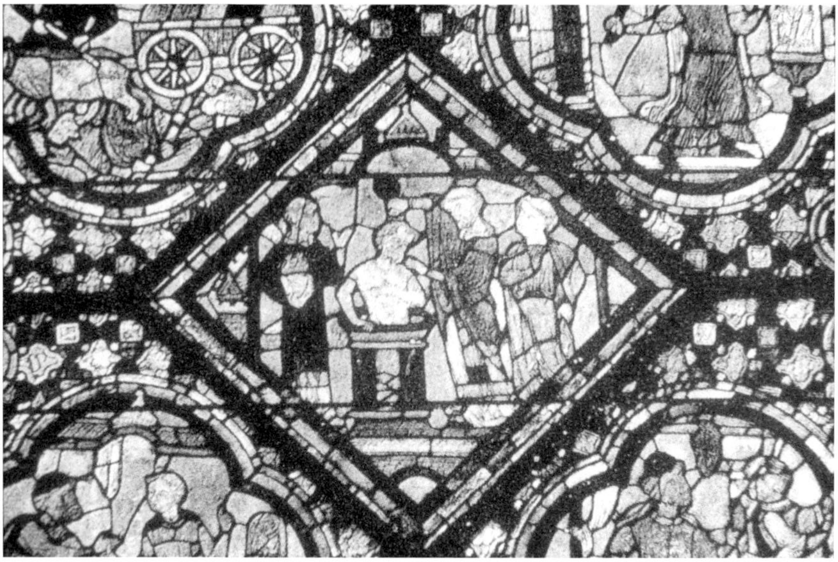

Figure 6. Baptism of the Jew, stained glass window in the ambulatory, Chartres Cathedral, 1210–1235 (Corpus Vitrearum no. 14, panel 19). Photo source: Colette Manhes Deremble, *Les vitraux de la Cathédrale de Chartres: Étude iconographique* (Paris: Comité du Corpus Vitrearum Français et Le Léopard d'Or, 1993).

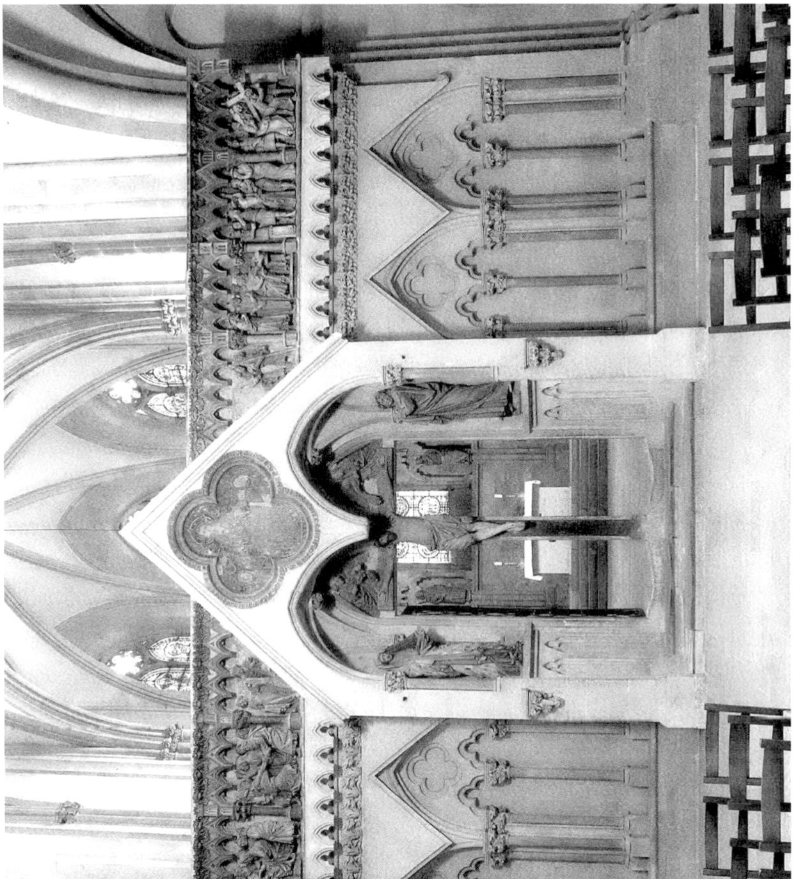

Figure 1. Full view of west choir screen, Naumburg Cathedral, ca. 1250. Author's photo.

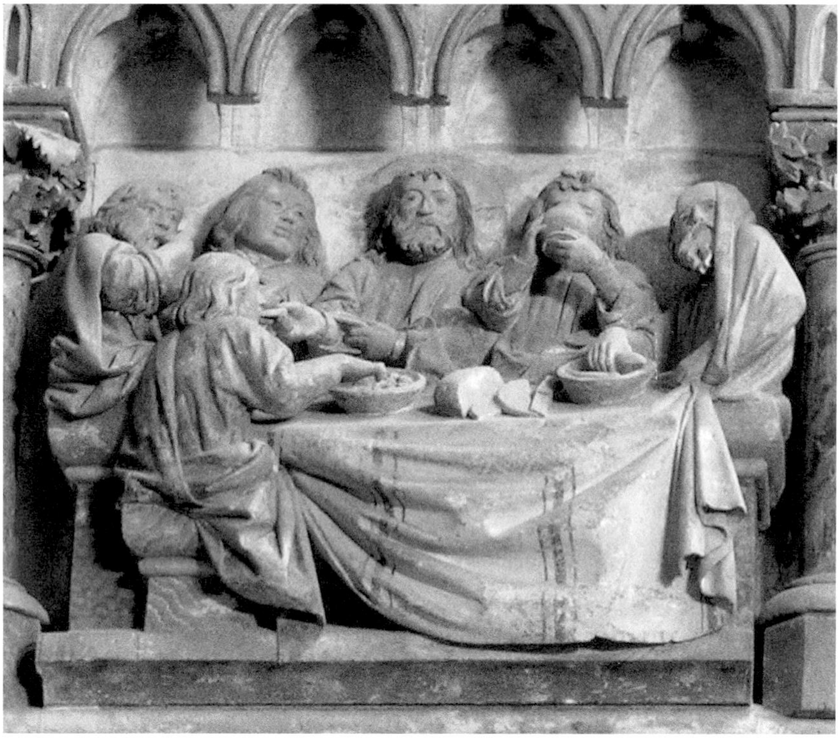

Figure 2. The Last Supper, relief on west choir screen, Naumburg Cathedral, ca. 1250. Author's photo.

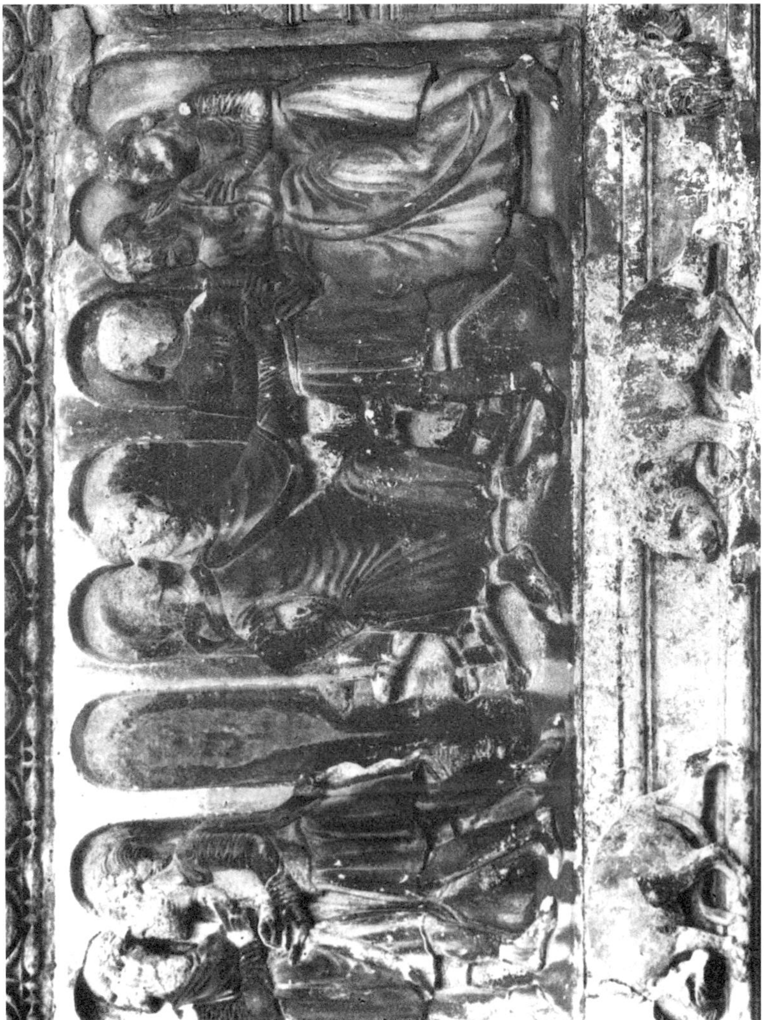

Figure 3. The Payment of Judas, west facade frieze at St-Gilles-du-Gard, ca. 1180. Photo: Réunion des Musées Nationaux/Art Resource, New York.

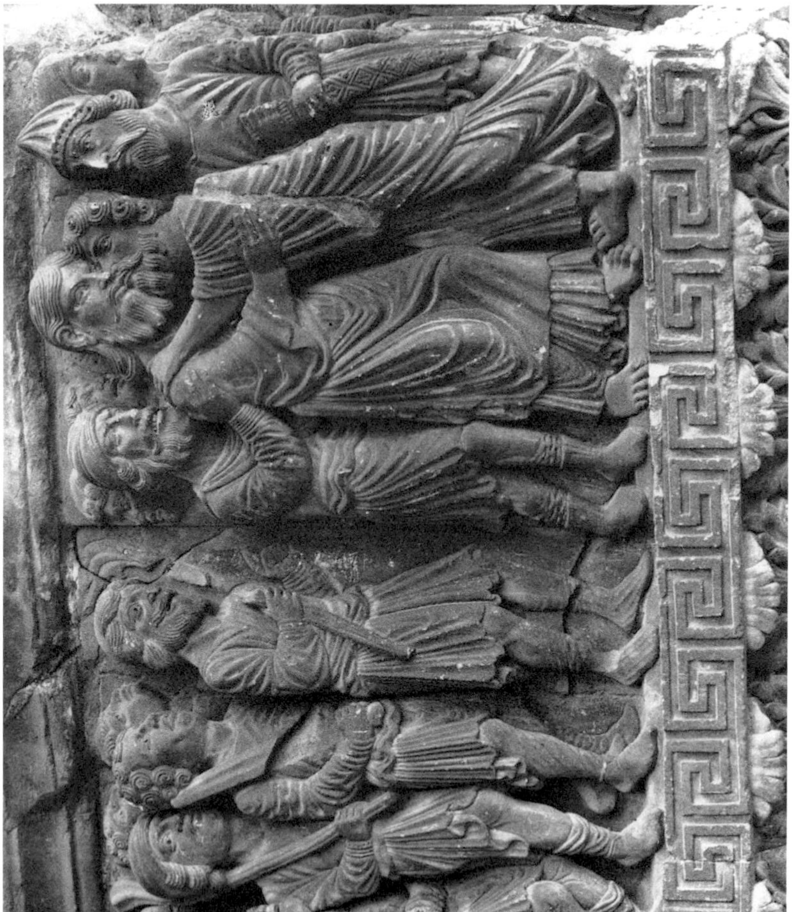

Figure 4. The Arrest of Christ, west facade frieze at St-Gilles-du-Gard, ca. 1180. Photo: Foto Marburg/Art Resource, New York.

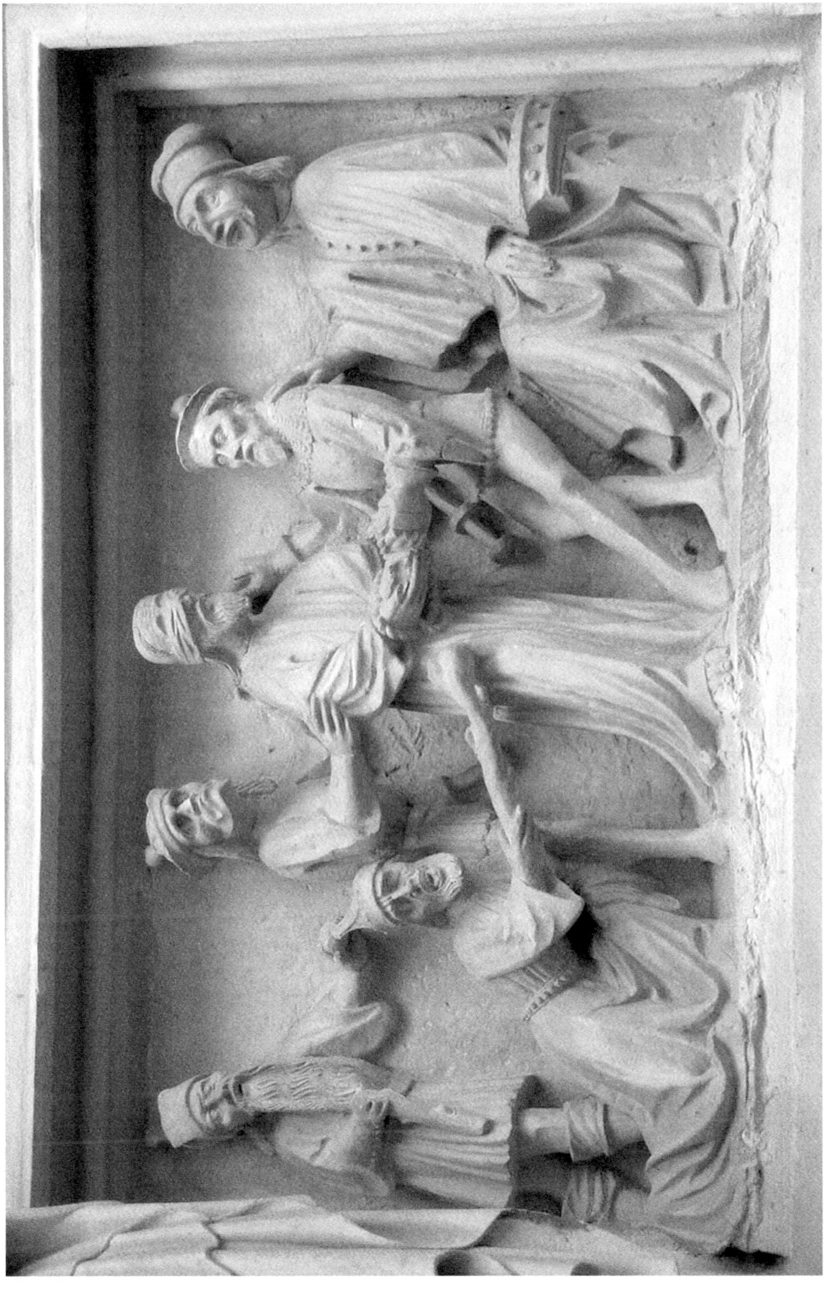

Figure 5. The Mocking of Christ before Caiaphas, relief on inner surface of south choir enclosure (facing crossing altar), Havelberg Cathedral, 1395–1411. Author's photo.

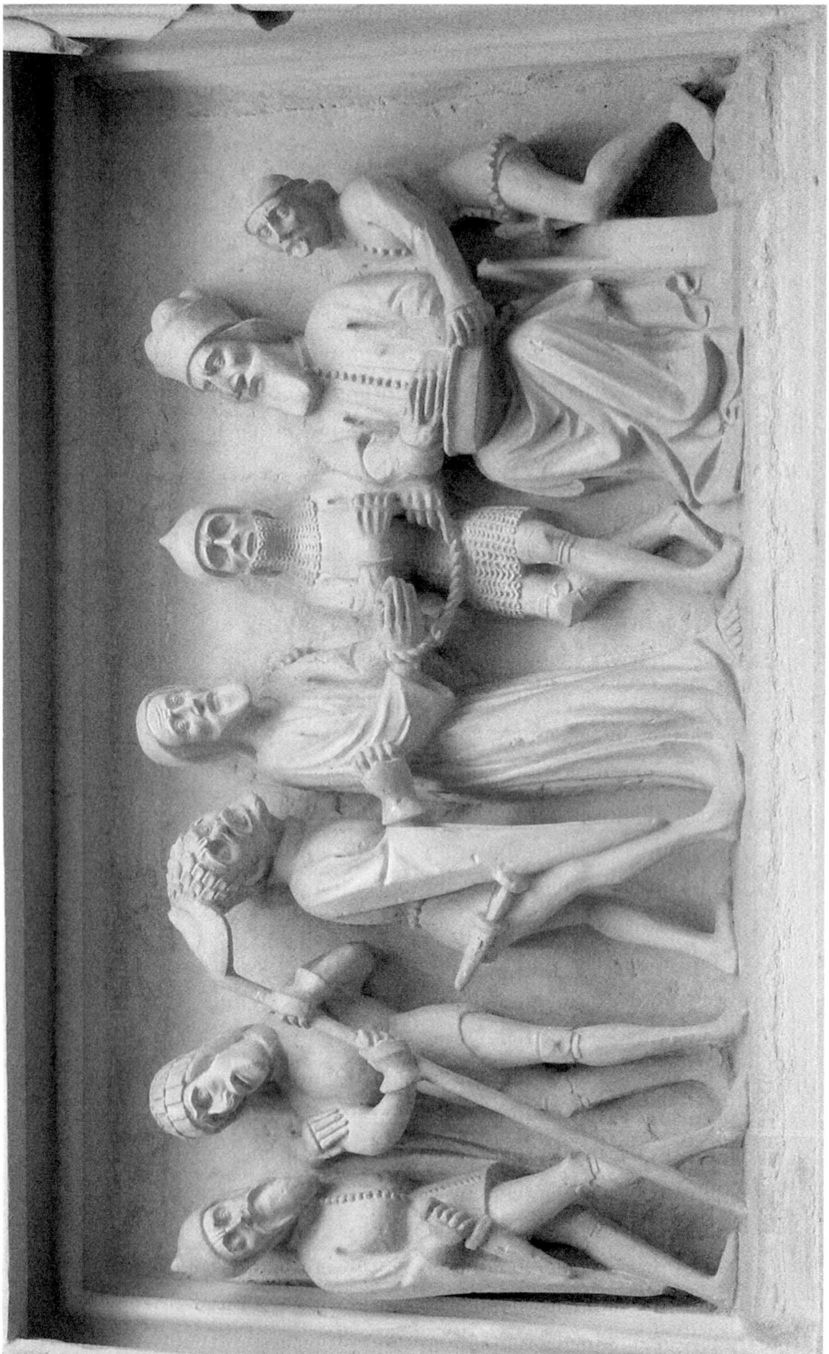

Figure 6. Christ's Trial Before Pilate, relief on inner surface of south choir enclosure (facing crossing altar), Havelberg Cathedral, 1395–1411. Author's photo.

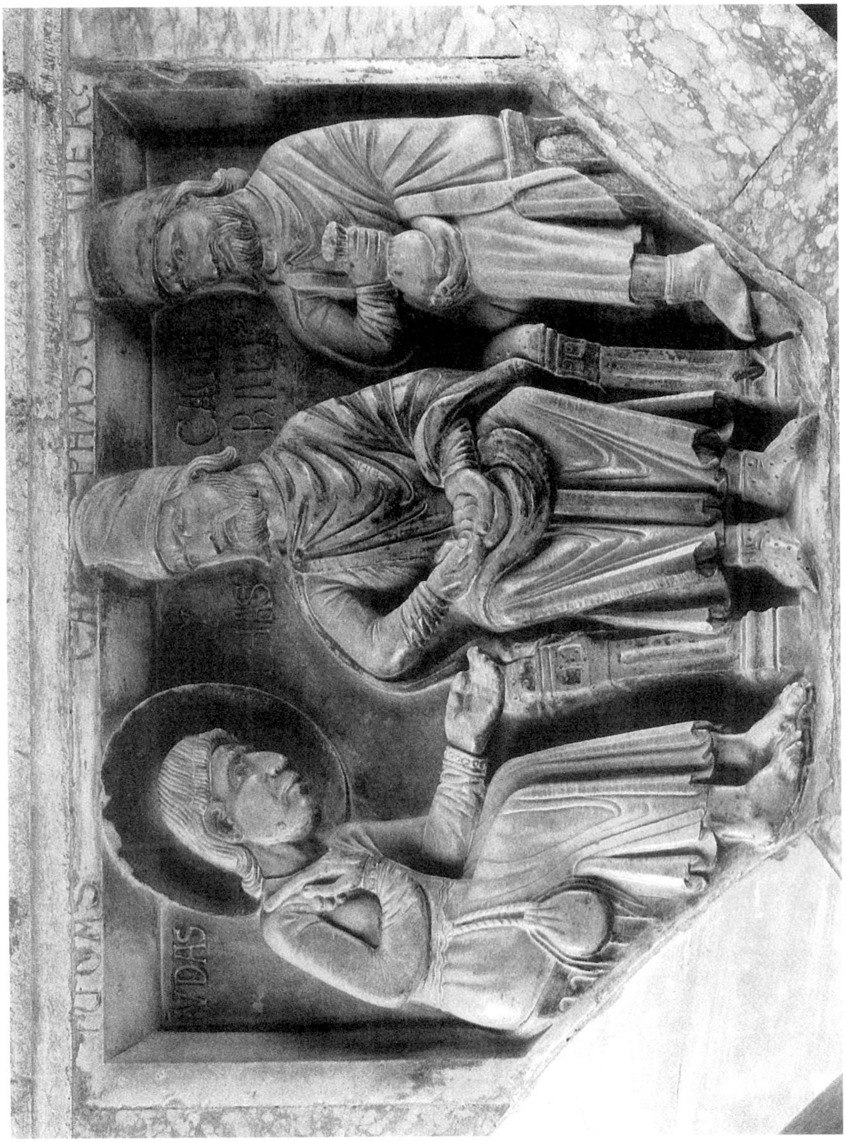

Figure 7. The Payment of Judas by Caiaphas, relief on lower back wall of choir screen, Modena Cathedral, ca. 1180. Photo by Ghigo Roli, in *Il Duomo di Modena/The Cathedral of Modena: Atlante fotografico*, ed. Chiara Frugoni (Modena, 1999), vol. 2: 678, plate 1322.

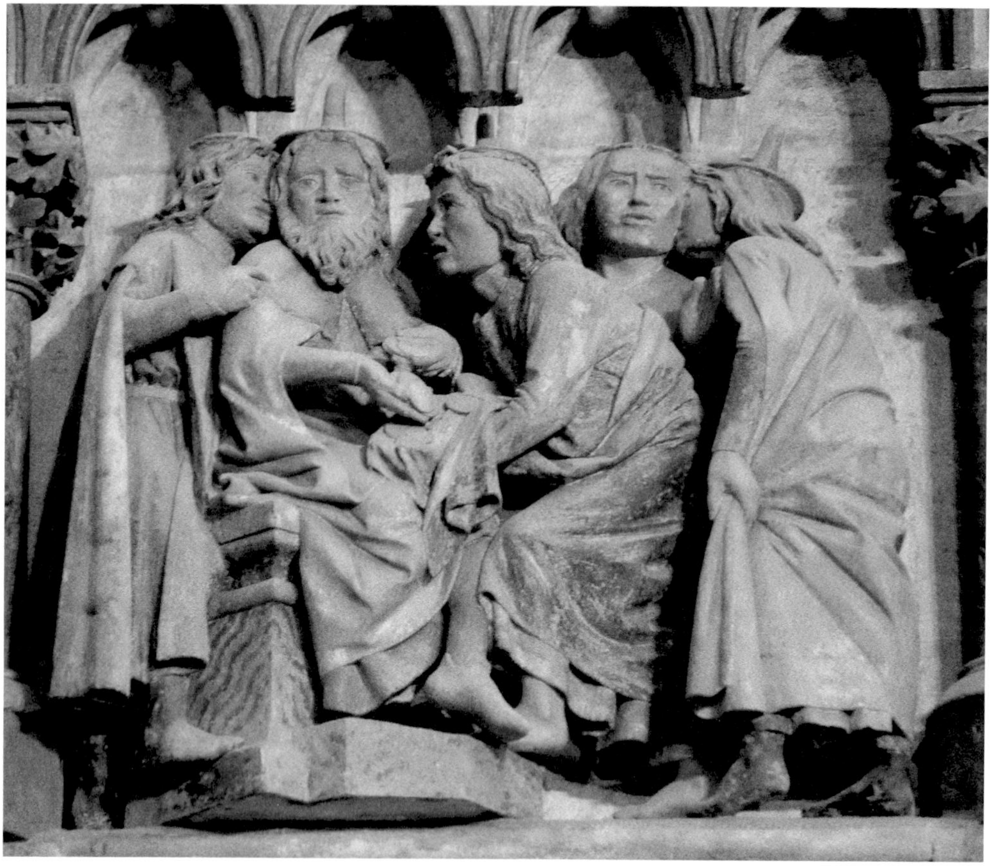

Figure 8. The Payment of Judas by Caiaphas, relief on west choir screen, Naumburg Cathedral, ca. 1250. Author's photo.

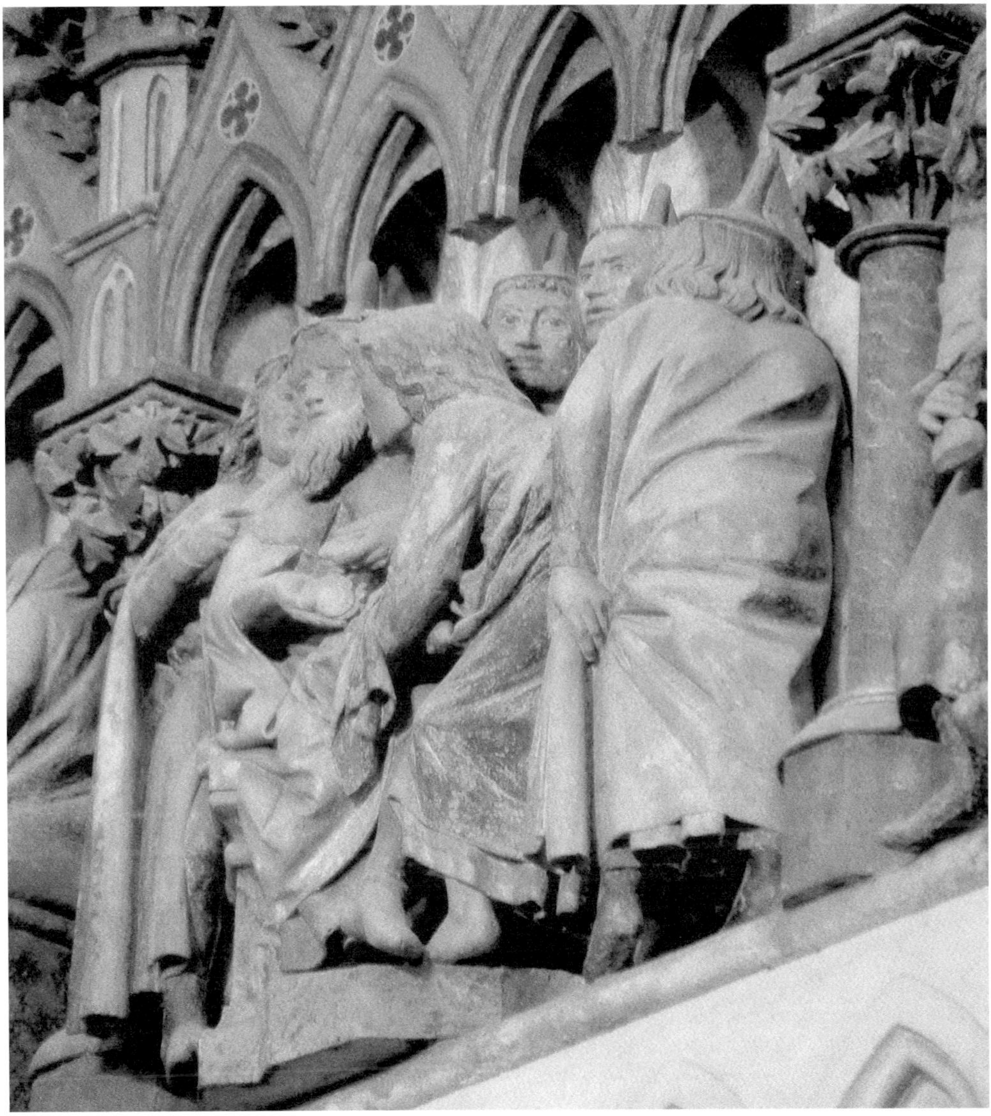

Figure 9. The Payment of Judas by Caiaphas (oblique view), relief on west choir screen, Naumburg Cathedral, ca. 1250. Author's photo.

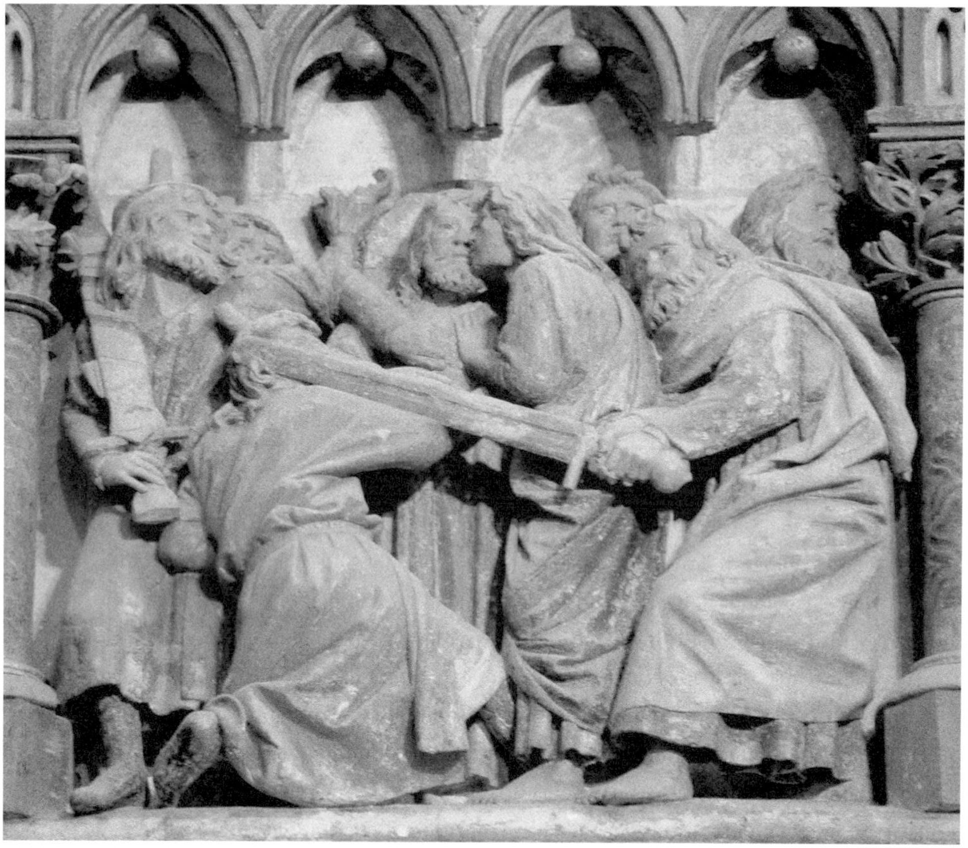

Figure 10. The Betrayal and Arrest of Christ, relief on west choir screen, Naumburg Cathedral, ca. 1250. Author's photo.

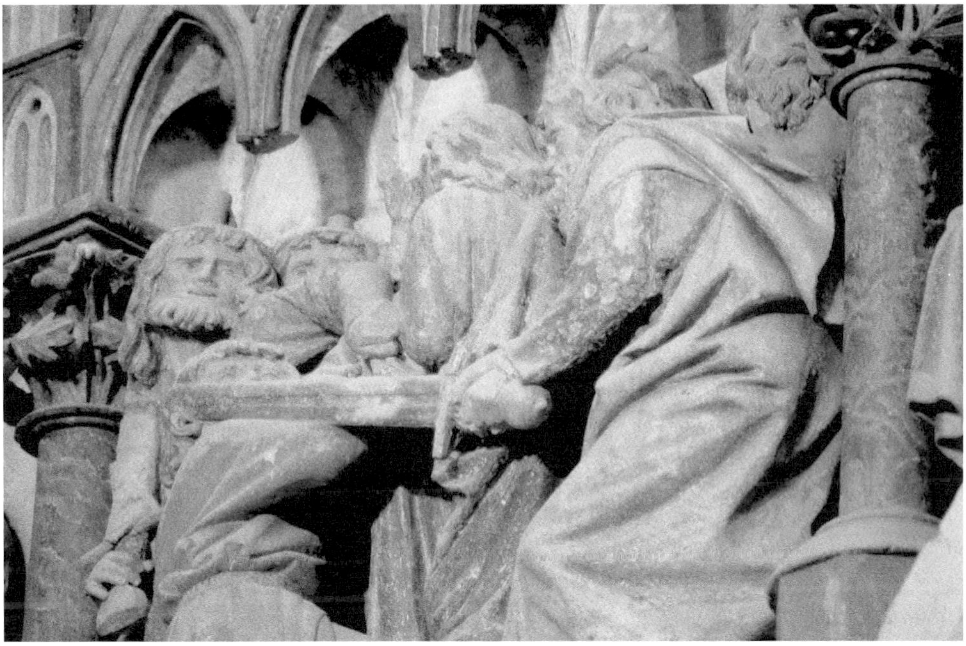

Figure 11. The Betrayal and Arrest of Christ (detail of chief captor), relief on west choir screen, Naumburg Cathedral, ca. 1250. Author's photo.

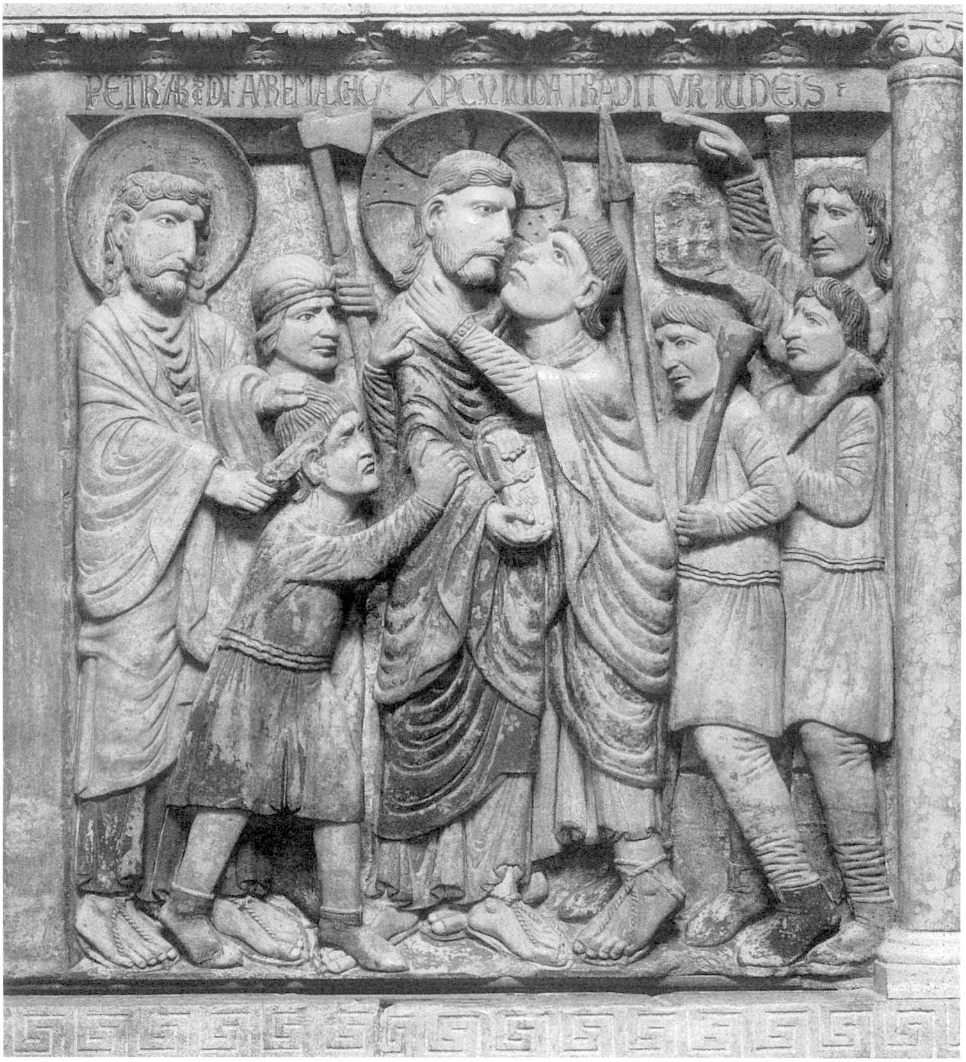

Figure 12. The Betrayal and Arrest of Christ, relief on choir screen, Modena Cathedral, ca. 1180. Photo by Ghigo Roli, in *Il Duomo di Modena/The Cathedral of Modena: Atlante fotografico*, ed. Chiara Frugoni (Modena, 1999), 669, plate 1311.

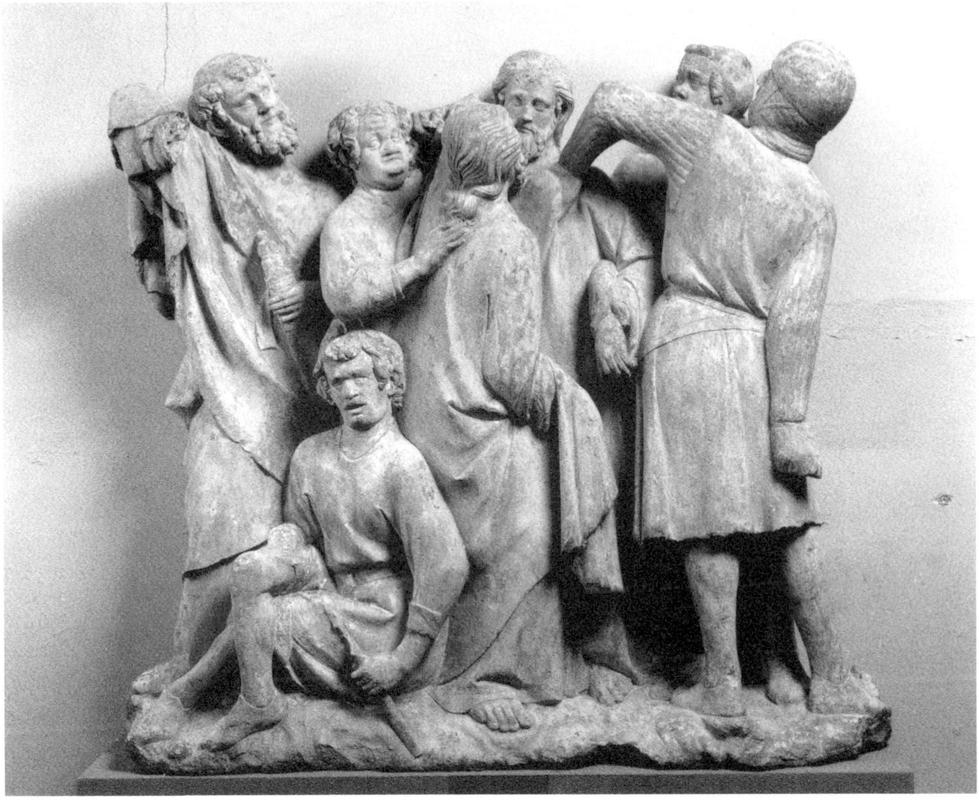

Figure 13. The Betrayal and Arrest of Christ, stone relief from the former choir screen of Amiens Cathedral, ca. 1260. New York, The Metropolitan Museum of Art (17.120.5). Photo courtesy of The Metropolitan Museum of Art.

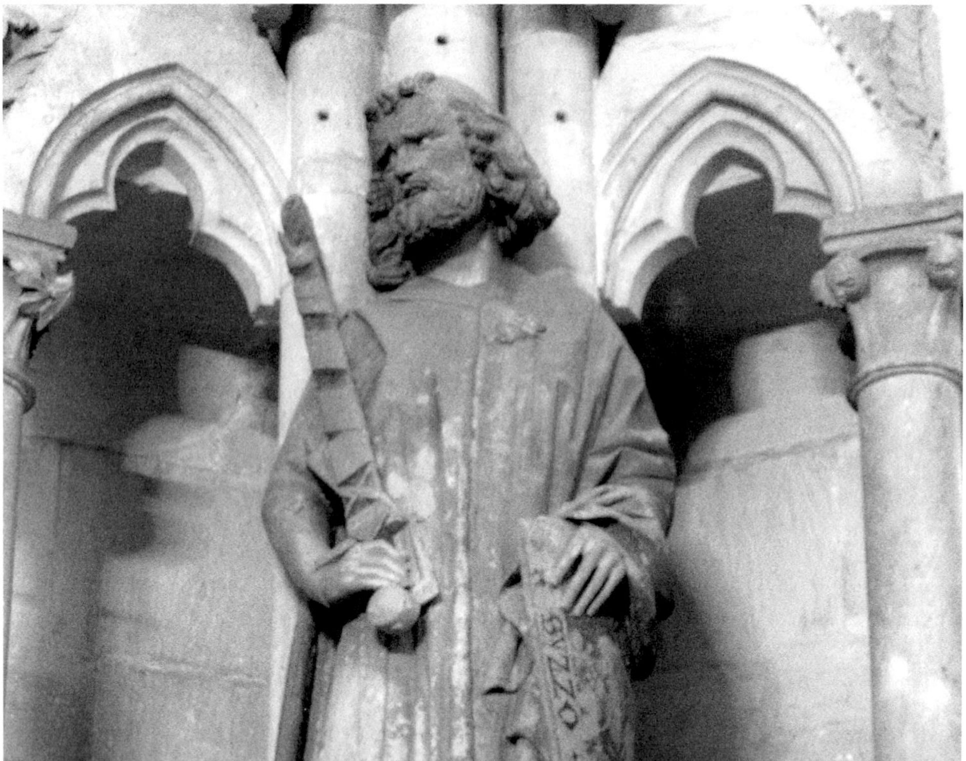

Figure 14. Donor statue of Thuringian count Sizzo, west choir, apse, Naumburg Cathedral, ca. 1245–55. Author's photo.

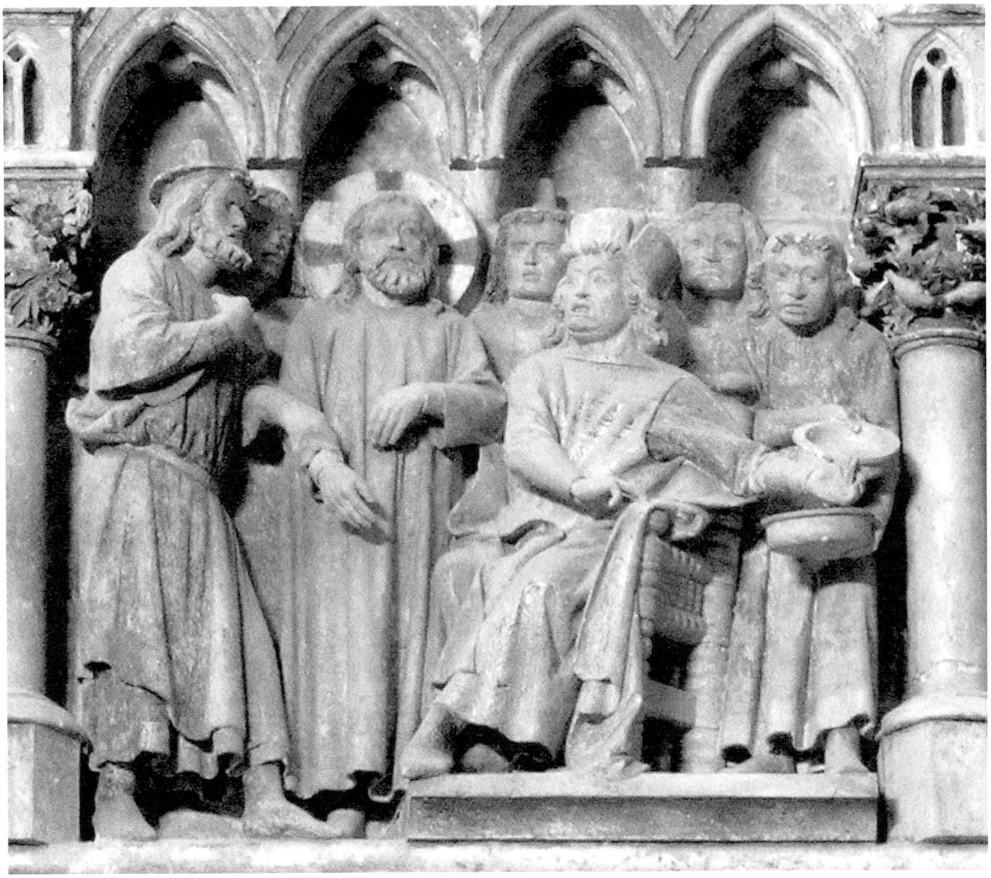

Figure 15. Christ's Trial before Pilate, relief on west choir screen, Naumburg Cathedral, ca. 1250. Author's photo.

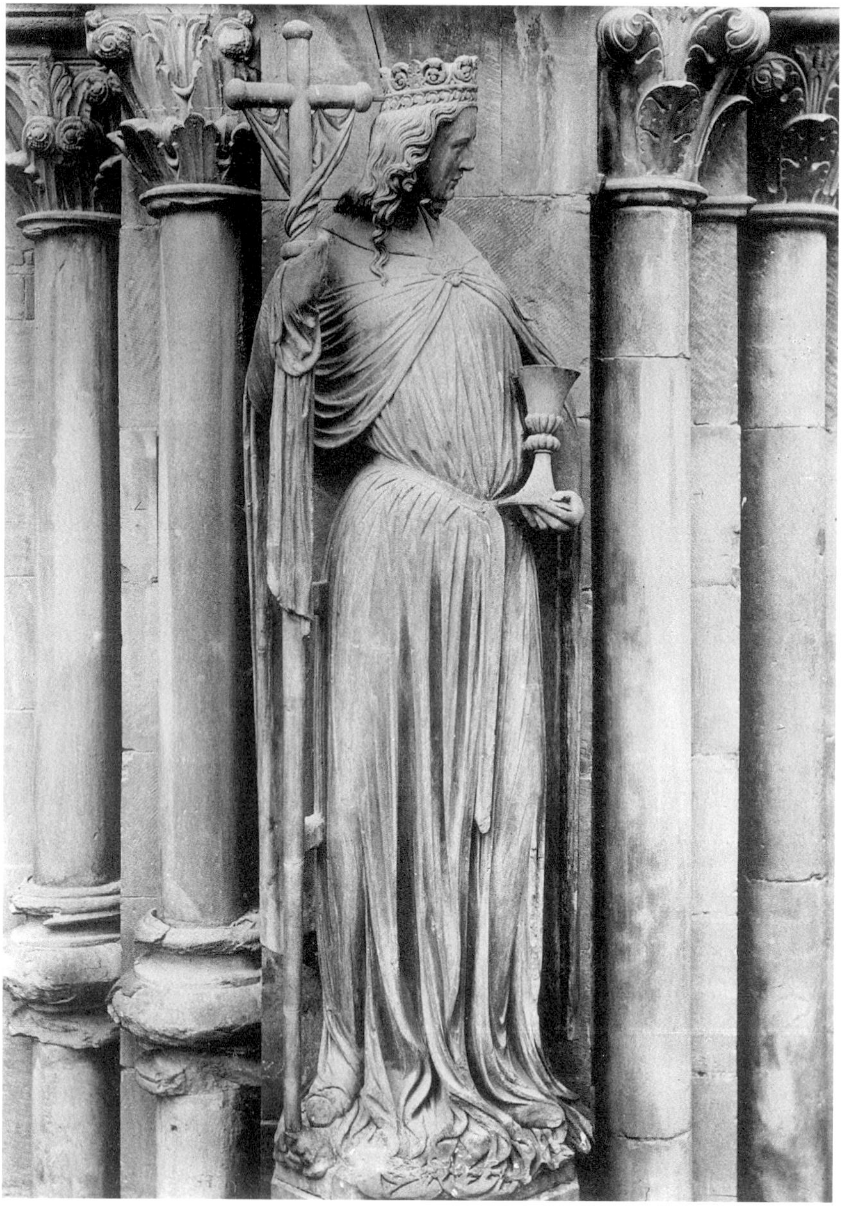

Figure 1. Ecclesia, south transept façade, Strasbourg Cathedral, c. 1225–1235. Photo: Foto Marburg/Art Resource, NY.

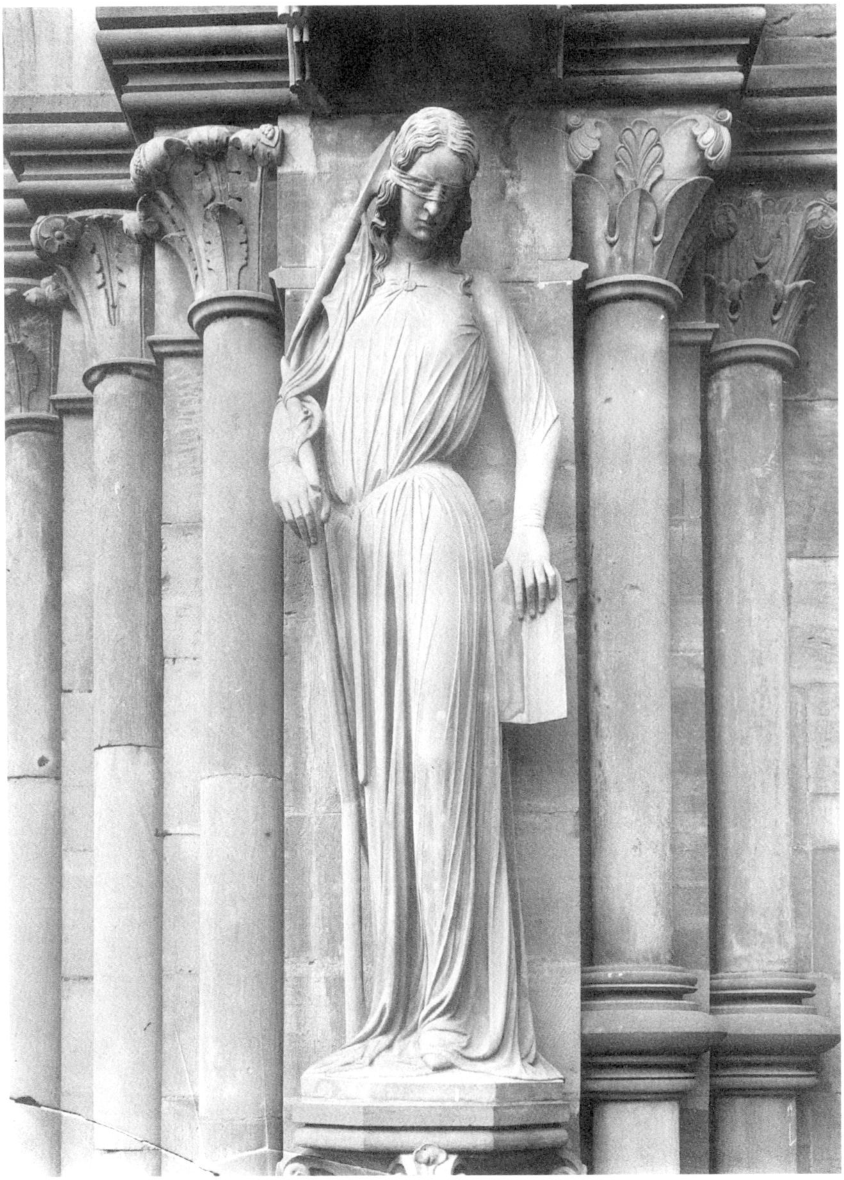

Figure 2. Synagoga, south transept façade, Strasbourg Cathedral, c. 1225–1235. Photo: Foto Marburg/Art Resource, NY.

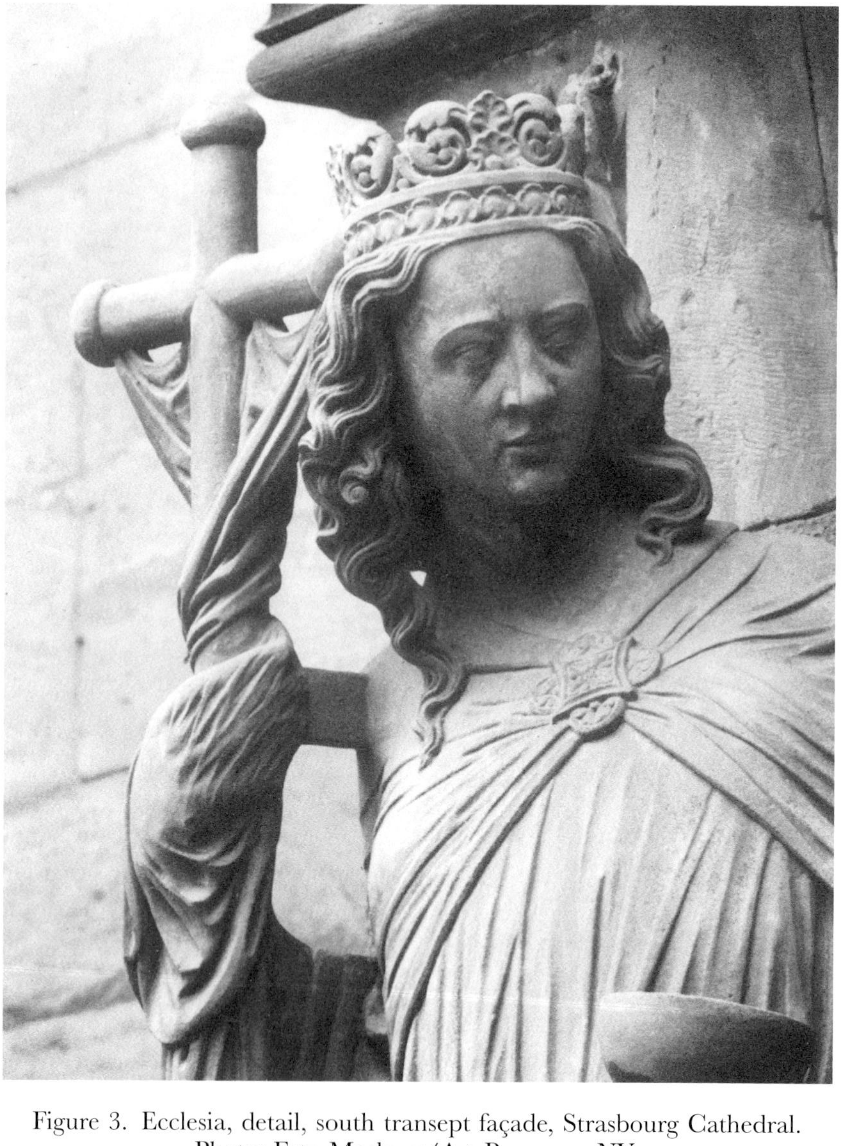

Figure 3. Ecclesia, detail, south transept façade, Strasbourg Cathedral.
Photo: Foto Marburg/Art Resource, NY.

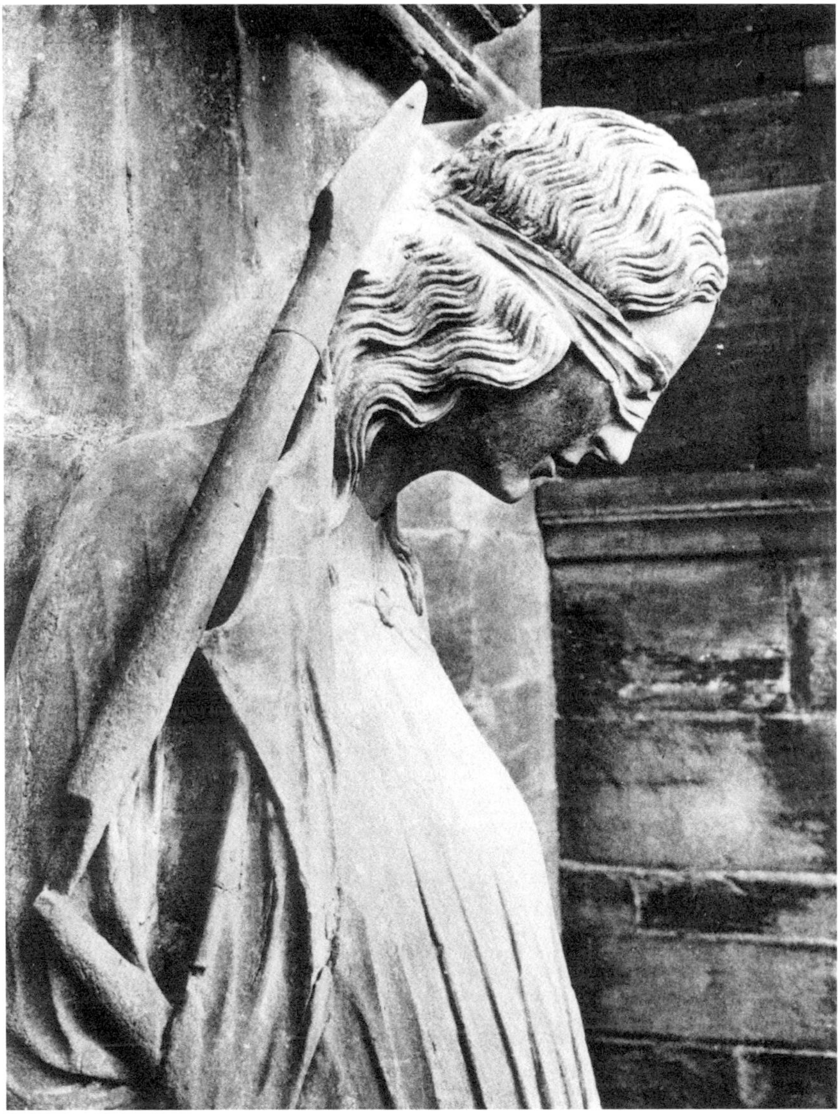

Figure 4. Synagoga, detail, south transept façade, Strasbourg Cathedral. Photo: Foto Marburg/Art Resource, NY.

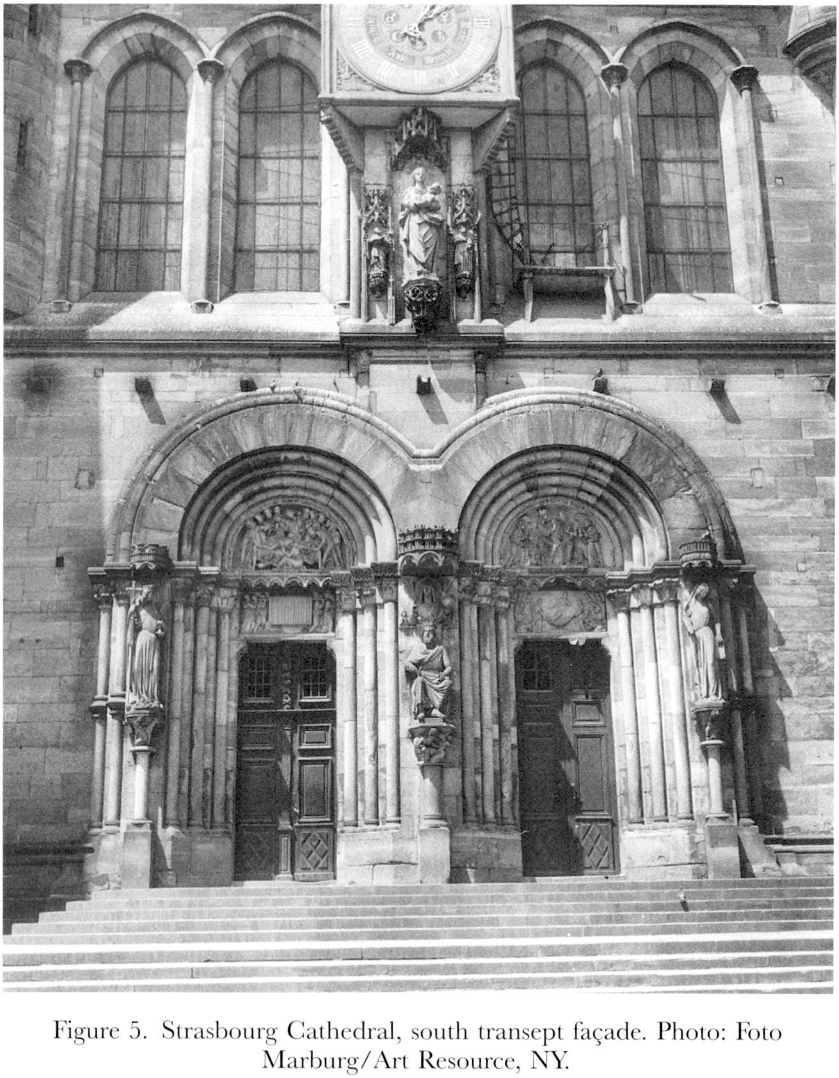

Figure 5. Strasbourg Cathedral, south transept façade. Photo: Foto Marburg/Art Resource, NY.

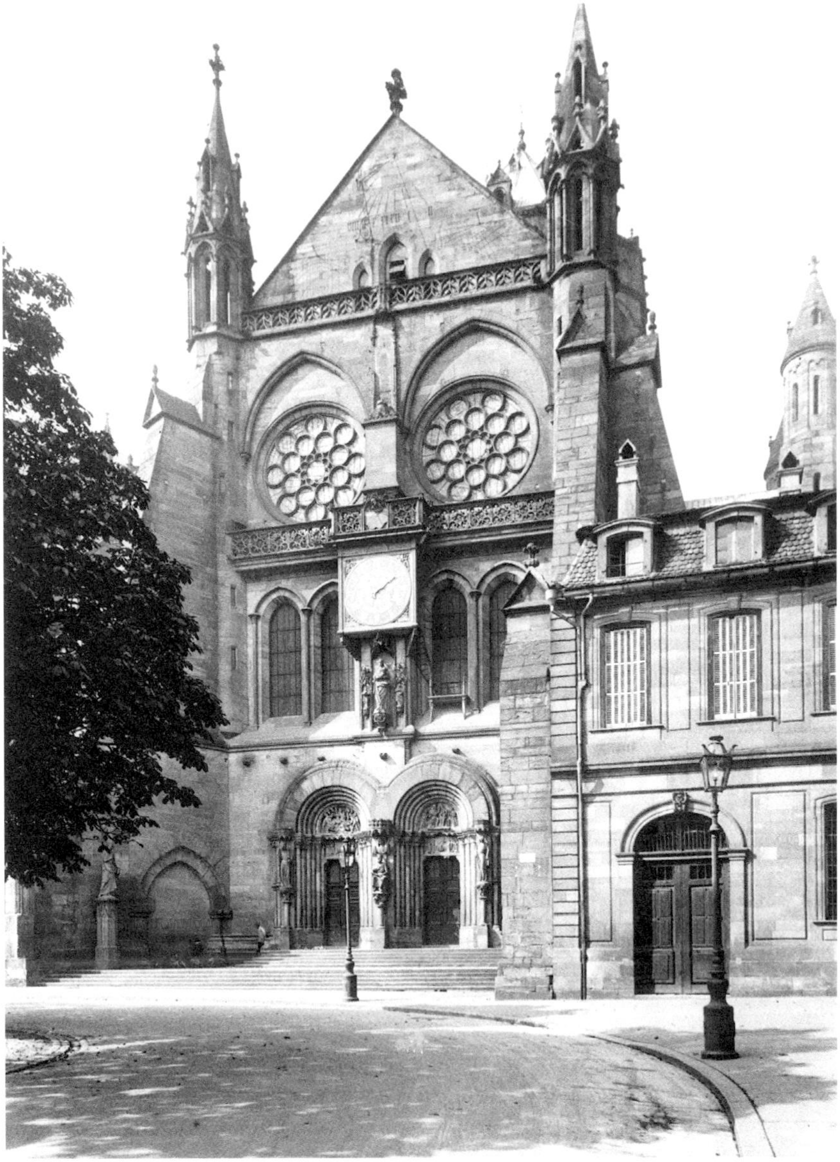

Figure 6. Strasbourg Cathedral, southern flank of east end. Photo: Foto Marburg/Art Resource, NY.

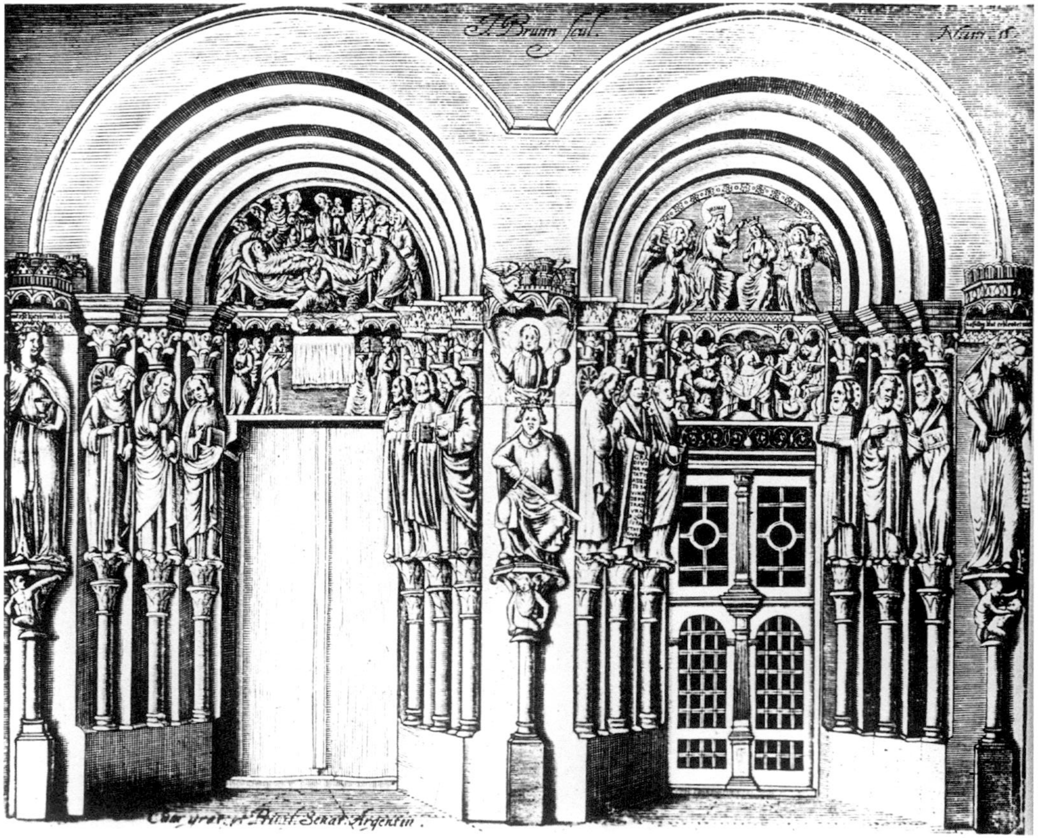

Figure 7. Isaac Brunn, South façade of Strasbourg Cathedral before modern damage and alterations, engraving, c. 1617, published in Oseas Schadaeus, *Summum Argentoratensium Templum, das ist Aussfürliche und Eigentliche Beschreibung des viel künstlichen, sehr kostbaren und in aller Welt berühmten Münsters zu Straßburg* (Strasbourg, 1617), pl. 6. Photo: Foto Marburg/Art Resource, NY.

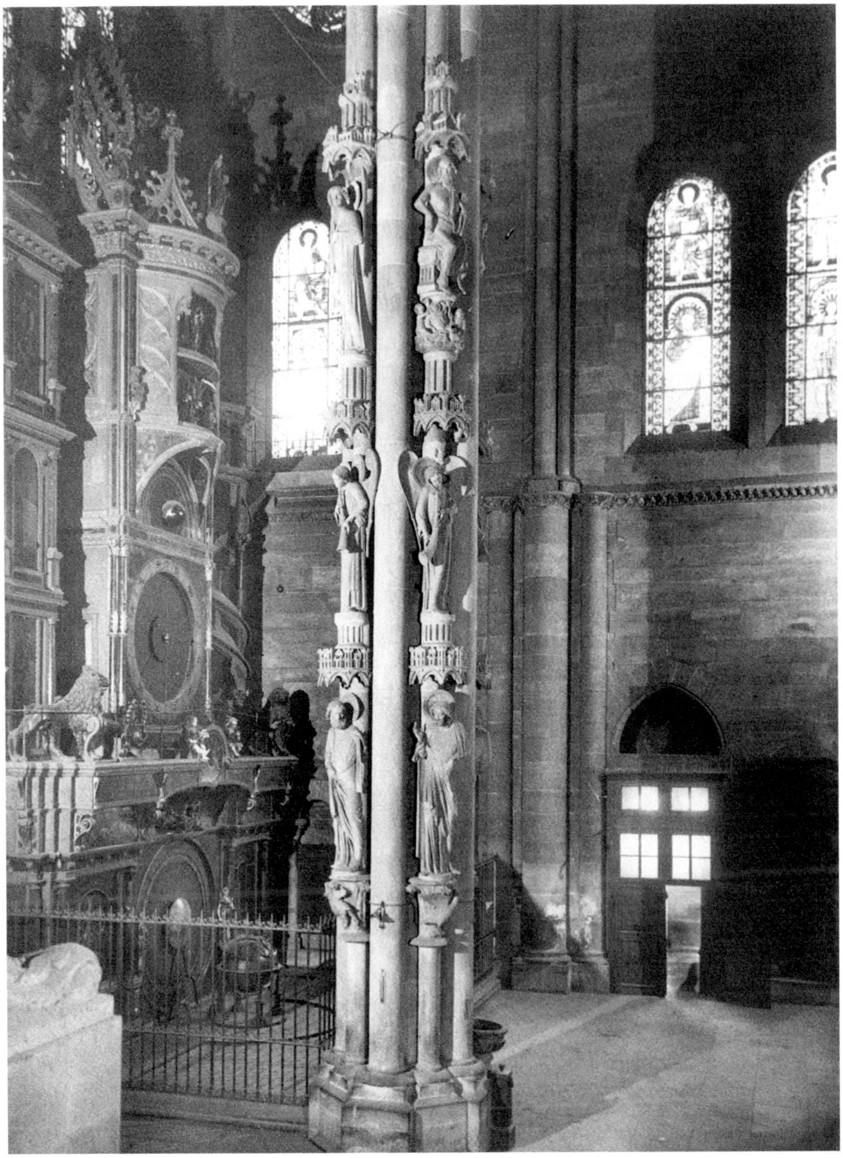

Figure 8. Pillar of Angels, south transept, interior, Strasbourg Cathedral, c. 1225–1235. Photo: Foto Marburg/Art Resource, NY.

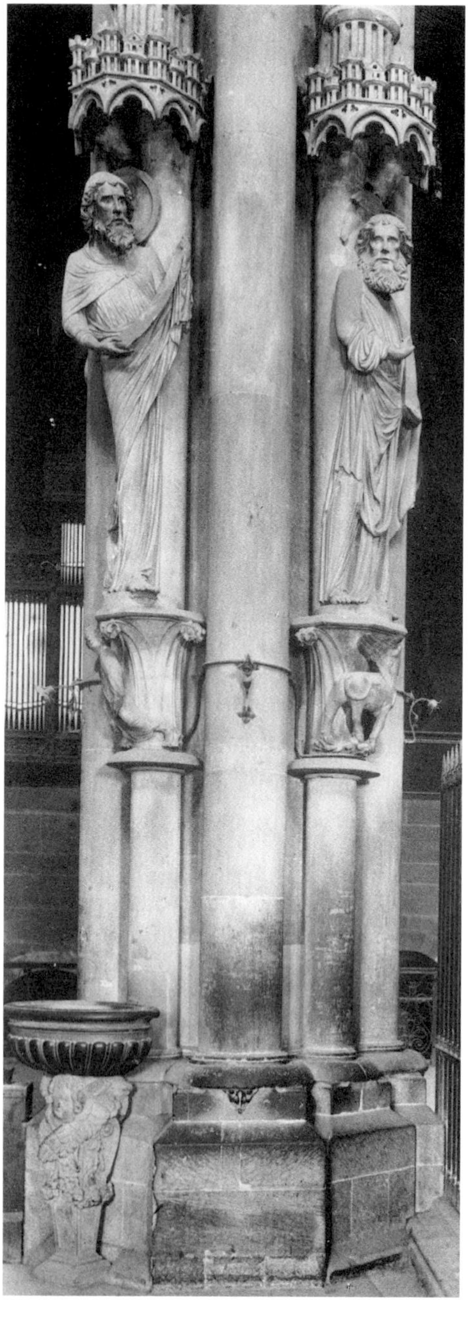

Figure 9. Matthew and Luke on Pillar of Angels, south transept interior, Strasbourg Cathedral. Photo: Foto Marburg/Art Resource, NY.

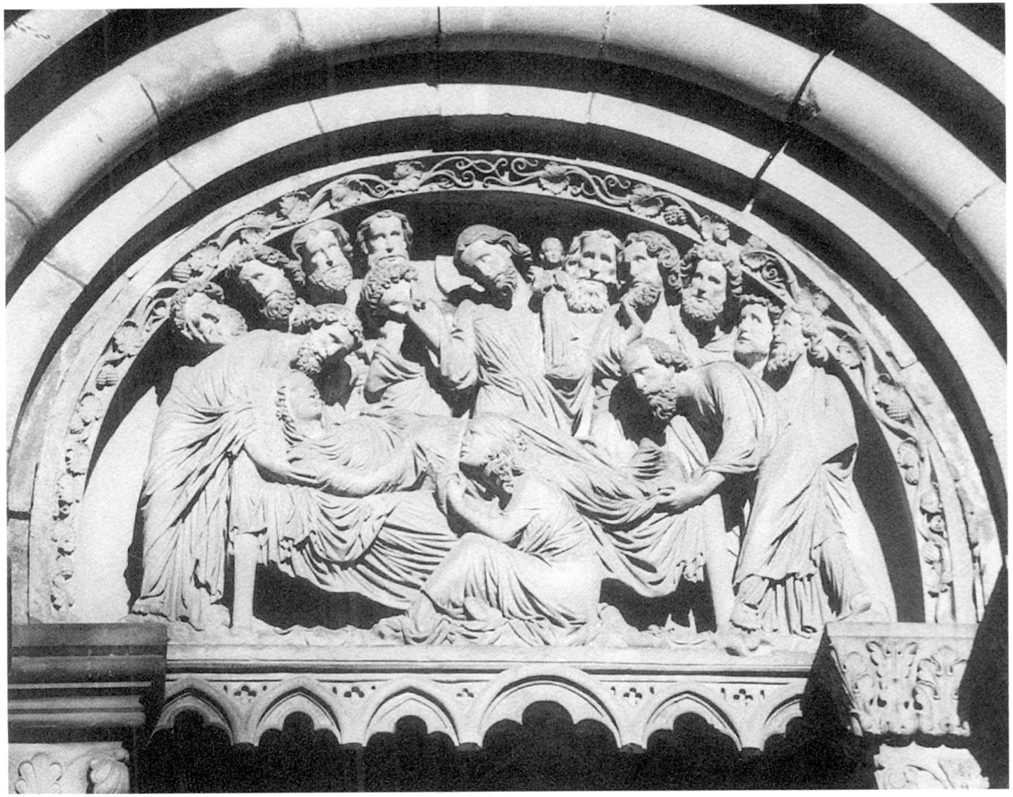

Figure 10. Dormition of the Virgin, left tympanum, south transept façade, Strasbourg Cathedral, c. 1225–1235. Author's photo.

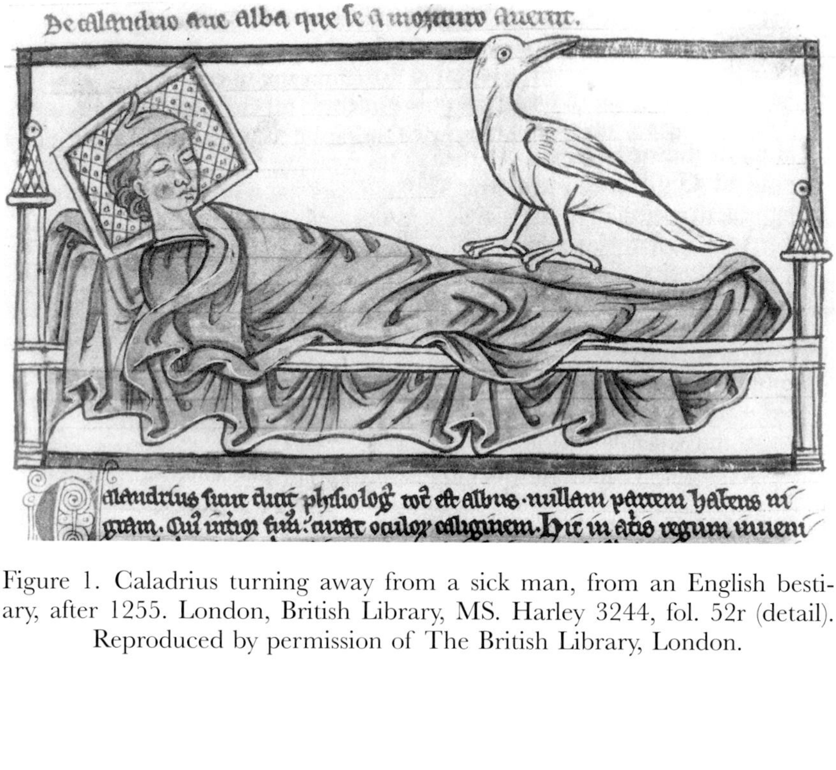

Figure 1. Caladrius turning away from a sick man, from an English bestiary, after 1255. London, British Library, MS. Harley 3244, fol. 52r (detail). Reproduced by permission of The British Library, London.

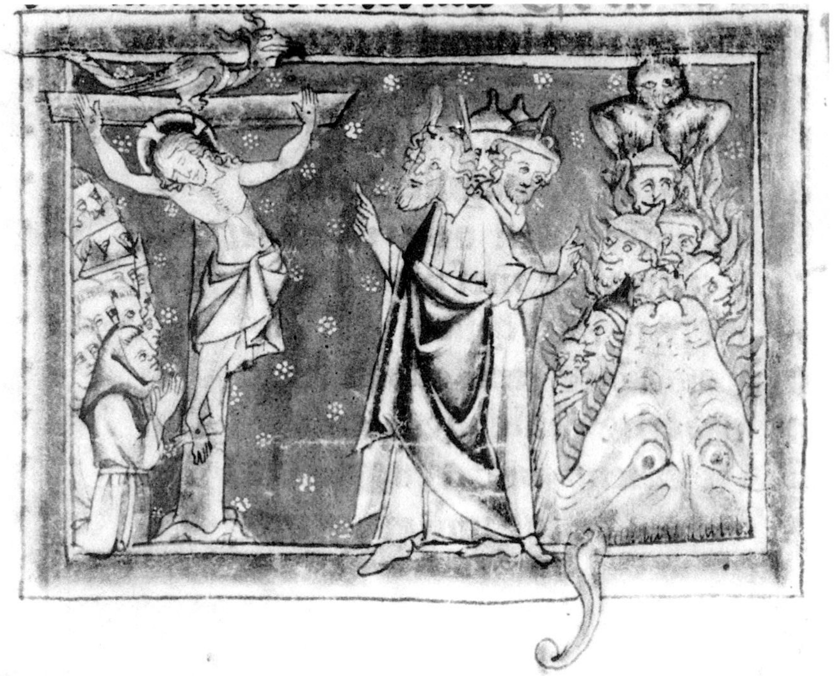

Figure 2. Crucifixion with clerics, Moses and Jews (commentary image for the caladrius), from an English copy of the *Bestiare* of Guillaume le Clerc (London or Oxford), 1265–70. Paris, Bibliothèque Nationale, MS. fr. 14969, fol. 9r (detail). Reproduced by permission of the Bibliothèque Nationale de France.

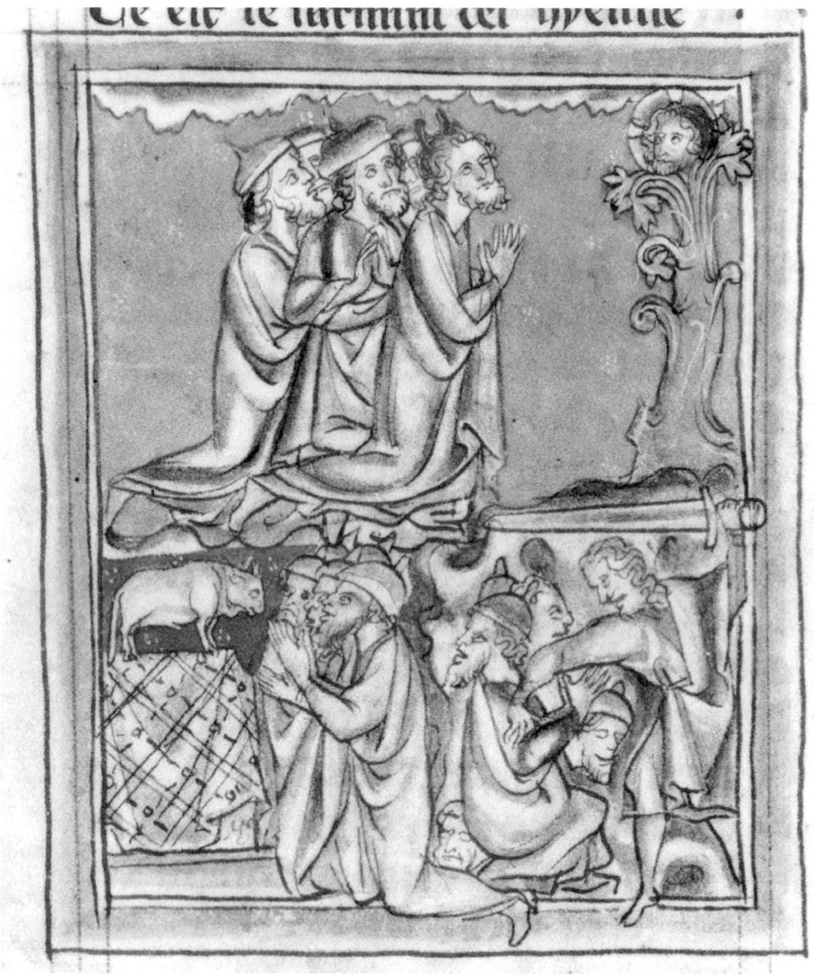

Figure 3. Moses and Israelites before the Burning Bush; Jews worshipping the Golden Calf (commentary image for the hyena). French 14969, fol. 29r (detail). Reproduced by permission of the Bibliothèque Nationale de France.

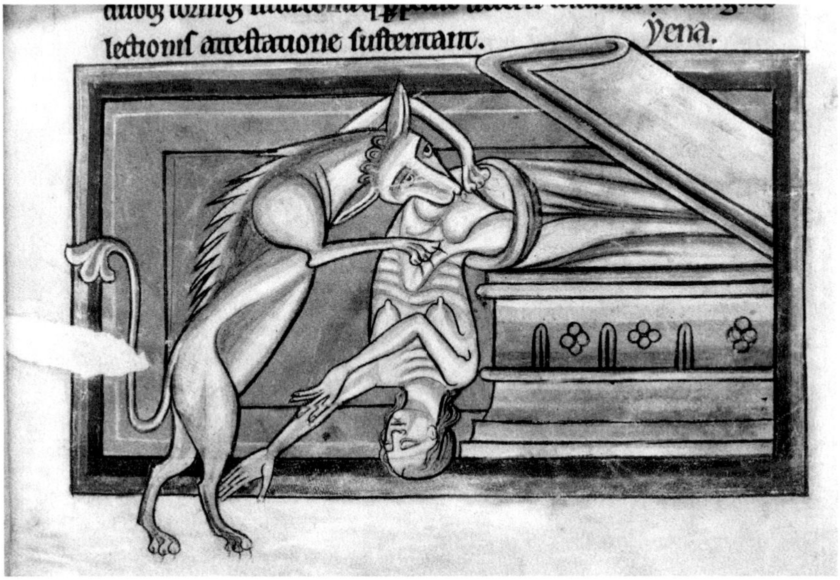

Figure 4. Hyena violating a female corpse, from an English bestiary (Salisbury?), c. 1230–40. London, British Library, MS. Harley 4751, fol. 10r (detail). Reproduced by permission of The British Library, London.

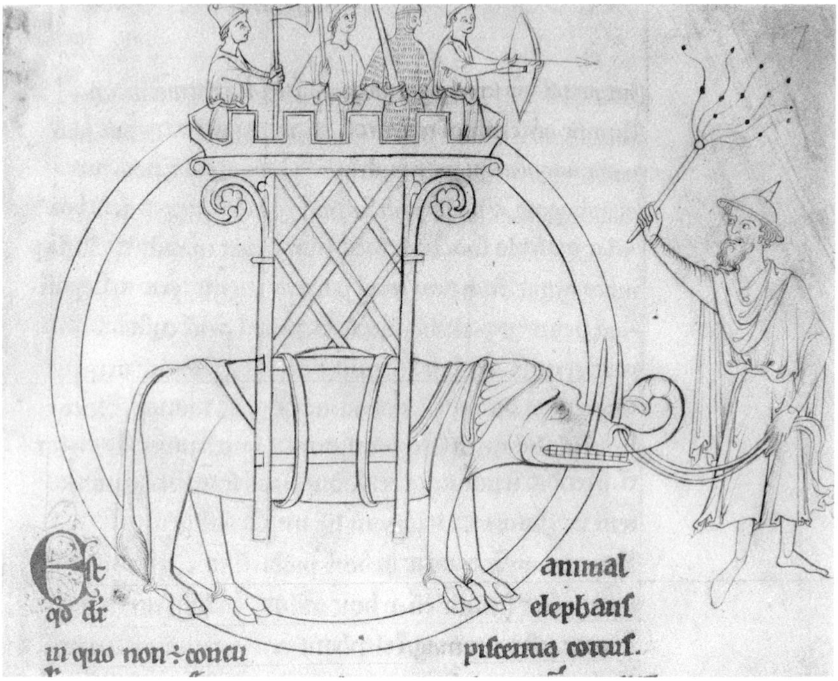

Figure 5. Elephant driven by a Jewish manhout, Bestiary, North Midlands (?), 1200–1210. Cambridge, University Library, MS. Ii.4.26, fol. 7r (detail). Reproduced by permission of the Syndics of Cambridge University Library.

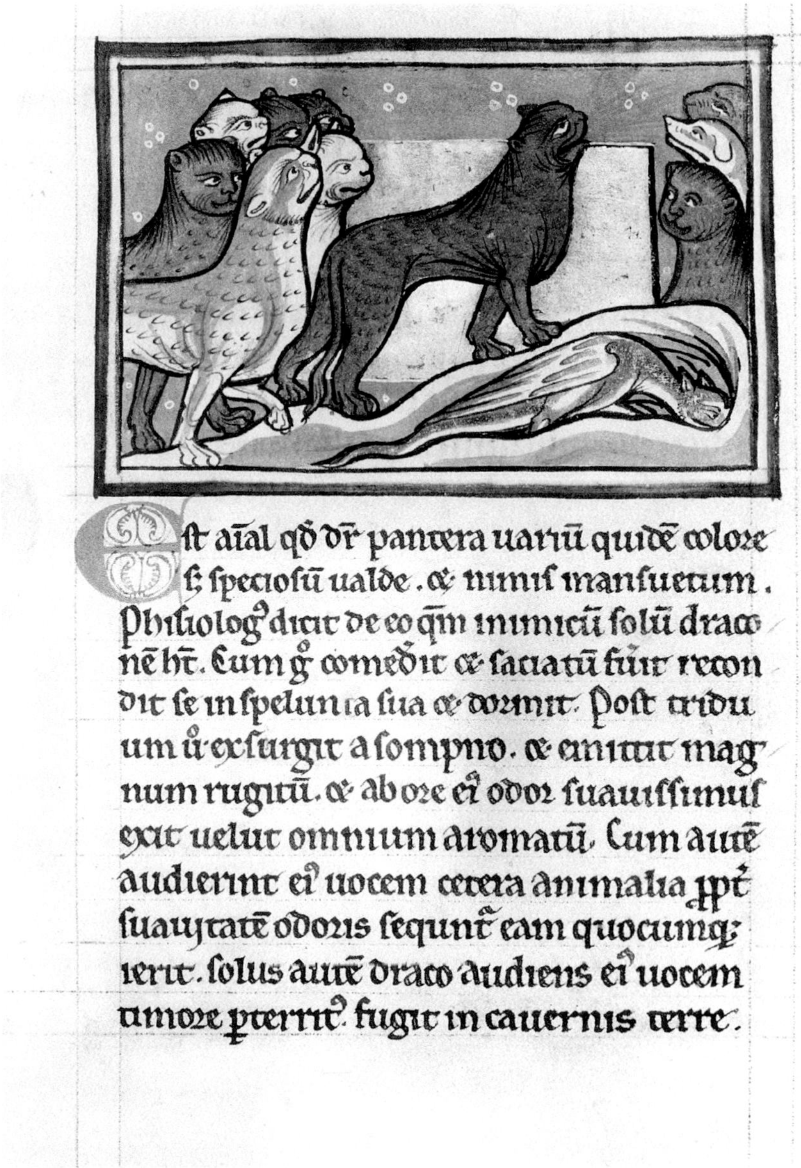

Est aĩal qđ dr̃ pantera uariũ quidẽ colore
s; speciosũ ualde. & nimis mansuetum.
Phisiolog dicit de eo qm inimicũ solũ draco
nẽ hr̃. Cum g comedit & saciatũ fuit recon
dit se in spelunca sua & dormit. Post tridu
um ũ exsurgit a sompno. & emittit mag
num rugitũ. & ab ore ei odor suauissimus
exit uelut omnium aromatũ. Cum autẽ
audierint ei uocem cetera animalia ppt
suauitatẽ odoris sequnt eam quocumq;
ierit. solus autẽ draco audiens ei uocem
timore pterrit fugit in cauernis terre.

Figure 6. Panther and followers, from an English bestiary (Lincoln?), c. 1185. New York, Pierpont Morgan Library, MS. M. 81, fol. 21r. Reproduced by permission of The Morgan Library, New York.

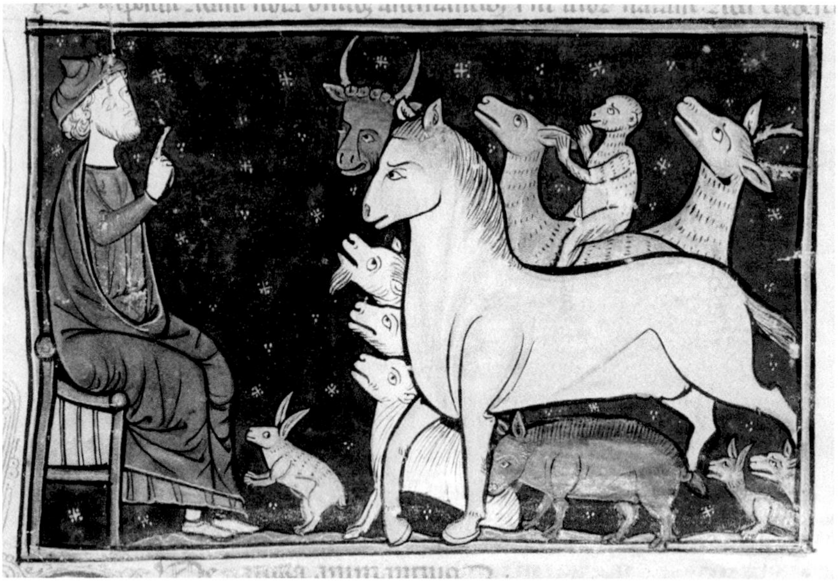

Figure 7. Adam naming the animals, from an English bestiary (York?), c. 1270–90. London, Westminster Abbey Library, MS. 22, fol. 4r (detail). Reproduction copyright: Dean and Chapter of Westminster.

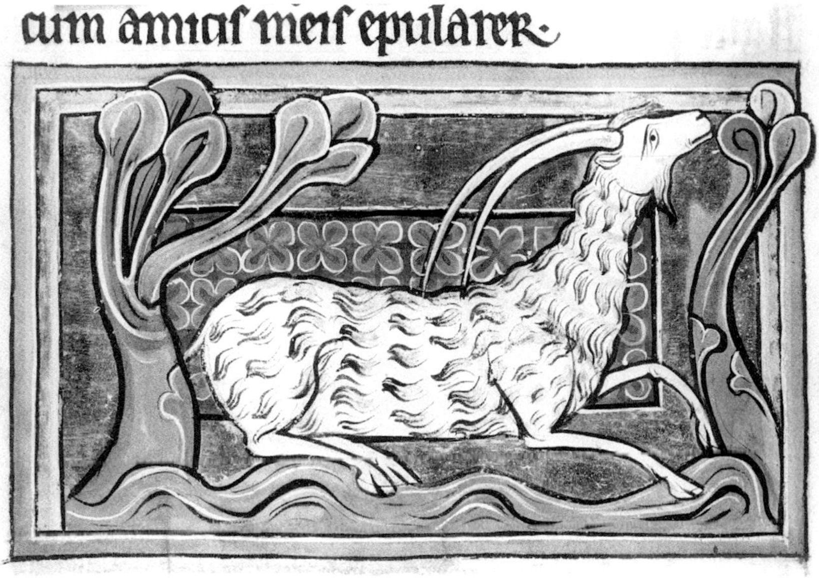

Figure 8. Goat. Oxford, from an English bestiary (Salisbury?), 1240–50. Bodleian Library, MS. Bodley 764, fol. 36v (detail). Reproduced by permission of The Bodleian Library, University of Oxford.

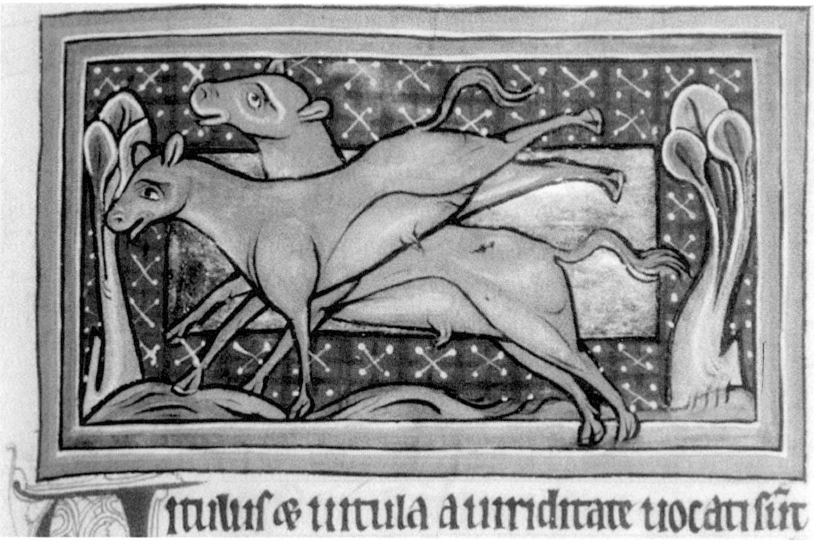

Figure 9. Calves of the Old Law and the New Law. Bodley 764 (as for fig. 8), fol. 42r (detail). Reproduced by permission of the Bodleian Library, University of Oxford.

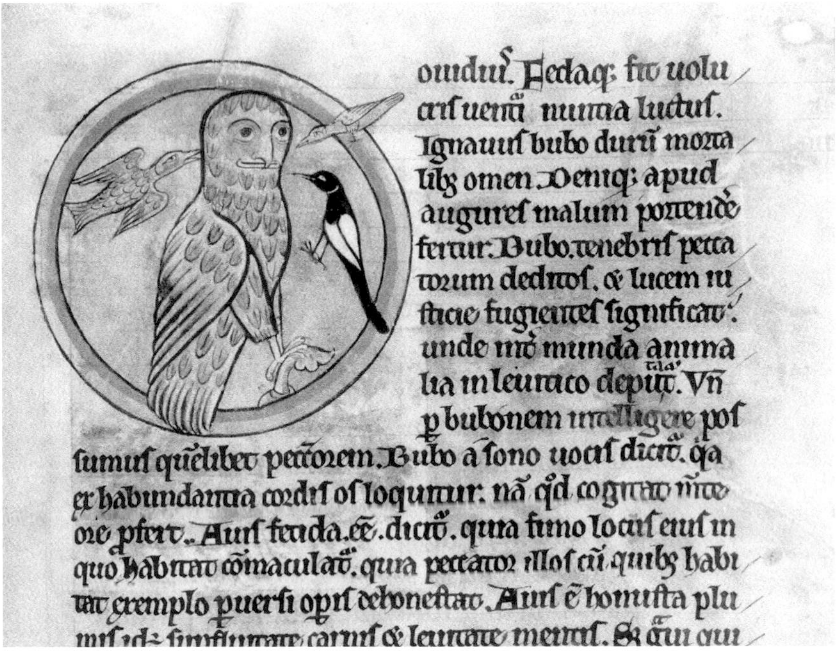

Figure 10. Owl attacked by other birds. Harley 4751 (as for fig. 4), fol. 47r (detail). Reproduced by permission of The British Library, London.

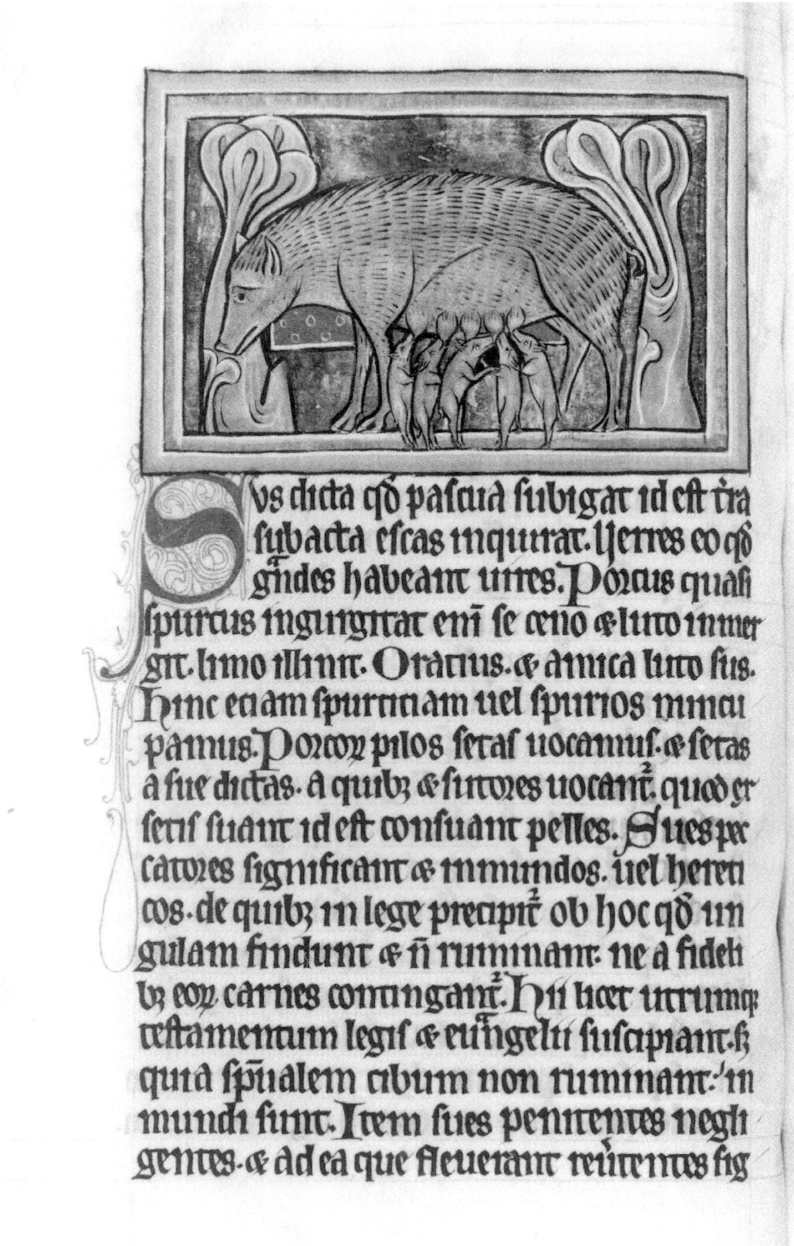

Figure 11. Sow suckling piglets. Bodley 764 (as for fig. 8), fol. 37v (detail). Reproduced by permission of The Bodleian Library, University of Oxford.

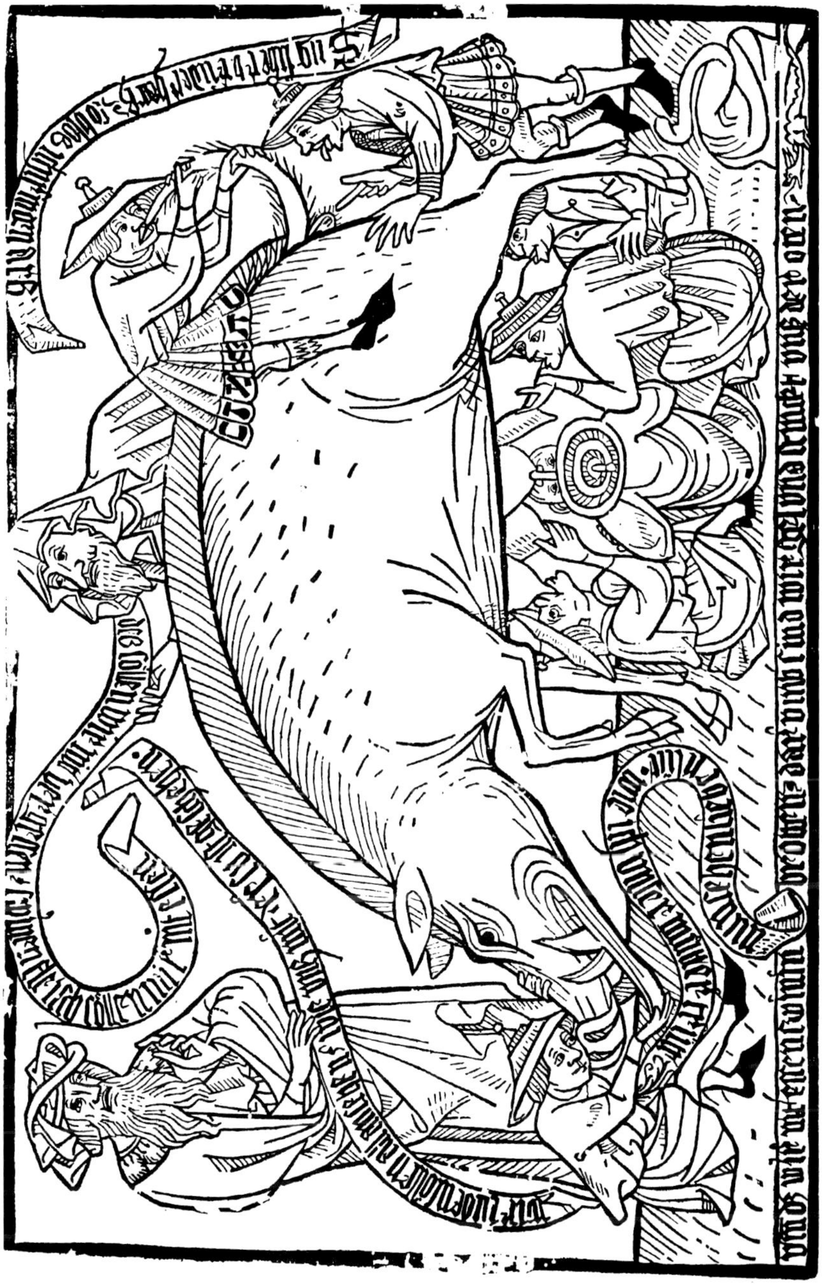

Figure 12. Anonymous German (Breisach), *Judensau*, woodcut, mid-fifteenth century. Reproduced by permission of the Staatliche Graphische Sammlung, Munich.

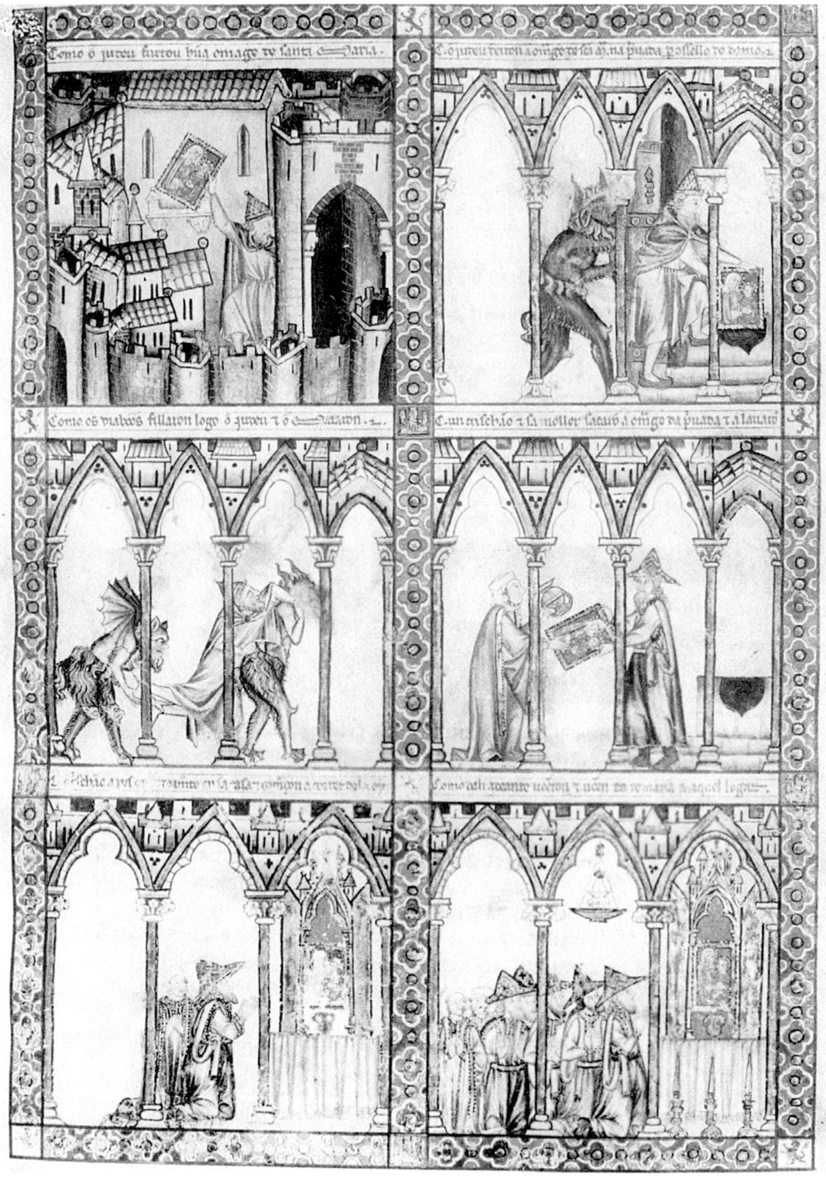

Figure 1. "How Holy Mary Got Even with the Jew for the Dishonor He Did to Her Image," *Cantigas de Santa Maria* (illustration for *cantiga* 34), late thirteenth century. Escorial, MS T.I.1, fol. 50r. Permission of the Instituto Amatller d'Art Hispanic.

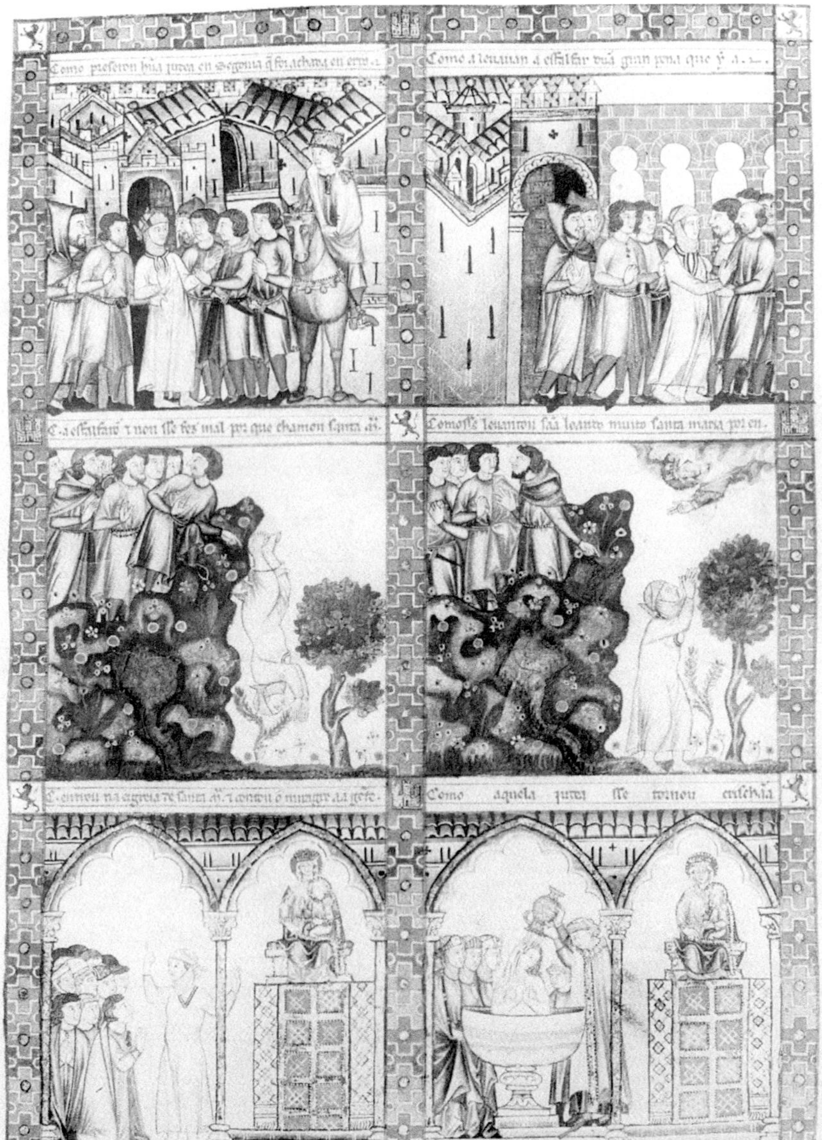

Figure 2. "How Holy Mary Saved From Death the Jewess Who Was Thrown Over a Cliff in Segovia," *Cantigas de Santa Maria* (illustration for *cantiga* 107), late thirteenth century. Escorial, MS T.I.1, fol. 154r. Permission of the Instituto Amatller d'Art Hispanic.

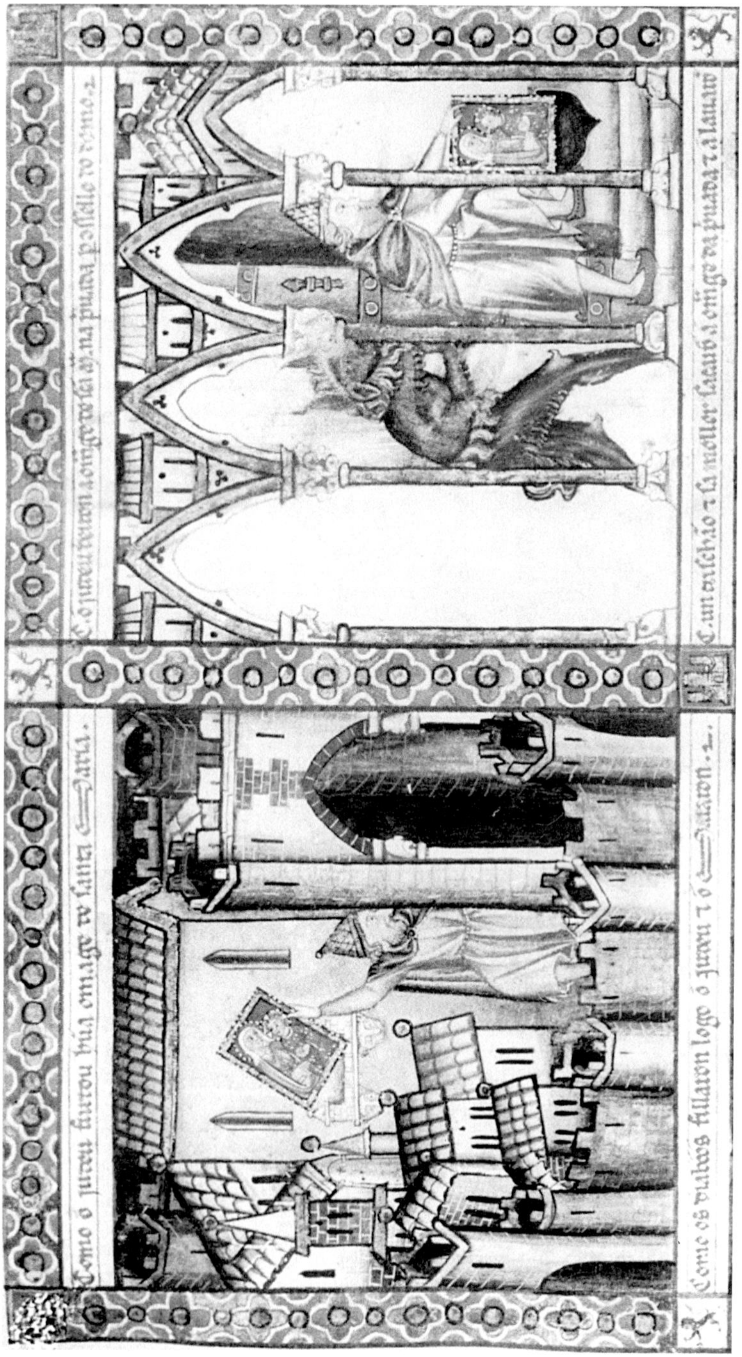

Figure 3. The Jew Stealing the Virgin's Image, *Cantigas de Santa Maria* (detail of illustration for *cantiga* 34), late thirteenth century. Escorial, MS T.I.1, fol. 50r. Permission of the Instituto Amatller d'Art Hispanic.

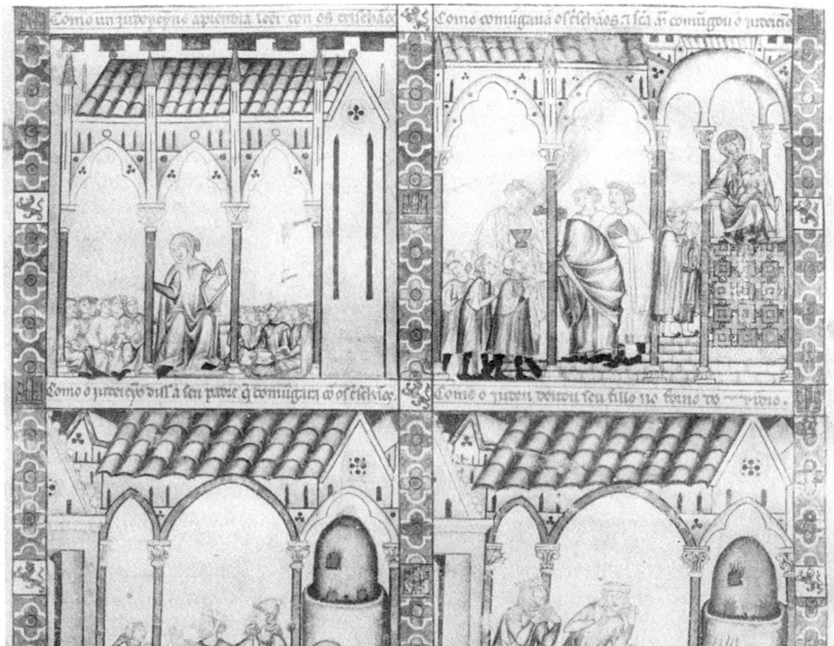

Figure 4. "How Holy Mary Saved from Burning the Son of the Jew, Whose Father Had Thrown Him into the Furnace," *Cantigas de Santa Maria* (illustration for *cantiga* 4), late thirteenth century. Escorial, MS T.I.1, fol. 9v. Permission of the Instituto Amatller d'Art Hispanic.

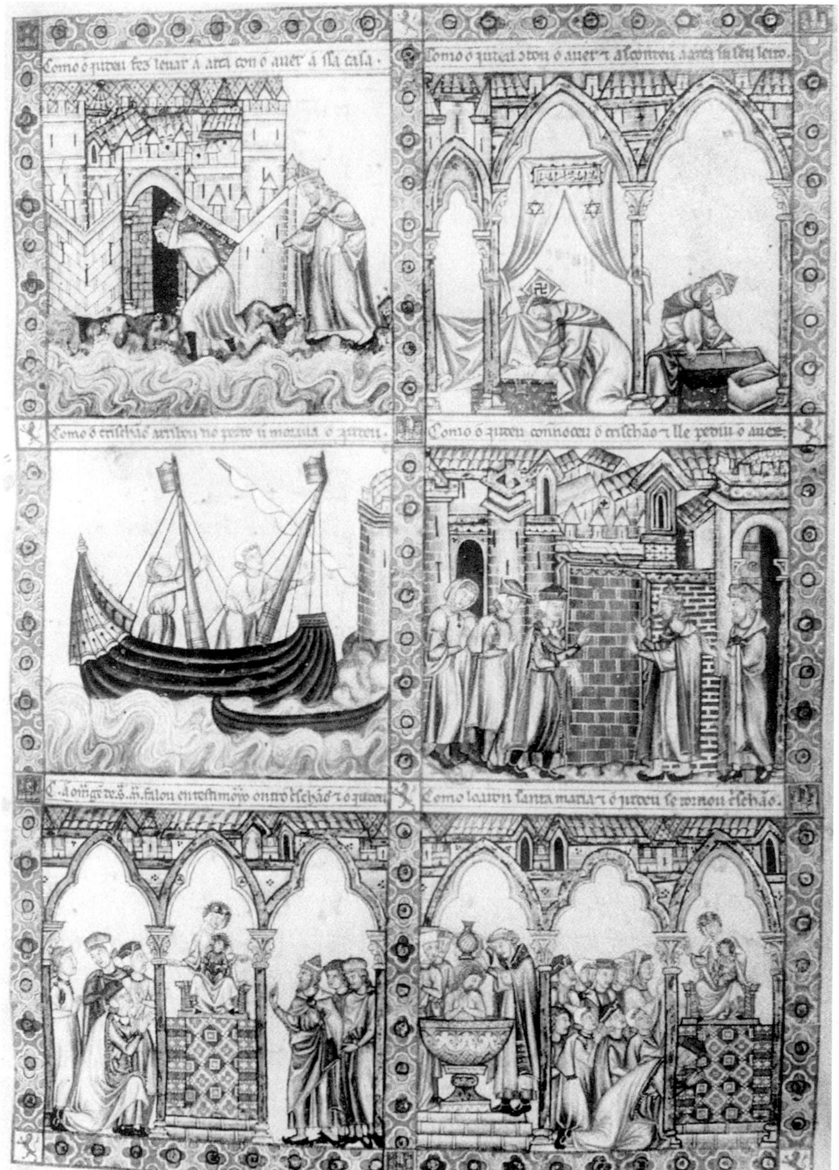

Figure 5. "How the Statue of Holy Mary Served as Witness Between the Christian and the Jew," *Cantigas de Santa Maria* (illustration for *cantiga* 25), late thirteenth century. Escorial, MS T.I.1, fol. 39r. Permission of the Instituto Amatller d'Art Hispanic.

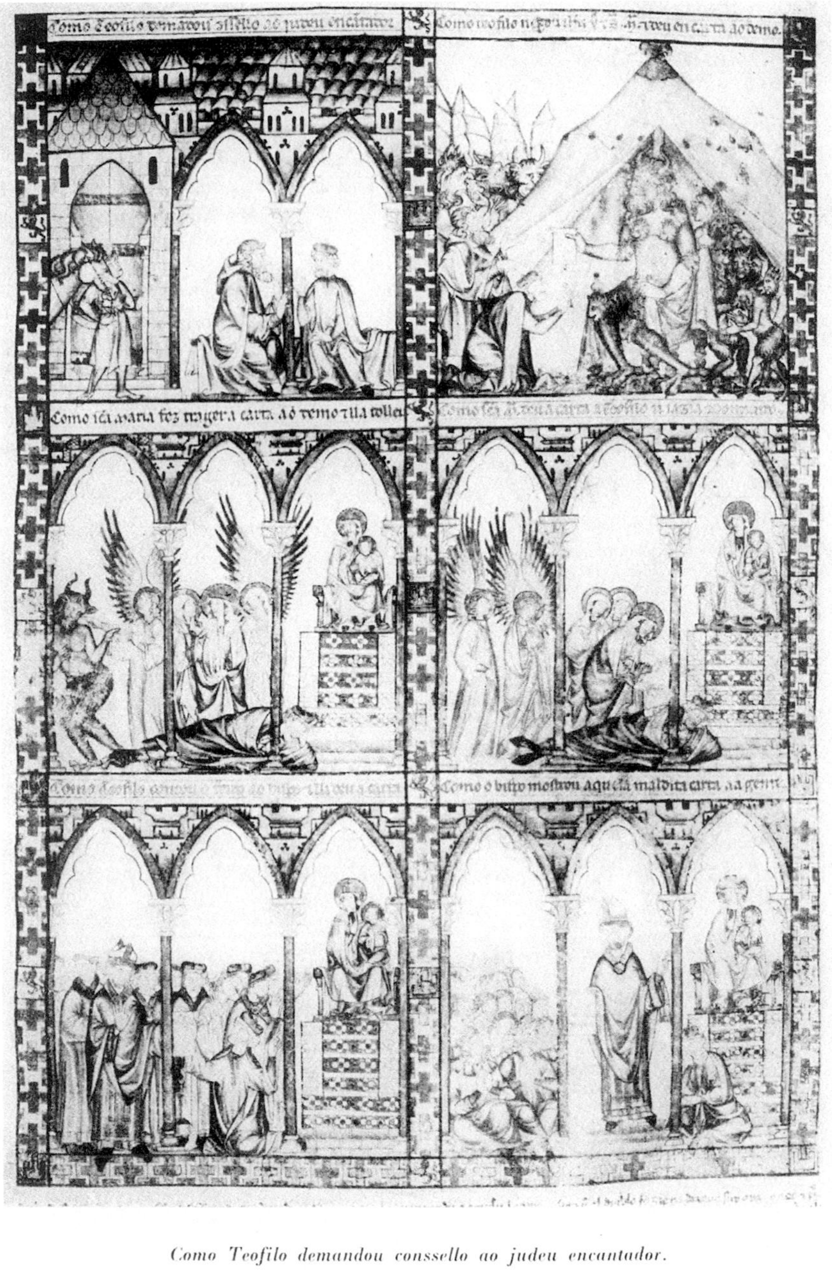

Como Teofilo demandou conssello ao judeu encantador.

Figure 6. "How Holy Mary Made Theophilus Recover the Letter Which He Had Signed With the Devil, Promising to Become His Vassal," *Cantigas de Santa Maria* (illustration for *cantiga* 3), late thirteenth century. Escorial, MS T.I.1, fol 8r. Permission of the Instituto Amatller d'Art Hispanic.

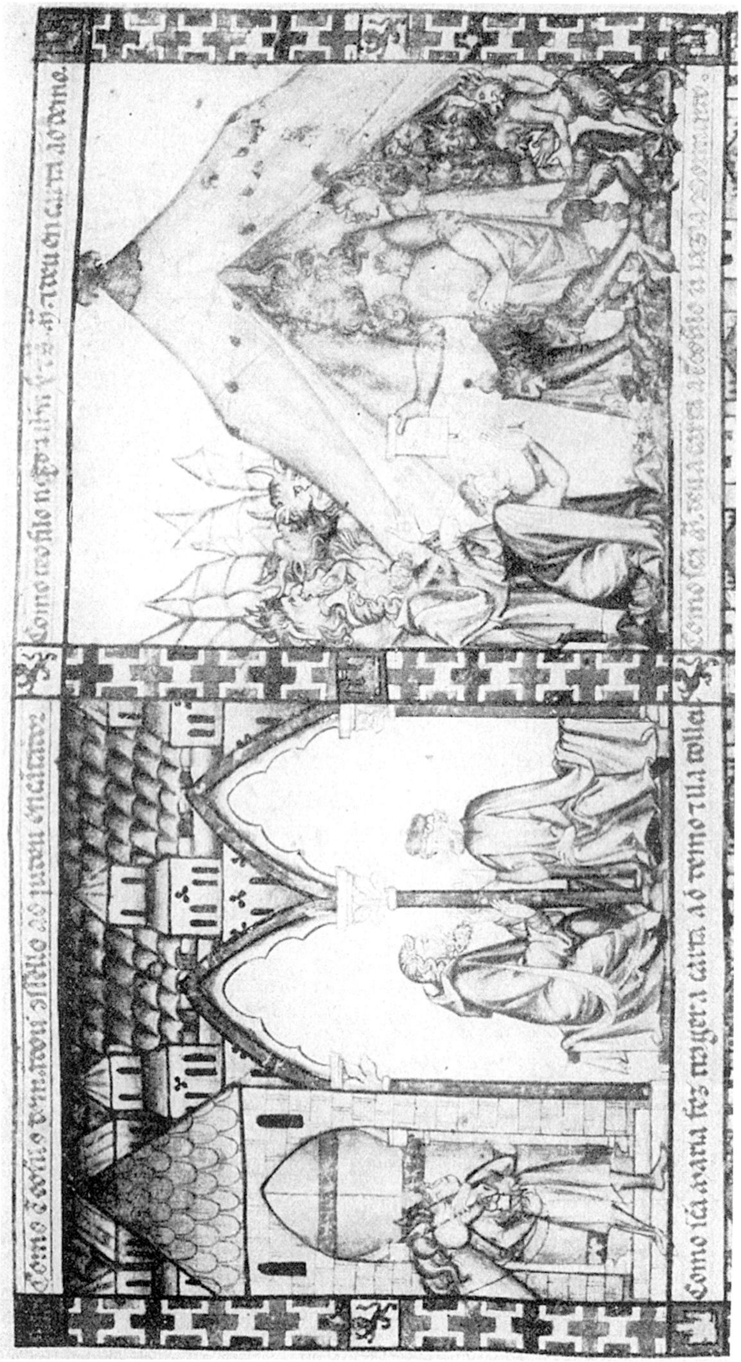

Figure 7. Theophilus making a pact with the Devil, *Cantigas de Santa Maria* (detail of illustration, for *cantiga* 3), late thirteenth century. Escorial, MS T.I.1, fol. 8r. Permission of the Instituto Amatller d'Art Hispanic.

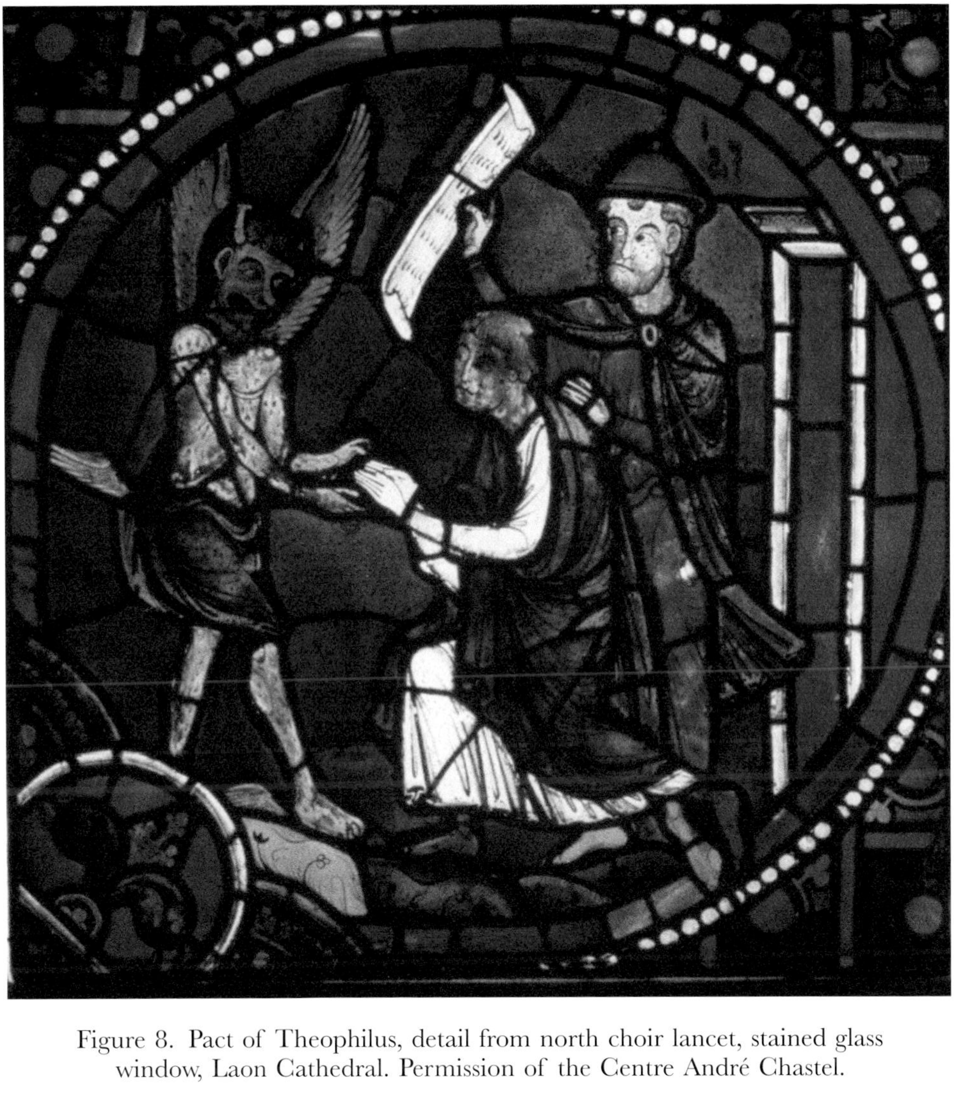

Figure 8. Pact of Theophilus, detail from north choir lancet, stained glass window, Laon Cathedral. Permission of the Centre André Chastel.

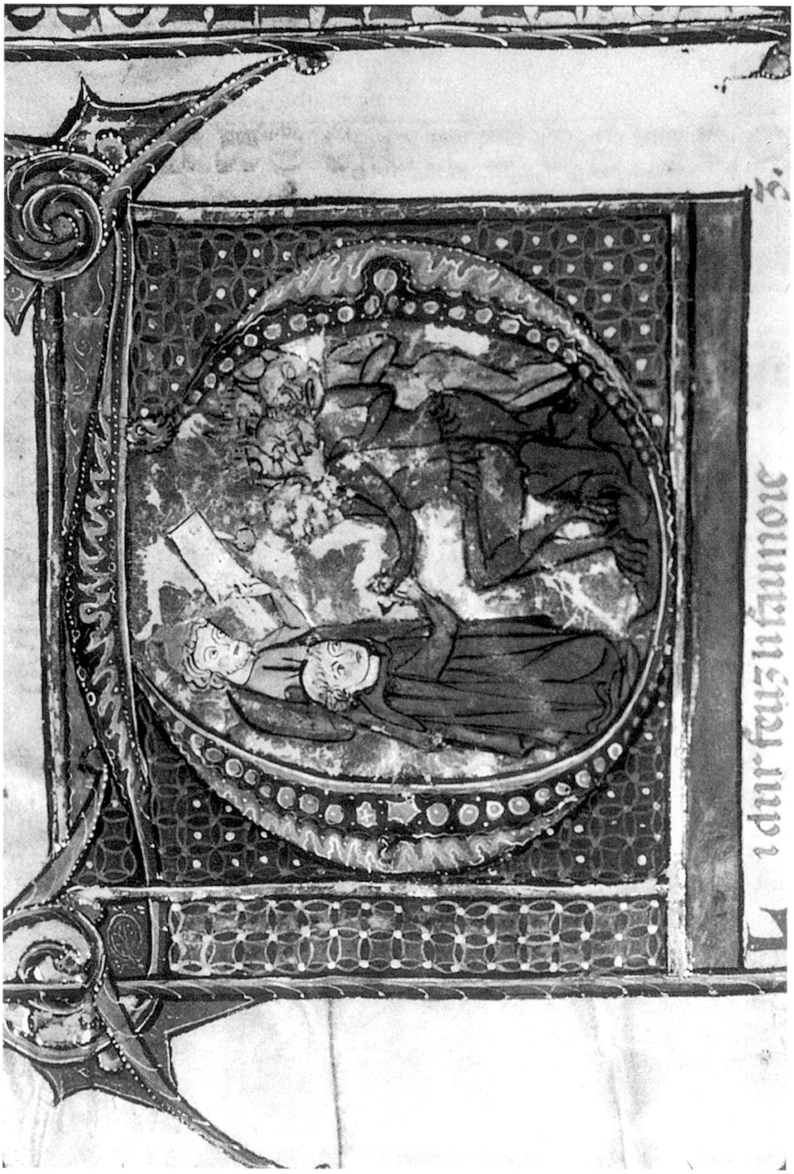

Figure 9. Initial depicting the pact of Theophilus, Besançon, Municipal Library, MS 551, fol. 7v. Institut de Recherche et d'Histoire des Textes (CNRS), by permission of the Bibliothéque Municipale de Besançon.

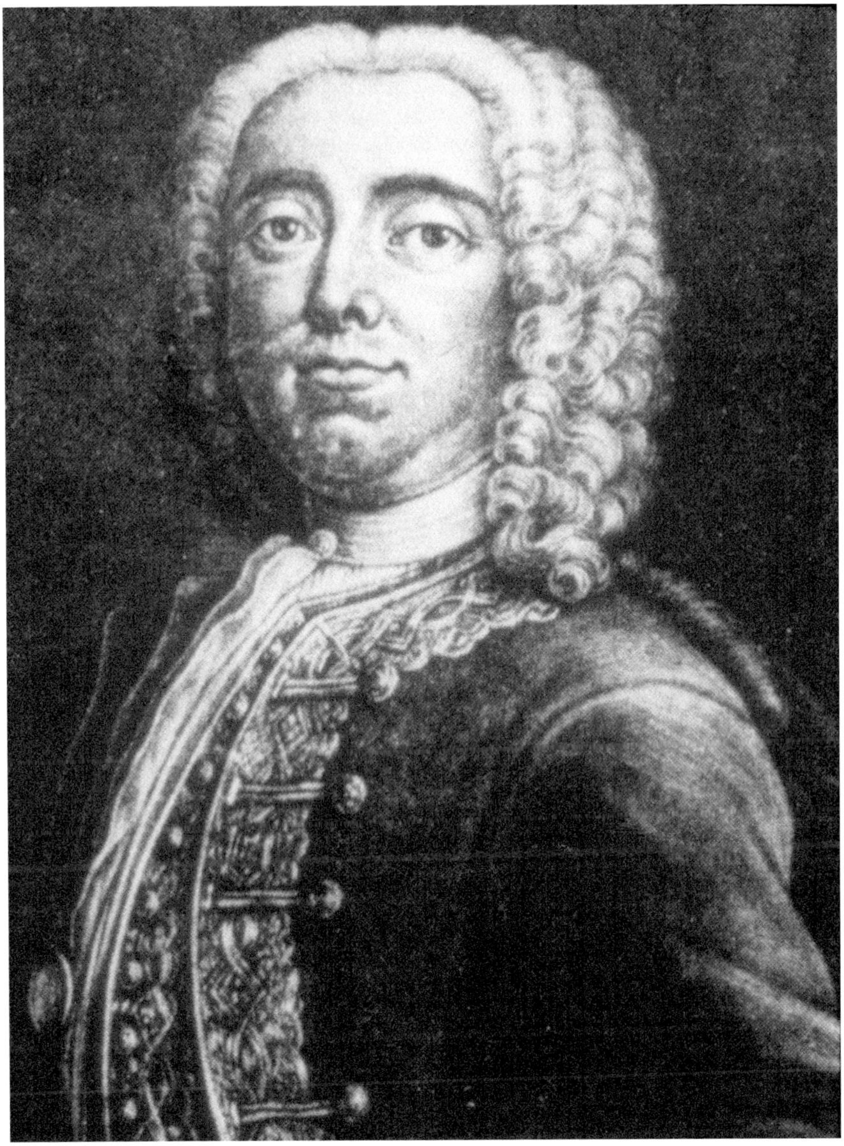

Figure 1. *Joseph Süss Oppenheimer*, 1738, mezzotint. Formerly in the Collection of Alfred Rubens, London.

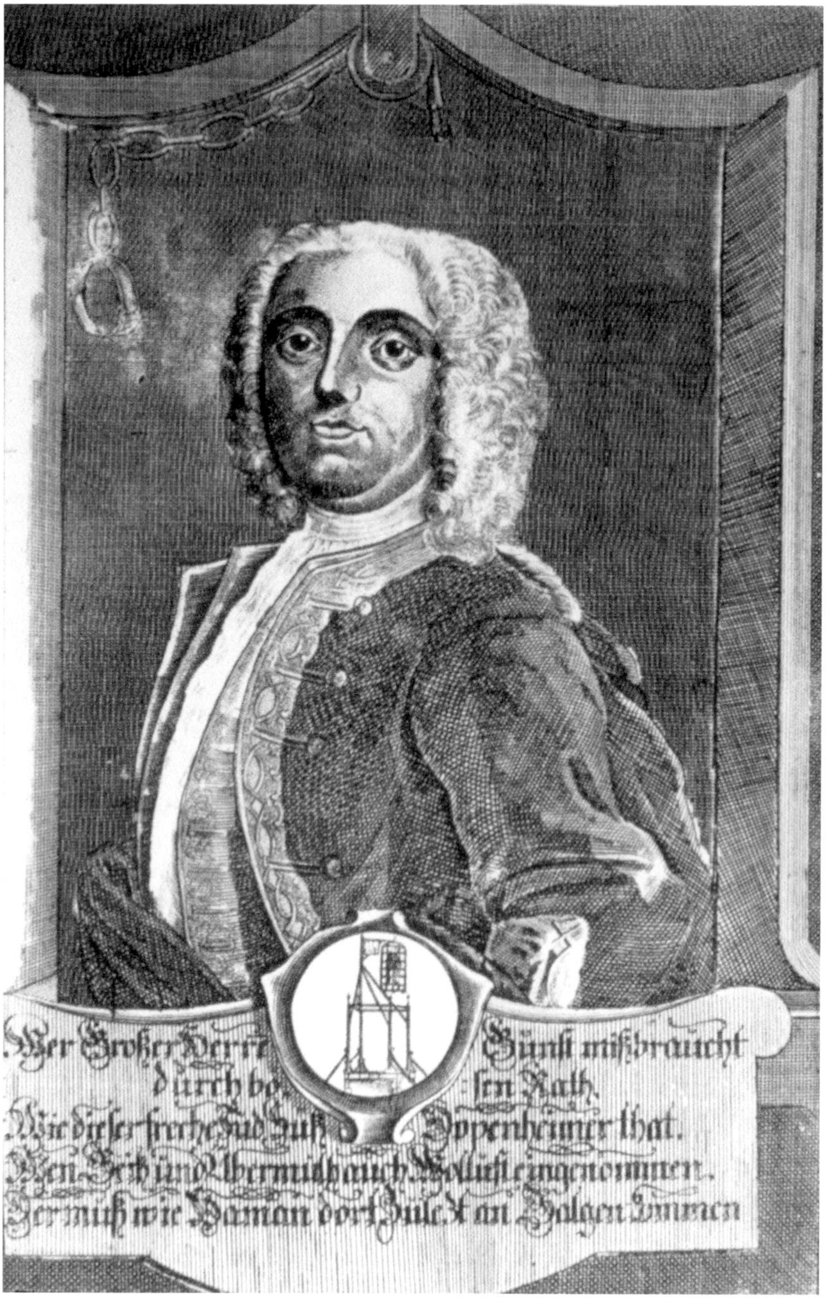

Figure 2. *Portrait of Joseph S. Oppenheimer*, Stuttgart (?), 1738, etching, 33.3 × 21.7. Nuremberg, Germanisches Nationalmuseum, HB 8513.

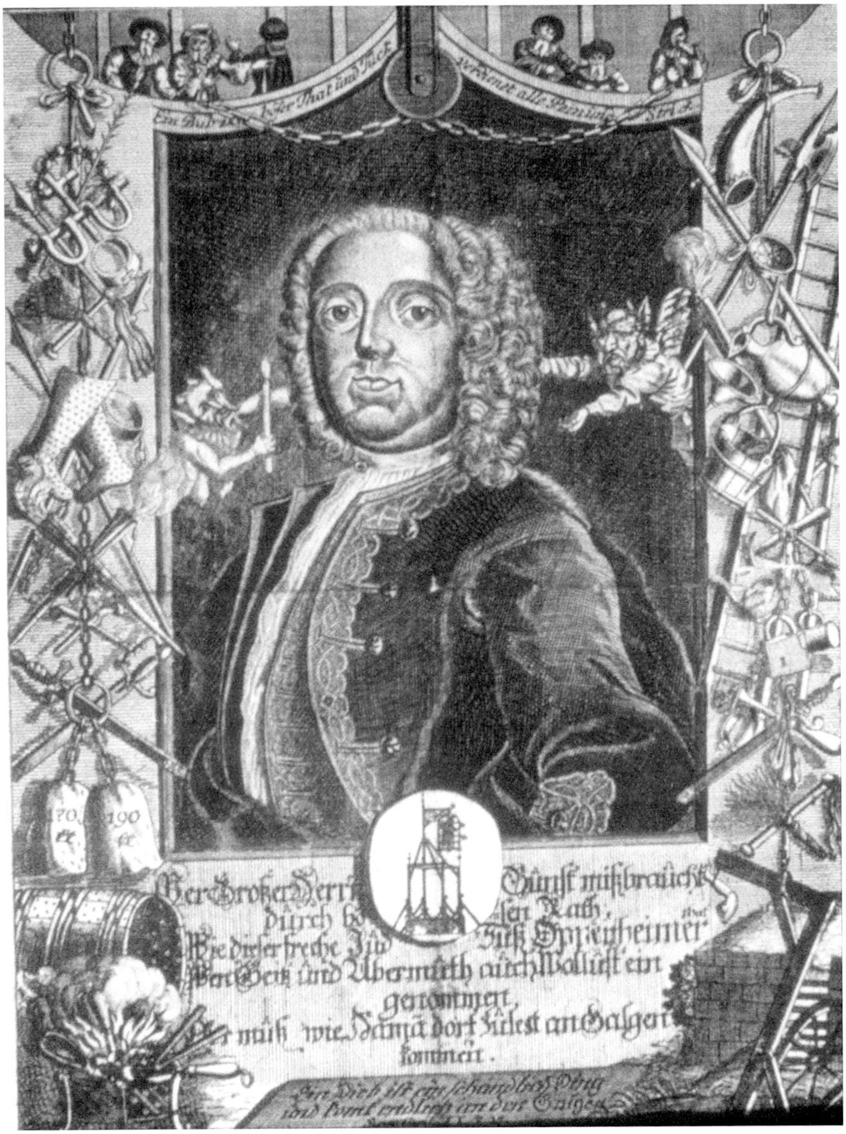

Figure 3. *Wer grossen Herrn missbraucht durch bösen Rath*, Stuttgart (?), 1738, engraving 41 × 30.5 cm. The Moldovan Family Collection.

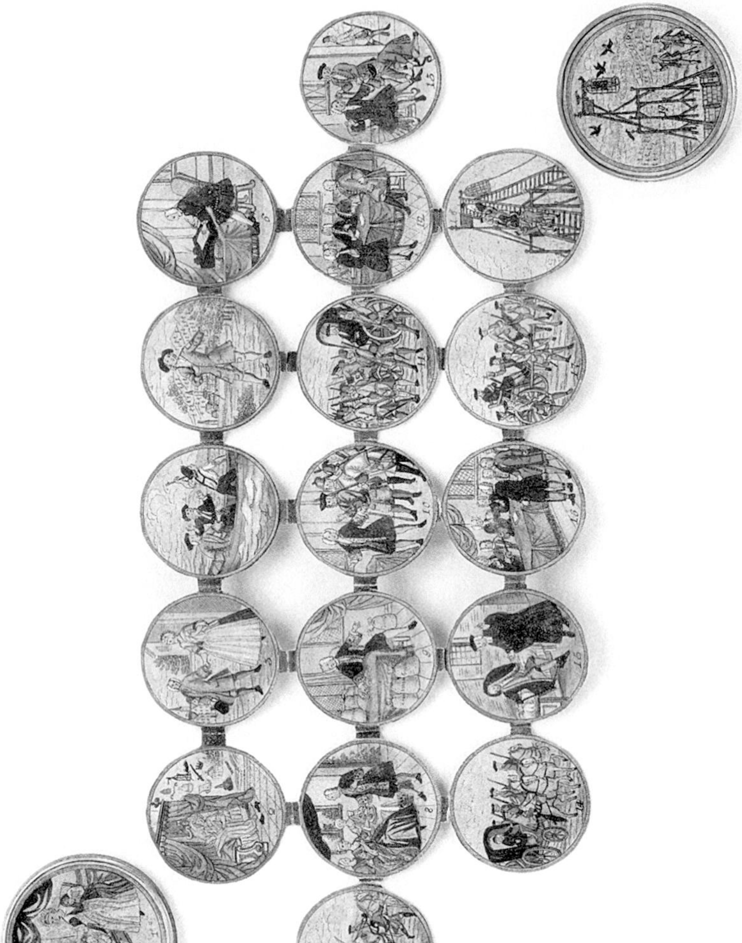

Figure 4. *Spottmedaille or Schraubtaler* of Jud Süss, Stuttgart (?), 1738, Silver, parchment and gouache, 4.2 cm. in dia. Collection of Mr. and Mrs. Bill Stern.

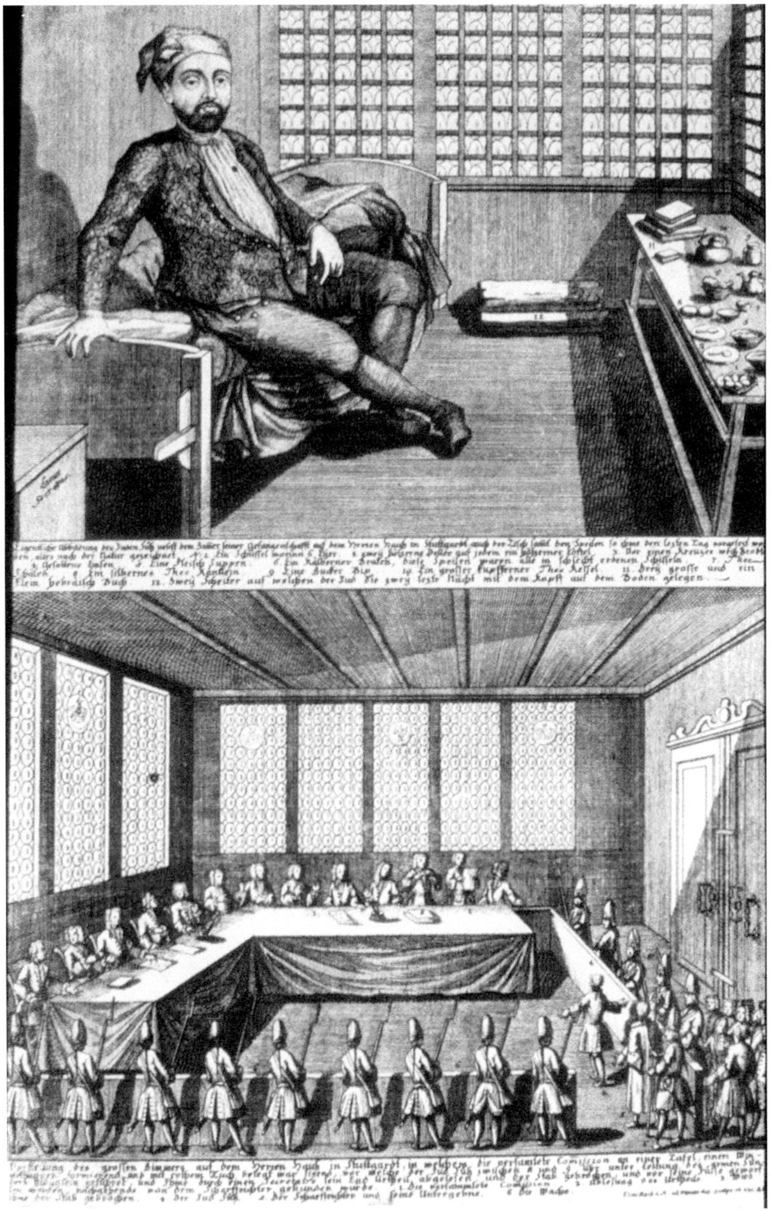

Figure 5. Elias Baeck (1679–1747), *Wahrhaffte und gründliche Relations was sich in den letzten Studen*...*Juden Joseph Süss Oppenheimer*, Augsburg, 1738, engraving, 17.5 × 28.5 cm. The Leo Baeck Institute.

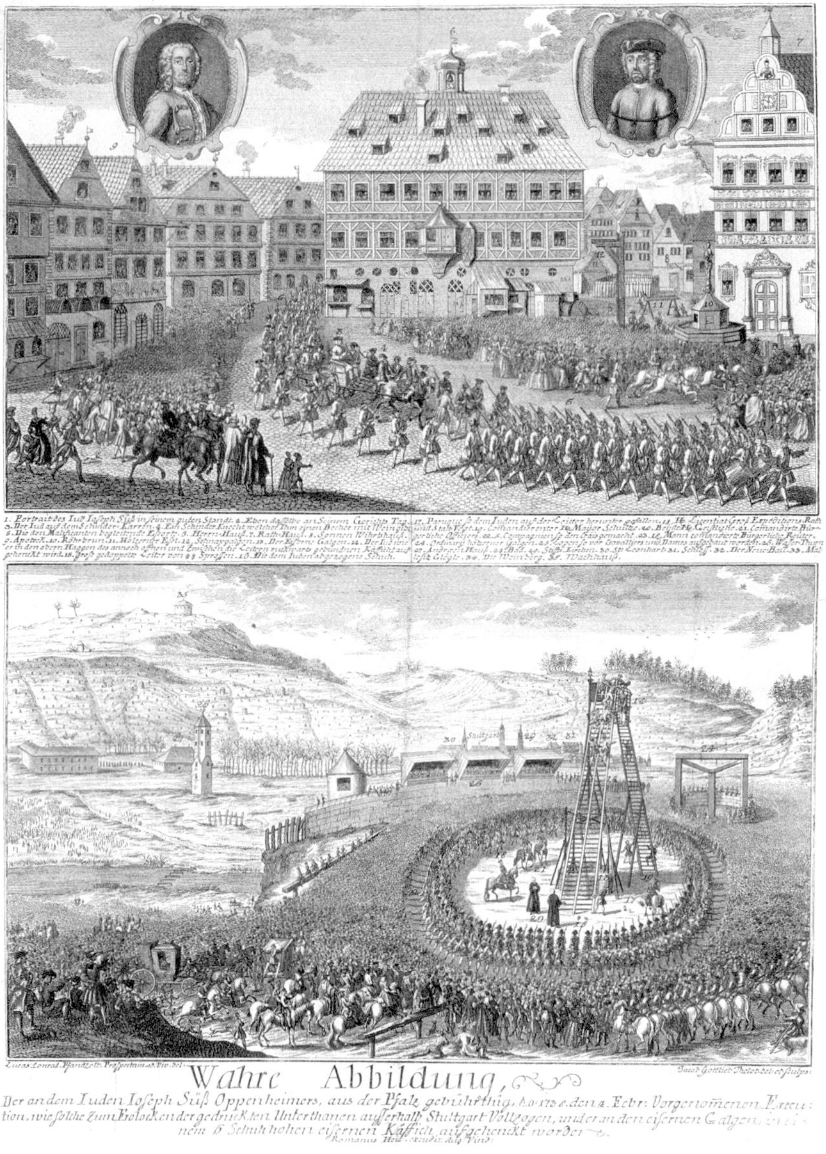

Figure 6. Jacob Gottlieb Thelot (1708–1760), *Wahre Abbildung*, Stuttgart, 1738, colored engraving on copper, after a design by C. L. Pfandzelt (1716–1786), 22.4 × 32.6 cm. The Moldovan Family Collection.

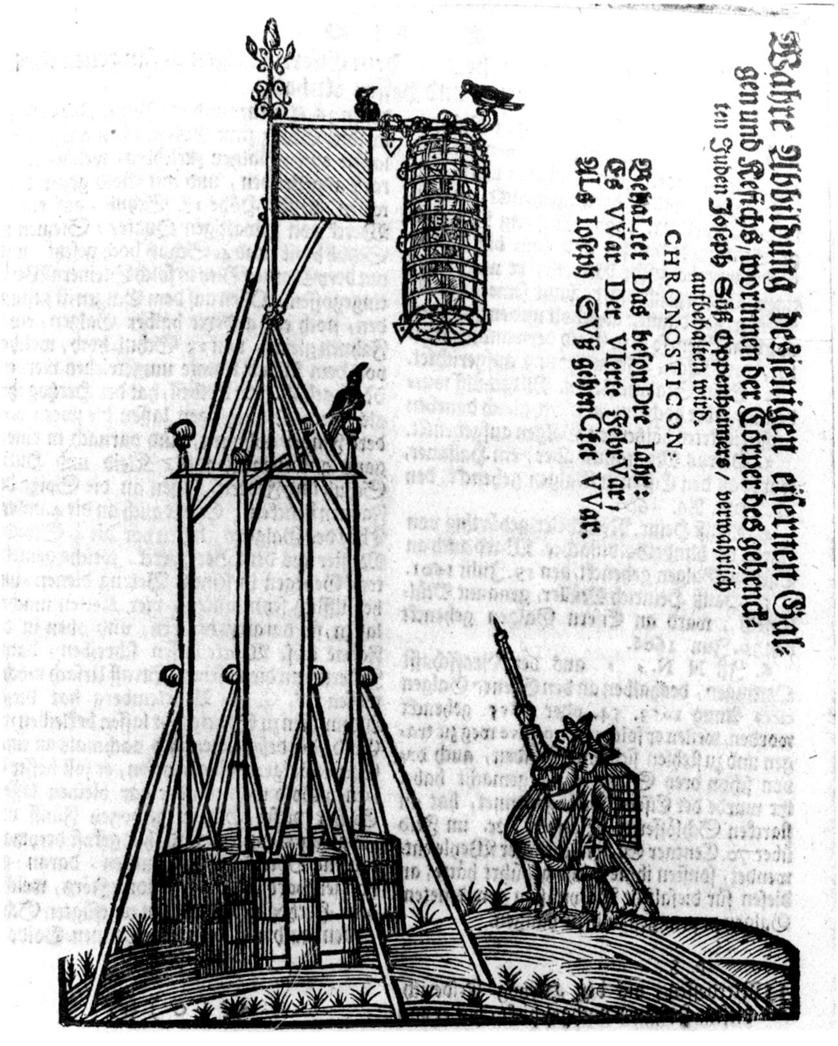

Figure 7. *Galgen des Joseph S. Oppenheimer, Poetischer Entwurff*, 1737, woodcut. Courtesy of The Library of the Jewish Theological Seminary of America.

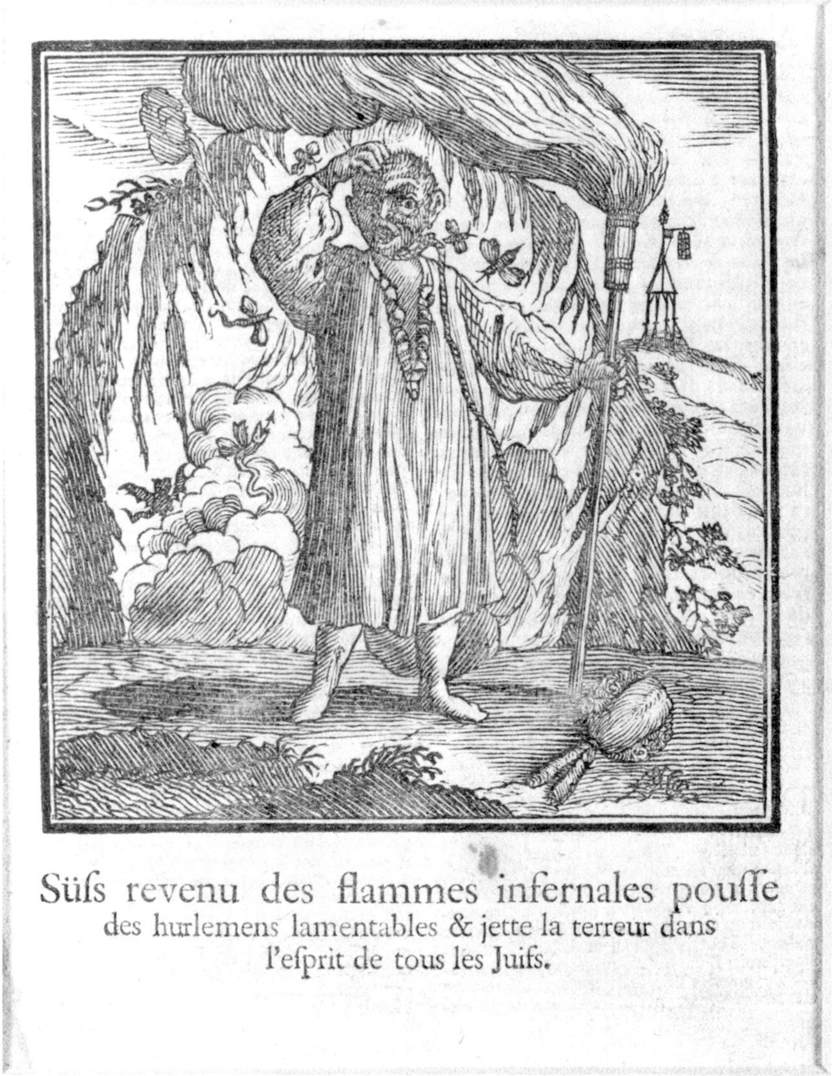

Figure 8. *Süss revenu des flammes infernales*... *Suite de la relation curieuse des choses les plus remarquable arrivées en Europe*, Basel, 1738–47, engraving 18 × 15.8 cm. Collection of Daniel Friedenberg.

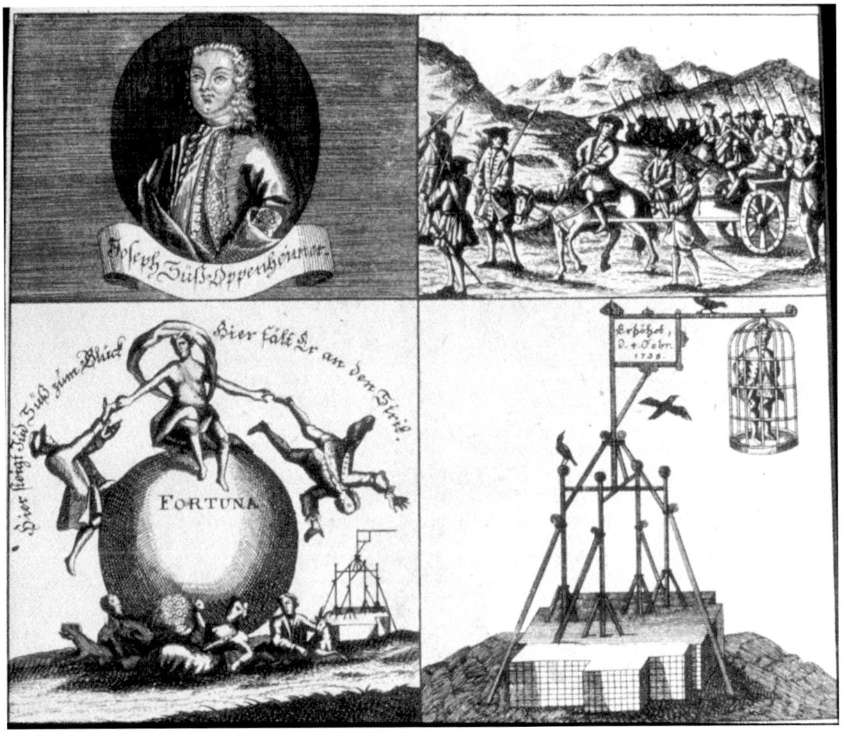

Figure 9. *Rise and Fall of Jud Süss*, engraving, 16.7 × 19 cm., from Arnoldo Liberio, *Volkommene Historie und Lebens-Beschreibung* (Frankfurt and Leipzig, 1738). Private Collection.

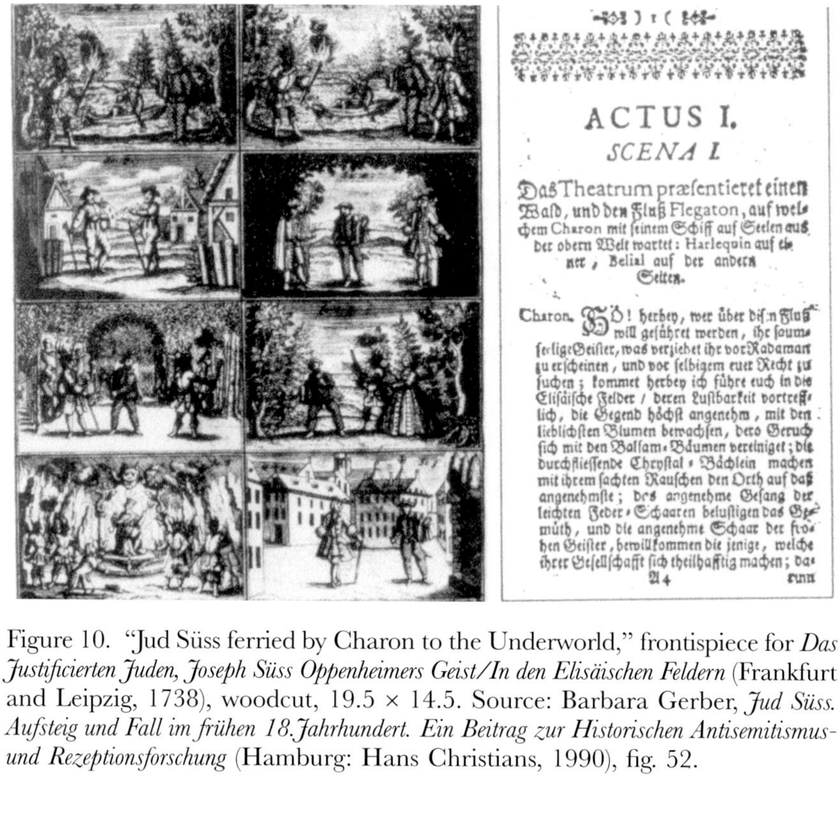

Figure 10. "Jud Süss ferried by Charon to the Underworld," frontispiece for *Das Justificierten Juden, Joseph Süss Oppenheimers Geist/In den Elisäischen Feldern* (Frankfurt and Leipzig, 1738), woodcut, 19.5 × 14.5. Source: Barbara Gerber, *Jud Süss. Aufsteig und Fall im frühen 18.Jahrhundert. Ein Beitrag zur Historischen Antisemitismus- und Rezeptionsforschung* (Hamburg: Hans Christians, 1990), fig. 52.

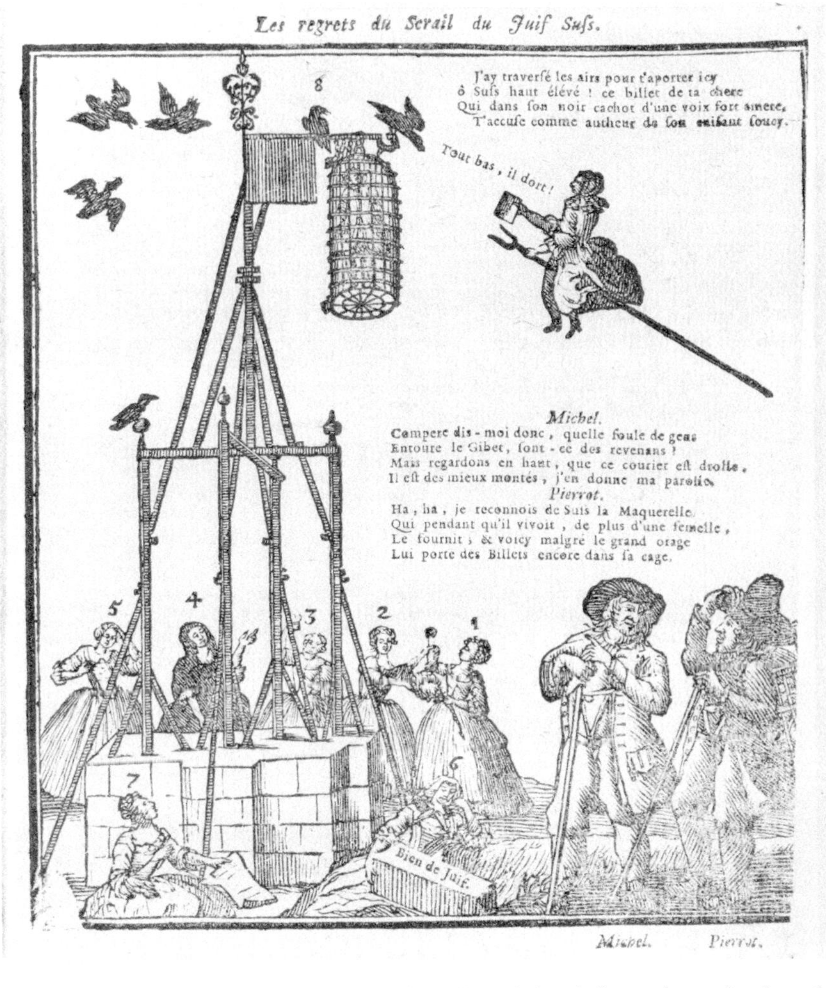

Figure 11. *Les Regrets du Serail du Juif Süss, Suite de la relation curieuses des choses les plus remarquable arrivées en Europe* (Basel, 1738–1747), engraving, 18 × 15.8 cm. Collection of Daniel Friedenberg.

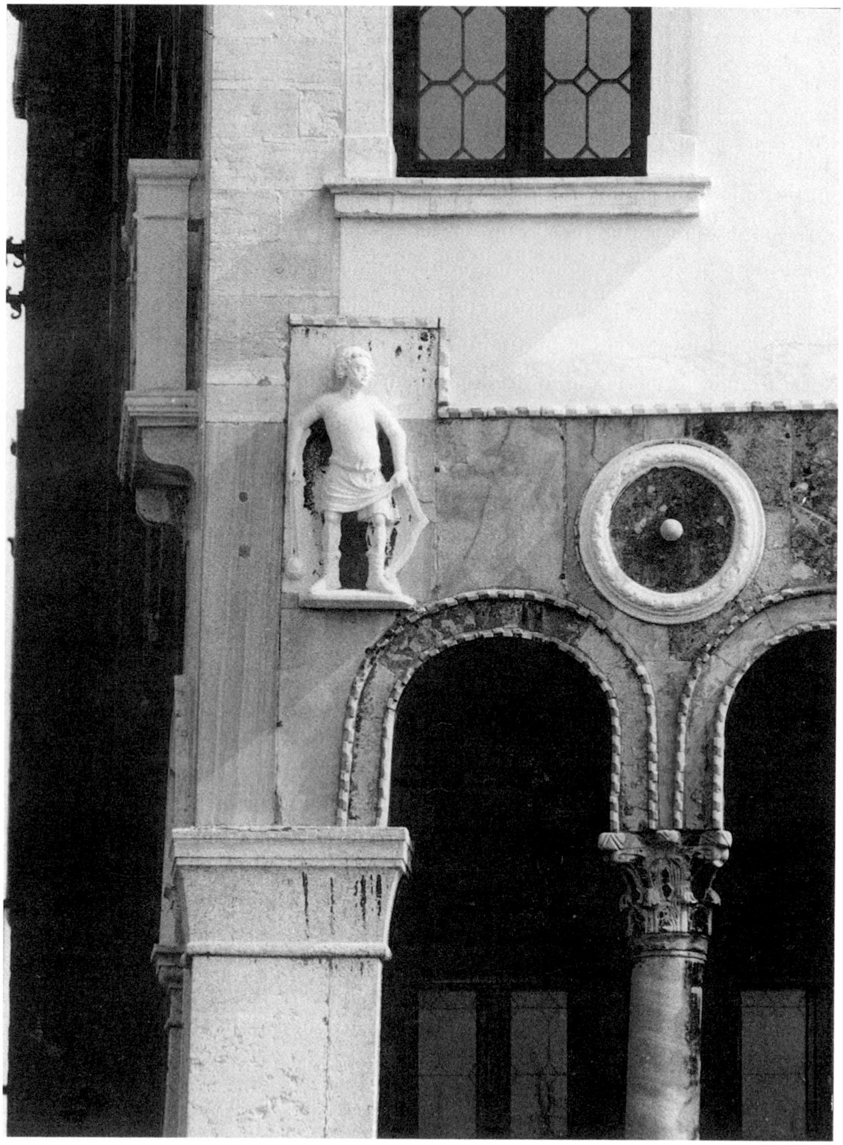

Figure 1. David, Palazzo Loredan (Corner-Pisciopia), Venice, c. 1363–1365, stone, about 50 × 120 cm. Photo by Oswaldo Böhm, Venice.

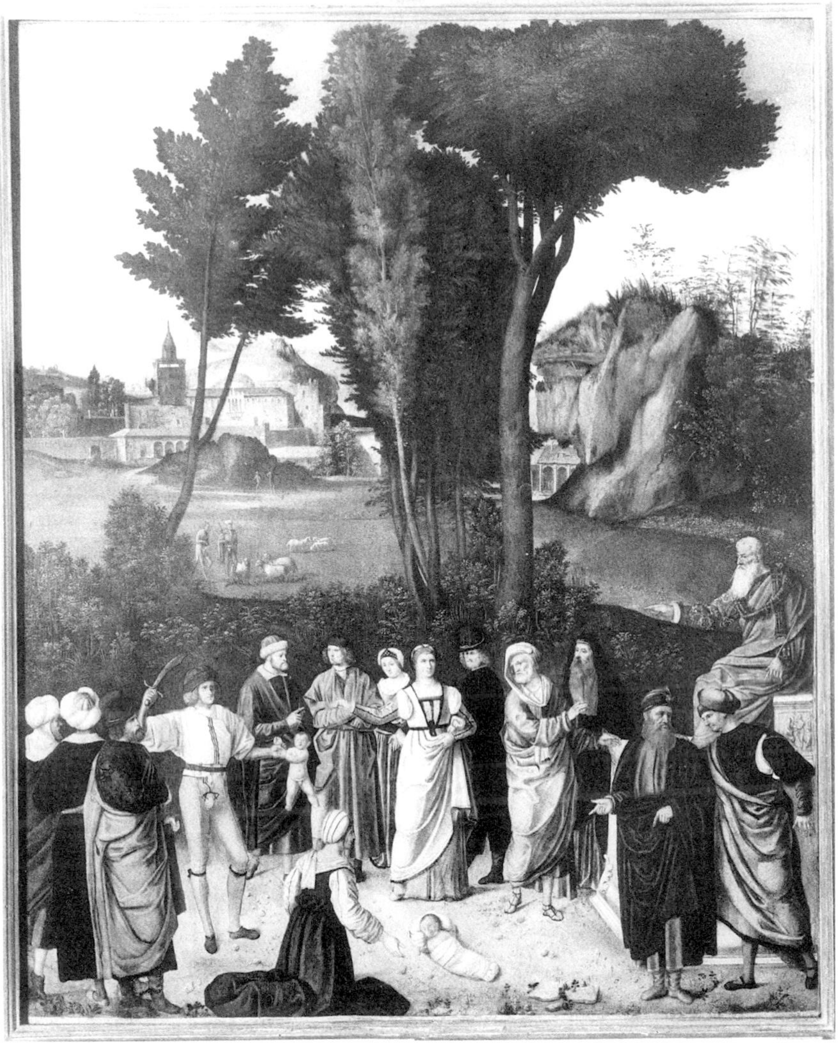

Figure 2. Giorgione, *Judgment of Solomon*, oil on panel, 89 × 72 cm. Uffizi Gallery, Florence. Reproduced by permission of Soprintendenza ai Beni Artistici e Storici di Firenze, Prato, Pistoia. Photo by Alinari.

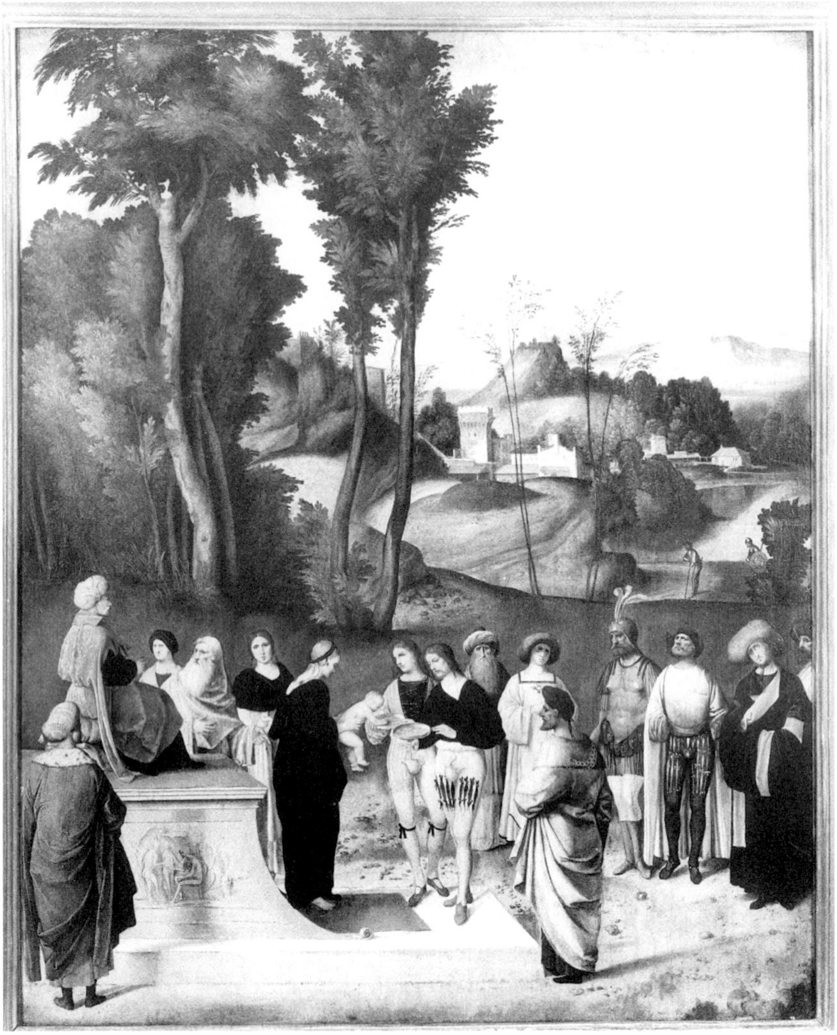

Figure 3. Giorgione, *Trial of the Infant Moses*, oil on panel, 89 × 72 cm. Uffizi Gallery, Florence. Reproduced by permission of Soprintendenza ai Beni Artistici e Storici di Firenze, Prato, Pistoia. Photo by Alinari.

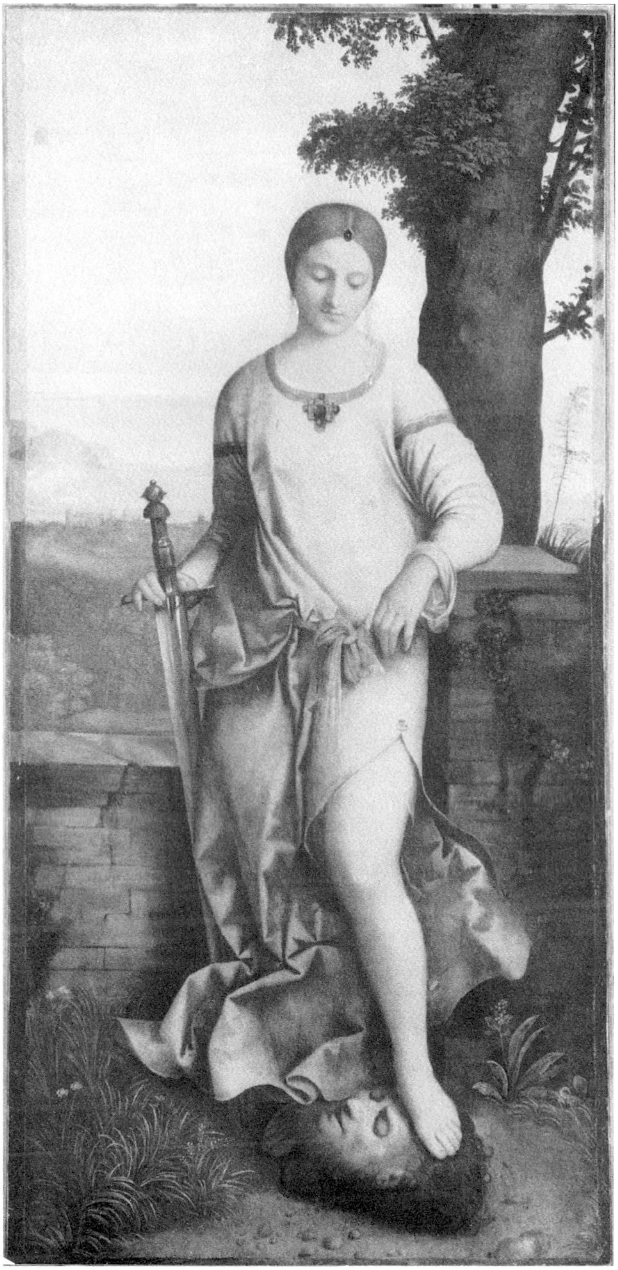

Figure 4. Giorgione, *Judith*, oil on panel transferred to canvas, 144 × 67 cm. State Hermitage Museum, St. Petersburg. Reproduced by permission of the State Hermitage Museum, St. Petersburg.

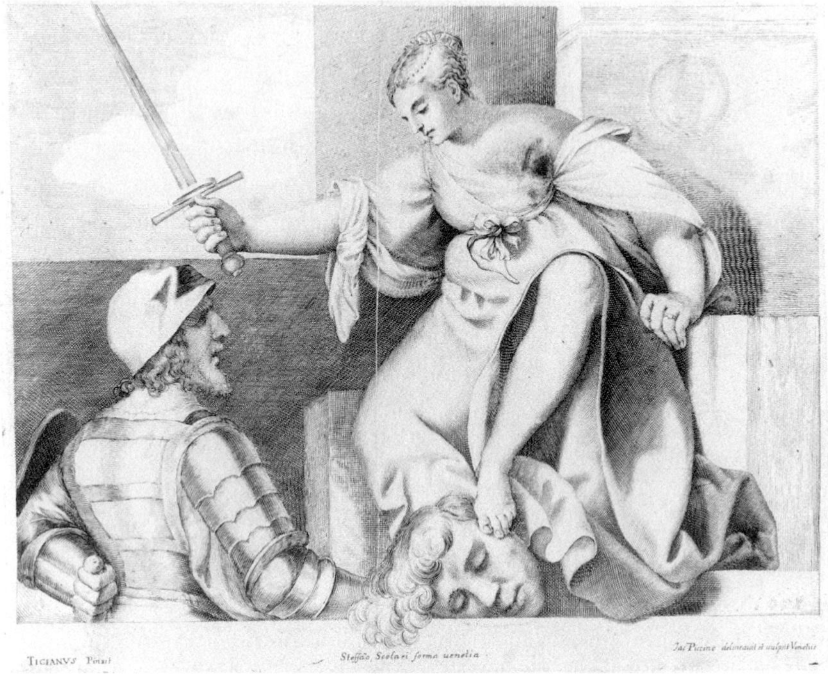

Figure 5. Jacopo Piccini after Giorgione and/or Titian, *Judith as Justice*, engraving, 30 × 36 cm. Author's photo.

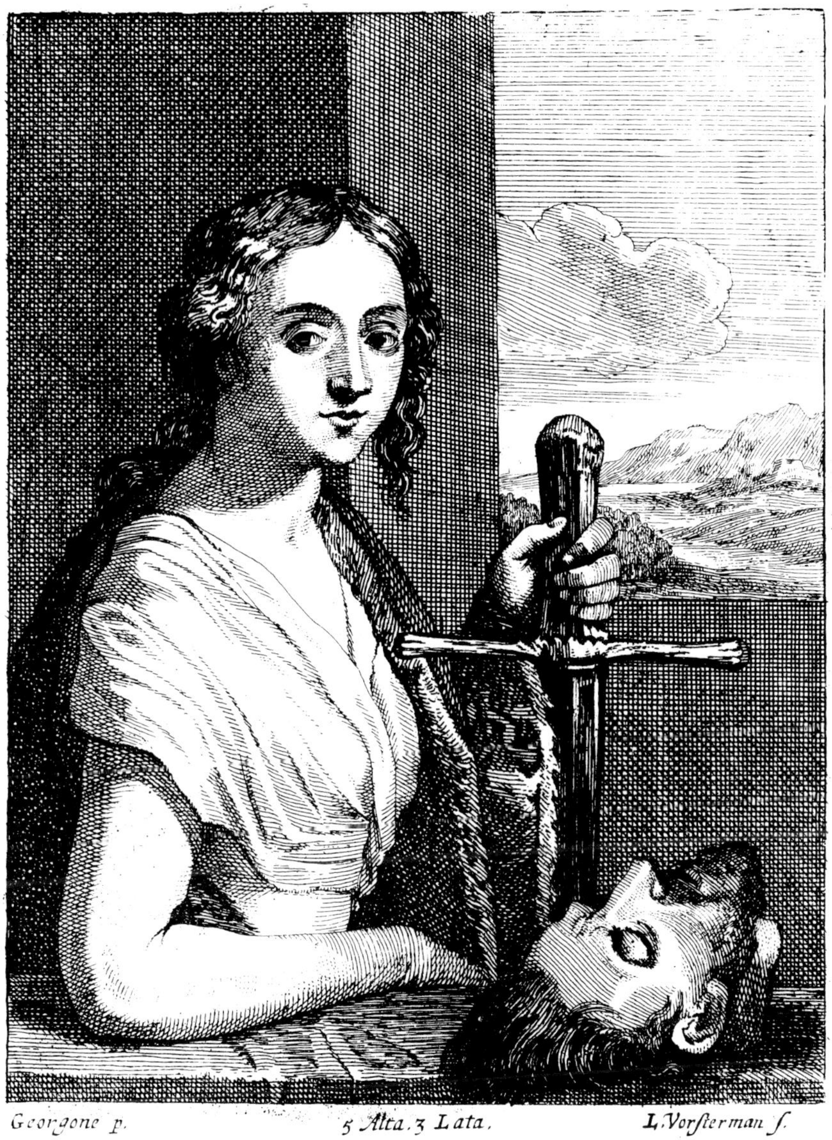

Figure 6. David Teniers after Giorgione (?), *Judith*, engraving (by Lucas Vorsterman II), 13 × 10 cm., from the *Theatrum Pictorium* (1660). Reproduced from the Collections of the Library of Congress.

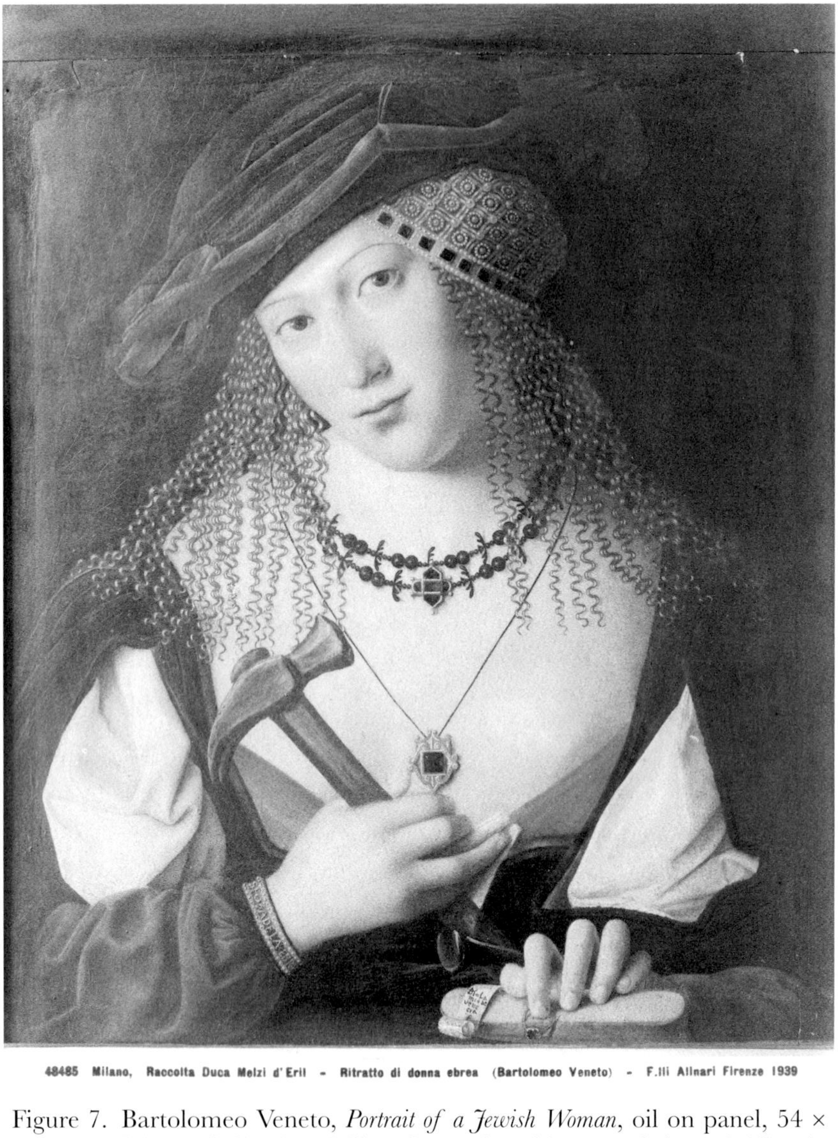

48485 Milano, Raccolta Duca Melzi d'Eril - Ritratto di donna ebrea (Bartolomeo Veneto) - F.lli Alinari Firenze 1939

Figure 7. Bartolomeo Veneto, *Portrait of a Jewish Woman*, oil on panel, 54 × 41.5 cm. Private Collection, Milan. Reproduced by permission of Alinari.

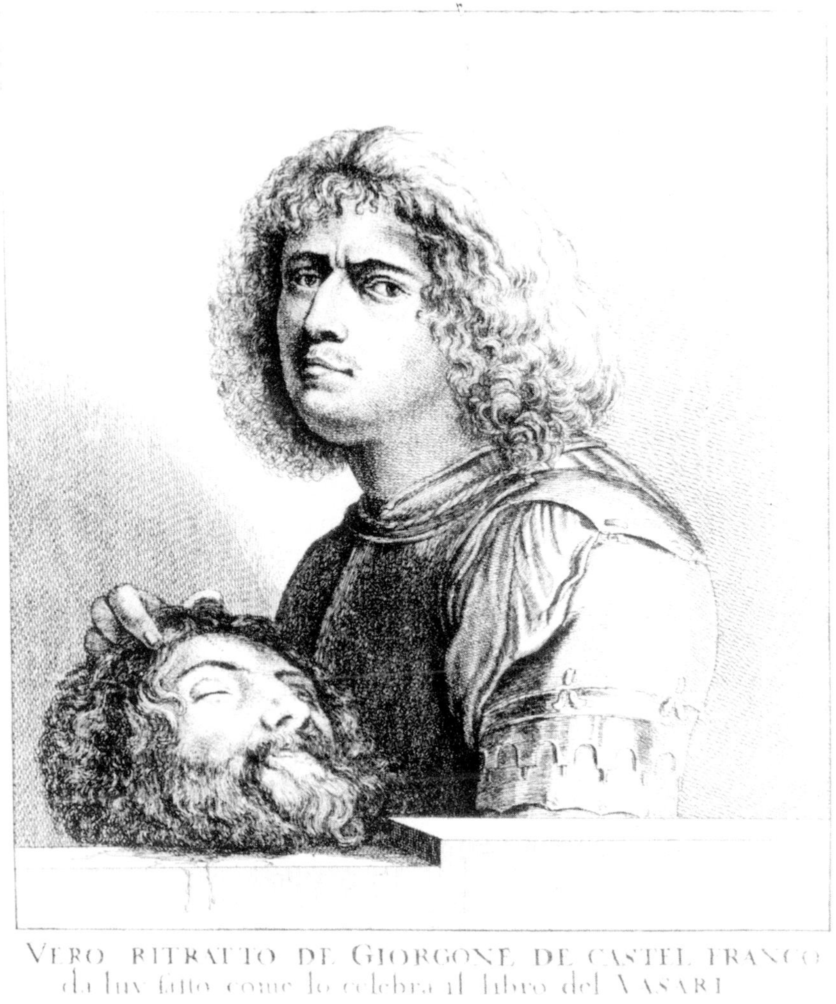

Figure 8. Wenzel Hollar after Giorgione, *Self-Portrait as David*, etching, 26 × 19 cm. Author's photo.

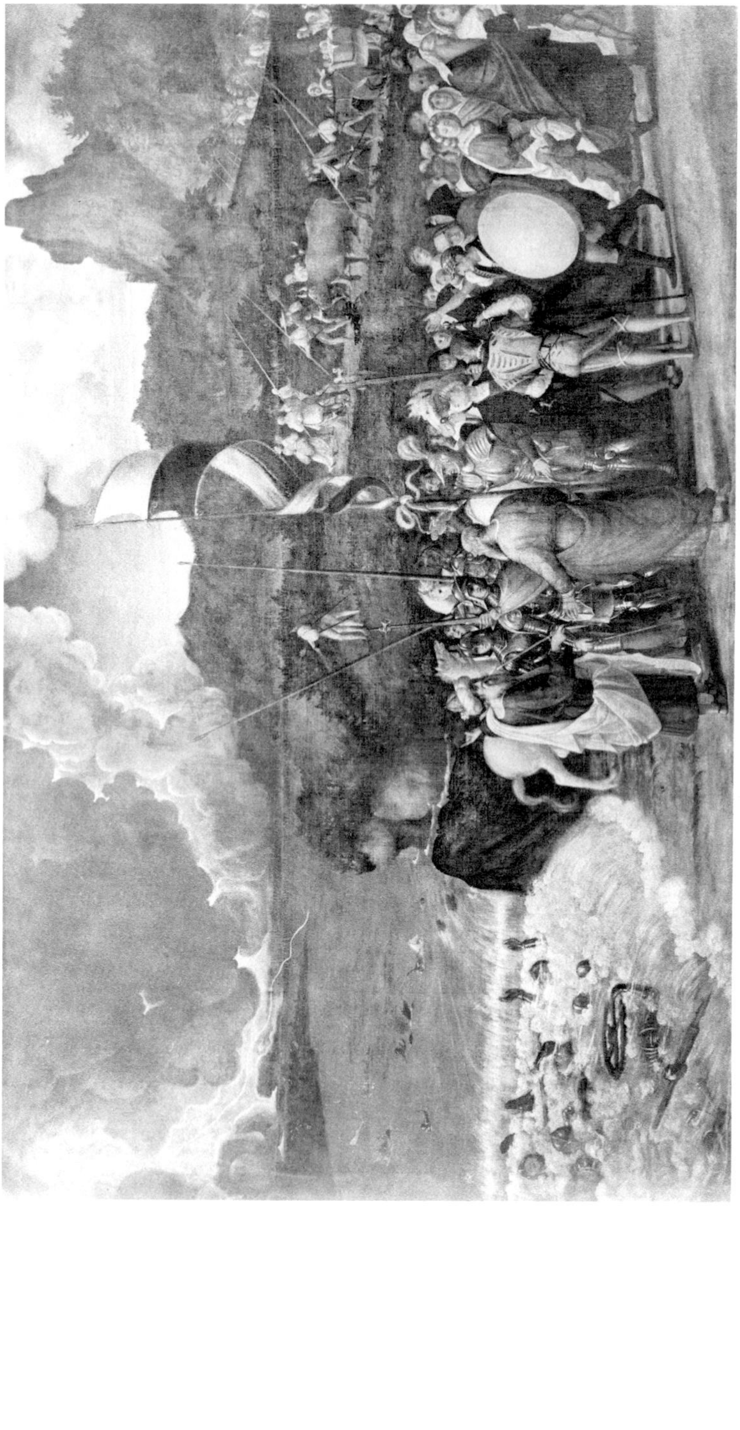

(Ed.ne Alinari) P.e 2.a N.o 13284. VENEZIA - Palazzo Ducale. Il passaggio del Mar Rosso. (Previtali Andrea, già att. a Tiziano.)

Figure 9. Andrea Previtali, *Crossing of the Red Sea*, oil on canvas, 130 × 210 cm. Gallerie dell'Accademia, Venice. Reproduced by permission of the Soprintendenza Speciale per il Polo Museale Veneziano. Photo by Alinari.

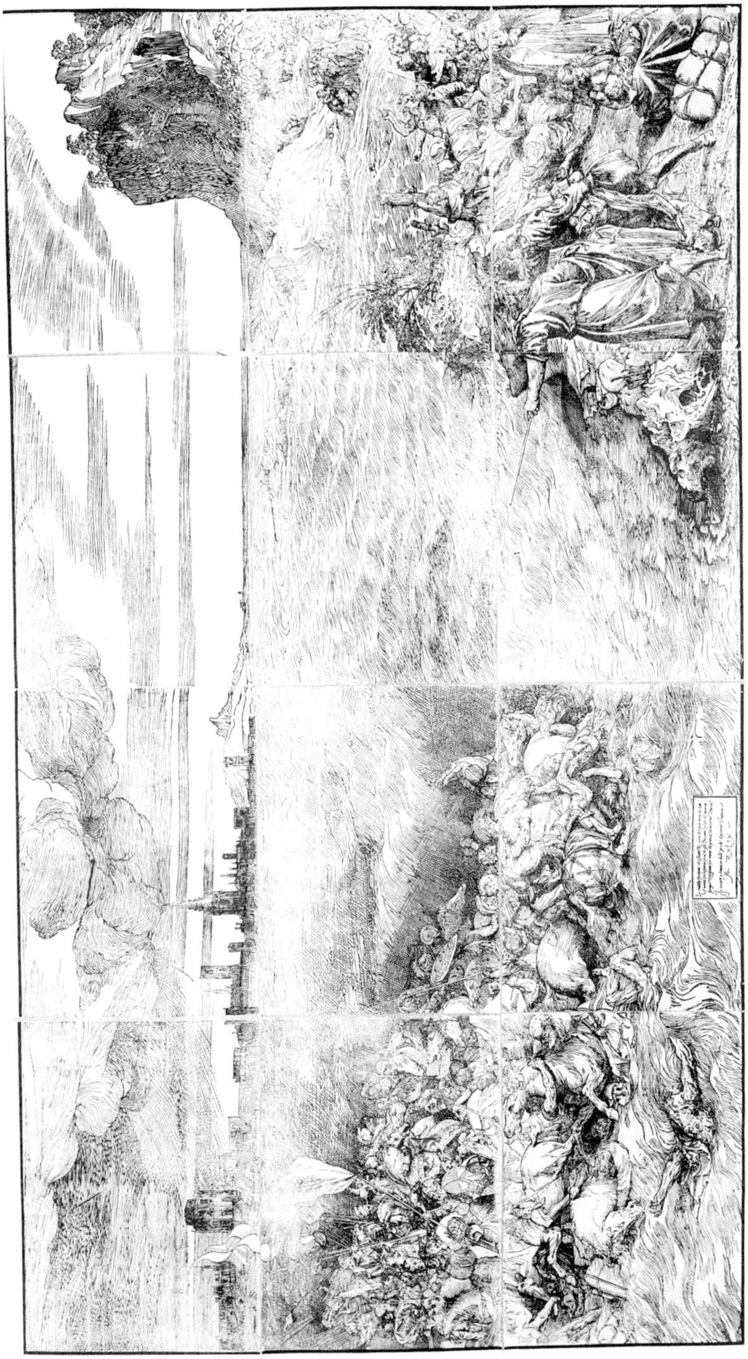

Figure 10. Titian, *Crossing of the Red Sea*, woodcut, 123 × 222 cm. Author's photo.

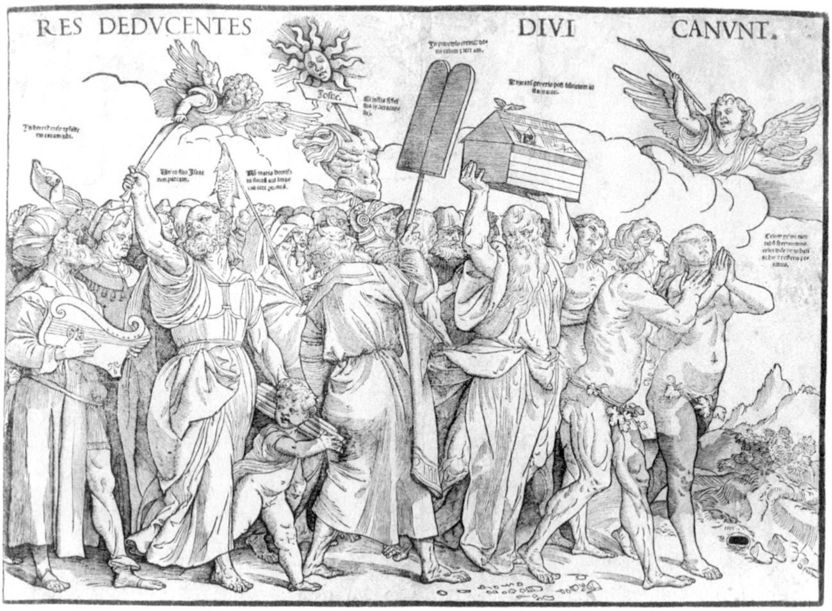

Figure 11. After Titian, *Triumph of Christ* (detail of far right section), woodcut, about 39 × 53 cm. Author's photo.

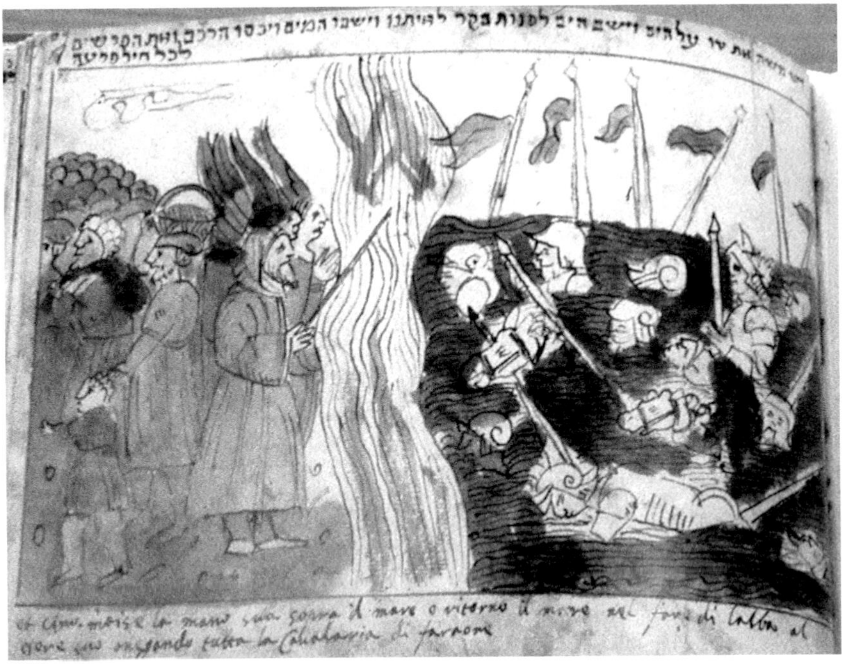

Figure 12. After Moisè dal Castellazzo and daughters, *Crossing of the Red Sea*, watercolor, about 15.5 × 25 cm. Formerly in Warsaw, Library of the Jewish Historical Institute, Codex 1184, no. 88. Reproduced by permission of the Library of the Jewish Historical Institute, Warsaw. Author's photo.

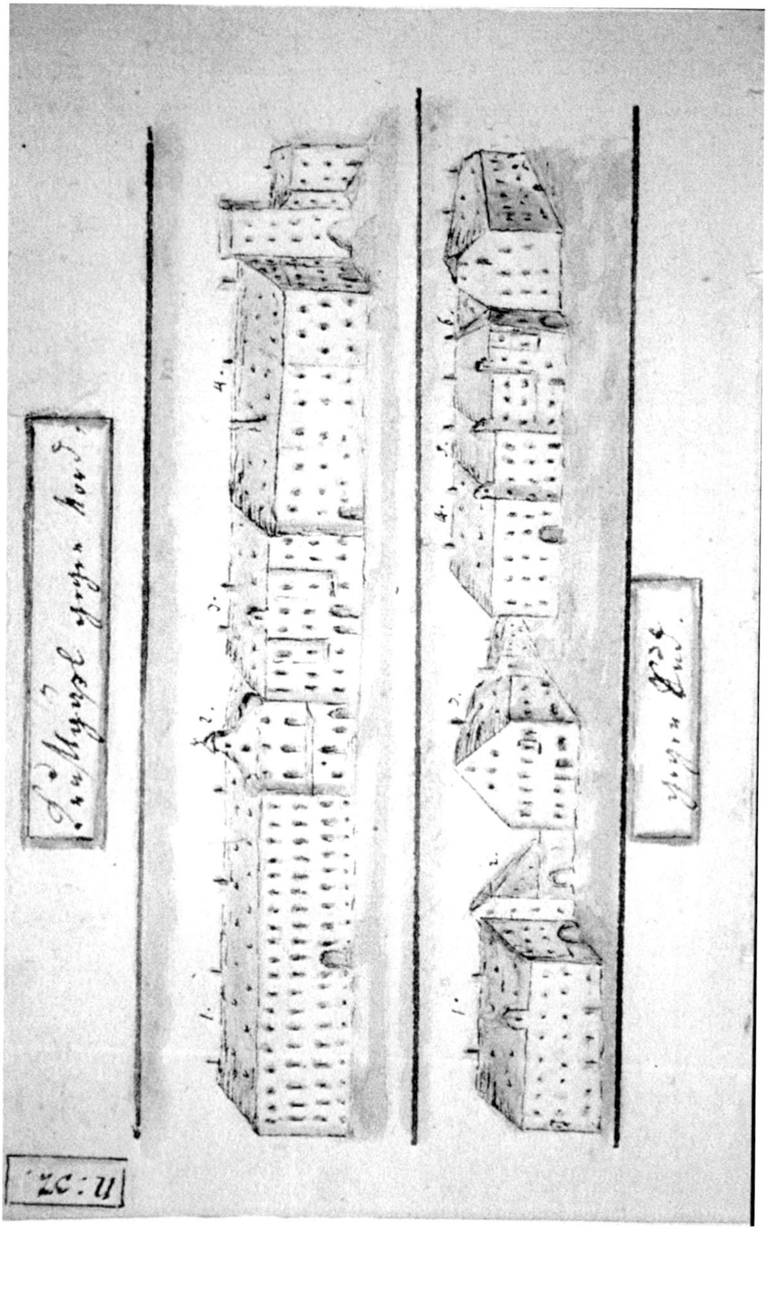

Figure 1. Johann Paul Stimmelmayr, View of Gruftgasse 1, pen and ink drawing, c. 1800, for his inventory of Munich houses and streets. Source: Gabriele Dischinger and Richard Bauer, eds., *München um 1800. Die Häuser und Gassen der Stadt. Gezeichnet und beschrieben von Johann Paul Stimmelmayr* (Munich: Beck, 1980).

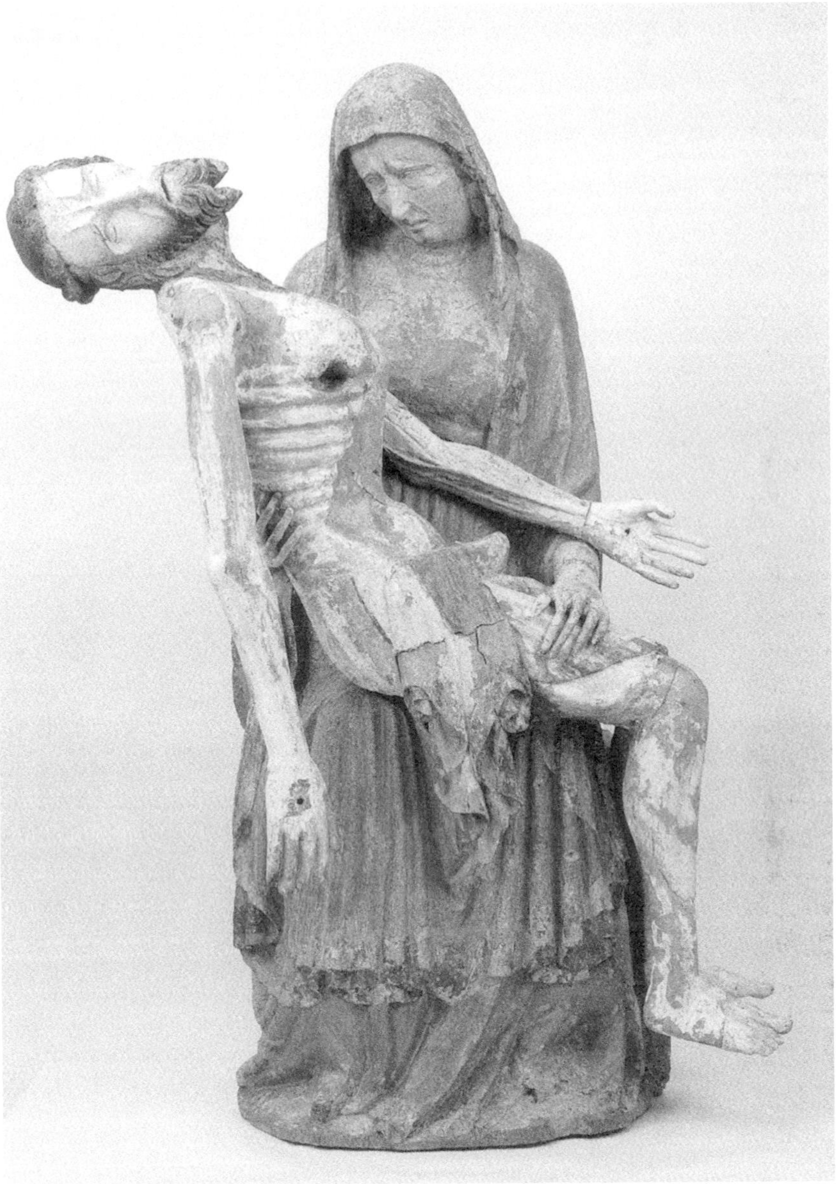

Figure 2. Franconian or Thuringian, *The Salmdorf Pietà*, c. 1340, limewood, 186 cm. H. Salmdorf, Katholische Pfarrkirche St. Mariä Himmelfahrt. Photo courtesy of Bayerisches Landesamt für Denkmalpflege, Munich.

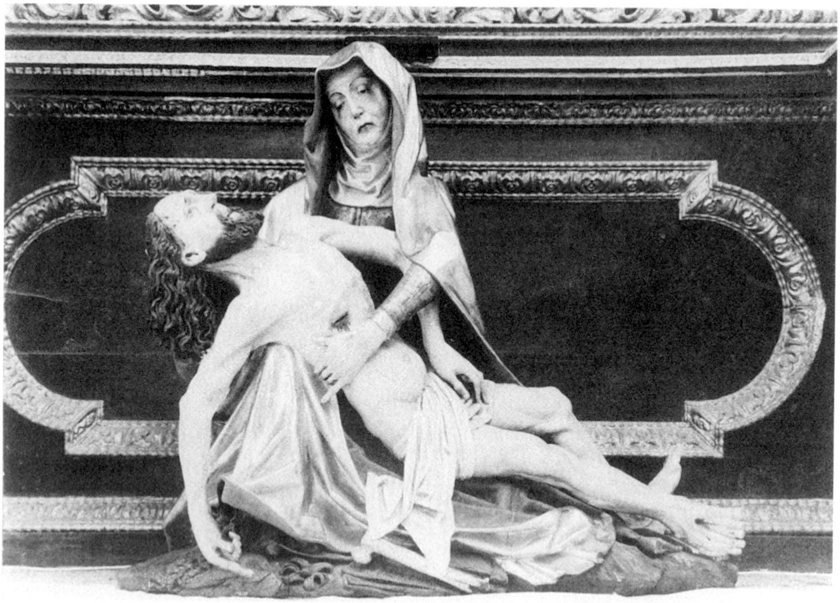

Figure 3. Erasmus Grasser, *Pietà*, 1510, wood with new polychrome and gilding, 86.5 × 94.5 cm., Wallfahrts- und Klosterkirche zum hl. Rasso, Grafrath/Amper. Photo courtesy of Bayerisches Landesamt für Denkmalpflese, Munich.

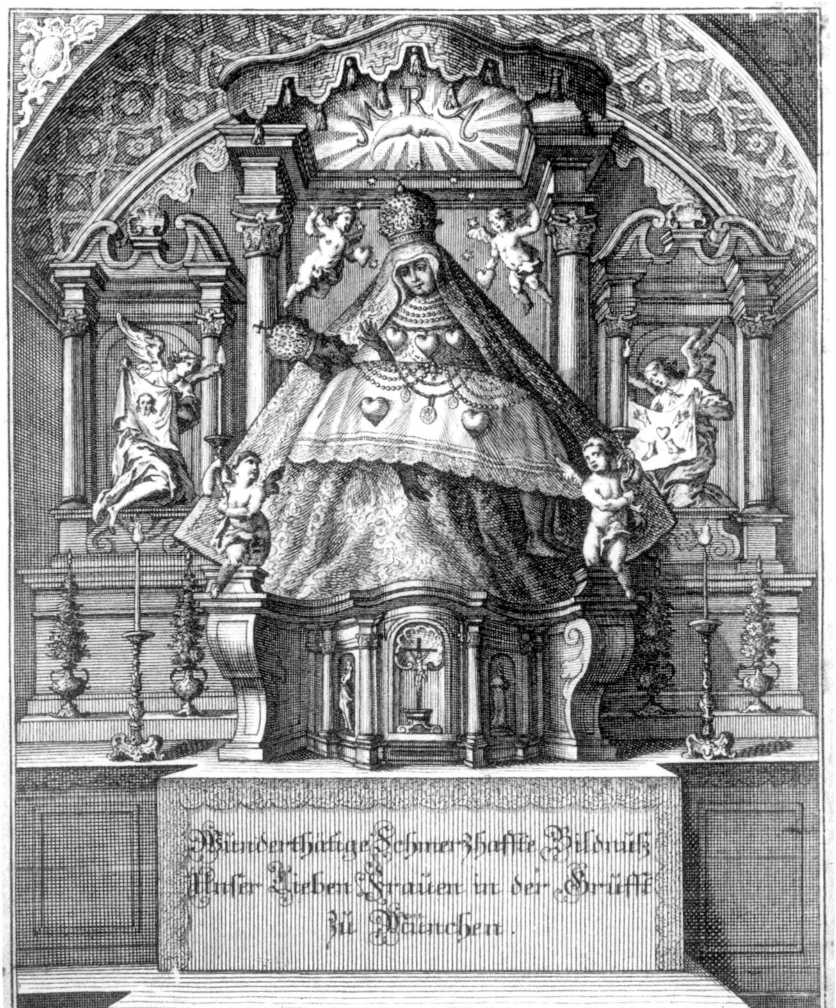

Figure 4. Johann Baptist Klauber, *Wunderthätige Schmerzehaffte Bildnuß Unser Lieben Frau in der Grufft zu München*, c. 1760, engraving 18.2 × 14.5. Munich, Stadtmuseum, Inv. nr. 37/1916.

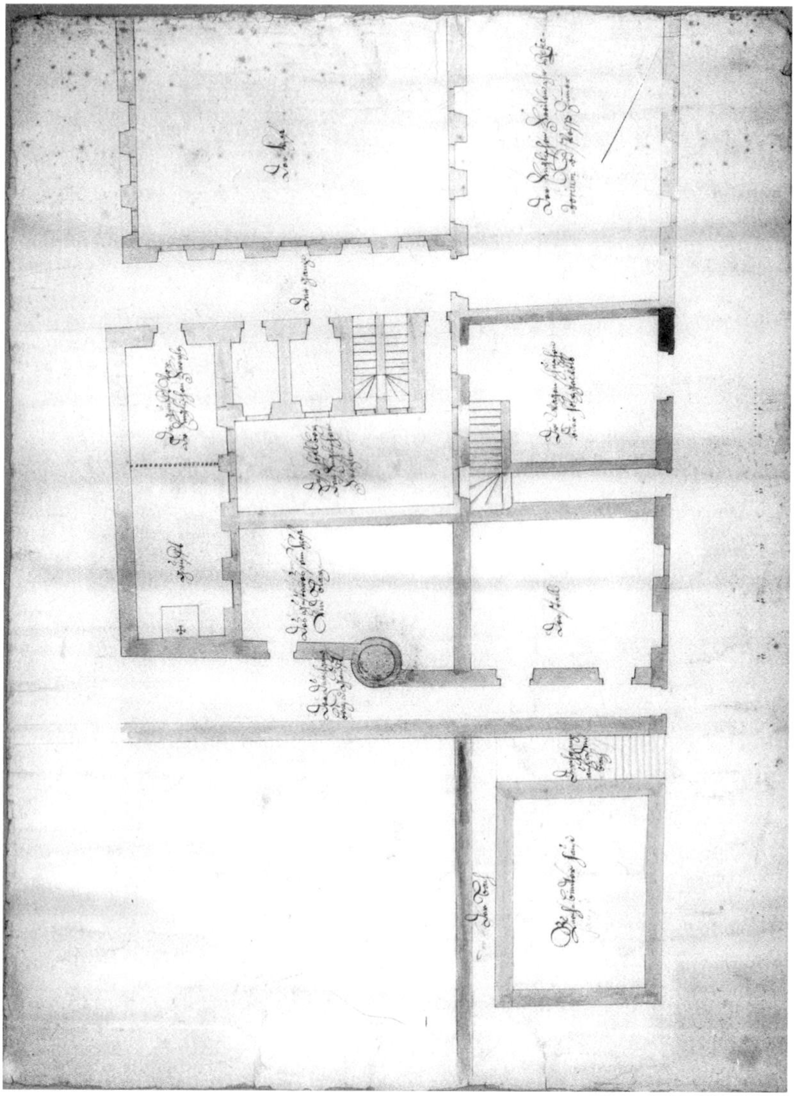

Figure 5. Plan of 1696, showing layout of former Gruftkirche, and city-block between Schrammergasse and Gruftgasse. Munich, Hauptstaatsarchiv, Abt. I, Plansammlung, Nr. 8542.

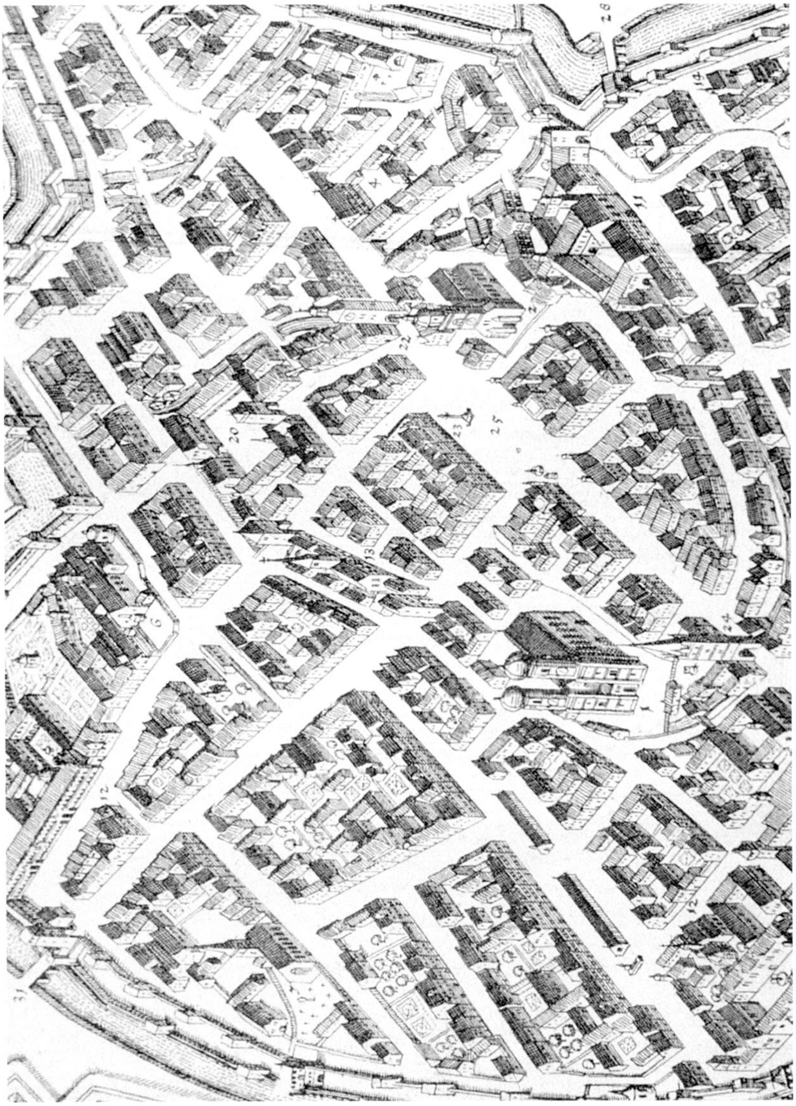

Figure 6. Matthäus Merian the Elder, City-plan of Munich (detail), engraving from *Topographia Bavariae*, 2nd edn. (1647).

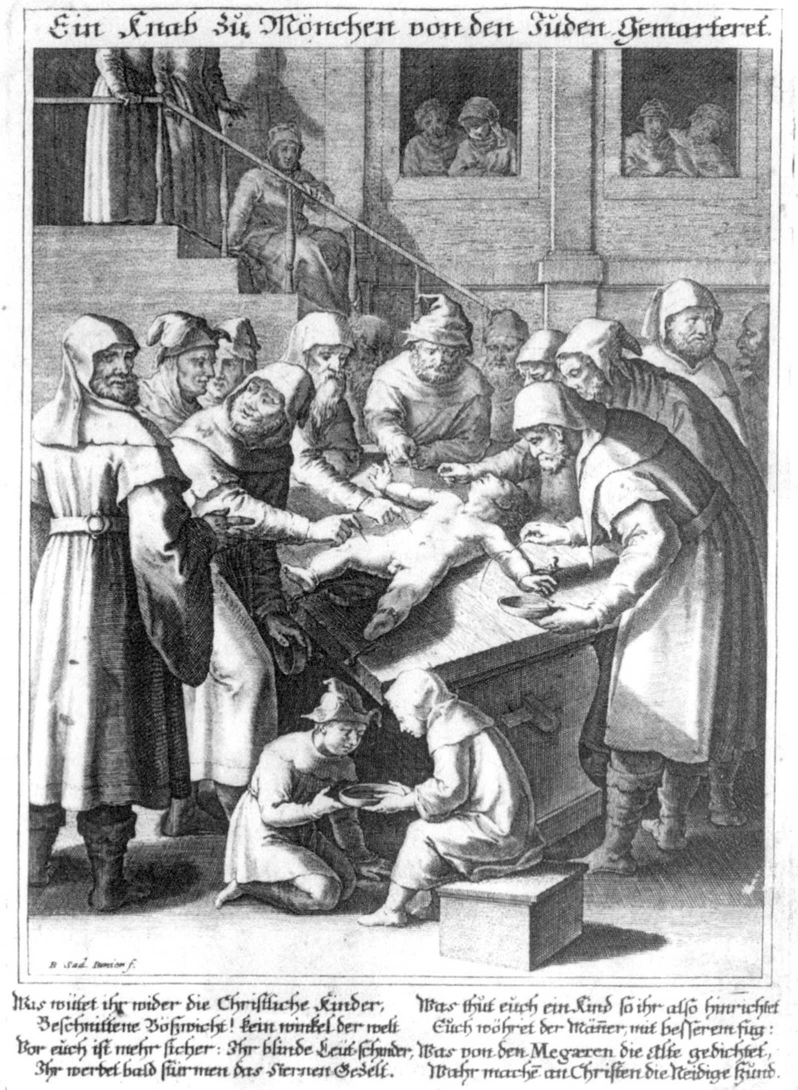

Figure 7. Raphael Sadeler the Elder (d. 1632), "A young boy martyred in Munich by the Jews" (1285), engraving from Matthäus Rader's *Bavaria Sancta*, orig. publ. in 3 vols. (Munich, 1615–27). Nuremberg, Germanisches National Museum, Graphische Sammlung, Sig. HB 31001.

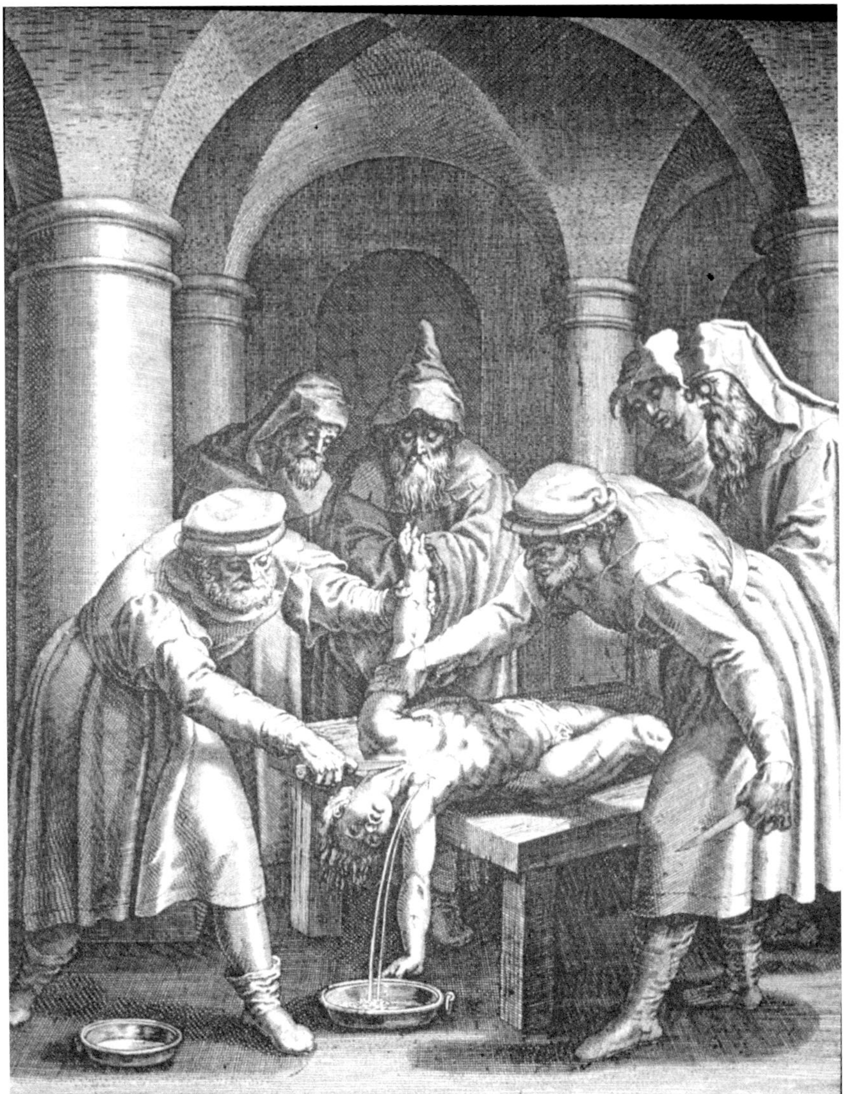

Figure 8. Raphael Sadeler the Elder (d. 1632), "Saint Heinrich, a boy murdered by the Jews in Munich," engraving from Matthäus Rader's *Bavaria Sancta*, orig. publ. in 3 vols. (Munich, 1615–27). Photo: Author.

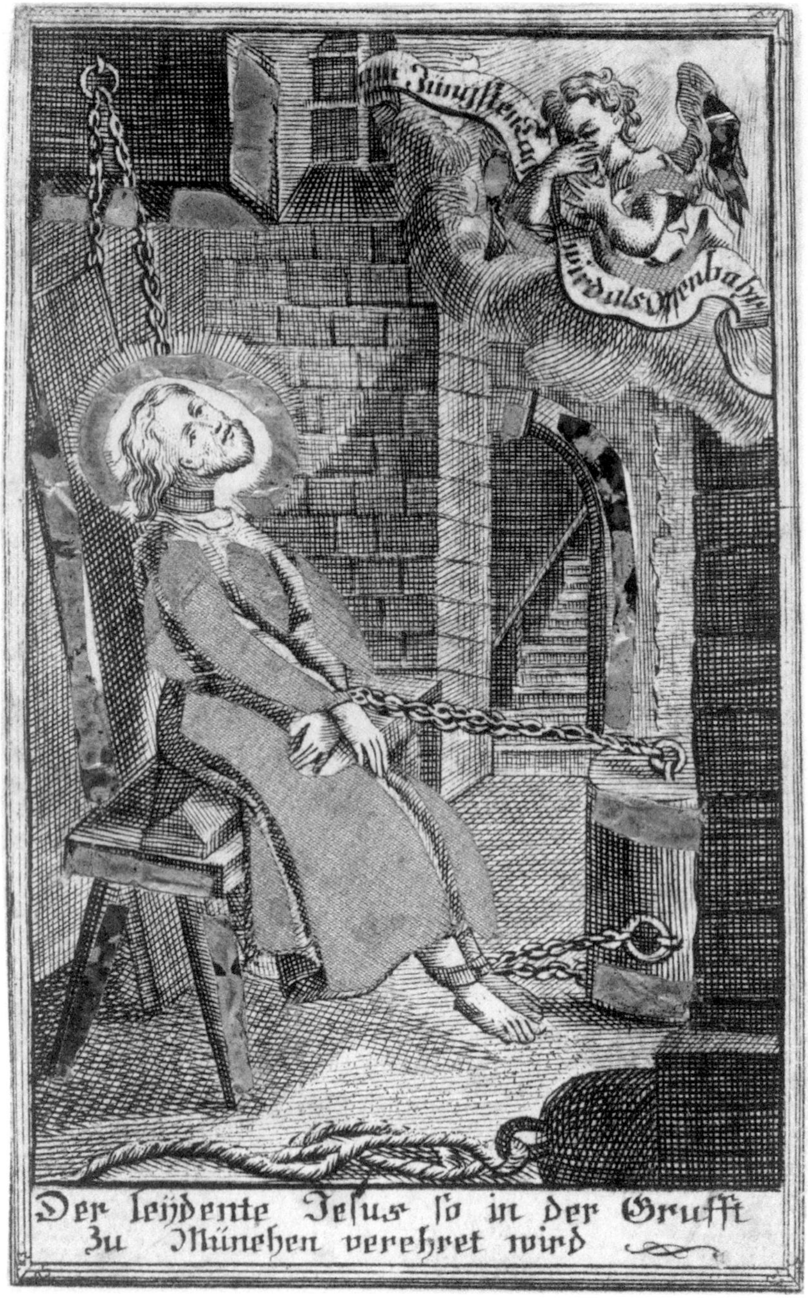

Figure 9. Anonymous German, *The Secret Passion of Christ in the Gruft in Munich*, c. 1790, hand-colored engraving with gold leaf, 10.7 × 6.6. Munich, Stadtmuseum, Inv. nr. 36/1062.

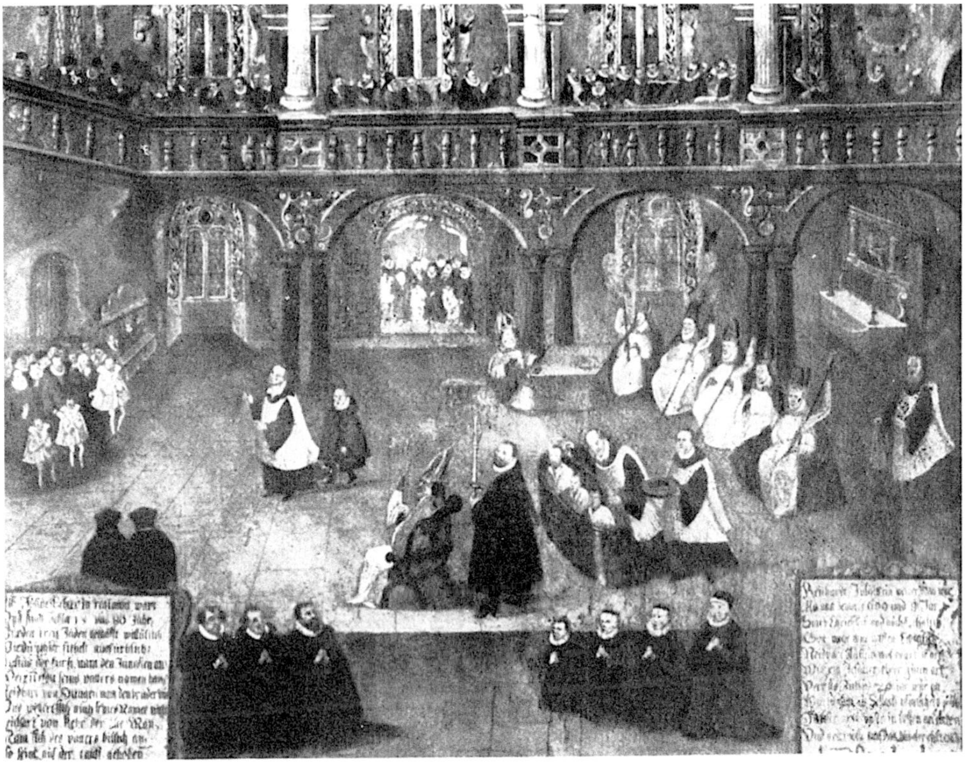

Figure 1. Baptism of three Jews in the presence of Bishop Echter von Mespelbrunn at the occasion of the consecration of the chapel of the Julius Hospital in 1580, from a painting of 1611, destroyed in 1944. Photo: Bayerisches Landesamt für Denkmalpflege.

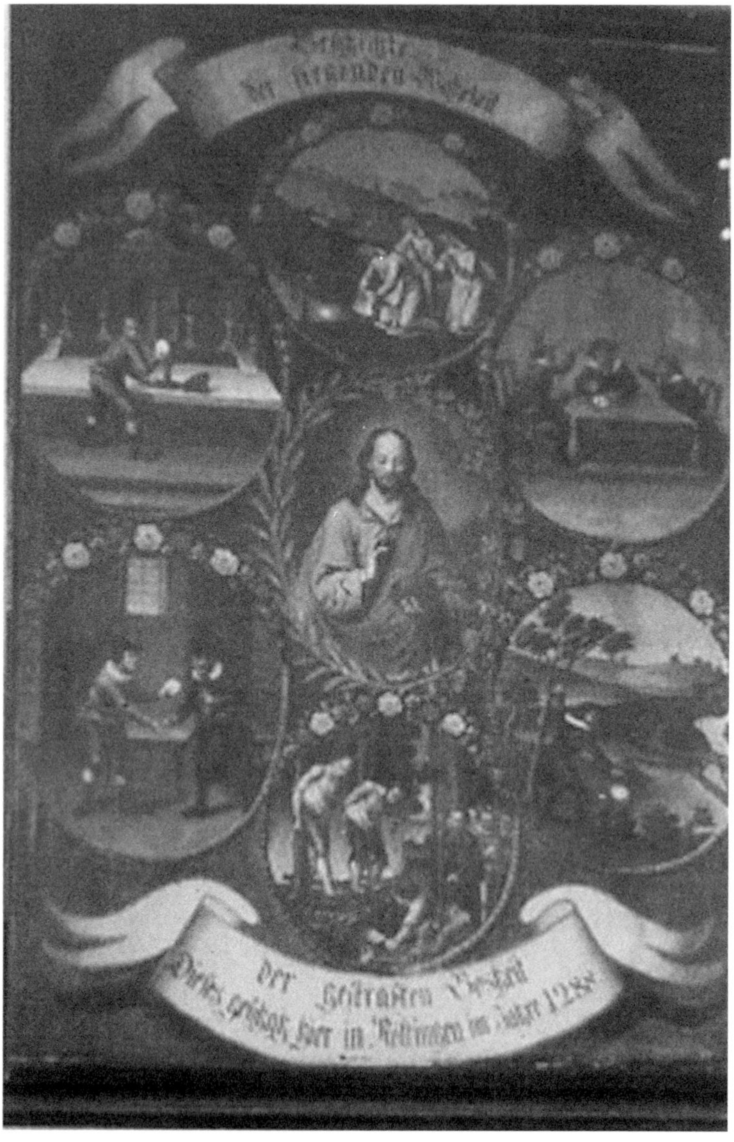

Figure 2. Legend of the alleged host desecration in Röttingen on the Tauber, painted panel, late eighteenth century. Catholic Parish Church, Röttingen on the Tauber. Photo: Hochschule für Jüdische Studien, Heidelberg.

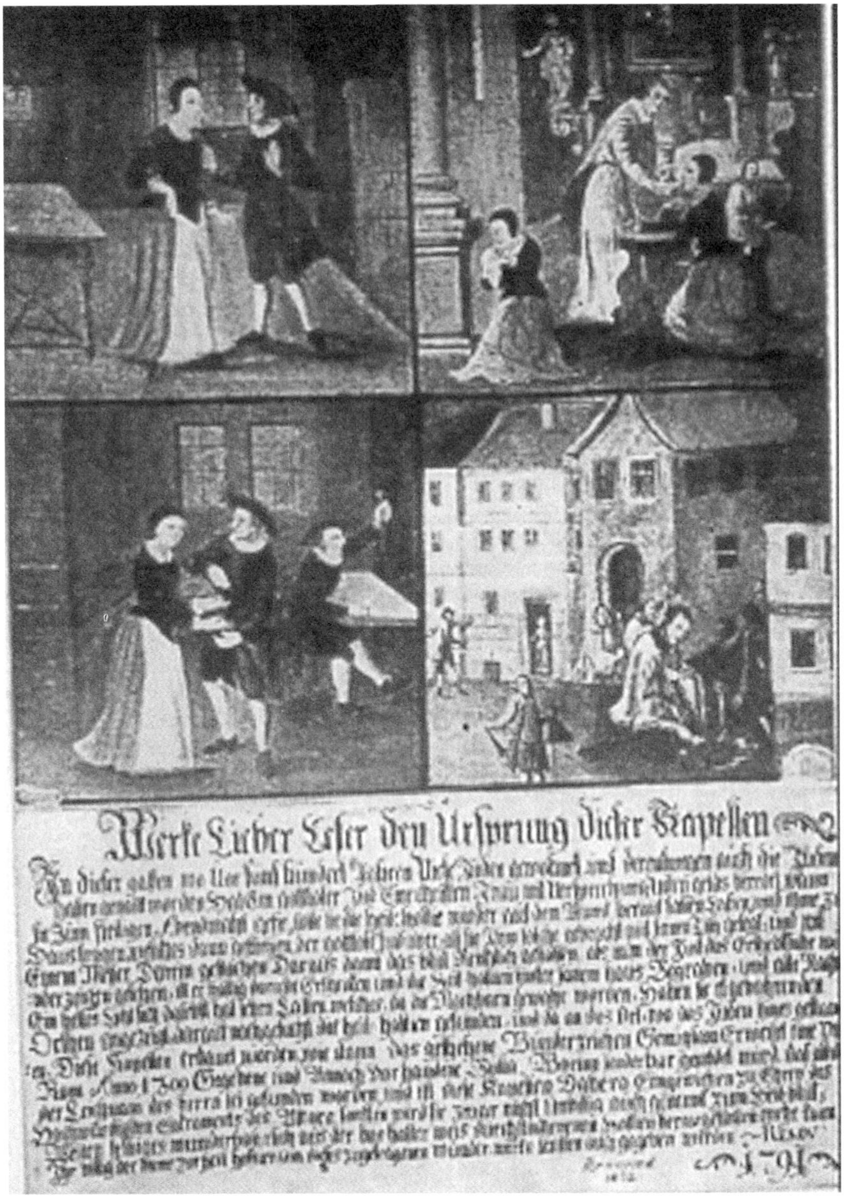

Figure 3. Legend of the alleged host desecration in Lauda, ex-voto painting in the chapel of the Holy Blood, Lauda, renovated 1781 and 1822. Source: Joachim Hahn, *Synagogen in Baden-Württemberg* (Stuttgart 1987), fig. 4.

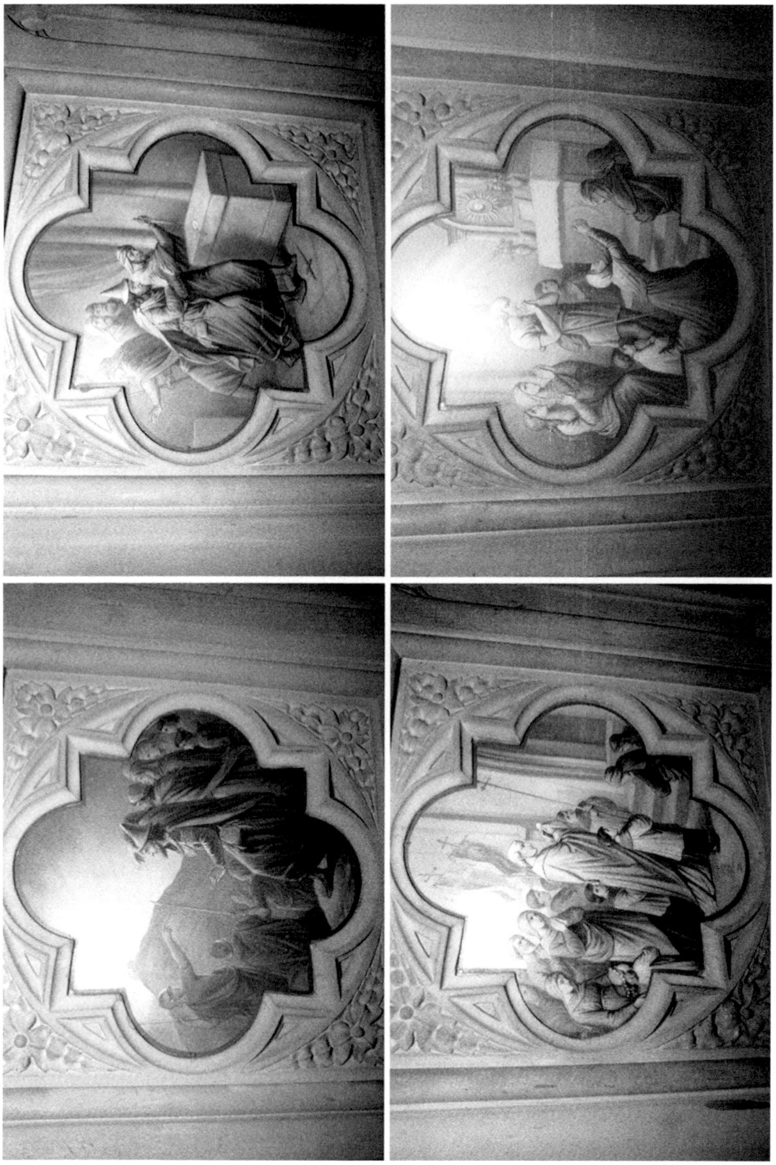

Figure 4. Legend of the alleged host desecration in Iphofen, four painted scenes place from the so-called Heilig Grab Altarpiece, renovated c. 1892, Catholic Parish Church of the Holy Blood, Iphofen. Photos: Mitchell Merback.

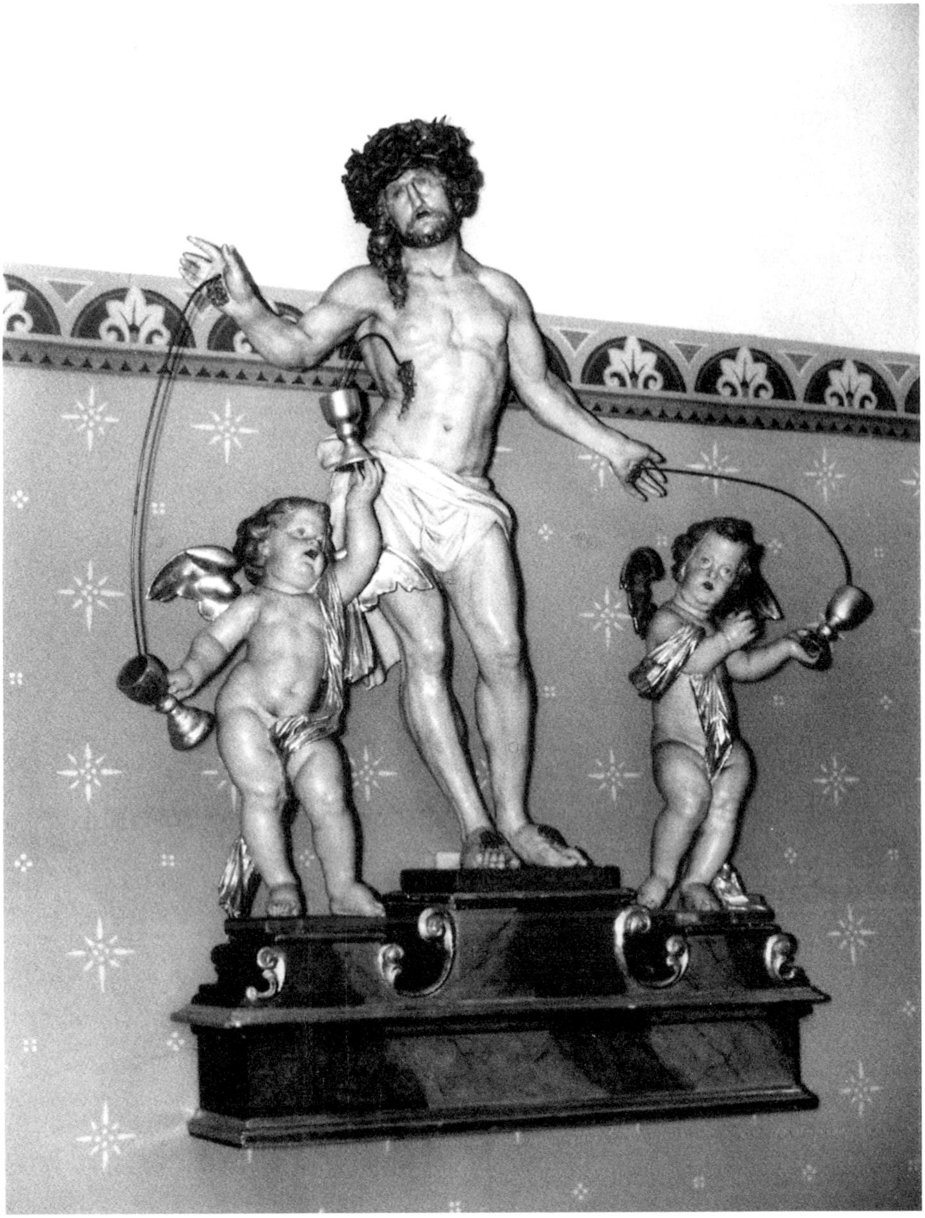

Figure 5. South German, *Christ as the Source of Salvific Blood*, formerly part of the Heilig Grab Altarpiece, Fraconian stone, ca. 1730–1740. Catholic Parish Church of the Holy Blood, Iphofen. Photo: Mitchell Merback.

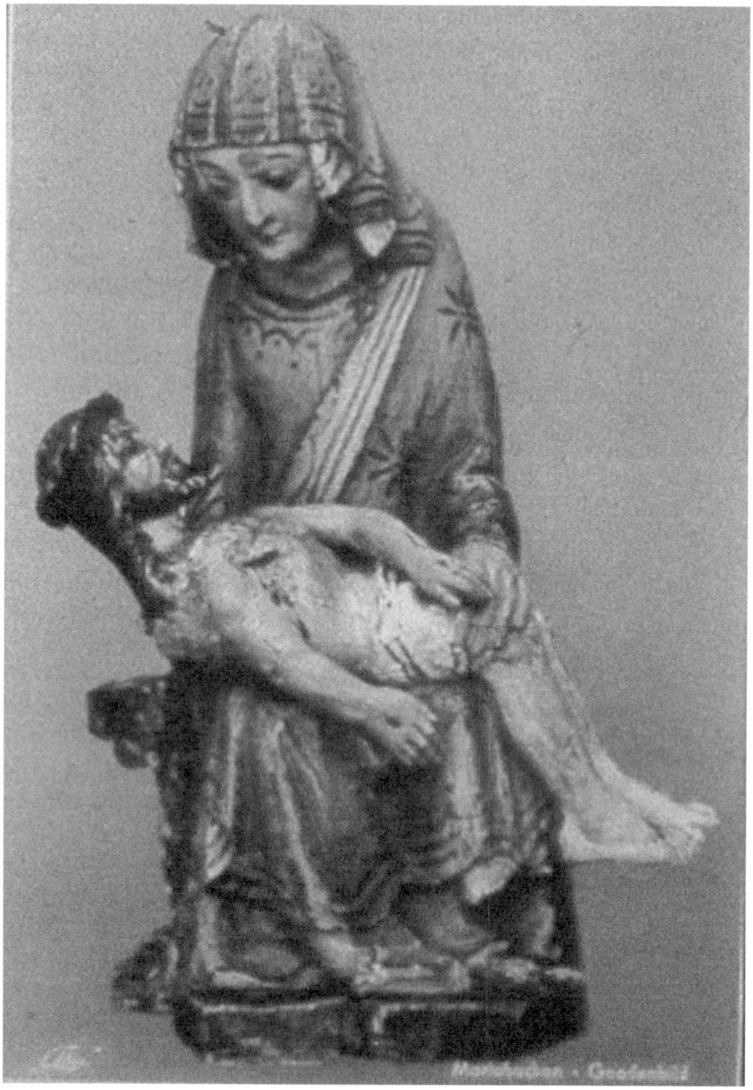

Figure 6. German, *Pietà*, from the Chapel of Maria Buchen on the Main, ca. 1395, wood with later additions and restorations, repainted in 1883. Source: Alfons Ruf, *600 Jahre Maria Buchen* (Lohr am Main, 1995), p. 17.

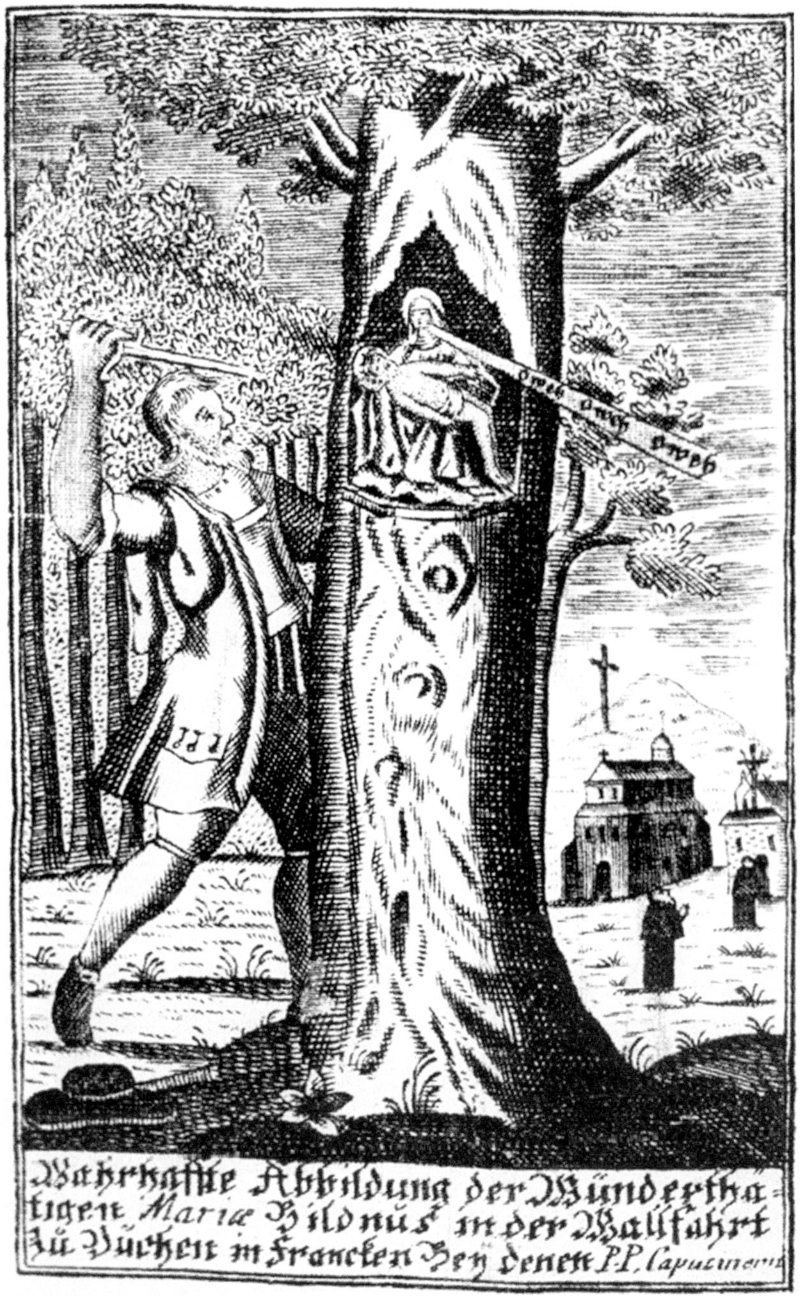

Figure 7a. Legend of Maria Buchen: the Jew attacks the Pietà, copper print on silk, after 1726. Source: Alfons Ruf, *600 Jahre Maria Buchen* (Lohr am Main, 1995), p. 34.

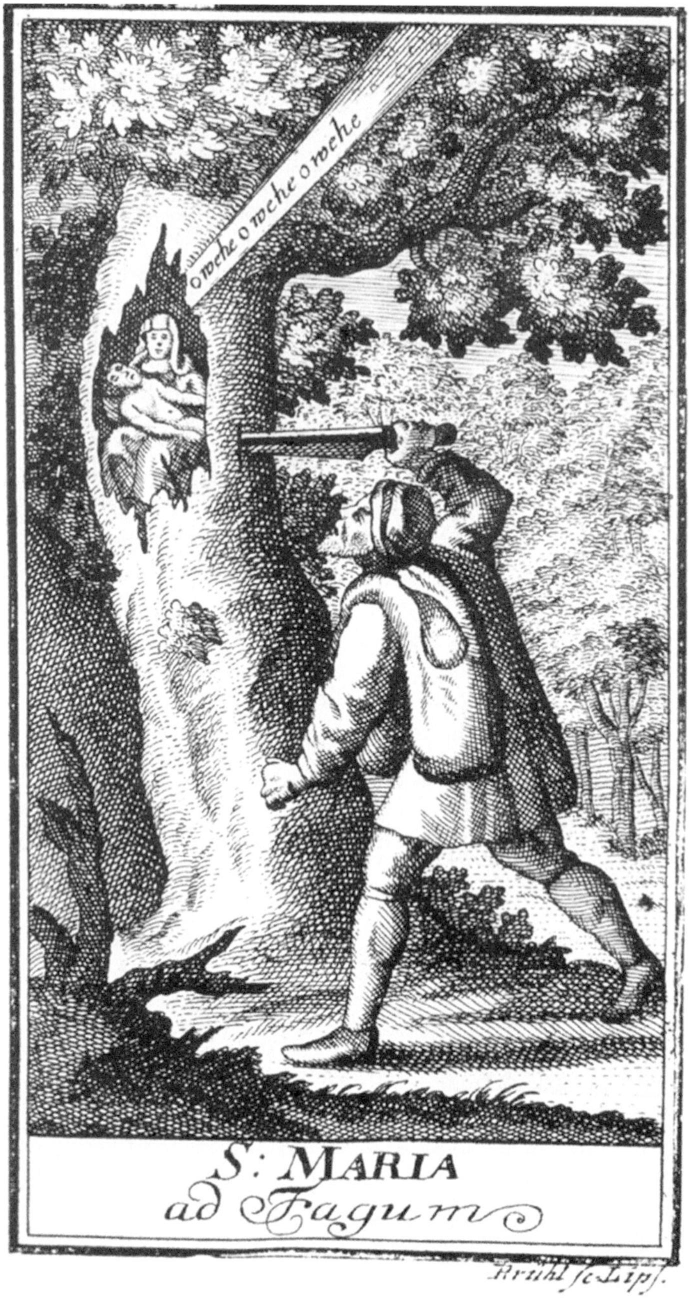

Figure 7b. Legend of Maria Buchen: the Jew attacks the Pietà, copper print on silk, second half of the eighteenth century. Source: Alfons Ruf, *600 Jahre Maria Buchen* (Lohr am Main, 1995), p. 34.

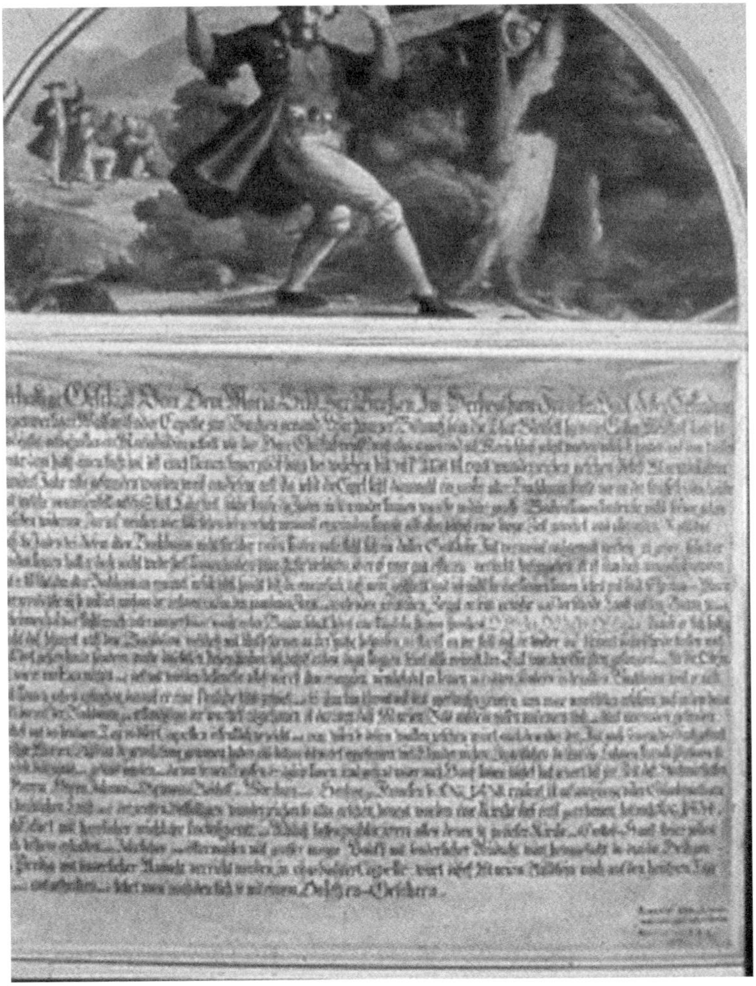

Figure 8. Johann Bernhard Sätz, Jew attacking the Pietà of Maria Buchen, oil on canvas, 1698. The text panel underneath was composed under the auspices of Bishop Julius Echter in 1613 and reports the miraculous finding of the Pietà. Source: Alfons Ruf, *600 Jahre Maria Buchen* (Lohr am Main, 1995), p. 14.

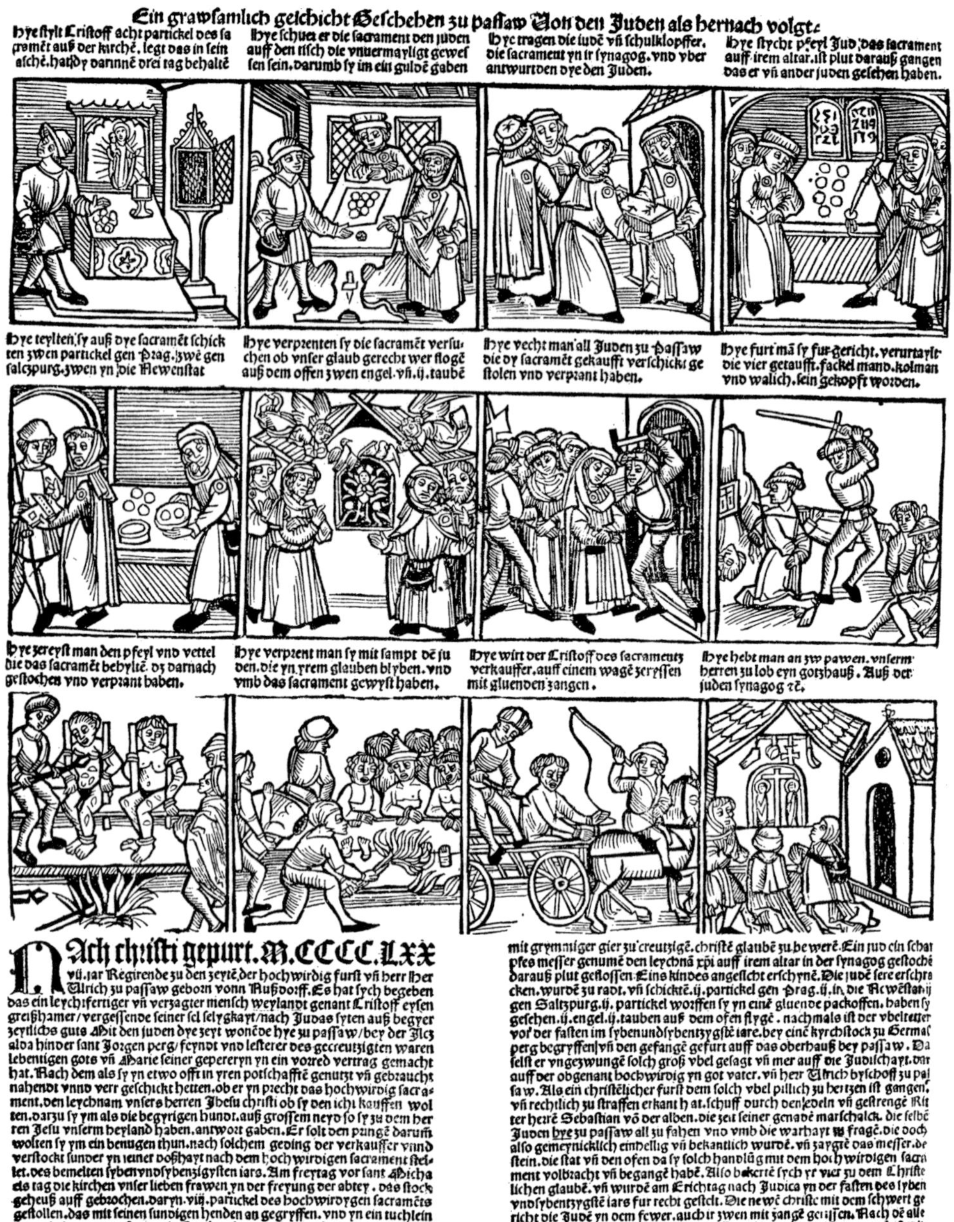

Figure 9. South German, *Ein grawsamlich geschicht zu Passau von den Juden*...; woodcut broadsheet illustrating the host desecration at Passau (Nuremberg: Caspar Hochfeder, ca. 1498). Munich, Staatliche Graphische Sammlung, Inv. 118307.

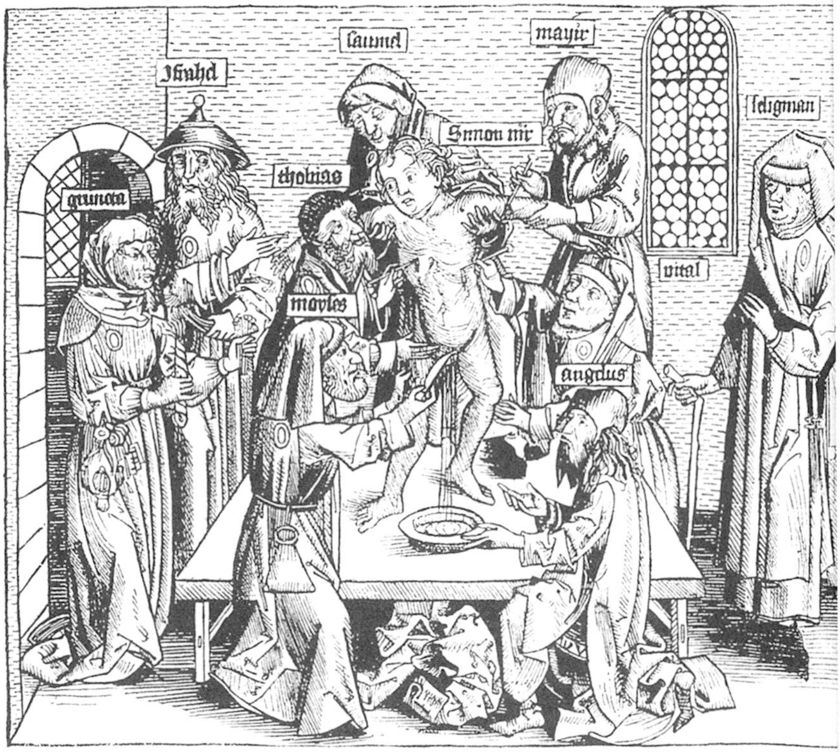

Symon das sellig kindlein zu Trient ist am .xxi. tag des Mertzen nach der gepurt Cristi. M.cccc.lxxv.iar.in
heiligen marterwochen in der statt Trient von den iuden getödt vnd ein martrer Cristi worden.dann al
die iuden in derselben statt wonende ir ostern nach irem sytten begeen wolten vnd doch kein cristenlichs plůt z
gepauch irs vngesewrten prots hetten do brachten sie diss kindlein verstolens in Samuelis eins iuden hawe
in solcher gestalt.an dem dritte tag vor ostern vmb versperzeit sasse diss kindlein vor seins vaters thür in abw
sen seiner eltern do nehnet sich Thobias ein iüdischer verreter zu disem kindlein das noch nit dreymal zehen mo
nat alt was.dem redet er mit schmaychlenden wortē zu vnd trůg es pald in das haws Samuelis. Als nw d
nacht herfiele do frewten sich Samuel Thobias Vitalis Moyses Jsrahel vnd Mayer vor der synagog vbe
vergiessung cristenlichs plůts.Nw entplösseten sie das kindlein vnd legten ime ein facieletlein vmb sein helßlei
das man es nit schreyen hören möcht vnd spanneten ime sein ermlein auß.schnytten ime erstlich sein mälich gli
lein ab vnd auß seinem rechten wenglein ein stücklein vnd stachen es allenthalben mit scharpffen spitzigen st
cheln heftlein oder nadeln.einer die hend der ander die füßlein haltende.vnd als sie nw das plůt grawsamlic
gesamelt hetten do hůben sie an lobsang zesingen vnd zu dem kindlein mit hönischen bedroewortten zesprech
Nym hin du gehangner Jhesu also haben dir ettwen vnsser eltern gethan.also sollen alle cristen in hymel. au
erden vnd meer geschend werden.dieweil verschied das vnschuldig mertrerlein.die iuden eyletē zum nachtma
vnd assen von dem plůt das vngesewerte zu schmahe Cristo vnßerm hayland vnd wurffen dē totē leichnā i
ein fliessends wasser nahent bey irem haws vnnd hielten ir ostern mit frewden.Die bekümerten eltern suchte
ir verlorns kindlein.das funden sie vber drey tag in dem fluss.Als solchs an Johanssen von Salis den edel
burger von Brixien kaiserlicher rechten doctor vnd deßmals öbersten pfleger gelanget do hieß er nach den iud
greiffen vnd sie mit marter anzichen.also das sie nach ordnung ansagten wie sie dise mißtat begangen hett er
vnd darauff warden sie mit gepürlicher straff außgetilgt.Als der leichnam auff befelhe Johāssen hinderbach
bischoffs daselbst bestattet wardt do fieng er alßpald an in wunderzaichen zescheinen vnd auß allen cristenlic
en gegenten zu dises heilliges kindes grab ein zulawff zewerden.dauon dañ dise statt nicht kleine auffung vnn
zunemung empfunden hat.vnd die burger daselbst haben disem leichnam ein schöne kirchen auffgerichtet.

Figure 10. Michael Wolgemut and workshop, Ritual murder of Simon of Trent in 1475, woodcut from Hartmann Schedel's *Nuremberg Chronicle* (Nuremberg, 1493), fol. ccliii verso.

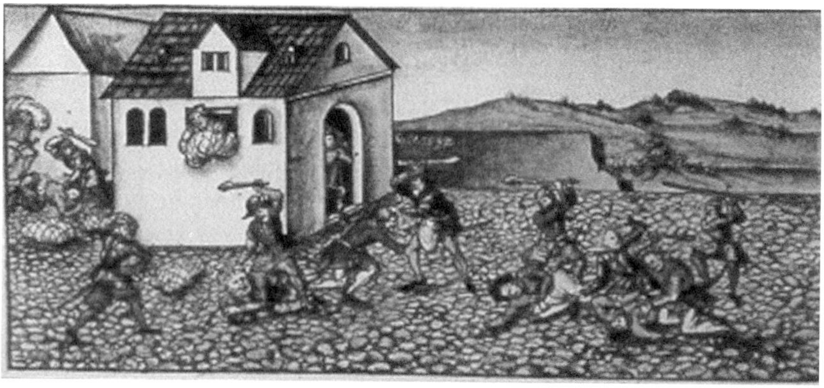

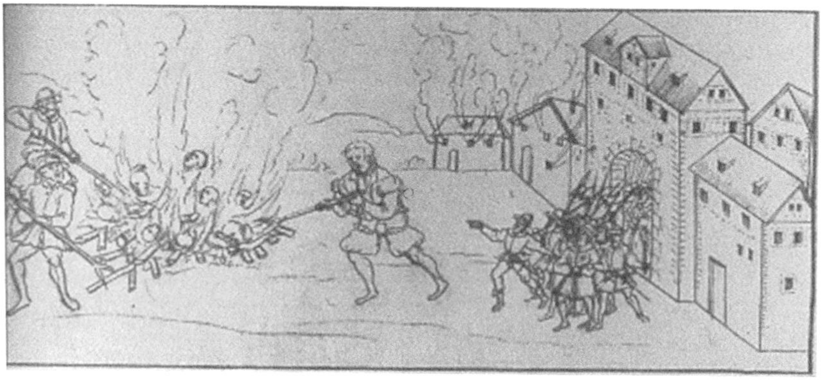

Figure 11a–11b. 11a) Georg Mack, Anti-Jewish Pogrom in Lower Franconia in 1336, illustration from copy of the Lorenz Fries chronicle, produced by order of Bishop Echter von Mespelbrunn. Universitätsbibliothek Würzburg, Cod. M.ch.f.760, fol. 257b. Source: Gottfried Mälzer, *Die Fries-Chronik des Fürstbischofs Julius Echter von Mespelbrunn* (Universitätsbibliothek Würzburg, 1989), fig. 106. 11b) Burning of the Jews in 1349 in Würzburg, unfinished illustration in the copy of the Lorenz Fries chronicle, produced by order of Bishop Echter von Mespelbrunn. Universitätsbibliothek Würzburg, Cod. M.ch.f.760, fol. 274b. Source: Mälzer, *Die Fries-Chronik*, fig. 113.

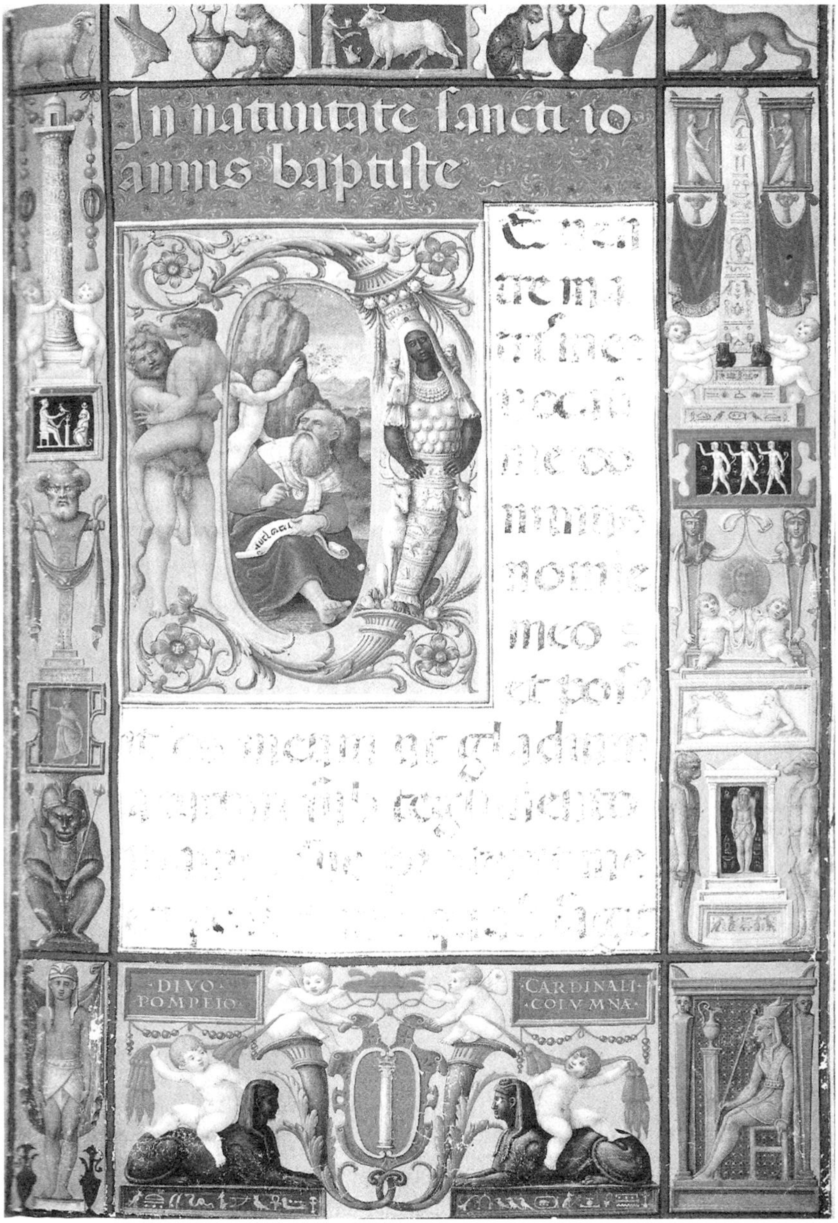

Figure 1. Giulio Clovio, Illuminated page in the Missal of Cardinal Pompeo Colonna, ca. 1532. Manchester, John Rylands Library, Latin Ms. 32, fol. 79.

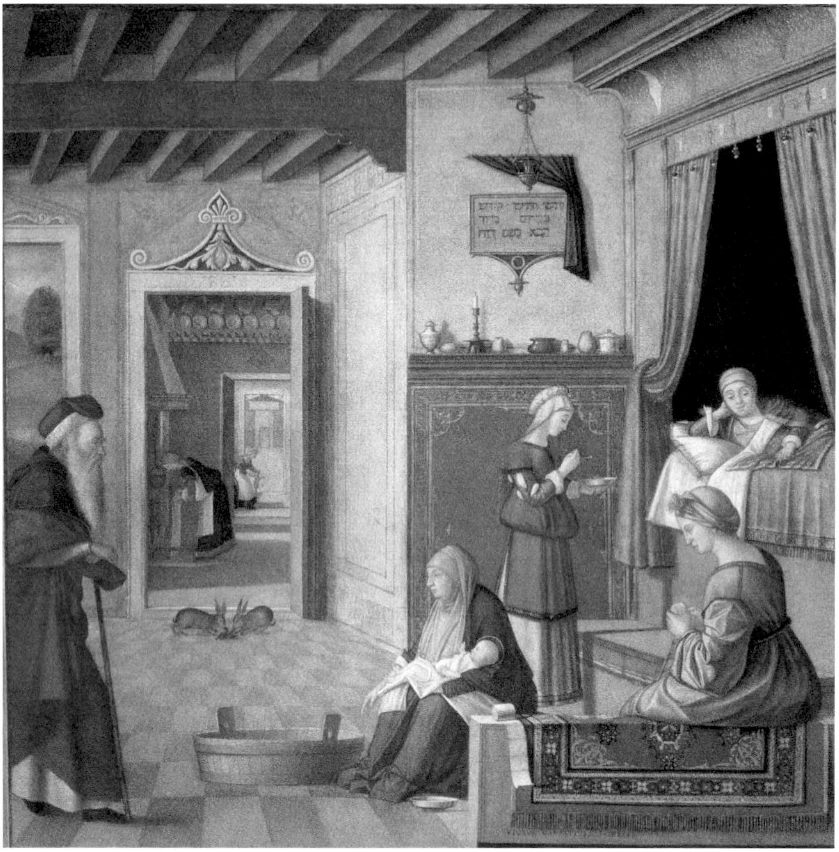

Figure 2. Vittore Carpaccio, *Birth of the Virgin*, 1504, tempera on canvas, 126 × 129 cm. Bergamo, Accademia Carrara. Photo: © 1991. Photo Scala, Florence.

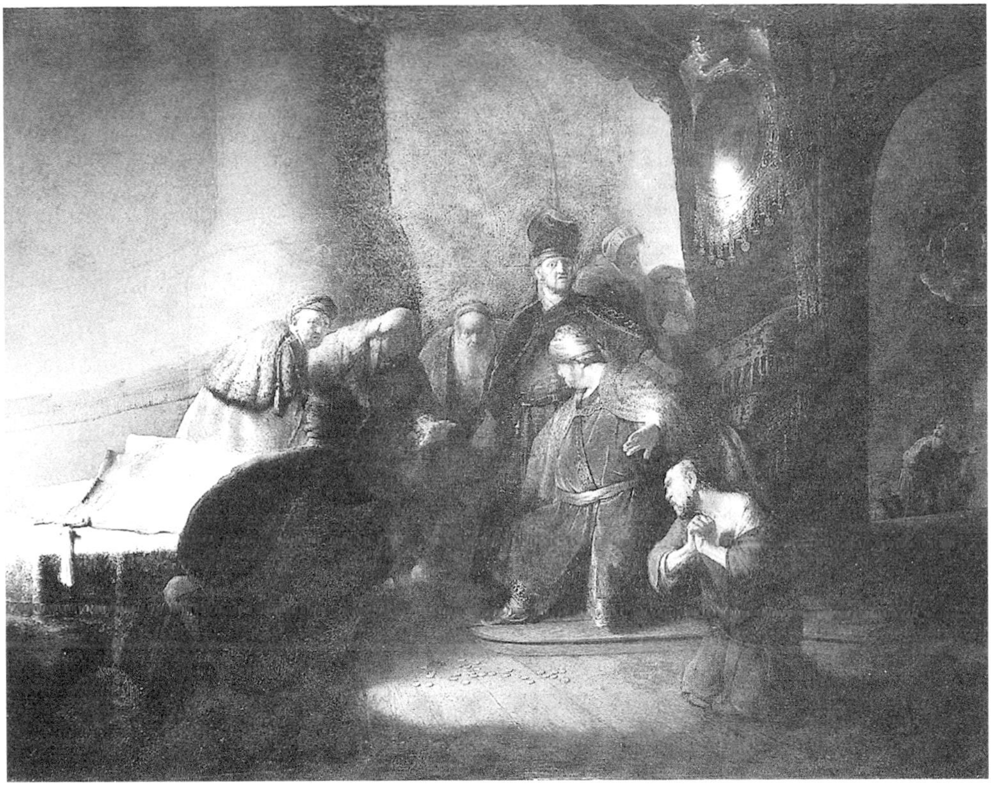

Figure 3. Rembrandt, *Repentant Judas Returning the Thirty Pieces of Silver*, 1629, panel, 79 × 102.3 cm. England, Private Collection.

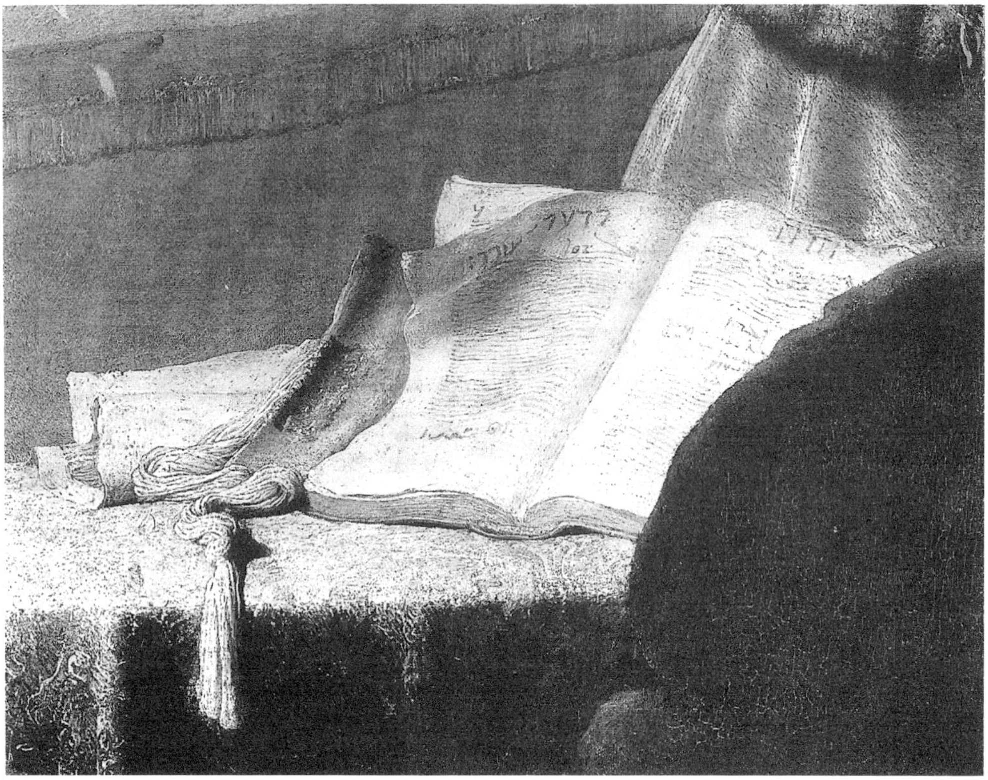

Figure 4. Rembrandt, *Repentant Judas*. Detail of fig. 3: open book with Hebrew and Syriac words.

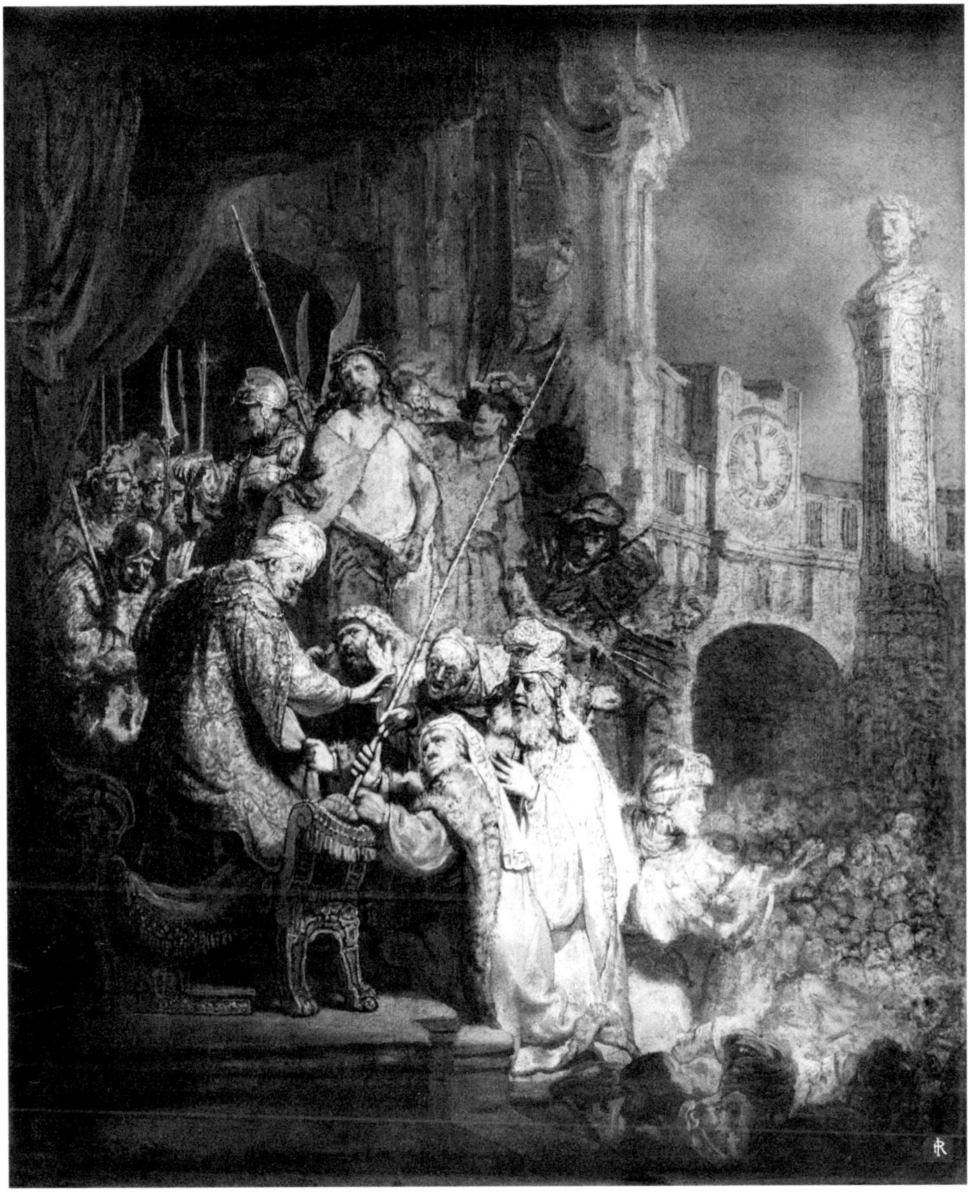

Figure 5. Rembrandt, *Christ before Pontius Pilate and the People*, 1634, paper attached to canvas, 54.5 × 44.5 cm. London, National Gallery. Photo: Alinari/Art Resource, NY.

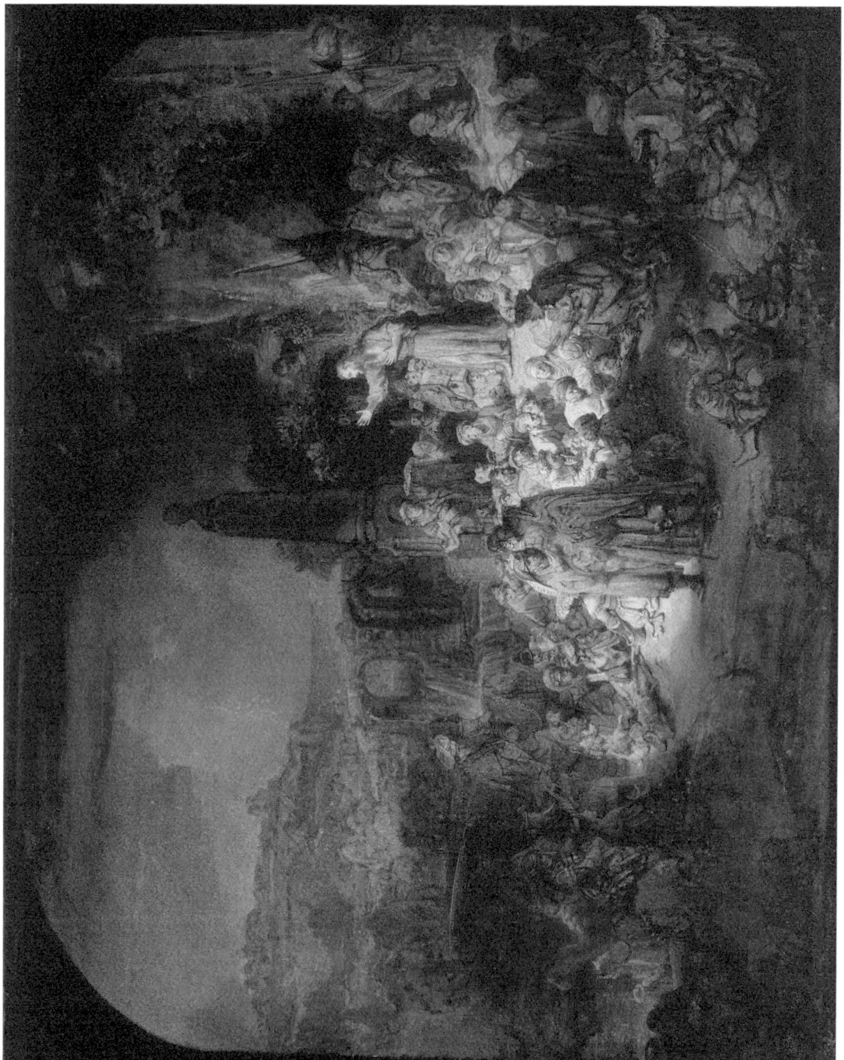

Figure 6. Rembrandt, *St. John the Baptist Preaching in the Desert*, 1634/35, canvas on panel, 62.7 × 80.1 cm. Berlin, Gemäldegalerie, Staatliche Museen. Photo: Bildarchiv Preussischer Kulturbesitz/Art Resource, NY.

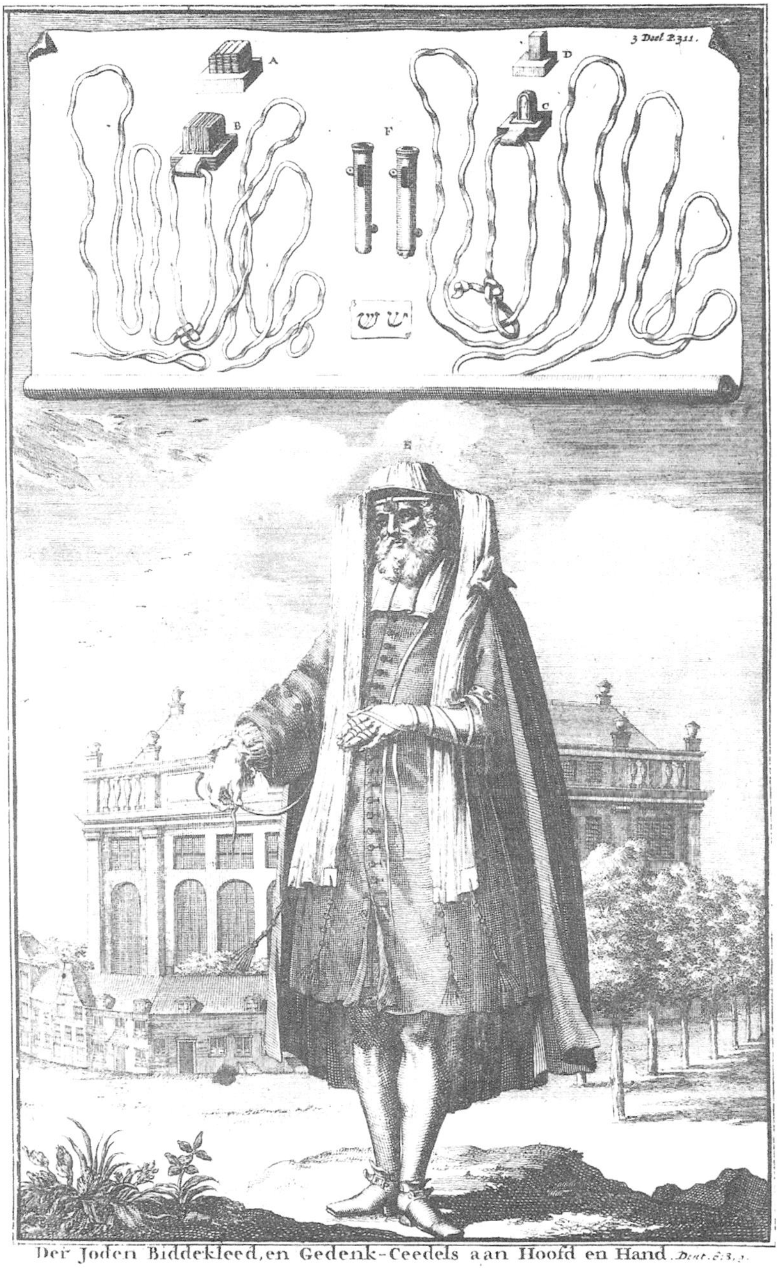

Figure 7. Jan Luyken, "The Jew's Praying Shawl and Phylacteries worn on the Hand and Head," etching, 32.5 × 19.5 cm., from W. Goeree, *Mozaïse Historie de Hebreeuwse Kerke*, vol. 3 (Amsterdam, 1700). Courtesy of The Library of The Jewish Theological Seminary, New York.

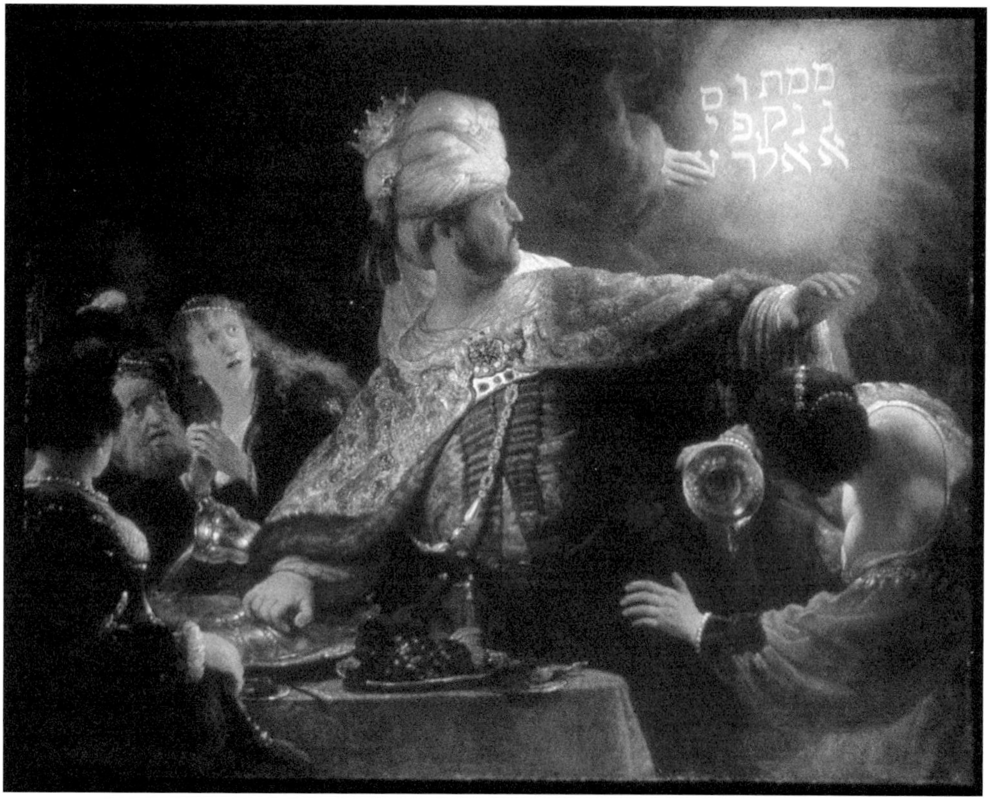

Figure 8. Rembrandt, *Belshazzar's Feast*, ca. 1635, canvas, 167.6 × 209.2 cm. London, National Gallery. Photo: Art Resource, NY.

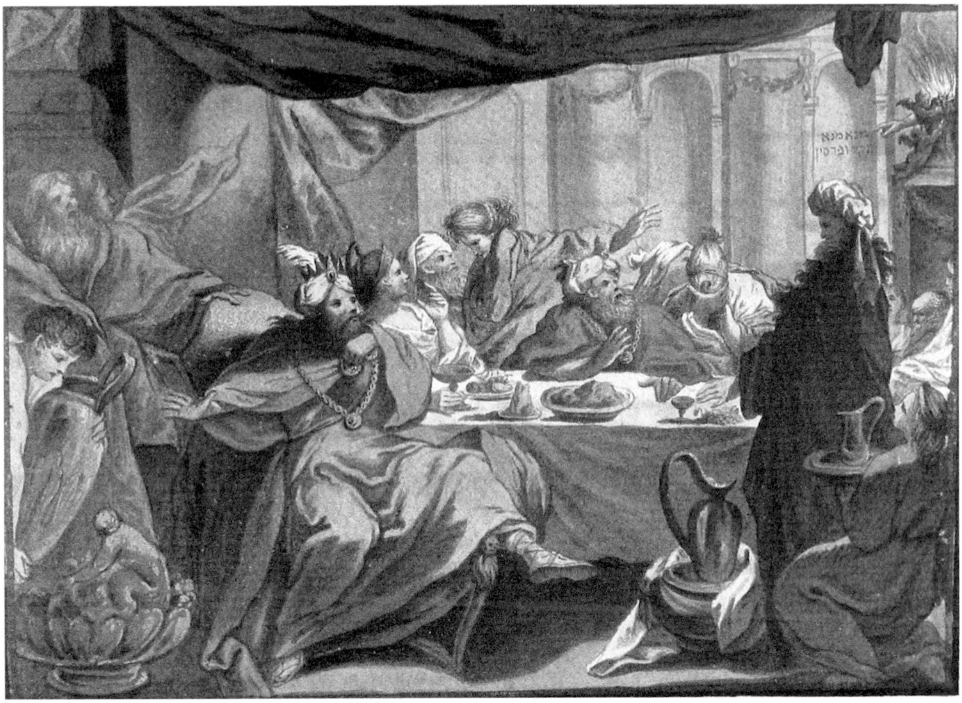

Figure 9. Judah Leib ha-Cohen, *Belshazzar's Feast*, miniature in a Passover Haggadah, Copenhgen, 1769. Darmstadt, Hessischen Landes- und Hochschulbibliothek, Cod. Or. 7.

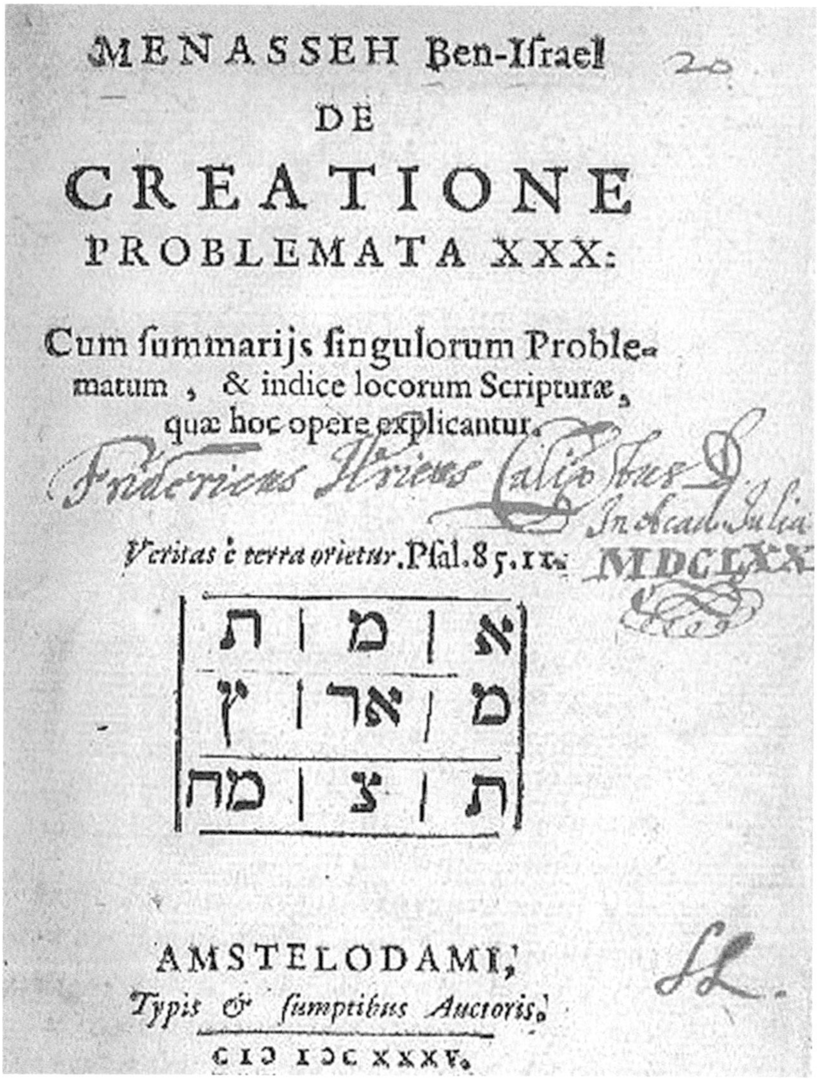

Figure 10. Title page of Menasseh ben Israel, *De Creatione Problemata XXX*, Amsterdam, 1635, with the Printer Device of Menasseh. Tel Aviv, Gross Family Collection.

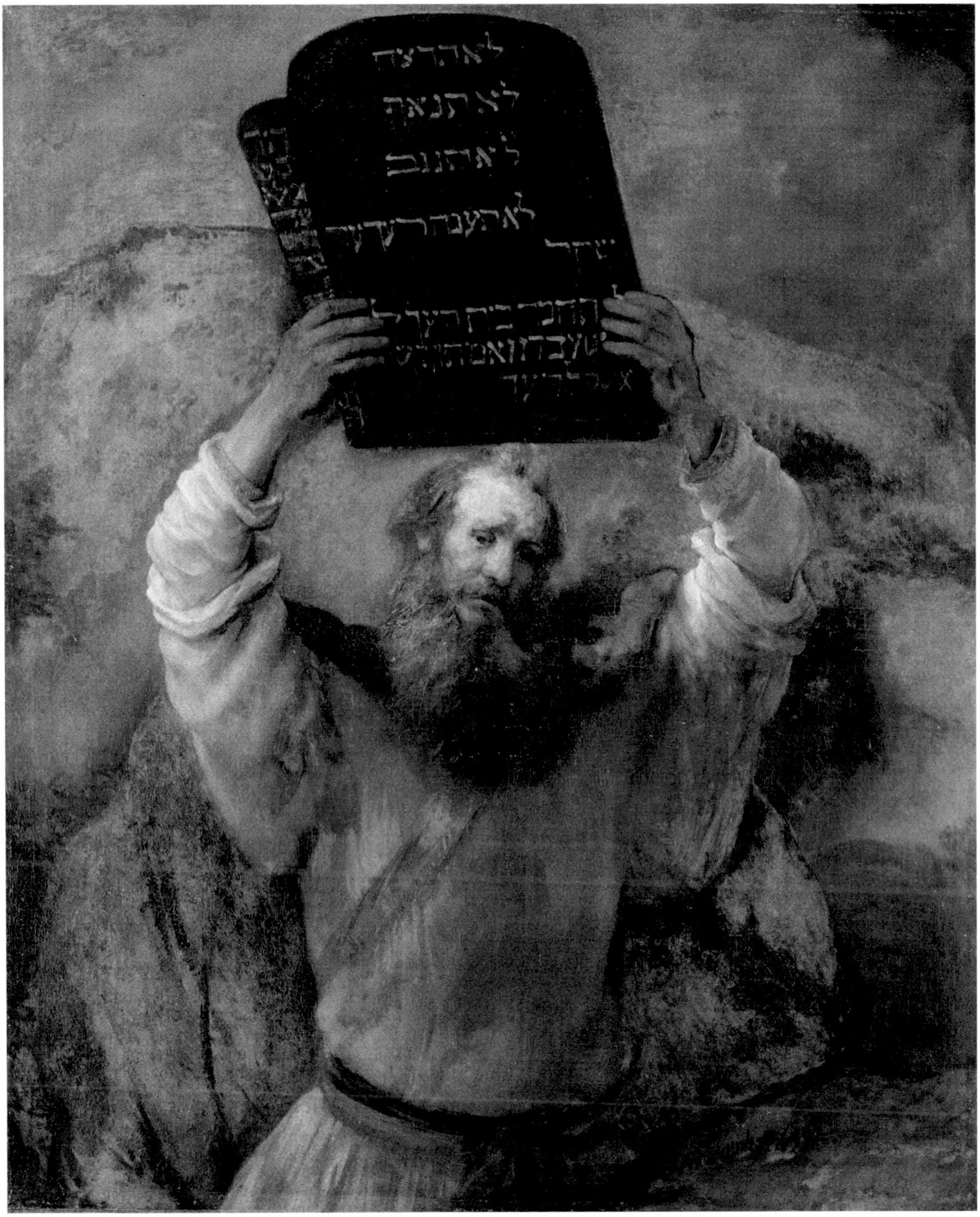

Figure 11. Rembrandt, *Moses Holding the Tablets of the Law*, 1659, canvas, 168.5 × 136.5 cm. Berlin, Gemäldegalerie, Staatliche Museen. Photo: Preussischer Kulturbesitz/Art Resource, NY.

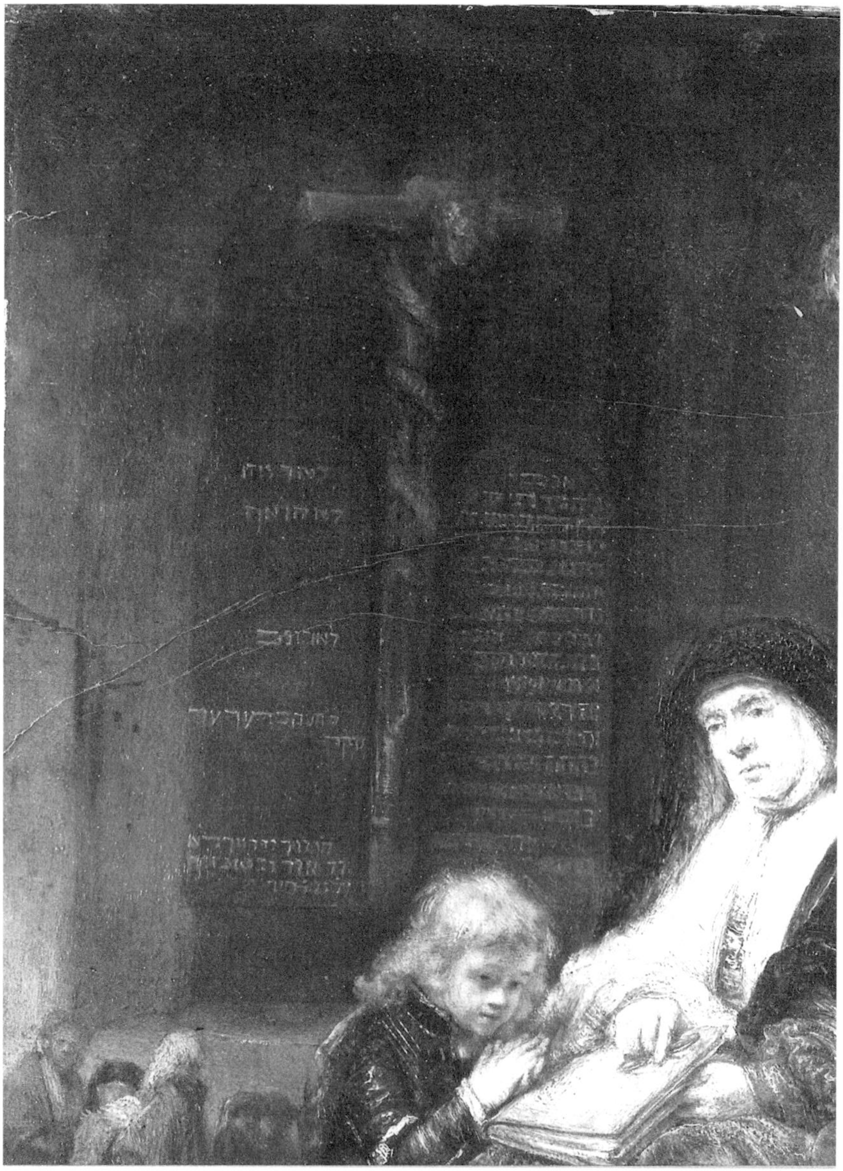

Figure 12. Pupil of Rembrandt, *Hannah and Samuel at the Temple* (detail), 1650, panel, 40.6 × 31.8 cm. Duke of Sutherland Collection, on loan to the National Gallery of Scotland, Edinburgh. By permission of His Grace, Duke of Sutherland.

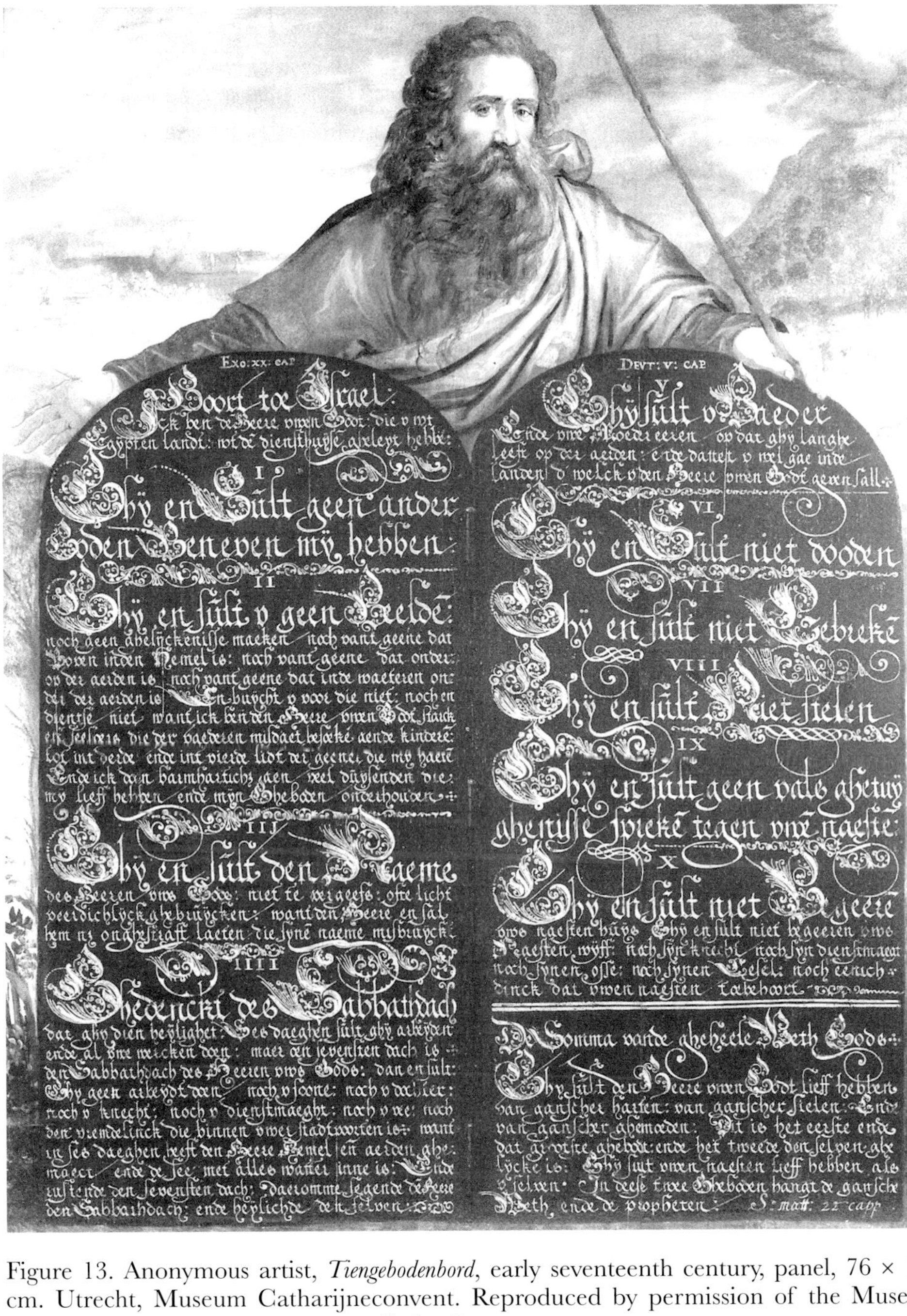

Figure 13. Anonymous artist, *Tiengebodenbord*, early seventeenth century, panel, 76 × 110 cm. Utrecht, Museum Catharijneconvent. Reproduced by permission of the Museum Catharijneconvent.

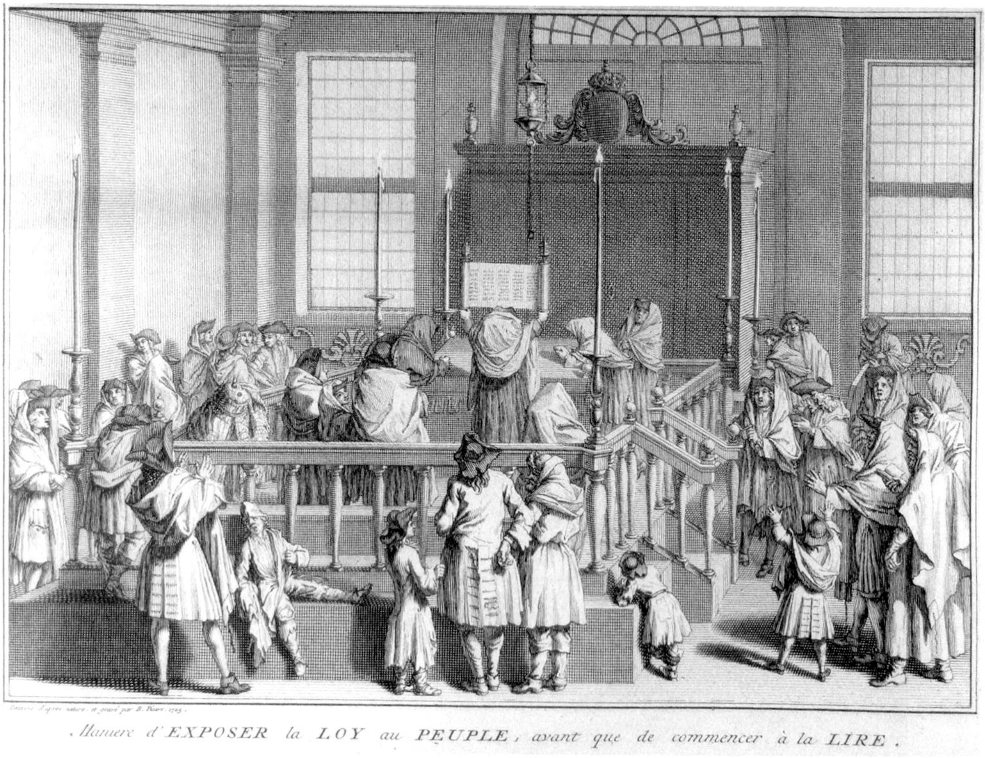

Figure 14. Bernard Picart, *Presenting the Torah to the People*, etching, from Picart, *Céremoniés et coutumes religieuses de tous les peuples du monde* (Amsterdam, 1723). Tel Aviv, Gross Family Collection.

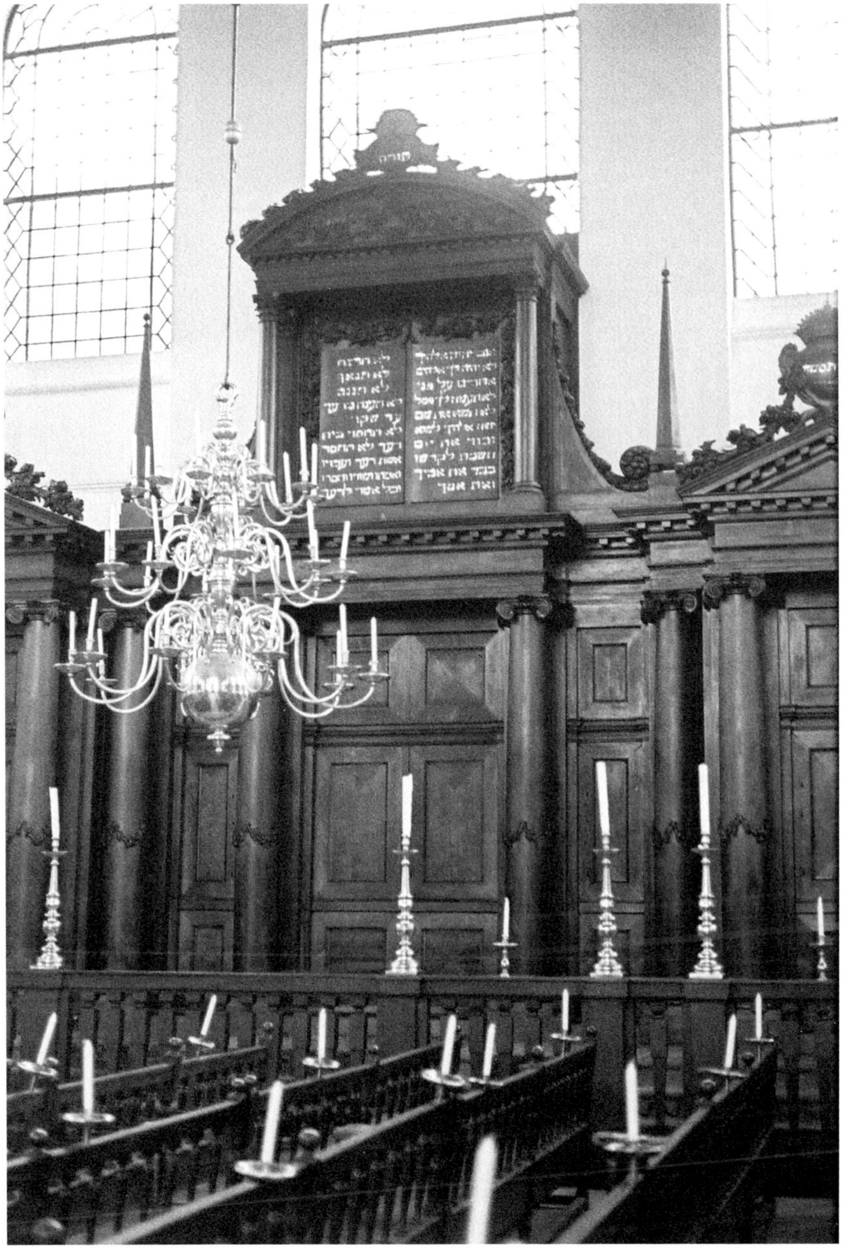

Figure 15. Detail of the Torah Ark with engraved Decalogue, Portuguese Synagogue (The Esnoga), Amsterdam, 1675. Photo by Willy Lindwer.